Inclusive Recreation

Programs and Services for Diverse Populations

Human Kinetics

Editor

Human Kinetics

Library of Congress Cataloging-in-Publication Data

Inclusive recreation: programs and services for diverse populations.
   p. cm.
   Includes bibliographical references and index.
   ISBN-13: 978-0-7360-8177-1 (hard cover)
   ISBN-10: 0-7360-8177-1 (hard cover)
   1. People with disabilities--Recreation--United States. 2. People with disabilities--Recreation--United States--Planning. 3. Recreation--Law and legislation--United States. 4. Inclusive education--United States. I. Human Kinetics (Organization)
   GV183.5.I54 2010
   790.196--dc22

2009047649

ISBN-13: 978-0-7360-8177-1

The Web addresses cited in this text were current as of August 2009, unless otherwise noted.

Acquisitions Editor: Gayle Kassing, PhD; **Developmental Editor:** Ragen E. Sanner; **Assistant Editor:** Anne Rumery; **Copyeditor:** Julie Anderson; **Indexer:** Betty Frizzell; **Permission Manager:** Dalene Reeder; **Graphic Designer:** Joe Buck; **Graphic Artist:** Yvonne Griffith; **Cover Designer:** Keith Blomberg; **Photographer (cover):** Photo courtesy of Camp Riley Children's Foundation. Photographer: Jamie Sutter. **Photographer (interior):** © Human Kinetics, unless otherwise noted in the text. **Chapter opening photos noted here:** Photo courtesy of Camp Riley Children's Foundation (pages 3 and 119); photo courtesy of Tom Watkins (page 137); © BananaStock (page 19); © Simon Jarratt/Corbis (page 61); © Photodisc/Getty Images (page 81); photo courtesy of Monika Stodolska (page 93); Realistic Reflections/Getty Images (page 177); photo courtesy of Ronald Davis (page 193); photo courtesy of NCPAD (page 209); AXIS Dance Company, photo by Margot Hartford (page 233); photo courtesy of Aquatic Therapy & Rehab Institute, 866-462-2874, atri@atri.org, www.atri.org (page 249); photo courtesy of Cindy Dillenschneider (page 279); photo courtesy of Bradford Woods (page 303); photo courtesy of NCA (page 331). **Contributor photos noted here:** Photo courtesy of Clopper Almon (Joan Almon); photo courtesy of Cindy Burkhour (Cindy Burkhour); photo courtesy of Indiana University Photographic Services (Shu Cole); photo courtesy of Tracey Crawford (Tracey Crawford); photo courtesy of Brendan Meehan (Ronald W. Davis); photo courtesy of Rodney Dieser (Rodney Dieser); photo courtesy of Cindy Dillenschneider (Cindy Dillenschneider); photo courtesy of Ken Jacques Photography (Torie Dunlap); photo courtesy of Indiana University Photographic Services (Alan Ewert); photo courtesy of Rick Green (Frederick Green); photo courtesy of California State University, Fresno (Jody Hironaka-Juteau); photo courtesy of Terry Long (Terry Long); photo courtesy of Pam Morris (Pamala V. Morris); photo courtesy of California State University, Fresno (Nancy Nisbett); photo courtesy of MaryBeth Pappas Baun (MaryBeth Pappas Baun); photo courtesy of Erik Rabinowitz (Erik Rabinowitz); photo courtesy of Amy Rauworth (Amy Rauworth); photo courtesy of Terry Robertson (Terry Robertson); photo courtesy of Richard Scholl (Kathleen G. Scholl); photo courtesy of Kathlyn Steedly (Kathlyn Steedly); photo courtesy of Matthew Marcinkowski (Monika Stodolska); photo courtesy of Sheila Swann-Guerrero (Sheila Swann-Guerrero); photo courtesy of Indiana University Photographic Services (Alison Voight); photo courtesy of Stephanie West (Stephanie West); photo courtesy of Brent Wolfe (Brent Wolfe). **Art Manager:** Kelly Hendren; **Associate Art Manager:** Alan L. Wilborn; **Illustrator:** Keri Evans; **Printer:** Total Printing Systems

Printed in the United States of America   15 14 13 12 11 10 9

The paper in this book is certified under a sustainable forestry program.

Human Kinetics
P.O. Box 5076
Champaign, IL 61825-5076
Website: www.HumanKinetics.com

In the United States, email info@hkusa.com or call 800-747-4457.
In Canada, email info@hkcanada.com.
In the United Kingdom/Europe, email hk@hkeurope.com.

For information about Human Kinetics' coverage in other areas of the world, please visit our website: **www.HumanKinetics.com**

Tell us what you think!
Human Kinetics would love to hear what we can do to improve the customer experience. Use this QR code to take our brief survey.

E4767

Contents

Preface

Inclusive recreation gives everyone an opportunity to participate in and enjoy leisure and recreation activities. Given America's expanding and diverse population, park, recreation, and tourism professionals are on the front line to enhance the quality of life in their communities through health-enhancing and rewarding activities. *Inclusive recreation* is an all-encompassing term for programs and services for people of all ages, abilities, cultures, ethnicities, genders, races, and religions.

Inclusive Recreation: Programs and Services for Diverse Populations is an undergraduate course textbook for students pursuing careers in recreation, parks, leisure, or tourism. This comprehensive textbook provides foundational theory and practical applications to prepare you for a wide variety of recreation activities through the inclusion lens.

About This Book

This book addresses what entry-level recreation, leisure, and tourism providers need to know and be able to do to ensure the participation of diverse populations. By reading the book, you will gain awareness of best practices for providing access and accommodations for people of all abilities, genders, ages, and cultures who participate in recreation, leisure, and tourism activities. Every professional, be it recreation professional, inclusion specialist, or certified therapeutic recreation specialist, can develop the skills and talents to make inclusion part of his or her organization.

A team of professors and professionals who are leaders in the inclusive recreation field guide you from theories to today's best practices used in inclusive recreation. These experts provide a comprehensive view of inclusion so that it can be implemented system-wide throughout your agency or organization.

Here are some of the features of this book:

- Disability and diversity awareness, language, and strategies for including all individuals in recreation activities
- Universal design principles and processes for facilities and programs to provide access and accommodation

- Chapters on inclusive recreation and leisure activity areas
- Best-practice examples from different sectors

Reading this book will help you do the following:

- Become diversity conscious by using appropriate disability and diversity communication skills and strategies
- Explore universal design principles applications in facilities, programs, and services to provide inclusive experiences
- Learn how inclusion strategies work within specific recreation types of programming and services
- Survey best practices and examples of inclusive recreation from across the world

Organization

Inclusive Recreation: Programs and Services for Diverse Populations has four parts that present a comprehensive view of inclusion, theories and concepts, what constitutes inclusive facilities and programs, and applications of inclusion best practices in recreation activity areas.

Part I, Foundations of Inclusive Recreation, introduces you to inclusion, its history, cultural competence, theories, concepts, and models.

Part II, The Inclusion Process for Recreation and Leisure: Access and Training for Clients, Staff, and Volunteers, teaches you about inclusion processes, diverse groups and individuals with disabilities, and staff training.

Part III, Applying Inclusive Practices in Recreation and Leisure, teaches you about universal design principles and how they extend through facilities and programs.

Part IV, Inclusive Recreation and Leisure Programs and Services, explores specific recreation program and service areas such as play and playgrounds; inclusive sports; fitness, physical activity, and wellness; arts, crafts, and culture; aquatics; outdoor activities and camps; adventure and challenge courses; and travel, tourism, and amusements.

Special Features

Each chapter contains a Spotlight on Inclusive Programs or a Professionals in Action feature, offering insight on a best-practice program or professional who has contributed to inclusive practices in many ways. A focus on international perspectives provides a glimpse at how inclusive practices work in selected countries: Australia, Brazil, Canada, Japan, and the United Kingdom.

This comprehensive textbook also works in conjunction with online ancillaries including an instructor guide, test package, presentation package, and student resources. The student resources extend learning and provide assignments, Web links, and other resources to help students pre-pare to be a part of inclusive recreation within any community.

Inclusion for All

Inclusive recreation is an important theme in the 21st century that will continue to grow and develop through recreation, leisure, and tourism. Using an inclusive lens that welcomes and supports everyone is an important component of developing our communities and our world. Many important pioneers have led the inclusion movement to where it is today. The future of inclusion will be written by you, as you meet the next challenges in your organization and community.

Foundations of Inclusive Recreation

Introduction to Inclusion

Jody H. Hironaka-Juteau, EdD, CTRS, RTC

> California State University, Fresno

Tracey Crawford, CTRS, CPRP

> Fox Valley Special Recreation
> Association

The act of observing and reflecting on our own practices can be an enlightening experience, enabling us to see ourselves more clearly and to formulate ways of working that are more effective and that enhance the lives of people.

—E.T. Stringer

Learning Outcomes

After completing this chapter, learners will be able to do the following:

- Define *inclusion*.
- Identify terms associated with inclusion, such as *diversity, culture, prejudice,* and *stereotype*.
- Describe the benefits of inclusion.
- Describe barriers to inclusion.

The diversity of our communities requires leaders who have an awareness of themselves and of others. This allows leaders to anticipate the needs of others in the community, including those from different socioeconomic groups, racial or ideological backgrounds, and cultural backgrounds and those with various abilities. Without this insight, leaders could make decisions that create uncomfortable and unwelcoming environments. Self-awareness is critical as we journey forward as lifelong learners. The ability to develop and promote inclusion is a wonderful and worthwhile journey wherein we learn and grow with others. Recreation offers unique opportunities where all people can and should be included!

What Is Inclusion?

Inclusion is a cultural characteristic whereby that culture is characterized by attitudes and behaviors that are open and accepting of all people. It is a term used to capture a sense of belonging, value, and respect. This chapter starts the basic framework for defining inclusion. All people have the right to choose what they would like to do for recreation as well as with whom and where they would like to recreate. However, people who come from diverse groups have limited access to the full range of recreation opportunities within their communities. Some of the barriers preventing access are attitudinal or physical, and some involve lack of education or training. Lack of experience with inclusion practices could cause leaders to inadvertently promote segregated environments, where the right to choose and the right to be a part of the community are absent. The concept of inclusive recreation is based on providing opportunities and choices for people from diverse groups to participate with their peers. Complete inclusion is achieved when a person is physically included in the space or environment and all of the necessary adaptations, accommodations, and supports are in place to allow social, cognitive, and emotional inclusion.

First Impressions

Look around the classroom and find a partner whom you have not met yet. Now without saying a word, just by looking at her, answer the following questions about that person. How old is she? What does she like to do for fun? What is her ethnicity? What kind of music does she like to listen to? Now take a deep breath and exchange the answers with your partner.

Within in the first few minutes of meeting someone, you determine whether you like that person. This assessment could be based on what the person looks like, how she acts, what she sounds like, how she smells, or her age, her race, gender, or perceived ability. In other words, your assessment is based on any feeling or image that you retain after meeting with this person. Whatever this feeling or image, it determines your first impression of that person.

Was it difficult to communicate your first impressions out loud to your partner? Were you true to your first impression or did you alter your answers? A first impression is instinctive; it is your gut reaction to a person or a situation. If you altered your answers, why? What stopped you from sharing with your partner your gut responses to the questions?

It is human nature to form a first impression of someone upon meeting him. The point of this exercise and this discussion is to open your mind to how your first impressions affect your judgment and interactions with a diverse group of people who are not like you.

When you hear the word *inclusion*, what is your first impression? What image, what thought, what belief, or what action comes to your mind? What is your picture of inclusion? Stop right now while the image, thought, story, or action is fresh in your mind's eye and write it down or draw it.

Take a look at what you created and answer the following questions:

- Was the image, thought, belief, or action one of acceptance?
- Was it positive or negative?
- Did it lead you to tolerance or intolerance?
- Do you believe it has formed your current beliefs of inclusion?
- Whatever the image, from where did it come?

From these initial impressions, your philosophy of inclusion is built.

Definition of Inclusion

Inclusion is a process. This process includes providing opportunities for choice and the necessary support to ensure that engagement is fun, is enjoyable, and matches skills with challenge. Inclusion is about creating environments for meaningful engagement. Inclusion is not a one-time event or a program offered for a specific time period, nor is it a separate service. Inclusion is the process of learning, preparing, experiencing, and growing with each person, with each family, and in each recreational opportunity. For the participant, inclusion is being invited to typical opportunities with friends and family and being welcomed as an equal participant. It is having the necessary support in place to be successful. Inclusion is learning and preparing to address the needs, interests, and abilities of all people to support their experience and growth. It is not a place but a state of being. Recognizing that inclusion is important for all, effective leaders not only provide opportunities for choice but also provide essential support that cultivates connectedness and engagement. Everyone deserves to be included and to freely choose to participate.

Although this text is designed to expand your understanding of inclusive recreation, the broad concept of inclusion is not limited to recreation. Inclusion applies to all aspects of life where participation and engagement are possible and where appropriate modification and support that draw on individual abilities and potential are provided. Thus, inclusion is not about providing limited opportunities because we believe it is a nice thing to do or because we feel obligated. Inclusion is a way of being with others that is welcoming, is respectful, and values experience, knowledge, and abilities. Inclusion is a mind-set and a process (Da Gama et al., 2003). Just as the authors do, you will continue to learn new things about inclusion every day.

You must have a working definition of inclusion as you move forward in this text. It is helpful to understand terms associated with inclusion, which will deepen your awareness of inclusion. Additional terms we have not mentioned include *diversity, culture, prejudice,* and *stereotype.*

• *Diversity* refers to various human qualities that are present in others but are different and outside the groups to which we personally belong. Examples include age, ethnicity, race, gender, sexual orientation, and physical abilities. These are referred to as primary dimensions because they cannot change. Qualities that can be changed include marital status, religious beliefs, occupation, parental status, education, income, and military status, just to name a few (University of Maryland, 1995). Although such descriptors are often used out of convenience to group a large number of people into a particular category, we must remember that we are still referring to individual people. Leaders must take time to assess individual preferences, interests, and abilities.

• *Culture* can be described as patterns, beliefs, or practices that are expressed by or are expressions of a particular group. Each of us belongs to a variety of groups. As such, our personal interactions, decisions, behaviors, and the like reflect and are influenced by our culture. People may have beliefs, patterns, or practices that come from the various groups to which they belong. Recognizing that some cultural traditions may be very similar to or very different from their own, effective leaders foster a culturally aware and sensitive environment that is welcoming and inclusive.

• *Prejudice* involves drawing conclusions without examining the facts or having predetermined thoughts that lead us to unfairly pass judgment. Sometimes the assumptions that we make about people or situations are correct and sometimes they are not. Our assumptions can lead to unfounded suspicion or even hatred of a particular group of people for their real or imagined social characteristics. This could include holding a preconceived idea about a person based on her race, religion, sexual orientation, or any group to which she belongs.

• *Stereotype* is an oversimplification of attributes or characteristics that are used to label people from a group or culture. This could include a fixed belief or assumption about people who belong to a specific group. For example, a stereotype based on ethnicity may be that all people of Asian heritage are quiet or excel in mathematics and science. Although some people of Asian heritage may have these characteristics, they do not necessarily apply to all Asian people.

Why Inclusion?

Our vision of the future is one of unity in the community. The blending of people who differ from each other enhances everyone's quality of life. As people from diverse groups are included in our community, access to recreation and leisure opportunities becomes very important. Out of such opportunities, relationships will develop, people will enjoy each other, and the quality of life for all in the community will be improved by what each person has to offer the other. Through inclusion, we recognize other people's unique gifts, abilities, and talents and learn to appreciate how such diversity contributes to the dynamic communities in which we live. We see difference and uniqueness as assets, not liabilities. We approach, not avoid. We accept, not reject. We open our minds, our hearts, and our doors!

Inclusion allows us to individually and collectively develop into the supportive, knowledgeable, and effective leaders we are capable of becoming. As such, it is valuable to understand core concepts that will serve as a foundation for fostering inclusive environments.

Philosophical Basis for Inclusion

The philosophical basis for inclusion is an individual and very personal journey. No one will take the exact same journey; hence, no one will have the same inclusion philosophy. Who you are determines what you think. In other words, your philosophy is a compilation of all of your first impressions, your life experiences, your education, your environment, your community, your friends, your family, and the world in which you live.

You must acknowledge three core concepts to fully embrace inclusion. The first core concept addresses the definition of inclusion noted earlier in this chapter.

The second core concept is always putting the person first in our language, our planning, and our minds. A person who has a disability is still first and foremost a person. He has hopes and dreams, and he has struggles that he will win and lose every day just like everyone else. The person with a disability has a condition that will limit his ability to do some things some of the time. The disability does not limit his personal growth and what he will accomplish in life. Think of a person's disability as a personal characteristic that helps to define who he is. For example, when using person-first language you would describe a fellow student in class as Johnny, a freshman, who is from Ethiopia, plays on the tennis team, and has Asperger's syndrome. Do not label a person by his disability. He is not his condition; he is a unique person.

Apply this concept to all people. Don't see a "homeless person": See a person who doesn't have a home. Don't see a "senior citizen"; see a person who is elderly. All of us are people first!

The third core concept is that no one is exempt. The groups to which we belong can change over time based on our life's journey: We may experience changes in educational or marital status, religion, citizenship, or socioeconomic status. Thus, we must recognize that diversity knows no boundaries. For example, someday someone you love and care about may be affected by a disability . . . and that person could be you!

© Brand X Pictures

Look past the categories in which you might put someone; see the person before you as an individual with hopes, dreams, and struggles just like your own.

Anything that you do from this day forward to make inclusion a reality for a person with a disability, or any person who comes from a diverse group, will come back to serve you personally some day.

As you start on your journey of personal development and face your own life experiences, the three core concepts discussed in this chapter will give you a firm base of understanding on which to build your own philosophy of inclusion.

Inclusion as a Choice

Sometimes we become overloaded with all of our responsibilities, such as school, work, and family. What do you do when you have an opportunity to have nonscheduled, free time? What does free time look like for you? Jot down your thoughts.

Now, imagine you have finally acquired your precious free time and you happen to have cerebral palsy and cannot drive yourself anywhere. Does that change your plans at all? What does your free time look like now? What if your best friend has a traumatic brain injury and is prone to aggressive outbursts? Does that change your plans? Next, imagine yourself in your future work setting. You volunteer to be on the committee that plans employee social activities, and you notice that on the agenda for the next meeting is the annual family Christmas party. You know that some employees do not celebrate Christmas and some do not celebrate any religious holidays. How might this awareness affect the discussion at the meeting? You know that some employees do not have family members, and some identify as lesbian or gay. What thoughts come to mind about how to create an event that is welcoming to all?

Overview About Diversity Laws

A brief overview of three key legislations related to diversity is valuable in understanding the significance of inclusion. A more in-depth examination of diversity-related laws appears later in the book.

The Civil Rights Act of 1964 was landmark legislation in the United States that outlawed racial segregation in schools, public places, and the workplace. First introduced in a civil rights speech by President John F. Kennedy in June 1963, this law prohibits discrimination based on race, color, and national origin in programs and activities receiving financial assistance from the federal government.

The Rehabilitation Act of 1973, specifically section 504, is the first major piece of civil rights legislation related to people with disabilities. It ensures people with disabilities basic civil rights protection against discrimination. Programs receiving federal funding, such as municipal recreation departments, public schools, state institutions, and the like, must offer people with disabilities equal opportunity for participation.

The Americans with Disabilities Act (ADA) is a sweeping civil rights law passed in 1990. It was intended to eliminate discrimination in all aspects of life for the millions of Americans with disabilities. It opened doors and enabled people with disabilities to choose where and when they recreate and with whom. There is value in all aspects of the recreational experience: every sight, sound, touch, taste, and smell; however, the true value is determined by the person, not the professional. The ADA is known as the federal mandate that provided equal access to recreational opportunities for all people.

Understanding and developing inclusive practices is an ongoing journey. These key laws provide a glimpse into where we have been and offer anchors for subsequent legislation intended to ensure equitable treatment, access, and services to all people.

Demographics

According to the Census Bureau's 2005-2007 American Community Survey, approximately 41.3 million people or 15.1% of the United States population age 5 and older and not residing in institutions reported having a disability. This includes physical disabilities (9.4%), mental disabilities (5.8%), sensory disabilities (4.3%), and self-care disabilities (3%). For adults 65 years and older, the prevalence of disability was the highest: 41%. This is more than triple that of the 16- to 64-year-old group (12.3%) and six times greater than 5- to 15-year-olds (6.3%). At the same time, it is important to note that the majority of people older than 65 (59%) do not have a disability.

Sixteen percent of the U.S. population older than 25 have not graduated from high school, and 27% have education at a bachelor's degree or higher. More than 6% of Americans older than 16 years are unemployed. Nearly one tenth of families (9.8%) live below the poverty level and a similar number (10.4%) are civilian veterans. For people 15 years and older, 10.5% are divorced and nearly three times that number (30.4%) have never married.

Of a population of 298.7 million, Americans identify their race as white (74.1%), Hispanic or Latino (of any race) (14.7%), black or African American (12.4%), Asian (4.3%), American Indian and Alaska Native (0.8%), Native Hawaiian and other Pacific Islander (0.1%), and other race (6.2%). Approximately 6.1 million or 2.1% of Americans identify as having two or more races, and 19.5% of Americans speak a language other than English at home. These demographic data show that people are diverse in many ways. We must not make assumptions about who a person is or is not based what we see or do not see.

Professional Competence and Responsibility

Professional competence means that you can perform the essential tasks of your job as a result of your education and training and your professional work experience. Learning is a lifelong journey, and professional competence is more than completing a college degree, showing up to work every day, or attending a workshop or two a year. As a professional, it is your responsibility and privilege to continually expand your knowledge and deepen your understanding of best practices and then better practices. This comes from taking risks and stepping outside of your comfort zone to gain new experiences and enhance your skills as an advocate for inclusion and advocates for recreation.

Are you ready, willing, and able to take personal responsibility for becoming a competent inclusion professional? Are you ready to embrace the concept that inclusion is a right and a choice that each person must make? Are you willing to accept the challenge of implementing the inclusion process, knowing that it is a unique and personal journey for each person, professional, and family involved? Are you able to keep an open mind, even when you are faced with challenges that will force you to question and explore your personal and professional beliefs and philosophies?

Here are six strategies that professionals can use to be more inclusive.

1. "You are welcome to register." Provide welcoming language that encourages recreation for people of all abilities and background throughout recreation department materials and program brochures. Include a statement regarding the Americans with Disabilities Act in the recreation department brochures. Provide customer service training for the recreation department's front desk and recreation staff; this training should emphasize the philosophy of the agency regarding inclusion and its willingness to provide recreational opportunities for everyone.

2. "Let's talk about what you need." The registration form should provide a way for people to indicate that they require special accommodations to participate in the recreation program.

3. "We will assess the situation to support you." When someone requests special accommodations, staff must contact the person or her family to identify specific needs to begin the inclusion process. The staff member may recommend observation and assessment of the person.

4. "Recreate and enjoy." Following the observation and assessment, staff will indentify and implement needed accommodations. Accommodations may be in the form of extra staff, sign language interpreters, adaptive rules and policies, behavior management support, disability awareness training, and any other services necessary to include in the person in the program.

5. "We will be there to observe and evaluate." Recreation staff should conduct scheduled observations throughout the inclusion placement, using a standardized observation form that the agency has created. The observation may indicate that the types of accommodations provided need to be adjusted. Any barriers identified during the observation process must be addressed.

6. "Let's communicate as a team." The inclusion team consists of the recreation supervisor, the program leader, the participant, and, if necessary, a family member. The family can invite anyone who may be beneficial to the inclusion process to become part of the inclusion team. These can include the participant's teachers, friends, caregivers, and therapists. The inclusion team must constantly communicate the participant's successes and be prepared to address any barriers that may occur. The inclusion team works together to discuss the participant's involvement in the program. This includes not only highlighting the participant's strengths and the successful aspects of involvement but addressing any barriers or areas in need of improvement as well.

The inclusion journey is like a roller coaster: It is thrilling, yet scary. Anticipation builds before you take action. The ride often includes twists, turns, loops, and pauses, but it will always start moving again. Becoming ready, willing, and able to embrace inclusion as a professional means preparing for the roller-coaster ride. You will walk in with your eyes open and with clear expectations because you have prepared for the ride.

Who Should Be Included?

To whom are we referring when we discuss inclusion? Inclusion refers to everybody. Each of us deserves to be included from the very beginning and not as an afterthought. Think about a time when you were left out, chosen last, overlooked, or ignored. How did you feel? How did it affect your perception of yourself or others? Conversely, how did you feel when you were included? What impact did inclusion have on you? Although inclusion refers to everyone, there are some groups of people to whom leaders must give particular attention to ensure inclusion.

These groups include people with disabilities and people from diverse groups.

People With Disabilities

Each of us has strengths as well as weaknesses or areas that are less developed. Often, abilities that are more developed help to make our weaknesses less noticeable. Although leaders must recognize that everyone has abilities as well as disabilities, an awareness of various disability groupings is important to understand what types of support or modifications are needed to provide an inclusive environment.

According to the Americans with Disabilities Act, a person with a disability is one who has a mental or physical impairment that substantially limits one or more major life activities, who has a record of such impairment, or who is regarded as having such impairment. The major life activities to which the ADA refers are those a person does in the course of a typical day, such as walking, speaking, seeing, hearing, dressing, feeding oneself, working, learning, recreating, and engaging in other daily physical or mental activities (U.S. Department of Justice, 1990). This can include people with visual or hearing impairments, spinal cord injuries, amputation, multiple sclerosis, stroke, brain injury, cerebral palsy, autism, and diabetes, just to name a few. Mental illness, emotional illness, mental retardation, development disabilities, and chemical dependency are other conditions covered by the ADA.

Diverse Groups

Leaders must be attentive to people who come from diverse groups to ensure that environments are welcoming and inclusive. As previously noted, diversity refers to primary and secondary dimensions including, but not limited to, age, ethnicity, race, gender, sexual orientation, physical abilities, socioeconomic status, education, religion, occupation, parental status, and military status. Leaders must recognize that the people with whom they work come from diverse backgrounds, and this diversity affects each person differently. By getting to know a person and her interests, abilities, and preferences, leaders can create working relationships and environments that welcome and embrace diversity.

Community leaders who learn what individual recreation needs exist within the community can develop programs that appeal to many people.

Barriers and Benefits of Inclusion

Inclusion is a process: It is a journey, not a destination. Along the journey, there will be highlights and lowlights. We also know that there will be myriad insights! Some of the most salient insights for the authors have surfaced when we were faced with barriers; reflecting on the benefits and values of inclusion restored our energy and replenished our motivation to continue the journey.

Barriers

One may assume that a key barrier to inclusion would be that which makes a person diverse. For example, a person with a disability, a person who is experiencing temporary homelessness, a person who is older than 65, a person who identifies as transgender, or a person who is biracial may appear to have limitations or challenges that affect his ability to fully participate. Often, however, the real barriers to inclusion are the negative attitudes of others who lack exposure to or interaction with people from diverse groups. It is not surprising that we may be fearful of what is different or what we have yet to experience. Through education and interaction with people from diverse groups, we can begin to notice and appreciate the similarities within the differences that we share and break down barriers that keep us apart.

Some typical barriers include the following

- *Transportation:* These barriers restrict a person's access to recreational and leisure activities. Lack of accessible transportation is one of the biggest barriers experienced by people with disabilities and can cause the greatest degree of frustration. Some people have public transportation options; however, scheduling and expense often prevent people with disabilities from accessing these transportation services.

- *Structural:* These barriers restrict a person from free and independent movement from one place to another. Inclusion starts at the point at which your patron arrives at your facility, that is, the parking lot, and leads to the place where the program is held.

- *Economic:* Some people with disabilities cannot access recreational and leisure activities because of the expense. It is costly for people with disabilities to make their homes accessible, find accessible transportation, receive medical care, and seek therapy, and the additional expense of recreation may be beyond their means.

- *Social and attitudinal:* These barriers are caused by attitudes or personal beliefs of people without disabilities based on their prejudices regarding a particular disability, diverse groups, or people with disabilities in general.

- *Psychological:* These are barriers maintained by people with disabilities themselves. Psychological barriers exist when people have learned to believe that they are not capable. These barriers may be created out of fear of not being able to participate in a particular recreational and leisure activity. Fear and anxiety are experienced by all people, but for people with disabilities, fear is compounded by societal attitudes that people with disabilities are unable to or should not participate in recreational and leisure activities. These attitudes can lead a person to believe that she just can't participate in activity and doesn't even want to try.

- *Communication:* Many people with hearing impairments, visual impairments, and speech and language impairments or disorders cannot easily access information. Another consideration is language barriers between different cultures and countries; participants might speak a language or dialect that is different from the leader's or may use similar words in different ways.

- *Programmatic accommodations:* These barriers exist when needs of people with disabilities are not taken into consideration in the planning of a program, activity, or event. You are not expected to know every accommodation needed for every person accessing your program, but you must communicate with the person and, if necessary, her family or caregiver. This creates a team approach in providing the necessary accommodations for that person.

Inclusion itself can sometimes be a barrier to productive and meaningful opportunities. Although there are myriad benefits of inclusion, there are times when noninclusive programs are beneficial. Some people may feel more comfortable discussing issues of concern with others who share a common experience. For example, a person with bipolar disorder may thoroughly enjoy playing in the community softball league that is inclusive and open to all while at the same time value the supportive and open dialogue that she experiences during a noninclusive mental health support group held at that same community center. To be in the company of others

Susie Lund

Background Information

Education BA Elementary and Special Education, University of Idaho

Career Information

Position Inclusion Director at the Family YMCA of Blackhawk County, Waterloo, Iowa

What I Like About My Job I have the privilege to help children with disabilities participate in recreation and leisure activities throughout our community. The key to our success is having partner agencies that are committed to including people with disabilities in their programming. I love my job because I have such a variety of responsibilities: meeting with families, working with our partner agencies, training staff, and working with children and youth. The challenges of my job are the attitudinal barriers that I face each day regarding people with disabilities.

who share common challenges and who can help identify useful strategies to overcome such challenges has benefits, too. Therefore, inclusion is not an "either/or" or an all-or-nothing situation. Inclusion is a way of being. Inclusion recognizes similarities and difference and celebrates them in a welcoming manner.

Benefits

One of the most famous phrases in the U.S. Declaration of Independence is "life, liberty, and the pursuit of happiness." These inalienable rights cannot be taken away, violated, or transferred from one person to another. Yet how often are people excluded, deprived of independence, provided with limited choices, offered little or no support to pursue their dreams, or deprived of the opportunity to find what is most meaningful in their lives?

Inclusion provides opportunities to develop greater awareness and sensitivity to similarities and differences of people who come from diverse groups. In turn, professionals develop a deeper appreciation of their own abilities and limitations, their strengths and struggles, that are the direct result of their own diversity. The resulting empathy can spur the creation of new environments that are designed to welcome diversity.

At a time when embracing difference in our society is more difficult for some groups than others, inclusion provides the opportunity for

us to see firsthand the benefits of interacting with various people; hear diverse perspectives, firsthand accounts of people's abilities, and personal stories of mistreatment as a result of one's diversity; and learn to be an ally, providing much-needed support and advocacy. Through inclusion, we become better friends, more effective allies, and more compassionate human beings.

How Do You Do It?

Inclusion is a constant, ongoing process of actions and steps. These steps include assessment of the person and the program, implementation of accommodations that the person needs to be able to participate, observation of the person's progress, determination of any changes that need to be made, and documentation of the person's outcome. Inclusion involves identifying steps to take to support a person with disabilities within a recreational program. There is no one way to implement inclusion that will work for everyone. Chapter 4 goes into greater discussion of processes that can be used to develop inclusive programming.

It is critical to have an inclusion process so that you recognize a barrier that can hinder the ongoing movement. By knowing where you are in the inclusion process, you are better equipped to navigate around any barrier that you may encounter so that you can move to the next step of inclusion.

Summary

As you get ready to embark on the journey that lies ahead, take time to reflect on the exercise at the beginning of this chapter on first impressions. What now are your second impressions of inclusion? How are these similar to or different from your first impressions? What can you commit to do next to support inclusion efforts?

Effective leaders know that their understanding of inclusion will continue to evolve, and these leaders regularly engage in reflection. As a result, the vision for "unity in the community" becomes more clear as we work together to create communities that are welcoming to all people.

Discussion Questions

1. Think about the various diverse groups to which you belong. What are your perceptions about how others view you related to these groups? How do you see yourself? In what way are these similar or different?

2. What does diversity mean to you? How does your own diversity provide you with insight into creating inclusive environments?

3. Are there situations where using person-first language is easier or more difficult? In what ways can you gain additional practice or experience?

4. What does inclusion mean to you? As a future leader, what do you look forward to most in creating inclusive environments?

>> Spotlight on Inclusive Programs

Bradford Woods

Bradford Woods hosts a variety of camps during the summer and is regarded as one of the best residential camping facilities in the Midwest for youth and adults with disabilities and specific medical needs such as physical disabilities, cancer, sickle cell anemia, Down syndrome, hearing impairments, and craniofacial differences. Camp partners include Riley Children's Foundation, Riley Hospital for Children, Little Red Door Cancer Agency, HEAR Indiana, and the Muscular Dystrophy Association. The therapeutic recreation program area at Bradford Woods offers week-long (summer) and weekend (fall, winter, and spring) residential camp programs for children with specific health care needs and their families. Overnight programs have fulfilled the recreational and therapeutic requirements of both children and adults with disabilities and chronic illness for more than 50 years.

Bradford Woods is a national and international leader in the application of universal design principles. Its facilities are designed for all participants despite their ability level. *Universal design* is defined by the National Center on Accessibility (NCA) as the design of products and environments to be usable by all people, to the greatest extent possible, without adaptation or specialized design. Many examples of universal design are found on the grounds of Bradford Woods. These include its nationally known amphitheater, switchback trail, universal high ropes course, climbing tower, and Olympic-sized

Photo courtesy of Camp Riley Children's Foundation. Photographer: Jamie Sutter.

Through inclusion we become better friends, more effective allies, and more compassionate human beings.

pool. Program directors are trained in recreational therapy practices, hold advanced degrees, and are certified therapeutic recreation specialists through the National Council for Therapeutic Recreation Certification (NCTRC). Support staff are typically students in a medical field, such as therapeutic recreation, occupational therapy, physical therapy, child life, art therapy, social work, music therapy, and nursing, as well as premed and first-year medical programs.

All therapeutic recreation programs and services focus on meeting the individual needs of participants. Low staff-to-participant ratios promote engagement, empowerment, and fun. Staff are well trained in person-first language, disability awareness, and medical and personal care and are supported by medical professionals such as nurses, doctors, and recreational therapists. The therapeutic recreation staff at Bradford Woods conduct therapeutic programming for at-risk youth, families, and adults with disabling conditions, and an equine-based therapy program is conducted through Agape Therapeutic Riding Resources. Staff in these programs collaborate on research projects in the social sciences and disability, instruct university classes in recreational therapy, and host practicum and internship students in the fields of therapeutic outdoor programming and recreational therapy. Pro-grams include Camp Riley (Riley Hospital for Children) and other specialty camps for children and adults with disabilities. Here is an overview of the camp's programming:

Camp Riley

Camp Riley is sponsored by the Riley Children's Foundation, philanthropic arm of the Riley Hospital for Children, and was originated in 1955. For a child, fitting in and making friends have great meaning. But when a youngster has a disability, connecting with a circle of friends and facing daily tasks can seem insurmountable. At Camp Riley, every child is encouraged to move beyond her limitations to accomplish greater independence. For many children with physical disabilities, Camp Riley is their first and only opportunity to experience a traditional camp environment. Campers gain confidence and thrive because every activity is accessible and encouraged. From swimming and horseback riding to learning valuable independent life skills, anything is possible at Camp Riley. With affiliations with Riley Hospital for Children and Indiana University School of Medicine, Camp Riley provides premiere 24-hour medical care during every camp session.

Here's what kids say about Camp Riley:

Spending the summer surrounded by kids made going back to school easier. I can stand up for myself now.
> –Katie Wooten

Camp is fun because you get to do activities you think you can't do at home. When camp is over, I don't want to go home because it's fun!
> –Catherine Wyman

Camp Riley challenges you. It's much more physical than a lot of other camps.
> –Cara Evans

Camp Riley has changed my life. I know who I am now.
> –Kohn Ashmore

The thing I remember most is the feeling I got from being around other kids who all shared feelings of insecurity, self-doubt, and shame. For two weeks in the summer, we could all feel like we were just "normal" kids. We were accepted, we excelled, we were cared for and cared about.
> –Suanne Jeffries

The one thing I want kids to take away from Camp Riley is self-confidence. I'm here to help kids believe in themselves.
> –Daniel Ryder

(continued)

My cabin was filled with girls who were like me. I am looking forward to going back to camp to see my friends.
　　　　—Markesha Jones

I had a better outlook on life whenever I came home from Camp Riley. I would make an extra effort to take care of myself and others. When you're not the only one with a disability, you learn to just be yourself.
　　　　—Brad Shaffer

Camp Riley Sessions

Newcomer's Day

Newcomer's Day lets new Riley campers and families have a trial run with a visit to Bradford Woods (home to Camp Riley). It's extremely important that campers see the staff and facilities prior to attending camp and that families get firsthand information and reassurance about their children's experience. New Camp Riley families tour the property and participate in typical camp activities; parents attend informational sessions, ask questions, and express concerns about sending their child to camp for the first time.

Riley 1

Ages 8 to 18 with physical disabilities

Discover new activities and master familiar ones like swimming, art, sports, music, games, campouts, and horseback riding (special release form required) in this 1-week traditional camp experience. Every day is packed with a broad range of interests, cultures, and environments. This session is geared toward campers who benefit from a 1-to-1 staff-to-camper ratio. Come and explore all that camp has to offer!

Riley 2

Ages 8 to 18 with physical disabilities

A 1-week camp offering traditional camp activities such as horseback riding, creative arts, nature activities, challenge day, fun at the pool, archery, overnight campout, and much more. This session is designed for campers who thrive in a 1-to-2 staff-to-camper ratio.

Riley 3

Ages 8 to 18 with physical disabilities

This 2-week session is ideal for campers who want to challenge themselves in sports and outdoor adventures and who have attended a 1-week Riley camp in the past. Campers participate in traditional camp

activities such as swimming, archery, horseback riding (special release form required), arts, and waterfront fun, focusing on cooperating with others, working together, and making friends. Visits from the Indiana Four Wheel Drive Association and Indiana High School Football All-Stars fill the days with excitement. This session is specifically designed for campers who are ready for a longer camper experience and thrive in a 1-to-3 staff-to-camper ratio.

Venture

Ages 15 to 18 with physical disabilities

This 2-week session is designed for older campers who want to focus on developing leadership, social, and independent life skills through elements of challenge, leadership, and service in addition to experiencing traditional camp activities. Campers participate in a 24-hour "immersion experience," a campout to develop and implement individual and group goals. Campers plan and implement activities for younger campers and participate in a service project. Venture campers participate in Pursuits of Excellence, an intensive 36-hour experience devoted to personal challenge, goals, and service to others. These experiences may be on or off site, such as caving, camping, and raft-building. Campers dance the night away at the Venture Prom. This session is designed for campers who are ready for a longer camp experience and thrive in a 1-to-3 staff-to-camper ratio.

Top It Off

Ages 17 and 18 with physical disabilities

This 2-week session is for older, veteran campers seeking new challenges. Working as a team, campers spend their first few days planning and preparing for a trip across Indiana. Using fully accessible transportation, campers hit the road to explore central, northern, or southern parts of the state. The trip may include activities such as rafting, tubing, visiting amusement parks, meeting the disability service representative at a local university (such as Notre Dame or Indiana

University) for a tour, and camping at state and public campgrounds. This trip broadens each camper's view of independence, self-advocacy, and public accessibility. This session is designed for campers who are ready for a longer camp experience and thrive in a 1-to-2 or 1-to-3 staff-to-camper ratio.

Kan-Du

Ages 8 to 18 with both physical and cognitive disabilities

See, smell, and touch all that the woods have to offer in this award-winning camp session that gives campers who need one-on-one attention and medical care a chance to experience the great adventures of camp. Campers explore the environment using their five senses with stimulating activities involving the outdoors, the pool, the barn, art, and the unique "sensory cave." This session is specifically designed for youth with cognitive and physical functioning levels assessed between 0 and 48 months and who thrive in a 1-to-1 staff-to-camper ratio.

Riley Specialty Camps

These camps are sponsored through the Riley Hospital for Children's Clinics with support from the Riley Children's Foundation.

Camp About Face

Ages 8 to 18 with craniofacial differences

One of the few camps in the United States designed for children who have been born with a cleft palate or lip as well as other, more rare anomalies of the face and skull. This camp is sponsored by the Cranial Facial Clinic at Riley Hospital for Children and is designed to serve children by promoting development of new skills while increasing self-confidence. Interaction with others with similar social and medical experiences in a traditional summer camp setting helps campers to grow socially.

This camp hosts a leadership academy the weekend prior to the start of camp for older adolescents and young adults to develop self-awareness, interpersonal skills, and leadership skills by leading selected activities for younger campers, keeping a journal, and continuing relationships with adult mentors after camp.

Camp Independence

Ages 8 to 18 with sickle cell anemia and other blood disorders

Camp Independence is sponsored by the Hematology/Oncology Clinic at the Riley Hospital for Children. This camp gives children an opportunity for a traditional camp experience under the watchful eye of doctors, nurses, and social workers.

Camp Hi-Lite

Ages 8 to 22 years with Down syndrome

Camp Hi-Lite was named as a result of many campers saying, "That was the highlight of my year!" This camp serves 70 children and young adults who have Down syndrome and is sponsored by the Developmental Pediatric Clinic/Ann Whitehall Down Syndrome Program at the Riley Hospital for Children.

Indianapolis Agency-Supported Camps

These camps are supported by well-respected agencies in the greater Indianapolis area.

Camp Little Red Door

Ages 8 to 18 who are affected by cancer

Camp LRD is sponsored by the Little Red Door Cancer Agency. This camp provides a traditional camp experience for children with cancer in an atmosphere that has been described as "high energy." These campers can bring a friend or sibling to experience all that camp has to offer.

Camp LRD has a leadership academy during the weekend prior to the start of camp for older, more experienced campers. This 3-day training session teaches campers about leadership, communication, and social skills. These campers can put their new skills into practice by mentoring younger campers during the traditional week of camp.

MDA Camp

Ages 8 to 18 with muscular dystrophy

This fun-filled camp, sponsored by the Muscular Dystrophy Association, hosts 90 campers. During this 7-day experience, campers participate in traditional camp activities such as horseback riding, creative arts, adventure activities, and special events. Each camper is paired with a counselor for the entire week.

HEAR Indiana Leadership Camp

Ages 8 to 18 with a hearing impairment

This camp is designed for 30 to 50 campers who have a hearing impairment and use spoken language to communicate. Therapeutic goals of this camp include increasing independence, confidence, and self-esteem

(continued)

and enabling campers to confidently communicate needs.

Bradford Woods Open Enrollment Camps

These programs are sponsored by Bradford Woods and hosted by Bradford Woods.

Adult Summer Retreat

Ages 18 and older

Adult campers with varying degrees of cerebral palsy and other disabilities enjoy a week of relaxation and socialization with newly acquired and long-standing friends. This 4-day camp is a relaxing vacation for 40 campers, filled with live music events, casino night, pontoon rides on our 110-acre (0.44 km) lake, cooking classes, and lounging by the pool. Many of these campers have attended camp at Bradford Woods for 20 to 40 years.

Adult Weekend Camps

Ages 18 and older

These camps are for adults who have attended our pediatric camping program. Many of these campers have attended camp for 20 to 40 years. Weekend camps take place four times a year in a variety of settings on the property. The manor, a turn-of-the-century universally accessible mansion, is the setting for a holiday retreat. The Agape Lodge Retreat is at a quaint lodge, and two other camps are hosted in the typical camp cabins used in summer. During these weekends, campers help cook meals and clean up after meals. Campers can practice meal planning, make a budget, handle money, and visit a grocery store. Campers are empowered to choose all activities they participate in and are encouraged to offer ideas for activities and to even lead a program if desired. Empowerment, socialization, and healthy leisure lifestyles are promoted.

Riley Reunion

Ages 8 to 18 who attend a summer camp at Bradford Woods

Campers have varying degrees of disability and diagnosis.

This Friday-to-Sunday weekend camp is designed for campers and staff to reunite for a beautiful autumn weekend at Bradford Woods. A fall harvest theme is the tradition with trick or treating, dressing up in costumes, and having a lot of fun while working on independence and social skills.

Camp Programming Overview

Nature and Outdoor Living Skills

This combined program teaches campers about their environment, the interdependency of humans and nature, and ways to protect the environment. Campers learn outdoor skills and how to be safe in the woods. All indoor and outdoor activities can be adapted to fit the campers' needs and abilities.

Recreation

All campers can participate and compete in various games, including traditional and nontraditional games and activities. All of these games and activities can be adapted in many ways to fit the abilities and needs of the campers.

Creative Arts and Music

This program allows campers the freedom to express their creativity and imagination through drawing, painting, drama, music, and writing. Creative arts programs allow time for the campers to go at their own pace and to do as much as they can independently. These programs take place in many different areas of camp. All of the activities can be adapted to fit the needs and abilities of the campers.

Waterfront

Waterfront is a program that allows campers to experience freedom and new activities in the pool and lake. Activities include boating, swimming, water games, and more. All activities can be adapted to fit the abilities and needs of the campers.

Horsebarn

This program is a partnership between Bradford Woods and Agape Therapeutic Riding Center and is designed to introduce the campers to horses and other domesticated barn animals. The program allows campers to learn and develop skills in horseback riding. This program provides campers with various activities that will tie in with barn life. Horseback riding and activities can be adapted to fit camper's needs and abilities.

Adventure Challenge

Adventure Challenge provides activities that allow campers to challenge themselves. They learn how to depend on and communicate with other campers and staff. This program entails many different elements, games, and initiatives, all of which can be adapted to fit campers' needs and abilities.

Challenge Day

Challenge days are a time for campers to challenge themselves emotionally, physically, or socially. Some challenges include swimming across the lake, climbing Cardiac Hill, shadowing a member of the Leadership Team for the day, or cooking. Challenges are individual to the camper, but sometimes they are completed as a cabin.

Courtesy of Camp Riley Children's Foundation.

Photo courtesy of Camp Riley Children's Foundation. Photographer: Jamie Sutter.

Campers gain confidence and thrive because every activity is accessible and encouraged.

Inclusive Recreation History and Legislation

Rodney Dieser, PhD
University of Northern Iowa

Kathleen G. Scholl, PhD, CTRS
University of Northern Iowa

" *This country will not be a good place for any of us to live in unless we make it a good place for all of us to live in.* "

—President Theodore Roosevelt

›› Learning Outcomes

After completing this chapter, learners will be able to do the following:

- Explain why it is important for professionals in leisure services to understand the history of inclusive recreation for people with disabilities.

- Articulate how recreation was used historically to humiliate people with disabilities and how hospitals were places that confined people with disabilities.

- Identify how Jane Addams and Hull House programs provided early inclusive programs in human and leisure services.

- Demonstrate the positive aspects of the deinstitutionalization movement in the United States.

- Identify how recreation programs, facilities, parks, and the tourism industry have been affected by the outcome of recent judicial cases related to inclusive recreation.

- Explain the normalization principle and outline the similarities and differences between Nirje's and Wolfensberger's perspectives.

Understanding the history of a professional field, such as inclusive recreation, has three important roles in contemporary professional practice (Dieser, 2008). First, understanding past successes and failures helps contemporary professionals avoid repeating past mistakes, learn from past successes, and predict the consequence of individual and organizational action. Second, understanding the history of a profession provides a professional identity. Sylvester (1989) underscored that a professional field without history is like a person without a memory—without sources of identity drawn from a meaningful past, purposeful direction is less likely. Why is inclusive recreation important? What is the difference between inclusive recreation and special recreation? Should community parks and recreation departments provide programs for people with disabilities? These questions, and many more, can be answered when a professional identity is developed. Third, historical research creates and shapes current perceptions of reality. Understanding how people with disabilities were marginalized and abused in the past can shape contemporary leaders' commitment to provide inclusive recreation services.

The development of social movements and values often takes a long time. Although social development can occur through strategic planning by individuals, communities, governments, and institutions (Midgley, 1995), social values and movements, such as inclusive recreation, often develop from discursive, interdisciplinary, irrelevant, and irrational locations, such as the summing influence of social events, political decisions, popular opinion, class values, economic realities, academic research, and different bodies of learning (Foucault, 1998). This chapter highlights the development of inclusive recreation by outlining discursive and dominant social values that influenced the development of inclusive recreation, such as the societal perceptions and treatment of people with disabilities in ancient Greece and 18th-century America, and by discussing the history of legislation and social policy in the United States.

Evolution of Inclusion

Throughout history and in different countries, people from differing minority groups (e.g., people with disabilities, people from different ethnic backgrounds) have been treated in different ways. Regrettably, most historical research indicates that in the United States, people with disabilities and people from minority backgrounds were treated in troubling and abusive ways. As this chapter highlights, recreation was often used in an ugly manner to humiliate people who were considered different from the mainstream. It has only been in the past 50 years that recreation has been used in an inclusive manner to support people with disabilities and people from minority backgrounds. This section briefly explains how people with disabilities were perceived and treated in ancient Greece and pre-1900s North America and from the 1900s to the present in the United States.

From Ancient Greece to Pre-1900s North America

Historical research, writings, poetry, and art give us a glimpse of how past cultures and societies perceived and treated people with disabilities. Scant historical research suggests that inclusive recreation occurred for people with disabilities during ancient Greek society. For example, Avedon (1974) listed some early forms of inclusive recreation for people with special needs, such as in ancient Rome, where people with disabilities were taken from their dark cells, brought into sunshine, and provided with music, poetry, games, and movement. In contrast, a solid body of historical research suggests that recreation was used to humiliate and abuse people who were different from societal norms, such as people with disabilities, under the framework of amusement and entertainment. Historical observations seem to have much research evidence: In ancient Greek society until fairly recently, people with disabilities were used for amusement and for economic reasons and were banished from mainstream society. For example, Weir (1984) reported that children with disabilities in ancient Greece were regularly strangled, drowned, buried in dunghills, potted in jars to starve to death, or exposed to the elements (with the belief that the gods had the responsibility of saving exposed infants).

There is much greater historical evidence regarding how people with disabilities were perceived during the Renaissance in Italy (14th-17th centuries) and the Age of Reason in Europe and America (17th-18th century). Foucault (1965) wrote that during both eras, people with disabilities and people with mental illness were expelled from society. During the Renaissance, people with disabilities and mental illness were excluded from society under the banner of folly and sent out on a ship of fools to other lands. During the

Age of Reason, people with disabilities were confined to hospitals. However, the hospitals did not function as medical institutions oriented toward health; rather they were prisons. Foucault highlighted, for example, that in 1656 the Hospital General in Paris had confined 1 in every 100 people for economic reasons. Hospitalization caused people with disabilities to lose their rights, which created large groups of people whom the wealthy class could use for low-cost labor. Evans (1983) underscored how people with disabilities were banished from mainstream society, used for amusement, and exploited to make profit at the Bethlehem Royal Hospital. In particular, people with disabilities were exhibited for a price of about a penny every Sunday, which created annual revenue in 1815 of £400 (indicating an audience of approximately 96,000 that year). The visitor's curiosity was aroused by an attendant who would get inmates to perform dances and acrobatics with a few flicks of the whip. Entry was free on every Tuesday, and visitors liked to watch antics of a sexual or violent nature. Likewise, during the Age of Reason people with disabilities were often viewed as people without reason and as animalistic creatures (e.g., Foucault wrote of the *gryllos,* an animal with a human face consumed by desire) (Foucault, 1965). Using people with disabilities as entertainment was also reported among some Egyptian pharaohs and wealthy men of the Roman Empire (Welsford, 1935); Philip IV of Spain had a substantial group of people with disabilities who performed amusing acts (Evans, 1983).

A few examples show that recreation was used for inclusion or as part of a curative process during the Age of Reason. For example, concerts were provided at the Glasgow Royal Asylum for Lunatics to help people with disabilities and special needs gain some degree of self-determination (Bullock & Mahon, 2000). Foucault (1965) noted that movement, such as walking, running, and sea voyages, had a "normalizing" effect and helped people with disabilities gain stability in society.

1900s United States to the Present

Since the 1900s, governmental agencies, volunteer and nonprofit organizations, and private human services, along with other interdisciplinary movements and values, have contributed to a societal movement to provide services for people with disabilities (Richie & Alperin,

2003). Governmental services went from creating prisonlike hospitals to protect the public from "dangerous" people with disabilities to advocating on behalf of people with disabilities. However, the changes have been slow, and the history of the perceptions and treatment of people with disabilities in the United States is shameful and ugly.

In the early part of the 1900s, people who were different—such as people with disabilities or people from ethnic minority backgrounds (e.g., American Indians)—were banished from American society by being institutionalized and were viewed as dangerous and animalistic creatures or as economic objects. Trimble (1981) underscored how counseling and psychiatric interventions were used to banish American Indian people and assimilate them into "whitestream" culture. Likewise, people with disabilities were valued in certain industries that needed unskilled, low-wage workers (e.g., to clear forests for the forest industry) (Evans, 1983). People with disabilities were viewed as a social and economic burden, a parasitic and predatory class who were a menace and a danger to society because they had "criminal tendencies" (Evans, 1983).

The dominant societal discourse that people from minority groups should be excluded from society, including expert opinions of scientists and professionals, was the ideological vehicle that continued the institutional movement and drove the early-1900s practice of forced sterilization on people with disabilities in the United States. By 1926, 23 states had mandatory forced sterilization laws, and in 1927 the Supreme Court upheld the constitutionality of forced sterilization (Bullock & Mahon, 2000). An estimated 50,000 people with disabilities, or those labeled as defective, were sterilized in the United States between 1925 and 1955 (Evans, 1983). Bullock and Mahon (2000) underscored overcrowding and dehumanizing aspects of institutions during the first half of the 1900s; for example, it was common in institutions for people to wear soiled clothes for days at a time. As such, people with disabilities would often walk around institutions unclothed, thus reinforcing the stereotype and stigma that people with disabilities were deviant. Dower (1986) outlined how racist journalistic coverage of expert opinion of scientists during the Second World War (e.g., *Chicago Tribune, New York Times, Washington Post)* underscored the belief that Asian Americans should be excluded in society because they were subhuman (monsters, monkeys).

During the early part of the 1900s, some professionals, including community recreation leaders, advocated for inclusion of people who were outside of whitestream normality (e.g., immigrants, people of different ethnic and racial background, people with disabilities) and resisted the dominant societal view that people from minority groups should be hidden from society and confined to prisonlike hospitals and institutions. One such group was the women (and few men) at Hull House, with Jane Addams, a pioneer in community recreation (Edginton et al., 2006; McBride, 1989), as its leader. In September 1889, Jane Addams, Ellen Gates Starr, and Mary Keyser opened Hull House—a settlement house in a poor district of Chicago. Hull House, as most settlement houses, established agencies in city slums where residents provided human services and engaged in social action on behalf of people with special needs, including people with all types of disabilities (Schram & Mandell, 2000). In 1908, Addams (1908/2002) presented a powerful argument at the National Education Association conference that children with disabilities needed to be included in all aspects of society, and she provided case studies demonstrating how successful inclusive practices helped people with disabilities, their families, and the community. Numerous case studies and personal narratives describe how Jane Addams helped immigrants from different nationalities and ethnicities become included and integrated into mainstream society (see Bryan & Davis, 1990; Polacheck, 1989). Jane Addams advocated that people from all minority backgrounds be accepted and integrated into mainstream society and that recreation be used as one medium to foster inclusion. Dieser's (2005, 2008) historical research demonstrates how Jane Addams and Hull House programs used expressive arts, reading, social activities, and leisure education in an inclusive manner to help people from minority backgrounds.

During the 1950s, a social movement began to sweep throughout the United States to humanize institutions, and in the late 1960s and early 1970s, there was a societal move toward deinstitutionalization—the movement of people with disabilities and special needs out of institutions and into the community.

One of the important aspects of this movement was the development of the theoretical framework of inclusion and inclusive recreation—the normalization principle.

It is thanks to social movements from the past that people with disabilities living today enjoy greater acceptance and protective laws.

The Normalization Principle

The normalization principle was developed during the deinstitutionalization movement of the late 1960s and early 1970s and is a conceptual cornerstone to inclusive recreation, special recreation, and therapeutic recreation service (Bullock & Mahon, 2000; Howe-Murphy & Charboneau, 1987; Pedlar & Gilbert, 1997; Sylvester et al., 2001). The normalization principle provides the theoretical scaffolding for the development and implementation of numerous leisure education programs to benefit people with disabilities through inclusive recreation (e.g., Bullock & Howe, 1991; Mahon et al., 1996; Searle et al., 1995, 1998).

The principle of normalization was first defined by Nirje (1969, 1972) during the late 1960s and 1970s. Shortly after Nirje presented his ideas on normalization, Wolfensberger (1972) presented a reformulation of Nirje's work and defined *normalization* as the "utilization of means which are as culturally normative as possible, in order to establish and/or maintain personal behaviors and characteristics which are as culturally normative as possible" (p. 28). Wolfensberger and Thomas (1983) developed an evaluation system based on Wolfensberger's (1972) definition of normalization, called the program analysis of service system (PASS), in which individuality and personal autonomy were chief indicators that persons with disabilities were acting in a normalized manner. Wolfensberger (1983) extended his academic work on the principle of normalization to develop social role valorization. Wolfensberger (1985) argued that (1) normalization principles should use culturally normative means to offer persons with disabilities life conditions at least as good as that of the average person and (2) social role valorization incorporates the recognition that persons with disabilities should follow a social role that is valued by the majority of people in a society.

One concern pertaining to Wolfensberger's normalization principle is that it is not cross-culturally sensitive because the valuing of social roles is based on the majority of people (dominant culture) in a society rather than the regular circumstances and ways of life of the communities and cultures to which people with disabilities belong (Dieser et al., 2005). Perrin and Nirje (1985) highlighted how Wolfensberger's normalization principle advocated normative standards of behavior to which people with disabilities, regardless of culture, must conform if they are to be valued by the dominant culture in society, whereas Nirje's original work is based on egalitarian values that emphasize respect for cultural difference. Wolfensberger's normalization principle can be viewed as an inclusive approach where people with disabilities from different racial and ethnic backgrounds (e.g., African Americans) become assimilated into white culture. The following quotation from Perrin and Nirje underscores the normative white-centered approach of the Wolfensberger framework:

> At a PASS workshop held in Toronto in 1974, numerous examples along the lines [of normative standards of behavior] were presented. A black woman in attendance finally said: "You aren't talking about normalization, you are talking about making people [with disabilities] into upper-middle class whites!" . . . Wolfensberger's model of normalization in our view is excessively concerned with the notion of mentally handicapped people "passing" in society. (p. 72)

Perrin and Nirje's cross-cultural sensitivity to the normalization principle has led other professionals and academics to develop more cross-culturally inclusive recreation practices. For example, Hutchison and McGill (1998) argued that Wolfensberger's model of normalization focuses on understanding what a dominant culture values and that the model also suggests that successful integration requires people with disabilities to make personal adjustments that are valued by the dominant culture. Fox and van Dyck (1997) wrote that Wolfensberger's culturally normative concept of normalization brings differentiated people (e.g., American Indians) into a dominant set of values and structures of a white, nondisabled, individualistic society. For example, Peregoy and Dieser (1997) pointed out that many inclusive recreation programs require people with disabilities to maintain eye contact or develop independence but that the behaviors of eye contact and independent leisure functioning are primarily cultural behaviors that white people deem important (looking downward and not making eye contact is normal, respectful nonverbal behavior for people from American Indian backgrounds).

Dieser and colleagues (2005) wrote that to make inclusive recreation more cross-culturally sensitive, recreation leaders should abandon

Wolfensberger's model of normalization and instead embrace Nirje's normalization principle. This principle indicates that leaders should make available to persons with disabilities patterns of life and conditions of everyday living that are as close as possible to or indeed the same as the regular circumstances and ways of life of their communities (Nirje, 1992). To learn more about cultural competencies in inclusive recreation, see chapter 3 in this book and read about the therapeutic recreation multicultural competencies outlined by Peregoy and Dieser (1997), which follow.

Inclusion Recreation Leaders' Cultural Values and Biases

Attitudes and Beliefs

1. Recreation leaders must possess self-awareness and sensitivity to their own cultural heritage. Leaders must
   - identify cultures to which they belong,
   - understand the cultural heritage of interventions used,
   - challenge their attitudes and beliefs that do not support valuing of differences,
   - articulate positive aspects of their own heritage that provide strengths in understanding differences, and
   - understand the cultural heritage of recreation and leisure activity.
2. Recreation specialists must be aware of how their own cultural background and experiences influence their attitudes, values, and biases about psychological processes. These specialists must
   - identify the history of their culture,
   - identify social and cultural influences on their cognitive development, and
   - articulate the beliefs of their own culture and religious groups as they relate to differing cultures and the influence of those beliefs in a helping relationship.
3. Recreation leaders should recognize the limits of their multicultural competencies. Leaders must
   - recognize when and how their attitudes, beliefs, and values interfere with providing the best service to a client;
   - identify training that contributes to expertise in therapeutic recreation practice; and

- provide real examples of cultural situations in which they recognize their limitations and refer the client to more appropriate services.
4. Recreation specialists must recognize their own discomfort with differences between themselves and their clients in terms of race, ethnicity, and culture. Specialists must
   - recognize their sources of comfort and discomfort,
   - identify differences, and
   - communicate acceptance of and respect for differences.

Knowledge

1. Recreation practitioners must learn about their own racial and cultural heritage and how it personally and professionally affects their definitions and biases. Practitioners must
   - have knowledge regarding their heritage,
   - recognize their family's and culture's perspectives of acceptable and unacceptable codes of conduct, and
   - recognize their family's and culture's perspectives of recreation and leisure.
2. Leaders must understand how oppression, racism, discrimination, and stereotyping affect them personally and in their work. They must
   - identify their identity development and
   - be able to define *racism, prejudice, discrimination,* and *stereotype.*
3. Recreation specialists should understand their social impact on others. These specialists should
   - define their communication style and describe their verbal and nonverbal behaviors,
   - describe the behavioral impact of their communication styles on clients that are different from themselves, and
   - provide an example of an incident in which communication broke down with a client from a different culture.

Skills

1. Recreation practitioners must seek educational, consultative, and training experiences that improve their understanding and effectiveness in working with culturally different populations. These professionals must

- be able to describe objectives of at least two professional development activities that pertain to multiculturalism,
- develop professional relationships with helpers (both inside and outside of therapeutic recreation) from differing cultural backgrounds,
- maintain an active referral list and engage in professional and personal growth activities pertaining to working with clients from different cultures, and
- consult with other professionals regarding issues of culture.

2. Leaders must constantly seek to understand themselves as racial and cultural beings and to develop a nonracist identity.

Reprinted, by permission, from J.J. Peregoy and R.B. Dieser, 1997, "Multicultural awareness in therapeutic recreation: Hamlet living," *Therapeutic Recreation Journal* 31(3): 174-188.

Inclusion Recreation Leaders' Awareness of Clients' Worldview

Attitudes and Beliefs

1. Recreation practitioners must be aware of their own negative and positive emotional reactions to other racial and ethnic groups that may prove detrimental to the therapeutic relationship. Practitioners must
   - identify their common emotional reactions about people different from themselves,
   - identify how emotional reactions observed in themselves can influence effectiveness in therapeutic recreation intervention, and
   - be able to describe at least two examples of cultural conflict between themselves and culturally different clients.

2. Recreation specialists must be aware of the stereotypes and preconceived notions that they may hold toward other racial and ethnic minority groups. These professionals must
   - recognize their stereotyped reactions to people who are different from themselves,
   - consciously attend to examples that contradict stereotypes, and
   - recognize assumptions made concerning different cultures.

Knowledge

1. Recreation leaders must be knowledgeable about groups with whom they work. These leaders must be aware of the life experiences, cultural heritage, and historical backgrounds of the culturally different clients. In addition, recreation leaders must
   - be able to identify differences in nonverbal and verbal behavior of different cultural groups,
   - be familiar with at least two models of minority identity development,
   - understand the historical implications of contact with dominant society for various ethnic groups, and
   - be able to identify within-group differences of cultures.

2. Inclusion recreation leaders must understand how race, culture, and ethnicity can affect personal choices, help-seeking behaviors, recreation and leisure behaviors, and disorders. These professionals must
   - be able to draw on the literature to describe and provide examples of how different therapeutic recreation approaches may or may not be appropriate for a specific culture and
   - be able to describe one system of personality development and how this system relates or does not relate to at least two culturally different populations.

3. Practitioners must know about sociopolitical influences that impinge on the life of people from racial and ethnic minorities. Practitioners must
   - understand the implications of concepts such as internalized oppression, institutional racism, privilege, and the historical and current political climate regarding immigration, poverty, and welfare;
   - be able to explain the relationship between culture and power;
   - understand the unique position, constraints, and needs of those clients who experience oppression;
   - identify current issues that affect different cultures in legislation and social climate; and
   - understand how documents and affirmative action legislation affect society's

perceptions (both positive and negative) of different cultural groups.

Skills

1. Inclusion recreation leaders must become familiar with research relevant to their discipline that affects racial and ethnic groups. These professionals must
   - be knowledgeable of recent research regarding relevant topics (e.g., mental health, education, recreation and leisure, therapeutic recreation) related to different cultural populations;
   - complete workshops, conferences, and in-service training regarding multicultural skills and knowledge; and
   - be able to identify professional growth activities.
2. Recreation specialists must become actively involved with members of minority groups outside of the helping setting (e.g., community events, social functions) so that these specialists' perspective of minorities is more than just an academic exercise. Specialists must
   - be able to identify at least five multicultural experiences in which they have participated within the past 3 years and
   - actively plan experiences and activities that will contradict negative stereotypes and preconceived notions they may hold.

Reprinted, by permission, from J.J. Peregoy and R.B. Dieser, 1997, "Multicultural awareness in therapeutic recreation: Hamlet living," *Therapeutic Recreation Journal* 31(3): 174-188.

As social attitudes toward people with disabilities changed and the theoretical development of inclusive recreation progressed, inclusive recreation services began to increase across the United States as a result of the deinstitutionalization movement. For example, in the late 1960s and early 1970s, the Cincinnati Recreation Commission established inclusive recreation services for people with disabilities (see www.cincinnati-oh.gov/crc/pages/-5721-). The commission's goal is to provide opportunities for inclusion that reduce physical, programmatic, and attitudinal barriers.

Legislation in the United States and Its Influence on Inclusive Recreation

To understand why it is important for all people to be a part of and have access to community recreation programs and facilities, let us reflect on the relevant and significant accessibility legislation in the United States during the 20th century. As previously explained in this chapter, minority groups have historically been invisible within American life. For example, people with disabilities and elderly people were often unable to support themselves and were forced to be physically, socially, and economically dependent on others to care and speak for them. Even when marginalized people had family, friends, or professionals who truly cared for them, society in general viewed people with disabilities or elderly women and men in a paternal manner with biased assumptions, often institutionalizing them in special living facilities or hospitals, resulting in stigmatization and marginalization from the larger society (Calasanti et al., 2006; Zames-Fleischer & Zames, 2001).

The American system of law and litigation is unique. This legal system is based on the idea of separation of religious and secular spheres of authority, as was sought by early settlers who left Europe in order to worship freely. This concept of different spheres of authority would later lead to the idea of the separation of governmental powers into three coequal branches of government: executive, legislative, and judicial (Bogus, 2001). One aspect that makes the American legal system unique is that "the founders not only made the judiciary an independent branch of government; they consciously laid the foundation for federal courts to assume the power of judicial review—that is, to declare invalid laws enacted by Congress or state legislatures when, in the courts' judgment, violated the Constitution" (Bogus, 2001, p. 49). Civil rights disputes that require legal or equitable remedy are brought before either a state or a federal court. Given that the third branch of government determines the meaning and applicability of state or federal laws, litigation (lawsuits) plays an important role in American democracy and the incremental process of social change.

Federal legislation consists of acts passed by the U.S. Congress that are either signed into law by the U.S. President or subsequently passed by Congress after a presidential veto. The following section is a selected chronology of significant federal legislation and Supreme Court cases (see tables 2.1 and 2.2) that have affected the access of minority groups to American institutions and amenities such as public schools, transit services, hotel and restaurant accommodations, entertainment venues, employment opportunities, and recreation facilities.

For more than 90 years, the approval and interpretation of various federal legislative acts have increased marginalized people's physical and social access to their community, specifically affecting access to the workplace, school settings, housing opportunities, and recreation facilities

and programs. Unfortunately, inaccessibility continues for many people, particularly those with disabilities, as a result of society's disability-related ignorance and prejudices, which are deeply rooted in cultural attitudes. Like those before you who have set legislative precedent, you can design recreation facilities and programs to accommodate all people.

1918 to 1950

During the early part of 20th century, disabled veterans returning from World Wars I and II made disability visible in American life. Thousands of soldiers returned home with disabilities, and the U.S. Congress passed rehabilitation legislation in response to the soldiers' need to return to the workplace. The Smith-Sear Veterans Vocational

Table 2.1 Chronology of Selected Inclusion Legislation

Year	Legislation	Description of the act
1918	Smith-Sear Veterans Vocational Rehabilitation Act	Provided services for vocational rehabilitation of veterans disabled during World War I.
1920	Fess-Smith Civilian Vocational Rehabilitation Act.	Patterned after the Soldiers Rehabilitation Act; program for all Americans with disabilities for primarily vocational services; only for persons with physical disabilities.
1924	Indian Citizenship Act	Granted U.S. citizenship to all Native Americans.
1964	Civil Rights Act	Prohibited discrimination solely on the basis of race, religion, ethnicity, national origin, and creed (gender was added later) in public accommodations and employment as well as in federally assisted programs.
1967	Age Discrimination in Employment Act	Protected individuals who are 40 years of age or older from employment discrimination based on age.
1968	Architectural Barriers Act	Prohibited architectural barriers in all federally owned or leased buildings.
1972	Title IX	Prohibited exclusion, discrimination, or the denial of benefits, on the basis of sex, of any educational program or activity provided by schools or other institutions receiving federal financial assistance.
1973	Rehabilitation Act	Prohibited discrimination in federal programs and services and all other programs or services receiving federal funds.
1975	Age Discrimination Act	Prohibited discrimination based on age in programs or activities that receive federal financial assistance.

(continued)

Table 2.1 (continued)

Year	Legislation	Description of the act
1975	Education of All Handicapped Children Act	Required free, appropriate public education in the least restrictive setting. Later renamed the Individuals with Disabilities Education Act (IDEA).
1981	Telecommunications for the Disabled Act	Mandated telephone access for deaf and hard-of-hearing people at public places like hospitals and police stations. All coin-operated telephones had to be hearing aid–compatible by January 1985.
1986	Air Carrier Access Act	Prohibited airlines from refusing to serve people simply because they were disabled and from charging people with disabilities more for airfare than nondisabled travelers.
1988	Technology-Related Assistance Act for Individuals with Disabilities	Authorized federal funding to state projects designed to develop consumer-driven, statewide service delivery systems that increase access to assistive technology devices and services to individuals of all ages with disabilities.
1988	Civil Rights Restoration Act	Expanded the reach of nondiscrimination laws within public and private institutions, not just in the particular program or activity that received federal funding.
1990	Americans with Disabilities Act	Provided comprehensive civil rights protection for people with disabilities. Closely modeled after the Civil Rights Act and Section 504, the law was the most sweeping disability rights legislation in history.
1990	Individuals with Disabilities Education Act (IDEA)	Congress renamed the Education of the Handicapped Act and reauthorized programs to improve support services to students with disabilities, especially in the areas of transition (to adult life beyond high school) and assistive technology.
1994	Technology-Related Assistance for Individuals with Disabilities Act	Congress reauthorized the 1988 "Tech Act." The 1994 amendments emphasize advocacy, systems changes activities, and consumer involvement.
1998	Assistive Technology Act	Reaffirmed that technology remains a valuable tool to improve the lives of Americans with disabilities. Also affirms the federal role in promoting access to assistive technology devices and services for individuals with disabilities. Purpose is to support capacity building and advocacy activities designed to assist states in maintaining permanent, comprehensive statewide programs of technology-related assistance.
2004	Individuals with Disabilities Education Act of 2004	Amended the 1997 law. The new law preserves the basic structure and civil rights guarantees of IDEA but also makes significant changes to the law.

Based on A Chronology of the Disability Rights Movements. Online: http://www.sfsu.edu/~hrdpu/chron.htm

Rehabilitation Act and the Fess-Smith Civilian Vocational Rehabilitation Act, with its periodic amendments, made treatments and rehabilitation available after World War I, the Korean War, and the Vietnam War. These amendments helped civilians as well (Welch, 1995). Although Native Americans fought for the U.S. Army in World War I, the 14th Amendment did not apply to many indigenous people within U.S. borders. Unlike black soldiers, who were organized in segregated military units, American Indian soldiers were integrated throughout the Army. This assimilation of Native Americans who fought in World War I in part led to the Indian Citizenship Act of 1924 granting American citizenship to all American Indians born in the United States (Camurat, 1993).

Racial segregation of black people was the norm across the United States, especially in public schools, for the first 6 decades of the 20th century. In 1954, the case *Brown v. the Board of Education of Topeka, Kansas,* was heard by the

Table 2.2 Selected U.S. Supreme Court and District Court Cases That Influenced Inclusion of Individuals With Disabilities in the Community

Year	Lawsuit	Ruling
1954	*Brown v. Board of Education*	Supreme Court ruled that separate schools for black and white children are unequal and unconstitutional. This decision became a catalyst for the Civil Rights Movement.
1968	*Miller v. Amusement Enterprises, Inc*	Overturning a 1966 ruling, Fifth Circuit Court ruled that places of entertainment are prohibited from practicing racial discrimination under Title II of the Civil Rights Act. This case advocates inclusion rather than exclusion as a means of eliminating discrimination.
1972	*Mills v. Board of Education*	U.S. District Court ruled that the District of Columbia cannot exclude children with disabilities from the public schools. Similarly, the U.S. District Court for the Eastern District of Pennsylvania, in *PARC v. Pennsylvania,* struck down various state laws used to exclude children with disabilities from the public schools.
1974	*Halderman v. Pennhurst*	Filed in Pennsylvania on behalf of residents of Pennhurst State School and Hospital, this Supreme Court case highlighted conditions at state schools for people with mental retardation. It became a precedent in the battle for deinstitutionalization, establishing a right to community services for people with developmental disabilities.
1976	*Cherry v. Mathews*	U.S. Court of Appeals ruled that federal government was obligated to develop and promulgate a comprehensive regulation under Section 504 to prevent discrimination against persons with disabilities nationwide.
1976	*Disabled in Action of Pennsylvania, Inc. v. Coleman*	"Transbus lawsuit" ruling from U.S. Court of Appeals required that all buses purchased by public transit authorities receiving federal funds meet Transbus specifications (making them wheelchair accessible).
1979	*Southeastern Community College v. Davis*	Supreme Court ruled that under Section 504 of the Rehabilitation Act of 1973, programs receiving federal funds must make "reasonable modifications" to enable the participation of otherwise qualified people with disabilities. This decision was the court's first ruling on Section 504, and begins to establish reasonable modification as an important principle in disability rights law.
1985	*City of Cleburne v. Cleburne Living Center*	Supreme Court ruled that localities cannot use zoning laws to prohibit group homes for people with developmental disabilities from opening in a residential area solely because its residents are disabled.
1993	*Sacramento City Unified School District v. Holland*	9th Circuit Court affirmed the right of children with disabilities to attend public school classes with nondisabled children. The ruling was a major victory in the ongoing effort to ensure enforcement of IDEA.
1995	*Helen L. v. Snider*	U.S. Court of Appeals ruled that continued institutionalization of a disabled Pennsylvania woman, when not medically necessary and where there was the option of home care, was a violation of her rights under the Americans with Disabilities Act of 1990. Disability rights advocates perceived this ruling as a landmark decision regarding the rights of people in nursing homes to personal assistance services.
1999	*Olmstead v. L.C. and E.W.*	Supreme Court decided that individuals with disabilities must be offered services in the most integrated setting.

Based on A Chronology of the Disability Rights Movements. Online: http://www.sfsu.edu/~hrdpu/chron.htm

U.S. Supreme Court. The Court unanimously decided that segregation of children in public schools solely on the basis of race, even though the physical facilities of the segregated schools and other factors may be equal, deprived the children of the minority group equal educational opportunities and therefore was unconstitutional given equal protections of laws guaranteed by the 14th Amendment of the U.S. Constitution. This Supreme Court decision did not require desegregation of public schools by a specific time or abolish segregation in other public areas, such as restaurants, recreation facilities, and restrooms (Cozzens, 1995). This court decision, however, was the foundation of later legislation such as the Civil Rights Act of 1964, the Americans with Disabilities Act of 1990, and Title IX.

1964

There are similarities between the 1960s Civil Rights movement and other antidiscrimination legislation. After nearly a decade of nonviolent protests aimed at abolishing acts of racial discrimination against African Americans, Dr. Martin Luther King said it best on August 28, 1963 in his speech "I Have a Dream." Dr. King declared his vision of a just and inclusive society for all people. On July 2, 1964, Congress passed the Civil Rights Act guaranteeing basic civil rights for all Americans, regardless of race. The Civil Rights Act of 1964 required that recipients of federal funds, employers, and places of public use could not discriminate based on race, religion, or national origin. The first lawsuit to bring recreation facilities within coverage of Title II of the Civil Rights Act occurred in 1966 when a Louisiana mother, Patricia B. Miller, sued Amusement Enterprises for refusing to admit her children to Fun Fair Park because they were African American (Civil Rights Acts, 1969). The court's ruling upheld the purpose of the Civil Rights Act to eliminate discrimination as a broad national policy and provide a framework to increase "contacts between blacks and white during leisure pastimes" (p. 689). Unfortunately, when signed into law, the Civil Rights Act did not address discrimination based on disability status, sex, or age, but the act later served as the basis of the Americans with Disabilities Act, Title IX, and the Age Discrimination Act. As reflected by the Miller case, the purpose of inclusive recreation is to bring people of differing abilities together and increase their interaction with each other to enhance understanding of others' differences.

1968

The idea of equal environmental access for all people is the basis of the Architectural Barriers Act of 1968. This act set out accessibility standards and guidelines for agencies, organizations, and businesses to design facilities and programs that include people with disabilities in all facets of parks, recreation, and tourism. In the mid-1960s, discussion on what constitutes a disability or a barrier began with the passage of the Architectural Barriers Act, which required "any building constructed or leased in whole or in part with federal funds must be made accessible to and usable by the physically handicapped" (Architectural Barriers Act of 1968, p. 718). This act was not initially effective in enforcing accessible design standards in new construction or remodeled federally funded buildings. It did, however, establish the foundation for later efforts to provide physical accessibility, such as the Transbus Lawsuit in 1976. Based on the belief that transportation is essential for social participation, the ruling on *Disabled in Action v. Coleman* mandated that city buses be wheelchair accessible.

1972

Before 1970, women and girls were severely limited and virtually excluded from technical and academic high school and college courses such as auto mechanics, wood shop, science, and business. Only 1 in 27 high school girls played varsity sports in 1972. Today, 1 in 3 girls participates in high school sports. Since 1971, females participating in college sports increased by 456% (Lopiano, 2000; Thomas, 2008). Title IX of the Educational Amendments of 1972 ensures equal program access for women and men. Any federally funded educational institution must provide women with educational treatment, opportunity, and resources equal to those provided for men for most of its programs and activities. Although high school and collegiate athletics programs have the greatest influence on the public's impression of this act, the legislation provides women with access to areas of education such as academic study (e.g., math, science, medicine, and law), health care and dormitory facilities, nonsport activities and school clubs, and any other program or activity of alleged or historical gender inequality. There are a few program exceptions, such as social fraternities and sororities and gender-specific youth clubs like the Boy Scouts and Girl Scouts.

1973

The Rehabilitation Act of 1973 was a revision of the Vocational Rehabilitation Act Amendment of 1965. This act addressed the concept of equal access of people with disabilities through the removal of architectural, employment, and transportation barriers and further supported the rights of persons with disabilities through affirmative action programs established through Title V. There were four sections within Title V: 501, 502, 503, and 504. Sections 501 and 503 focus on affirmative action and nondiscrimination in employment by federal agencies, including federal government contractors and subcontractors. Section 502 established the Federal Architectural and Transportation Barriers Compliance Board, also known as the Access Board, to enforce the standards set under the Architectural Barriers Act of 1968. Today, the Access Board is the leading source of information on accessible design for built environments, transit vehicles, telecommunication equipment, and electronic and information technology. Americans with Disabilities Accessibility Guidelines have also been established for restaurants, libraries, hotels, motels, developed outdoor recreation areas, play facilities, and sports facilities. Specific guidelines for recreation facilities such as amusement rides, boating facilities, fishing piers and platforms, miniature golf course, golf courses, exercise equipment, bowling lanes, shooting facilities, swimming pools, wading pools, and spas can be found at www.access-board.gov/recreation/index.htm.

The power of the Rehabilitation Act of 1973 was its language, especially in Section 504. Key language in that section states, "No otherwise qualified handicapped individual in the United States, shall, solely by reason of his handicap, be excluded from the participation in, be denied the benefits of, or be subjected to discrimination under any program or activity receiving federal financial assistance." This act laid the groundwork for change but once again did not address the specific regulations necessary for implementation. Regulations for enforcement were still needed by the U.S. Department of Health, Education and Welfare (DHEW).

The spirit of inclusive recreation provides people from different backgrounds and abilities the opportunity and resources necessary for community relations, social contacts, educational advancement, and cultural enrichment that are considered the societal norm (Cohen, 2001).

Individuals picketing at the U.N. Plaza in front of the Federal Building in San Francisco, California on April 5, 1977.

Anthony Tusler, www.AboutDisability.com

Realizing the connection between social accommodations denied because of race and physical accommodations denied based on disability, James Cherry, a white student with a severe disability, started writing letters to DHEW in 1973 requesting assurances of Section 504 regulations. After 2 years of "an unresponsive response," Cherry filed a lawsuit against DHEW Secretary David Matthews. On July 19, 1976, a district court issued an order requiring that DHEW develop and enforce regulations for Section 504. The judge did not impose a specific deadline, however, and on the day that Jimmy Carter took office as President, David Mathews' appointment expired and Joseph Califano was appointed as secretary of Health, Education and Welfare (Zames-Fleischer & Zames, 2001).

In 1977, 4 years after Section 504 was passed, meaningful regulations had yet to be signed by the U.S. Secretary of Health, Education and Welfare. The American Coalition of Citizens with Disabilities (ACCD) announced that nationwide demonstrations would take place in 10 major U.S. cities if regulations were not signed by April 4, 1977. Joseph Califano, the U.S. Secretary of Health, Education and Welfare at the time, refused to sign meaningful regulations for Section 504. On April 5, 1977, disability rights activists demonstrated for the immediate signing of Section 504 regulation assurances. It was a dramatic event, particularly at the San Francisco Office of the U.S. Department of Health, Education and Welfare, where more than 120 demonstrators refused to disband. The San Francisco sit-in lasted until May 1, 25 days. Prompted by the belief that the provisions of Section 504 were an absolute and unequivocal civil right of those with disabilities, this action became the longest sit-in at a federal building to date. The historic demonstrations were successful and the regulations were finally signed (Cone, 1996). When asked what influenced this juncture in disability legislation, Frank Bowe, the director of ACCD in 1978, stated,

For a long time I had trouble answering that question because so many different factors and influences seemed to have combined to make it happen. Then, sometime later in 1977, I happened to be reading a book about the black civil rights movement, and I found the answer to that question. . . . This advisor [to Martin Luther King] said, "People think that revolutions begin with injustices. They don't. A revolution begins with hope." If you think about that, and you move back to the Spring of 1977, then you will understand that the reason disabled people came together and demonstrated as they did the Spring of that year was because they had hope." (Zames-Fleischer & Zames, 2001, p. 55)

1975

The Age Discrimination Act of 1975 and the Age Discrimination in Employment Act of 1967 (ADEA) set forth important civil rights legislation that intersects race, ethnicity, gender, class, and sexuality. These laws intend to eliminate age-related discrimination and inequality in federally funded programs and in employment. As a society, we have recognized social imbalances in race and gender and we need to think critically about how age also serves as an organizing principle of power and social grouping. Age inequality is different than race and gender equality, given that we typically do not change our race or gender, and age also serves as a social organizing principle as membership and power to a particular age group shift over a lifetime (Calasant et al., 2006).

In 1975, there were also notable lawsuits that led to passage of Education for All Handicapped Children Act of 1975 were *Pennsylvania Association for Retarded Children v. Commonwealth of Pennsylvania* in 1971 and *Mills v. Board of Education* in 1972. These rulings struck down all previous laws in Pennsylvania or the District of Columbia that excluded children with dis-

The Power of 504

Readers of this chapter are invited to watch *The Power of 504,* an 18-minute documentary video of the 1977 San Francisco sit-in at www.npr.org/programs/wesun/features/2002/504/.

abilities from public schools. These cases also set a precedent that educational services must be provided based on a child's need and not on the school's financial capacity for such services. In 1975, Congress passed the Education for All Handicapped Children Act, obligating public schools to provide a free and appropriate public education for children with disabilities. This legislation specified that every child has a right to education and introduced the concept of mainstreaming to ensure that education for children with disabilities takes place in the "least restrictive environment" and whenever possible in the same environment as children without disabilities unless a satisfactory level of education cannot be achieved given the nature of the child's disability.

In 1979, Francis Davis brought suit against Southeastern Community College for denying her acceptance into a nursing program based on the fact that she was deaf. The college alleged that the applicant was not "otherwise qualified," because even if she was provided accommodations for her hearing impairment, she would be unable to safely participate in the clinical training program. The court found no discrimination by the school, ruling that Davis' disability "did in fact prevent her from safely completing the program and performing in a nursing profession" (Brinckerhoff, Shaw, and McGuire, 1992, p. 419). However, the Supreme Court did conclude that the college did not have to lower standards to accommodate a person with a disability but that a program must make reasonable accommodations for a person who is otherwise qualified.

1980s

Activism among people with disabilities continued with a focus on the concept of "independent living," which stressed the development of services and resources that help people with disabilities to live and participate in their community in the same manner as people without disabilities. Precedent for independent living was set in 1974 with *Halderman v. Pennhurst*, which showed the nation the conditions that institutionalized people faced, and the ruling established the right to community services. The Telecommunications for the Disabled Act of 1981, Air Carrier Access Act of 1986, and the Technology-Related Assistance Act for Individuals with Disabilities of 1988 were a few of the acts passed during this decade that increased community and travel

access. Today, the development of technological devices continues to reduce physical and attitudinal barriers in all facets of parks, recreation, and tourism opportunities.

1990 to 2004

Closely modeled after the Civil Rights Act and Section 504, the Americans with Disabilities Act was landmark disability rights legislation that mandated that local, state, and federal governments and programs be accessible; that businesses with more than 15 employees make reasonable accommodations to workers who are disabled; and that public accommodations such as restaurants and stores make reasonable modifications to ensure access for persons with disabilities in the public. In terms of providing recreation services, "reasonable modification or accommodations" are considered individualized techniques and resources used to enhance program participation for a person with a disability without fundamentally altering a program. The ADA also mandated access in public transportation, communication, and other areas of public life. The intent of this act is for the full participation, inclusion, and integration of people with disabilities in society.

In 1990, the Education for All Handicapped Children Act was renamed the Individuals with Disabilities Education Act (IDEA). The act required that children and youth who receive special education and related services have educational goals and objectives designed to meet their individual needs. Other accomplishments directly attributable to IDEA include educating more children in their neighborhood schools, rather than in separate schools and institutions, and improving rates of high school graduation, postsecondary school enrollment, and post-school employment for youth with disabilities. IDEA has also supported the preparation of students for vocational success through new and improved transition programs.

In 1989, Rachel Holland's parents requested that Rachel, who had mental retardation and tested with an IQ of 44, be placed in a regular kindergarten classroom. Sacramento School District rejected the request and proposed a segregated placement for Rachel. While the district court was rendering an opinion for this 1993 case, *Sacramento City Unified School District v. Holland,* Rachel was enrolled in regular classes at a private school until the second grade. In assessing whether the school district was obligated to provide an inclusive placement, the courts asked the following questions: What are the academic and nonacademic benefits of inclusion? Does the presence of a child with a disability detract from the education of other children? Is the cost of services so unreasonable as to impair the other children in the district? The court found that Rachel had made substantial progress in the regular classroom and that there had been no detrimental effect on the regular education program, supporting the parents' request for a full-time placement of their child in a regular classroom with some modification to the curriculum and with the assistance of a part-time aide (Zames-Fleischer & Zames, 2001).

Finally, the Individuals with Disabilities Education Act of 2004 amended the 1997 version of this law. The new law preserved the basic structure and civil rights guarantees of IDEA but made significant changes to the law, calling for states to establish individual performance goals for children with disabilities that align with "adequate yearly progress" school objectives necessary under the No Child Left Behind Act of 2001.

Judicial Cases That Have Influenced Access to Recreation for People With Disabilities

Since 2001, the courts have heard a handful of disability lawsuits related to the provision of recreation services and facilities (see table 2.3). To meet the needs of people with disabilities for equality of opportunity in sports, tourism, hospitality, and outdoor recreation, the Americans with Disabilities Act outlines five areas of required access and accommodations:

- Title I pertains to employers with 15 or more workers.
- Title II applies to public entities, such as state and local government including public transportation systems.

Table 2.3 Recent Litigation Related to Recreation

Year	Litigation	Ruling or Settlement
2001	*PGA Tour, Inc. v Martin*	Supreme Court ruled that allowing Casey Martin to use a golf cart was not a modification that would fundamentally alter the nature of the PGA Tour. Therefore, the PGA Tour is prohibited from denying individuals equal access to its tours based on disability.
2005	*Spector v. Norwegian Cruise Line Ltd.*	Supreme Court ruled that foreign cruise ships must follow ADA if they are sailing in U.S. waters and docking at U.S. ports.
2005	*Tucker v. State of California of Parks and Recreation*	1998 lawsuit, heard by San Francisco District Court, alleged a denial of access to California State Parks due to access barriers. Settlement: Implementation of the Barrier Removal Plan Agreement, which includes a specific number of accessible trails including access to all of the park's recreational, educational, and interpretive programs.
2007	*Smith et al. v. Hotels.com*	Lawsuit, heard by California Superior Court for Alameda County, alleged discrimination against people with disabilities by refusing to guarantee reservations for wheelchair-accessible room. This lawsuit was the first of its kind in the United States. 2009 settlement: Hotels.com and Expedia.com will add features to their online travel reservation systems so that millions of travelers with disabilities can use their online services to search for and reserve hotel rooms that have the accommodations they need.
2008	*Celano v. Marriott International*	2005 lawsuit sought an injunction requiring Marriott to provide accessible golf carts at each of the golf courses it owns, operates, or contracts for usage. Judge of U.S. District Court of Northern District of California did not direct Marriot to provide the carts but told both sides to work out details to settle the case. Ocean Colony, which owns and operates a golf course in Half Moon Bay, California, was sued in conjunction with Marriot and agreed to provide two accessible golf carts at the Half Moon Bay Golf Links.

- Title III applies to private sector places where people meet or conduct business.
- Title IV applies to providers of telecommunications and information technology services.
- Title V contains supplemental provisions that clarify that both states and Congress are covered by all provisions of the ADA (DBTAC, n.d).

The goal of the ADA is access or modification to ensure the full and equal enjoyment of goods, services, facilities, programs, or accommodations, such as in the use of an accessible golf cart as decided in *PGA Tour, Inc. v. Martin* in 2001 or the recent *Celano v. Marriott International* decision. Barriers to the community participation of people with disabilities include institutional, educational, economic, and physical. The greatest barrier that any stigmatized or marginalized group faces is an attitudinal barrier.

Dennis Cannon, an early advocate for accessible public transportation, stated it best in his 1980 testimony before the U.S. Commission on Civil Rights. Mr. Cannon believed that if uninformed or negative attitudes were not a barrier for people with disabilities, then

> "when we perceive a problem such as transportation or accesses to recreation facilities or programs, the involved parties would sit down and work out a simple engineering or accommodation solution. The fact that authentic communication, assessment, and simple problem solving do not occur even when there is, indeed, a simple engineering or accommodation solution available is due to the attitudinal barrier of individuals or organizations, and not to the physical barrier." (Zames-Fleischer & Zames, 2001, p. 69)

Congressional laws reflect who we are as a society, and litigation raises questions and debate as to whether our laws have become misaligned with the rights that Americans believe they have. The social dynamic that occurs with review of Americans civil rights continues to have a transformative effect on our society (Still & Williams, 2005).

Summary

Understanding the history of a field, such as leisure services and inclusive recreation, is important because contemporary parks, recreation, and tourism professionals can learn from the past and be in a better position to provide beneficial outcomes. In the dark and hidden past, recreation was used to abuse, humiliate, and marginalize people outside societal norms. This history should not be forgotten, so that contemporary leisure professionals feel an ethical obligation to go beyond minimal standards in providing inclusive services.

An overview of civil rights legislation highlights that leisure professionals need to be aware of the importance of inclusive recreation services; however, we hope that readers will go beyond minimal standards and learn about cross-cultural dimensions of inclusive recreation. For example, leisure professionals should go beyond the minimal laws of the Civil Rights Act, Title IX, the Age Discrimination Act, and the Americans with Disabilities Act and focus on the spirit of these laws so that in-depth and broad inclusive services are provided. Likewise, leisure professionals need to learn about the social and cultural background of different groups of people so that cross-culturally appropriate inclusive recreation is provided.

Discussion Questions

1. Why is understanding the history of a field, such as inclusive recreation, important for contemporary professions in leisure services?

2. Explain how historically recreation was used to humiliate people with disabilities.

3. Explain why hospitals were places that confined people with disabilities.

4. Explain how people with disabilities were used as economic objects. To this end, provide actual examples of how this occurred during (a) the Age of Reason and (b) the deinstitutionalization movement in the United States.

5. Explain how Jane Addams and Hull-House provided some early inclusive programs in human services and leisure services.

6. Explain the positive and negative aspects of the deinstitutionalization movement in the United States.

7. Explain in your own words the spirit and intent of the Americans with Disabilities Act. What previous legislation helped shape the content of this particular piece of disability legislation?

8. How have recreation programs and facilities, parks, and the tourism industry been affected by the outcome of recent judicial cases?

9. What groups of people are discriminated against in mainstream society today? Is any legislation pending or are lawsuits under review that are specific to these groups of people?

10. Explain the similarities and differences between Nirje's and Wolfensberger's normalization principle.

11. Explain how the normalization principle has the theoretical standard or theory that created inclusive services and inclusive recreation.

Spotlight on Inclusive Programs

Public Policies of Sport and Leisure in Brazil

Rejane Penna Rodrigues, Leila Pinto, and Arianne Reis

National Secretary of Development of Sport and Leisure, Ministry of Sports in Brazil

To manage public policies in Brazil, it's necessary to know some of our country's characteristics. Brazil is the largest country in South America, with a population of more than 169 million habitants, of whom 81% live urban areas and 19% in rural areas. Brazil has 315,000 indigenous people, distributed among 562 indigenous territories and quilombo communities formed by descendants of refugee slaves. Today these indigenous people, like their ancestors, live in a precarious situation.

Even though Brazil has great natural wealth, the greatest biodiversity on the planet, and the world's largest forest, the Amazon forest, and even though the Brazilian economy—which is based on agriculture, livestock, fisheries, and mining—is strong, social problems here do not differ from those of other developing countries. Major Brazilian cities have pockets of poverty caused by displacement of people who seek work in construction and believe they will have a better life in cosmopolitan areas.

One of the challenges of public policy in Brazil is inspiring public participation in demanding laws that guarantee human rights and social rights, because we cannot speak of public policy outside of the relationship between state and society. Citizens need to seek a better quality of life and participate in democracy by attending national councils and conferences, a practice that has increased in Brazil in recent years.

Social rights are defined in Article 6 of the Federal Constitution of 1988, which states, "There are social rights to education, health, work, housing, leisure, security, social welfare, the protection of maternity and childhood, assistance to destitute" (Brasil, 1988).

Recognizing the economic and social inequalities in Brazil, but also enhancing the richness of its cultural diversity and respecting differences, the Brazilian government has implemented social policies that seek to include more people.

In 2003, still at the beginning of the first administration of the President Luiz Inácio Lula da Silva, the federal government created a specific body for sports and leisure: the Ministry of Sports. In 2004 the Ministry of Sports held the First National Conference of Sports with the theme Sports, Leisure and Human Development, involving 83,000 people throughout the country.

Since then, the Ministry of Sports has worked to ensure access to all Brazilian sports and leisure. Its main programs are designed to use sport as a practical tool for social inclusion, contributing to citizens' health and well-being, reducing inequalities, and redeeming values and principles. The Ministry of Sports is addressing these issues through various programs: the Program Sport and Leisure of the City (PELC), the Law of Incentive to Sports, the Second Time Program, the Bolsa-Athletes Program, the Program Painting the Freedom, and the Program Painting the Citizenship (Ministério do Esporte, 2009).

Program Sport and Leisure of the City (PELC)

To develop a proposal for public and social policy that meets the needs of recreational sports and leisure of the population, the National Bureau of Development of Sports and Leisure, part of the Ministry of Sports,

Photo courtesy of Rejane Penna Rodrigues.

Program Sport and Leisure of the City provides access to physical activities and games for persons of all ages and abilities.

created the Program Sport and Leisure of the City (PELC, 2009)

In addition to providing access to physical activities, games, and tricks for persons of all ages and abilities, PELC stimulates social coexistence, trains managers and community leaders, promotes research and socialization of knowledge, and advocates that public policy treat sport and leisure as the rights of all.

PELC began in 2003, in the office of the National Secretary of Development of Sports and Leisure, and mainly focuses on training and community development, triggered by the promotion of sport activities and leisure.

PELC seeks to generate new values rooted in the principles of intergenerational, collective work. The program uses actions and actors from different fields—sports, education, health, social development, and culture—to improve quality of life for a broad and more complex segment of the population (Ministério do Esporte, 2008)

PELC sponsors the following projects:

- PELC All Ages: Created to involve all ages (children, adolescents, young adults, adults, and elderly people) as well as people with disabilities and special educational needs in sports, entertainment, and recreational activities; developed by agreements with partners of the Ministry of Sports.

- PELC Healthy Life: Developed to provide sports, entertainment, and leisure activities that are appropriate for people 45 years and older; developed by partner agreements with the Ministry of Sports.

- PELC Pronasci: Created to help socially and economically vulnerable young people (ages 15-24 years) challenge injustice, social exclusion, and violence; improve their quality of life; and recover self-esteem through sports, recreation, and leisure activities appropriate for this age group; developed by partner agreements with the Ministry of Sports (PELC, 2009).

- PELC Network Cedes: Established to set up a national system of sports information and documentation, implementation of research policies in recreational sports and leisure, and promotion and dissemination of scientific events and publications (Rede Cedes, 2009).

Law of Incentive to Sports

The Law of Incentive to Sports (11.438/2006) allows individuals and businesses that sponsor or make donations to projects and sports to deduct these contributions from their income taxes by 1%. Projects are presented by the bodies to the Technical Commission of the Ministry of Sports, which evaluates them (Lei de Incentivo ao Esporte, 2009).

Second Time Program

The program is for children and adolescents in primary and secondary schools who are exposed to social risks. The program promotes access to sport and related activities in public spaces or community schools, with the main focus on sport education.

The Second Time Program works through partnerships between the Ministry of Sport and state and local governments, nongovernmental organizations, and national, international, public, private, and nonprofit groups (Programa Segundo Tempo, 2009).

Bolsa-Athletes Program

For highly talented athletes who have no sponsors, the Ministry of Sport provides financial support through the Bolsa-Athlete Program. This program

(continued)

aims to increase sponsorships for elite athletes, so they can devote time to training and competing and can fully develop their sporting careers.

Athletes interested in participating should verify whether they meet all prerequisites determined by law for their category of scholarship-athlete. After that, they must submit their application at the program site or by mail, by the date established by the Ministry of Sports (Programa Bolsa Atleta, 2008).

Program Painting the Freedom

This program promotes the resocialization of prisoners while in the prison system through the manufacture of sporting goods; this work provides a salary, gives the prisoners work experience, and can result in reduction of the prison sentence (Programa Pintando a Liberdade, 2009).

Program Painting the Citizenship

Program Painting the Citizenship provides people at social risk with jobs in factories that manufacture sports equipment, thus increasing the income of residents in poor communities and providing entry into the labor market. Income depends on production. The products made in the factories (balls, bags, nets, shirts, caps, and flags) are used by the Second Time Program, by the Program Sport and Leisure of the City, and in schools and social agencies throughout the country and abroad (Programa Pintando a Cidadania, 2009).

Award for Social Inclusion in Brazilian Sports and Leisure

In making this award, the Ministry of Sports recognizes scientific initiatives, technology, and pedagogy that influence public policy regarding social inclusion in sport and leisure. The award is sponsored by the Ministry of Sports on the agenda of Brazilian science and technology in partnership with social sectors (Prêmio Brasil de Esporte e Lazer de Inclusão Social, 2009)

The award has five categories:

Regional awards

Category 1: dissertations, theses, and independent research

Category 2: papers by graduate students and experts

Category 3: reports of public policy experience

National awards

Category 4: tests

Category 5: new media

Many programs of the Ministry of Sports maintain relationships with other federal agency programs, such as the Ministry of Education, the Ministry of Culture, the Ministry of Social Development and Combating Hunger, the Ministry of Justice, and the Ministry of Health, creating a multi-agency policy network.

This is a brief presentation of public policies for sport and leisure developed by the Ministry of Sports of Brazil. Space limitations have prevented in-depth discussion of our programs; further information can be obtained at www.esporte.gov.br or by sending an e-mail message to rejane.rodrigues@esporte.gov.br.

References

Brasil. (1988). *Constituição da República Federativa do Brasil.* www6.senado.gov.br/con1988/CON1988_05.10.1988/CON1988.htm

Lei de Incentivo ao Esporte. (2009). http://portal.esporte.gov.br/leiIncentivoEsporte.

Ministério do Esporte. (2008). Brincar, Jogar, Viver: Lazer e intersetorialidade com o PELC. Vol. 1, no. 1.

Ministério do Esporte. (2009). http://portal.esporte.gov.br.

PELC. (2009). http://portal.esporte.gov.br/sndel/esporte_lazer.

Prêmio Brasil de Esporte e Lazer de Inclusão Social. (2009). http://portal2.esporte.gov.br/premiobrasil.

Programa Bolsa Atleta. (2008). http://portal.esporte.gov.br/snear/bolsa_atleta.

Programa Pintando a Cidadania. (2009). http://portal.esporte.gov.br/pintando.

Programa Pintando a Liberdade. (2009). http://portal.esporte.gov.br/pintando.

Programa Segundo Tempo. (2009). http://portal.esporte.gov.br/snee/segundotempo.

Rede Cedes. (2009). http://portal.esporte.gov.br/sndel/esporte_lazer/cedes.

Building Cultural Competencies

3

Pamala V. Morris, PhD
Purdue University

" *People don't get along because they fear each other. People fear each other because they don't know each other. They don't know each other because they have not properly communicated with each other.* "

—Martin Luther King, Jr.

Learning Outcomes

After reading this chapter, learners will be able to do the following:

- Define the term *culture* and its characteristics in the United States and Canada.
- Clarify the concept of culture as a foundation for clearer thinking and discussion about one's own cultural assumptions as well as the dominant culture.
- Understand the levels of culture and their relationship.
- Identify the mechanisms of cultural change.
- Understand cultural influences on recreation and leisure.
- Define *cultural competence* and understand its importance in the field of recreation and leisure.
- Understand the importance of addressing cultural issues in serving a diverse clientele.
- Describe three dimensions of cultural competence; knowledge, awareness, and skill development.
- Discuss the relevance of Bennett's developmental model of intercultural sensitivity (DMIS).
- Understand the application of the Intercultural Development Inventory in relation to the DMIS.

There is a growing sense of urgency for citizens of the 21st century to increase their understanding of people from diverse cultural and ethnic backgrounds. From misunderstandings to intercultural conflicts, frictions exist within and between cultures. With rapid changes in global economy, technology, transportation, and immigration policies, the world is becoming a small, intersecting community (Diller & Moule, 2005). People find themselves in increased contact with people who are culturally different, working side by side with them. In the workplace and the community, different cultural beliefs, values, and communication styles are here to stay. It is not enough for people to become aware of and sensitive to cultural difference. Our changing world requires individuals as well as organizations to begin that visionary journey to become culturally competent.

Cultural competence is a process whereby people develop competencies in multiple ways of perceiving, evaluating, believing, and doing in order to communicate and interact effectively in diverse environments. This process is especially important for and in the best interest of those who provide services to the general public, such as recreation and leisure practitioners.

The demographics of the United States and Canada are dramatically changing, and central to these changes is a significant increase in diversity of ethnicity and culture. Significant demographic changes have been a trend since the early 1980s and are referred to as the "diversification" of America (Atkinson et al., 1993). The subsequent statistics convey the dramatic demographics well. Between 1980 and 1992, the relative percentages of population increase for ethnic groups were as follows: Asians and Pacific Islanders 123.5%; Hispanics 65.3%; Native Americans, Eskimos, and Aleuts 30.7%; African Americans 16.4%; and non-Hispanic whites 5.5%. These percentages represent not only a sizable increase in the actual numbers of people of color in the United States but also a significant decline in the relative percentage of whites from almost 80% to less than 75%. If this trend continues, it will not take many generations before non-Hispanic whites are a numerical minority of the population (Healey, 1995, p. 12).

Let's take a closer look at the projections related to Healey's prediction. For example, it is estimated that in 2020, the relative percentages will be non-Hispanic white 64%, Hispanic 17%, African American 13%, and Asian 6%. Although Native Americans and American Indians are projected to remain less than 1% of the population, actual numbers will probably triple during this period. It is estimated that by 2060, non-Hispanic whites will represent less than 50% of the U.S. population, and by 2100 Hispanics alone will represent 33% of the population and nonwhites 60% of the population.

Changes in population are primarily due to the increase in immigration and birthrates; however, because of large-scale immigration to the United States and Canada, we have witnessed important societal transformations, and these likely will continue. Immigration will have not only socioeconomic consequences but cultural implications as well. People will eat differently, dress differently, dance differently, think differently, and communicate differently because of immigration.

Immigration is reshaping societies across the world and will affect the lifestyle of every person. *Lifestyle* is defined here as "the distinctive behavioral expression of a characteristic pattern of values and beliefs" (Horley, 1992, p. 206) and as "the distinctive pattern of personal and social behavior characteristics of an individual or group" (Veal, 1993, p. 247). It has been suggested that an acceptable definition of lifestyle should also incorporate "intentional behavior or purposive activity" (Horley, 1992). In other words, people and groups will have some conception of what they seek to accomplish and the behavior that must be exhibited to achieve a specific outcome.

These lifestyle changes will have a direct impact on the way the general public identifies and participates in activities of necessity and activities of leisure. Lifestyle consists of, but is not limited to, a person's hobbies, interests, recreation and cultural activities, and work. It is crucial for professionals in the field of recreation and leisure to have a holistic picture of people's interests. A broader profile of customers will allow recreation professionals to tailor their services. Public sector recreation managers can provide better services by learning about how customers spend their leisure time. With general lifestyle information, recreation managers can better identify what services they should provide or expand. Wherever there is a need to design more effective outreach, communication, education, marketing, advertising or sales strategies, lifestyle information can be helpful. This is especially true when the information provided, about the services and programs offered, is targeted to match people's routine activities, interests, and needs (Gobster, 2002). Researchers studying the recreation and leisure field started to examine people's activities and interests in the late 1970s under the umbrella of "specialization" (Bryan, 2000). Since then research into specialization (and lifestyles) has broadened from looking at differences within a specific group (e.g., bird-watchers, immigrants, married couples, golfers; Bryan, 2000; Kalmijn & Bernasco, 2001; Petrick et al., 2001; Scott & Thigpen, 2003; Stodolska, 2000) to differences between specific groups (e.g., African American vs. Latino urban park users, skiers vs. snowboarders, participants who are blind vs. those who are low vision or sighted; Gobster, 2002; Vaske et al., 2000; Wolffe & Sacks, 1997).

This chapter introduces two major concepts, culture and cultural competence, the latter of which is also referred to as intercultural competence. In the context of the chapter, *cultural* and *intercultural* are interchangeable terms. All people have a culture that shapes their worldview and affects every aspect of their life. Understanding our own culture first and then the culture of others helps us understand why people behave in certain ways, how people perceive reality, what people believe to be true, what people build and create, what people accept as good or bad, and how people communicate and interact with other people. Culture influences communication, and communication influences culture: Different cultures may have different meanings for the same word or symbol, and many words and symbols have no direct translation. Therefore, vocabulary, slang, and dialects can cause people to misinterpret verbal messages and nonverbal gestures during daily interactions with people whom they consider different. This misinterpretation and misunderstanding can lead to the exclusion of people or groups of people who are culturally or linguistically different. If we are going to relate to and interact with clients from different cultural backgrounds, we must develop our ability to effectively communicate across cultures by moving toward cultural competence.

The principles for cultural competence outlined in this chapter apply to recreation and leisure practitioners in the United States and Canada in particular. To provide practical guidance, the discussion is confined to increasing cultural competence to benefit the practitioner as well as clients from culturally and linguistically diverse backgrounds, with an emphasis on developing culturally relevant programs for recreation and leisure pursuits.

Conceptualization of Culture

What is culture, and how does it affect our everyday lives and lifestyles? This question has intrigued scholars across many academic disciplines for decades. In the early 1950s, more than 160 different definitions of the term *culture* were identified (Kroeber & Kluckhohn, 1952). The term *culture* originates from the Latin word *cultura* or *cultus*, as in *agri cultura*," which means "cultivation of the soil." As Frielich (1989) noted, "Later, the word culture grabbed a set of related meanings: training, adornment, fostering, worship. . . . From its root meaning of an activity, culture became transformed into a condition, a state of being cultivated" (p. 2). People who were knowledgeable in history, literature, and the arts were said to possess culture. Today, culture refers to a diverse pool of shared knowledge, realities, and norms that make up the learned systems of meanings in a distinct society. These learned systems of meanings are shared and transmitted through everyday interactions among people within a particular culture and passed from one generation to the next. Culture has become a vehicle for groups of people to survive and adapt to their environment.

Culture is a way of life of a group of people, the behaviors, beliefs, values, traditions, and symbols that they accept, usually without thinking about them, and that are passed along by communication and imitation from one generation to the next. Culture consists of a host of interrelated dimensions, such as race, religion, ethnicity, age, gender, sexual orientation, socioeconomic status, geographic location, view of time, recreation and leisure activities, food preparation, communication patterns, and family structures (see table 3.1 on page 42). The intricate interaction between these dimensions shapes how people define themselves and has a profound impact on relationships and relationship building. Culture is something that people usually do not think about on a daily basis. In fact, many people think that culture is something that is possessed only by people of color or people from other parts of the world. Culture is an enigma. It contains both concrete and abstract components and is a multifaceted phenomenon.

Table 3.1 Cultural Considerations

Cultural aspect	Anglo-American perspective	Culturally different perspectives
Family name	• Father's surname is usually used.	• Father's and mother's surnames are used. • Family name may be written first, followed by the given name.
Family	• Nuclear families are the norm. • Marriage contracts can be terminated. • Families are usually small. • Families are based on partnerships. • Families are child centered.	• Extended families are the norm. • There are a variety of family arrangements. • Children are subordinate to parents. • Older children care for younger siblings. • Authority is delegated by maleness and age.
Social distance	• People keep a moderate distance for conversation. • People value their own space.	• People maintain close distance for conversation. • Close physical contact is welcome.
Age orientation	• Culture is youth oriented. • Young people think independently and make decisions.	• Elders are respected. • Tradition is important.
Education	• Education is universal. • Education is formal and technical. • Education increases social mobility and security. • Education is pragmatic. • Schools stress verbal fluency and application to life. • The teacher is an authority figure or surrogate parent. • The emphasis is on evaluation.	• Education is for those with high aspirations. • Education enables people to feel comfortable in mainstream society. • Education is an obstacle course to be surmounted. • Learning and doing are integrated. • Education stresses affective and psychomotor skills.
Individuality	• An individual shapes her own destiny. • Self-reliance is important. • A hero is a person of action. • People are self-disciplined.	• Anonymity is the norm. • People accept group sanctions. • People are dependent on others—families and peers. • Humility is valued.
Work achievement	• People work to make material and spiritual acquisitions. • Money is a symbol for success, intelligence, and power.	• People work to satisfy present need and physical survival. • People follow ways of their parents in terms of occupation. • Workers share a group spirit of achievement. • The workplace stresses cooperation. • The status quo is accepted. • Manual labor is respected.
Time	• People are conscious of time. • Society is governed by the clock and calendar. • People like routines. • The culture is future oriented. • People value efficiency and speed.	• People are concerned with joys of the present. • There is little concept of wasting time. • People control time. • People are more important than time.
Touching	• Touching is acceptable in some situations.	• Touching may be a sign of acceptance in some groups but in other groups may be offensive for religious or other reasons.

Cultural aspect	Anglo-American perspective	Culturally different perspectives
Smiling	• Smiling shows pleasure and acceptance. • Smiling is considered a sign of disrespect if one smiles when being reprimanded.	• Smiling is used to hide embarrassment and to show respect. • Smiling is used to interrupt conversation.
Eye contact	• Making eye contact shows interest in what is being heard. • Making eye contact shows honesty and demonstrates respect.	• Eye contact may be indirect in conversation. • Indirect eye contact is a sign of respect.
Work habits	• Independence is preferable to dependence. • Work is competitive.	• Dependence is sometimes acceptable. • Cooperation is preferred to competition. • Hard work is valued.
Teacher's role	• The teacher is respected.	• The teacher is highly respected. • The teacher is honored.
Teaching strategies	• Teacher-directed lessons and work are familiar.	• Teacher-directed activities are familiar. • The lecture method is commonly used.
Noise tolerance	• Silence is preferred to noise.	• Noise tolerance is high. • Noise shows enthusiasm. • Noise is preferable to silence.
Waiting one's turn	• Not waiting for one's turn in line and in conversation is considered impolite.	• People do not necessarily form an orderly line. • Getting service by getting the attention of the clerk may be acceptable. • Interrupting in conversation may show enthusiasm and interest. • Waiting may also show respect.
Use of language	• Language is used for direct communication. • Language is concise and clear. • Language is organized linearly.	• Language may be used to express feelings. • Language may be used to show status within a group. • Organization of language may be nonlinear, circular, or zigzag.
Listening style	• People listen to one person at a time.	• People are capable of listening to more than one person at a time even while talking.
Discipline	• Consequences should fit the misconduct. • Punishment is logical.	• Punishment may be effective. • Punishment may involve shaming. • Punishment may cause loss of face.

Chart compiled using information from a cultural chart by Yvonne Cadiz; a cultural chart by The Intercultural Development Research Association in Training Module III, "Recognizing Cultural Differences in the Classroom"; and a cultural chart by Louise Hart, Robin Matthes, and Verna Nelson in *Caring and Preparing to Meet the Needs of the Limited-English-Proficient Student* for Hillcrest Elementary School, Orange County Public Schools (John B. Martin, Principal).

Reprinted, by permission, from G. Kassing and D. Jay, 2003, *Dance teaching methods and curriculum design* (Champaign, IL: Human Kinetics).

These dancers have their own specialized language that they use with each other, their own norms and rituals. Every group, such as the one pictured here, operates in a cultural context where a common language is used to communicate effectively and work is carried out in unity to deliver a desired outcome.

Culture is both adaptive and maladaptive. Culture is the main reason for human adaptability and success (Kottak, 2008). People learn to adapt to their environment just as other mammals rely on biological means of adaptation (e.g., a chameleon will adapt to its surroundings by changing colors). People adapt to environmental stress in many different ways, such as traveling to warmer climates during winter months to offset the effects of the cold. Culture can also be maladaptive in that same environment, that is, it may endanger a person's health to the point of life-threatening conditions. For example, moving to and living in a warmer climate may be more comfortable, but the increased exposure to the sun could result in certain health risks.

Cultures are all-encompassing and dynamic systems that are constantly changing. Can you name one thing that is not encompassed by culture? The answer is no! All people have culture, and culture affects all aspects of our lives and lifestyles. Culture is powerful and is central to life. It is more than the food you eat, the way you dress, your language, your communication style, your work ethic, where you live, your ethnicity, and when, where, and how you worship.

Culture is education, the media, sports, music, mountain climbing, picnics in the park, visits with relatives, and more. It affects everything that you do, say, or imagine. To understand the ways that people view the world and their corresponding values and beliefs, we first need to understand the multidimensional nature of our own culture. Every human being must discern the breadth and depth of the individualized self in the quest to shed new light on the ethnic and racial selves of others.

Cultures Have a Shared Knowledge

As multifaceted phenomena, cultures are characterized as something that people learn and share. Cultures are symbolic, nature-oriented, integrated patterns of systems, and they can be both adaptive and maladaptive.

Culture is a learned, not inherited, trait. It is derived from our social environment and not through our genes. People are born and grow up being exposed to every aspect of their environment. The process by which people are socialized and by which they learn cultural traditions, norms, values, beliefs, and behaviors is called *enculturation*. Culture in particular is transmitted through learning and language. Learning or learned behavior can mean almost anything: what and where people eat, the way people dress, the way people speak. Whenever people brush their teeth, cross their legs, listen to music, attend a religious or secular gathering, and participate in recreation or leisure activities, they are exhibiting conscious and unconscious behaviors.

When people are born, they learn certain behaviors from their parents; later their interactions branch out to include siblings, grandparents, babysitters, peers, teachers, the media, and other sources of information. The world of technology enables people to reach out to a world community where the enculturation process deepens and enriches experiences. Enculturation is both a conscious and an unconscious conditioning process where people, from birth to death, achieve competence in their own culture, internalize their culture, and become thoroughly socialized. People internalize their dreams and expectations, the rules and requirements, not just for the larger society seen as a whole, but also for every specific demand within the whole. Society does whatever is necessary to aid any one of its members in learning proper and appropriate behavior for any given social setting and in meeting the demands of any challenge. Consequently, people learn respect for the symbols of the nation by reciting a pledge of allegiance and singing the national anthem. People learn to love and to befriend certain other people. They learn to work, relax, and become aware of their own rights, obligations, and privileges as well as the rights of others.

Culture is shared and transmitted throughout society in our day-to-day interactions and passed down from generation to generation. This transmission is a critical aspect affecting how people learn and share their culture with others. The process of sharing begins at birth and is a continuous life process. Sharing is conscious and unconscious. People share through cultural traditions such as stories, myths, ceremonies, rituals, and celebrations that are passed on through oral and written forms of communication. As members of a world community, people are able to share with a broad spectrum of people across the globe. Our sharing has no limits or boundaries. Advanced technology enables people to interact across cultures whenever they want or need to.

Cultures Have a Shared Reality

Cultures are integrated patterns of systems that consist of an assortment of interrelated traditions, values, beliefs, and customs. Culture is a series of cultural traits, individual items in a culture, such as a particular value, belief, tool, or practice. These cultural traits integrate to form cultural patterns defined as coherent sets of interrelated traits. For example, our values, beliefs, customs, traditions, communication styles, and institutions form patterns. Our traits are so connected and interrelated that if one trait is modified or altered, a new cultural pattern will emerge. A good example of this is the increasing cost of fuel, where fuel is a culture trait that has resulted in recent lifestyles changes. In the past, people with an average to high income could travel freely to different vacation spots to rest and relax. They were less concerned about the mode of transportation or the cost of hotels and restaurants. However, today people are forced to look at different vacation spots, alter their recreation and leisure activities, and use modes of transportation such as carpooling or riding the bus. The high cost of fuel has affected our lifestyles. A new cultural pattern has emerged as a result of one change within our system. Of course, the following is by no means an exhaustive list, but the new pattern includes eating out less often, reevaluating vacation spots, making fewer trips to the mall, and using community resources (e.g., parks) for inexpensive or even free recreation pursuits.

Beliefs and Values

The beliefs and values that a person holds influence how she processes the world around her. Cultures contain their own sets of beliefs and values that members of a culture work within.

Beliefs have been defined as a set of fundamental assumptions that people hold dearly without question. These beliefs can revolve around questions as to the origins of human beings and the concepts of time, space, and reality.

Values play an important role in shaping perspectives and prescribing the cultural lens that people in any society use to view the world. *Values* are combinations of attitudes that generate action or deliberate choice to avoid action (Kniker, 1977). In other words, values determine a person's choices and are the foundation for the actions people choose to take or avoid. Values are abstract ideas, positive or negative, that represent a person's beliefs about ideal modes of conduct and ideal terminal goals (Rokeach, 1972). People use their values to pass judgment on people from other cultures.

Cultures teach their individual members to share certain values. These shared values or set of characteristics are considered core values, which are defined as key, basic, or central values that integrate each culture and help distinguish it from others. Many of the core values that have permeated the American culture for generations can be found within the U.S. Constitution, such as rights to freedom of speech, press, religion, assembly, and private association and the rights to life, liberty, property, and the pursuit of happiness. Different sets of values can be found as patterns of attitudes and behavior in other cultures.

Symbols

Culture uses symbols to help people understand and interpret their surroundings as well as the actions and utterances of other members of their society. To understand a culture, we must have in-depth knowledge of the values and meanings of its core symbols. A symbol is something verbal or nonverbal in a language or culture that comes to stand for something else. There is no obvious, natural, or necessary connection between the symbol and that which it symbolizes (Kottak, 2008). These interpretations form a shared cultural system of meaning (i.e., understandings shared, to varying degrees, among members of the same society).

Symbols are often linguistic. There are also myriad nonverbal symbols, such as flags, which stand for various countries. Another example is the use of holy water as a symbol of Roman Catholicism. The association between a symbol and what is symbolic is revered and has become an integral part of rituals within the Roman Catholic culture (Kottak, 2008).

Orientation to Nature

A culture's orientation to nature is the role people assign to their natural environment. Orientations to nature have much to do with how we conduct our day-to-day lives; therefore, nature is at the center of our existence and survival. Cultures may seek to master nature, accept and be subjugated by it, or live in the most effective harmony with it. Humans from the beginning have been besieged by natural elements: wind, floods, fire, cold, earthquakes, hurricanes, famine, pests, and predators (Trompenaars & Hampden-Turner, 1998). Survival has meant acting against and with the environment in ways to render it both less threatening and more sustaining (Trompenaars & Hampden-Truner, 1998).

People interact with their environments daily as a way to survive. People have to eat, but culture teaches what, when, where, and how to eat. As an example, in Japan, people are taught to drink green tea during each meal and to eat a serving of salad at breakfast, whereas for many British people eating fish for breakfast is the norm. In the United States and Canada, people eat a variety of different foods for breakfast.

Cultures Have Shared Norms

Cultural norms are the collective expectations of what constitutes proper or improper behavior in a given situation (Olsen, 1978). These norms direct the scripts that people and organizations follow in certain situations. Although cultural beliefs and values are deep seated and invisible, norms can be readily inferred and observed through behaviors (Ting-Toomey, 1999). Cultural traditions, beliefs, and values intersect to influence the development of collective norms in a culture. The average person has limited awareness of different cultural norms and rules that are prescribed as well as hidden. With limited awareness of each other's cultural differences, people can undoubtedly fall into unintentional situations of conflict. Two or more people engaging in some type of interaction may not be aware of violating another culture's norms and values.

Levels of Culture

As a result of the increased diversification of society in the United States and Canada, it is necessary to understand the different levels of culture that exist. Cultures can be larger or smaller than nations, so cultures can be defined in terms of three different levels: international culture, national culture, and subculture or microcosm.

International culture extends beyond and across national boundaries. Because we live in a world community, many cultural traits and patterns across nations have become international in scope and flavor. This internationalization has spread through technology, immigration, colonization, and the expansion of multinational organizations. For example, the United States, Canada, Great Britain, and Australia share certain culture traits as a result of shared linguistic and cultural heritage from British founders.

National culture refers to experiences, beliefs, customs, values, and norms shared by people who have been socialized within the same nation (e.g., the United States or Canada); however, within each nation there are subcultures or microcosms of the national culture.

The term *microcosm* has a more positive tone than *subculture* because the prefix *sub* connotes "lower than," which can be offensive and devaluing in nature. Microcosms are the diverse cultural patterns and traditions associated with smaller groups that exist within the same nation (i.e., individuals, family structures, organizations, institutions, regions, socioeconomic groups, religious groups, and any other cultural unit). The microcosms within nations have shared cultural traits and patterns as well as traits and patterns that are specific or unique to a group member; however, as a result of this uniqueness within and between groups, culture is usually contested. In other words, because different groups in society hold different values and beliefs, they often struggle with each other over whose ideas, values, and beliefs are more acceptable. Although people who live in the same society (e.g., a nation) share cultural traditions, cultures have internal diversity. This internal diversity provides the basis for the discussion in this chapter.

Culture Is Analogous to an Iceberg

An iceberg is a useful and effective metaphor to help us understand cultural interactions, cultural perspectives, and cultural conflicts. As an iceberg floats in the water, you can see a little of it, in the same way that you can see how people behave on the surface. When you look at a person or a group you really only see and hear the outer layer or surface culture, consisting of their cultural artifacts (e.g., fashion, trends, pop music, art, language) and verbal and nonverbal symbols. However, the most important part of our culture, the part below the waterline that cannot be seen, is invisible to the human eye and is referred to as *deep culture*. The iceberg metaphor demonstrates that approximately 10% of who people are as individuals can only be seen above the waterline. The top of the iceberg is supported by a much larger part, approximately 90%, that is below the waterline and, therefore, is invisible. Thus, the 90% of culture that cannot be seen is the powerful foundation on which the visible aspects of culture are constructed. The deep layers (e.g., traditions, beliefs, values) are hidden from our view.

The visible parts of culture are just expressions of its invisible parts. Unfortunately, people cannot immediately see the foundations or building blocks these parts rest upon. Therefore, it is difficult at times to understand and interact with people from different cultural backgrounds and experiences. Too often, this lack of understanding can cause individuals and groups to unintentionally or intentionally exclude others.

The key is to develop an inquiring mind, one that seeks to become aware of the part of culture that lies below the surface or waterline. Once people become aware of how they have internalized the patterns of their cultural upbringing and experiences, they are better able to comprehend the value and significance of their own cultural heritage and worldview as a starting place for understanding others who are culturally different.

Culture of Domination

Every society contains cultural influences that affect the way people live and communicate. One cultural influence that has had a positive or negative impact on individuals as well as groups is the culture of domination. The culture of domination is the extent to which individuals and groups of people exercise power over others. Power is defined as the ability to control or exert authority. Some people have power as a result of personal characteristics (e.g., charismatic personalities). Others have power because of wealth, influence, or personal connections. How is this culture of domination developed?

One of the most pervasive paradigms instrumental in developing a culture of domination has been ethnocentrism. Ethnocentrism is a tendency to view one's own culture as superior and to apply one's own cultural standards when judging the behavior and beliefs of other cultures. Ethnocentrism contributes to social solidarity, a sense of value and community among people who share a cultural tradition (Kottak, 2008). People maintaining this paradigm may regard the behavior of others as weird, immoral, and unacceptable. Ethnocentrism promotes assimilation where people from other cultures are expected to go through an adaptive process in which they blend into the mainstream culture. This way of

Cultures can change, adapt, and grow to take in new traits from other cultures, such as the practice of yoga, which originated in India but has become a widely accepted exercise for people all over the world.

thinking and behaving can have a negative effect on people who have little or no power and can result in exclusion.

One contrasting viewpoint is cultural relativism. Cultural relativism advocates being nonjudgmental, understanding different cultural and ethnic value systems, and considering them as equal. This viewpoint has been challenged because it infers that ethical and moral actions of different cultures warrant respect regardless of whether they are acceptable in our own culture. What do you think?

Instruments of Cultural Change

Cultures are not static: They are dynamic systems. One instrument of change is diffusion or borrowing of traits between cultures. Diffusion can be direct, indirect, or forced. An example of direct diffusion is the result of cultures' trade agreements (i.e., importing and exporting goods). One example of indirect diffusion in today's society is the sharing and spreading of cultural traditions through the mass media and advanced information technology. Diffusion is forced when a culture of domination is prevalent and the dominant culture imposes its customs on

people who are subjected to societal oppression and subordination (Kottak, 2008).

Acculturation is another instrument of change that affects our society. Acculturation takes place when people adapt to a new environment and have continuous direct contact. In acculturation, both cultures share and each group retains its unique identity.

Globalization is instrumental in changing culture. Globalization includes diffusion, acculturation, and immigration; it promotes change across boundaries, helping nations of people understand that they live in a world that is interconnected and interdependent.

Theoretical Framework

Two theories can serve as guidelines for understanding who we are and how we see the world and make sense of it: cultural identity development and the constructivist theories. The cultural identity theory refers to the process of learning to identify with larger groups such as families, peers, and interest groups and understanding their way of life. Our identities are shaped from birth until we die. A wide range of socializing factors contribute to a person's cultural identity development: families, peer groups, religious and spiritual groups, and the media. The list of socializing factors is by no means exhaustive. Identity development is not a straightforward process and will vary from group to group and person to person. How did you see yourself and others when you started school? How has your identity continued to evolve through adolescence and now your college years? The following key assumptions are important to keep in mind as your cultural identity continues to develop:

- Increasing mobility of people throughout the world will continue to affect the development of cultural identities.
- Identity development evolves through sequential shifts or stages of consciousness toward greater complexity, inclusiveness, and differentiation.
- The goal of identity development is liberation from internalized oppression or internalized domination.
- Individual interactions within groups as well as between groups are affected by differences in levels of consciousness or world views.

Constructivist theory, based on scientific study, is derived from the field of epistemological psychology and describes how people construct their reality and make sense of the world. Constructivist theorists have proven that people construct their own understanding and knowledge of the world through experiencing things and reflecting on those experiences. When we encounter something new, we have to reconcile it with our previous ideas and experiences, maybe changing what we believe or maybe discarding the new information as irrelevant. As individuals, we actively create our own knowledge; therefore, our knowledge grows when we ask questions, explore, and assess who we are and what we know.

Bennett's developmental model of intercultural sensitivity, discussed in the next section, is grounded in constructivism. Bennett used concepts from cognitive psychology and constructivism as he organized the data collected from years of observation into the six developmental stages of increasing sensitivity to cultural difference.

Model of Intercultural Sensitivity

There are many widely used cultural and intercultural developmental competence models in the field of intercultural communication. One most widely used model is Bennett's developmental model of intercultural sensitivity (DMIS). The DMIS is a stage model developed by Dr. Milton Bennett as a framework to explain the experience of people he observed over the course of months and years in intercultural workshops, classes, exchanges, and graduate programs. The underlying assumption of the model is that as one's experience of cultural difference becomes more sophisticated, one's competence in intercultural relations potentially increases. (See figure 3.1.)

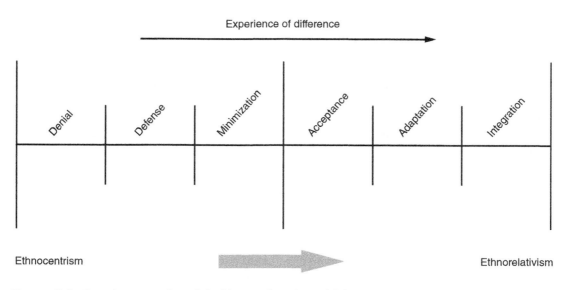

Figure 3.1 Developmental model of intercultural sensitivity.

Reprinted, by permission, from M. J. Bennett, 1986. "A developmental approach to training for intercultural sensitivity," *International Journal of Intercultural Relations* 10(2): 179-196. © Milton J. Bennett. www.idrinstitute.org.

Dr. Bennett identified two distinct levels within the model, ethnocentric and ethnorelative, and six stages or worldviews that fall along a unidirectional continuum. Both distinct levels each contain three stages: denial, defense, and minimization for the ethnocentric level; and acceptance, adaptation, and integration for the ethnorelative level. Bennett assumed that each stage was indicative of a particular worldview structure and that certain kinds of cognitive processing, attitudes, and behaviors would typically be associated with each such configuration of worldviews. In other words, the DMIS is not a model of attitude change or of skill acquisition. Rather, it is a model of the development of worldview structures along a continuum.

The first distinct level in the DMIS is ethnocentric, meaning that one's own culture is experienced as central to reality in some way. At this level there are three stages or worldviews: denial, defense, and minimization. In the denial stage, one's own culture is experienced as the only real one, and consideration of other cultures is avoided by maintaining psychological or physical isolation from differences. In the defense stage, one's own culture (or an adopted culture) is experienced as the only good one and is experienced as universal, so that despite acceptable surface differences with other cultures, deep down those cultures are seen as essentially similar to one's own. With the minimization stage, the worldview overgeneralizes similarities between self and other, allowing cultural differences to be trivialized and therefore considered harmless. Minimization acts as a kind of transition between the polarization of difference in the defense stage and the nonevaluative recognition of difference in the acceptance stage (Bennett, 1998).

The second distinct level in the DMIS is ethnorelative, meaning that one's own culture is experienced in the context of other cultures. At this level Bennett identified three stages or worldviews: acceptance, adaptation, and integration. In the acceptance stage, other cultures are experienced as equally complex but different constructions of reality. In adaptation, one has the ability to shift perspectives in and out of another cultural worldview; therefore, one's experience potentially includes the different cultural experience of someone from another culture. Integration is considered one's experience of self and is expanded to include the moments in and out of different cultural worldviews.

The ethnocentric stages can be seen as ways of avoiding cultural difference, either by denying its existence, by raising defenses against it, or by minimizing its importance. The ethnorelative stages are ways of seeking cultural difference, either by accepting its importance, by adapting one's perspective to take it into account, or by integrating the whole concept into a definition of one's identity (Bennett, 1986, 1993).

Intercultural Development Inventory

Using the theoretical framework of the DMIS, Bennett constructed the Intercultural Development Inventory (IDI) to measure the orientations toward cultural differences. The IDI is a 50-item (with additional demographic items) paper-and-pencil measure of intercultural competence. The IDI meets standard scientific empirical criteria for the valid and reliable measurement of constructs as those described in the developmental model of intercultural sensitivity. The inventory is not to be confused with the model itself. Rather, its major purpose is to provide an empirical method for assessing or profiling respondents in terms of the general orientations toward cultural differences (Hammer et al., 2003). Do you have a strategy in place that will help you engage in opportunities to experience cultural difference?

Process and Development of Cultural Competence

Developing cultural and intercultural competence is an ongoing and challenging process. Like gaining any other competency or skill, developing cultural sensitivity and skill requires intentional effort and practice. A culturally sensitive person needs to learn more about how communication style and perspectives are influenced by cultural upbringing and lived experiences.

Unless people understand how culture influences communication, they may be unable to effectively communicate with others who are culturally and linguistically different. As an important part of this ongoing process, people need to have a deep understanding of self in relation to cultural difference; therefore, this section defines cultural competence, its importance, and its dimensions.

What Is Cultural Competence and Why Is It Important?

As noted previously, the concept of individuals' and organizations' becoming culturally and interculturally competent is an ideal toward which to strive. The definition of cultural competence is quite simple: the ability to effectively and appropriately communicate and interact in diverse environments. Cultural competence is a "set of congruent behaviors, attitudes, and policies that come together in a system, agency, or among professionals and enable that system, agency, or those professional to work effectively in cross-cultural situations" (Cross, 1988, p. 13). It is not a new idea. It has been called "ethnic sensitivity practice" (Devore & Schlesinger, 1981), "cross-cultural awareness practice" and "ethnic competence" (Green, 1982), and "ethnic minority practice" (Lum, 1986) by human service providers. Cultural competence has also been referred to as "intercultural communication" (Hoopes, 1972) by those working in international relations and as "cross-cultural counseling" (Petersen et al., 1989) and "multicultural counseling" (Ponterotto et al., 1995).

People in the 21st century will find it difficult to function if they are psychologically bound by outdated and narrow assumptions about their neighbors. To thrive, even to survive, in this complicated world, people need to learn how to function in many different cultural contexts, to recognize and respect different histories and perspectives, and to work together to create a more just world that can take care of all its people, its living creatures, and its land (Derman-Sparks, 1993).

A variety of dimensions of cultural and intercultural competence could be addressed here, but I have identified three very important dimensions that have emerged from the literature as being significant and critical for people beginning their journey toward competence. Knowledge, awareness, and skills are the three dimensions discussed in this section.

Knowledge

An effective and culturally competent system must begin with a set of unifying values, or what might be called assumptions, about how to best educate diverse communities. These values share the notion that being culturally different is positive, that education or program development must be responsive to specific cultural needs, and that appropriate interactions must be offered in a manner that empowers people. A culturally competent system achieves the following (Cross et al., 1989):

- Respects the unique, culturally defined needs of represented populations.
- Acknowledges culture as a predominant force in shaping behaviors, values, and institutions and that culture has an impact on education.
- Views natural systems (family, community, church, healers) as primary mechanisms of support for diverse populations.
- Recognizes that the concepts of family, community, and the like are different for various cultures and even for subgroups within cultures.
- Understands that ethnic minorities are usually best served by persons who are part of or in tune with their cultures.
- Educates members of society in the context of their social status, which creates unique educational issues for them, including issues related to self-esteem, identity formation, isolation, and assumptions about the role of recreation and leisure.
- Recognizes the thought patterns of non-Western people.
- Respects cultural preferences that value process rather than product and harmony or balance within one's life rather than achievement.
- Recognizes that taking the best of both worlds enhances the capacity of all.
- Understands when values of nondominant cultures are in conflict with dominant society values.

The basic assumptions mentioned here are not necessarily focused on the skill areas that people need to become culturally competent. Therefore, two critical skills, communication and conflict management, are addressed later in the section on skills.

Awareness

Awareness and acceptance of differences comprise the first step that individuals and organizations should take when moving toward becoming culturally competent. It is impossible to appreciate and understand other cultures if you lack a deep understanding of your own culture. One very important skill area for individuals and organizations is self-awareness. "Many people never acknowledge how their day-to-day behaviors have been shaped by cultural norms and values and reinforced by families, peers, and social institutions. How one defines *family*, identifies desirable life goals, views problems, and even says hello is influenced by the culture in which one functions" (Cross, 1988, p. 2). Increasing self-awareness is not an easy task because it requires us to probe deeper into our own ethnic and personal values and beliefs and increase our understanding of the complexity of layered identities and multiple ethnic cultural group memberships. This task will be a lifelong journey as we grow and evolve.

Understanding cultural effects on participation in recreation and leisure is an important aspect of awareness. The diversification of the United States and Canada will continue to affect communities and organizations. There will be an increased need for recreation and leisure professionals to develop programs and activities for different cultures (Godbey, 1991). Ignoring cultural variation as a result of a lack of contact with various cultures outside of our own is a process of being culturally encapsulated (Pedersen, 1994). Parks and recreation education programs that ignore cultural variation in curriculum development and program design contribute to the process of cultural encapsulation.

The U.S. National Park Service has become aware that ethnic minorities are largely absent from most major national parks. Goldsmith (1994) suggested that the absence of ethnic minorities is related to three variables:

- Famous parks are isolated from culturally diverse population centers.
- Visitation has been traditionally confined to upper-class, select groups.
- Ethnic minorities do not see themselves mirrored in park service employees.

The National Park Service (NPS) has become aware of the lack of ethnic minorities visiting national parks and has implemented strategies to increase the visitation of these groups. The history of the National Park Service illustrates cultural encapsulation. Culturally relevant programs and more diverse employees in park and recreation education programs may help prevent cultural value conflicts. Until recently, the National Park Service evaded alternative realities of ethnic minorities, and training programs mirrored the values of dominant groups in American society. However, in the last couple of decades, there has been a concerted effort by NPS to shift the traditional paradigm of cultural encapsulation to implementation of culturally relevant programs. For example, parks now include culturally relevant sites such as Japanese interment camps and there is an ongoing effort to highlight approximately 25 sites within the National Park System that preserve and interpret African-American history. In addition to these contemporary initiatives, the former NPS director under Reagan and Bush was black and is now serving as an advisor to President Obama.

Skills

Skill development is an important component of cultural competence. Multicultural skills allow people to effectively apply the multicultural awareness and knowledge they have internalized. Central to those skills is the ability to communicate across cultures and understand how culture influences the content as well as the verbal and nonverbal aspects of communication.

Function of Language

Cultural value orientations drive the use of language in everyday life. Language infiltrates the social experience within a culture so intensely that neither language nor culture can be understood without knowledge of both. To understand a culture deeply, we have to understand the culture's language. To understand language in context, we need to understand the fundamental value and belief systems that drive the use of particular language under certain situations. Language is the key to the heart of culture. It consists of two components: verbal and nonverbal communication.

Verbal As discussed earlier in this section, communication is a key ingredient in becoming culturally competent. Culture affects communication and communication affects culture. Through communication, culture is created, passed down, and modified from one generation to the next. Communication is necessary to define cultural experiences. Cultural communication shapes the implicit theories we have about appropriate human conduct and effective human practices in a given sociocultural context (Ting-Toomey, 1999).

Ryan Benson

Strength is not determined by physical capacity; it comes from an indomitable will.

Background Information

Education

Associate degree in physical education and sports studies at Vincennes University

Credentials

*Certified personal trainer *CPR/first aid certified

Career Information

Position Fitness manager

Organization Complete Fitness Solutions

Job Description My job is to educate members about the benefits of exercise and nutrition and help them create a healthy lifestyle. This entails everything from creating meal plans, constructing fitness plans, and helping people deal with the emotional stresses that stem from believing that they are not physically fit. I recommend and sell individualized personal training programs and pair members with the most qualified and compatible personal trainer based on their needs.

Career Path Upon graduation from college, I began my career as a personal trainer at Bally Total Fitness. I quickly developed a reputation as a high-energy trainer whose top priority was results for the clients. In a matter of months I became the head trainer and began developing a client base that became a very useful networking tool and advanced my career in the health and fitness field. A couple of years later I was offered the opportunity to become an assistant manager with L.A. Fitness/Body of Change. After continuing to produce at a high level and establish myself in the Indianapolis market, I was then offered

the position of personal training manager with Anytime Fitness. These years of continuing education, hands-on training, and skills learned have led me to where I am today.

What I Like About My Job I love everything about my job. My primary reason for choosing this occupation was that I love to help people. Seeing the joy on a person's face who has not only lost weight but added years and quality to her life gives me a feeling of euphoria. A fitness club is the ultimate working environment. I'm able to do the things I love to do and have fun doing them.

Career Ladder This is definitely an intermediate stop on my career ladder. Now that I am a fitness manager of one club, my next goal is to become an area manager and manage multiple clubs within a market. From there I hope to someday start my own fitness club and continue helping people for years to come.

Advice to Undergraduate Students Choose something that you have passion for. If your passion is to help people and teach them about the benefits of exercise and staying active, this is the area of study for you. Having a passion for what you do can be the difference between choosing a job and pursuing a career.

Global communication is here to stay. With the technology available today, we can no longer expect to live our lives communicating only with people in our communities. Anyone who cannot effectively communicate with people from a variety of cultures will be at a great disadvantage.

Communicating with people from different cultures sometimes poses quite a challenge.

Misunderstandings and inadvertent offenses are commonplace. For example, problems can arise easily between employees, clients, and administrators when one or more people disregard, or are not aware of, some of the differences in cultural communication styles (Gudykunst & Kim, 1992). How can communication be improved in organizations or among individuals?

Consider the following key issues in effective intercultural communication as you interact with people of different cultures:

- There are some basic differences in the ways people of different cultures communicate, such as through different uses of words, voice pitch, and nonverbal communication (body language).
- Within each culture, there are individual differences in the way people communicate.
- In communicating with someone of a different culture, you must consider the person's cultural background.
- You need to be flexible in your communication style if you want to relate positively to people of different cultures.
- There are limits to how much someone should try to shift his communication style to be like someone who is culturally different.
- Openness, caring, and mutual respect for the dignity of people are essential qualities for effective communication, regardless of cultural differences.
- There are great advantages to being knowledgeable, respectful, and open toward others who are culturally different from you.

Nonverbal Communication Most researchers would agree that the most powerful form of communication is nonverbal. Approximately, 90% to 93% of our communication is nonverbal. Nonverbal communication is defined as the nonlinguistic behaviors or attributes that are consciously encoded and decoded via multiple channels. Nonverbal messages are the nonlinguistic aspects of communication that carry powerful emotional meaning. They provide the context for how the accompanying verbal message should be interpreted and understood. Consequently, a nonverbal message can create more conflict between two people than a verbal message. Nonverbal communication consists of, but is not limited to, eye contact, interpersonal space, touching, facial gestures, and other kinds of body movement.

Barriers to Intercultural Communication

Improving cross-cultural communication in your organization can be challenging for several reasons. Many people spend most of their time with others who share their culture, race, or ethnicity. People tend to feel most comfortable and safe when they are with people similar to themselves. As people form groups based on similarities, they may unintentionally create barriers and exclude people who are different from them. People from different groups may feel like outsiders and be hesitant to approach.

There are six stumbling blocks or barriers to effective cross-cultural communication: assumption of similarities, language differences, nonverbal misinterpretations, preconceptions and stereotypes, tendency to evaluate, and high anxiety (Barna, 1994). Being aware of the six stumbling blocks is the first step in avoiding them, but it isn't an easy task. It usually takes willingness, training, and openness to a new way of thinking and responding.

- Assumption of similarities is the first stumbling block. Many people assume that people are all the same. The thought that people are all the same is comforting and reduces the discomfort of dealing with diverse people. Too many people naively assume that there are sufficient similarities among peoples of the world to make communication easy. They expect that simply being human and having common requirements of food, shelter, and security make everyone alike. Unfortunately, many people overlook the fact that the forms of adaption to these common biological and social needs and the values, beliefs, and attitudes surrounding them are vastly different from culture to culture.
- Language differences, the second danger, are not surprising. Diversity of different spoken languages, vocabulary, syntax, idioms, slang, and dialects all cause difficulty, but the person struggling with a different language is usually cognizant of the challenge. However, a greater language problem is the variation in meanings from culture to culture of different words.
- Nonverbal misinterpretation is another barrier to communication. It is common for people to misinterpret observable nonverbal signs and symbols, such as gestures, eye contact, postures, and other body movements. People from different cultures experience different sensory realities. They see, hear, feel, and smell only that which has some meaning or importance to them. They abstract whatever fits into their personal world of recognition and then interpret it through the frame of reference specific to their own culture. But it is possible to learn the intent of these

observable messages, usually in informal rather than formal ways.

• Preconceptions and stereotypes can result in exclusion of others. Stereotypes help to reduce the threat of the unknown by making sense of the world through a person's cultural lens. This is one of the basic functions of culture: to lay out a predictable world in which the person is well grounded and oriented. Stereotypes are stumbling blocks for communicators because they interfere with the objectivity of viewing others who appear to be different. They are not easy to overcome in ourselves or to correct in others, even with the presentation of factual information. Stereotypes persist because they are firmly established as myths or truisms by one's own national culture and because they sometimes rationalize prejudices.

• Tendency to evaluate is the fifth stumbling block and a deterrent in understanding persons of differing cultures. People have a tendency to evaluate, to approve or disapprove, the statements and actions of other individuals or groups. Rather than try to comprehend thoughts and feelings from the perspective of the other, a person evaluates the situation through an ethnocentric worldview, judging people based on his or her own culture or way of life.

• High anxiety or tension, often referred to as stress, is considered a serious stumbling block. Anxiety and tension are very common in cross-cultural interactions because so many unknown factors exist. Anxiety and tension also go hand in hand because people usually cannot experience mental anxiety without physical tension. It is acceptable for people to have a certain degree of tension as well as positive attitudes to prepare them to meet challenges with energy. However, too much anxiety or tension requires some form of relief, which too often comes in the form of defenses, such as the skewed perceptions, isolation, or anger.

Strategies for Bridging Intercultural Communication Barriers

Intercultural communication is about dealing with people from other cultures in a way that minimizes misunderstandings and maximizes a person's potential to create strong, positive relationships. As discussed in the previous section, it is easy to understand how barriers can result in confusion and misunderstanding and, as a result, exclusion of others who are culturally or linguistically different. This section discusses strategies to help people overcome these barriers and reduce misunderstandings when communicating interculturally. Strategies discussed include conflict resolution, different conflict management styles, and active, mindful listening skills.

Conflict Resolution Intercultural miscommunication and misattributions often underscore intercultural conflict. People coming from two contrasting cultural communities bring with them different values assumptions, expectations, verbal and nonverbal habits, and interaction scripts that influence the conflict process. *Intercultural conflict* is defined as the perceived or actual incompatibility of values, norms, processes, or goals between a minimum of two cultural parties over content, identity, and relational and procedural issues (Ting-Toomey, 1999).

The following are some ways to constructively resolve conflict:

• Agree upon a common goal of resolving the conflict so everyone wins—look for common ground.
• Demonstrate respect for the other person.
• Be open with your thoughts and feelings.
• Do not attack or blame the other person.
• Listen to the other person with an open mind.
• Value differences in viewpoint.
• Identify and understand your own and others' conflict management styles.

Conflict Management Styles Everyone has a conflict management style. Understanding your own and others' styles can be helpful in understanding and resolving conflict. Effective conflict management depends, to a large degree, on being mindful that your communication style is one of many and that it is not better, just different. In embracing cultural dilemmas, we may choose to avoid the conflict or get angry and blame others.

The following are typical conflict management styles:

• *Avoidance:* The Avoider would rather not address conflict at all and is most comfortable ignoring or delaying issues and repressing her own feelings and needs. This is a lose–lose style, because the conflict goes unaddressed and teamwork and productivity are usually negatively affected.

- Competition: The Competitor tries to win the conflict at all costs, usually at the expense of the other person. This is a win–lose style, in which one person may get what he or she wants whereas the other person loses. Although this style produces short-term victories, in the end it damages productivity because it hurts people's relationships.

- Adaptation: The Adaptor is most comfortable giving in to the other person's needs, sacrificing his or her own goals. This is a lose–win style that appears cooperative but can be detrimental in the long run because it does not produce a win for all parties.

- Cooperation: The Cooperator tries to find a solution that meets everyone's needs. In cooperation, the issues are fully explored, all parties state their needs, and people work together to find creative solutions in which everyone benefits. This is a win–win style.

Mindful Listening to Resolve Conflict Active and mindful listening is critical in managing a difficult situation. Acquiring new information in conflict negotiation means that both parties have to learn to listen mindfully to each other even when they disagree. Both parties have to learn to listen responsively, which means attending closely with our "ears, eyes, and a focused heart, to the sounds, tones, gestures, movements, nonverbal nuances, pauses, and silence in a given situation" (Ting-Tooney, 1999, p. 220).

Applications of Culture

In today's society, culture as a term and as a concept is used liberally among people in general and by professionals in every discipline (Kottak & Kozaitis, 2008). The term is used loosely in everyday conversation between people who talk about different cultures of people migrating, especially from other countries. Students who study abroad do so to learn about another culture. If you hold any type of position in the workplace, more than likely you are involved in training programs and workshops where discussions of organizational culture ensue. Most corporate cultures were established when the vast majority of workers were white and male; however, today's employees are more diverse. It is managerially prudent to ask whether the culture that served well in the past can serve the organization well in the present and the future (Thomas, 1991). Organizations, agencies, corporations, industries, institutions,

and Fortune 500 companies are recognizing the importance of managing diversity and creating a welcoming, inclusive environment. Businesses are looking for new markets, termed *cultural niche marketing*. Culture is receiving more attention than ever before. From workplace to classroom to community diversity, different cultural beliefs, values, and communication styles are here to stay.

Culture as a term and concept relative to issues of diversity requires organizations to develop new paradigms that will result in creating new positions to hire diversity specialists or consultants. The charge will be to change the culture of the organization to benefit a more diverse workforce.

As for those in the field of recreation and leisure, a major implication of the rapidly changing demographics is a drastically different clientele. More and more, professionals will be compelled to work with people from diverse cultures. Job announcements will increasingly state, "experience with diverse populations required" and "fluency in a second language preferred" (Diller & Moule, 2005). It will not be sufficient to simply direct new clients into traditional programs and organizational structures or to hire a few token people of color. It will be necessary to embrace a more inclusive cultural environment. This will require professionals to acquire new knowledge, increase cultural awareness, and embrace an evolving skill set needed to communicate effectively and appropriately across cultures.

Cultural Influences on Recreation and Leisure

At this point we must discuss an important cultural variable that affects how effectively people interact with each other: individualism versus collectivism. Cultures that have been identified as using a collectivistic perspective emphasize the welfare of the group, cooperation and conformity, and interdependence. Cultures identified as collectivistic include Latino, Asian, and Native American (Axelson, 1985; Marin & Marin, 1991; McAdoo, 1993). People from these cultures prefer more personal contact from practitioners, provide more socially acceptable responses to questions, and attempt to avoid conflict by hesitating to offer an alternative point of view in a group discussion. Cultures that are more individualistic emphasize independence, pursuit of personal objectives, and competition. The dominant culture defined as white, Anglo-Saxon, and Protestant has been described as individualistic culture in this way (Katz, 1989). However, these assertions regarding different cultural groups are not intended to stereotype a particular group because an infinite number of differences exist among any given ethnic group.

The values of individualistic and collectivistic cultures may influence communication styles. Communication styles among individualistic cultures are characterized as direct, open, frank, and even confrontational. Assertive expression of thought and feeling is emphasized in individualistic cultures. Among collectivistic cultures, just the opposite is the case, where the preferred style of communication is nonverbal and indirect and where communication that may lead to confrontation is avoided. What impact does this information have on recreation and leisure?

Managers and planners need to develop more sophisticated and comprehensive tools that will enable them to better serve existing users; identify potential users; more fully understand and address a diversity of interests, needs, and preferences; and successfully market facilities and services. Cultural issues are relevant and need to be addressed within every core area or function with the administrative practice (e.g., budgeting, program and strategic planning, staffing, and supervision; Pope et al., 2004). Gaining a deeper understanding of cultural influences on lifestyles is not an option in the field of recreation and leisure but rather a necessity for the growth of the profession.

Promoting Cultural Competence in Recreation and Leisure

It seems clear that if the remarks presented in this chapter have merit, then some very definite implications for recreation and leisure professional training and education in the area of cultural competence would follow. In the United States and Canada, the focus on culture is valuable. Every day people hear about cultural differences and about social problems whose solutions require creative thinking and multiple perspectives. Anyone working for an agency, organization, or institution that serves the public constantly deals with people from different social classes, ethnicities, gender identities, abilities and disabilities, ages, and generations. Attorneys, teachers, social workers, and service providers can all do a better job if they understand the social differences that exist in diverse environments.

Knowledge about traditions, values, and beliefs of most social groups within a diverse society is important in planning and developing programs that affect those groups. Attention to social background and cultural categories helps ensure the welfare of affected groups, communities, and neighborhoods. Experience in planned social change, whether it is a community in the United States or Canada or an economic development project overseas, shows that a proper social study should be done before a project or policy can be implemented. When local people want the change and it fits their lifestyle and traditions, change will be more successful, beneficial, and cost effective (Kottak, 2008).

Recreation and leisure professionals must understand the cultural fabric that prevails in a diverse society and how this fabric manifests itself in the lifestyle of all citizens. Professionals in the field will need to confront their own biases honestly and work hard to overcome them. Through this process, recreation and leisure specialists will come to terms with their own cultural ideologies, values, and beliefs and understand how these are actualized in marketing strategies, program development, and general outreach and personal interaction with clients. This exercise of self-analyses and self-discovery is not a disclosure of the malignant ideology of Western societies but an exercise of becoming culturally accountable and responsible.

Recreation and leisure professionals will be expected to be earnest in their acknowledgment and appreciation of cultural diversity. A preprofessional should be able to discern the integrity of differing cultural orientations. It will be important to learn to distinguish between expressions of cultural integrity and expressions that are simply unacceptable. Those in our field should learn to acknowledge and appreciate that certain expressions of cultural integrity may at times be inappropriate or maladaptive for certain programs but that the expressions nonetheless have integrity. Professionals and preprofessionals must receive practical experiences in how to effectively infuse cultural manifestations into pedagogical contexts that are appropriate for traditional and new clients.

Summary

Demographics in the United States and Canada are changing radically, increasing the diversity of these societies. Drastic changes are occurring in the number of immigrants and people of color, and there is a noticeable decline in the percentages of white people. An increased demand for service providers and recreation professionals to work in diverse environments with culturally and linguistically different customers is inevitable.

To adequately serve this diverse customer base, we must be aware of and sensitive to issues of diversity that affect our ability to communicate effectively across cultures, but this awareness is not enough. We must move beyond our own self-interest and value the importance of all cultures as we deliver services to all segments of the population.

This new paradigm, new vision, must be grounded in and based on the concept of cultural competence, the ability to effectively communicate and interact with people who are culturally and linguistically different. This vision calls for individuals and systems to live and work with diverse people and communities and to educate and serve them. This vision takes a systems perspective that values difference and, as a result, is responsive to diversity at all levels of an organization, that is, policy, governance, administrative, workforce, provider, and customer or client. In particular, cultural competence is the attention to the needs of culturally and linguistically different groups and the integration of cultural attitudes, beliefs, and practices into more effective outreach, communication, education, marketing, advertising, and sales strategies. It is the continuous promotion of skills, practices, and interactions to ensure that services are culturally responsive and competent. Culturally competent activities include developing skills through training, using self-assessment tools, and implementing goals and objectives to ensure that governance, administrative policies and practices, and program development are responsive to diversity within the populations served.

The kind of education and learning that have been the topic of discussion in this chapter are long-term and ongoing. Such an education is as much process as content, tends to be cumulative in nature, and—as Cross and colleagues (1989), Sue and colleagues (1992), and Bennett (1993) have pointed out—is highly developmental, meaning that the learner goes through predictable stages of growth, emotion, and change. Keep in mind that this chapter is only the beginning of the journey. What happens next is up to you!

A final thought for you to ponder:

> The communicator cannot stop at knowing that the people he is working with have different customs, goals, and thought patterns from his own. He must be able to feel his way into intimate contact with these alien values, attitudes, and feelings. He must be able to work with them and within them, neither losing his own values in the confrontation nor protecting himself behind a wall of intellectual detachment. (Robert Harrison, 1966, p. 4)

Discussion Questions

1. How will beginning a journey toward cultural competence (improving cross-cultural communication, teamwork, conflict management, open-mindedness, critical thinking) affect your career plans?

2. What will be your most difficult challenge as you work on increasing your own cultural competence?

3. What are three challenges that will test your cultural competence and why?

4. Because the reality we experience is based on a particular system of symbols, how do we tend to view members of other cultures? What special efforts are needed to overcome the tendency to treat people of different cultures as less worthy than we are?

5. Historically, people in the United States and Canada have been rather indifferent to the dangers of inadvertently offending others. Why do you think this has been the case?

6. Explain how communication and culture are interrelated.

Everybody Gets to Play

Carolyn McClelland, Coordinator National Initiatives

Canadian Parks and Recreation Association

Keri Hoffman, Manager National Initiatives

Canadian Parks and Recreation Association

Disclaimer: Production of the Everybody Gets to Play Community Mobilization Tool Kit has been made possible through a financial contribution from the Public Health Agency of Canada. The views expressed herein do not necessarily represent the views of the Public Health Agency of Canada.

The Everybody Gets to Play national initiative—2008 winner of the World Leisure International Innovation Prize—was developed by the Canadian Parks and Recreation Association (CPRA) to help make recreation accessible to children in low-income families, providing them with the same opportunities for healthy growth and social development that average families may take for granted.

Making sure that children have fair access to recreation is part of a national and global commitment. Canada endorsed the 1989 United Nations Convention on the Rights of the Child, which says, "The child has the right to rest and leisure . . . play and recreational activities." Canada's National Children's Agenda states, "As a nation, we aspire to have children who are as physically and emotionally healthy as they can be, with strong self-esteem, life skills and enthusiasm."

About 1.1 million or 1 of 6 children in Canada live in poverty (Campaign 2000). Despite the country's strong economic performance in recent years, child poverty continues to increase. There are many reasons. The changing makeup of the population is one. The numbers of new Canadians, members of visible minorities, and Aboriginal peoples are increasing. The latter often fall into the lowest income groups. Divorce rates continue to rise, and single-parent families are among the poorest in Canada.

Making sure that kids have a chance to play may seem like an odd way to address poverty, but CPRA's research indicates that it's actually a powerful technique. Some benefits are obvious; sports and

Reprinted, by permission, from Canadian Parks and Recreation, Carolyn McClelland and Keri Hoffman.

physical activity can help children build strong bodies, self-esteem, and social skills. Some are less apparent; initiatives to improve recreation opportunities for the young can encourage volunteerism in communities, break down barriers between cultural groups, build civic pride, contribute to environmental awareness, and even reduce crime and the cost of social services.

Many recreation facilities and programs in Canada have longstanding policies to subsidize recreation for people who cannot afford it. But, as CPRA discovered, affordability is only the tip of the iceberg. Transportation to distant facilities can be expensive and time consuming. New Canadians often spend some years in low-income jobs. Language, culture, or feelings of isolation may prevent children from participating. Racial discrimination is a problem for Aboriginal youth and members of visible minorities. The list goes on.

It's easy to be overwhelmed by the complexity of the problem, but supporters of the principles behind the Everybody Gets to Play initiative aren't daunted. Every community has its own characteristics to deal with—local recreation practitioners only have to focus on local issues. And they don't have to do it alone.

The centerpiece of the initiative is a Community Mobilization Tool Kit and 1-day workshop designed to help recreation practitioners and other community leaders mobilize their communities and develop sustainable programs that will deliver measurable results. Practitioners are being given the resources to build the case for accessible recreation, evaluate

(continued) ⟩⟩

community needs and resources, identify and enlist partners, develop outcome-based plans for action, measure and report results, and share successes with other communities.

As the Everybody Gets to Play initiative grows, CPRA is working to provide new supplemental resources to recreation practitioners. One of these resources is titled Nutrition and Healthy Eating, which aims to provide recreational practitioners with information about links between poverty, health, and food security; an understanding of the nutritional needs of children and youth; and assistance on finding additional information on these topics. This resource will provide a detailed directory of nutrition-related strategies that are targeted to or inclusive of low-income families.

A resource in conjunction with the Everybody Gets to Play initiative is an Aboriginal strategy. CPRA is assessing the needs and interests of practitioners when engaging Aboriginal populations in recreation opportunities in urban settings. Information will be shared concerning the realities, challenges, and potential strategies in engaging Aboriginal communities in recreation opportunities.

To find out more about this initiative, visit www.everybodygetstoplay.ca or contact cpra@cpra.ca.

References

Campaign 2000. (2002). *Report card on child and family poverty in Canada*. www.campaign2000.ca/rc/rc02/NOV02reportcard.pdf.

Based on Campaign, 2000, Report Card on Child and Family Poverty in Canada, 2002.

Inclusion Concepts, Processes, and Models

4

Terry Long, PhD

Northwest Missouri State University

Terry Robertson, PhD

Northwest Missouri State University

" *You don't ask everybody to conform to the same system. You ask the system to include everybody.* "

–Gerard Etienne

Learning Outcomes

After reading this chapter, students will be able to do the following:

- Identify the elements of the inclusion process.
- Explain the nature and purpose of conceptual models.
- Explain how models can be useful to recreation professionals.
- Identify and explain at least three prerequisites for inclusive recreation.
- Identify three potential frameworks for developing an inclusive recreation program.
- Explain and apply various traditional models of inclusion.
- Explain and apply the CITI model of inclusion.

This chapter is about models of inclusion. Models are symbolic representations used to explain or describe a concept, process, or system. They are also frequently used to represent the ideal, or the best. Terms like *role model* or *model citizen* are used describe people who serve as behavioral examples for how others in our society might want live their lives.

Models also tend to be little things that are used to represent big things. For example, a plastic model of our solar system, a doll house, or the model cars you may have put together as a child are tiny representations of the real thing. Because they are small and easy to view, these miniaturized versions have the advantage of demonstrating the overall characteristics of something that would otherwise be inconvenient or impossible to see. Through these models we learn and understand the world around us.

Some models are literal representations of an object, whereas others are made up of symbols or words that represent a more abstract concept or process. The models in this book tend to be the latter, and they typically involve diagrams and drawings intended to represent what it means to provide an inclusive recreation experience. These models are meant to guide those of us who wish to build successful inclusive recreation programs. When you look at these models, realize they represent real participants, professionals, and programs. Try to imagine what these programs might be like. If there is a part of the model that you cannot understand and visualize, ask your instructor to discuss this part of the model and what it represents. This process will help these models come to life for you and have meaning.

Before exploring the models of inclusion that are presented in this chapter, we need to clarify several related concepts. These concepts are considered to be prerequisites to inclusion. A prerequisite is something that is required before a condition or behavior can occur. Some examples include learning to stand before you can walk, passing driver's education before you get your driver's license, or working 30 years before you can retire. We all deal with these kinds of requirements every day. They seem troublesome, but in most cases they are meant to ensure safety, preparedness, quality, or entitlement. Several prerequisites must be in place for successful inclusion.

Prerequisites to Inclusion

For inclusion to be possible, professionals must be skilled at providing participants with access to facilities and programs. Professionals must also be skilled in identifying and implementing appropriate accommodations and adaptations in a manner that does not trivialize activities or patronize participants. Failure to address these issues will undermine efforts to create an inclusive recreation environment, whereas their presence can greatly enhance the recreation experience for participants. The following section discusses each of these prerequisites for inclusion in more detail.

Accessibility

Several conditions can be considered as prerequisites to providing a quality inclusive recreation experience. The first is accessibility. As discussed in chapter 2, the Americans with Disabilities Act (ADA, 1990) requires that access to public recreation facilities be provided. In truth, the development of guidelines, policies, and public knowledge regarding this requirement is an ongoing and never-ending process. It is critical that recreation professionals understand not only access requirements but also available tools and strategies for maximizing access. Physical access is best provided through universal design, where the built environment supports all people regardless of whether they have a disability (see chapter 8 for more on universal design).

Access pertains to both the physical environment and the programs provided within that environment. Participants with disabilities have a right to participate in programs alongside their fellow community members, as do people from all ethnic, racial, cultural, and religious backgrounds. Without access, there is no inclusion.

Accommodation

Appropriate provision of needed accommodations is a second prerequisite to inclusion. Accommodation is used here to refer to the removal of barriers that otherwise might prevent participation and, ultimately, inclusion. In education settings, an accommodation is differentiated from other modifications by the fact that performance requirements are not lowered for the student, meaning that she must still take the same exams and meet the same performance expectations as students who do not receive accommodations. This principle can be applied to the recreation setting, in that accommodations involve barriers that are outside of the skills or abilities necessary to perform a particular activity. For example, hearing is not typically an inherent part of swimming, but accommodations may be necessary for communication with a deaf participant. Accommodations for a deaf participant might include an interpreter for swimming lessons or a starting light for a competitive swimmer. Once in the water, the deaf participant has the potential to swim as well as others without any further accommodation or adaptation. Likewise, cultural or religious accommodations may be necessary, such as providing interpreters, arranging for kosher meals, or making exceptions in regard to traditional dress codes for aquatic facilities.

Adaptation

Adaptation is the third prerequisite for inclusion. Adaptation has been defined as "the art and science, used by qualified professionals, of assessing and managing variables and services so as to meet unique needs and achieve desired outcomes" (Sherrill, 2004, p. 7). Technically, accommodation would fall under this definition as well, meaning that an accommodation is a particular type or area of adaptation. Unlike accommodation, adaptation is used here to refer to the alteration of variables directly related to the participant's ability to perform the activity at hand. For example, use of flotation devices and modification of stroke technique are adaptations related to swimming. Rules and regulations can be adapted, or modified, as well as the activity environment (e.g., two-bounce rule in tennis, alteration of field surfaces). The nature of a recreational activity may need to be modified because of religious or cultural factors (e.g., rules and

Photo courtesy Ragen E. Sanner.

Accessibility, accommodation, and adaptation are necessary to help make experiences, like gardening, open to all.

norms associated with mixed-gender activities for adolescents).

Adaptations will not be necessary for all participants, but every recreation professional should be trained and skilled in identifying and implementing appropriate adaptations. Adaptations should be made only when necessary so that participants are able to take part in activities in the most normalized, integrated, and independent manner possible.

From Access to Inclusion

Understanding inclusion requires an understanding of access, which consists of two elements. The first is access to facilities. Physical access was described earlier and is explored further in chapter 9. The second element is program accessibility, which is a specific requirement under the ADA (1990) and is an inherent element of most civil rights legislation. Anderson and Kress (2003) described program accessibility as "providing supports and accommodations so people with disabilities can pursue their leisure choices, beyond making the space physically accessible" (p. 31). Through this process, people with disabilities are ensured their right to access. Still, program access does not guarantee inclusion.

Access begins to evolve into inclusion when activities are delivered in the most integrated setting. The ADA requires that public recreation be provided in the most integrated setting, meaning that people with disabilities have the right to participate in recreation programs in a setting in which "interaction between people with and without disabilities is provided to the maximum extent feasible" (ADA, 1990). Under this guideline, programs offered to the general public must accept registrants who meet the programs' essential eligibility guidelines or guidelines that all participants must meet regardless of disability (e.g., age, residency, gender, behavioral guidelines). For registrants who meet these guidelines, the provision of inclusive programs is required by law, and only under certain circumstances described in the ADA can participation be restricted or denied in a program offered to the public (see the Essential Eligibility Requirements and Accommodation Limitations sidebar on page 64).

Inclusive recreation experiences have the potential to create truly rewarding and memorable life moments for all involved. The idea that the ADA (1990) or other legislative requirements can "mandate" this experience is inherently flawed, because the value of inclusive recreation

Essential Eligibility Requirements

These are the basic program requirements that all people must meet to participate in a program. These include things like age, registration deadlines, residency, and minimal skill levels. All participants, whether they have a disability or not, must meet these requirements. Thus, a child who is over the age limit for the program cannot participate, regardless of the fact that he has an intellectual disability.

Limitations of Required Accommodation

There are four basic situations when an accommodation can be refused.

- Significant financial hardship or burden
- Significant administrative burden
- Changes inherent nature of activity
- Danger to self or others

Program providers must be able to document the existence of any such limitations. Policies and procedures pertaining to determining any such limitations should be reviewed by legal counsel. The extent of financial and administrative burdens should be considered in the context of the overall agency, not specific program budgets and resources.

---

comes from the genuine social experience of the participant, not mere presence. This idea of social inclusion goes beyond physical presence at an activity; inclusion means that people positively experience the activity. Several models that promote social inclusion are presented later in this chapter, but the topic warrants a bit of discussion at this point. Essentially, all of the benefits that one gets from participating in recreation and leisure should be equally available to all people. Included among these benefits are opportunities for friendship, belonging, contribution, competition, success, failure, and genuine shared experiences. Interpersonal interactions with others should be as genuine as possible. Traditionally marginalizing traits become meaningless and disappear from the immediate thoughts of all participants. In other words, everyone is thinking about the game, or the campfire or concert, and nobody is paying attention to Susie's wheelchair or Joey's skin color. For social inclusion to become the norm, society must change in terms of how people understand what it means to be a human being and what characteristics should or should not be used as evaluative criteria. Great strides have been made toward simply viewing people as people, but we have a long way to go.

Public Perceptions Inclusion

Legal mandates over the past 40 years have helped shift society's perceptions and treatment of women, cultural and racial minority groups, people who are gay or lesbian, and persons with disabilities away from an expectation of segregation and unequal treatment and toward an expectation of inclusive and equal treatment of all society members. Gradually, beliefs and behaviors have shifted as laws enacted as a means of eliminating discriminatory treatment pushed American culture toward inclusion in all realms of life.

One consequence of this legally enforced compliance, particularly in regard to inclusion, was the tendency for those responsible for developing and implementing programs to focus on minimum legal requirements and head counts rather than the underlying philosophy of inclusion. Furthermore, the growing pains associated with compliance within a society that was unprepared for inclusion further encouraged a focus on physical inclusion rather than social or emotional inclusion. In the case of ADA, the task of retrofitting facilities to be compliant was viewed by many as a daunting financial nightmare. Ultimately, reasonable expectations were established, but financial and administrative costs were still present. This culture shock has wavered as the necessity of considering ADA requirements has become the norm, but many still view ADA as a burden rather than a blessing, especially in the realm of program access.

Fortunately, recent attention has been placed on implementing humanistic and ecological philosophies of inclusion that highlight the social and dynamic nature of people and society. At the core of this movement is the acknowledgment of the impact that attitudes can have on the inclusion process. Attitudes of participants with and without disabilities or differentiating characteristics, as well as attitudes of program staff and society in general, can have a significant impact on participant experience and program effectiveness. Attitudes are a key element of successful social inclusion, opening the door to genuine and accepting relationships. In contrast, negative attitudes and beliefs (e.g., racism, elitism, ethnocentrism, or pity) can be significant barriers in moving from legal compliance to social inclusion.

Addressing Attitudes

As we begin our discussion of models that are useful in the understanding of inclusive recreation services, a good place to start is with the concept of attitude. For the participant who is somehow differentiated from others (e.g., race, religion, disability), attitude related barriers, whether from their own attitudes or the attitudes of others, can deter inclusion. Attitudes are learned tendencies or dispositions toward an object or person that produce consistently positive or negative reactions (Fishbein & Ajzen, 1975).

An example of a framework for understanding the role that attitude plays in determining behavior is the theory of planned behavior (Ajzen, 1991). A model depicting the nature of this theory is displayed in figure 4.1. Note that three factors determine a person's intention to behave in a certain manner. The first of these three factors is a person's attitude toward the behavior. Attitudes are driven by behavioral beliefs; for example, if a person believes that all

humans should be treated equally, he or she will have a disapproving attitude toward any ridicule or discrimination of a person who is perceived as different. Thus, influencing a person's beliefs can impact attitude, intention, and, ultimately, behavior toward other people.

Several other factors come into play in determining whether or not an attitude or intention will result in behavior. For example, subjective norms, or perceived social pressures, are the second major determinant of intention. Our beliefs regarding social expectations will determine how influential the perceived subjective norm is on intentions. Peer pressure is a classic example of this aspect of behavioral intention (e.g., to be accepted by the group, I must tease people who are seen as different or as outsiders, even though I believe it is wrong to do so).

The third determinant of intention is perceived behavioral control, which is made up of a person's beliefs regarding their ability to control the outcome of, or successfully perform, a behavior. For example, if an individual sees herself as incapable of persuading her peers that teasing is wrong, it is unlikely she will have any intention to stand up to them when they encourage her to tease another person.

Note that a person's actual behavioral control mediates whether or not an established intention results in an actual behavior. In other words, intentions only become a reality when a person actually has the skills, resources, and other prerequisites necessary to successfully complete a behavior.

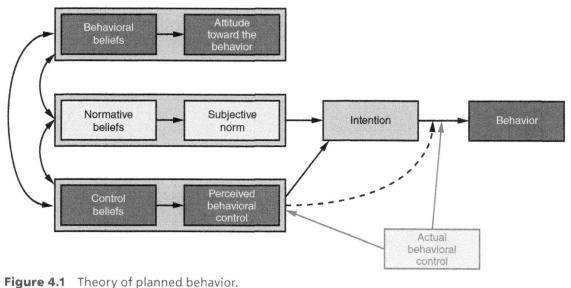

Figure 4.1 Theory of planned behavior.

Reprinted from *Organizational Behavior and Human Decision Processes,* Vol. 50, I. Ajzen, pgs. 179-211, copyright 1991, with permission from Elsevier.

This is an important point because it suggests that influencing attitudes and intentions as a training strategy for staff should be accompanied by opportunities to master skills necessary to successfully turn intentions into behaviors. Otherwise, well intended efforts to foster inclusion may result in failure or, even worse, undesirable consequences such as insult, embarrassment, or patronization (e.g., talking extremely loudly or slowly to a blind person, a person who speaks a different language, or a person who just looks different than others would be unnecessary and unhelpful and would demonstrate a lack of awareness).

Obviously, attitudes alone do not ensure that a person will behave in a certain way, but they are a starting point for influencing behavioral tendencies. One way to change negative attitudes is to provide positive personal contact or interaction between those who hold the negative attitudes and the people toward whom those attitudes are held (Bullock & Mahon, 2001). Dattilo (2002) suggested seven actions that profession-als can use to foster positive attitudes toward inclusion, particularly in regard to inclusion of persons with disabilities (see figure 4.2). Using strategies such as promoting joint participation and fostering cooperative interdependence, professionals can use positive experiences to challenge negative attitudes. Take a few minutes to examine these strategies and how they might be implemented. Think about why this action would be beneficial.

Attitudes of participants can be a barrier to their own inclusion as well. An unwillingness to trust others or a lack of self-confidence can create barriers for a participant. Attitudes such as these stand in the way of participants' self-determination (Dattilo, 2002; Deci & Ryan, 1985, 2000). Achieving self-determination increases a person's learning and perceptions of competence, whereas a lack of self-determination is associated with disengagement (Dattilo, 2002). Maximizing self-determination is, therefore, a second attitude-related approach to facilitating

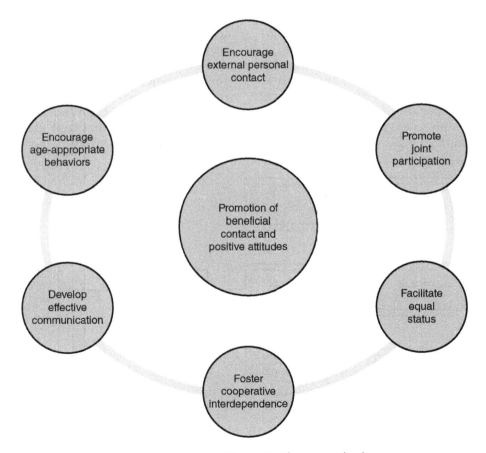

Figure 4.2 Actions promoting positive attitudes toward others.

Adapted, by permission, from J. Dattilo, 2002, *Inclusive leisure services: Responding to the rights of people with disabilities*, 2nd ed. (State College, PA: Venture), 54.

social inclusion. Dattilo suggested six strategies for facilitating self-determination.

- Provide opportunities for choice.
- Promote communication.
- Respond to preferences.
- Foster active participation.
- Encourage empowerment.
- Expand repertoires and increase competence.

Focus is placed heavily on empowering participants who have disabilities through the provision of choice, active participation in preferred activities, and skill development; however, these techniques are again relevant to other groups. For example, teaching immigrant children how to play American football expands their repertoire of sport skills, increasing their competence and the likelihood of acceptance by their peers on the local football team. See Dattilo (2002) for ideas on how to implement these techniques.

This information on attitudes does not alone provide a comprehensive process or model for inclusion. Attitudes are only briefly presented in this chapter but should be considered within the context of broader inclusion models. We now turn toward a more comprehensive examination of how inclusion can be achieved in the recreation environment.

Process of Inclusion

Discussion of processes and models can get a little confusing. Again, models are symbolic representations, whereas a process is a series of steps or interrelated tasks that are systematically arranged to create a product or outcome. A process, such as how to get your first job, can be represented by a model (see figure 4.3). In addition, there may be more specific processes involved within a broader process. For the hopeful job applicant, the process for finding a job includes several other, more specific processes that need to be mastered

within the context of the overall process. Specific tasks such as conducting Internet job searches, preparing for interviews, and negotiating terms are all unique processes, but they also have to be conducted in the appropriate order within the overall job search.

Thus, models can be used to represent or describe processes, including the inclusion process. Here, several frameworks for the inclusion process are discussed and represented through graphic depictions (models). Some are fairly specific and focused, whereas others are broader. Each model is useful and communicates a different perspective of inclusion.

Anderson and Kress Inclusion Process

Anderson and Kress (2003) presented a step-by-step framework for implementing the inclusion process. Focusing on the nuts and bolts of inclusion, this process is based on the original work of Wagner and colleagues (1994). The process involves seven steps that provide a balance between the general and the specific. This balance allows for the process to be applied to a variety of settings or scenarios while still providing a specific framework for the provision of inclusive programs.

Step 1—Program promotion

Step 2—Registration and assessment

Step 3—Accommodations and supports

Step 4—Staff training

Step 5—Program implementation

Step 6—Documentation

Step 7—Evaluation

The Anderson and Kress model has significant applicability to the day-to-day practice of recreation agencies that are striving to create an inclusive culture. The first step, program promotion, informs the community of this

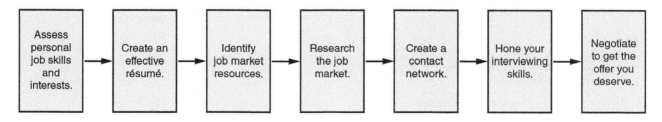

Figure 4.3 Example of a visual depiction of a process.

culture and invites people to become a part of it. This is accomplished by providing information to groups in the community through accessible media outlets. *Accessible* in this case can refer to the size or type of print (including Braille), the language in which the information is presented, or the symbols and statements that communicate that the environment is accessible and inclusive. Commercials, advertisements, or brochures can include images that depict a broad array of people.

Registration and assessment, which comprise step 2, are equally important. The registration process should be inclusive, using the same rules and procedures for all people. Registration needs to be accessible, whether participants register online, by mail, or in person. In addition, registration is an opportunity for participants to indicate that an accommodation will be necessary for their participation. Anderson and Kress (2003) suggest that a statement similar to the following one be included on the registration form: "Does the participant require any accommodations or have any needs of which we should be aware?" Once the participant indicates the need for accommodations, it is appropriate to contact this person to discuss the details of his request.

Step 3, accommodations and supports, is complex and is probably best accomplished when specific processes are laid out in regard to how these services can be provided. The term *accommodations* is used here to refer to adaptations, such as those pertaining to equipment or materials, skill requirement, procedures or rules, space, and team or group formation (Anderson & Kress, 2003; Schleien, Ray, & Green, 1988). This differs slightly from the definitions presented earlier regarding accommodation and adaptation; however, the point is that once the need for accommodation is apparent, the recreation professional must devise an appropriate strategy for facilitating optimal participation. The second part of this task is providing supports, which can involve several techniques for additional staff supervision or peer support. This can include providing an assistant for the participant, assigning peer partners, or using volunteers to provide coaching or support (Anderson & Kress, 2003). Accommodations and supports often are intertwined, such as when the programmer adjusts activities to introduce a cooperative element into activities (e.g., partner tag, cooperative relay races).

Step 4, staff training, is critical to providing quality inclusive experiences on a consistent basis. Table 4.1 outlines critical content areas for staff training and guidelines for conducting training, as identified by Anderson and Kress (2003).

Once staff are trained and ready to provide any identified accommodations and supports, steps 5 (program implementation), 6 (documentation), and 7 (evaluation) can be carried out. Programming should include an ongoing effort to monitor and adjust program activities in a

Table 4.1 Critical Staff Training Topics and Guidelines

Staff training content areas	Staff training guidelines
• Importance of inclusion	• Conduct training on an ongoing basis.
• Disability awareness activities	• Ensure that training is consistent.
• People-first language	• Include all leaders, instructors, and additional staff.
• Simulations and experiential activities	• If appropriate, and by choice, invite participants, parents, and guardians to provide input or take part.
• Scenarios: "What would you do if . . ."	• Ensure that new midstream hires are brought up to speed on the inclusion process.
• Staff roles	
• If possible, important issues regarding each participant, but only if necessary	
• Personal care assistance (if provided)	
• Training for peers without disabilities	

Based on L. Anderson and C.B. Kress, 2003, *Including people with disabilities in parks and recreation opportunities* (State College, PA: Venture).

manner that fosters social inclusion. This process is enhanced through program observation, regular meetings with staff and participants, and open communication with parents and guardians (Anderson & Kress, 2003). Documentation not only facilitates the inclusion process and, ultimately, the progress of the participant but also allows for communication between staff members and formative (ongoing) evaluation. Evaluation can be summative also, or conducted once the program is complete. Evaluation should include multiple sources of information, including the participant, the staff, and, when relevant, parents or guardians. Evaluation should also include those participants without disabilities and their parents or guardians, because they are a part of the inclusive environment and also receive services (Anderson & Kress, 2003).

JCC Programming Cycle

The St. Paul Jewish Community Center has developed a Programming Cycle for Inclusion (Nolan, 2005). This six-phase model is very similar in content to the inclusion process of Anderson and Kress (2003) and is depicted as an ongoing cycle in figure 4.4.

Two points are critical when considering this model. First, the phases of the model are cyclic, meaning that the process is conducted repeatedly, allowing for consistent redirection of goals and processes based on observed effectiveness. Second, agencies using this model are expected to reach out to other agencies or services within the community to create a community-wide network of inclusive services.

The St. Paul JCC, which served as the pilot in the development of this model, is part of a consortium of organizations (temples, synagogues, schools, and social service agencies) and attributes the success of the program to this key factor. Under this model, the lead inclusion staff member, often a certified therapeutic recreation specialist, does not work directly with clients. Instead, this person facilitates the inclusion process through training, supervision, and occasional assistance of inclusion staff. This concept of an inclusion specialist or coordinator has gained popularity and is reflected in several of the models described next. Likewise, the idea that inclusion is contingent on a broader system or community that extends beyond the recreation center is further developed within these models.

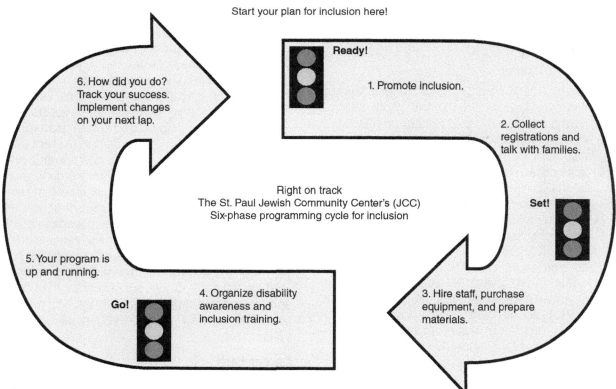

Figure 4.4 JCC programming cycle.

Reprinted, by permission, from C.V. Nolan, 2005, *Best practices of inclusive services: the value of inclusion* (Bloomington, IN: National Center on Accessibility, Indiana University–Bloomington). Available www.ncaonline.org. Figure courtesy of Beth Gendler, CTRS.

Thomas "Andy" Fernandez

If we are going to learn to live together, we must learn to play together.
   —Nike

Background Information

Education MA in recreation from the University of Northern Colorado

Credentials

*Certified Therapeutic Recreation Specialist, NCTRC *Certified Parks and Recreation Professional, NRPA

Special Awards

*City of Eugene Human Rights Award (2007) *National Therapeutic Recreation Society Presidential Citation (2002, 2000) *National Therapeutic Recreation Society New Professional of the Year Award (1999) *Nevada Recreation and Park Society Program Excellence Award F.L.O.A.T. (1997) *1997 NRPA PacSW Region Program Excellence Certificate Award F.L.O.A.T. (1997) *City of Las Vegas Employee of the Month (1996) *Nevada Recreation and Park Society Program Excellence Award Project D.I.R.T. (1996)

Special Affiliations

*Oregon UCEDD/OHSU CPC Member *Nevada Advisory Council on Children With Special Health Care Needs *U.S. Senator John Ensign's Disability Task Force *University of Nevada/Reno, instructor *University of Northern Colorado, adjunct faculty *Lakeside Chapter of Disabled Sports USA board member, former president, and treasurer *National Recreation and Parks Association Congress 2004, local host committee and accessibility chair *Nevada Recreation and Park Society, former therapeutic recreation committee co-chair, scholarship committee *National Therapeutic Recreation Society, Pacific Southwest regional director, state/regional advisory council director, local host committee/ NRPA 2001 liaison, awards committee, marketing committee, membership committee, SRAC Pacific/Southwest regional director, Paralympic liaison representative, 1996 Paralympics World

Photo courtesy of Andy Fernandez.

Congress *National Institute on Recreation Inclusion steering committee, 2008 local host, 2002 program chair, awards committee *University of Northern Colorado recreation program advisory board *Colorado Therapeutic Recreation Society president, legislative committee chair

Career Information

Position Interim division manager in the city manager's office in Eugene, Oregon

Size of Organization The city manager's office has 1,600 employees and serves the approximately 165,000 residents of Eugene.

Job Description I direct and coordinate CMO division activities with those of other divisions, departments, and outside agencies and organizations and participate on intergovernmental teams, representing the city of Eugene before other agencies. I also provide professional staff assistance to the assistant city manager; oversee, prepare, and present staff reports and other documents; and deliver presentations to the city council's budget committee and other boards, commissions, and community organizations. I analyze large, complex, and controversial issues, often interdisciplinary, assess courses of action, and develop recommendations to city management, city council, and community. My job also requires me to manage, direct, and organize support activities for a variety of program areas, including support for the work of the commissions supported by the division and to supervise staff, city work plans, and priorities related to human rights, accessibility, diversity, and sustainability.

Career Path On the way to Eugene, I specifically chose positions with premier agencies that would give me the opportunity to gain valuable experience in community TR: University of Arizona Adapted Athletics, The Breckenridge Outdoor Education Center, The City of Boulder EXPAND Program, The City of Las Vegas Adaptive Recreation and as the creator and supervisor of The City of Reno Inclusion Services; each one with more progressive responsibility.

The path to my current position was part challenge and part opportunity to test and develop my skill set in a new arena. I applied for this position outside of therapeutic recreation in order to enhance my work with people with disabilities from within a broader social equity and public policy scope. Before this assignment, I was the adaptive recreation manager for the Library, Recreation, and Cultural Services Department of the city of Eugene. In that position, I was given additional duties as assigned that connected me with staff and work groups outside of my division and department. Those relationships helped me get a big picture view of the work of the larger organization and how I might contribute.

What I Like About My Job   I enjoy the opportunity to test my existing leadership skills and to develop new leadership and management skills. It's also satisfying to have an impact on public policies.

Career Ladder   This was an interim assignment—kind of like enrolling in an intense one-year educational program—so I have considered it a rung on the ladder. However, the ladder doesn't always have to go up.

Advice to Undergraduate Students   Acquire skills that translate to a broad range of positions. Don't worry too much about specialization. Consider career development in any position you take. For example, here in Eugene there are many key staff with degrees in therapeutic recreation who are now in positions outside of the field: planning, training, and development; athletics, youth, and family services; outdoor adventure; human resources; and the city manager's office. However, all of them have the same core set of transferable skills that they learned studying recreation for people with disabilities.

For example in Eugene, the recreation division manager studied therapeutic recreation and applies the knowledge of multidisciplinary teams to his management of a wide variety of programs. Managers of the youth and family and athletics sections of the recreation division utilize their therapeutic recreation background to provide inclusive recreation opportunities that are both culturally competent and nationally recognized.

A special point to consider and take note of is that the city employees who were trained as therapeutic recreation professionals and now work outside of recreation but still use the core fundamentals learned from therapeutic recreation in their new positions. The city's performance and development manager is tasked with coordinating all the central training and continuing education for the organization. This includes the Americans with Disabilities Act and all diversity and human rights trainings. In addition to this function of her job, she is also a trained facilitator who has applied assessment, counseling, and listening techniques to group problem solving and goal planning. Our strategic planner for the police department, also a former therapeutic recreation professional, uses her program planning skill set to design, implement, and evaluate ongoing performance measures for a department with a completely different mission and purpose. So those prepared in therapeutic recreation have become so widely appreciated and accepted for the skills and knowledge they bring that the doors to other opportunities have become wide open.

Cincinnati Model for Inclusion

One of the most popular models of inclusion is the Cincinnati model. This model is referred to here as a content model rather than a process model because it focuses on what inclusion involves but does not describe a specific process for how this content should be delivered or arranged. The strength of such a model is its acknowledgment that inclusion is more than just a linear set of tasks; rather, inclusion is a dynamic and ongoing cultural phenomenon that is difficult to encapsulate in a drawing. At the same time, the model has the limitation of being less specific in regard to guidelines or actions for practice. Fortunately, guidelines for how to effectively accomplish each of these elements are available in the literature, some of which are explored in other sections of this book.

The Cincinnati Recreation Commission (CRC) has a long history of programs for people with disabilities, going back to 1967, but the commission's more recent efforts toward inclusion have garnered extensive attention as well (Montgomery & Kazin, 2005). After the passing of ADA in 1990, the CRC began educating their employees about disabilities and the process of inclusion. Through these efforts, the Cincinnati model for inclusion was developed, as were several therapeutic recreation divisions. The teams who staff these divisions serve a purpose similar to that of the lead inclusion staff member in the JCC programming cycle. The CRC inclusion teams, each of which consists of an inclusion coordinator and an inclusion specialist, work within their designated regions to facilitate the delivery of inclusive recreation services through existing programs.

In addition to promoting the concept of the inclusion team, the Cincinnati model reflects several key service delivery components (i.e., inclusion content). The inclusion teams work with community center staff and volunteers in their designated regions to provide services through these components, which include the following:

- Inclusion support within community centers
- Disability awareness program
- Staff training
- Internal and external marketing
- Advocacy
- Integration
- Regional representation on an inclusion counsel

Note that these components are a bit broader than the steps associated with the process models and are more easily tied to the broader community and culture. Although still somewhat similar to the specific tasks associated with process models, these content areas tend to address a broader ecological system. The remaining models to be discussed focus on an even broader perspective, with heavy emphasis on building inclusive culture throughout ecological systems that include and interact with the recreation environment. A more detailed discussion of the components of the Cincinnati model can be found at www.ncpad.org/fun/fact_sheet.php?sheet=66.

Inclusion Systems Models

The presented process and content models focus primarily on the parts of an inclusion program and how they work together to produce an out-come. These models are very useful in the practical planning and implementation of inclusion. One criticism of these models is that they fail to consider the importance of the broader ecological system or environment. The following section presents several broader "systems" models that are very helpful in communicating the broader philosophy of inclusion and identifying an array of internal and external factors that affect the inclusion process. At the same time, these models lack the detail related to operations that is provided by the process and content models. As such, it is beneficial to use models at both the micro and macro level when working to create an inclusive recreation environment.

I-Triad Model

Many times, the most effective models are the simplest ones. Deborah Chavez (2000) has presented a model for cultural inclusion referred to as the I-triad. This model involves three steps to consider when developing a strategic plan to inclusion: invite, include, and involve (see figure 4.5). Examples for each step are given next, but the real value of this model is in the philosophy that it represents in regard to systems change.

The first step is to invite all people to use your service. This is done by reaching out to all

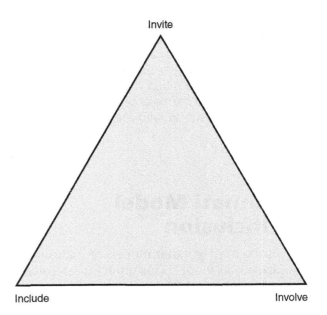

Figure 4.5 The I-triad.

Reprinted, by permission, from D. Chavez, 2000, Invite, include, involve! Racial groups, ethnic groups, and leisure. In *Diversity and the recreation profession: Organizational perspectives*, edited by T. M. Allison & I. E. Schneider (State College, PA: Venture), 179-191.

groups through advertisements, publications, visits, and any other means possible. Critical to this process is that you reach out in a way that is consistent with the norms and expectations of those you are trying to reach. There are several ways to invite:

- Print brochures or other materials in different languages, including Braille.
- Portray diversity in the photos included in brochures and advertising.
- Advertise through media that cater to certain groups (e.g., Spanish-language newspaper).
- Visit churches, support groups, or social clubs that cater to certain groups.

The second step is to include a diverse array of people in your programs. This step seems obvious, but it requires purposeful effort and planning. Here are several suggestions:

- Provide a multilingual public announcer and interpreters at events.
- Program cultural activities or other events and programs that are of interest.
- Personally greet people as they arrive at events.
- Ask individual people whether their needs are being met and how you can help.
- Ask for opinions on how programs or services might be improved.
- Ask for feedback regarding satisfaction with quality of programs.
- Conduct these information-gathering activities both inside and outside of your agency.

Third, involve a diverse group of people in the ongoing operations of your agency. This means that not only are the participants diverse but so are those who work to provide the inclusive recreation experience. Hiring a diverse staff takes inclusion beyond the symbolism portrayed on the cover of a brochure and creates an agency system that truly operates as an inclusive mechanism. To accomplish this step, use the following strategies:

- Hire staff who are diverse in regard to race, gender, and disability.
- Hire a diverse array of supervisors, managers, and directors.
- Recruit a board of directors that is made up of a diverse group of people.

An important point regarding the I-triad is that even though "invite, include, and involve" are referred to as steps, they really should be simultaneous and ongoing efforts. If anything, step 3 would be the most effective starting point, because engaging a diverse array of people in the strategic planning and leadership of the agency will empower accomplishment in the other areas. Again, the examples are useful, but they are somewhat meaningless if inclusion does not saturate the agency environment to the point that differences are valued rather than questioned.

Together We Play Model

The Together We Play (TWP) service delivery model is the first model presented here that directly addresses the broad ecological system that encompasses the participant (see figure 4.6). Described as an ecological approach, the model was created to address links between social service agencies, general recreation service providers, parents, and participants in a manner that facilitates successful participation in community recreation (Scholl, Dieser, & Davison, 2005; Scholl, Smith, & Davison; 2005).

The TWP model is also somewhat unique in its origins, as it was the result of a grassroots, or "bottom-up," approach. A coalition of concerned citizens in northwest Iowa worked together to identify barriers and resources pertinent to inclusive recreation services. The result was a collaboration between multiple agencies whose primary goal was to "offer children and youth with and without disabilities the same recreation education, and social opportunities by connecting people to community resources among agencies, thereby avoiding duplication of services" (Scholl, Dieser, & Davison, 2005, p. 300). Through community foundation funding (United Way: Vision Inclusion, Community Foundation, & R.J. McElroy Trust), a certified therapeutic recreation specialist was hired as a full-time inclusion director and given the task of coordinating the collaboration. The efforts of these agencies and individuals led to the development of the TWP model.

At the center of the model is a box representing inclusion services, which are coordinated by a certified therapeutic recreation specialist (CTRS). This box is surrounded by four circles. The circles each contain two elements: the party being served and the services to be provided. Note that the participant is not the only responsibility of

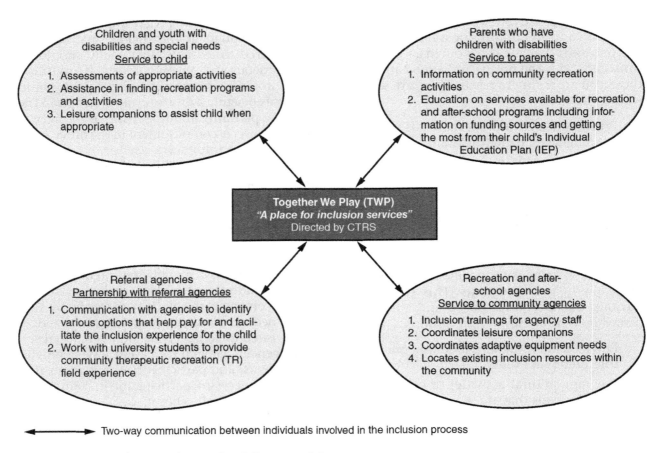

Children and youth with disabilities and special needs
Service to child

1. Assessments of appropriate activities
2. Assistance in finding recreation programs and activities
3. Leisure companions to assist child when appropriate

Parents who have children with disabilities
Service to parents

1. Information on community recreation activities
2. Education on services available for recreation and after-school programs including information on funding sources and getting the most from their child's Individual Education Plan (IEP)

Together We Play (TWP)
"A place for inclusion services"
Directed by CTRS

Referral agencies
Partnership with referral agencies

1. Communication with agencies to identify various options that help pay for and facilitate the inclusion experience for the child
2. Work with university students to provide community therapeutic recreation (TR) field experience

Recreation and after-school agencies
Service to community agencies

1. Inclusion trainings for agency staff
2. Coordinates leisure companions
3. Coordinates adaptive equipment needs
4. Locates existing inclusion resources within the community

◄──────► Two-way communication between individuals involved in the inclusion process

Figure 4.6 Together We Play service delivery model.

Reprinted, by permission, from K. Scholl, J. Smith, and A. Davidson, 2005, "Agency readiness to provide inclusive recreation and after-school services for children with disabilities," *Therapeutic Recreation Journal*, 39(1): 50.

the CTRS. Parents, referral agencies, and community agencies (e.g., recreation and after-school agencies) are all beneficiaries of inclusion services under this model. The CTRS works to fulfill services such as coordinating the acquisition and use of adaptive equipment for recreation centers, providing information on community recreation activities to parents, assisting referral agencies in securing funding for participation, and arranging leisure companions for children with disabilities.

The manner in which the model was developed created several significant strengths within the model and the resulting program. The sense of ownership resulting from involving several agencies led to a broad array of funders. A total of 15 different agencies contributed funds between 2001 and 2005 (Scholl, Dieser, & Davison, 2005). In addition, the ecological approach to service delivery was enabled by the bottom-up approach to planning. Only through open communication and exchanging of ideas can such a complex and dynamic system be considered. The TWP model

is similar to other models in this chapter in that it recommends employing an independent inclusion specialist or inclusion team and advocates a systems approach. Although these two elements would be considered best practice by most inclusion experts, the most valuable element of the model may be the creators' suggestion to use the bottom-up approach. Doing so builds a sense of moral ownership within the community and creates a culture where inclusion is valued.

Supportive Recreation Inclusion Model

A second model that is based on the idea that people and their environments are interconnected (i.e., ecological theory) is the supportive recreation inclusion (SRI) model (Devine, O'Brien, & Crawford, 2004). This model, like the TWP model, emphasizes the importance of considering the participant's entire world when attempting to provide an inclusive experience.

Examples of systemic factors that can affect the inclusion process include attitudes of the community toward the participant, availability of public transportation, and resources available to the recreation provider (Devine, O'Brien, & Crawford, 2004).

The SRI model consists of four components. Like the TWP model, the SRI model was designed in the context of inclusive services for persons with disabilities. The labels depicted in this figure have been slightly modified to reflect that this model can have a broader application. The parentheses within each component label represent the terminology used by the original authors.

Each of these four components can be analyzed in regard to strengths and barriers, and recommendations for support services can be made to address any areas of need. Devine and colleagues (2004) identified potential support services as including "recreation program assessments, leisure skills training, adaptation of recreation program components, service provider training, or inclusion follow-up evaluations" (p. 212).

Again, the strength of this model is not in these specific support services (as they have been identified in other models) but in the fact that they must be conducted at various levels within the ecological framework of the participant. The four components of the SRI essentially map out this ecological framework.

The first component is the individual. When addressing this component, the recreation professional works together with the individual in designing an inclusion plan to "match (the) individual with recreation programs in their community" (Devine, O'Brien, & Crawford, 2004, p. 212).

The second component is support systems. Support systems include immediate and extended family, friends, and caregivers who are able to support the individual in her daily functioning. A sibling or friend who is able to drive a participant to recreation programs and assist her during the program would be considered an element of this support system. This example illustrates the importance of assessing support systems and using this information to develop an inclusion plan. Likewise, ignoring this aspect of the participant's life will surely have a negative impact on her experiences.

The third component is the actual recreation service provider. This component involves an "analysis of the recreation organization's philosophical, administrative, programming, and resource components" (Devine, O'Brien, & Crawford, 2004, p. 213). Specific strategies for addressing needs in this area can then be implemented, such as awareness training for staff or facility modifications to address accessibility issues. As was the case in the I-triad model and the TWP model, a thorough evaluation of the recreation agency, beginning with the core philosophy, is a critical component to ongoing and pervasive inclusion of all people.

The final component is the community at large. This is the broadest of the four components, representing various ecological factors in the community such as health care services, transportation, providers of goods and services, education, and government services and policies (Devine et al., 2004). Understanding these macrosystem elements is critical to developing the most effective plan for using resources and addressing barriers to recreation participation. Failure to consider these factors often creates additional barriers. For example, scheduling programs for evening hours, after many bus routes are shut down for the day, undermines an inclusion plan that involves participation in this program. Likewise, failure to understand how program participation can be funded or subsidized through medical insurance or tax-reducing medical savings accounts limits the opportunities available to the participant.

CITI Model

If access equals influence, as some have asserted (Boyte, 2000; Boyte et al., 1999), then the implied hierarchy from physical to programmatic and then to social access can lead to an opportunity for inclusion and the associated experience. An "independent essence experience" becomes possible, which is more than access, more than accommodation, and more than having a physical or social presence. It allows one to truly be a part of the situation and the experience. The individual is integrated into the essence of the experience. Essence refers to the attributes that define the experience. Thus, inclusion allows a participant to become an essential, or defining, part of ongoing activities and the surrounding culture, both internally (as experienced by the participant) and externally (as experienced by others). The participant and the surrounding culture have an independently positive and symbiotic relationship in which inclusiveness is essential and fundamental (Ellis, 1993; Robertson & Long, 2001, 2002).

The CITI model is based on this assumption that access can lead to inclusion but only when additional circumstances are present. The CITI model is an attempt to provide a framework for measuring and understanding the presence or absence of these circumstances within communities. The model is the broadest presented so far, going beyond recreation agencies and their partners to a level that considers societal conditions as a whole.

The model was aptly named the community inclusion target indices (CITI) model by Dr. David Compton (the chair of the World Leisure Commission on Access and Inclusion from 1998 to 2004).

The CITI model was originally presented at the Fifth World Leisure Congress in Bilbao, Spain, in 2000 by Robertson, Chambers, and Holmes and then again by Robertson and Long at the Third National Inclusion in Recreation Institute (NIRI) in Las Vegas, Nevada, in 2002. Originally conceived as a measurement instrument, the model now resembles a five-ringed archery target (see figure 4.7). The center, or bull's-eye, is representative of an essence, or inclusive, experience. The concentric rings represent the extent to which inclusion is present, with greater levels of inclusion represented as you move from outside to inside the ring.

The model also suggests that inclusion should be measured in regard to three distinct dimensions: individual experiences (person), community support and resources (environment), and circumstances (situations). Likewise, the most effective effort to create and foster inclusive experiences involves considering the person, the environment, and the situation.

Within each of the three dimensions, specific indicators can be measured, plotted, and portioned out. The dots depicted in figure 4.7 show how individual indicators would be plotted as a means of examining overall inclusion. Each individual indicator is scored on a 0 to 10 standardized scale, with 10 being within the bull's-eye and 0 falling outside the outer ring of the target.

Rather than listing specific indicators that should always be used within the CITI model, the developers of the model recommended that indicators be chosen based on the particular context of how and where the model is being applied. The CITI model can be catered to fit specific community needs or concerns. Listed here are examples of possible indicators for each dimension of the CITI model.

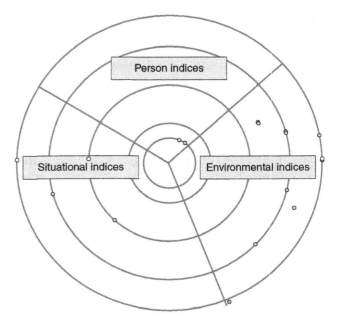

Figure 4.7 When plotting CITI model indicators, the extent of inclusion is indicated by the extent to which the plotted indicators cluster around the bull's eye.

Person
- Socioeconomic status
- Personal data (e.g., age, gender, race)
- Domain assessment (e.g., psychosocial, physical, intellectual, spiritual)
- Interest and motivation

Environment
- Funding base (e.g., taxes, fees)
- Community data (e.g., size, density, composition)
- Transportation (e.g., system ratings, classification)
- Weather zone (e.g., planting zone, water resources)

Situation
- Acute versus chronic condition(s)
- Inclusion (e.g., access or inclusion networks in place)
- Multiple systems (e.g., public, non-profit, for-profit)
- Ability or independence (e.g., knowledge, skill, experience levels)

These profiles have several possible applications. The broadest application is to assess the overall culture of inclusion within the identified community. This information allows for strategic planning in regard to how to address gaps or barriers related to inclusion throughout the community and in the context of the current situation. Eventually, standardized scales might be developed that would allow for community assessments to be compared across cities and for the establishment of benchmarks regarding best practices for building inclusive programs and communities. The measurement of the CITI model would allow recreation agencies and other service providers to track the possible impact that their programs and procedures might have on their local community. The profile is applicable at the micro level, because understanding the community, situational factors, and characteristics of individual participants allows for a true systems approach to developing inclusion plans and providing individualized services (Robertson, 2004).

Summary

This chapter has explained a variety of concepts, processes, and models that have been developed and put into place as a means of fostering inclusion in recreation settings.

With so much support in place, it is important to remember the notion of prerequisites to inclusion. Examining attitudes, especially our own, is critical even before we begin thinking about how to provide inclusive experiences and environments. As mentioned at the beginning of this chapter, for inclusion to be possible, professionals must be skilled at providing participants with access to facilities and programs. This includes identifying and implementing appropriate accommodations and adaptations in a manner that does not trivialize activities or patronize participants. Failure to address these issues will undermine efforts to create an inclusive recreation environment, whereas addressing them can greatly enhance the recreation experience for participants.

These prerequisites, along with the structured frameworks of the presented processes and models, can be used to facilitate true inclusive experiences among all participants. Professionals must be familiar with these models and apply them in appropriate situations, because each has a particular focus.

Although we are legally and morally bound to provide experiences, environments, and service opportunities that are as inclusive as possible, individual participants may still seek segregated opportunities. People with disabilities are citizens and consumers of our profession. The choice is still theirs. Inclusion is an ongoing process and ultimately a culture, not an event. It takes time, practice, and patience. It is essential and fundamental to modern service provision and it starts with you.

Discussion Questions

1. If you were assigned the task of developing a disability awareness campaign on campus, and one of your primary goals was to promote positive attitudes toward people with disabilities, what strategies could you implement? How do these strategies align with the theory of planned behavior and other information pertaining to attitudes presented in this chapter?

2. Review the Anderson and Kress inclusion process presented in this chapter. Discuss the following questions.

   a. What strategies could be used to promote inclusive recreation programs in your community?

   b. Discuss the importance of confidentiality in the registration process. How would you handle the gathering of confidential information?

   c. What content areas should be included in staff inclusion training? How would you prioritize these areas, and are some more important than others?

   d. Why is it important to adapt the recreation environment only when absolutely necessary?

   e. What are some programming-related strategies for promoting inclusion.

3. Which model do you see as most relevant to your future as a recreation professional? Can you think of situations where each model would be useful?

4. The summary of this chapter mentions that inclusion is a choice. Can you think of situations where participants might prefer a segregated environment? Can this choice be made without discriminating against others who want to join you (what's the difference between self-segregation and discrimination against others)?

National Center on Physical Activity and Disability Community Inclusion Model—City of Reno Inclusion Plan

One of the inclusion supervisor's first duties was to develop a comprehensive plan that addressed programs, opportunities, and services for persons with disabilities throughout the department. Following a system of research and investigation, planning, implementation, and evaluation, 1- and 5-year inclusion plans were created to be incorporated into the mission, business plan, and master plan of the Parks, Recreation, and Community Services Department. Following is the outline of that plan:

Program Purpose

To include persons with disabilities in the provision of excellent parks, recreation, and community opportunities that enhance our community.

Desired Outcome 1

Ensure that all parks, recreation, and community services programs and services are able to include persons with disabilities.

- Strategy A: Create a model of inclusion that allows for each program or service within the department to be responsible for the choices, opportunities, and participation of persons with disabilities.
- Strategy B: Provide persons with disabilities access to all city-sponsored or contracted special events.
- Strategy C: Ensure accessible and barrier-free facilities, parks, and features.
- Strategy D: Improve staff qualifications and training opportunities regarding inclusion, therapeutic recreation, and persons with disabilities.
- Strategy E: Develop a marketing plan that informs citizens with disabilities about the department's services, facilities, and programs and invites people to participate.

Desired Outcome 2

Develop the inclusion office into a resource for the Parks, Recreation, and Community Services Department to address the recreation, leisure, and inclusion needs of participants with disabilities.

- Strategy A: Provide support to managerial and supervisory staff on budget and funding issues related to inclusion.
- Strategy B: Create a leisure education program that introduces and informs participants with disabilities of department programs, classes, and services.
- Strategy C: Develop an inclusion management and personnel plan for part-time specialized staff, therapeutic staff, and interns that addresses the needs of the department to provide recreation services, opportunities, and programs for persons with disabilities.
- Strategy D: Provide quality assurance of services through periodic review and documentation.

Desired Outcome 3

Facilitate the growth of a continuum of recreation opportunities, programs, and services that meet the needs of persons with disabilities within the Truckee Meadows.

Strategy A: Establish and support current and future partnerships and collaborations with area agencies and organizations to ensure a continuum of programming for persons with disabilities in the Truckee Meadows.

Implementation

The implementation of this plan requires the support and approval of numerous organizations and people and all of the divisions with the department, each of which has an important role in the inclusion of people with disabilities within the community. The body of the plan includes realizable steps, convening parties, timelines, and budget for each desired outcome.

Evaluation

This inclusion plan is subject to approval by the department director, is reviewed by the Access Advisory Committee and the Recreation and Park Commission, and will be adopted by the city council as part of the department master plan.

The department and the Access Advisory Committee will conduct an annual review. The inclusion business plan will be evaluated as part of the PRCS 1- and 5-year budget process.

Reprinted, by permission, from NCPAD. Available:
http://www.ncpad.org/fun/fact_sheet.php?sheet=95&view=all&print=yes&PHPSESSID=0

PART

II

The Inclusion Process for Recreation and Leisure

Access and Training for Clients, Staff, and Volunteers

Marketing Inclusive Recreation Experiences

Stephanie West, PhD

Appalachian State University

Erik Rabinowitz, PhD

Appalachian State University

> *This may seem simple, but you need to give customers what they want, not what you think they want. And, if you do this, people will keep coming back.*
>
> –John Ilhan

Learning Outcomes

After completing this chapter, learners will be able to do the following:

- Explain the difference between a marketing orientation and a sales orientation.
- Identify and describe the four characteristics that differentiate a service from a good.
- Identify and describe the seven elements of the marketing mix.
- Explain the purpose of market segmentation and when to use each of the three types of market segmentation.
- Identify and describe the three recognized approaches to pricing a service.
- Identify and describe the five basic types of promotional efforts.
- Explain how the "servicescape" of a service may affect a participant's experience.
- Identify and describe the specific roles of the two groups of people who are essential to the provision of a service.
- Identify and describe the two basic types of skill sets needed by service staff.
- Identify and describe some of the common evaluation methods used for evaluating a service.
- Identify and describe the five dimensions of service quality.

In 2000, as many as 54 million Americans, or nearly 20% of the population, had a disability or activity limitation (U.S. Census Bureau, 2000). Other groups of people who may feel marginalized and unwelcome at traditional programs include those whose race, gender, age, body shape, or sexual orientation is different than that of typical program participants. Effective marketing is key to the provision of inclusive recreation services. This chapter summarizes the value of developing a service that best meets the needs of participants, including those from diverse groups. Specific components discussed in the chapter include the elements of a service that distinguish it from a product and the seven components of an inclusive marketing mix that are essential to the development of a well-received service. The chapter concludes with information on the value of evaluations in the marketing process and the five dimensions of service quality with which most people evaluate services.

Inclusive Marketing to Meet Needs

Many people have the misconception that marketing refers to the promotion of a product whereby you convince others to purchase your product. Perhaps this was once the case. Many people also still believe that salespeople should not be trusted and will do anything, including lying about their product, to make a sale. Although marketing has roots in sales, a sales orientation with a focus on influencing consumers to buy your product has been replaced by a marketing orientation in which you develop a product to meet consumer needs (Pride & Ferrell, 2008).

If the most effective method for selling a product is to develop the product so that it meets the needs of consumers, it makes sense that recreation services should also be designed to best meet the needs of those who use them. People who use products are typically referred to as consumers. Although consumers include people who use services, in recreation we also refer to consumers as participants, clients, or guests. In an inclusive environment, marketing includes family, caregivers, and the community.

Inclusive Services as Products

In the recreation profession, our products are services rather than goods. Services are activities performed by another party and are traditionally thought to differ from goods in four ways. The four characteristics that differentiate a service from a good are intangibility, simultaneity, heterogeneity, and perishability (Zeithaml et al., 2005). Intangibility refers to the lack of tangibility of a service; as a performance, it cannot be held or touched. For example, a person cannot touch an experience like an Alaskan Porcupine River Canoe Expedition offered by Wilderness Inquiry. Simultaneity is another characteristic because services are simultaneously consumed while they are provided. Intangibility and simultaneity prevent services from being evaluated prior to purchase and make it difficult to communicate the benefits of services to potential customers.

The heterogeneity of services reflects differences in services attributable to their reliance on the performance of people. As such, no two services will be exactly alike. Challenges associated with heterogeneity therefore arise from limitations in quality control. For example, every canoe trip will be different than the previous ones. Finally, perishability suggests that services cannot be stored for later consumption, leading to difficulties in synchronizing supply with demand for services. Thus, even if a beeper ball game (see www.tukandu.org/What%20is%20Beeper%20Ball.htm) was excellent this time, it may not be the next time. Similarly, service providers must instill greater confidence with consumers than those who sell products because services cannot be returned or resold.

Marketing Mix for Inclusive Services

The development of a product (e.g., canoe) or service (e.g., guided canoe trip) to meet the needs of consumers or participants is accomplished through the manipulation of elements that are under the control of the person, agency, or business responsible for developing it. These elements are known as the marketing mix. For products, the traditional marketing mix consists of product, price, place, and promotion, frequently known as the four Ps. An expanded marketing mix, however, has been adopted by service marketers and includes people, physical evidence, and the process of assembly (Zeithaml et al., 2005). This section focuses on how each of the seven elements of the marketing mix for services can be used in providing inclusive recreation services (see figure 5.1).

Figure 5.1 The seven Ps of inclusive marketing.

Inclusive Product, aka Service

This text focuses on recreation services as the product (i.e., service) being provided. Perhaps the most important factor contributing to the development of a service to meet the needs of participants is developing a service for all. Market segmentation is the division of the market into smaller, identifiable markets consisting of people with similar wants or needs as a result of comparable sociodemographic, lifestyle, or behavioral characteristics.

Rather than using an undifferentiated approach to market segmentation and providing a single service for every available participant, recreation leaders may find another approach to market segmentation is to use either a differentiated or a concentrated approach. A differentiated approach provides different services for different groups of people (target markets), whereas a concentrated approach focuses on a single service for a specific

target market. Service providers can develop recreation services that use any of the following approaches:

- A concentrated approach that focuses primarily on people with disabilities; for example, special recreation associations, like the South Suburban Special Recreation Association (www.sssra.org), provide year-round recreation opportunities for people with disabilities.

- A differentiated approach that focuses on people with disabilities as one of several target markets, such as most city and parks and recreation programs do. For an example, see the City of Miami Parks and Recreation Web site (www.miamigov.com/cms/parks).

- An undifferentiated approach that provides completely inclusive services by accommodating those with special needs but otherwise providing services at the same level as everyone else. A significant movement in this area is the inclusion of universal design components. An example is removing all steps to a recreation center's main entrance and replacing them with a sloping ramp that is easier for all users. More examples of universal design can be found at the Center for Universal Design Web site (www.design.ncsu.edu/cud/), and information on minimum design standards can be found at www.ada.gov/stdspdf.htm. An advantage of universal design is that a person with a disability is not singled out but instead is one of many participants. From a marketing perspective, however, concentrated and differentiated approaches are more visible to the public in terms of input in perceptions.

Inclusive Pricing

Given the intangibility of a service and the related inability to evaluate it prior to purchase, price is especially significant as an indicator of service quality. There are three recognized approaches to pricing: cost-based pricing, competition-based pricing, and demand-based pricing (Fisk et al., 2007). In cost-based pricing, the price of the service is based on the cost to provide the service. If a profit is needed, the participant might be charged a fee equal to twice the cost of providing that service. In this case, however, the price of the service is still dependent on the cost of provision. Competition-based pricing takes into consideration what the competition is charging. A service can be priced less than that of a competitor in an attempt to win business by appealing to the price sensitivity of participants, or the service could be priced more than a competitor so as to convey a greater value. With demand-based pricing, service prices are established based on what the market will bear according to the principles of supply and demand. When demand is high, prices increase, whereas low demand leads to lower prices.

Although it is illegal to charge a greater amount for a service than what is otherwise charged, you can, however, anticipate such needs and adjust fees for all participants based on this expense. The key here is that integrating costs into marketing that directly target people with disabilities or other differences is not relevant because these differentiating factors should not be a factor in determining fees for a specific marginalized group. It is relevant, however, in regard to overall, undifferentiated fees or costs.

Therefore, when considering that the expenses of providing inclusive services must be absorbed into the fees of all participants rather than adjusted for each individual's accommodation needs, it is especially important to consider the role of nonmonetary costs and their impact on marketing.

Before establishing the price of a service, consider the role of nonmonetary costs and the perceived value of the service. Nonmonetary costs are those costs that are not considered directly in the price but may have a substantial impact on the perceived value of a service. Typical examples include travel costs (such as gas, fees for parking, toll roads, or bus fares) and travel time necessary to get to and from the service, the amount of effort to be able to participate in a service, and the opportunity foregone in order to participate in the service. For people with disabilities, going to a recreation center for exercise could be viewed as time-consuming, inconvenient, and uncomfortable, thus having high nonmonetary costs. However, these nonmonetary costs could be reduced if recreation professionals were prepared to meet the needs of these people. This would increase the value of a service, defined as the result of benefits received minus burdens endured. Burdens include the price of the service as well as the nonmonetary costs of using the service whereas the benefits received are the outcomes of using the service.

Inclusive Promotion

Many people use the terms *marketing* and *promotion* interchangeably. However, they are not synonymous. Rather, promotion is one of the seven key components in marketing. So promotion is marketing, but marketing is not necessarily promotion. Although marketing is the development of a product or service to meet the needs of consumers or participants, promotion is the intentional communication of that product or service to its customer base. Although different names may be used, there are five basic types of promotional efforts: advertising, publicity, direct contact, sales promotion, and public relations (Pride & Ferrell, 2008).

Advertising is the public promotion of a service through public media, such as newspaper, radio, or television. Typically, advertising is intentional, requires a fee, and is in the control of the agency placing the advertisement rather than the media outlet. So when an agency places an advertisement in the newspaper, the agency indicates exactly how the ad will look (a half page ad in color), where the ad will be located in the newspaper (e.g., page 1 or page 8), and what day or days the ad is to run. Including people with disabilities in advertisements and recognizing diverse groups in advertising (e.g., TV ads that have subscripts for people with hearing impairments, Web sites that are designed for people with visual impairments) clearly communicate to the public that your program welcomes people of all abilities and cultures. Without such advertisements, many people with disabilities and their families will assume that your program is like many others that have turned them away. Target marketing to people with inclusive needs might be as simple as running an advertisement in a trade journal such as *Sports 'n Spokes* (www.pvamagazines.com/sns/).

Publicity involves the dissemination of information, but unlike advertising, publicity tends to be free and in the control of the press rather than the agency. So although an agency might write a press release about an event, the newspaper may choose to not use it, to make small mention of it (such as placing just the facts in the announcements section of the paper), or to run an entire feature article. Other examples of publicity include in-house newsletters or flyers. Publicize your offerings in a variety of community institutions and organizations (e.g., public and private schools, cultural organizations, churches) that serve people from diverse groups. When preparing materials, consider your target market. For example, you may want to increase the font size to accommodate elderly people and those with visual impairments. There may be a small cost associated with buying the paper and making these materials, but these costs are negligible and the agency does not need to contract with a media source. One of the secondary benefits of inclusive programming is the increased media coverage for an agency that can result when the media sees their programs as newsworthy.

Direct contact is often referred to as direct sales in the case of products. However, not all services are sold. Direct contact, therefore, involves communicating directly with potential participants and is used frequently in the recreation setting. Efforts to be inclusive through direct contact with potential participants might include having staff attend local community group meetings for diverse populations where they can talk with individuals, their families, or caregivers about how they might use your services. For example, those unfamiliar with how to play beeper baseball

© Photodisc/Getty Images

Use advertising, publicity, direct contact, sales promotion, or public relations so that people will use the programs you offer.

may want to talk to someone about it before they commit themselves to becoming a participant. Beep ball is an inclusive softball game designed to be played by people both with and without visual impairments. The ball and bases give off beeping sounds to allow players to locate them. Players without visual impairments wear masks. (For more information on beeper ball, see http://everything2.com/index.pl?node_id=1673653.)

Recreation professionals often believe strongly in their ability to meet the needs of their customers and, as such, are frequently seen recruiting participants or encouraging current participants to increase their involvement. Meeting the needs of diverse customers may entail hiring people with special skills, abilities, and language proficiencies. For example, Royal Caribbean Cruise Line, a private cruise line, goes above and beyond the requirements of the Americans with Disabilities Act by having two interpreters on board any ship in which a guest notifies her travel agent that she requires such services. Rather than receiving a salary, both interpreters cruise free while providing the interpretive services and receive an additional free cruise they may use at their convenience. Recreation agencies interested in capitalizing on the impact of direct contact can try using a snowball technique where they have people from a particular group recruit for the agency by bringing a friend to an agency program.

Sales promotion involves using items or activities to help spark interest and generate involvement above and beyond what the service alone might achieve. Examples include coupons, giveaways, or special events that celebrate a milestone. For example, two people might get in for the price of one, or caregivers might be admitted free of charge.

The area of public relations is the least tangible of the five types of promotion and entails providing a positive community image. An organization can accomplish this by examining its physical environment (parking lot, building entrance, inside all the rooms), information and materials (pamphlets, flyers), communication (telephones, TTY, assistive listening device, sign language interpreters), and staff and volunteers' attitudes about disabilities, all of which can improve or hurt your public relations (NCODH, 2002). Examples include hiring people with disabilities and including these people in promotion materials. You can also include a script at the bottom of a Web page, like this: "We are committed to providing facilities, programs, and services that are accessible to everyone, including those with disabilities, and we are willing to make reasonable adjustments to meet your needs. If you have a disability and would like to suggest any changes that would be helpful to you, we would be happy to hear from you."

Inclusive Place, aka Location

Although place for a product is where it is purchased, place for a service includes both where it is purchased and where the service takes place. For example, a store or your hotel might sell tickets to go canoeing, but you need to either drive or take a shuttle to the river where the trip begins. As such, it is important to consider the physical evidence of inclusion at both locations. See the following for more details on how physical evidence relates to the place or location of a service.

Physical Evidence of Inclusion

The tangible aspects of a service that communicate physical evidence include the service environment and the image of the agency as represented by its promotion and service staff. The physical evidence of a service environment is like the packaging of a product in that it communicates quality to the participant. The service

setting, also known as "servicescape," includes both its physical exterior and interior and is affected by design, smell, sounds, lighting, and ambience. Specific attributes of these features that should be considered in the development of an appropriate servicescape include signage, parking, landscaping, layout, air quality and temperature, restrooms, waiting rooms, curb cuts, ramps, accessibility, and offices.

Ideally, every component will assist service performance by enhancing participant flow and encouraging the accomplishment of goals by both participants and staff; beyond the legal requirements of ADA compliance. In addition to enhancing service performance, a well-designed servicescape helps to differentiate the services from the services of competitors, communicate which target market the service has been designed to serve, facilitate socialization, and communicate roles, behaviors, and relationships among and between participants and staff. Care should be taken to ensure that all aspects of the service, even those beyond the setting, communicate an appropriate message, including paperwork, staff attire, publicity materials, and company vehicles. For example, registration paperwork for a summer camp might be proactive and include a space for necessary accommodations rather than require the person bring these needs to the attention of camp management.

In recreation, our physical evidence is often the facility in which we offer our services. These facilities can communicate either acceptable or unacceptable access and quality to the participant. In the example in chapter 12, there are two layouts for a workout facility: one that offers successful flow in terms of inclusion (figure 12.1b) and one that does not (figure 12.1a). From this example, we can see physical evidence being applied. In figure 12.1a, you can see that the person who uses a wheelchair has significant difficulty communicating with check-in desk staff. However, in figure 12.1b, service quality is improved by simply adjusting the height of the check-in desk. In addition, figure 12.1b demonstrates how access to equipment is increased for those in wheelchairs by simply moving some of the equipment, thereby improving flow.

Inclusive People

The two groups of people who are essential to the provision of a service are participants and staff. It is important to recruit appropriate participants identified through market segmentation. Choosing the right participant for your service involves selecting those who are identifiable, reachable, and in large enough numbers to ensure long-term success. Given the simultaneity of a service, participants are integrally involved during the consumption of services. As such, other participants can also influence a participant's interaction with a service. Thus, participants need to be educated on how to help themselves, help others, and interact properly with other customers and staff. For example, if you don't have enough challenged individuals in your community who want to play wheelchair basketball, you might recruit and train able-bodied volunteers to participate as well.

On the other hand, a misbehaving customer creates a negative environment for other participants. While it may be difficult to screen out customers who may misbehave during your recruitment of participants, you can train staff on how to minimize the situation by noticing signs of escalating misbehavior and addressing the misbehavior in a timely fashion. Once suitable participants have been recruited, they need to be trained. For example, participants at a karaoke party might need to know how to select a song or how to operate the microphone to minimize speaker feedback. Such training can improve customer-to-customer and staff-to-customer interactions, and a participant who knows how a service is to be used is much more self-sufficient and efficient than one who is unfamiliar with this information. Volunteers at a dance are more helpful to creating a positive environment if they know how to dance with someone who is in a wheelchair. Finally, whenever possible, customers should be rewarded for their contributions in helping other customers or staff. A few kind words may be all that is necessary, for example, "Thank you, Joe, for showing Sarah how to pick a song."

Staff are the second group of people critical to a service and include both paid employees and volunteers. Regardless of whether a staff member is paid, proper steps to managing staff effectively include hiring intelligently, training intensively, monitoring incessantly, and rewarding inspirationally (Fisk et al., 2007). Each of these steps requires attention to technical skill and social skill sets. Technical skills involve the ability to perform a specific skill, such as belaying the wheelchair for a person with quadriplegia. Social skills, on the other hand, involve the ability to

© Jeff Greenberg/age fotostock

Participants knowledgeable in the procedures at a program can help other participants to have a positive experience.

interact positively with other people. In the case of belaying a person with quadriplegia, it might involve the ability to make the person feel safe and willing to reach slightly beyond her comfort zone to experience growth. Sixteen U.S. states have offices of disabilities and health services (e.g., the North Carolina Office of Disability and Health, or NCODH). In many cases, these offices will send a professional to your facility to train your staff on preparing technically and socially for working with diverse groups. Find out whether your state government has an office like this.

Inclusive Process of Service Assembly

The process of service assembly entails smoothly connecting individual activities that comprise the service. These activities allow participants and staff to accomplish their goals. Each activity must be conducted efficiently and effectively and then ordered together with the others to provide an optimal experience for participants. Often, as in figure 12.1, *a* and *b* the physical layout of a facility enhances or impedes a smooth process of assembly. One way that service providers can reassure participants about the service they have purchased is to include steps in the process of assembly that are visible to participants. For example, you can give anxious family members or caregivers a brochure you have developed for a summer camp to explain the steps you have taken to provide an inclusive camp experience.

Inclusive Evaluation

Given that service providers need to understand how they are meeting or failing to meet the needs of their participants, evaluation is especially important for services that are prone to intangibility. Evaluations should be conducted for each of the seven components of the marketing mix as well as for each of the five areas that comprise service quality. Opportunities for evaluation exist among customers, staff, facilities, and processes. Common evaluation methods include soliciting feedback or complaints from customers, soliciting feedback from staff, evaluating customer requests, conducting need-based or posttransaction surveys, hiring mystery shoppers, making comparisons with successful competing agencies (also known as benchmarking), and practicing management by walking around.

Among diverse groups, some people may not be intellectually or physically able to participate in an evaluation without slight modifications. You must go beyond basic facility and program modifications aimed at facilitating inclusion and consider how even the manner with which you collect participant feedback influences your ability to be inclusive. For example, if you determine what new programs to offer or facility improvements to make based on participant feedback from a written or online survey, the results may not appropriately represent those with intellectual challenges. Survey questions may need to be modified for a lower comprehension level or asked verbally to more accurately communicate with this population. Caregivers are sometimes helpful in soliciting feedback from clients. Caregivers can either rephrase the questions on an individual basis or provide their opinions based on their personal interactions with a person who is intellectually challenged.

Inclusive Service Quality

The quality of a service must be evaluated. Service quality is the participant's appraisal of the service. People have been found to evaluate service quality in terms of five dimensions: reliability, assurance, empathy, tangibles, and responsiveness (Zeithaml et al., 2005). Reliability suggests that participants can count on consistent delivery and performance of a service. Camp Little Giant was one of the pioneers in camping for people with disabilities and has reliably provided continuous summer camp programming since 1952. Recreation agencies with a history of success are encouraged to demonstrate this success in their advertisements or on facility signage. Another method for demonstrating reliability is to allow prospective participants and their family members or caregivers access to previous evaluations of service performance. Calculating retention rates and sharing them with clients can be an effective means of communicating reliability.

Assurance conveys a message to participants that the service will be performed well. Displayed certifications, such as the following, provide physical evidence of assurance:

- Certified Parks and Recreation Professional (CPRP)
- Certified Therapeutic Recreation Specialist (CTRS)
- Degrees of staff (e.g., BS in recreation)
- Agency accreditation with a national body (e.g., Commission for Accreditation of Park and Recreation Agencies [CAPRA], Certified Playground Safety Inspector [CPSI])

The presence of appropriate inclusive facilities provides physical evidence of assurance as well. Some state governments will help agencies improve their physical accessibility for clients. The North Carolina Office on Disability and Health offers a free on-site inclusion training workshop, during which staff from that office conduct an accessibility assessment and help the agency develop a plan of action to remove potential barriers. Including positive testimonials from previous participants helps to assure potential participants and their significant others that they can trust an agency.

Empathy refers to whether agencies and staff who offer a service seem to understand the feelings of participants. If the check-in desk at a hotel is too tall, an empathetic staff member might move out from behind the desk when someone who is using a wheelchair approaches. Agencies can improve empathy among staff by providing sensitivity training. In addition to seeking support from state disability and health offices, agencies can request assistance from professional experts, local colleges and universities, or other agencies that have more experience with diverse groups. For example, the coordinator of public school special education classes might offer suggestions about how to improve a local playground beyond the legal requirements of ADA.

Tangibles are those aspects of a service that can be evaluated, such as setting, equipment, and staff. Tangibles in an inclusive art program used by soldiers with upper-limb impairments or amputations might include special brushes or jars that do not require the use of hands or fingers.

Responsiveness entails reacting quickly to meet the needs of participants. Being proactive, rather than reactive, in the provision of inclusive facilities and programs suggests that your agency is responsive to the needs of participants with physical and mental challenges. An easy-to-implement strategy is to place a sign at the entrance to a privately owned facility that states, "This facility voluntarily complies with Title III of the ADA, but additional suggestions or modifications are welcomed."

Summary

Effective marketing is key to providing inclusive recreation services that facilitate participation by all kinds of people. Those who develop a service must consider how best to meet the needs of diverse participants. Services are similar to products in many ways except that services are more likely to be intangible, heterogeneous, and perishable and are more likely to be consumed while simultaneously being produced. Seven components of an inclusive marketing mix are essential to the development of a well-received service: product (i.e., service), price, place, promotion, physical evidence, participants, and process of assembly. The development of an effective service requires monitoring. Thus, you must evaluate your service and consider how well the service addresses the five dimensions of service quality (reliability, assurance, responsibility, empathy, and tangibles).

Discussion Questions

1. Identify a recreation agency with which you are familiar and describe how it addresses the five dimensions of service quality.

2. Describe the seven elements of the marketing mix as they apply at a recreation agency with which you are familiar.

3. Identify the five basic types of promotional efforts and describe how a recreation agency that you are familiar with uses each of them.

4. Describe the servicescape for a recreation agency with which you are familiar and how you think it affects its participants' experiences.

5. Describe a situation where you have seen a staff member who was technically proficient but lacked the social skills necessary for her job.

Laura Pate

It's not the critic who counts. Not the person who points out where the strong stumbled or where the doers of great deeds could have done them better. The credit belongs to those who are actually in the arena. Whose faces are marred by dust and sweat and blood. Who strive valiantly, who err and come up short again and again. And who, while daring greatly, spend themselves in a worthy cause so that their place may not be among those cold and timid souls who know neither victory nor defeat.

> –Theodore Roosevelt

Background Information

Education

*BS in business administration from UNC–Chapel Hill *BS in leisure studies from Appalachian State University *MS in education from Southern Illinois University at Carbondale

Credentials

*Wilderness First Responder *Lifeguard *WEA National Standard Program Instructor

Special Awards

*Outstanding Alumnus (2008) *Recreation Management Program, Appalachian State University

Special Affiliations

*American Camp Association *Association for Experiential Education

Career Information

Position Director of North Carolina Programs, SOAR, Inc.

Organization Information SOAR is an outdoor and experiential education program using 10-, 12-, 18-, and 26-day expedition-style adventures with youth diagnosed with attention-deficit/hyperactivity disorder or learning disabilities. Programs are coed, students are between the ages of 8 and 18, and groups consist of seven to eight students with two staff members. Course sites include the North Carolina Smokies, Florida Keys, Wyoming, and California's Big Sur. Activities include rock climbing, whitewater rafting, backpacking, orienteering, llama treks, horsepacking, mountain biking, caving snorkeling, scuba diving, surfing, and sea kayaking.

Organization's Mission SOAR is a private, nonprofit corporation dedicated to a two-fold purpose:

*First, to provide adventure-based programs and experiential education services to individuals and families dealing with learning disabilities or attention-deficit\hyperactivity disorder

*Second, to provide experiential education services and adventure-based wilderness programs to school-aged youth

SOAR embraces a commitment to service that is evident in the professional and community involvement of its staff members.

Size of Organization SOAR has two base camps—one in Balsam, North Carolina, and one in Dubois, Wyoming. We also conduct off-site courses in California, Florida, and Costa Rica. SOAR is a certified North Carolina nonpublic school that conducts semester programs in the fall and spring. SOAR serves approximately 600 students during the summer and around 40 fall and spring semester students per year. SOAR employs 18 full-time administrative and semester staff, 6 seasonal semester staff, and approximately 80 seasonal summer staff.

Job Description Program planning and development for North Carolina summer courses. Staff recruitment and hiring. Protocol development and documentation. Risk management assessment and planning. Accreditation compliance management. North Carolina summer staff training and supervision. Oversight of permitting process for public land usage. Assistance with outdoor classrooms. Lectures and educational presentations.

Career Path Obtained undergraduate degree in recreation in 1988; spent 10 years working in a field capacity for youth-at-risk wilderness programs;

obtained master's degree in education in 1996; became program director for Connecticut Wilderness School in 1996; became program director for SOAR in 1998; became director of North Carolina Programs for SOAR in 1999.

What I Like About My Job   I enjoy planning and adventure programs, training and supervising staff, and interacting with kids.

Career Ladder   I've been with SOAR for 10 years now and I do not anticipate leaving any time soon!

Advice to Undergraduate Students   Obtain as much practical field experience as possible, particularly prior to entering graduate school or administrative positions. Work for a variety of organizations to discover your niche and to capitalize on your strengths. Continue to grow as a professional by learning new skills, attending conferences and workshops, and staying up to date on the latest peer practices.

Personal Statement   Every day I am happy to be able to help young people discover their gifts and strengths through the use of the outdoors and through experiential education. No other venues for learning are as powerful as the outdoors and adventure activities.

Providing Leisure Services for Diverse Populations

6

Monika Stodolska, PhD

University of Illinois at Urbana-Champaign

We all live with the objective of being happy; our lives are all different and yet the same.

—Anne Frank

⟫ Learning Outcomes

After completing this chapter, learners will be able to do the following:

- Describe the diverse demographic characteristics of American society.
- Identify demographic conditions and trends regarding racial and ethnic minorities, women, people living in poverty, people who are homeless, and older adults.
- Recognize the unique factors that shape the recreation patterns of various identified demographic groups.
- Identify factors that affect provision of leisure services to these unique populations.
- Identify optimal strategies to provide recreation services to minority groups.

American society has changed rapidly in recent years. The American population is aging, and every year millions of newcomers from Latin America, Asia, and other continents are becoming part of the American mosaic. As the same time, American society includes a number of other groups, such as many women or people in poverty, whose lives are conditioned by lack of socioeconomic resources, lack of time, and strenuous conditions of employment. Such factors shape people's everyday lives, including their ability to participate in leisure activities of their choice.

In this chapter we focus on four subgroups of the American population: ethnic and racial minorities, women, people who live in poverty (including those who are homeless), and older adults. We discuss the major sociodemographic characteristics and factors that affect the recreation participation of people from these groups, and we provide suggestions for how they should be served by recreation professionals.

Race and Ethnicity

Racial and ethnic minorities constitute a significant portion of the American population. While some of these families have resided in the United States for generations, others have immigrated into this country in recent years. In many cases they differ from the mainstream American population with respect to their socioeconomic characteristics and their culture, including their leisure participation patterns.

Defining Race and Ethnicity

Although some groups of people, for example, those of Creole, African, Russian, or Hispanic heritage, constitute minority populations in the United States, many people have problems in distinguishing which of these groups are considered ethnic versus racial minorities. This confusion stems from the fact that the concepts of race and ethnicity are not fully understood.

An ethnic group has been described as a group of people sharing similar culture, including family arrangements, religion, language, dress styles, art, value systems, and recreation patterns. They often share a common descent, political unity, or allegiance to a common leader, religion, language, or territory (Anderson & Frideres, 1981; Berry, 1958). There are external and internal aspects of ethnic identity. *External aspects* refer to observable behaviors such as maintaining ethnic traditions, speaking a common language, and participating in ethnic personal networks, institutional organizations, voluntary organizations (clubs and societies), and functions sponsored by the ethnic community (e.g., dances, picnics, and concerts). *Internal aspects* of ethnic identity refer to images, attitudes, and feelings (Isajiw, 1990). A person's ethnic identity is a composite of the view he has of himself as well as the views that other people hold about his or her ethnic identity (Barth, 1969). Thus, for example, a person who immigrated to the United States from Cuba at a very young age may consider himself an American, but the mainstream society may perceive and label him as Cuban-American or Latino.

According to Hutchison (1988), "Race is based on socially constructed definitions of physical appearances" (p. 18). Floyd (1998) questioned why phenotypic characteristics such as skin color, hair color, or texture would matter when it comes to recreation participation. He argued, however, "Phenotypic characteristics demarcate social boundaries and structure social interaction. . . . The meaning society ascribes to the phenotype and the societal rewards and privileges allocated to persons based on their phenotypic characteristics can have a profound effect on leisure choices and constraints. Race, as a social construct, matters because of its stratification implications" (p. 11).

Changing Sociodemographic Makeup of the United States

In the 20th century, the United States was transformed from a country composed mostly of Caucasians to one whose population represents a wide range of racial and ethnic minorities. *Caucasian* is the traditional term used to describe the white population. According to the last census, however, Latinos are also classified as whites. To avoid confusion, in this chapter we use the term *Caucasian* to denote people of non-Hispanic white descent, and we use it interchangeably with the term *mainstream white*.

At the beginning of the 20th century, the American population was 87% Caucasian, but more than 100 years later Caucasians account for less than 75% of American residents. Currently, Hispanic Americans (primarily Mexicans,

Puerto Ricans, and Cubans) constitute the largest minority group in the United States, accounting for 14.8% of the population, or approximately 44 million people (American Community Survey, 2006a). African Americans account for 12.4% of the American population (approximately 37 million people), and Asian Americans account for 4.4% of the total population (approximately 13 million people; American Community Survey, 2006a). America's ethnic landscape also includes a rapidly growing South Asian population (with India and Pakistan being the largest source countries), an Arab population, a sizeable Jewish population, and people from other ethnic groups, including those of European origins, such as Italians, Russians, and Poles.

The most recent projections from the U.S. Census Bureau forecast that in 2050, Caucasians will account for barely half of the U.S. population, the proportion of Hispanic Americans will increase to 25%, and African Americans will remain at approximately 13%. If these projections materialize, today's minority groups will constitute tomorrow's "average American citizens" and, thus, the culture of the mainstream, including its leisure patterns, will significantly change.

The growth of the ethnic minority population in the United States can be attributed to two major factors.

First, immigration has accounted for more than one-third of the growth of the minorities since 1980 (Martin & Midgley, 2003). In 2007, more than 38 million immigrants lived in the United States, which constituted 12.6% of the American population (Terrazas & Batalova, 2008). The majority of immigrants came from Latin America. The top source countries of immigration included Mexico (30.8% of all immigrants to the U.S.), followed by the Philippines (4.5%), India (3.9%), and China (excluding Hong Kong and Taiwan; 3.6%). It is estimated that approximately 12 million immigrants reside in the United States illegally (Terrazas & Batalova, 2008). Undocumented immigrants make up 30% of the nation's foreign-born population.

The second major reason for the rapid increase in the minority populations in the United States is higher fertility rates among some minority women. Many of the minorities come from countries where large families are the norm. Moreover, many minority women, particularly those of Hispanic background, tend to have their first child at a younger age than Caucasian women, which contributes to a larger total family size (Pollard & O'Hare, 1999).

Spatial Distribution of Ethnic and Racial Minorities in the United States

Members of ethnic minorities and recent immigrants in particular show distinct residence patterns. African Americans are primarily concentrated in southern and southeastern states: Georgia, South Carolina, Alabama, Mississippi, and Louisiana. Hispanic Americans are primarily concentrated in the southern and southwestern states: Texas, New Mexico, Arizona, and California. Asian Americans are primarily concentrated in Hawaii, California, Nevada, Washington, and Alaska. Native Americans are primarily concentrated in Arizona, New Mexico, Oklahoma, Montana, South Dakota, and Alaska (see figures 6.1-6.4 on pages 96-99).

This spatial concentration of minorities in the United States is changing because of high rates of immigration to this country. Most new immigrants continue to cluster into large, mostly coastal metropolitan areas, such as Los Angeles, New York, San Francisco, Chicago, Miami, and Houston. These metropolitan centers are home to more than 60% of all foreign-born residents; however, this spatial distribution of minorities has changed rapidly. Now the states with traditionally lower concentrations of immigrants, such as Nevada, Utah, Colorado, and Nebraska, and southeastern states of Arkansas, Tennessee, North Carolina, South Carolina, Georgia, and Alabama, are experiencing the most significant increases in the number of immigrants. They are attracted to these states by the available jobs in the manufacturing sector, construction, and agricultural industry (e.g., poultry).

Moreover, although many immigrants choose large metropolitan centers as their destinations, many of them, and Hispanics in particular, now tend to increasingly settle in small towns where it is easier to obtain jobs. Whereas populations of big cities have been diverse for centuries, new immigrants completely change the makeup of small towns and communities.

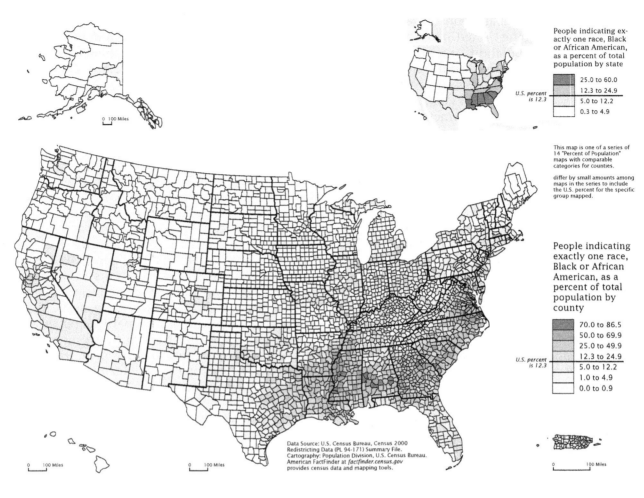

People indicating exactly one race, Black or African American, as a percent of total population by state

U.S. percent is 12.3

- 25.0 to 60.0
- 12.3 to 24.9
- 5.0 to 12.2
- 0.3 to 4.9

This map is one of a series of 14 "Percent of Population" maps with comparable categories for counties.

differ by small amounts among maps in the series to include the U.S. percent for the specific group mapped.

People indicating exactly one race, Black or African American, as a percent of total population by county

U.S. percent is 12.3

- 70.0 to 86.5
- 50.0 to 69.9
- 25.0 to 49.9
- 12.3 to 24.9
- 5.0 to 12.2
- 1.0 to 4.9
- 0.0 to 0.9

Data Source: U.S. Census Bureau, Census 2000 Redistricting Data (PL 94-171) Summary File. Cartography: Population Division, U.S. Census Bureau. American FactFinder at *factfinder.census.gov* provides census data and mapping tools.

Figure 6.1 African Americans in the United States.

Reprinted from Mapping census: The geography of U.S. diversity, p. 39. Available: http://www.census.gov/population/www/cen2000/atlas/pdf/censr01-106.pdf

Overall index site: http://www.census.gov/population/www/cen2000/atlas/index.html

Socioeconomic Profile of Ethnic and Racial Minorities in the United States

Ethnic and racial minorities are characterized by different socioeconomic patterns than the mainstream population. In particular, the household incomes and employment patterns of members of minorities differ from those of mainstream whites. Recreation providers need to be familiar with these characteristics because they have a significant effect on recreation styles and constraints on leisure faced by ethnic and racial minorities.

Although many minorities have enjoyed a degree of emancipation and an increased economic and political power in recent years, some groups remain largely disfranchised. As the census data show, African Americans and Hispanics still lag behind mainstream whites in terms of median household income. The median household income in the United States for all households in 2006 was $48,451 (Webster & Bishaw, 2007). Asian American households had the highest median household income ($63,642), followed by mainstream whites ($52,375), Hispanics ($38,747), and African Americans ($32,372).

Employment patterns vary among racial and ethnic groups. Asians and non-Hispanic whites are more often employed in management, professional, and related occupations, whereas African Americans and Hispanics are prominent in production, transportation, and material-moving

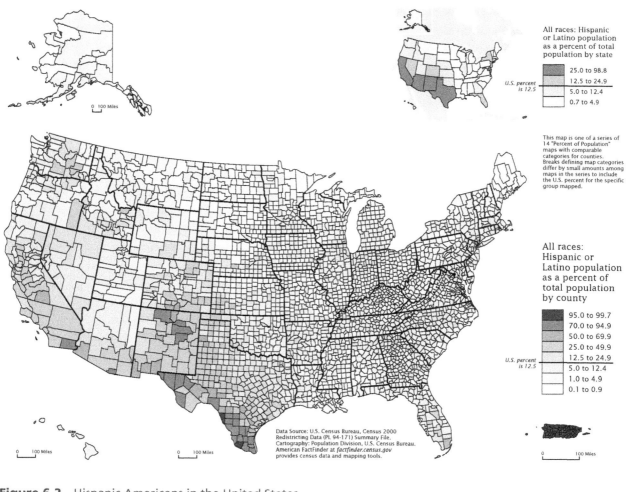

Figure 6.2 Hispanic Americans in the United States.

Reprinted from Mapping census: The geography of U.S. diversity, p. 93. Available:
http://www.census.gov/population/www/cen2000/atlas/pdf/censr01-111.pdf

Overall index site: http://www.census.gov/population/www/cen2000/atlas/index.html

occupations. In other words, African Americans and Hispanics have lower incomes than mainstream whites and Asians, have higher poverty rates, and are employed in more physically strenuous occupations. These circumstances lead to a unique set of constraints on leisure for these groups, which are described later in this chapter.

Segregation Among Ethnic and Racial Minorities

Many ethnic and racial minority groups still face large degrees of segregation in their residential, employment, and leisure patterns. In fact, many urban areas are more ethnically and racially segregated now than they were 10 or 20 years ago. Moreover, in many cities there exist "ethnic niches" in the labor market. Ethnic minority

members specialize in certain jobs, some of which are obtained through personal networking within their ethnic community.

Many members of ethnic and racial minorities are significantly ethnically enclosed during their leisure time. Research has shown that the primary leisure companions of many members of ethnic and racial minorities are people from their own ethnic groups. For example, students often segregate themselves along ethnic lines during their lunch hour activities, and employees often interact with people of the same ethnicity or race during company-sponsored leisure outings (e.g., picnics, barbecues, holiday parties; Stodolska, 2007). Other examples of ethnically enclosed free-time activities include playing sports and games with people of the same ethnic group and traveling with people

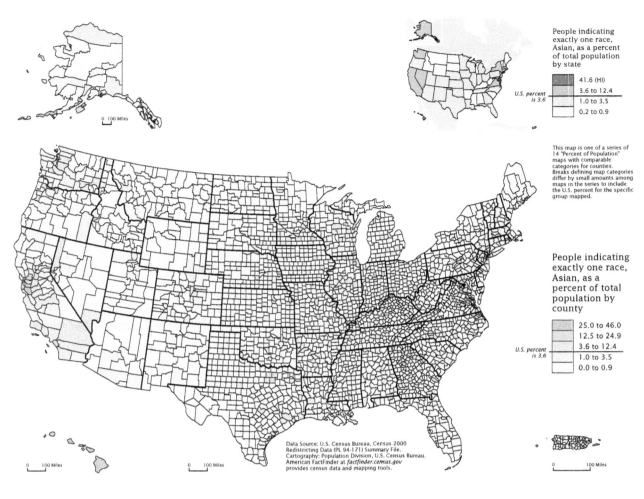

People indicating exactly one race, Asian, as a percent of total population by state

U.S. percent is 3.6

- 41.6 (HI)
- 3.6 to 12.4
- 1.0 to 3.5
- 0.2 to 0.9

This map is one of a series of 14 "Percent of Population" maps with comparable categories for counties. Breaks defining map categories differ by small amounts among maps in the series to include the U.S. percent for the specific group mapped.

People indicating exactly one race, Asian, as a percent of total population by county

U.S. percent is 3.6

- 25.0 to 46.0
- 12.5 to 24.9
- 3.6 to 12.4
- 1.0 to 3.5
- 0.0 to 0.9

Data Source: U.S. Census Bureau, Census 2000 Redistricting Data (PL 94-171) Summary File. Cartography: Population Division, U.S. Census Bureau. American FactFinder at *factfinder.census.gov* provides census data and mapping tools.

Figure 6.3 Asian Americans in the United States.

Reprinted from Mapping census: The geography of U.S. diversity, p. 63. Available: http://www.census.gov/population/www/cen2000/atlas/pdf/censr01-108.pdf

Overall index site: http://www.census.gov/population/www/cen2000/atlas/index.html

of the same ethnicity. Commonly mentioned explanations for the ethnic enclosure in leisure include comfort level, similar experiences, common culture, lack of English-language skills, discrimination or exclusion by the mainstream, and fear of the unknown. Members of ethnic and racial minorities may find that limiting leisure contacts to members of their own ethnic group provides psychological and emotional comfort as well as certain tangible economic benefits (e.g., establishing business-related contacts with other people from the same group). On the other hand, these self-imposed limitations could have negative consequences such as delayed assimilation, difficulties in securing employment (lack of professional networks among the mainstream), and hindered advancement in the mainstream workplace (Stodolska, 2007).

Leisure Participation Patterns and Styles

Research has shown that many minority members prefer participation in different leisure activities than those chosen by mainstream whites, and even when minority members participate in the same activities as mainstream whites, they often do it slightly differently. For instance, African Americans have been shown to participate less in outdoor recreation than mainstream whites and to have a preference for urban activities such as social interactions, sports and fitness activities, visiting malls, and attending clubs (Shinew et al., 2004; Washburne, 1978).

Low frequency of participation among African Americans in outdoor recreation has been attributed to lack of socialization to such activities and

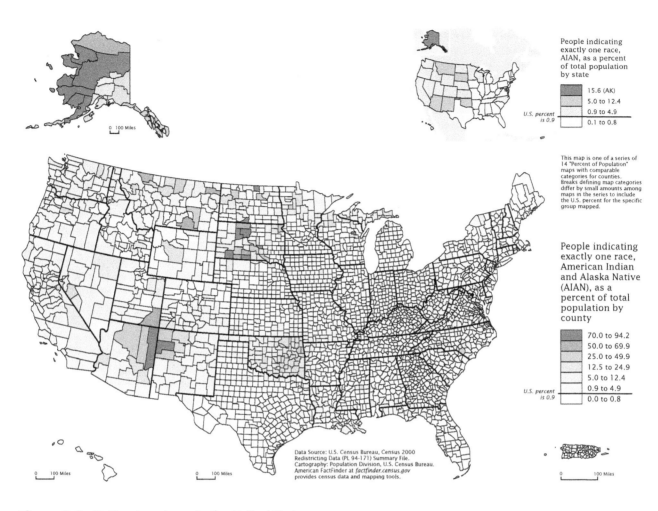

People indicating exactly one race, AIAN, as a percent of total population by state

	15.6 (AK)
	5.0 to 12.4
	0.9 to 4.9
	0.1 to 0.8

U.S. percent is 0.9

This map is one of a series of 14 "Percent of Population" maps with comparable categories for counties. Breaks defining map categories differ by small amounts among maps in the series to include the U.S. percent for the specific group mapped.

People indicating exactly one race, American Indian and Alaska Native (AIAN), as a percent of total population by county

	70.0 to 94.2
	50.0 to 69.9
	25.0 to 49.9
	12.5 to 24.9
	5.0 to 12.4
	0.9 to 4.9
	0.0 to 0.8

U.S. percent is 0.9

Data Source: U.S. Census Bureau, Census 2000 Redistricting Data (PL 94-171) Summary File. Cartography: Population Division, U.S. Census Bureau. American FactFinder at *factfinder.census.gov* provides census data and mapping tools.

Figure 6.4 Native Americans in the United States.

Reprinted from Source: Mapping census: The geography of U.S. diversity, p. 51. Available:
http://www.census.gov/population/www/cen2000/atlas/pdf/censr01-107.pdf
Overall index site: http://www.census.gov/population/www/cen2000/atlas/index.html

dislike for the outdoors because of the history of discrimination and violence that took place in natural areas (Johnson et al., 1998). Conversely, mainstream whites have been shown to have a strong preference for outdoor, adventure recreation (e.g., hiking, camping, kayaking, fishing, mountain biking), exercise activities, and winter sports.

Differences in recreation patterns between the mainstream whites and members of ethnic and racial minorities have been explained by different preferences, values, and socialization patterns (the ethnicity theory) and unequal access to socioeconomic resources (the marginality theory; Washburne, 1978).

Styles of recreation participation among ethnic and racial groups also vary. For example, Hispanic Americans have been shown to participate in many recreation activities in large, multigenerational, and family-oriented groups. Average Hispanic barbecue parties are usually large (at least six people), participants spend 5 to 6 hours at the location, and they prepare food on-site (Cronan et al., 2008; Gobster, 2002; Tinsley et al., 2002).

The average party of mainstream whites is much smaller (two to four people); participants bring prepared food and spend 1 to 2 hours at the location. Moreover, when using city parks, mainstream whites, Asians, and African Americans often prefer active uses such as bicycling or jogging and running, whereas Hispanic Americans are known for their social and passive uses of outdoor locations.

The large size of the average recreation party among Hispanic Americans has led to some leisure constraints for these people. For example,

Picnicking allows Hispanic American families to spend time together and reinforce family cohesiveness.

the small sizes of campgrounds, designed to accommodate smaller parties of mainstream whites, negatively affect participation patterns of Hispanic Americans and many South Asian groups (Irwin et al., 1990).

Research also shows that although many minority groups have a preference for well-developed recreation areas (e.g., with tap water and flush toilets), mainstream white recreationists often prefer less developed places (e.g., undisturbed natural environment with few or no amenities; Irwin et al., 1990).

Motivations for Participation in Leisure

While for many members of the American mainstream, primary motivations for engaging in leisure activities include having fun, relaxing, improving their health, or spending time with the family, members of ethnic and racial groups often display some additional motives for taking part in recreation. For instance, research shows that many Hispanic Americans participate in leisure to reinforce family cohesiveness (Shaull & Gramann, 1998), whereas Native Americans visit outdoor recreation sites to maintain spiritual contact with nature (McDonald & McAvoy, 1997). Many immigrants read newspapers in their native language, watch ethnic TV, and participate in activities of ethnic clubs to maintain contact with the culture of their homeland (Kim et al., 2001; Stodolska, 2000), whereas other immigrants watch mainstream American TV and travel across the United States to learn the English language and familiarize themselves with culture of their new country (Allison & Geiger, 1993)

Constraints on Participation in Leisure Typical to Racial and Ethnic Minorities

Members of ethnic and racial minorities, and immigrants in particular, experience many constraints on leisure that are not typical to mainstream Americans. Moreover, members of minorities may experience many of the same constraints as the mainstream Americans but with increased intensity.

Language problems are the most often mentioned leisure constraint among immigrants (Doherty & Taylor, 2007; Rublee & Shaw, 1991). Consider the fact that in Miami, three-quarters of residents speak a language other than English at home and 67% of those are not fluent in English. Such immigrants may have problems finding out about recreation opportunities, communicating with the staff of recreation agencies, and signing up for programs.

Many activities to which immigrants were used to in their home country may not be available in the United States, whereas others may be offered in a different form. Immigrants may also have to deal with broken social networks, given that many of their friends and family members have remained in their home country (Stodolska & Santos, 2006).

Those who reside in the United States illegally are not able to acquire a driver's license and thus may be constrained by transportation problems and by the lack of documents often necessary to sign up for recreation programs and to travel.

As has been discussed previously, many members of ethnic and racial minorities are disadvantaged socioeconomically and thus are constrained by the lack of financial resources to participate in leisure activities. Just consider the costs of signing up for many sport activities, the costs of the apparel, club fees, and transportation costs. Moreover, because of the disadvantaged position of many minority members, they often work long hours at physically demanding jobs and are constrained by the lack of time and physical stamina necessary for active recreation.

Many predominantly minority communities are troubled by safety problems and the poor maintenance of local recreational facilities. Natural environments suitable for recreation are often scarce in such neighborhoods, and those that are available are often poorly maintained and unsafe.

Cultural differences can constrain recreation participation. The necessity to take care of younger siblings in large families, lack of culturally appropriate child-care services, some religious restrictions on mixed-gender interactions, and preference for wearing clothing that restrict recreation participation of members of some religious minorities may constrain leisure participation (Rublee & Shaw, 1991; Stodolska & Livengood, 2006; Tirone & Shaw 1997).

Members of ethnic and racial minorities often experience discrimination in leisure settings (Blahna & Black, 1993; Floyd & Gramann, 1995; Philipp, 1999). This discrimination can be perpetrated by other recreationists, staff of recreation agencies, park rangers, police, or local residents. It happens often that minority members are harassed in parks, pools, playgrounds, and on beaches in "white" neighborhoods; are told that there is no available space on almost empty campgrounds; are stared at; are subject to derogatory remarks; and are even physically attacked. As a result, minority members might avoid certain recreation places or activities, visit locations with other members of the group for protection, or derive diminished pleasure from participation.

Provision of Leisure Services for Ethnic and Racial Minorities

Although the numbers of ethnic and racial minorities in many communities across the United States are rapidly increasing, many recreation agencies are poorly prepared to serve their diverse customers. Agencies need to follow certain steps to ensure that they meet the needs of a diverse clientele and that minority participants are satisfied with their recreation participation:

- Recreation agencies should keep track of the demographic changes in the makeup of their constituents. Demographic changes rarely happen overnight, and usually agencies have ample time to review their activity offering, hire and train staff, and modify their facilities if necessary. Agencies should monitor the changing ethnic and racial makeup of their communities and occasionally review census data to verify any trends that they may have observed.

- Recreation agencies should conduct periodic surveys of the recreational needs of their constituents. Agency directors need to find out what activities their customers or potential customers would like to participate in, what kind of facilities they would like to use, and the most common barriers to recreation they have experienced. Such surveys need to examine the needs, preferences, and barriers not only of the existing customers but also of other members of the community. After all, some people may not be visiting recreation facilities because of the things that are not being offered, because they are not aware of the existing offerings, or because they have experienced other constraints.

- Once the agency has established that the community does include a sizable number of ethnic and racial minorities, the agency director should consider expanding the agency's activities and services and promoting them in culturally appropriate ways.

  - Promotional materials should be reviewed periodically. Do they represent the diverse constituents well? Are they written in the language that the users and potential users speak? Have the services been advertized in a variety of ways and in places frequented by people in the community (brochures, radio spots, local newspapers, community centers, churches, schools)?

• The agency director should consider whether the staff includes people of the same or similar ethnic or racial backgrounds as the users or potential users. Are minority members represented at all levels of the agency, both in managerial positions and in positions that involve direct contact with customers?

• The agency director should evaluate whether staff effectively communicate with existing or potential customers. Do staff members speak the language of the existing or potential users? Do staff members possess cultural understanding of the needs of the group they intend to serve?

The racial and ethnic makeup of American society is changing rapidly. Recreation professionals need to be adequately prepared to embrace the opportunities and address the challenges that this diversity brings to the provision of recreation services.

Gender

In 2006, there were almost 152 million women living in the United States. They outnumbered men by approximately 4.5 million (50.76% vs. 49.24%), particularly in the older age categories (American Community Survey, 2006b). Although there are more women than men in the United States, and thus they cannot be described as a minority group, the leisure behavior of women is affected by a unique set of motivations and constraints that agencies must take into account when providing recreation services to women.

Socioeconomic Profile of Women in the United States

In 2006, 71.5% of women were in labor force, compared with 83.2% of men (American Community Survey, 2006b). Despite women's gains in labor force participation, women's earnings are still significantly lower than those of men (see figure 6.5). For example, in 2006, only

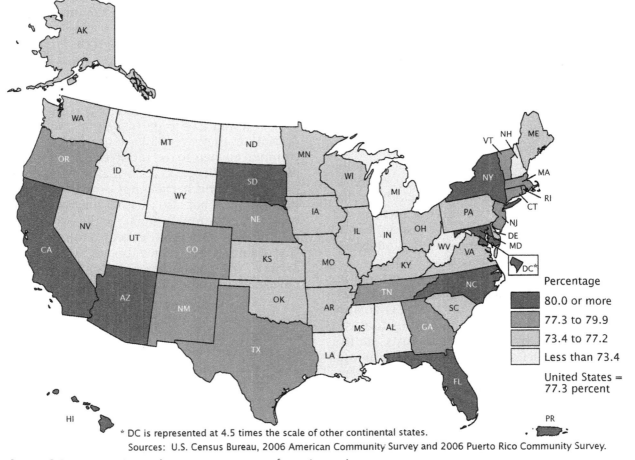

Percentage

- 80.0 or more
- 77.3 to 79.9
- 73.4 to 77.2
- Less than 73.4

United States = 77.3 percent

* DC is represented at 4.5 times the scale of other continental states.

Sources: U.S. Census Bureau, 2006 American Community Survey and 2006 Puerto Rico Community Survey.

Figure 6.5 Women's earnings as percentage of men's earnings.

Reprinted from B.H. Webster and A. Bishaw, 2007, *Income, earnings, and poverty data from the 2006 American Community Survey.* American Community Survey Reports, (ACS-08). (Washington, DC: U.S. Census Bureau) 15.

9.3% of women reported earnings of $75,000 or more, compared with 20.4% of men (American Community Survey, 2006c). At the same time, women earned 77 cents for every 1 dollar earned by men. The discrepancy between the earnings of men and women was the highest in south central, Midwestern, and west central states and the lowest in California, Arizona, South Dakota, Florida, North Carolina, New York, Maryland, and Washington, D.C.

Of the 120 million women age 15 and older residing in the United States in 2006, 51% were married, 26.2% were single, 10.9% were divorced, 9.4% were widowed, and 2.4% were separated (U.S. Census, 2006c). Hispanic women had the highest fertility rates among all racial and ethnic groups. In 2004, with an average of 2.3 births, Hispanic women were the only group above the replacement rate (the number of births that exceeded the level required for natural replacement of the population—about 2.1 births per woman; Dye, 2005). African American and non-Hispanic white women had fertility levels below the replacement rate, ranging from about 1.8 to 1.9 births per woman (Dye, 2005).

Differences in Leisure Patterns Between Men and Women

Differences in recreation behavior between men and women can be related to psychological and biological characteristics (e.g., different body build, strength) and to societal role expectations. In this section, after we review the research on gender and leisure by Henderson (1990, 1996), Henderson and colleagues (2002), and Henderson and Hickerson (2007), we focus on the ways social factors affect women's leisure patterns.

Research shows that women's leisure time is fragmented. Women seldom find major blocks of time for leisure in their lives but tend to "steal" free time as they can. Women do not compartmentalize their lives the way that men do and thus, women have leisure whenever they have an opportunity. Women often schedule leisure around domestic activities. How many times have you seen your mother or another female family member prepare dinner or do other domestic tasks while other people are watching TV, socializing, and having fun?

Women also often double up their activities, doing something considered leisure, such as watching TV, while also doing housework, such as cooking or ironing. Portable TVs installed in the kitchen have been a feature of many houses

Girls playing soccer at the University of Illinois campus.

for years. Companies such as GE and Whirlpool install TVs in refrigerators so (mostly) women who are preparing meals or doing other tasks can catch their favorite shows. For instance, Central-park Whirlpool refrigerators are equipped with Internet access that can control MP3 devices, DVD players, cell phones, and digital photo albums from a hub built into their door. They have been designed to "turn kitchens into command centers" in new houses where kitchens "have increasingly become the focal point for entertaining and family gathering alike" (Crave, 2007).

Research also shows that women who have more roles to undertake (e.g., wife, mother, employee, volunteer) are less likely to have personal leisure time. Women who are employed outside of their home have the least leisure; however, they value it more. Moreover, paid work that may constrain women's leisure can also enhance it in many tangible ways. Women employed outside of their home have more resources to spend on leisure and often feel entitled to leisure for themselves.

Leisure of many women is organized around family obligations. Many women perceive themselves as family members first and as individuals second. They are often more concerned for others than for their own interests and welfare. TV commercials are full of ideas of "nutritious breakfast on the go" that women may catch in their car after dropping their children off at school or taking care of a "hectic house" in the morning. Many women also perceive their leisure as their family's leisure or their family's leisure as their leisure. For instance, many mothers spend their "free hours" accompanying their children to playgrounds, taking them on trips, or driving them to games and other activities. Is this leisure time or work time for these women?

Research shows that for both men and women, leisure participation declines with age; a steep decline among women is particularly visible in late adolescence and early adulthood. The decline is related mainly to changes in opportunities, time, perceptions about recreation, and responsibilities.

Findings of research also show that differences in leisure and sport participation exist not only between men and women but also *among women* based on age, class, ethnicity, and other characteristics. Although opportunities for women's participation in many sports have increased following the passage of Title IX in 1972, many groups of women are still significantly constrained in their participation in active recreation.

It has been shown that leisure may be a context for the empowerment of women (e.g., through participation in unconventional activities) as well as a context for the victimization and disempowerment of women (e.g., pornography). Similarly, leisure may be an avenue for conformity to social roles (e.g., taking care of others during social occasions) as well as resistance to those roles.

Constraints on Participation in Leisure Typical to Girls and Women

Women and girls may experience certain constraints on leisure that do not apply to men. Women may also experience many of the same constraints as do men but with increased intensity. For instance, research by Shaw (1994) and others shows that women are more constrained than men with regard to household obligations and family commitments. These constraints are clearly related to family life cycle—they are most pronounced for young mothers. With marriage women gain more roles, their obliga-

tions increase, and personal free time becomes a second priority.

There is also evidence that many women are disadvantaged with regard to time for leisure. They have less time for leisure compared with men because of household obligations and family commitments. This constraint is particularly pronounced for women who are employed in the labor market and experience a "second shift" at home. Balancing work and household obligations imposes additional stress on women. Constant feelings of being rushed have negative effects on the quality of women's leisure and may lead to deterioration of their health, exhaustion, and lack of energy. However, being employed outside of home can also have many benefits—it gives women more disposable income and empowers them.

It has been suggested (Shaw, 1994) that because of the ethic of care, women usually take care of the needs of others first, thus neglecting their own leisure needs. Women are usually the primary caregivers in the family, and family commitments often take precedence over women's personal needs. Ethic of care has been described as the major constraint that reduces women's enjoyment of leisure; however, for some women, the ethic of care may also be a source of identity and power within a family.

In general, women experience more economic (monetary) constraints than men. This applies to stay-at-home mothers, who often do not have any personal income and have to rely on income provided by their husbands. However, it also applies to women employed in the labor market, who have lower earning power than men. Economic constraints are also evident when women report lack of transportation as a constraint on leisure participation. Economic constraints are particularly pronounced for low-income, unemployed women, single parents, and women who belong to ethnic and racial minorities.

Safety and fear of violence are frequently mentioned by women as important constraints on their leisure. Fear affects where and when women participate in leisure (e.g., they may avoid visiting parks at night) and with whom they participate (they may avoid participating alone). Fear of violence may not necessarily prevent participation in desired activities but can negatively affect the quality of experience. Women often have to be on alert and to plan ahead in terms of getting safe transportation and securing leisure companions.

Body image or the so-called "beauty myth"—the excessive concern about physical appearance—may constrain leisure of women. Low body image, especially if coupled with low self-esteem, may reduce participation in certain activities, such as swimming or aerobics, among women and girls concerned about their "less than perfect looks" (James, 2000). Low body image can also reduce enjoyment of these activities.

Gender stereotyping of activities can constrain the leisure behavior of girls and women. The fact that some activities are considered to be appropriate for men only and some appropriate for women may prevent women from participating in activities such as wrestling, bodybuilding, or hunting.

As some people claim, gender role expectations are more restrictive for women than they are for men, even within the sphere of leisure experience. Social norms make women primarily responsible for the care of children as well as aging parents and grandchildren. This can prevent women's participation in leisure and sport.

Findings of research reviewed by Henderson and Hickerson (2007) concerning constraints on women's and girls' sport and leisure participation also suggest that there are as many within-gender differences in leisure constraints as there are between-gender differences. Variables such as age, income, and family structure are mediating factors that affect constraints for women. However, constraints to leisure may be more acute for women who are members of nondominant groups.

Provision of Leisure Services for Girls and Women

Recreation and sport have many benefits for girls and women, including improved mental and physical health, increased self-esteem and a sense of empowerment, and development of social networks. However, many girls withdraw from sport participation at the time when such benefits are most needed, whereas adult women's participation is constrained by a number of factors that we have already discussed. Recreation agencies need to address a number of issues to ensure that girls and women are provided with services that they desire and that they can obtain full benefits from participation. Bialeschki and Henderson (2000) provided a number of suggestions for how recreation agencies can successfully provide recreation services to girls and women:

- Recreation agencies should focus on specific needs and interests of girls and women as well as on causes of their nonparticipation or underparticipation.
- Recreation providers should consider both positive (e.g., the role of sport as a tool of empowerment) and negative aspects of recreation participation (e.g., recreation activities that further gender stereotypes).
- Recreation agencies should offer women and girls settings that are inclusive, nonthreatening, and supportive.
- Girls should be provided with access to recreation programs that allow them to further their interests beyond what society expects of them. Recreation should provide girls with means to resist gender-stereotyped societal messages, overcome fear of body changes, and gain a sense of control over their lives.
- Girls should have access to no-cost, informally supervised places where they can have a sense of their own place and engage in activities of their choice.
- Staff of recreation agencies should focus on activities that girls cease to participate in when they reach adolescence and on the causes of the high dropout rates.
- Staff of recreation agencies should create programs that provide opportunities for meaningful identity development and a sense of belonging rather than programs that emphasize winning at all costs.
- Programs and facilities used by girls and women should be planned with issues of perceived safety in mind.
- Recreation agencies should consider messages sent when they offer traditional activities socially identified as gender specific (e.g., football for boys, ice-skating for girls).
- Recreation organizations with a focus on inclusive and equitable recreation should provide a wide range of choices for all people—both men and women. Both boys and girls should be offered an opportunity and a supportive environment to participate in recreation programs of their choice.
- Recreation service providers should increase visibility of programs designed for girls, effectively provide information about such programs, staff their agencies with female

role models, adopt policies for inclusion, and offer girls opportunities to develop their leadership skills and gain a sense of control over their lives.

Poverty and Homelessness

One group of people who tend to be significantly disadvantaged when it comes to leisure opportunities are those of lower socioeconomic status and those who are homeless. Regardless of their gender, racial and ethnic background, age, or ability status, these are the people who have the least material resources to devote to recreation participation. Thus, recreation service providers need to pay special attention to ensure that members of this group are provided with recreation opportunities in an age when consumerism and pay-for-service models tend to regulate provision of leisure services.

Poverty

The U.S. Census Bureau defines poverty using a set of monetary income thresholds (U.S. Census, 2007a). The thresholds represent the annual amount of cash income minimally required to support families of various sizes. If a family's total income is less than the family's threshold, then all members of that family are considered to be in poverty. Monetary income does not include noncash benefits such as public housing, Medicaid, employer-provided health insurance, and food stamps. The official poverty thresholds do not vary geographically, but they are adjusted for inflation using the Consumer Price Index. Thresholds vary according to size of the family and ages of the members. In 2006, the poverty threshold for a single person less than 65 years of age was $10,288 and for a person more than 65 years of age $9,669. The poverty threshold for a family of three with one child less than 18 years of age was $16,227 and for a family of four with two children was $20,444 (U.S. Census, 2006a).

Number and Characteristics of People in Poverty

The poverty rate in 2006 was 12.3% (U.S. Census, 2007b), meaning that 36.5 million people in the United States were living in poverty. Poverty rates were the highest for African Americans (24.3%), followed by Hispanics (20.6%), Asians (10.3%), and mainstream whites (8.2%).

In 2006, 10 states in the southern and central United States (Appalachian belt and Washington, D.C.) had the highest poverty rates, at more than 16%. The lowest poverty rates, below 11%, were recorded in the northeastern states of New Hampshire, Vermont, Massachusetts, Connecticut, New Jersey, Virginia; in Minnesota and Alaska; and in Wyoming, Utah, and Nevada (see figure 6.6).

Constraints on Participation in Leisure Typical to People in Poverty

A multitude of issues related to lower incomes can affect people's leisure and recreation patterns. The first and the most obvious one is the lack money for purchasing recreation and sport equipment, paying club membership fees, or purchasing apparel.

Lack of discretionary income, however, can also influence people's recreation in less obvious ways. Many people of low income do not have transportation to and from recreation sites. They do not have cars, or have old and unreliable cars, or cannot afford car insurance or gas for "unnecessary" trips. Although those who live in cities with well-developed transportation systems can travel to many recreation locations by bus or subway, many sites such as forest preserves or sport complexes are located on the edges of communities and are not accessible by public transportation. People who live in small towns and rural areas are even more constrained, because public transportation is often completely unavailable. Transportation problems make cross-country travel and tourism out of reach for many people with low incomes.

People who live near or below the poverty level often hold physically strenuous jobs, which leave them too exhausted to engage in any physically active types of leisure. Long and unstable work hours that make it difficult to plan for organized types of leisure, the necessity to hold several jobs concurrently, and problems with taking time off add to the burden that affects these people's leisure. Many people in low-wage positions with high employment turnaround rates are afraid to take time off, because it might give their employers an excuse to hire somebody else for their position.

People with low incomes often reside in communities that are not conducive to outdoor recreation. Crime problems, lack of or poor maintenance of facilities, and lack of quality natural environments make participation in many types

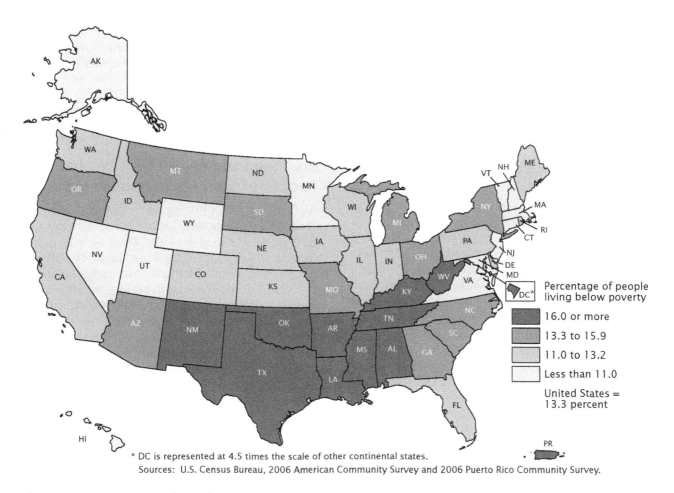

* DC is represented at 4.5 times the scale of other continental states.
Sources: U.S. Census Bureau, 2006 American Community Survey and 2006 Puerto Rico Community Survey.

Figure 6.6 Percentage of people in poverty.

Reprinted from B.H. Webster and A. Bishaw, 2007, *Income, earnings, and poverty data from the 2006 American Community Survey.* American Community Survey Reports, (ACS-08). (Washington, DC: U.S. Census Bureau) 22.

of leisure difficult. Such problems particularly affect women, who might be afraid to go out after dark or to take their children to poorly maintained and crime-ridden parks, as well as youth who lack facilities and programs for active leisure.

People who live near or below the poverty line often have large families and include a disproportionate number of single women with children. In addition to working many hours and having financial problems, such women are often constrained by extensive household obligations and problems finding appropriate and affordable child care that would make leisure possible.

Poverty is also correlated with health problems and disabilities that make obtaining highly paid employment difficult. Health issues create an additional barrier to leisure that must be negotiated to allow for participation.

People who live near or below the poverty line are unaware of many leisure opportunities and lack access to affordable leisure options. High rates of computer illiteracy exclude such people from using the Internet for comparison shopping and learning of cheap leisure opportunities available through online sources. People who do not have access to the Internet are forced to rely on often-overpriced services of travel agencies and have less information about leisure programs and leisure destinations that are increasingly being advertized on line. Leisure pastimes such as hobbies are more difficult to engage in when people do not have access to information that is being shared through the Internet and through online-based interest communities.

Poverty is often intergenerational. Research shows that there is much continuity in our leisure behavior and that activities we participate in when we are young are often carried over to our adulthood and retirement years (Freysinger, 1999). Children who grow up in underprivileged families are socialized to a narrow repertoire of leisure activities. The lack of exposure to different leisure options during formative years constrains leisure participation among adults who lack the skills or information about pastimes that were not popular in their families. Active and outdoor leisure pursuits are the activities that are most restricted by the lack of prior socialization.

Discrimination constrains leisure pursuits among people who live near or below the poverty line. More affluent participants may look down on those who cannot afford quality equipment or who are perceived to be "out of place" in some leisure venues or locations. A young person from an underprivileged background who is admitted on scholarship to a prestigious school may be looked down upon by his or her peers who are socialized to different leisure activities and leisure spending patterns. Children and adolescents who cannot afford brand-name apparel are often too embarrassed to participate in many activities for the fear of ridicule from their more affluent counterparts. Such reasons for the reluctance to participate in some activities, including sports, might be difficult to detect by parents and recreation service providers. Nevertheless, they constitute important and quite pervasive constraints on leisure participation, particularly among people in their formative years, who are sensitive to the image they hold among their peers.

Participation in leisure activities that are not normative to the peer group may be restricted by the fear of disapproval from people of the same socioeconomic class. It is well documented that many members of racial and ethnic minorities are reluctant to participate in activities that are perceived to be outside of their cultural domain by fear of condemnation and exclusion from their own peer group. Concern about being perceived as "acting white" has been shown to constrain leisure participation among African American youth (Philipp, 1999; Woodard, 1988). Similar processes might be observable among people from underprivileged socioeconomic backgrounds who might be afraid of being labeled as snobs if they show a desire to participate in "upper-class" activities.

Last, poverty is often correlated with psychological states of depression and low self-esteem, which can decrease the desire to participate in active, out-of-home leisure activities that require higher organizational involvement and social interaction.

The constraints discussed here contribute to specific leisure activity patterns typical to many people of low socioeconomic standing. They are characterized by overreliance on passive, home-based leisure activities such as watching television, reading, listening to music, and socializing informally. Rates of physical and outdoor pastimes among such populations are quite low, and so is the participation in activities that require high outlay of resources.

Provision of Leisure Services for People of Low Socioeconomic Status

As Dawson (2000) poignantly commented, "In contemporary society, leisure is more consumption of goods and services than at any other time in history" (p. 108). Thus, lack of ability to pay for services is an important constraint that prevents many people from taking full advantage of leisure opportunities. Serious constraints on participation in leisure and recreation activities experienced by the poor can be at least partially overcome if disadvantaged people are provided with appropriate help in using services and programs that are being offered. Who should provide such help? Government recreation services and facilities initially were designed to provide for the needs of people of low socioeconomic standing (Cross, 1990). However, in practice, people of low socioeconomic classes have increasingly been excluded from the offerings of government organizations by continuously rising prices of leisure services. It is commonly the case that people of low socioeconomic standing cannot afford to enroll their children in basketball classes, swimming lessons, art programs, and soccer leagues. Such activities are increasingly becoming reserved for affluent members of the middle class. Given the scarce public-sector resources available, philanthropic organizations, not-for-profit agencies, and churches now increasingly provide low-cost recreation services.

Dawson (2000) developed an important list of suggestions that should facilitate provision of leisure services to people of low socioeconomic standing:

- Conduct ongoing needs assessments to collect information about the needs of poor members of the community and to build a relationship between the community and the service provider.
- Make a long-term commitment to serve the disfranchised members of the community. "One-shot" or sporadic efforts are unlikely to make real progress in serving the needs of the poor.

- Provide sufficient resources to serve the needs of citizens from low socioeconomic classes. These resources include reduced fees, appropriately trained staff, help in transportation, and equipment.

- Make people from disadvantaged groups aware of recreation opportunities available to them but, at the same time, make sure that leisure providers are aware of the needs of disfranchised communities and have open lines of communication with the needy constituents.

- Involve participants of low socioeconomic status in program planning and delivery to ensure that they develop a sense of ownership over the programs offered to them.

Homelessness

According to the Stewart B. McKinney Act (1994), "a person is considered homeless who

> lacks a fixed, regular, and adequate nighttime residence; and . . . has a primary night time residency that is: (A) a supervised publicly or privately operated shelter designed to provide temporary living accommodations . . . (B) an institution that provides temporary residence for people intended to be institutionalized, or (C) a public or private place not designed for, or ordinarily used as, a regular sleeping accommodation for human beings." The term 'homeless individual' "does not include any individual imprisoned or otherwise detained pursuant to an Act of Congress or a state law" 42 U.S.C. § 11302(c) (National Coalition for the Homeless, 2007a).

How Many People Are Homeless?

It is very difficult to estimate the number of homeless people in the United States and in any other country. In most cases, homelessness is a temporary circumstance. Homeless people can live in shelters, on the streets, in vacant homes, and in overcrowded residences of their friends and relatives. As a result of methodological constraints, most studies are limited to counting people who live in shelters or who are easy to locate on the streets. This approach underestimates the true extent of homelessness. Despite these measurement problems, there are several national estimates of homelessness. According to the National Law Center on Homelessness and Poverty, approximately 3.5 million people, including 1.35 million children, are likely to experience homelessness in a given year (National Coalition for the Homeless, 2007b). This means that approximately 1% of the U.S. population experience homelessness each year. Other studies estimate the numbers of homeless people at between 2.3 and 3.5 million, including between 900,000 and 1.35 million children (Urban Institute, 2000).

Why Are People Homeless?

There are several reasons for the increased numbers of homeless people. Because of a number of factors, including a decrease in the number of manufacturing jobs and a move toward more temporary and part-time-employment, the value of the minimum wage has been eroding for many years. Declining wages have put housing out of reach for many workers. It is estimated that as many as 26% of people residing in shelters are employed but cannot afford housing (National Coalition for the Homeless, 2007c).

At the same time, the opportunities for public assistance have declined in recent years. For instance, Temporary Assistance to Needy Families (TANF) benefits and the Supplemental Nutrition Assistance Program (SNAP) (previously called the Food Stamp Program) combined are below the poverty level in every state (National Coalition for the Homeless, 2007c). Affordable housing and housing assistance programs have also become very scarce and contribute significantly to rising homelessness rates. Subsidized housing is so limited that less than one in four TANF families receives any type of housing assistance. Moreover, the strong U.S. economy prior to the economic crisis that began in 2008 led to increased rents, putting housing out of reach of many Americans. More recently, rampant foreclosures have caused many people to lose their homes.

A number of other factors often lead to homelessness, such as unexpected job loss, lack of savings, and problems obtaining employment. When people who lack affordable health care insurance experience sudden illness or disability, their medical bills often put them in debt and lead to eviction (National Coalition for the Homeless, 2007c). Mental illness, addiction disorders, and domestic abuse increase a person's likelihood of becoming homeless (see the next section).

Who Are the People Who Are Homeless?

The homeless population is very diverse. It is estimated that single men comprise between 51% and 61% of the homeless population, families with children between 30% and 33%, and single women approximately 17% (National Coalition for the Homeless, 2007a; Smith & Smith, 2001). The homeless population is estimated to be 42% African American, 39% mainstream white, and 13% Hispanic (National Coalition for the Homeless, 2007a). It is estimated that California and New York are the two states with the most homeless people (Smith & Smith, 2001).

Domestic violence is among the primary causes of homelessness among women. Moving to a shelter is often the only choice for poor women who live in abusive relationships. A 2003 survey of homeless mothers in 10 locations across the United States found that 25% of respondents had been physically abused in the last year (National Coalition for the Homeless, 2007a).

Approximately 16% of homeless people suffer from mental illness (National Coalition for the Homeless, 2007a). It is difficult to estimate the prevalence of addiction disorders among homeless adults. The estimates that are available place the number somewhere between 25% and 30%, although rates as high as 65% have been reported. Podymow and colleagues (2006) estimated that alcoholism affects between 53% and 73% of homeless adults and that the incidence of heavy alcoholism (>20 drinks a day) is high. Others argue, however, that such high prevalence rates are due to overrepresenting long-term male shelter users and assessing their lifetime rather than current measures of addiction (National Coalition for the Homeless, 2007a).

Leisure and Homelessness

The main role of shelters is to provide a safe place for occupants to sleep, eat, and wash. Homeless shelters often provide a range of other services, including job training and placement, support groups, substance (i.e., drugs or alcohol) abuse treatment, assistance with mental health disorders, assistance with housing search, workshops on money management skills, resume writing, interview preparation, literacy programs, computer trainings, and legal counseling. Leisure activities often play a secondary, although important role in the activities provided by shelters.

Benefits of Leisure for People Who Are Homeless
People who reside in homeless shelters experience significant amounts of anxiety, depression, and stress, including chronic stress, related to their overall financial, legal, and family situations and to living in the shelter community

(Klitzing, 2003, 2004). Many people who reside in shelters have had run-ins with the law, have experienced physical and sexual abuse, have had long-standing relationship problems, are in recovery from substance abuse, and are separated from their children, who remain in foster care. Living in shelters provides its own share of problems related to conflicts over living space, theft, dealing with shelter regulations, and co-existing with people who often relapse in their substance abuse and provide temptation to those who try to remain "clean" (Klitzing, 2003, 2004).

Leisure activities can provide diversion and distraction, respite, and relief from stress (Klitzing, 2004). They help people maintain physical and mental well-being, improve self-esteem, and relax; they entertain, occupy free time, and provide alternatives to substance abuse (Dawson, 2000; Klitzing, 2003, 2004).

Many shelters organize activity groups such as fiber arts, cooking, painting, or pottery classes. Involvement in those activities helps people build a sense of success through skill mastery, develop positive relaxation techniques, and express feelings and explore trauma issues through art projects. Moreover, participants give back to the community through working on projects that are donated to hospitals or nonprofit organizations.

Recreation activities undertaken outside of the shelter help people stay connected and integrated with the outside community, help people maintain a sense of normalcy, build confidence, improve social interaction skills, and teach norms of appropriate social behavior (Dawson, 2000).

Provision of Leisure Services for People Who Are Homeless
The majority of leisure activities undertaken in homeless shelters are passive in nature: watching television, listening to music, reading books, doing crossword puzzles, journaling, playing computer games, studying the religious books, practicing fiber arts, knitting, or cooking. Leisure activities that foster socialization are particularly important. Interacting with others through phone calls and e-mail is common, and so are informal chatting, spending time with children on a playground, and reading to children. Klitzing (2004) found that porches were the most often used places in the shelter where women sat, chatted, listened to music, and "watched the world go by."

Shelters rarely give people an opportunity to be alone, and thus spending time alone is often highly valued by shelter residents. Women interviewed by Klitzing (2004) reported that they valued reading a book in a quiet bedroom or even spending time in a shelter basement "with their own thoughts."

Physical activities, although not as common as passive pastimes, are also undertaken by shelter residents. These activities include walking, yoga classes, bowling, dancing, and other physical exercise (Klitzing, 2003).

It is important for shelter occupants to break the monotony of shelter life and participate in activities outside of their place of residence. Those who can afford it sometimes take shopping trips to local malls, go to movies or restaurants, and use "overnights" to stay with their friends outside of the shelter (Klitzing, 2004). Shelters also organize dinner groups for homeless women; softball teams for homeless men; after-school recreation programs for homeless children; trips to theaters, museums and sporting events; and visits to community facilities such as pools and playing fields (Dawson, 2000).

These are some of the recreation activities undertaken by homeless people who reside in shelters. As has been mentioned, however, a large percentage of homeless people are not served by local shelters and reside on the streets, in abandoned houses, or with their friends or relatives.

Such people are hard to reach and, depending on their situation, require different help when it comes to providing recreation opportunities.

Aging

People in the United States are living longer than ever before. Average life expectancy at birth increased from 47.3 years in 1900 to 77.8 years in 2004 (Health United States, 2006). Sparked by the increase in life expectancy and other factors, the population of older adults (65 years and older) in the United States increased significantly during the 20th century, from 3.1 million in 1900 to 37.2 million (or 12.4% of the population) in 2006 (He et al., 2005; U.S. Census, 2006d). It is expected that by 2030, the number of older people will reach 72 million and represent nearly 20% of the total U.S. population (He et al., 2005). The population of the oldest old (those 85 years of age and older) is growing particularly rapidly. It was 34 times larger in 2000 than in 1900 (He et al., 2005; see figure 6.7.).

Leisure is known to provide numerous physical and mental health benefits to people of all age categories and to older adults in particular. In light of these demographic changes, leisure service providers across the United States and other developed countries are increasingly facing

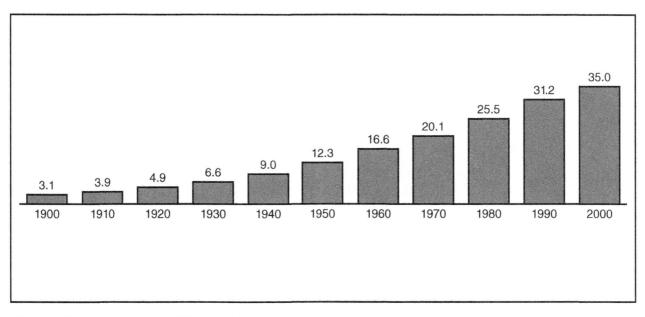

Figure 6.7 Population aged 65 and older.

Reprinted from W. He, M. Sengupta, V.A. Velkoff, and K.A. DeBarros, 2005, 65+ in the United States: 2005. In *Current population reports* (Washington, DC: U.S. Census Bureau), 9.

the challenge of providing services to older adults who are more educated and healthier than ever before.

Socioeconomic Profile of Older Adults in the United States

In 2006, women outnumbered men in older age categories, constituting 58% of people more than 65 years of age (U.S. Census, 2006d). More than 85% of older adults were mainstream whites. African Americans made up only 8.3% of the older population, whereas 6.3% of older Americans were Hispanic (U.S. Census, 2006d).

In 2006, 13.9% of people more than 65 years of age were employed (U.S. Census, 2006d). Social security provided the largest share of income for many older people, followed by earnings and asset incomes.

The population of older adults, in general, is concentrated regionally. In 2005, Florida had the highest proportion of people more than 65 years of age (17%), followed by West Virginia and Pennsylvania (approximately 15% each). Conversely, the lowest proportions of older adults were in Alaska (6%), Utah, Georgia, Colorado, and Texas (each below 10%; see figure 6.8).

Leisure Behavior of Older Adults

Leisure behavior patterns, motivations, and constraints on leisure change with advancing age. Some of these changes are caused by biological maturation of our bodies, whereas others stem from our changing roles and responsibilities and the perceptions on the part of society that prescribe which activities are appropriate for certain age groups.

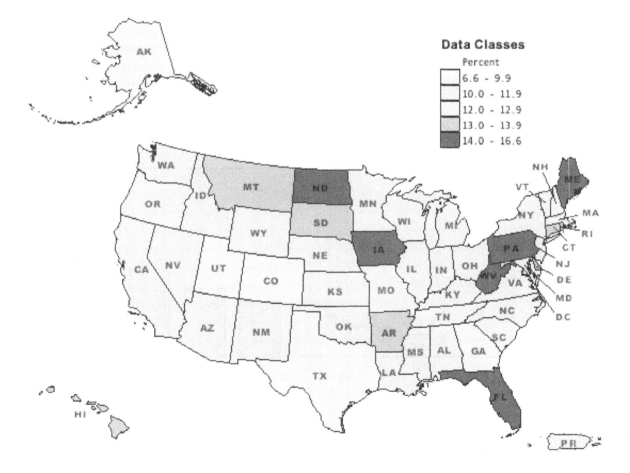

Figure 6.8 Percentage of population aged 65 and older.

Reprinted from U.S. Census (2005). Age and sex distribution in 2005. Available: http://www.census.gov/population/pop-profile/dynamic/AgeSex.pdf

There is usually more continuity than change in leisure participation over the life span (Freysinger, 1999). In other words, participation in activities to which we were socialized as children or teenagers is likely to carry over to our adult years. For instance, people who were socialized to physically active pastimes early in their lives are likely to be active in their older years, and those who developed a preference for outdoor activities will maintain a preference for such activities later in life. Older adults are known to discontinue or replace participation in some activities in later years because of a variety of constraints they experience (Iso-Ahola et al., 1994). If such changes take place, however, activity replacement is likely to take place within the already existing leisure repertoire and developed leisure patterns (Iso-Ahola et al., 1994). For instance, those who were active in strenuous winter mountain sports such as downhill skiing may replace them with the cross-country variety, and those who liked to backpack in mountains may still visit such locations but may stay in more comfortable accommodations and take less strenuous, shorter, and better maintained routes for their walks. As we age, we are also likely to return to activities that were part of our leisure repertoire in younger years but in which participation has been limited by constraints such as lack of time. This can explain an increase in participation in hobbies and other home-based activities among older adults, including knitting, cross-stitch, gardening, doing crossword puzzles, cooking, and reading (Iso-Ahola et al., 1994).

Aging leads to many changes in leisure participation among older adults by imposing constraints that were not present earlier in their lives. These constraints are related to physical changes, changing socioeconomic status (e.g., decrease in income among many older people), new roles and responsibilities (e.g., the necessity to take care of aging parents), loss of independence regarding living arrangements and transportation, and shrinking social networks (e.g., loss of spouse, children moving away). However, leisure and recreation can play significant roles in helping older adults deal with some of the negative changes associated with aging. Leisure activities can serve a therapeutic role by strengthening the cardiovascular and musculoskeletal systems, exercising mental capacities to delay the onset of dementia, preventing loneliness and depression, alleviating boredom, and helping people maintain social contacts.

Although aging has significant effects on people's leisure motivations, constraints, styles, and participation patterns, its effects are moderated by other characteristics of older adults. One's race, ethnicity, gender, socioeconomic status, ability status, and sexual orientation interact with age to determine recreation patterns, expectations regarding leisure participation, and opportunities to participate in leisure.

Factors That Affect Leisure Behavior of Older Adults

Two main groups of factors shape the leisure behavior of older adults. One of them is related to biological changes that all people go through. The other set of considerations is related to people's changing roles and responsibilities, the social transitions that are related to the process of aging, and the expectations posed by the broader society on older adults.

Biological Aging There are significant variations in the rate of physical change among older adults. Although diseases such as diabetes or stroke functionally impair some people early in their lives, other people remain relatively healthy and active well into old age. Regardless of the variations in the rate of change, each of us experiences similar changes in our organs as we grow older.

Our senses, including vision and hearing, become less acute in midlife. Vision usually begins to decline in our 40s and hearing loss begins in our 20s (Hawkins et al., 1996). As vision and hearing acuity decrease, people begin to experience difficulties with equilibrium and develop problems with maintaining balance. Loss of vision, hearing, touch, temperature sensation, smell, and taste influence the quality of our lives and can impair our everyday functioning as well as participation in leisure activities.

As people move into their old age, they begin to experience a decrease in their physical strength, flexibility, and endurance (Freysinger, 2000). Muscle mass and strength decline with age. The elasticity of connective tissue such as ligaments, cartilage, and tendons also declines, resulting in decreases in joint function (Hawkins et al., 1996). In the process known as osteoporosis, bones lose calcium and other minerals and become more porous and prone to breakage (Hawkins et al., 1996). Age-related changes in the musculoskeletal system lower people's strength, reduce range of motion, increase stiffness and pain, slow down their movements, and increase susceptibility to injuries (Hawkins et al., 1996). These changes limit older people's participation in leisure activities that can involve falls and injuries (many sports) and activities that require fine motor function, repetitive flexing of joints, and significant strength or endurance.

Older adults also experience changes in their cardiovascular and respiratory systems. Support tissues and airways harden and stiffen; bronchial tubes degenerate, reducing the amount of air being moved in and out of the lungs; and the reserve capacity of the lungs decreases (Hawkins et al., 1996). Because of age-related changes, people may not be able to participate in activities that put stress on their respiratory system and may not be able to spend time outside during hot weather and in places with high air pollution. With age, maximal function and efficiency of the cardiovascular system decline. The heart muscle becomes less elastic and the walls of the heart thicken (Hawkins et al., 1996). The weight of the heart increases, leading to increased pumping force and thus elevated blood pressure. Such changes put significant constraints on participation in many physical activities; however, active leisure can improve the function of the cardiovascular system and thus is highly recommended for older adults.

The nervous system, which consists of the brain, spinal cord, and peripheral components, undergoes changes with aging (Hawkins et al., 1996). Brain decreases in weight and size, and the number of neuron cells declines (Hawkins et al., 1996). One of the consequences of loss in the number of neuron cells and neuron functioning is reduced reaction time (Hawkins et al., 1996). As a result, older adults may need more time to learn new material or to react to stimuli, thus affecting their participation in leisure activities such as team sports, motor sports, and activities that involve new technologies.

Social Construction of Aging Many age-related modifications in people's leisure participation are caused not by the biological changes in their bodies but by their shifting roles and responsibilities, by the events or transitions that take place when they are in certain age groups, and by the responses of society to their aging process.

Despite many changes in the roles and responsibilities that are expected of people in their life course, research shows that there is a significant uniformity in ages at which people take on and leave certain roles (Freysinger, 2000). Accord-ing to Kelly and Godbey (1992), there are three major periods of the life course: preparation, establishment, and culmination. The final major period of life—the culmination—is usually subdivided into two subperiods: active aging and frailty.

Physiologically, active aging begins when the processes of aging constrain activity and require significant adaptations (Kelly & Godbey, 1992). Psychologically, active aging starts when a person accepts that he or she has entered into the final stage of life. In this life stage, most older adults have some caregiving responsibilities for their parents and relatives who enter frailty, and many older adults care for their grandchildren to some extent. Retirement provides older adults with increased time for leisure, although financial resources may be strained for many of these people. Most older adults in this life stage are married, and their spouses and other family members remain their primary leisure companions. Leisure activities are centered on the family and social interactions and include many home-based pastimes, travel, and involvement in community organizations. Participation rates in sport, physical exercise, and outdoor recreation usually decline in this life stage (Kelly & Godbey, 1992).

Frailty comes when a person loses the ability to live independently. Frailty can be a gradual process or may occur suddenly because of health problems (e.g., stroke) (Kelly & Godbey, 1992). Married women usually go through the trauma of loss of their spouse and, as a consequence, need to adjust their lifestyle patterns and social networks. Leisure can help people during the grieving process by providing a context for social interactions and reaffirmation of social support. Most people in this life stage also need to give up driving a car and thus lose much of their independence and ability to travel to and from leisure activities. The frailty period is associated with marked loss of physical and mental abilities and decreased social networks. The role of leisure in this life period is to help maintain meaningful relationships, to relieve boredom and occupy time for those who are homebound, and, most important, to help people maintain mental, physical, and social competencies (Kelly & Godbey, 1992).

Leisure service providers should be familiar with the timing of social roles that people under-take in different life stages, because these roles affect the time and money people spend on leisure participation as well as their leisure preferences, motivations, and constraints (Freysinger, 2000).

Provision of Leisure Services for Older Adults

In the 21st century, it is increasingly acceptable for older adults to engage in activities that extend beyond the roles traditionally prescribed to people in their age group. Many older adults travel extensively, learn new skills, and attempt things they have postponed. Unfortunately, much of the activity participation among older adults is still guided by the stereotypes and prejudices deeply engrained in our society that define what activities are appropriate for people in this age group, what older adults are capable of, and how they should be served. Because of these stereotypes, older adults who, for example, date or engage in sports may be considered immature or unnecessarily endangering their health. People in older age categories are often steered toward activities that are considered appropriate for their age (e.g., gardening, bingo, church participation), thus restricting the range of leisure options available to them.

Older people may be prevented from participation in their desired pastimes by recreation service providers who assume that seniors are incapable of or uninterested in participation or who are ill at ease interacting with people who have hearing and vision impairments, slow reaction time, or other disabilities (Freysinger, 2000). Such restrictions are particularly detrimental to leisure engagements among older adults who live in institutionalized settings and who are dependent on the leisure offerings of the local service providers.

Those who provide leisure services to older adults must take into account the following issues:

• There is a tremendous diversity in the experience of aging and in the skills and abilities of older adults (Freysinger, 2000). Leisure service providers must consider the needs and abilities of their constituents rather than focus on their chronological age. In other words, leisure service providers should not assume that just because of their age people are incapable of or not interested in participating in certain leisure and recreation activities (Freysinger, 2000).

• Regardless of their age, people have common desires—they want to enjoy themselves, be recognized by others, and spend time with others in meaningful ways. Research shows that because of meaningless and trivial activity offerings, only a small proportion of older adults participate in senior centers (Freysinger, 2000). Traditional activities organized for older people such as bingo games and arts and crafts may not necessarily be high priorities for older adults. Recreation service agencies should look beyond their traditional service offerings and provide older adults with interesting and mentally and physically challenging activities such as educational programs, trips to interesting destinations, skill classes, or competitions.

• Recreation service providers should consider social needs of older adults who face death of the spouse and waning friendship circles. Possibilities for development of new friendship networks that would provide moral and physical support for home-bound older adults need to be considered. Technology, if appropriately adjusted and introduced to older individuals may become particularly important in such cases.

• Recreation service providers should consider providing appropriate opportunities for older adults who want to contribute to their families and communities through their leisure engagements (e.g., volunteering, fine arts and crafts). Recreation and leisure services can help to resist, challenge, and transform stereotypical and oppressive images of age and aging (Freysinger, 2000). Recreation service providers can change societal beliefs about the interests and abilities of older adults by providing them with activities that are challenging and offering opportunities for learning and affiliation (Freysinger, 2000).

• By providing stimulating and meaningful activities, recreation service providers can play a critical role in improving health and well-being of older adults.

Leisure Behavior of Older Adults in the Future

The social and economic implications of the aging of the American population are a concern for policy makers, the private sector, and leisure service providers. The transition of the baby boomers to retirement has triggered heated debates about possible modifications to Social Security, Medicare, and disability and retirement benefits (He et al., 2005).

Today's older adults are healthier, are more educated, have better incomes, and have higher

Older adults enjoying a walk in the park.

expectations regarding leisure service delivery than preceding generations. People who are moving into retirement age have been socialized to a variety of leisure pursuits that were not common among their parents and grandparents and have expectations regarding their retirement age that have not been seen among people retiring in previous years. Retirement is no longer viewed as the period preceding one's death but rather as a time one can devote to fulfilling dreams and making up for the time previously devoted to building careers and raising families. These changing characteristics of older adults and their high expectations will challenge recreation service providers who are charged with meeting the leisure needs of this group.

The changing marital and family patterns in the United States are likely to affect the types of support available to people of older age (He et al., 2005). Although in previous generations daughters and daughters-in-law were mostly responsible for the care of the oldest old, current low fertility rates and geographic movement of the younger and older generations may mean that many older adults do not have access to social networks that previously conditioned their leisure. This trend will need to be addressed by leisure service providers, who may have to provide services to an elderly population with different social support structures and residential patterns.

The population of older adults in the next several decades will be significantly more diverse than the older adults who are currently being served by recreation service providers. This population will include an increasing number of racial and ethnic minorities, many of whom will attach different meanings to leisure activities and will be accustomed to different leisure patterns.

Summary

The American population is changing rapidly. In the decades to come it will likely become more racially and ethnically diverse and will include a larger proportion of older adults than at any point in recent history. Moreover, the global economic downturn that began in 2008 is likely to affect all aspects of the everyday life of Americans, including their leisure behavior.

There exist numerous minority groups whom we have not been able to discuss in this chapter. People with disabilities, people of alternative sexual preference, and members of religious minorities are among millions of Americans whom you will serve as recreation professionals. Recreation practitioners need to stay informed about the changing makeup of American society and the special needs, interests, and constraints on recreation participation of diverse segments of the population. American society has been built on diversity and draws its strength from the many minority groups who make up the uniquely American mosaic. Our goal as recreation professionals should be to embrace this diversity and promote the ideals of tolerance and inclusion in the recreation settings and programs and in other aspects of life.

Discussion Questions

1. What could be the social, political, cultural, and economic consequences when large numbers of new immigrants settle in nontraditional destinations, such as small towns?

2. What sports are particularly popular among African Americans, Mexican Americans, Puerto Ricans, Pakistani and Hindu Americans, and Chinese Americans?

3. What effect will the increasing racial and ethnic diversity of the United States likely have on the recreation and leisure industry in the next 20 years?

4. Do you think certain constraints, such as body image, gender stereotyping of activities, and gender role expectations, can also constrain leisure and sport participation among men? Can you provide examples of leisure and sport activities in which men may feel constrained to participate due to these factors?

5. In which leisure activities might participation be particularly constrained for people of low socioeconomic status?

6. What will be the social, political, cultural, and economic consequences of the aging of the American population?

7. How is aging of the American population likely to affect recreation and leisure industry in the next 20 years?

ACCESSRecreation

Rick Green, PhD, CTRS

Professor of Therapeutic Recreation

Director of ACCESSRecreation
University of Southern Mississippi

Overview of the Program

ACCESSRecreation is the service learning laboratory of the recreation program at the University of Southern Mississippi. The mission of ACCESSRecreation is to provide progressive and inclusive recreation services for people in Hattiesburg, Mississippi, and throughout the state, to provide students in recreation an opportunity to learn through application, and to provide education and training services in inclusive recreation to students, parents, and professionals throughout Mississippi and the Southeast.

ACCESSRecreation is supported in part by funding from the Mississippi Council on Developmental Disabilities and the City of Hattiesburg Recreation Department.

Examples and Current Status

During the 2008-2009 school year, ACCESSRecreation offered the following programs:

- VSA arts (formerly Very Special Arts): For the past 6 years, ACCESSRecreation has hosted the VSA arts program as an inclusive program for all children. The program has grown to involve more than 600 children, of whom 10% to 20% have a disability.
- Accessible Sports and Recreation Club: ACCESSRecreation serves as the home of an official student sports and recreation club on campus. The purpose of the club is to promote access to sports and recreation for students with disabilities and their nondisabled friends.
- Power Soccer: ACCESSRecreation hosts the local power soccer club and schedules regular practices and games in the Hattiesburg area. Power wheelchairs are available for use by nondisabled participants.
- Wheelchair Tennis: ACCESSRecreation sponsors the local wheelchair tennis team. Practices and

nonsanctioned competitions are open to all. Additional support for the tennis program is provided by a grant from the United States Tennis Association.
- Golf: ACCESSRecreation hosted an inclusive golf instructional camp in June and July 2009.
- Support: ACCESSRecreation provides trained support staff for people who request assistance in local recreation activities.
- The 7th Annual Tri-State Conference on Recreation Inclusion: ACCESSRecreation hosts the annual conference on recreation inclusion, which draws participants from four states (Mississippi, Alabama, Louisiana, and Georgia). Additional support for the conference is provided by the Mississippi Protection and Advocacy System, the T.K. Martin Center on Technology and Disability at Mississippi State University, and the Alabama Council on Developmental Disabilities.

Brief History

ACCESSRecreation was established in 2000 as the Service Learning Laboratory for the USM Recreation Program. Since that time, ACCESSRecreation has worked with local agencies to provide recreation services to people with disabilities, provided service learning opportunities for students, and served as a local resource for training on inclusive recreation in Mississippi. Since 2000, more than 400 students in recreation, therapeutic recreation, exercise science, and sport coaching programs have received training and hands-on experience with inclusive recreation. Initial funding for the program was provided by a grant through the Mississippi Council on Developmental Disabilities. ACCESSRecreation is currently supported through funding by the Mississippi Council on Developmental Disabilities and the City of Hattiesburg Recreation Department.

Staff Training for Inclusion

Kathleen G. Scholl, PhD, CTRS

University of Northern Iowa

Torrie Dunlap, CPLP

National Training Center on Inclusion,
Kids Included Together

" *Leadership and learning are indispensable to each other.* "

–John F. Kennedy

Learning Outcomes

After completing this chapter, learners will be able to do the following:

- Explain the interconnections between people and their communities through an ecological perspective.
- Identify what a recreation agency can do to create community or system change.
- Identify the inclusion practices that help recreation service providers build on the strengths and abilities of people who are disabled.
- Provide examples of simple and respectful accommodations that facilitate access to a recreation activity for a person with a disability.
- Explain how using community resources and collaborating with others are related to inclusion advocacy.
- Articulate why agency mission statements, admission policies, and enrollment processes can make or break the inclusion process.
- Explain why ongoing inclusion training is important for all recreation professionals.

You may know or occasionally meet a person with a disability or someone who is racially or ethnically different than you. As a recreation provider, you have the potential to facilitate recreation opportunities that will help this person to grow, develop, and interact within the community. In fact, an important purpose of inclusive recreation is to help people from diverse backgrounds establish or strengthen community connections. Quality recreation services start with your interest and willingness to serve a variety of people with a broad array of abilities. This chapter (a) outlines an inclusion framework that includes the role of the recreation provider training as part of a social system within the recreation service delivery process, (b) explains the salient knowledge that recreation providers need to facilitate inclusion, and (c) lists the primary steps to begin inclusive recreation opportunities at your agency. To change how an organization conceptualizes and then constructs, delivers, and monitors recreation services for people with disabilities, we must start by examining the interrelationship between a person and their social environment.

Ecological Approach to Inclusive Recreation

What do we mean by an ecological approach to inclusive recreation? Social ecological theory (see figure 7.1) is based on the assumption that people and their environments are interconnected, that there is continuous interaction, both direct and indirect, between people and the environment in which they live. Social ecology theory defines the environment by its social organizations, such as family relationships, school settings, peer groups, social class, religious affiliation, or culture and society (Bronfenbrenner, 1979; Howe-Murphy & Charboneau, 1987). Social organizations are categorized into four types of nested environmental systems, with bidirectional influences within and between each system. As people interact with these systems, they shape and change each other. The four nested systems include these:

- *Microsystem*: the immediate environments in which a person has direct contact (family, school or work, peer group, and neighborhood)

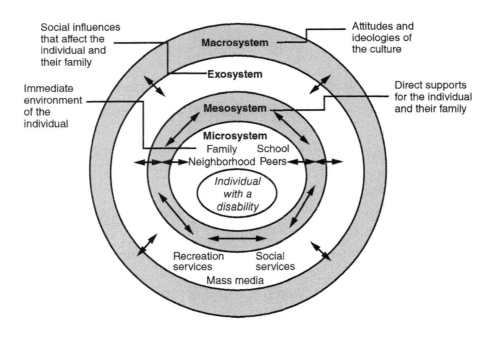

Figure 7.1 The social ecology model.

Based on U. Bronfenbrenner, 1979, *The ecology of human development* (Cambridge, MA: Harvard University Press).

- *Mesosystem*: a system of connections between immediate environments (e.g., a child's home and school, other parents and a child's friends; a recreation center and the neighborhood)
- *Exosystem*: external environmental settings that only indirectly affect a person's social interaction or development (e.g., recreation staff meetings and the agency's policies, city council meetings, human services departments, mass media, legal services)
- *Macrosystem*: the outermost system of a person's environment, which represents the larger cultural context (e.g., societal values, attitudes, ideologies, customs, laws, national economy, political culture, and social class)

This ecological viewpoint is not a new concept. Thirty years ago, the *Therapeutic Recreation Journal* (1979) published a special issue on the topic of mainstreaming people with disabilities into the community. More than 20 years ago, Howe-Murphy and Charboneau (1987) explained how therapeutic recreation specialists should take an ecological perspective and examine how the economic, technological, and social patterns in our society affect people with disabilities. An ecological approach assumes that interdependence (opposed to independence) is paramount, for no person is totally independent, an island unto himself. People bring their own set of skills and abilities, but the assets that exist within the community and the system at large are as important to individual achievement (Kretzmann McKnight, 1993). The ecological perspective considers that the environment is faulty and may need modification to provide the maximum support possible to "enable the individual with a disability an opportunity to attain a healthy interdependence" (Howe-Murphy and Charboneau, 1987, p. 20).

Conversely, a client-oriented model of intervention perceives that a person with a disability possesses deficits or problems and is the target for individually focused behavior change strategies, while neglecting the environmental effects of a disability (Stumbo & Peterson, 2009). A client-based approach is part of the ecological model, yet there are times when a broader perspective is required to meet a client's needs. As discussed in chapter 2, some people have traditionally been separated from society by institutionalization or segregated programs, thereby preventing parks and recreation personnel from gaining the professional skills needed to provide inclusion recreation services.

Applying ecological theory helps recreation professionals consider the social influences that affect recreation services. Enabling different groups of people to access and participate in recreation programs and become visible members of their community may require some agencies to make a deliberate social shift. To accomplish this, recreation service providers must identify and understand the arrangement and interdependencies of the social system components that encompass the delivery of their community programs and practices.

Who Facilitates the Inclusion of People With Disabilities in a Recreation Setting?

If people and their environments are indeed interrelated, then everyone within recreation services has a responsibility and a role in providing recreation opportunities for all people. All recreation professionals must be earnest and assume leadership to initiate the necessary changes and capacity-building efforts within their agencies and their communities. Recreation providers who are unaware of the needs of people with disabilities can unintentionally create barriers for these people, denying their freedom of choice in leisure and recreation preferences (Scholl et al., 2006). Using the tenets of ecological theory, the supportive recreation inclusion model (Devine et al., 2004) outlines the role of recreation services to provide inclusive recreation within the context of a larger social system.

Supportive Recreation Inclusion Model

The supportive recreation inclusion (SRI) model outlines components for designing less restrictive leisure environments and providing the maximum support possible to empower people with disabilities to attain interdependence within a recreation setting. The four components of the

SRI model are (a) the needs and interests of the person with a disability, (b) that person's support systems, (c) recreation service providers; and (d) the community at large (Devine et al., 2004, p. 212).

The initial focus of inclusive recreation is to improve the capacities of the person who is interested in participating in a recreation program with other people in her community. To enable successful inclusion, the provider must understand the strengths and weaknesses of the client's support system. A person's support system may include friends and neighbors, people from school or support groups, or others within the community. Successful inclusion also requires that the provider understand the client's financial limitations, her caregiver's abilities, and her family's and caregiver's attitudes toward inclusion. A certified therapeutic recreation specialist (CTRS) hired by a hospital, school, or recreation agency could also be considered a support system for either the person with a disability or the recreation provider. A CTRS is a person who has a degree in therapeutic recreation, or in recreation with a concentration in therapeutic recreation, and has passed a written certification exam by National Council for Therapeutic Recreation Certification (NCTRC). A CTRS can design an inclusion plan based on an activity and recreation analysis, in cooperation with the client and recreation program staff. An inclusion plan can include activities such as training the recreation instructor or the participant's peers in adaptations and accommodations, securing a companion or aide to help the client participate in the program, or purchasing adaptive recreation equipment to facilitate participation. A CTRS assists with initial implementation of the inclusion plan and conducts observations and follow-up visits to evaluate and possibly revise the plan (NCTRC, n.d.).

Another support system for the recreation provider is an inclusion specialist who may or may not be certified as a CTRS. An inclusion specialist may be someone who works in a recreation setting or an inclusion specialist may be a special education teacher within a formal education setting who works as an advocate for students up to 22 years of age who are involved in inclusive education programs (Cameron, 1994). This specialist is involved in the development of a child's Individualized Education Plan (IEP), which is designed to meet the unique educational needs of the child. The IEP is tailored to the individual student's needs as identified by the evaluation process and helps teachers and related service providers understand the student's disability and how the disability affects the learning process. In other words, the IEP describes how the child learns, how the child best demonstrates that learning, and what teachers and service providers should do to help the child learn more effectively. For a child who needs additional services outside of school time, recreation is one of many related services that schools can provide and list on a child's IEP (Küpper, 2000). More is said about collaborating with colleagues, families, and school districts later in this chapter.

Recreation service providers, camp counselors, recreation leaders, recreation supervisors, directors of recreation, parks, aquatic center directors, and sports program administrators are all vital links in the inclusion process, yet the level of preparedness of recreation personnel to provide inclusive recreation services remains moderate (Scholl et al., 2006). Recreation providers should continue to build their capacity and comfort level in providing recreation opportunities for all participants including those with disabilities (Cameron, 1994). For inclusion to be successful within the recreation agency from the top down, the recreation director or administrator must analyze the recreation organization's philosophical, administrative, programming, and resource components. For example, an accurate understanding of attitudes and competencies among recreation staff is helpful when an administrator assesses the agency's strengths and limitations regarding inclusion (Devine et al., 2004). Scholl and colleagues' (2006) study of recreation agencies' use of inclusion support services confirmed the findings of Devine and McGovern (2001) that recreation agencies need information on current ADA regulations and assistance in marketing their recreation programs to people with disabilities. Scholl and colleagues (2006) also reported that recreation agencies desire help in locating financial resources to pay for inclusion assessments and evaluations. Analyzing the community at large, including examining attitudes toward inclusion, compliance with the ADA, physical accommodations, and services that support inclusion, will inform the recreation service provider about attitudinal, programmatic, or administrative barriers that must be addressed to facilitate recreation inclusion.

Camp counselors and other personnel who interact directly with clients should be capable and prepared but also should be able to make clients comfortable in their recreation experience.

The community at large represents the exosystem of the SRI model and includes educational institutions, government agencies, health care and human service providers, transportation providers, and commercial organizations. An agency's policies influence the extent to which members of the exosystem provide money and the authority to guide the organization's objectives, which in turn influences the ability of the agency to provide services (McDonnell & Elmore, 1987). According to this model, all systems (individuals, families, recreation organizations, and the community) have reciprocal influences on each other; however, the attitudes and ideologies of all systems are represented by the macrosystem of the model. Community agencies and organizations that are unwilling to provide activities and services for diverse groups of people will undoubtedly influence the recreation organization and support services.

Ecological Model

Using the ecological model as a framework to identify needs and to create community change or "systems change" involves developing the capacity of your recreation program to make an impact at the microsystem or individual level. To create change at the community level involves "a revision in the ways that people and institutions think, behave, and use their resources to fundamentally affect the types, quality, and degree of service delivery to children and their families" (Melaville et al., 1993, p. vii). Community change can be more difficult to produce than individual-level change because of the multiple levels of community systems and multiple stages of the recreation programming process, but if your community capacity-building efforts are successful, they will make your community the best possible place to live (Community, n.d). To create community change through recreation programming, you must identify the following:

1. The efficiency and effectiveness of your agency's recreation program delivery processes for people with disabilities.

2. Availability and usability of your agency's resources. This includes acquiring the resources needed to deliver recreation services to different groups of people and ensuring that the resources are accessible,

integrated, and used effectively. If individuals, their family members, and staff do not know how to use the resources effectively, the resources will do little to benefit the community.

3. Develop agency policies to effectively distribute and redistribute resources, regulate behavior, create or modify procedures, and evaluate both intended and unintended consequences. For example, allocate funding for specific programs or services that directly affect children or adults with disabilities (Community, n.d.).

Inclusive recreation involves looking at your programs and resources and thinking about how you can affect the lives of all people in your community. The ecological approach to inclusive recreation highlights the multiple interconnections between people and their communities. Recreation professionals need to examine the way their programs are delivered and the way they conduct business to make significant and sustainable changes in the manner in which minority groups are served. The next sections of this chapter describe how your agency can increase the diversity of the people you serve.

Importance of Training

Many recreation providers believe that they do not have the training necessary to serve people with disabilities in their programs. People are fearful of what is unfamiliar to them, and many of us have not interacted with people with disabilities in education and community life. Training in inclusion can help us understand disability and learn specific techniques for supporting people of all abilities in recreation activities (Mulvihill et al., 2004). More important than the knowledge of specific types of disabilities is the understanding that people with and without disabilities are more alike than they are different. All people have areas of strength and areas that challenge them, and the same is true for people with disabilities. Knowing how to build on strengths and make accommodations for areas of challenge is the centerpiece of inclusion. To provide inclusive services you must commit to the following practices: (a) communicate respect for all people; (b) examine your own biases and beliefs about others; (c) learn how to make respectful accommodations; and (d) collaborate with your colleagues, community agencies, school districts,

and participants' families. A way to get started in understanding disability and inclusion is to practice using person-first language.

Use Language to Communicate Respect

People are often stymied in interacting with people with disabilities, or discussing disability at all, by the language and terms. It can be difficult to know how to respectfully refer to a person with a disability. We have all heard negative and deficiency-based language in the media and in our own communities. Pejorative slang terms like "retard" and "lame" are used colloquially among young people in America. The media frequently use outdated terms like *handicapped, crippled,* and *wheelchair bound.* People also have trouble referring to those without a diagnosed disability and use terms like *able-bodied, nondisabled,* and *healthy.* Providers of recreation must not allow a lack of language to keep them from interacting with people with disabilities.

Using person-first language is a general rule for communicating respect for people with disabilities (see table 7.1). The key is to always put the person before the disability. In other words, you can refer to *people with disabilities* instead of *the disabled,* or to *a child with autism* rather than *an autistic child.* People with disabilities are multifaceted human beings whose qualities reach far beyond the label of a disability. No one wants to be classified by one trait, and we all want to be acknowledged and understood for our complete personalities, interests, and experiences.

There are exceptions to the use of person-first language, notably in the deaf community where people prefer to be referred to as *deaf* rather than a *person who is deaf.* Some adults with autism also prefer to be referred to as *autistic.* Make a sincere effort to use language that is respectful to others, and also to respect the preferences of people with disabilities. In most cases, it is more precise to refer to a person by their name rather than a trait.

Using person-first language, you can also refer to those who do not have a disability as *people without disabilities.* In your own journey to inclusion you will likely hear the term *typically developing* used to describe children without disabilities. This term is most often used when referring to very young children, who do have a set of developmental benchmarks that tend to be met along a specific timeline (i.e., rolling over, sitting up,

Table 7.1 People-First Language

Say	Instead of
People with disabilities	The handicapped or disabled
Paul has a cognitive disability (or a diagnosis of cognitive disability).	He is mentally retarded.
Kate has autism (or a diagnosis of autism).	She is autistic.
Ryan has Down syndrome (or a diagnosis of Down syndrome).	He's Down's.
Sara has a learning disability (or a diagnosis of learning disability).	She is learning disabled.
Bob has a physical disability (or a diagnosis of physical disability).	He is a quadriplegic; he is crippled.
Mary is of short stature; Mary is a little person.	She's a dwarf; she's a midget.
Tom has a mental health diagnosis.	He is emotionally disturbed; he is mentally ill.
Nora uses a wheelchair or mobility chair.	She is confined to a wheelchair; she is wheelchair bound.
Steve receives special education services.	He's in special education.
Tonya has a developmental delay.	She's developmentally delayed.
Children without disabilities	Normal or healthy kids
She communicates with her eyes or a device.	She is nonverbal.
Customer	Client, consumer, recipient
Alice has a congenital disability	Alice has a birth defect.
He has brain injury.	He is brain damaged.
Accessible parking, accessible hotel room	Handicapped parking, handicapped hotel room
She needs . . . or she uses . . .	She has problems; she has special needs.

Excerpted from Kathie Snow's "People First Language" Article, www.disabilityisnatural.com; used with permission.

crawling, developing language). Children who meet these standards in the accepted timeline are called typically developing. You can also refer to children as *children without disabilities* or *peers without disabilities*. Of course, you may not need to refer to a disability at all and can refer to Adam, the 9-year-old with freckles and red hair who loves soccer.

Using person-first language helps you communicate respect for people with disabilities, but it can also guide your own interactions with people with disabilities. When you put a label on a person like "autistic" or "developmentally delayed," you limit your own opportunity to experience everything this person has to offer. If you characterize a person as "autistic" you may inadvertently stereotype her in your mind and

expect a certain set of behaviors or responses. You may not give yourself the chance to learn that this person is also an accomplished pianist or loves the same TV show that you do.

When practicing inclusive language, it is also important to eliminate uses of stereotypical and derogatory language as they apply to various cultures and communities of people. There are phrases and slang terms that are derogatory to groups of people, and in some cases have become a part of our lexicon. Referring to a group of rambunctious children as *wild Indians* is promoting a stereotype. Characterizing something as *gay* or *lame* is a derogatory use of language and negatively affects a group of people. Training on the use of appropriate and respectful language should be mandatory for all staff.

Examine Your Own Biases

Archaic terms influence our biases and beliefs about people and disability. Our cultural backgrounds come with a set of beliefs about disability (Lynch & Hanson, 1998). We may have experiences from childhood that affect our beliefs about disability. A lack of experience interacting with people with disabilities can lead to a bias about people with disabilities (Anderson & Kress, 2003). All of these factors must be examined when working in a recreation setting where you will serve all people who live in a community. In the same way that using outdated language can convey disrespect for people with disabilities, an inherent bias toward people with disabilities will be evident in your service delivery. Do you believe that people with physical disabilities, who may use wheelchairs for mobility, cannot play on the basketball team? What evidence do you have to support this bias? If you hold this as a bias and you receive a call from a person who uses a wheelchair for mobility and would like to play a team sport like basketball, you may limit her opportunities without even knowing that you are doing so. You may guide her toward a wheelchair basketball league held across town, which would not only limit her opportunity to play on your recreation team but also prevent other team members from getting to know this person. If you can be honest about your biases and beliefs, you will be more able to react openly to each situation you encounter. You will be more willing to explore ways to support the inclusion of people with disabilities in the programs that you offer.

There are certainly other personal biases and beliefs that can be explored, especially in terms of ethnicity, age, socio-economic status, and sexual orientation. What personal beliefs might you hold about people based on their age, whether it be young people entering the workforce or the elderly wishing to access recreation programs? Do you have biases related to race that may be deeply rooted to a childhood experience? A commitment to examining individual biases and assumptions can contribute to creating a truly inclusive environment in a recreation program.

Make Respectful Accommodations

The Americans with Disabilities Act (1990) requires public programs to make "reasonable modifications" to include people with disabili-

ties. If you follow the spirit of the law, rather than the letter of the law, and learn to make respectful accommodations, you will provide the best possible service to all of your participants. By making the accommodation respectful, you value the inherent right of each person to participate in the life-enhancing activities that you offer. By being respectful, you model for others, both children and adults, the appreciation of differences.

An accommodation is an individualized support that promotes access to learning, recreation, leisure, or work. Accommodation frequently entails modifying expectations you have for the participant. An accommodation might involve providing additional support, for example, changing the ratio of adults to children in a summer camp. An accommodation might mean lengthening the time you provide someone to complete an activity or modifying the activity so that the person with a disability can partially participate. Accommodation might entail shortening the length of time the person participates by changing the schedule or allowing a participant to be excused from part or all of an activity. An accommodation should be made if it will physically, socially, or emotionally support the inclusion of the person with a disability in an activity (Dunlap & Shea, 2004).

People without disabilities likely benefit from accommodations at some point in their lives. Surely you have been in a situation where you would have benefited from having material presented in a different way, being given more time to finish an activity, or receiving even just a little amount of assistance for the task. You may have a temporary or lifelong disability that requires accommodation or you may have used crutches after an ankle sprain or leg break. Your family and friends probably made some accommodations for you so that you could continue to participate in the activities of your daily life. It is no different when making accommodations for people with disabilities in your recreation programs.

Accommodations should be provided only when they are necessary to facilitate access to the activity or learning opportunity. The accommodation should be faded or eliminated if the person no longer requires the accommodation, or requires less of an accommodation, to be successfully involved in the activity. Accommodations should be explained to other participants in the group as needed; however, accommodations need not be justified or explained as a privilege.

Accommodations are not exceptions to program rules but rather are features that allow a participant to function successfully within program boundaries.

Staff working in recreation programs need to know how to design accommodations for people with a variety of ability levels. Information about accommodations can come first from the participant (in the case of adults) and from the family (in the case of children). Although you cannot ask about the nature of a person's disability or ask for a medical diagnosis, you can ask about the person's strengths, interests, and areas in which he may need some support. You can solicit ideas for accommodations by explaining the activity to the participant or his family (e.g., "We offer a hiking program every Saturday for a month where we meet at the base of the trail at 8 a.m. and hike 4 miles on mostly flat, unpaved surface. We take a break at the 2-mile mark for water and stretching, and we have a trail guide who notes points of interest for the group"). Sometimes, inviting the participant or family members to visit the program environment is the best way to get information about necessary accommodations. Your goal is to promote successful participation in the activity, and accommodation supports participation (Frazeur Cross et al., 2004).

Collaborate With Your Community

As part of your organization's training plan, you will need to identify and learn to make appropriate accommodations for your participants. Training will likely extend past the classroom walls as you reach out into the community and your clients' *microsystem* and *mesosystem,* as you will recall from the beginning of this chapter. You can get suggestions for accommodations from others who work with your client, providing that you have her permission (or her family's permission) to speak with any teachers or specialists. In the case of a child with a disability, the classroom teacher can be a valuable source of information on accommodations and will provide consistency between the school day and recreation setting. This consistency will enhance a child's participation in the program, will support her positive behavior, and will help her feel safe and supported (Couchenour & Chrisman, 2004).

Colleagues can be a resource in your efforts to design accommodations for participants. Be sure that you protect a participant's confidentiality and hold any conversations about the participant in a private location where others will not hear you. Your colleagues can provide you with new ideas for accommodations and also help

›› Professionals in Action

Nili Mathews

Background Information

Education   BA in recreation and leisure studies with an emphasis in therapy from San Francisco State University

Credentials   Certified therapeutic recreation specialist

Career Information

Position   Program Specialist

Organization   Kids Included Together (KIT)

What I Like About My Job   I get paid for my passion! There is nothing better than being able to work at your life's passion. I am fortunate enough to train and educate out-of-school providers about including children with disabilities in their programs. One of my favorite things about training is watching people learn and demonstrate acceptance for *all* children as part of their community. I also get to travel all over the nation, taking the philosophy and importance of inclusion to all who will listen. Every time I train a group, I learn from participants at the same time they learn from me. I also conduct a training of trainers on our curriculum, which allows KIT to empower agencies all over the map on the best practices of inclusion.

you when you believe that an accommodation has stopped working and you need to fade or redesign the strategy. Your colleagues may have worked with the same participant and can offer suggestions based on the person's interests and strengths. Regular staff meetings can be used to communicate information about accommodations and behavioral strategies.

Reaching out to your community is a vital part of creating an inclusive environment. Community resources are valuable in a variety of ways. You may access the services of the local Braille Institute to translate your materials into braille for a participant who is blind. You may contact your local Deaf Community Services to inquire about American Sign Language (ASL) interpreters who are available to work in your program. Perhaps you will contact a local Easter Seals or United Cerebral Palsy chapter and ask a member of its speaker's bureau to address your staff, volunteers, or board of directors. You can also use community resources as referral agencies for your program and as a method of outreach. Each organization likely distributes a newsletter to its constituents. You may be able to list your upcoming events in the newsletter to reach out to families of children with disabilities. The local school district can also be a valuable community resource. Ask school administrators for support in reaching out to children who are receiving special education services, or ask special education teachers to review materials or work in your program during their holiday and summer breaks.

As you collaborate with families, colleagues, community agencies, and school districts, you will become an advocate for inclusion. Your efforts to ensure that people with disabilities have access to recreation programs will likely provide leadership for others and could create a more inclusive community. Your efforts will certainly increase the level of collaboration in your community, and people with disabilities may gain more opportunities for participation as a result. Inclusion is process, not a program, and you can lead the way in your agency by providing modeling for your colleagues, communicating openly with families and other agencies, and celebrating successes. These efforts will also likely increase systems coordination in your community and could ensure that families receive more integrated services. For instance, to receive services to which they are entitled, people may have to make a series of time-consuming phone calls as they are referred and re-referred by agencies that specialize in one area of service. When a commu-

nity is linked together to provide services, even in an informal way, a family can call any number of agencies and receive information.

Where to Begin the Inclusion Process

Successful inclusion depends on an agency-wide commitment to serving all people. All levels of staff and volunteers must adopt an inclusive philosophy. This new way of thinking can transform an organization into one that is truly reflective of the community it serves and accepting of all people.

Ensure That Your Mission Statement Welcomes All

A critical piece of organizational transformation is the development of a mission statement that welcomes all people (Miller & Schleien, 1999). Examine your current mission statement. Does it accurately reflect your desire to serve people of all abilities? Is it clear, concise, and welcoming? If you are unsure what message your statement is delivering, ask a few participants to review it and give you some feedback. Generally, the use of the word *all* will convey your moral philosophy.

Here are some examples of inclusive mission and values statements:

- From national organizations:
  - Inspiring and enabling all young people to realize their full potential as productive, responsible, and caring citizens. (Boys & Girls Clubs of America)
  - We are dedicated to improving the quality of human life and to helping all people realize their fullest potential. (YMCA)
  - (Core Value) We are inclusive, welcoming children, youth and adults regardless of race, religion, socioeconomic status, disability, sexual orientation or other aspect of diversity. (Camp Fire USA)
- From after-school and recreation programs:
  - We provide engaging, innovative, high-quality theater education and productions for children of all cultural heritages, ages, abilities and levels of interest.
  - To provide learning and recreational experiences for children at all stages of development.
  - We are committed to serving all children and meeting their needs for social interaction and educational enrichment.

If you decide that your mission statement needs revising, you must begin a thoughtful process that includes the key stakeholders of the agency. Mission statements often come with a long history and are meaningful to staff and volunteers who have experience with the organization. You will need to respect the history of the mission statement and work to build consensus among stakeholders. One way to accomplish this is to convene a focus group of people from the different facets of your organization. Lead them through a process to determine what core services the agency provides. Then, discuss the agency's purpose (e.g., to teach life skills through participation in team sports). Be sure that the statement is not exclusionary and invites participation from all. Once you have created a mission statement that includes all, you will have developed a vision for a caring, respectful community that welcomes people with diverse abilities.

Once you have an inclusive mission statement, do not keep it a secret. Display the mission statement in a visible place in all facilities, include it in every piece of print material, and locate it prominently on your Web site. Many organizations publish their mission statement on business cards and letterhead stationery as a way to constantly advertise their philosophy. The mission statement should be familiar to every staff member.

A complement to an inclusive mission statement is a separate inclusion statement that can be printed in all registration brochures. This will more directly invite people with disabilities to participate in the programs you offer. If families know that your agency is committed to inclusion, they will be more likely to provide you with valuable information regarding accommodations. The inclusion statement may be something like "we welcome children of all ability levels in our day camps." This will let parents know that they will not be turned away when they call or visit to register for your programs.

Examine Your Admission Policies

Once you are sure that your agency mission statement communicates an inclusive philosophy, look at your admission policies. Are your policies rigid, or do they use mostly skill-based requirements? An example of a rigid policy is that children may not use flotation supports in the pool. Some children will never be able to swim without the support of flotation devices, because

Accommodating a child's needs can allow him to fully participate in activities.

of low muscle tone or poor gross motor skills, but would benefit greatly from the opportunity to be in the swimming pool with their peers without disabilities. An accommodation to support inclusion would be to allow a child to use a flotation device. An example of a skill-based requirement is that children must perform a solo song or dance in order to participate in the community talent show or play production camp. An accommodation to facilitate inclusion could be that the child participates in the performance in another way, perhaps as a technical assistant. Your agency must have policies related to admission and enrollment and must adhere strictly to them whenever possible. In designing policies, ensure that you are not excluding groups of people by demanding prerequisite skills.

Design an Intake and Enrollment Process

Inclusion has the best chance of success when a thoughtful and respectful intake process is in place. This process will likely include staff members at several levels in an agency, including the administrative assistant or registrar, program director, and program instructors or leaders. The intake and enrollment process helps a family to feel welcomed by your agency and allows them to provide you with information and resources that will be valuable in your efforts to include a person with a disability. Families are a critical component in facilitating inclusion (National Child Care Information Center, 2003). Establishing a positive rapport with a family prior to the start of the program will enhance communication if challenges arise.

The process will likely begin with a phone call of inquiry from a parent. Be sure that the staff member who answers the phone is aware of the agency's commitment to inclusion. Many times parents are turned away at the first phone call because the person they speak to has not undergone training for inclusion. The staff member who takes the call should be able to provide the parent with information about the program, dates and times, fees, and payment schedules. This staff member will determine whether there is space available in the class and, if not, will put the participant on a waiting list. You are not required to open up a space in a class or camp that is closed in order to include a child with a disability, but you cannot deny a space if there are openings (Dunlap & Shea, 2004).

The first contact with a family may be through a registration or enrollment form. There should be a statement on the registration form that asks whether a participant needs an accommodation because of a medical condition or disability. You cannot ask for a diagnosis but should ask open-ended questions that will help you determine what types of supports will need to be in place. You may also want to include a place on the registration form for a family to let you know about any cultural concerns they have related to their participation in your program (e.g., food substitutions if meals or snacks are provided).

The next step is to invite the parent and participant to visit the program, preferably during program hours. This is an opportunity for a family to see the facility, get more information about the activities offered, and provide program staff with suggestions for accommodations. For the program staff, this is a time to find out about the family's goals for the child in the program, learn more about the strengths and interests of the child, and determine what areas may be challenging and need accommodation or additional support. This is also a time to let the family know that all information about the child will be kept confidential by program staff and that information will only be given to staff members on a need-to-know-basis. Encourage families to put important information about medications and food restrictions in writing, and keep this information in a secure location.

Here are some sample questions to include in the intake process:

- Safety
  - Does your child have allergies?
  - Will you provide medications and instructions for administering medication?
  - Does your child require a special diet? What are her preferred snacks and eating schedule?
  - What should we do if the child has a seizure or goes into diabetic shock?
  - Is the child a flight risk (i.e., does he run away)?
  - Who are your emergency contacts and physician, and what hospital should we send your child to in case of emergency?
- Special Interests and Talents
  - Friendships: What are his friends like and what do they like to do together?
  - Hobbies: What does he like to do at home in his free time?
  - Interests: What are her favorite books, games, and television shows?
  - Talents: What is he really good at?
  - Goals: What goals do you have for your child in this program?
- Development
  - Physical: How does the child move? Does he require any adaptive equipment?
  - Emotional: What does he do when he is upset? What helps to calm him down?
  - Social: How does she communicate? Does she use words, pictures, or gestures?
  - Self-help: Does he need assistance when using the toilet? Are there specific things that he needs help with (opening his lunch or blowing his nose)?
- Your Child and Our Program
  - What are his favorite types of activities?
  - What are some of her fears (dogs, the dark)?
  - Do any particular sounds or smells bother him?
  - Does he mind being close to other children and people?
  - What kinds of accommodations can we make to help her be successful in our program?

Ask questions that will help your staff interact in a positive way with an individual who has special needs. What kind of emotional assistance might he need? What are his communication styles and preferences?

The site visit is a good opportunity to establish a plan for ongoing communication with the parent. Decide whether you will use a daily written log, phone calls, or e-mail or will chat at the drop-off or pickup point. Be sure that the method is convenient for both you and the family, and respect the family's privacy by speaking out of earshot of other participants and their families and keeping logs and e-mails private.

The site visit will give parents an idea of what accommodations may be necessary to support successful inclusion. Be thorough in your descriptions of program activities and show the environments in which they take place. Ask open-ended questions: "What do you see that you think your child will really enjoy?" "How can we adjust the environment to meet her needs?" Be a good listener and take notes if necessary, but don't ask the parent to fill out lengthy forms that parents of children without disabilities are not asked to complete.

If the participant uses assistive technology or has other specific needs, consider asking the family to orient the staff to the equipment. A parent may be willing to visit a staff meeting and demonstrate how to use a piece of equipment or may share specific information about the child with the program staff.

Evaluate Your Facility and Program Offerings for Inclusion

For inclusion to become a part of your program, all members of the staff must understand what accessibility means in terms of both facilities and programs. Inclusion is everyone's responsibility (Anderson & Kress, 2003). Planning for inclusion involves job responsibilities at every level of an organization: administrators who create budgets and policies that allow for inclusion, directors and coordinators who design thoughtful intake and enrollment processes for families and instruct program staff on accommodations, marketing personnel who depict inclusion in print materials and promotional photos, and facilities and custodial staff who ensure that program environments are conducive to inclusion. Entrances and public areas should be welcoming to families and take into account a variety of methods of communication. Families and participants need to be able to both enter your facility and take advantage of your program offerings once inside. Is the reception desk accessible? Are alternate forms of communication provided for registration or check-in? Examples of alternate forms of communication include large-print materials, computer with screen reader, braille, and languages other than English.

It is important to have a "top down, bottom up" strategy in an organization so that inclusion is consistent and pervasive. In the context of organizational structure, the term *top down, bottom up* refers to how decisions are made and executed. In a "top down, bottom up" approach, the staff at the executive level make decisions and disseminate them to the staff at lower levels. A "bottom up" approach is when staff at the frontline level can affect decision-making. To ensure "top down, bottom up" is to be sure that everyone working in an organization has the information and knowledge of the philosophy of inclusion so that service delivery is seamless for participants. Custodial staff may question why they need to receive training on inclusion, but their role will be important, especially if you are including a person who is blind or visually impaired and depends on the consistency of furniture in the environment. If custodial staff are aware of your agency's commitment to inclusion, they can make decisions about the physical spaces that reflect the moral philosophy of inclusion. This may mean that they reposition trash receptacles to provide access for those using wheelchairs. Or it may mean they do not hose down sidewalks when they know children with limited mobility will be in camp. Front desk staffers who understand inclusion will be open to using TTY (teletypewriter) systems to take registration from participants who are deaf and will make parents of children with disabilities feel welcome in their first interaction with the agency. Support from program leaders will ensure that all members of staff receive the training and support they need to provide the best possible programs for the widest range of people.

Commit to Ongoing Training

A high rate of staff turnover is common in programs that take place outside of school hours (Yohalem & Pittman, 2006). Ongoing training is vital to ensuring the consistency of inclusive practices in an agency. The Massachusetts After-school Research Study (MARS) found that programs with more highly trained staff, particularly at the levels of program director and direct service, were rated significantly higher in overall program quality (Intercultural Center, 2005). Training that is most successful goes beyond merely raising awareness of disability and inclu-

sion and includes activities to increase knowledge and skill (Mulvihill et al., 2002).

Ongoing staff training can take many formats and should be rooted in the following efforts:

- Ensure that new hires are oriented on inclusive practices of the agency.
- Provide ongoing support to staff and information on new techniques.
- Keep a commitment to inclusion at the forefront of business practices.

Methods for staff training can include live presentations to staff at regularly scheduled meetings or special training events, job coaching provided by a supervisor or senior staff member, technical assistance provided by outside consultants, Internet research on specific disabilities or behavior support strategies, attendance at conferences, and online training.

Every new employee should be oriented on inclusion and the agency's philosophy, policies, and procedures related to inclusion. Formal staff orientations can be combined with other efforts seasonally when large numbers of people are hired at once. Late spring, when summer camp staff are hired, is a good time for an orientation to inclusion. Orientation for new employees throughout the year can take place through one-on-one meetings with a mentor or senior staff member, by having new employees review the operations manual, or through enrolling new staff in a distance learning course using the Internet. New staff should understand the agency's intention to provide service to all people and how employees can support inclusion through their own position. Sharing stories about successful inclusion in your organization can be a good way to communicate the value of inclusion to new hires. Newsletter articles, thank-you letters from families, and agency scrapbooks can all show the benefits of inclusion.

Seasoned staff will also need ongoing training and support for inclusion. As the agency progresses in its journey to inclusion, new challenges will arise that training can address. Enrollment of participants with specific types of disabilities may require that staff undertake specific training. As the agency moves toward meaningful inclusion for all, participants with more significant disabilities will be more likely to enroll. Once staff members have experience with basic inclusion techniques, they will want to explore a more intentional approach to social inclusion and friendship development among the participants. This type of ongoing training can be provided in a group setting using disability service agencies from the community or organizations that specialize in inclusion. A way to create sustainability for inclusion is to assign some seasoned staff members to present training during staff meetings. These staff members can research a topic that is timely using books, journals, the Internet, or live interviews and then present the information to the group. Online training can keep seasoned staff motivated.

All levels of staff will to need to revisit their commitment periodically to ensure that inclusion remains an integral part of business practices and organizational identity. Gathering time-limited advisory groups, made up of people with and without disabilities who use the agency's services, can be a good way to review program policies and procedures to ensure inclusiveness. Asking families of children who have been included to speak to staff and volunteer groups about their experience can help staff renew their commitment to serving people of all abilities. Satisfaction surveys distributed to participants and their families will help staff refine processes related to inclusion. Keep staff enthused by supporting their attendance at inclusion-related conferences, finding local opportunities for training, and searching the Internet for new information regarding disability and inclusion. Make discussion about inclusion a regular part of staff and department meetings so that ongoing progress can be evaluated by staff.

Summary

Recreation providers are part of a larger social system that offers services to community members. As society changes and evolves, recreation professionals must evaluate the way that they think about service delivery, continually question whether they are using their resources as effectively and efficiently as possible, and envision ways to include all people in programs and activities. To enhance community life for people with disabilities, recreation providers can start by observing that people are more alike than different, even if they walk or communicate with the use of an assistive device. To expand recreation services to a broader audience, adopt and model a philosophy of respect of all people and use your resources to include people with disabilities in your program activities. Review organizational policies and procedures, facilities, and programs, and provide ongoing inclusion training for staff so that they feel competent and up-to-date on best practices for program and behavior modifications and on state and federal regulations in order to build local community capacity to make their town the best possible place to live.

Discussion Questions

1. How are you connected to your community at the micro-, meso-, and exosystem levels? How does the cultural context of your community affect your recreation opportunities and experiences? Does your community draw on diverse traditions?

2. What are your biases related to people with ability or cultural differences? How have your past experiences (or lack of experiences) informed your beliefs?

3. What are some ways that recreation agencies can provide training to their staff members, keeping in mind limited professional development budgets and time constraints? How can community resources be used for staff training?

KIDS—The Disabled Children and Young People's Charity

KIDS is a national charity in Great Britain working toward a vision in which all children and young people with disabilities realize their aspirations and their right to an inclusive community that supports them and their families. KIDS provides a wide range of services in seven British regions and promotes inclusive play and leisure for children and young people through workforce development and support.

KIDS runs a number of inclusive playgrounds and projects including the Playwork Inclusion Project (PIP) funded by the Department for Children, Schools and Families. PIP is coordinated by KIDS National Development Department and was complemented by another project, the Young People's Inclusion Network (YP-in) funded until the end of 2008. The YP-in project worked directly with young people with disabilities, looking at the barriers they face in accessing inclusive leisure, and produced online guidance information. For further information on these projects, e-mail pip@kids.org.uk or go to www.kids.org.uk

KIDS

6 Aztec Row
Berners Road
London N1 OPW
Tel: +44 (0)207 359 3073
www.kids.org.uk

Photo courtesy of Luke Tchalenko 2008.

Participants at KIDS Hayward Adventure Playground in north London.

Reprinted, by permission, from KIDS.

PART III

Applying Inclusive Practices in Recreation and Leisure

Universal Design in Recreation

Cindy Dillenschneider, MS Ed

Northland College, Ashland, Wisconsin

Cindy Burkhour, MA, CTRS, CPRP

Access Recreation Group, LLC

"Universal Design is the design of products and environments to be usable by all people, to the greatest extent possible, without the need for adaptation or specialized design."

–Ron Mace

» Learning Outcomes

After completing this chapter, learners will be able to do the following:

- Discuss the difference between minimum ADA compliance design characteristics and universal design characteristics.
- Identify program and facility design strategies that ensure full inclusion of all people of all abilities.
- Explain why universal design of recreation programs and facilities should consider such varied factors as gender, cultural background, physical and cognitive ability, and economic ability.
- Explain the relationship between civil rights legislation and socially responsible design of recreation programs and facilities.

Including all people in all recreation experiences is the right thing to do, and in many cases it is the law. Recreation providers have a moral, ethical, and legal responsibility for serving all people in the community. But a variety of obstacles can get in the way, such as environmental barriers, programmatic barriers, and social barriers.

Before we can remove the things that get in the way of full and equal participation by all people, we must understand what the obstacles are and develop a plan to remove those barriers. We then need to make policy and procedural changes so that inclusive, universally accessible recreation becomes a way of doing business. We need to consider universal design concepts up front in the planning and design process for all programs, services, and facilities. Including everyone and using universal design then become forethought rather than an afterthought. We make decisions to purchase only equipment that is designed for accessibility, like picnic tables and benches, so people of all abilities can have equal opportunities to recreate together; we plan every aspect of our programs so the greatest range of people feel invited and encouraged to join in the fun. In this chapter we introduce you to the principles of universal design and the legal history and mandates that have shaped the inclusive recreation movement. We then share practical examples of how to apply the concepts to all recreation programs, services, and facilities to create truly inclusive and universally accessible recreation experiences for people of all abilities.

Universal Design Defined

The concept of universal design appeared in the 1970s in the field of architecture. An architect in the United States, Michael Bednar, recognized that everyone would benefit from environments where barriers did not exist (Institute for Human Centered Design, 2008). This concept began to move architecture beyond design that provided access to people with disabilities to design that was more universal, one that would enhance usability for all people throughout the life span and for all ordinary life experiences.

A keen look at typically built environments prior to the mid 1990s reveals a level of expectation around physical and cognitive ability that was not inclusive of a significant portion of the population. The environment was built to accommodate an "ideal" average human (Government

Photo courtesy of Cindy Burkhour.

It is important not only to identify barriers but to involve people with disabilities in the process so that they have a voice in identifying what problems exist and what improvements could be made.

of Alberta, 2003), without modification for any exception. Facilities were built with entrances that required everyone to use stairs, toilet stalls were too narrow and too small to accommodate people who used wheelchairs or who were accompanied by a baby in a stroller, and signs required the ability to read the language to understand information as commonly needed in locating a restroom. As a result of awareness raised by those who embraced the concept of universal design, a series of changes began to reshape our environment. We began to see "universal" symbols (Osborne, 2001) such as male or female pictograms that eliminated the need to read to gain commonly needed information. Buildings were designed to be accessed by people who used wheelchairs. Usability within public spaces was enhanced through newly designed devices such as faucets that were turned on or off through the use of motion detectors and through design sensitivity such as providing information counters, telephones, and water fountains accessible to people of varied heights and usable from a standing or seated position.

Universal design typically applies to the process of creating architecture and products where barriers to use are eliminated during the design phase. Attention on the front end of design results in a final product or facility that is usable by the broadest range of people as possible throughout the life span. Consider the difference between universally designed buildings with family-friendly and wheelchair-accessible restrooms and buildings retrofitted to accommodate people who use wheelchairs and adults with infants. The universally designed restroom is spacious, with a floor plan that positions stalls, sinks, and changing tables in a manner to allow ease of maneuvering, whereas the second often requires users to perform difficult maneuvering around others just to access the toilet facilities, and some restrooms may not be usable at all by people who use wheelchairs, scooters, or other mobility devices. Universal design for facilities and products is guided by a set of principles (see table 8.1) conceived and developed by the Center for Universal Design (1997). Recreation providers who participate in facility design or

Table 8.1 Principles of Universal Design

Principle	Brief description
Equitable use	The design is useful and marketable to people with diverse abilities.
	Guidelines
	1a. Provide the same means of use for all users: identical whenever possible, equivalent when not.
	1b. Avoid segregating or stigmatizing any users.
	1c. Make privacy, security, and safety equally available to all users.
	1d. Make the design appealing to all users.
Flexibility in use	The design accommodates a wide range of individual preferences and abilities.
	Guidelines
	2a. Provide choice in methods of use.
	2b. Accommodate right- or left-handed access and use.
	2c. Facilitate the user's accuracy and precision.
	2d. Provide adaptability to the user's pace.
Simple and intuitive use	The design is easy to understand, regardless of the user's experience, knowledge, language skills, or current concentration level.
	Guidelines
	3a. Eliminate unnecessary complexity.
	3b. Be consistent with user expectations and intuition.
	3c. Accommodate a wide range of literacy and language skills.
	3d. Arrange information consistent with its importance.
	3e. Provide effective prompting and feedback during and after task completion.

(continued)

Table 8.1 *(continued)*

Principle	Brief description
Perceptible information	The design communicates necessary information effectively to the user, regardless of ambient conditions or the user's sensory abilities. Guidelines 4a. Use different modes (pictorial, verbal, tactile) for redundant presentation of essential information. 4b. Provide adequate contrast between essential information and its surroundings. 4c. Maximize "legibility" of essential information. 4d. Differentiate elements in ways that can be described (i.e., make it easy to give instructions or directions). 4e. Provide compatibility with a variety of techniques or devices used by people with sensory limitations.
Tolerance for error	The design minimizes hazards and the adverse consequences of accidental or unintended actions. Guidelines 5a. Arrange elements to minimize hazards and errors: most used elements, most accessible; hazardous elements eliminated, isolated, or shielded. 5b. Provide warnings of hazards and errors. 5c. Provide fail safe features. 5d. Discourage unconscious action in tasks that require vigilance.
Low physical effort	The design can be used efficiently and comfortably and with a minimum of fatigue. Guidelines 6a. Allow user to maintain a neutral body position. 6b. Use reasonable operating forces. 6c. Minimize repetitive actions. 6d. Minimize sustained physical effort.
Size and space for approach and use	Appropriate size and space are provided for approach, reach, manipulation, and use regardless of user's body size, posture, or mobility. Guidelines 7a. Provide a clear line of sight to important elements for any seated or standing user. 7b. Make the reach to all components comfortable for any seated or standing user. 7c. Accommodate variations in hand and grip size. 7d. Provide adequate space for the use of assistive devices or personal assistance.

product choice are strongly encouraged to refer to and apply these principles from the beginning of the planning phase and throughout project development. When properly implemented, universal design improves efficiency and lowers cost because everyone is able to use the facility or product with equal ease, thereby reducing or eliminating the need for specialized adaptation and retrofitting.

However, as understood by the founders of universal design, universality requires consideration of factors beyond facility or product usability. Universal design is used to create "a broadly inclusive environment that effectively blends a variety of design concepts, including accessibility, into a range of meaningful options for all users" (Rogers, 2000). Universal design also requires attention to how people who use a facility, product, or service see themselves engaging with that facility, product, or service. Social factors such as ethnicity, gender, and culture strongly influence perceptions of the individual and of others. For example, considering the perceptions of the individual, a person with a physical impairment is more likely to participate in a recreational rock climbing program if the recreation program posts images of people of all abilities engaged in climbing. Women and girls who follow specific religious or cultural practices of modesty are more likely to use the local pool when facility management does not discourage or preclude the use of swimsuits that provide head-to-ankle coverage. An extended family will feel welcome to camp at a park that equips one or more campsites with multiple picnic tables rather than only one table per campsite seating a maximum of six people. The perception of others is also influenced by the same images, leadership, and presentation. If we see a broader range of recreation participants effectively integrated in recreation programs we will develop attitudes that support inclusion. Rogers also stated, "In a universally designed program it is not evident that modifications have been made for a specific person or group." The more we design the entirety of our programs with universality in mind, the more likely we are to serve the greatest range of people to the greatest extent possible.

To understand the application of universal design specific to recreation programming, we can look at the eight principles of universal design for challenge course programs. See table 8.2 for the abbreviated listing.

Challenge course programs, like many recreation programs, depend on small-group inter-

actions. The principles established by Rogers address not only usability but also participant interaction. The principles call on us to design programs that, among other goals, are individually meaningful, encourage reciprocity, and are equitable across individual experiences. For programs to be individually meaningful, we cannot ask people to take a lesser role as a result of our inattention to universal planning. For example, it is not acceptable to assign a child with a disability the job of handing out personal flotation devices while everyone else gets to canoe. Reciprocity occurs when each person has a contribution that is genuinely valued by others and when each person's contribution to a group outcome is viewed by others as vital as every other contribution. Finally, equitability exists when each person is provided the supports needed to engage in substantive choice or self-determination, takes on similarly scaled challenges in relation to other participants, and attains similarly rewarding outcomes as other participants. For the recreation participant who wants to engage in a soccer program but who has no skills or experience, the recreation professional applying universal principles might suggest a program that teaches basic ball-handling skills and engages the participant in cooperative play rather than enrolling the participant in the competitive league where

Table 8.2 Principles of Universal Design for Challenge Course Programming

Principle	Brief description
Equitable experience	Course and program designs provide usable elements and meaningful experiences for each participant.
Goodness of fit	Elements are adjustable and program designs are flexible in order to meet the specific needs of individuals and groups
Engagement in process	The design encourages active involvement, reciprocity, and investment in the experience.
Experience perceptions	Participants interact with the design and experience in perceptible ways using all and any senses and sensory processes.
Scope of safety and risk	Each experience is designed with a range of risk options and safety features.
Economy and equity of effort	Over the course of a program, no one individual is expected to expend substantially more effort than others in order to complete the experience.
Dimensions and intended use	Designs are sized and scaled to facilitate intended processes and outcomes for all participants.
Agency commitment	Agency applies universal design principles and practices to all aspects of the program.

Guidelines for each principle can be found at www.indiana.edu/~nca/challenge/pro_universal_design.htm.
Reprinted courtesy of the National Center on Accessibility.

her skill development might consist of warming benches or carrying water.

Universal Design for a Just Society

In 1999, architect Leslie Kanes Weisman spoke of universal design as a "values-based framework for design decision making, based on an ethic of inclusiveness and interdependence that values and celebrates human difference and acknowledges humanity's debt to the earth" (Weisman, 1999).

The recreation provider who values and celebrates human difference will conceive of and design programs and facilities differently than would others who don't hold such an ethic. The provider will attempt to understand how people are influenced by differences such as age; gender and gender identity; ability; race, culture, and ethnicity; religious practices; economic ability; and historical recreation patterns. The information gathered will be used to build programs to accommodate a full range of human experiences. When we successfully incorporate this ethic, our programs will be truly open and inviting to people from the broadest range of ages, genders, abilities, and cultures.

As individuals, we are heavily influenced by our life experiences, and it is hard to imagine the life experiences of others or how these life experiences are different from our own. However, research in recreation patterns and values makes it evident that people from different backgrounds recreate differently (Outdoor Industry Foundation, 2005; U.S. Department of Interior, 2006; Winter, 2007). As recreation providers, we recruit assistance and gather information from people who have different life experiences to help us understand our facilities and programs from other viewpoints. This is similar to using interchangeable lenses on a camera or microscope. Each lens that we use takes into consideration another set of characteristics; one lens holds a perspective regarding changes caused by aging, whereas another lens holds characteristics of extended families. By combining what we learn from each viewpoint, we can design programs that serve the broadest range of people to the greatest extent possible without the need for retrofitting our programs with adaptations or specialized design. By considering universal design as socially responsible design, the recreation provider takes on the responsibility to create programs and facilities that eliminate common barriers and anticipate new ways of improving access and participation. Considering socially responsible, universal design, concentrate on the following questions regarding program access across user groups. Can every person in an experience be a full participant and be among people who are similar to and different from himself? Can every individual operate at a level of competence and independence based on her abilities and strengths? Can every person choose from a range of supports that facilitate his competence and independence? Does every participant have the opportunity to hold the same status and respect as all other members of the group?

Removing Barriers

The most obvious barriers to participation in recreation are those within the physical context of our programs. These may be barriers to or within natural spaces, physical facilities, access routes, transitions between environments, equipment, and communication. We are fortunate to have access to specific information and direction regarding design criteria as identified in documents such as the principles of universal design (see table 8.1), the Americans with Disabilities Act (ADA) accessibility guidelines, and more recently the U.S. Forest Service outdoor accessibility guidelines, the U.S. Forest Service trail accessibility guidelines published in 2006, and multiple documents from the National Center on Accessibility. Efforts to publish accessibility-related guidelines continue through the U.S. Access Board, the agency in charge of establishing and enforcing the guidelines of the ADA. The universal recreation access process described later in this chapter provides specific guidelines inclusive of people of all abilities developed for many recreation settings.

Less obvious but equally important are the social barriers brought about by stigma, cultural practices and beliefs, lack of awareness, and broader societal norms. It is difficult to provide concrete direction to bring about social acceptance, but theories and tested practices are available to guide the recreation professional.

Creating Physical Access

The act of creating physical access is guided by our ability to consider the range of conditions that may be experienced throughout the life span. At every age and life stage, humans experience the full range of abilities and limitations that are developmentally possible and a wide variation in physical capabilities such as strength, endurance, and coordination. Additionally, our access needs change based on our lifestyles and activities. Although some people experience great capacity in health and fitness, most of us experience short- or long-term impairments that limit our ability to access many environments. Consider for a moment how you might view physical access to your favorite recreation areas and events if you use a wheelchair rather than walk or vice versa, you were significantly taller or shorter than you are now, your vision was markedly better or worse than it currently is, or your coordination, strength, or endurance were cut in half or were doubled. In each case, whenever your abilities change, what you are easily able to accomplish also changes. Beyond ability, variations in lifestyle and activity affect physical access such as when you find yourself choosing ramps over stairways because you are pushing a stroller with a toddler, moving a cart full of groceries, or pulling a wheeled suitcase. At other times a lever action door knob or a power activated switch is more desirable than a round knob that requires you to have a free hand, particularly when you have an armload of books or basketballs. The section on the universal recreation access process in the latter part of the chapter provides the recreation professional with very specific suggestions regarding physical access.

Creating Cognitive Access

Cognitive access refers to abilities such as attending to important information and filtering out extraneous information, interpreting and using information, and comprehending language and communicated information. If you have ever travelled to a place where you don't understand the language, you will recognize how valuable multiple methods of communication delivery can be. In some ways, using techniques that enhance physical access also helps us to accommodate varied cognitive capacities. For example, when our programs are delivered through the use of multiple senses or multimedia, we are using strategies that help people learn and remember (Sousa, 2000). When we use universal symbols to communicate important information such as the location of accessible parking, we also enhance cognitive access by standardizing and minimizing the information to be comprehended and

interpreted. Research on universal design in learning will provide additional suggestions to increase the usability and conveyance of information to people who experience difficulties in cognitive processes and to people for whom English is a second language (Acrey et al., 2005).

Removing Social Barriers

Social acceptance plays a significant part in recreation participation and satisfaction. As recreation providers, we should consider ways to enhance our programs and facilities through the application of universal design to social contexts. A theory that can help us to remove social barriers is Abraham Maslow's hierarchy of needs. Maslow's hierarchy contends that a person is motivated to satisfy a continuum of needs that move from basic survival and safety to social belonging and finally to self-actualization (Ventegodt et al., 2003). Viewing the issue from another direction, Maslow postulated that various hardships or threats must be removed for the person to take the risk to engage in more socially involved and individually expansive actions.

Creating a Sense of Safety and Belonging

Universal design, in a social sense, calls on us to incorporate acceptance and appreciation of individual difference in our programs and facilities. This can include strategies to value and support differences that arise from age, culture, gender, and life stage as well as differences that are apparent in physical, cognitive, social, and emotional variation. These strategies should encompass the entire milieu of facilities and programs. What do prospective participants see when they walk into our facilities? Do images in marketing and in the facilities include people of varied ages, ethnicities, abilities, and genders? Are multilingual interpretation and signage provided? Are families and individuals encouraged to participate? Are participants with varied abilities welcomed and provided with appropriate support? What do participants experience regarding individual difference and variation? Are the staff aware, knowledgeable, and supportive of people who bring diverse perspectives? By intentionally designing programs to value and incorporate individual difference, we increase safety within programs and facilities by reducing risk of alienation, isolation, and emotional or physical injury.

As a recreation specialist, you must create an atmosphere where everyone is included and feels safe and appreciated so all participants can have fun together.

Creating an environment that is perceived by prospective participants as safe, both physically and emotionally, is a start. However, believing oneself to be safe is far from having a sense of being a valued member of the group, being liked or appreciated, or having something to contribute to the group or situation.

One of your many roles is to create an environment that promotes a universal appreciation for the unique contributions of each participant. You must set an example by valuing and appreciating the full range of personalities, skills, and backgrounds of your participants. Anticipate ways to welcome and incorporate the perspectives of people with different abilities, cultural backgrounds, ages and life stages, genders, socioeconomic classes, and ethnic orientations. Value equally the traits of physical prowess, humor, problem-solving skills, social inclusion, positive attitude, and all other factors that enhance the function of the group.

To enhance the social function and acceptance of participants, you can design programs by using tools such as the Full Value Contract designed by Project Adventure, described elsewhere in this text, and the seven strategies for fostering social integration described by Lais (2000). Lais identified group norm formation strategies that focus on potentials of individual members rather than on limitations or perceived limitations. He summarized the intent of these strategies as "establishing ground rules for how people treat each other, facilitating participant efforts to reexamine preconceived limitations and their own value system for measuring accomplishments, and initiating methods and approaches that enhance participation in achieving common group goals and needs." The seven strategies are as follows:

- Respect each person's dignity.
- Maintain open lines of communication.
- Establish patterns for integrated decision making.
- Emphasize the importance of contributions of all types.
- Focus on group challenges and activities.
- Delineate and delegate tasks.
- Develop symbiotic relationships among participants.

Creating a Sense of Empowerment

Beyond needing safety and a sense of belonging, we all need to have control over ourselves and to have a positive impact within our environment. Universally designed environments are planned to allow each participant to accomplish tasks, contribute to the success of the group, or make a positive difference. When designing programs, consider how participants will gain a sense of accomplishment and empowerment from their participation. What can you do to help participants understand and appreciate their contribution to the group, gain a sense of individual accomplishment, and believe they are contributing to the experience? A universally designed program will consider these social factors in the planning stage so that the outcomes are predictable.

Removing Programmatic Barriers

Program design consists of every plan and action taken prior to the arrival of your participants. Having considered the application of universal design to physical, cognitive, and social contexts of recreation, we also need to consider how our program design sets up or eliminates barriers.

The recreation professional must take a broad look at every aspect of program design to implement universal design effectively. Forethought should be given to language used in the program vision and mission statements, marketing images and delivery, methods and styles of communication, facility appearance, program scheduling, transit options, cost, staffing, program delivery methods, equipment availability, and all of the countless program specific details. Design of programs and facilities should be inclusive of and inviting to people of all abilities, cultures and ethnic groups, incomes, genders or gender identities, and spiritual and religious practices.

Universal program design requires use of inclusive language in multimedia, multilingual, and interpreted information presentation; images and meaningful inclusion of individuals and groups that demonstrate and promote diverse human engagement in all forms of recreation; programming that reaches and delivers to diverse economic and diverse cultural communities; knowledgeable and culturally diverse employees and volunteers who are trained to skillfully and sensitively engage participants with all levels and types of diverse abilities and backgrounds; equipment that allows participant choice regarding usability and preference; and awareness of and respect for cultural and religious traditions.

Choices made by providers of universally designed programs can help mitigate direct and indirect limitations to participation caused by limited public transportation systems, limited economic resources, and limited leisure time, which often significantly affect single-parent households and families of the working poor. Specific consideration should be given to clothing, physicals, or supplies that participants are expected to provide; program or activity fees; public or personal transportation availability and cost; time off work necessary to participate; parental permission necessary from families with divorced parents; and location of program delivery in relation to low-income communities.

Civil Rights Legislation as a Foundation for Universal Design in Recreation

Universal design developed concurrently with the passage of civil rights legislation, reflecting changing attitudes about people with disabilities in U.S. society. Sweeping legislative changes guaranteed access to facilities, services, and education. Today, it is reasonable for us to take this model further and look at how legislative history can help recreation providers apply an expanded interpretation of universal design to other aspects of human diversity.

Throughout the history of the United States, the populace has pursued civil rights for groups who have been discriminated against, through popular movements, constitutional amendments, and related enabling legislation that applies constitutional amendments to everyday life.

As members of a profession, we are responsible for abiding by legislation that protects the rights of individuals. As disconnected as the profession of recreation and the legislation protecting individual rights may seem, our engagement in socially responsible universal design in recreation facilities, programs, and services ensures, at the very least, the pursuit of happiness for all our participants. Because it is our professional duty to provide inclusive recreation services, and because the rights of individuals to these services flow directly from legislation, we must have a fundamental knowledge of laws that guarantee and protect these rights. Some of the more significant laws enacted to ensure the rights of various populations are included here for your reference.

Ability-Focused Legislation

Between 1968 and 1990, four critical pieces of legislation were passed that constitutionally affirmed the right of people with disabilities to take a full and equal role as participants in society. The following legislation laid the groundwork for full inclusion of people with disabilities.

- Architectural Barriers Act of 1968 and Section 504 of the Rehabilitation Act 1973: Combined, these two laws require buildings and services that are partially or fully funded with federal money to be accessible to and usable by people with disabilities.

- 1975 Education for Handicapped Children Act: This act established the right of children with disabilities to a free and appropriate public education. More recent versions of this act were named the Individuals with Disabilities Education Act (IDEA).

- 1990 Americans with Disabilities Act (ADA): The ADA made it illegal to discriminate against people on the basis of disability. The ADA specifically names recreation in the list of opportunities that must be made accessible to and usable by people with disabilities.

- Public Law 105-359: Signed into law in 1998, PL 105-359 established the intent of the federal government to guarantee people with disabilities access to federal lands. As a result, a study was conducted regarding ways to improve the access for persons with disabilities to outdoor recreational opportunities (such as fishing, hunting, trapping, wildlife viewing, hiking, boating, and camping).

The changes that occurred in civil rights legislation from the late 1960s to the 1990s show that people with disabilities have achieved significant gains. Accompanied by social movements such as universal design, these gains have moved beyond legislated rights to the recognition of disability and changing ability as part of typical human experience throughout the life span. This acceptance creates the opportunity for people with impairments to be valued for their humanity and their abilities rather than devalued as a result of society's perception of impairment as dehumanizing and debilitating.

Universal design can be viewed as a social movement. It is a movement to provide an entire milieu of facilities, products, curricula, programs, and media that are inviting to and usable by people of all abilities together in the same ways, so that all can enjoy the same experiences to the greatest extent possible.

It is easy to imagine designing recreation programs that are inclusive of people representing the full range of diverse characteristics embodied in our society. When we examine civil rights legislation as a foundation for the more inclusive concept of socially responsible universal design, we find a number of laws that guide our understanding of the limits to inclusion that have been, or currently are, pervasive in our society. And although it may seem that we should have moved beyond the point where the recreation provider needs to be aware of specific laws passed long before his or her birth, individuals within cultures tend to view their own norms and values as universal to people of all cultures. As recreation leaders steeped in our own cultural norms, we may unconsciously and unintentionally create program structures and strategies that are at best uninviting and at worst blatantly discriminatory toward people who have differing cultures. Therefore we may wish to look at the following laws as reminders of the other possible perspectives when establishing our own program structures.

Ethnicity, Cultural, and Social Legislation and Rulings

In addition to laws governing the whole of our population, laws pertaining to specific ethnic, cultural, and social groups have been enacted. These laws have sought to correct unjust situations that developed through the history unique to our nation.

- 1924 Indian Citizenship Act: This act granted the right of U.S. citizenship and all privileges of citizenship to Native Americans.

- 1954 *Brown v. the Board of Education of Topeka Kansas*: This Supreme Court ruling established that "separate educational facilities are inherently unequal." This court ruling established segregation as unlawful according to the constitution.

- 1964 Civil Rights Act: "Specifically, the Act bans discrimination in public accommodations and employment, and bars discrimination in federally funded programs on the bases of race, sex and national origin" (Reclaim Civil Rights, 2007).
- 1972 Title IX of the Education Amendments: This law prohibits educational programs and activities that receive federal financial assistance from discriminating against people based on gender (Reclaim Civil Rights, 2007).
- Age Discrimination Act 1975: The Age Discrimination Act bans programs and activities receiving federal financial assistance from discriminating against people based on age (Reclaim Civil Rights, 2007).
- Civil Rights Restoration Act of 1988: This act requires recipients of federal funds to comply with civil rights laws in all areas of their operation, not just the particular programs or activities that receive direct funding (Reclaim Civil Rights, 2007).
- Executive Order 13166—Improving Access to Services for Persons with Limited English Proficiency: This executive order signed in 2000 requires federal agencies to make their services accessible to persons who don't readily understand English (Reclaim Civil Rights, 2007).

Limits of Legislation

Civil rights legislation is enacted to correct long-term, pervasive discrimination against a specific group of people within society. Although this is often one step in securing equitable treatment, the positive impact is realized only when society accepts and acts on the intent of the legislation. Universal design is an excellent example of society's embracing and furthering the intent of antidiscrimination legislation.

Throughout its history, the United States has been in transition from a country where opportunities of access and participation in society were bestowed on privileged groups to one that recognizes the importance of citizen access and participation by all people regardless of ability or position in society. Recreation providers have a role to play in this transition and are uniquely placed to contribute and advance a more equitable society through universally designed programs, services, and facilities.

Applying the Universal Recreation Access Process

Now that you understand how the concepts of universal design evolved and the legal basis and mandates of nondiscrimination, we must discuss how to apply them in the planning, design, and construction of recreation programs, services, and facilities. The remainder of this chapter will provide an example of the application of universal design to a variety of recreation experiences and environment. Universally accessible environments are critical for successful inclusion of all people of all abilities in all types of recreation experiences.

To help create inclusive and accessible recreation facilities, the following process has been developed by Cindy Burkhour, director of the Access to Recreation Initiative (www.AccesstoRecreation.org) to guide recreation providers in making decisions that consider accessibility and inclusion up front in the planning and design processes, not as an afterthought. Funded by a $15 million grant from the W.K. Kellogg Foundation, the universal recreation access process is a set of activities to guide you in making design decisions to create recreation activity environments, elements, and spaces that truly are usable by all people of all abilities together. Universal recreation access means going beyond the minimal scoping (when, where, how many, how often) and technical (size, shape, space, physical characteristics) accessibility requirements of the Americans with Disabilities Act, which sets the minimum design standards for accessibility. Universal recreation access means that universally accessible recreation opportunities are easier to experience by people who have any type of ability limitation. It means that people with and without disabilities participate in the same recreation activity together in the same spaces, in the same way, enjoying the same benefits of that participation.

When designing a universally accessible recreation environment, use the following steps to ensure that you have considered access for people with a variety of disability characteristics.

Step 1 Learn about the minimum requirements of the ADA so you understand the least that is required by law. You can only go above and beyond the minimum if you know what that is and why it was set as the minimum standard. Several technical assistance documents are available that will help you better understand how people with disabilities use the recreation environment and explain the rationale behind the minimum requirements. Go to www.access-board.gov and download all the ADA requirements including the ADA Accessibility Guidelines (ADAAG), all final reports, and technical assistance documents for all recreation areas including amusement rides, boating and fishing, golf and miniature golf, play areas, swimming and wading pools, other aquatic facilities, spas, and exercise and sport facilities. Also download the Outdoor Developed Areas Final Report and proposed rule that covers outdoor trails, beaches, picnic areas, and camping as well as elements such as picnic tables, grills, and benches. Downloading all these documents to your hard drive makes it very easy to search for information by topic or key words. It is also helpful to order printed copies from the U.S. Access Board to take when you visit potential sites for projects.

Look for articles and other documents regarding creative design concepts that make the recreation experience more accessible. The National Center on Accessibility (www.ncaonline.org) is a great resource for information about accessible design characteristics. This center has conducted many research projects and studies on the effectiveness of many accessible design concepts and recreation products. Another resource is the National Center on Physical Activity and Disability (NCPAD, www.NCPAD.org), which has published many articles that highlight accessibility issues in recreation and physical activity and the needs of people with disabilities to be fully included in physical activity. Such documents can help you understand how people with a particular type of disability effectively participate in recreation and the kinds of modifications or adaptations that improve the experience.

Step 2 Consult people with disabilities in your community. The person with a disability who lives in your community is a great resource. Invite her to serve on your planning team, visit the site with you, review design concepts, and give you feedback. She knows what would make the recreation experience more accessible for her

personal use. Someone with a disability is not necessarily an expert in accessible design or the requirements of the law, but she can tell you what barriers would prevent her own full, enjoyable participation. Talk with people who have different types of ability limitations. Someone who does not see at all or has limited vision can give you great insight into techniques and strategies that can help him find his way around the recreation environment. Someone who walks with crutches or a walker can show the importance of accessible, clear spaces that accommodate her and her assistive device. Someone who has only one arm and hand that function can give you ideas on how to make things one-hand operable. A person who uses a wheelchair can help you understand the importance of level and firm surfaces with no drop-offs or steps. Disability-specific advocacy organizations and service providers such as Centers for Independent Living and Disability Networks are great resources for information and opinions.

Step 3 Analyze every aspect of the site and your design for ADA compliance and document how you have gone above and beyond the minimum requirements. Assessing every design feature of a project and site will ensure that you have really gone above and beyond minimum accessibility requirements. For example, look at every route for accessibility characteristics such as firm and stable surface, passage widths that accommodate someone walking next to or past someone who uses a wheelchair or walker, slopes that are gentle, level resting areas that are placed where there is an interesting view or interpretive information, and easy access to all the recreation experiences and to human comfort amenities in the facility, such as water fountains and restrooms.

Step 4 Make good design decisions from concept to layout, including amenities. Then make a commitment to do better than the minimum requirements of the law and make universally accessible design decisions that will benefit all people of all abilities. Several key characteristics of universally accessible recreation environments greatly affect usability and must be considered when evaluating the accessibility of a site or design: These include routes, spaces, reach ranges, operations, surfaces, clearances, views, and intuitive use, and way-finding. Table 8.3 provides a quick reference to the ADA minimum requirements for spaces, clearances, reaches, viewing, and operation. These are not specific to each type of recreation environment but rather are general minimum technical design requirements. You must consult the Americans with Disabilities Act Accessibility Guidelines to find specific scoping and technical requirement minimums for specific types of recreation environments.

The minimal technical requirements specified by the ADA are the building blocks of accessibility, meaning these access characteristics such as spaces and reaches are critical to create ease of use or quality of experience. Think about sitting at a picnic table. There should be enough space side to side (width) to accommodate a person seated in a wheelchair, allowing him to avoid scraping his wheel rims or knuckles on the bench seats on either side as he moves into the clear space at the table. He also needs to have enough space from the ground up to the underside of the table (height) to roll into the space without scraping the tops of his legs or the wheelchair armrests on the underside of the table. The legs of the table shouldn't get in the way of his foot rests or legs (depth) or prevent him from sitting beside someone who is seated on the picnic table bench.

Think about how to apply these basic access characteristics to the design of recreation facilities. Applying these design concepts in new construction design leads to better universal recreation access for all, and the ADA accessibility requirements also apply to renovations and alterations. The following examples of design concepts and decisions create universally accessible recreation environments that are easier to use by everyone together. These design concepts also include brief explanations of why or how the idea creates greater accessibility. Remember, these are only a few ideas and are by no means all or the only ways to create more universally accessible recreation environments; rather, these ideas are provided to prompt you to think inclusively and universally about the decisions you make and learn to apply the same thoughts and concepts to all other areas of recreation. When we learn to think about how someone with a disability uses something or moves about the environment, we can make thoughtful design

Table 8.3 General ADA Minimum Requirements for Spaces, Clearances, Reaches, Viewing, and Operation

Access characteristic	Technical requirement basic minimums
Clear width	36 in. (92 cm) minimum for most accessible routes
Maneuvering space	60 × 60 in. (153 × 153 cm) minimum with a level surface, at entries and change of direction
Surfaces	1/4 in. (6 mm) maximum change, slopes less than 5%, firm and stable
Transferable height	17-19 in. (43-48 cm) with transfer supports
Head clearance	80 in. (203 cm) high minimum and as wide as the route
Knee clearance	27 in. (69 cm) minimum height × 30 in. (76 cm) minimum width × 25 in. (63 cm) minimum depth
Clear space	30 in. (76 cm) minimum width × 48 in. (122 cm) minimum depth located at the element
Countertops and table-tops	34 in. (86 cm) maximum height
Viewing	Unrestricted viewing from 32 in. (81 cm) to 51 in. (130 cm)
Railing heights	34 in. (86 cm) maximum height
Reach ranges	48 in. (122 cm) maximum height for forward and side reach, 15 in. (38 cm) minimum for low reach above the finished floor
Operation	Operable with one hand; does not require tight pinching, grasping, or twisting to operate.

Based on data from ADAAG.

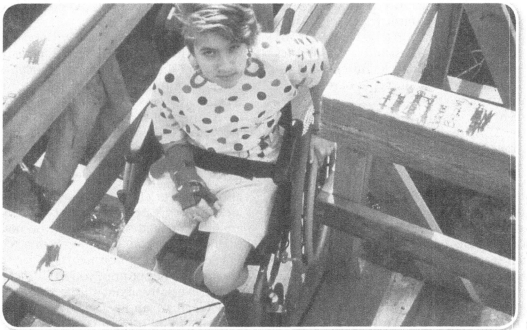

"You never want to have your child or anyone else's look at you like my daughter, Erin, was looking at me. I told her we could go to the playground, that the trail was accessible; I was wrong."

decisions to create facilities that all people of all abilities can use together.

Hiking Trails, Nature Trails, Walkways, Pathways

- Make trails wide enough so two people can walk side by side or people can pass without stepping off the trail.
- Use unitary trail surfaces like concrete, boardwalk, or asphalt or more natural surfaces like very small, crushed aggregate or screenings that have been "stabilized" or natural soils enhanced with soil stabilizers so the trail surface remains firm and stable with little need for maintenance. Concrete and asphalt can be colored so the surface blends into the natural environment, and surfaces can be stamped to look like boardwalk or dirt with animal tracks or fallen leaf prints.
- Use a contrasting color treatment of the surface and textured surface treatments such as brushed concrete at intersections or interpretive stations to cue people who have vision impairments that there is something to pay attention to at that spot. This type of visual and tactile cue can be helpful for people who have cognitive impairments, because it draws attention to a change.
- Make sure the cross-slopes (side to side) are nearly level, particularly where there is a change of direction on the route, and keep very gentle running slopes, with no steep slopes. If some sections with steep slopes are unavoidable, provide large (greater than 5 × 5 feet [1.5 × 1.5 meters]), level landing areas at the beginning and end of each steeper trail section and at all turns and intersections.
- Make sure all trails and routes are thoughtfully laid out to maximize the experience with minimal difficulty for all users. "Pick your way through the woods" in the most accessible route possible by looking for opportunities to achieve universal recreation accessibility that makes the experience more enjoyable by all people of all abilities together. Look for opportunities to lay out a route that has gentle slopes and level resting spots at interesting locations with a nice view or cooling shade. Easy slopes and resting areas are appreciated by families with children and older folks alike.

Picnic Areas and Picnic Elements Such As Pavilions, Picnic Tables, Grills, Fire Rings, Water Pumps

- Provide accessibility for all tables, grills, fire rings, and water pumps, so all people will be able to picnic at any table, cook on any grill, build a fire in any fire ring, and get water from any spigot. Remember, universally accessible designed elements are also usable by people who don't have a disability.

- Locate all elements on accessible routes. Place elements so all of us can get to them carrying our picnic basket, pulling our cooler on wheels, pushing a child in a stroller, or using a walker or wheelchair.

- Create level routes to picnic pavilions with no changes of level from pathway surface onto pavilion surfaces, and thoughtfully locate pavilions within easy access to accessible parking. It can be so frustrating to expend the energy to walk or roll to the pavilion and then not be able to get onto the concrete pad.

- Design wide routes and clear spaces, with firm surfaces, all the way around all elements so someone with mobility limits can easily move around the element (tables, grills). This is particularly helpful to parents who have a disability and need to cook the food or tend the kids who are seated all around a picnic table.

- Provide a variety of table styles: some with clear sitting space on one or both sides, some with extended table tops on one or both ends that allow people to sit side by side or across from others or at the head of the table. The interesting thing is that many people who don't have disabilities also like these tables; they put their hibachi on the extended top and their cooler underneath, or some choose to sit in a comfortable lawn chair in the accessible, clear space instead of on the hard bench that is difficult to climb onto.

- Include clear space all around each element, with firm level surfaces, and connect elements to a route so people can approach

Photo courtesy of Cindy Burkhour.

A wheelchair-accessible picnic table.

and use the grill or fire ring from the front, back, and either side; this also makes it easier to pull your cooler on wheels near the grill or the wagon with your firewood. A firm, level surface also reduces the chance that someone will trip over uneven surfaces and fall into a fire or onto a cooking surface. The accessible surface all the way around also gives you the opportunity to move out of the path of the smoke from a fire or grill.

- Design grills so users can lower and raise the cooking surface with only one hand, which is great for those who have paralysis on one side or only have one arm as well as for someone holding a platter of burgers or a beverage in one hand while moving the food closer to the heat or out of the flames.

- Include raised fire-building surfaces so you can place wood without leaning too far over from a standing or seated position. Not only are these easier to use but many campground rangers tell us this design reduces injuries from accidentally stepping into the cooling embers of fires built on the ground or in low fire rings, and the higher fire-building surface in accessible fire rings helps keep small children away from the fire surface. A well-designed fire ring with a raised fire surface also gets the flames up high enough to move smoke up and away from those seated around the fire because the flames are about knee height, again enhancing the campfire experience for everyone.

Fishing Dock or Pier and Observation or Viewing Decks

- Provide lowered rails all the way around or no rail at all so everyone can fish from anywhere. However, be sure to provide edge protection to prevent users from inadvertently rolling off. Provide multiple fish-landing openings on all sides of the dock. Also provide benches (all of which have backs and arm rests) so anglers can sit or stand to fish. Benches should have clear space at one or both ends to enable an angler in a wheelchair to sit next to another person who is sitting on the bench; this improves the opportunity to exchange "fish tales."

- Provide tackle box stands near the railing and make sure they are high enough and with clear space around them so an angler using a wheelchair can reach the items she

needs. If you place the tackle box stand next to a bench, do so only on one bench end (not both) and only on the end of some benches, leaving one bench end clear space for sitting side by side with someone in a wheelchair. These tackle box stands also make it easier to reach items for the angler who is standing to fish at the rail because he doesn't have to bend all the way to the ground, which is helpful for the angler who may not be as limber as he used to be. Also, providing these tackle box stands encourages anglers to not set their smelly equipment on the bench.

- Provide a variety of fishing opportunities such as overwater fishing from a deck or dock; shore fishing from firm, stable surfaces; and in-water fishing stations that have firm, stable, and accessible surfaces. Some people don't realize that anglers with disabilities, particularly those with mobility impairments, have the same interest as other anglers in a variety of fishing experiences.

Playgrounds

- Design playgrounds for all kids of all abilities. Include play areas that can be used by kids who don't walk, for example; ensure that participants can get to every level of the play structure in their wheelchair and reach every play component.

- Provide "on-deck transfers" so kids can leave a walker or transfer right out of their wheelchair onto the entry platform of the slide or climber.

- Design easy return routes from the "getting-off spot" back up to where a child left an assistive device; include either a transfer system or transferable play component that ends on an accessible route where the assistive mobility device can easily be brought to the child.

- Provide auditory and visual cues for kids who have limited vision that help them move safely around the play area. Include interactive activities that provide interesting and fun auditory experiences and don't require high levels of vision.

- Provide ramps and transfers that give kids with differing abilities choices of ways to move around the play area in ways that meet their individual needs and interests.

- Be sure all play components have both ramps and transfer access and return routes up to the decks where assistive devices have been left.

- Include ramps to every "getting-on spot" or activity spot of every play component so kids who can't transfer and move independently can reach the fun things.

- Provide a transfer system or transferable play component from the ground up to the main deck that is located near the exits of slides and climbers that are farthest from the ramp onto the structure.

- Use only unitary safety surfaces such as poured-in-place or rubber tiles, not any loose-fill materials like shredded rubber, wood chips, or engineered wood fiber or any other nonunitary surface material. Loose-fill materials require high levels of maintenance to keep them level, firm, and stable, and the loose material tends to migrate onto the unitary surfaces, creating changes of level obstacles. The other problem with a combination of surfaces is that edge treatments for the unitary surface often drop off sharply where they intersect the loose-fill surface, so when the loose-fill surface settles or gets kicked away at the intersection it creates a tip or trip hazard for all kids.

- Provide an on-deck transfer platform that has one open transfer side and one side with transfer steps located at every entry and exit point of every climber so kids climbing up can bump down to the deck to move to another component, because they may have left an assistive device at the ground, and so kids who climb down end up on a deck that is transferable height so they can transfer back into a wheelchair or stand up to their assistive device from a seated position on the transfer deck.

- Include a variety of things to manipulate that make noise or music, have high-contrast or bright colors, and games that two kids can play (this fosters social interaction). Provide braille and sign language panels to teach awareness of other ways to communicate. Include devices that are easy to operate with just one hand with a whole fist (i.e., that don't require tight pinching, grasping, or twisting to operate) so that all kids of all abilities can play together or alone if they choose.

- Provide different high-contrast colors for decks (that you walk on) versus transfers (that you sit, scoot, or crawl on) so kids with low vision can perceive a change in level.

- Locate play panels at heights so they can be used from a seated position or standing.

- Provide seating areas near the play area with shade so that parents and grandparents can be near for supervision and support yet comfortable and out of the action.

- Provide play panels in different languages which are reflective of the community culture.

Sports Fields and Courts

These include fields for soccer, football, and baseball and courts for tennis, basketball, boccie, and horseshoes.

- Provide accessible routes to both sides of all playing fields and all courts, not just end zones, so that coaches, players, and spectators have access to a variety of seating and viewing locations and areas to interact with the players when they are off the field of play.

- Design accessible seating spaces both at ground level and elevated if risers or bleachers are provided so all spectators have the same viewing opportunities and experiences and can sit with family and friends. Scatter these accessible seating spaces throughout all viewing areas and levels with companion seating on both sides of the space.

- Lower all service windows at all concession areas at the sports complex and provide menus in alternative formats such as large print or braille so everyone can independently get a snack.

- Provide wide gate openings into all court areas (tennis, boccie, basketball) and skate parks to accommodate sports wheelchairs which have a wider wheel camber.

- Design routes to both horseshoe pits and along both sides of the route between pits so players can play from either end, retrieve thrown horseshoes, and change ends during play.

- Provide level routes onto boccie courts with sitting benches at both ends where all players can rest.

Boardwalks

- Ensure wetland and water access.
- Provide wide boardwalks so two people can walk side by side or people can pass without moving off the boardwalk surface.
- Design edge treatment on elevated boardwalks to prevent inadvertent roll-off or step-off from the boardwalk surface.
- If there are side railings along the elevated boardwalk, provide all at a lowered height (less than the allowed maximum of 34 inches [86 centimeters]) to provide for easy viewing of the features along the boardwalk while again preventing inadvertent roll-off or step-off.
- Provide all interpretive information in a variety of formats such as auditory, large print, braille, tactile mapping and replication, and pictures.

Canoe, Kayak, and Boat Launches

- Provide a wide route to the launch site so people can hand-wheel or carry boats on a wheeled dolly to the launch, pulling the boat next to them if they are in a wheelchair; this extra width provides room for two people to carry a boat with one person on each side.
- Design accessible surface to water's edge and into the water at the launch.
- Provide gentle slopes for easier entry and exit when hand-wheeling a boat.
- Include a rack to stabilize the boat at a transferable height and a mechanism or roller system so the participant can move the boat into the water while seated in the boat.
- Provide transfer assistance such as overhead bars or slide board so someone can position her body weight over the center of the boat for a balanced entrance and exit.
- Provide a winch system so participants can pull the boat out of the water and back into the rack to an exit or transfer that leads to a transfer system on the dock or shore that people can use to transfer back into a mobility-assistive device.
- If there is a dock, provide a transfer system on the dock so someone seated on the dock can transfer to a boat in the water that is in a stabilizer rack.
- Provide adapted boats such as kayaks or sailboats available for use or rent if others have the opportunity to rent water craft.

- Design a shore station that has a platform (instead of a V rack) with a transfer system on the deck of the shore station, located next to a dock, so someone can roll or otherwise move onto the platform and lower it to the right level to transfer into a boat.
- All of these design ideas also make it easier for older people to move into boats safely and allow parents to help young children in and out of boats by sitting and scooting.

Campgrounds

- Make all sites and amenities accessible, not just some of the sites.
- Provide accessible surfaces on all sites. Surfaces don't have to be concrete or asphalt; there are other surfaces that blend with the natural environment.
- Include large spaces to accommodate side lifts on campers and vehicles.
- Design accessible tables, grills, and fire rings on all sites so all campers can enjoy meals and campfires on their own sites or when visiting with friends on other sites.
- Provide centrally located restrooms on easy routes from each site and provide single-user unisex shower and toilet facilities so that opposite-sex care providers (or parents of young children) can assist with personal care in a dignified and respectful manner.

Archery Range

- Ensure that all shooting stations can be used from a seated or standing position.
- Include accessible routes to the retrieval area for each target.
- Provide targets that are usable with crossbows and modified bows so hunters and archers with disabilities can use the targets.
- Include a backstop behind the target to limit retrieval distance of arrows that miss the target.
- Design large maneuvering spaces at all shooting stations to accommodate archers with shooting assistants or who use individual mobility-assistive devices.

Beaches and Waterfronts

- Design routes over the beach and into the water; these routes can be portable, such as temporary matting, which can be taken in and out for beach cleaning and dragging or in the off-season.

- Include beach routes that are wide enough for side-by-side walking and passing; this is good for a parent pushing a stroller while also holding the hand of a walking toddler.
- At the end of beach route have a "hanging out" area at the water's edge large enough to get off the route end; this allows grandparents and others who find walking in the sand difficult a way to get to the water to watch and interact with people who are in the water.
- Provide a transfer system at the water's edge so people can get to the ground level and into the water to play; this also helps families with young children who want an easy way to get to the water, and it gives the kids a surface to play on and lets them put their feet in the water without getting totally wet.

Swimming and Wading Pools, Spas, Aquatic Facilities

- Provide routes into the water.
- Design routes that are wide enough for side-by-side walking and passing.
- Provide a transfer system at water's edge so people can get into the water.
- At pools with zero depth or sloped entries or ramp access to the water, provide a water-access wheelchair so someone doesn't have to take her everyday chair into the water for access.
- At beaches and outdoor pools, provide some shaded areas for sun protection.

Nature Centers, Museums, Cultural Sites, Zoos

- Ensure that all interpretive information is in a variety of alternative formats such as auditory, large print, braille, and pictures.
- Use technology creatively, such as providing iPods for auditory descriptions (this gives the information directly to the person and won't disturb others), closed-loop assistive listening devices, and closed-circuit captioning of all interpretive presentations.
- Place all displays at heights that allow sitting or standing viewing for all people, including children.
- Ensure that all mechanisms are operable with one hand and do not require tight pinching, grasping, or twisting to operate.

Skiing and Sledding Hills

- Provide an accessible route to the top (no steps), maybe using a rope tow lift with the "magic carpet"; this is a carpet or mat-type surface that pulls the sled (with the participant in it) up the hill.
- Include a level surface for sled mounting at hilltop.
- If the location is staffed, provide ATV transport or have policy that allows personal ATV use by people with disabilities who can't get up the hill on their own.
- Include a transfer at hill bottom to help people get off the sled and get into a chair or reach a walker.

Camping Cabins and Yurts

- Provide a large, clear space and maneuvering spaces between all furnishings including when all are in use (beds, tables and chairs with people seated at the table); place shelves and wall hooks within reach of all users.
- Design a large, clear, thoughtfully located space for storage and use of typical portable items such as coolers, luggage, equipment, and food bins.

Labyrinths or Sensory Gardens and Walks

- Include unitary surfaces like concrete, boardwalk or asphalt, or crushed aggregate or screenings that have been stabilized or natural soils enhanced with soil stabilizers.
- Use contrasting color treatment of the surface and textured surface treatments such as brushed concrete at intersections or interpretive stations to cue people who have vision impairments that there is something to pay attention to at that spot.
- Design level cross-slopes (side to side) and very gentle running slopes with no steep sections. Include large (greater than 60×60 inches [152×152 centimeters]), level areas at all turns and intersections.
- Lay out the site to maximize the experience with minimal difficulty.
- Include plantings that provide sensory cues such as lavender at all intersections and turns and some plants in raised beds that users can touch to release fragrances.
- Ensure that all interpretive information is available in a variety of formats such as auditory, large print, braille, and pictures.

Restrooms

- Provide more than the minimum number.
- Design multiple unisex and single-user toilet rooms and units so opposite-sex caregivers can assist; these are good for parents of young children of the opposite sex so kids aren't sent alone into the multiuser restroom. If all the toilets are single-user rooms, then several are available for either sex to use at any time, so someone with a disability has as many options as anyone else. Another benefit of this design is that only one toilet room at a time is closed for cleaning, unlike the multi-user design where a whole gender's toilet room is closed.
- Locate restrooms near areas of activity such as play areas, beaches, and fishing piers.
- Ensure that all portable toilets are designed with accessibility in mind, again big enough for individual use or caregiver assist and also good for families with young children who need assistance.

Parking

- Provide more than minimum number of spots.
- Connect each accessible parking spot directly to an accessible route at the head end of the parking space that takes users to the park elements and not into the traffic flow behind the vehicle.
- Locate accessible parking spots near all the activity entrances (some near the beach, some near the playground, some near the bathhouse).

Summary

It all starts with planning and design. Universal design makes use easier for people with and without disabilities. The examples given here are just the tip of the iceberg of creative design ideas and concepts. To learn more about creative inclusive universally accessible recreation designs go to www.AccesstoRecreation.org. You can influence the development of universal design in all recreation spaces, places, and environments by requiring planners and designers to go above and beyond minimal ADA compliance to apply the principles of universal design and by holding construction contractors to quality construction practices that ensure accessible design characteristics. Make universally accessible design choices for all amenities so equipment and facilities that are accessible to and usable by all people of all abilities become the best practice standard and expectation in your system. Then just do it every time.

Discussion Questions

1. How can we use legislation to inform practices of universal design?
2. Describe physical, cognitive, and social barriers that exist in your community's recreation programs. What populations will be hindered by these barriers?
3. Explain how universal design strategies can be applied to be inclusive of people of different cultural backgrounds, ages, genders, and religions. Are there other underrepresented or underserved groups in your community? Describe ways in which they could be included by using universal design strategies.
4. Discuss challenges and solutions in the application of universal design strategies to be inclusive of all people.
5. Take a field trip to a park or recreation facility and identify which features meet only the minimum ADA design requirements and which features meet the principles of universal design.
6. Discuss how people without disabilities benefit from specific universal design characteristics in parks.
7. Discuss how universally accessible parks and recreation facilities enhance the programming opportunities for all people of all abilities.
8. Practice identifying universal design characteristics in conceptual design renderings as well as construction plan documents.
9. Develop a list of key stakeholders in your community who should always be included in the planning and design process to ensure that accessibility is always a forethought in this process.

Inclusive Recreation in Australia

Shane Pegg, PhD

School of Tourism
University of Queensland

Although there has been significant ongoing social and welfare reform in Australia, driven in part by deinstitutionalization in disability and mental health services in the early 1970s, the legislative and policy reform that followed in the 1980s has done much to promote inclusion in Australia (Pegg & Compton, 2004; Pegg & Darcy, 2007). For example, in passing the Disability Services Act (DSA) in 1986, the federal government enacted a piece of legislation that was to become the basis for actively encouraging all service providers to facilitate the successful integration of institutionalized people into the community (Molony & Taplin, 1990).

This shift in disability policy led to the enactment of other key pieces of legislation, such as the Queensland Anti-Discrimination Act in 1991 at the state level and the Commonwealth Disability Discrimination Act (DDA) in 1992, which have proven to be critical to the inclusionary process. Both of these acts were designed to protect people with disabilities from discrimination in employment, education, and access to premises used by the public; provision of services, goods, and facilities; accommodation; land ownership; activities of clubs; sport; and administration of commonwealth laws and programs (Handley, 2001). These acts also made it illegal to discriminate against people on the basis of physical, intellectual, psychiatric, sensory, and neurological or learning disabilities (HREOC, 2003). As a result of these pieces of legislation, the manner in which minority groups are addressed in Australia has radically changed from that of 30 years ago. No longer is it acceptable for people with disabilities to experience medicalized attitudes, institutional approaches, or segregated practices of service delivery (Goggin & Newell, 2005).

A number of authors (Culham & Nind, 2003; Florian, 1998) have argued that the concept of inclusion is far preferable to that of normalization, because inclusion stresses participation and positive integration of individuals rather than the potentially problematic concept of normalcy. The ramifications of successful inclusion are found in elements of diversity, respect, and a sense of belonging in a community (Thomas & Loxley, 2001). In the Australian setting, which is still far from perfect, it is nevertheless pleasing to report that many positive examples of such services and opportunities are now available in the community.

For example, Sailability is an organization that is certainly playing its part with respect to inclusion. Initially founded in Great Britain and established in Australia in 1991, it is an organization whose primary mission is to facilitate sailing for everyone, regardless of age or ability (Sailability, 2008). This organization provides a valued social and cultural context to leisure for people with disabilities in Australia and is a growing service organization accessed by people of all abilities. Sailability is a not-for-profit organization that operates through a combination of dedicated volunteers, community-based fundraising, and, when required, government funding for major infrastructure and other ongoing operational costs. Those people participating in the scheduled activities of Sailability

Photo courtesy of Simon Darcy.

The Sailability organization, and other like-minded marine-based operations in Australia, help make all marine environment activities available to people of all abilities. Here, Simon Darcy is hard at play getting ready to start a fishing trip.

(continued) ▶

prefer to view themselves as part of a broader community of people who simply enjoy the recreational sport of sailing. This is an important but salient point, because most of the people with disabilities involved with the organization perceive themselves as no different from anyone else in the community in that they seek to forge their own leisure identities through active engagement in a community-based recreation of their choosing. This agency is somewhat specific in nature, and it is worth noting the broader changes occurring throughout Australia regarding the marine environment. For example, the construction of appropriate pathways, jetties, and piers and the provision of ingress and egress points consistent with the notion of providing a continuous pathway of access are slowly occurring throughout Australia (Darcy, 2008). Although there is still much to be done, there is a growing recognition locally that the adoption of universal design principles in such settings benefits substantially more social groups than those for which the modifications were perhaps initially intended.

Other Australia-based initiatives worthy of particular mention include Cricket Victoria, which sponsors a series of annual carnivals in which different game formats have been established to suit all ability levels and to ensure that anyone in the community can enjoy cricket in a positive social setting. Following a similar line of thinking, the YMCA of South Australia has established Recreation Link-up, a service designed to enhance the quality of life of people with disabilities by supporting their active engagement in sport, arts, and other recreational activities. The service seeks to assist sports and recreation agencies in the broader community to provide a range of services including access to personal recreation planning, a recreation information phone and Web-based service, and awareness sessions about the service and its operations. Another land-based agency providing services underpinned by the concept of inclusion is Ausrapid. Although established first and foremost to provide services and support specifically for people with intellectual disabilities, the organization seeks to include any given person in the activities of generic sporting and recreation bodies located in the wider community at a level denoted by the ability and choice of the individual. Underpinning this effort is the organization's belief that positive ongoing involvement is crucial to the meaningful acceptance of people with an intellectual disability as valued citizens.

Although there is much to be proud of, much remains to be done with regard to inclusion. Although much evidence indicates that society's views of minority groups have changed quite markedly over the last few decades, far too many incidents still occur that raise real concern as to whether the majority of people truly appreciate the difference between segregated and inclusionary practices and whether all agencies truly support the process of inclusion. That stated, the wider acceptance of the social model of inclusion has done much to improve the quality of life of many Australians in recent times in that it has focused greater attention on the importance of the interaction between the environment and the individual. There is much more to be optimistic about than not when it comes to the ongoing evolution and development of inclusive recreation programs and services in Australia.

References

Culham, A., & Nind, M. (2003). Deconstructing normalisation: Clearing the way for inclusion. *Journal of Intellectual & Developmental Disability, 28*(1), 65.

Darcy, S. (2008). Disability access. In M. Lack (Ed.), *Encyclopedia of tourism and recreation in marine environments* (pp. 138-139). London: CABI.

Florian, L. (1998). Inclusive practice: What, why and how? In C. Tilstone, L. Florian, & R. Rose (Eds.), *Promoting inclusive practice* (pp. 13-26). London: Routledge.

Goggin, G., & Newell, C. (2005). *Disability in Australia: Exposing a social apartheid*. Sydney: University of New South Wales Press.

Handley, P. (2001). "Caught between a rock and a hard place": Anti-discrimination legislation in the liberal state and the fate of the Australian Disability Discrimination Act. *Australian Journal of Political Science, 36*(3), 515-528.

Human Rights and Equal Opportunity Commission (HREOC). (2003). *Don't judge what I can do by what you think I can't: Ten years of achievements using Australia's Disability Discrimination Act.* Sydney: Human Rights and Equal Opportunity Commission.

Molony, H., & Taplin, J.E. (1990). The deinstitutionalization of people with a developmental disability under the Richmond Program: I. Changes in adaptive behaviour. *Journal of Intellectual & Developmental Disability, 16*(2), 149-159.

Pegg, S., & Compton, D. (2004). Creating opportunities and insuring access to leisure and recreation services through inclusion in the global community. *Leisure/Loisir: Journal of the Canadian Association for Leisure Studies, 1-2*, 5-26.

Pegg, S., & Darcy, S. (2007). Sailing on troubled waters: Diversional therapy in Australia. *Therapeutic Recreation Journal, 41*(2), 132-140.

Sailability Online. (2008). www.sailability.org.

Thomas, G., & Loxley, A. (2001). *Deconstructing special education and constructing inclusion*. Birmingham, UK: Open University.

Designing Inclusive Experiences

Nancy Nisbett, EdD
California State University, Fresno

❝I am a part of all that I have met.❞
–Alfred Tennyson

▶▶ Learning Outcomes

After completing this chapter, learners will be able to do the following:

- Articulate the steps involved in creating an inclusive experience.
- Complete an activity analysis.
- List seven guidelines for making adaptations.
- Identify three areas of adaptation.
- Describe five management issues to be considered in designing an inclusive experience.
- Explain six behavior management strategies.

eeking through the window at the recreation center, what do you see? To your right is a group of 6-year-olds in a gymnastics class, practicing somersaults and cartwheels. To your left, a group of women are in a cooking class, whipping up baked goods that smell so good you are tempted to go inside. And in the back, a group of older adults in a yoga class are working on new poses to increase balance and flexibility. At first glance, all the participants are fully engaged, listening to the instructors, and interacting with their peers. These programs appear to be the same as the hundreds of programs that have gone on before them.

Now look closer. Did you notice the 6-year-old boy who uses a barrel mat when it is his turn to practice his somersault? Or maybe you could pick out the woman who is following the same recipe, only it is written in another language, or the older man in the yoga group who completes modified poses from a seated position in a chair. Only when we look closely do we notice the differences. The extra piece of tumbling equipment, the recipes in different languages, and the modified yoga poses all blend naturally into the backdrop of the class. All modifications are accepted as usual by the participants, and the instructors call no attention to them. Welcome to an inclusive experience!

This chapter provides you with the fundamentals to design your own inclusive program. In this chapter we explore what it takes to create an inclusive recreation program. The first part of the chapter focuses on creating the inclusive program to help you understand the program, its participants, and the activities themselves. The second part of the chapter concentrates on navigating the program management issues. Membership fees, site selection, program transportation, communication style, and behavior management techniques are explored as they relate to designing an inclusive program.

Creating an Inclusive Program

To create an inclusive program, you must understand the components of the program, including its purpose, the participants, and the activities. A clear understanding of all three components will allow you to create any adaptations necessary to ensure participation for all. In the following section, each of these three components is discussed. The section begins, however, with a discussion of positive attitude, an essential factor for any inclusive program.

Having a Positive Attitude

"We want you here!" The attitude an agency and individual leaders take in creating an inclusive environment can be the program's greatest strength. An inclusive program starts by creating a welcoming environment. At its foundation, the agency and its leaders need to convey to all participants that they are welcome in the agency's programs and services. A welcoming attitude is demonstrated in many ways:

- Using appropriate terminology in all interactions and written materials
- Showing genuine interest in making the experience positive
- Working to remove all barriers to full participation
- Remaining flexible and adapting activities
- Helping all participants to recognize everyone's similarities and differences
- Accepting differences
- Treating all participants with respect

By projecting a positive attitude, you create a strong program foundation. A message is sent to all participants that they are accepted in the program and that you will do your best to provide a high-quality experience for everyone.

Understanding the Program's Purpose

Your positive attitude indicates your willingness to provide inclusive experiences. Once you make this commitment, you must next determine the program's purpose. Is the purpose of the gymnastics class for 6-year-olds gross motor skill development, or is it to train the next Olympic champion? Is the purpose of Mom's Night Out to go to only the best (and most expensive) places in town, or is it to provide an opportunity for mothers of any income level to socialize? The answer to those questions will greatly affect the inclusiveness of the experiences you provide. Because the majority of recreation programs are designed for general skill development and socialization, this chapter focuses on those programs. If the purpose of the gymnastics class is gross motor skill development, does it matter if a participant cannot do a somersault by the end of the class? It shouldn't. If the older adult who uses a chair in yoga class is able to benefit from the modified poses, should it matter whether his poses look exactly like everyone else's?

But what about that training program for the Olympics? Because that program limits participation to only those with a superior skill set, many would argue that these programs cannot be inclusive. Later in this chapter we explore how simple adaptations can make all programs more inclusive, regardless of their purpose.

Understanding the Participants

With a positive attitude and an understanding of the program's purpose, you can begin creating an inclusive program by gaining a better understanding of the participants. One size does not fit all in our inclusive world or in any world. All of our participants, regardless of their ability, age, gender, income, or ethnicity, have their own strengths and challenges. One key to inclusive programming is to recognize both.

Understanding diverse populations is helpful for all leaders and is an important place to begin. To achieve a fully inclusive environment, however, you have to recognize the unique strengths and challenges of each participant. The agency's inclusion specialist or the program leader must talk with the participant and complete a needs assessment. This can be done through a preprogram interview or through a detailed questionnaire if an interview is not possible. The needs assessment should cover the following:

- What the participant wants to get out of the program
- Potential limitations and strengths (based on skills needed and requirements for the program)
- Adaptations used by the participant
- The participant's needs in terms of medications and health concerns
- Concerns and questions

The needs assessment is an opportunity to reinforce the agency's commitment to providing a positive experience. After the needs assessment is complete, the inclusion specialist should synthesize the information gathered and compare it with the skills required in the program (identified through an activity analysis, discussed in the next section). Adaptations can then be identified and that information can be shared with the program staff during staff training, as well as the participant, so that all needed accommodations are in place on the first day of the program.

Participants should feel empowered to act on their own preferences.

© Jeff Greenberg/age fotostock

Although the task of gathering information about participants often falls to the agency's inclusion specialist, typically a certified therapeutic recreation specialist, in agencies without an inclusion specialist this task would fall to the program leader or supervisor. Inclusion specialists are often used because of their knowledge of people from diverse populations and adaptation strategies. However, program leaders have an advantage in the information-gathering process as well. Although the leader may not have as much background information on participants from diverse populations, she is intimately familiar with the program and knows what skills and abilities are needed and where adaptations may need to be made. The second advantage to having the program leader conduct the interview is that the participant can meet the leader in advance and be assured that he or she is welcome in the program.

Understanding the participants requires an understanding of the concept of self-determination. Self-determination is defined as having control over one's life in the areas that are valued (Wehmeyer, 1998). People who are self-determined are empowered, understand their strengths and limitations, and are able to exert some control over their environment, effectively tackling the challenges of everyday life. To be self-determined means people are able to act on their own preferences, compare their skills with the skills required by the task, and implement a plan to address deficiencies. Participants in inclusive programs are empowered because they are able to engage in activities on their own, capitalizing on their abilities.

Understanding the Activity and Activity Analysis

Just as you reviewed the purpose of the overall program, you also need to consider the purpose of the individual activities done within the program. Why is the activity being done? Is it for skill development, team building, socialization, fun, competition, or practice? The purpose of the activity will be your guide to its design.

Understanding the purpose of the activity is the first step in activity analysis. An activity analysis is the process of breaking an activity down into its component parts. A thorough review of the activity allows the leader to understand the cognitive (thinking), emotional, physical, and social skills required to successfully engage in the activity as well as the contextual aspects of the activity. All steps of the activity analysis process are listed in table 9.1.

The specific skills required by an activity, as identified by the activity analysis, can then be compared with the participant's skills, which were identified through the preprogram interview. This comparison allows you to identify the areas where the participant may require assistance. Adaptations can then be identified to create a bridge between the required skills and a participant's abilities.

Making Adaptations

When do you make adaptations? Only when necessary: That is the short answer, anyway. We are often in such a hurry to help that we give more assistance than is necessary and make more

Table 9.1 Activity Analysis

Activity analysis area	Example
Purpose of the activity	Skill development, socialization, competition, practice
Cognitive skills needed	Counting, reading, matching
Emotional skills needed	Frustration tolerance, anger management, empathy
Physical skills needed	Gross motor skills, fine motor skills, stamina, balance
Social skills needed	Waiting in line, sharing, teamwork
Safety concerns	Sharp objects, open space, pool activity
Communication needed	Speaking, writing, listening
Personal needs	Toileting, eating, medications, dressing
Environment	Classroom, playground, woods, pool

adaptations than are needed. Although our desire to help is understandable, it often causes us to overlook the abilities of our participants and limits their participation.

The activity analysis will tell you when an adaptation is needed. Before spending time figuring out how to make the adaptation, ask the participant what will help her. As discussed previously in the self-determination section, in many cases participants already have their own adaptations in place and know best how to use their abilities. It is our job to listen and observe.

Whether the adaptation comes from the leader or the participant, it is important to consider the amount of autonomy the adaptation provides. Does the adaptation allow the participant to complete the activity on his own, or will he be dependent on someone else? To create an inclusive environment, you must provide the highest level of autonomy possible. Consider DJ's story.

DJ loves to fish; he happily spends many hours at the riverbank with his friends and joins the recreation department's summer clinic to learn about new types of bait and lures as well as to explore new fishing holes. DJ, however, has a form of muscular dystrophy that limits his ability to reach and restricts his ability to hold the fishing pole. It was important to find a method that would allow him as much autonomy in the process as possible. The answer for DJ, identified during an interview with DJ and his mother, was a fishing pole with an automatic reel that could attach to his power chair. The controls on the reel allow him to cast and reel in the line as well as bring the line within his grasp so that he can bait the hook and remove the fish. DJ needs assistance to attach the pole to his chair, but after that he is on his own.

Remember, the goal is to make sure all participants are fully included and benefit from their involvement. The following guidelines for adaptations are useful (Stensrud, 1993).

- Adapt only when necessary.
- Ask the participant what she needs.
- Tailor the modification to the participant.
- Be creative.
- Be realistic about the purpose of the activity and its requirements.

If other participants ask about the adaptation, respond briefly and in a straightforward manner. Whenever possible, include within this discussion the participant for whom the adaptation was made.

Focusing on Three Areas of Adaptation

Identifying the appropriate adaptation can seem overwhelming at first. Your preprogram interview and your activity analysis, however, will enable you, in consultation with the participant, to select adaptations with confidence. Adaptations can be made in three areas: equipment, rules and methods, and instructional aides. In each of these areas, adaptations can be created to focus on a person's strengths and address needs identified during the activity analysis. Examples of common adaptations are provided in table 9.2. Keep in mind, however, that adaptations are often as unique as the participants in your programs; allow the

Table 9.2 Examples of Common Adaptations

Skill Area	Adaptation		
	Equipment	Rules and methods	Instructional aids
Coordination	Provide larger equipment (balls, bats, targets).	Add extra strikes or attempts.	Add support for stability.
Vision or hearing	Use bright colors on equipment. Add sounds to equipment.	Reduce field size. Include multiple communication methods.	Provide alignment or placement assistance.
Cognitive ability	Use picture cards.	Simplify rules.	Offer extra assistance.
Physical skills such as the ability to walk	Modify equipment (shorter golf clubs, raised flower beds, bowling ramp).	Modify surfaces of playing fields. Reduce field size. Provide additional time.	Modify equipment setup.

activity analysis and your understanding of the participant to be your guides.

Equipment

In the preceding example, DJ's automatic reel allows him to independently engage in an activity he loves. Equipment adaptations can be found to enhance the independent recreation experiences of people of all ages. For example, for an older adult who enjoys gardening but has difficulty kneeling on the ground, a raised flower bed allows her to garden freely. Or consider the poker player who has had a stroke, limiting his ability to use his left hand. A card holder and automatic shuffler are the keys to his continuation in his poker club.

Equipment can be added or incorporated into an activity, as in the case of our fisherman, gardener, and poker player, and it can also be modified to assist in the performance of a task. For example, a beeper soccer ball can be used instead of a regular soccer ball by the player with limited vision; instructions and other written materials can be provided in any language; and a shortened golf club can be used by the person who plays golf from a seated position.

DJ's story provides an example of using equipment to enhance physical abilities. Equipment can also be used to boost social skills. For instance, signal lights can be used to cue participants to wait for their turn. Is it possible for equipment to be used to enhance cognitive and emotional abilities as well? Certainly. Automatic scorekeepers, such as in a game of bowling, are useful for participants who do not understand the rules of the game or who have difficulty with numbers; a bowling ball with a retractable handle can be used by a person with arthritis who may struggle with the finger holes. Finally, equipment can be used in contextual areas. For instance, you may find during the activity analysis that scissors are required; however, the age or impulsiveness of the participants raises concern about the safe use of the scissors. A common solution is to use safety scissors.

Rules and Methods

Rules and methods can be added or modified to focus on a person's abilities. A designated hitter, an extra strike, extra players, reduced playing areas, and payment plans are all included within this category. Consider wheelchair tennis. Allowing the ball to bounce twice before being returned is the main rule change separating wheelchair tennis from regulation tennis, because this rule allows the player to reach the ball. In an instructional skills course, such as painting, does it matter whether someone holds the brush in her hand or in her mouth, as long as she learns to paint?

Often the rules and methods that need to be adapted are standard agency-wide procedures. When and how dues or fees are paid, rules for dressing for games, and uniforms are examples of items in this category. At the local swim club, all swim team members were required to change in the locker room before practice. Kristi, a 25-year-old veteran, tried out and made the team. Because she used a prosthesis, Kristi felt more comfortable changing at home and arriving at the club ready to practice. She appealed to the swim coach for a rule change. After consulting with the club's board of directors, the club decided that where Kristi dressed would not affect her ability to be on the team, and the adaptation was approved.

Uniforms are another common area for adaptation under the rules and methods category. Although most recreational sports leagues require the use of uniforms, many participants cannot afford them. If uniforms are required, inclusive recreation programs need to identify cost-effective methods to provide those uniforms. Using sponsorships, developing a loan program, or instituting a program to work off the costs are all effective methods. However, cost is not the only factor to consider with uniforms. Kenny's story is a good example.

Kenny, an 8-year-old, was a participant in a weeklong musical theater day camp. Kenny learned the music and his lines alongside his peers and was looking forward to the big performance at the end of the week. The concern for his mother? The uniform. During the preprogram interview, the theater director explained all of the participants would be asked to wear red T-shirts (which would not be given to the participants until the day before the performance) and white shorts. Kenny's mother explained that Kenny had very particular preferences with clothing and only had five outfits he was willing to wear. Mom did not think she could get Kenny to wear the identified clothing, especially if the shirt was not coming until the last minute, meaning Kenny would not have any time to get used to it. The theater director, after reflecting on the purpose of the program, which was to introduce children to the theater and to provide an enjoyable experience, was not concerned that Kenny look exactly like everyone else. The theater director and Kenny's mother discussed the clothing Kenny was comfortable in and identified an appropriate outfit. As it turns out, Kenny was so excited about the performance that he wore the uniform with no complaints. His mother attributes Kenny's willingness both to his excitement and to the accepting attitude of the theater director. The lack of pressure to wear a certain outfit made the choice Kenny's.

Although wheelchair tennis and Kenny's story are examples of rule changes related to physical and emotional needs, Kristi provides an example of a rule change in a contextual area, the area of personal needs. A common adaptation addressing cognitive skills is simplifying the rules of a game, such as eliminating houses and hotels from a game of Monopoly. Many adaptations are possible to augment social skills. A recreational league basketball program in an ethnically diverse area, for instance, chose to increase socialization among players of different backgrounds by requiring each team roster to include an equitable mixture of people from various ethnicities.

Instructional Aides

In many cases, an instructional aide is necessary to promote full inclusion. Sign language interpreters, for example, augment communication for participants who are deaf. In children's programs, aides are often useful in shadowing participants with autism and attention-deficit/hyperactivity disorder (ADHD). The presence of the extra leader or aide, walking alongside the participant, increases the participant's focus and facilitates the development of social skills such as waiting in line and sharing. Aides can also be useful when working with participants with certain physical disabilities who need assistance to keep up with the group. Steven provides a good example, as described next.

Steven was a 6-year-old boy with Dandy Walker syndrome registered in an inclusive gymnastics program, two instructors with 12 students. With most of his hypothalamus gone, Steven's brain was unable to send messages to the rest of his body. As a result, although of average intelligence, Steven, at 6, had only recently learned to crawl, was being introduced to a walker, and was limited in his verbal skills. With limited trunk development, Steven had difficulty sitting up on his own. During the 8-week session of gymnastics, an aide worked with Steven one on one. She stabilized

An aide provides support for a camper during a hike in Bradford Woods.

his trunk while he sat with the group, supported him as he used his walker to move between stations, and, having been briefed by his mother on the signs he used, facilitated socialization between Steven and the other participants and the instructors.

At the end of the 8-week session, Steven's mom signed him up for the next session. She was noticing improvement in his trunk skills and he was using the walker more. The aide was there again, but after the second week, in consultation with the mother and the program leader, the aide began to reduce her direct contact. By the end of the second session, Steven was able to sit up by himself, was stable using his walker, and was initiating interaction with other participants. Steven enrolled again for a third session, only this time, in the preprogram meeting, both the instructor and Steven's mother agreed that no aide was needed. Steven was able to participate independently.

Although in many cases an additional paid staff member is necessary to provide individual assistance, in other situations a *buddy* can be identified from the participants already in the program. A buddy can be useful when one participant needs a minimal amount of assistance and providing that assistance would not interfere with the buddy's ability to fully participate in the program. Consider Shaun's story.

Shaun was a self-proclaimed ham. At age 10, he asked his mom to sign him up for an acting class at the local community center. For the class, the instructor decided to put on a play and assigned each participant a role. All participants had to learn new lines and stage directions each week. Shaun was excited about the play, but both he and his mother were concerned that he might have difficulty following the stage directions and reciting his lines as a result of his ADHD and speech impairment. When Shaun, his mom, and the instructor met, they decided the best option would be to assign a buddy to Shaun. Shaun's mother suggested Kim, another boy from the class with whom Shaun felt comfortable. The instructor contacted Kim and his parents, who agreed that Kim would be Shaun's buddy in the class. Kim had the same stage directions as Shaun, so when Kim moved, Shaun moved. This was not uncommon in the play, as several cast members had similar stage directions. Having a person to follow, and to encourage him when he forgot, assisted Shaun to focus. Kim's lines were also very similar to Shaun's and usually were said right before Shaun's lines. The instructor changed all the lines to match, helping Shaun to remember the lines and providing Shaun with the opportunity to mimic Kim, which his mother had identified as a way to assist with Shaun's speech.

Instructional aides, whether paid staff or peer buddies, can be used to enhance abilities in all areas of the activity analysis. This section has provided examples of using an instructional aide to augment cognitive, physical, emotional, social skills. Can you identify each adaptation?

Using an Inclusive Approach to Creating Adaptations

A method sometimes used in inclusive children's programs, although not commonly used in adult programs, is to include all program participants in creating the adaptations. Before initiating a discussion with the group, ask for the consent of the participant who requires the adaptations. Including the group in the adaptation process provides an opportunity to talk to the group about what makes us all similar and different. Additionally,

involving the group in the adaptation process increases their buy-in to the adaptations. Rebecca's story provides a good illustration of this concept.

Rebecca, a 10-year-old with autism, was enrolled in an inclusive 8-week summer day camp. Rebecca was fully included physically in the activities, but her limited communication abilities restricted her social involvement. Rebecca used a picture board for communicating her needs, but the existing pictures did not encompass the many activities and experiences at camp. Rebecca and her counselor brought the situation to the attention of everyone in Rebecca's group. Their solution was to create a new set of pictures, all based on camp activities. During their art session for the next 2 days, the whole group, including Rebecca, worked on the new pictures. For the rest of the 8-week camp, with the aid of her new pictures, Rebecca was fully engaged in the camp.

Fostering Socialization

As indicated in many of the previous examples, adaptations often result in an increased level of socialization. Because many people from diverse populations lack opportunities to socialize, inclusive recreation provides an important social

Campers socialize through partnered activities at an inclusive recreation summer camp.

environment. Depending on the purpose of the program, fostering socialization among the participants can be a direct outcome of the adaptation, as with Steven and Rebecca, or an indirect outcome of the adaptations, as with Shaun and DJ. The adaptation worked particularly well for DJ, because the controls on the reel brought the line close enough for DJ that he was able to bait his own hook. When the other boys and girls in the clinic saw how good he was at baiting, they lined up to have him bait their hooks too!

Navigating Program Management Issues

Understanding the activities and the participants and creating the appropriate adaptations are important for a successful program. Designing an inclusive program, however, is not just about the activities. A number of program management issues need to be considered to ensure an inclusive experience. Management issues include program fees, site selection, program transportation, communication methods, and behavior management techniques.

How Much to Charge

Hope has registered for the adult skiing clinic and requires a sit ski to participate. Can you charge Hope for the cost of the adaptive equipment? No! The fee Hope pays for the clinic is the same fee you charge everyone else. To manage the costs of accommodations, the agency has several options to consider. Many agencies establish a line item in the agency budget for accommodations. The costs of adaptive equipment and aides are pulled from this line. Other agencies raise the costs of all programs by a nominal amount (e.g., 50¢), which covers the cost of accommodations for all of their services. Agencies need to be creative in fulfilling their obligations to participants. Consider the following scenario:

Your agency is offering a 3-day cruise for seniors. Rhonda registers for the cruise and requests a sign language interpreter. You recognize your obligation to the participant and are willing to pay for the sign language interpreter (hourly wage plus accommodations on the cruise) to ensure Rhonda is fully included. However, because of a shortage of certified interpreters in the area, no one is available.

What can you do? One solution is to work with Rhonda to identify a friend or family member who might be able to interpret for her. If such a person is available and Rhonda is comfortable with this option, the agency can pay for the cost of the cruise for the person who will act as the interpreter, ensuring that Rhonda is able to engage in all of the planned activities.

Scholarships and Sliding Fees

Scholarships or similar grant programs are common in municipal and not-for-profit recreation agencies. If the mission of an agency is to provide services to the whole community, then it is incumbent upon the agency to identify mechanisms to ensure that the whole community has access to the programs and services. Given that agencies are increasingly moving toward fee-based programming, agencies need to have a system in place to ensure that programs and services are affordable.

Many agencies provide partial or full scholarships to cover program fees upon request of the participant, provided the participant meets the predetermined qualifications of the agency. Another system commonly used to reduce costs for participants is a sliding fee scale based on the income of the household. Here's a note of caution, however, regarding the second option. A household that includes a person with a disability or someone from another diverse population may encounter a number of expenses, identified in chapter 5, that are not typical of the average household. Determining fees solely by income may ignore these important considerations.

Site Selection

When selecting a program location, you must consider a number of factors. Barriers discussed in chapter 5, including transportation, signage, parking spaces, pathways, restrooms, water fountains, telephones, and controls, all need to be considered. For instance, if there is no elevator in the building, your program should be on the first floor. But what if your kitchen is on the second floor and you want to offer a cooking class? Is the class unavailable for anyone who cannot use the stairs?

You have several options. Your first option, of course, is to investigate other buildings that your agency may have available. A municipal recreation agency, for example, may have multiple community centers to choose from. A second option is to look at your community partners. Often arrangements can be made with a school, another recreation agency, or even a restaurant to use its kitchen. The third option is to consider

Amy Davison

Background Information

Education

*BA in leisure, youth, and human services and therapeutic recreation from the University of Northern Iowa
 *Master of Science from Western Illinois University

Credentials Certified Therapeutic Recreation Specialist

Career Information

Position Development Director

Organization Family YMCA of Black Hawk County

What I Like About My Job I work with the YMCA to write grant proposals and complete annual fundraising campaigns. I complete research for grant opportunities for program departments and work with YMCA program directors on new program initiatives. Every day poses different challenges in nonprofit agencies, and I have been fortunate to represent our organization in the community and develop many new collaborative efforts. I work on a variety of tasks, and no two days are the same.

how the class is taught. Depending on the purpose of the class and the type of cooking being done, it may be possible to have the participants meet in a room on the first floor to prepare the ingredients; which could then be transferred to the kitchen to be cooked. This solution would not work for all types of cooking classes, but the point is that there are solutions available if you are open to the options.

Program Transportation

Transportation becomes a program management issue if your program includes transportation of participants. Field trips during day camp and trips to the casino for older adults are common examples. In these cases, transportation must be accessible. Although you could send everyone else off in the bus and use an accessible van for the participant from a diverse population, the intent of inclusive programming is that all participants are fully included. That includes traveling together.

Communication Style

An inclusive approach to communication requires you to look at communication in a broader, more flexible way than you might be used to. Communicating with an inclusive audience requires the concurrent use of a variety of communication methods. For example, instead of giving instructions only verbally, incorporate verbal and written instructions as well as demonstration. Methods to consider include speech, the written word, pictures, demonstration, languages your participants use (including sign language), gestures, symbols, and body language. Incorporating multiple delivery methods can be difficult at first. However, you will quickly realize that using multiple methods of delivering information enhances understanding for all participants because we all learn differently.

Communication isn't just about delivering the message; receiving messages is just as important. Inclusive programming requires you to be respectful of participants' methods of communication and open to receiving messages in a variety of ways, whether through writing, pictures, signs, communication devices, interpreters, or speech that may be challenging to understand at first. Patience and a willingness to listen and understand are the keys. Through their actions, program leaders also model inclusive communication methods for all program participants, enhancing group communication and creating maximum opportunities for socialization. Earlier examples described how an instructional aide learned Steven's sign-based method of communication and taught it to the other participants and how Rebecca's group created new picture cards to enhance her communication with the others. As you practice these communication techniques, consider the suggestions provided in table 9.3.

Behavior Management

An important component in designing any recreation experience is effectively managing the behavior of all the participants. Behavior management is defined as a set of activities used by a leader to promote positive behavior and eliminate negative behavior. Behavior management strategies are used with individuals and with the entire group to create and maintain a productive group environment (see table 9.4 on page 170).

The goal behind behavior management is to create a structured, safe, and welcoming environment for everyone by eliminating counterproductive behavior and reinforcing prosocial behavior. Positive measures that reinforce desired behaviors should be used as much as possible, whereas negative consequences or disciplinary actions should be reserved for specific behaviors that are identified as vital to extinguish. Common behavior management strategies include these:

- Clear rules and expectations
- Consistency
- Respect
- Modeling of positive behavior
- Negative reinforcement
- Positive reinforcement

Recreation leaders can eliminate potential problems by establishing clear rules and expectations from the beginning and being consistent in their implementation. If participants understand the structure of a program and its rules and boundaries, and those rules make sense within the program context, participants are less likely to question or test the system. All rules and expectations, however, have to be fairly enforced to maintain equity among all participants.

Showing respect for the participants, through actions and words, is another mechanism the leader can use to diminish or eliminate

Table 9.3 Communication Suggestions

	Problem	Solution
Delivery	Information is too complex.	• Use simpler words. • Provide one piece of information at a time. • Use repetition. • Restate differently.
	Message is not received.	• Use multiple methods. • Eliminate distractions. • Allow additional time for message to be decoded. • Be sure participant is ready for your message. • Speak to the person, not to an aide or interpreter.
	Instructor is fearful or uncertain.	• Be confident! • Be yourself! • Use humor!
Reception	You have difficulty understanding the participant's speech or other method of communication.	• Be patient! • Ask person to repeat. • Repeat what you have heard and ask for confirmation. • Provide supplies for additional communication methods if appropriate (e.g., paper and pencil).
	Participant does not seem interested in communicating or is frustrated.	• Reinforce your willingness to communicate. • Be observant; look for nonverbal cues. • Use active listening skills. • Do not interrupt or fill in—wait for the person to finish (do not anticipate needs or person will not feel need to communicate).

Table 9.4 Behavior Management Techniques

Technique	Description	Considerations
Positive practice (Azrin & Besalel, 1999)	When error occurs, stop and practice correction successfully several times.	This practice avoids scolding and punishment. Misbehavior is interrupted immediately. Positive behavior becomes habit.
Response cost (Thibadeau, 1998)	Apply consequences for undesirable behaviors. Examples: • Losing recess for talking • Requiring payment of a fee for a late bill • Losing points or tokens for off-task behavior	Technique is relatively mild compared with aversive forms of punishment. Technique allows immediate feedback. Technique does not disrupt environment. When possible, consequences should be logically related to the causal behavior.
Shaping (Hall, 1975)	Teach complex behavior by rewarding successful progression through increasingly complex levels of the target behavior.	Leader analyzes tasks to determine levels. Leader must ensure that progressions are attainable. Examples include hitting a baseball and riding a bike.
Chaining (Hall, 1975)	Teach complex behavior by sequentially introducing and rewarding parts of the behavior.	Leader analyzes tasks to determine steps or parts. Leader must ensure that progressions are attainable. Technique can work backward or forward. For example, a dance instructor teaches step 1, then step 2, and finally step 3. Each step builds on the previous one.
Fading (Esveldt-Dawson & Kazdin, 1998)	Gradually remove external reinforcers.	Fading helps ensure that behavior is not indefinitely contingent on reward and helps shift the focus toward natural, intrinsic rewards.
Extinction (Hall & Hall, 1998a)	Ignore negative behaviors through techniques such as refusing to speak to or answer the person, looking away, turning your back toward the person, or removing yourself from environment.	Leader pinpoints behavior to change. Leader must measure behavior and set goal. Leader should practice ignoring behavior. Targeted behavior may first increase. Leader reinforces appropriate behaviors. Other people and staff must also ignore negative behaviors.
Modeling (Streifel, 1998)	Use prearranged models, or planned models, as a mechanism for learning through imitation.	Leader makes sure that the learner pays attention. Leader ensures that the learner is physically and cognitively capable of behavior. Leader must model clearly and consistently. Leader provides feedback and rewards.

Technique	Description	Considerations
Token economies (Ayllon, 1999)	Provide concrete reinforcers for appropriate behavior. Later, use a backup reinforcer.	Tokens must be easy to administer. Tokens must be administered immediately. Tokens must be hard to counterfeit. Leader must establish and always follow rules for exchanging tokens for rewards. Goal should be to fade out system.
Time-out (Hall & Hall, 1998b)	Decrease behavior by removing a person from the opportunity to receive attention or rewards for undesired behavior.	Leader must clearly explain undesired behavior and the specific consequence. Technique typically works best with 2- to 12-year-olds. Time-out area should be safe and free of reward. Time-out area should be easily monitored. Time-outs should last 2 to 5 min and no longer than 1 min for each year of age. Leader should add minutes for refusing to go to time-out or misbehaving in time-out, up to a maximum of 30 min. Time-outs may not be appropriate for kids with a history of self-stimulation.

*Additional information regarding the methods presented in this table can be found in the *How to Manage Behavior* series edited by Vance and Marilyn Hall and published by Pro Ed.

Reprinted, by permission, from T. Robertson and T. Long, 2007, *Foundations of therapeutic recreation* (Champaign, IL: Human Kinetics), 155 and 156.

behavioral issues. All participants need to know that the leader respects them and their contributions, strengths, and challenges. Leaders can demonstrate respect through their words, including the language they use and their tone of voice, as well as through actions such as being prepared, making sure everyone is involved, and treating everyone equitably. The leader can also model the positive behaviors he wishes to see from the participants. For instance, if one of the rules is to be a good sport and the leader is on the losing team, the leader can model good behavior by shaking the opposing players' hands and congratulating them on a well-played game.

Reinforcers, both positive and negative, are also commonly used as behavior management strategies. Negative reinforcements are designed to strengthen positive behavior by stopping or avoiding negative conditions as a consequence of the behavior (Geiser, 1976). For example, in an after-school program, completing homework correctly and expediently increases the amount of free time for the participants. Punishment, also commonly used as a behavior management technique, attempts to eliminate a behavior by attaching a consequence the participant views as unpleasant to the unwanted behavior. Demerit systems, points for negative behaviors, warning cards, and loss of privileges are all examples.

Positive reinforcers include encouragement as well as both intrinsic and extrinsic rewards (Lavay, French, & Henderson, 1997). Intrinsic rewards are internally motivating for the individual, such as praise. On the most basic level, an intrinsic reward is being told you are doing a good job, or realizing that the other participants like you and want to play with you because you are willing to share. Recognition of effort is also a good intrinsic motivator. Being named the outstanding teammate of the week for demonstrating good teamwork or becoming line leader as a reward for following directions are examples of the use of recognition as an intrinsic reward.

Extrinsic rewards, on the other hand, involve the participant receiving some type of outside motivator. Stickers, prizes, and food are common extrinsic rewards. While often used in recreation programs, extrinsic rewards, especially larger prizes and food, should be used with caution for several reasons. First, using food as a reward (e.g., rewarding cooperation with an ice cream cone) contradicts the important health messages that are embedded in recreation programs. Second, food allergies, special diets, and medications may prohibit some participants from taking part in the reward system. Healthy snacks should always be used as rewards, with alternative foods available so that everyone is eligible to receive a reward for their behavior. Finally, while its effect as a motivator is often short-lived, the extrinsic reward can often become the reason for doing the activity, defeating the intent of the program.

Summary

This chapter has looked at the necessary components to designing an inclusive recreation program. We explored elements of the program, including its purpose and activities, along with the individual characteristics of the participants. The reader was introduced to the process of activity analysis, guidelines for making adaptations, and different areas of adaptations. Management issues tied to inclusive programming were discussed as well, including program fees, site selection, program transportation, communication style, and behavior management.

Discussion Questions

1. As a program leader, you should take what steps to make your sure your program is inclusive?

2. Why are adaptations important in an inclusive recreation program?

3. Consider a recreation program you are familiar with. What elements discussed in this chapter does the program contain? What could be done to enhance the program's inclusiveness?

4. Which communication methods do you typically use? Which methods are most effective for you as a listener?

Break the Barriers

This section introduces you to Break the Barriers, a fully inclusive sport and performing arts agency in Fresno, California, and its cofounders Deby and Steve Hergenrader. Break the Barriers offers a wide assortment of programs, including gymnastics, martial arts, dance, swimming, sign language, and many more. Break the Barriers has been named a national role model for inclusion.

Birth of a Dream

Deby Mullen Hergenrader, daughter of Ice Capades performers, was born a true athlete. At the age of 10, she channeled her energies into gymnastics. By the age of 16, she had become a state, regional, and national gymnastics champion. When she reached the elite level, she was able to compete internationally and, but for an ankle injury in 1972, she may have competed in the Olympics.

With gymnastics in her blood, Deby turned to coaching other gymnasts, an activity she still enjoys today. Her dream, however, was not one of self-glory or trophies; it was something far deeper. It was born out of the shadows of another birth—that of Deby's sister, Kathy, a child with Down syndrome. It was a dream born not out of pity but rather out of challenge and foresight. Kathy had many opportunities to watch Deby perform her gymnastics routines and, through emulation, was able to excel within Special Olympics. Kathy's amazing achievements became a catalyst that began Deby's relentless efforts to create a common bond between persons of all abilities. This bond would be fused through sports.

Out of the Dream, Into Reality

Deby realized that in order for the desires of her heart to become realities, she would have to become immersed in the complexities of people with disabilities. She spent hours coaching adults who had different physical, neurological, and mental abilities. Then Deby married Steve Hergenrader, a former Yankees baseball player. Steve's interest and proficiency in gymnastics, coupled with his gift for working with children, and Deby's dream gave birth to the Fresno District Special Olympics Gymnastics Program.

Later, the Hergenraders found the perfect house in Fresno. It had a big room that they turned into a dance studio and a yard big enough to house gymnastics equipment, including old bed mattresses, a trampoline, balance beam, and a vaulting horse with a spring board. Steve and Deby named their new enterprise Gymnastics by Deby. They began using sign language to communicate with students who were deaf and hard of hearing and discovered that signing was part of the magic in the mixture that connected students of all abilities. The children listened better when they focused on the hand movements.

Breaking the Barrier

Barriers exist either to keep something out or to keep something in. Often one of the barriers that separate one person from another is the lack of opportunity to do anything in common together. Through the Hergenraders' inclusive sports and performing arts classes, students found common ground and barriers started tumbling down. Students of all abilities began to learn from each other. Students accomplished more than they had believed possible.

The atmosphere of the classes changed too. Competition became less important, and a feeling of being a supportive family grew. Without any advertising, these combined classes grew to include 200 participants from age 3 to adulthood. Soon a board of directors was formed of the students' parents, and Break the Barriers was officially incorporated as a nonprofit corporation in October 1985.

The Dream Lives On

The Barrier Breakers, formed in 1987, is a performing ensemble of students whose mission is to represent inclusion at its best while celebrating all abilities. Along the way these performers are softening hearts, opening eyes for awareness, and generating hope for all people. The team is a combination of performers, each with amazing abilities, who range in age from 6 years to adult. There are currently 58 performers on the team. Each performer has her or his own definition of triumph, a talent to show, and a mission to accomplish. Performing locally, nationally, and internationally, at such locations as the U.S. White House

(continued)

and in countries such as China, Romania, and South Africa, the Barrier Breakers spread the message of inclusion world-wide.

More than 3,000 students participate in the programs offered at Break the Barriers. The agency is continually adapting classes to meet the increasing demand for this unique program. From a backyard to a 32,000 square foot (9,754 square meter) facility, Break the Barriers continues to change the lives of people around the world. Break the Barriers is recognized as a national role model for inclusion and has broken barriers nationally and internationally. Together with sons Jared and Tyler, Steve and Deby Hergenrader have fostered a family of dedicated people who are instrumental in the tremendous success and acceptance of this program, making Break the Barriers a dream come true (History, 2008).

Reprinted with permission. To learn more, visit Deby and Steve at http://www.breakthebarriers.org.

Inclusive Recreation and Leisure Programs and Services

Play and Playgrounds

Cindy Burkhour, MA, CTRS, CPRP

Access Recreation Group, LLC

Joan Almon

Alliance for Childhood

" *Play, although it cannot change the external realities of children's lives, can be a vehicle for children to explore and enjoy their differences and similarities and to create, even for a brief time, a more just world where everyone is an equal and valued participant.* "

–Patricia G. Ramsey

Learning Outcomes

After completing this chapter, learners will be able to do the following:

- Identify accessible characteristics of play areas and individual playground components that comply with the minimum requirements of the Americans with Disabilities Act (ADA) and universal design concepts.
- Discuss the value of playing together for children with and without disabilities.
- Identify how universal design features in a play environment benefit all people of all abilities.
- Explain what play is and how it differs from adult-organized activities such as sports.
- Discuss the value of play for all children.
- Describe basic types of play and the need to create play environments that encourage multiple types of play.
- Explain the role of the playworker in supporting but not directing children's play.

Play is a deeply rooted activity that has been well studied in human beings, especially children. In its February 2009 issue, *Scientific American* featured a cover story titled "The Serious Need for Play" (Wenner, 2009). The article describes research showing that play reduces stress levels in children, builds strong social skills, and enhances intelligence and creative problem solving. Even play fighting is important and improves problem solving. The article posits that play has been part of the human experience for a very long time and is fulfilling essential evolutionary tasks. Remove play from children's lives and something essential is lost.

One researcher, Sergio Pellis, describes the importance of play this way: "A child who has had a rich exposure to social play experiences is more likely to become an adult who can manage unpredictable social situations" (p. 29). The article underscores the vital role of play, saying that children that do not play when they are young may grow into anxious, socially maladjusted adults.

In human beings the urge to play is very strong and lasts throughout one's life, as was noted by the well-known anthropologist Ashley Montagu. He described the work of many scientists as a continuation of their play as children: "The play aspect of their work has been often acknowledged by scientists and other creative individuals." Montagu described the central importance of play, saying, "Play has probably been the most important factor in the evolution of social behavior among vertebrates and . . . probably also of the mental and spiritual life of humankind." Montagu concluded, "The ability to play is one of the principal criteria of mental health" (Montague, 1981, pp. 155-156).

Play arises from within and is intrinsically motivated in contrast to adult work, which is generally motivated by outer needs—the need for a meal to be prepared, a roof to be repaired, or a salary to be earned. Although people often describe play as "children's work," this can lead to confusion if we attribute external motivation to play. We begin to think that play is important because it leads to a concrete goal. Play does lead to many positive outcomes, but they are not the reason children play. They play for the sheer enjoyment of the activity and to satisfy a deep urge or drive, similar to the urge to eat, drink, or sleep. All lead to important outcomes, but human beings exercise them to satisfy an immediate need. Play is the same and is fundamental to a healthy life.

What Is Play?

Defining play is like capturing water in your hand. You have it for a moment and then it flows away. Play is elusive. When you see it or experience it, you recognize it as play, yet it is hard to grasp or define. It's been said that defining play is as difficult as defining love. These are basic attributes of life and they are too vast to be contained in a simple definition.

Play can, however, be described, and a good description is provided by the "playworkers" in the British Isles. Playworkers oversee children's play and are deeply knowledgeable about it. They are also strong advocates for play, and one of their associations, Play Wales, helped the Welsh government formulate its policy for play, which says, "Play is a set of behaviors that are freely chosen, personally directed and intrinsically motivated. Play is performed for no external goal or reward, and is a fundamental and integral part of healthy development—not only for individual children, but also for the society in which they live." The organization clarifies this description as follows:

- *Freely chosen* means that children themselves choose when, how, and what to play. Play is not part of a set program and does not have any steps that need to be completed.
- *Personally directed* means children themselves decide the rules and roles they take within their play.
- *Intrinsically motivated* means that play is undertaken for its own sake and not performed for any reward, certificate, or status (Play, 2006).

This description sets play somewhat apart from playing video games and organized sports. Sandlot baseball, for instance, was initiated by the children and they set the rules, adapting them endlessly to the situation at hand. Today's sports programs are related but are significantly different in that they are run by adults and use fixed rules that the children do not create or adapt.

Video games, which are frequently considered to be a new form of play, have too much input from the programmers to be considered true, child-initiated play. The story line has been created by adults, and although children can adjust it they are not in charge of the game in the same way as when they create a game from scratch. The situation is similar with board games, card games, and other rule-based games. If the children are free to change the rules, the game becomes very playful. Otherwise, it may be a good activity in its own right but it is different from child-initiated play and should not be confused with it. By its nature, play is not competitive. No one wins in authentic play. Thus, if an activity has a winner and an air of competition, it may be a close kin to play but is not real play.

This line between child-initiated activity and adult-led activity is being explored in many settings that foster experiences for children, such as arts programs, children's museums, and outdoor learning programs. Program directors feel pressured to book every moment with planned activities to satisfy external pressures from parents, funders, and government agencies, yet many administrators and programmers know that children learn best if planned activities are balanced with child-initiated play and exploration.

In today's world, when children *are* able to initiate their own play, they are rarely left alone to follow it all the way through. Adults often believe that children will get more from play if the adult builds on the child's ideas and provides new information. Play becomes another means of teaching children. Adults usually do not recognize that when it comes to play children have a genius for knowing what they need and have a strong will to achieve it. In the process they learn an enormous amount. An adult may be able to add a light touch to the child's play, but if the adult adds anything more than that then the activity becomes the adult's play rather than the child's.

Adults have a role in children's play, but it is usually an invisible one. One reason that children were free to play outdoors for hours on their own in the past is that there were parents at home, usually mothers, who kept their eyes and ears open for the sounds of play, not only of their own children but also of the other children in the neighborhood. There was a network of safety around the children.

In today's world, play has largely disappeared, in part because parents aren't comfortable allowing children out on their own. Yet it is possible to provide a similar invisible network of safety so that elementary-age children can again have a chance to play on their own. This can happen when staff are trained to create safe but adventuresome areas for play in parks and zoos, in after-school programs, on school playgrounds, in camps, and in a host of other places where children gather for fun and recreation. Organized sports themselves can become much more playful, as one ice hockey coach learned when he gave

the children time to play their own game at the end of each coaching session. The coach left the ice and the children took over in the same way the coach and his friends had done as boys on the rivers and lakes of Chicago.

The playworkers in the United Kingdom provide a good model. They study play intensively and learn to create environments that allow for all types of play. They create safe play environments for children but allow as much risk-taking as they believe the children can handle. The playworkers then don a cloak of invisibility and stay outside the play as much as possible so that the children can initiate and direct their own play. The playworkers intervene when necessary and give assistance, but the emphasis is always on allowing children to take the lead in play. Playworkers understand that every child has a deep need to play, and this has to be satisfied if the child is to develop in a healthy and wholesome manner.

A beautiful aspect of play is that it dissolves differences between children. One sees this when children who speak different languages play together. They may not have a word in common but can play together for hours without difficulty. Likewise, when children of all abilities play together, differences tend to disappear. Penny Wilson, a playworker in London's adventure playgrounds and a specialist in inclusive play, describes a beautiful play situation in this way:

> I took a big bag of dressing up clothes into a park, and we were working with half a dozen children with complex needs. I opened the box up and all the children dived in and pulled out stuff, and there were flippers, and top hats, and sparkley dresses, and wings and—you couldn't imagine. It was a real mishmash of stuff. And they all dressed up in these mad outfits, and the children with disabilities couldn't be seen as being different from the other children." (P. Wilson, 2009)

Directors of park districts, zoos, children's museums, and other venues in the United States have become very interested in the playwork approach for their staff, and workshops and courses are developing across the country. Some of these specialize in inclusive play, others in outdoor play, and others in play and playwork in general. For further information about playwork and a fact sheet on play, playwork, and adventure playgrounds, see the Web site of the Alliance for Childhood: www.allianceforchildhood.org/playwork.

Creating safe but adventuresome play spaces for children is a challenge. One needs to comply with governmental standards for safety and at the same time give children opportunities for risk. Play is an evolving process in which children develop new capacities by confronting challenges. This is a critical process for developing capacities, such as self-control, problem-solving skills, and resilience. If the play arena is oversimplified, the children grow bored with it or take extreme risks such as jumping off the top of a swing set. For children to derive maximum benefit from play they need:

- "loose parts" (e.g., building materials, dress-up clothes, art materials) that allow children to alter the environment and make it suit their needs;
- as much risk as they can handle; and
- adults nearby who are watchful but not overly intrusive.

Most American playgrounds are designed to be as risk-free as possible for fear of accidents and litigation. In Europe, a different approach is taken and there are many "adventure playgrounds" where challenges abound; where children play with loose parts, simple play materials that can be used in dozens of different ways, to create their own environments; and in many cases where hammers, nails, and other tools are available for building huts and clubhouses. Such a "hammer and nails" playground exists in Berkeley, California, and has had a very low accident rate for more than 30 years (Adventure Playground, n.d.).

The Los Angeles area has two adventure playgrounds, one in Huntington Beach (Huntington Beach Adventure Playground, 2009) and one in Irvine (Adventure Playground, 2009), that are open in the summer and are equipped with loose parts and playwork staff. So there are a total of three such playgrounds in the United States. In contrast, London has 80 adventure playgrounds staffed with playworkers, and there are hundreds more throughout the British Isles, on the European continent, and in Japan.

Not only children are players. Adults are as well, although they are more likely to turn to rule-based play such as golf or other sports or hobbies rather than unstructured play. When they are given a chance to engage in creative play again, most adults are astonished to find that their playful spirit is alive and well, albeit

Children create their own play space.

somewhat inhibited at first compared with children, who play with relish and abandonment.

More and more adults are asking, What about us? How can we return to unstructured play? One answer is offered by David Hawkins and Karen Payne, who are developing Wild Zones in California and elsewhere. These are described as "places where adults, children and adolescents can playfully co-create new forms of public space that enliven people's connection with each other and with nature. . . . They differ from parks and nature reserves because they offer opportunities to alter the environment rather than leaving it untouched—places to build dens and forts and treehouses, make new pathways, mess around with water and mud, climb trees, create sculptures from natural materials, stage performances, invent games and other types of free play" (Wild Zones, 2008).

The movement to restore play is growing, and it is important that it be an inclusive movement that brings together people of all abilities, ages, genders, races, ethnic, and linguistic backgrounds. In the world of play, everyone is a player and differences that may matter elsewhere soon disappear.

Types of Play

Children engage in many types of play even within a single play session. A group of children may stalk through the woods with bows and arrows. They imagine themselves to be hunters on the path of game. They engage in large motor play and imaginative play; they develop small motor proficiency as they aim, point, and use their tools; they speak and negotiate with each other; and they observe nature and blend in with it. They also develop practical skills for life, in this case hunting, tracking, finding their way in the woods, and much more. Similarly when children play house, imaginative play takes place, there is a great deal of social interaction and negotiation over roles, and children learn skills as they bake, sew, build their houses, and rearrange them as needed.

Children use play as a primary means for exploring and developing their own thoughts, feelings, physical abilities, and social relationships. Sometimes their play is clear to adults and sometimes it is hard to decipher. Penny Wilson, the British playworker mentioned earlier, describes her work with Jan, a boy with autism spectrum disorder. One day as she observed Jan she saw him stop in his tracks, back up, and sway back and forth in an uncharacteristic rocking movement. He kept this up for a long time.

Penny moved behind him and copied his movements. Then she saw the wonder of what he was doing. As he walked past a tree he had caught the sun bursting with light around the trunk. "He had been so amazed and struck by the splendour of what he saw that he decided, without a second thought, to go back and see it again and again and again" (P. Wilson, 2009). Later, the playworkers met for their daily reflective session where they shared observations of the children. Many had shared the beauty of the sun and the tree with Jan and believed they would continue to view trees and light in new ways because of him.

Becoming sensitive to children's play and keeping the play types in mind helps one better observe play and make sense of the ever-changing scenarios the children create. Keeping the types in mind is also important when setting up a playground. Most modern playgrounds encourage large motor skills through climbing, sliding, and swinging, but children also need opportunities to play with smaller manipulative or loose parts and engage in imaginative play and other types of play.

Different types of play help children develop physical skills including strength, dexterity and eye–hand coordination, social capacities, use of language, self-knowledge and self-control, creativity, imagination, intellectual growth, and much more. There are many ways to divide play into types, but some of the main play types can be described as in table 10.1 on page 182.

One can add more and more categories as one watches children at play, for play is an incredibly varied and rich field of activity. It is ever-changing and very individualized. In addition to differences in play types, there are differences in play by gender and by age. In open-ended play or child-organized sports, it is easy to integrate children of different ages, genders, and abilities, for the play is very flexible and the ever-changing rules accommodate the needs of all the children.

Why Is Play So Important?

Play is a universal human activity that is found in children around the world. Although there are always individual differences in play behaviors,

Table 10.1 Main Types of Play

Type of play	Description
Large-motor play	Children love to climb, run, slide, swing, jump, and engage in every type of movement possible. Such play develops coordination, balance, and a sense of one's body in the space around it.
Small-motor play	Playing with small toys and activities like stringing beads, playing with puzzles, and sorting objects into types develops dexterity.
Mastery play	Children often repeat an action in play and persevere until they master it, such as making dozens of pretend birthday packages to learn to tie bows, or playing on a balance beam to become a circus performer.
Rule-based play	Kindergartners and elementary-school children enjoy the challenge of making up their own rules and the social negotiation involved in adapting the rules for each play situation.
Construction play	Building houses, ships, forts, and other structures is a basic form of play that requires skill and imagination.
Make-believe play	This broad category incorporates many other play types and is rich with language, problem solving, and imagination. It frequently begins with "Let's pretend" and goes on to include anything children might have experienced or imagined.
Symbolic play	Children take an object at hand and convert it into the toy or prop they need through a fluid process of fantasy or imagination.
Language play	Children develop mastery by playing with words, rhymes, verses, and songs they make up or change. They tell stories and dramatize them. They are fascinated by foreign languages, especially when they are presented playfully in story, verse, or song.
Playing with the arts	Children integrate all forms of art into their play, using whatever materials are at hand to draw, model, create music, and perform puppet shows. They explore the arts and use them to express their feelings and ideas.
Sensory play	Most children enjoy playing with dirt, sand, mud, water, and other materials with different textures, sounds, and smells. Such play develops the senses.
Rough-and-tumble play	This fundamental form of play is found in animals as well as human children. Animals know how to play roughly without injury by rounding their body gestures and not aiming for dominance. Children can be helped to do the same if their play becomes too aggressive.
Risk-taking play	Children extend their abilities through risky play and learn to master challenging environments. They generally know how far they can go without actually hurting themselves. Regrettably, most current play spaces are designed to be as risk-free as possible, giving children little chance to assess risks and set their own boundaries.

there are also remarkable similarities in children's play. What vary are the societal norms surrounding play. Most cultures recognize the importance of unstructured, child-led play and give children time to play alongside the time needed for school and for chores. In very poor areas children may be engaged in child labor, which clearly curtails their play time, but even then children are likely to use every opportunity for play.

Ironically, it is not only the poorest children who may not have time to play. In today's world the middle class and wealthiest are also denied play time in favor of a surfeit of adult-organized enrichment activities. These may be tutoring programs, sports programs, or simply a combination of too many different activities outside school. Play has also eroded in the United States through growing amounts of homework and hours spent in front of screens.

The average American child sits in front of television, computer, and video screens for 5 to 6 hours per day outside school (Henry J. Kaiser Foundation, 2005). Data from 2003 indicate that children ages 6 to 12 who went outdoors only spent about 4 hours *per week* outside. Even more disturbing, though, is that only 8% of

9- to 12-year-olds went out to play at all (Hofferth, 2008).

Children spend a growing amount of time with video games, and some adults see this as a legitimate form of play. But the games are so heavily loaded with a story line created by adults that the input of the children is minor in comparison. Likewise, most toys come with a strong story line developed in television shows or movies. Children have little opportunity to develop their own play stories with the objects. This is especially true of battery-operated and high-tech toys, which tend to do the playing for the child.

If play is of such central importance to children's overall development, what happens when children are deprived of play? Bob Hughes, a play-worker in England, writes that research connects play deprivation with heightened aggression, repressed emotions and social skills, and smaller brain growth. He adds that data about Romanian orphans who underwent extensive sensory and play deprivation show that these children experienced "severe learning difficulties, erratic behavior, and difficulty in forming bonds." Such findings are similar to those of animals that are play deprived. They become highly aggressive and show bizarre behaviors. They appear to lose touch with the social norms of their species (Play Deprivation, 2006).

Another ability that is eroding from a lack of play is children's ability to use their hands in constructive ways. As neurologist Frank Wilson (1998) points out in his book, *The Hand,* an unusually large part of the brain is linked to the hand and is stimulated when the hand is being used. Working with a keyboard or a mouse is not as stimulating as playing with loose parts or tinkering with machines, as children used to do.

A practical outcome of this lack of hand skills is described by Stuart Brown in his book *Play* (2009). He speaks of Cal Tech's Jet Propulsion Laboratory (JPL), which has been a leader in America's aerospace industry for seven decades. As older engineers retired in the 1990s, JPL found itself with a serious problem. Its young engineers were among the top students from Cal Tech, Stanford, and MIT, yet they lacked a vital skill: problem solving. They could conceive new ideas and develop models but did not know how to resolve the inevitable problems that developed with new approaches. JPL leaders discovered that engineers who had played and tinkered as children, taking apart things and putting them together again, were better able to solve problems than those who did not have a rich background in such play.

A growing recognition of the need for play and concern for its disappearance led the American Academy of Pediatrics to publish a far-reaching report in 2007 calling on pediatricians to discuss play with parents and help restore it to children's lives. The report says that "free and unstructured play is healthy and—in fact—essential for helping children reach important social, emotional, and cognitive developmental milestones as well as helping them manage stress and become resilient. . . . Whereas play protects children's emotional development, a loss of free time in combination with a hurried lifestyle can be a source of stress, anxiety and may even contribute to depression for many children" (American Academy of Pediatrics, 2007).

The American public is gradually recognizing the importance of play and the serious consequences of its loss. As time is again allotted for play, it is especially important that children of all abilities benefit. Many children with disabilities have been left on the sidelines of play in the past, and it is critical that they be given full opportunities to play with their peers. Their need for play to support their overall development is as fundamental as for all other children, and their capacity for play is as great.

Play is so fundamental to human life that it is considered a basic human right and is included in the United Nation's Convention on the Rights of the Child. Article 31 of the CRC recognizes "the right of the child to rest and leisure, to engage in play and recreational activities appropriate to the age of the child and to participate freely in cultural life and the arts." Unfortunately, the United States is one of only two nations that have not yet signed the CRC. There is growing interest, however, in its joining the 192 nations that have signed.

If play is recognized as a basic human right then it follows that it must be for *all* children without regard to their abilities, their socio-economic background, gender, ethnicity, race, or any other division that tends to separate us from one another. Play has the ability, like love, to erase lines, to reveal to us what we have in common. It enables children to develop a cultural competency so that they are at ease with all human beings. Playgrounds become a miniature world where children can build a society that recognizes individual capacity and social unity. It is very important that playgrounds foster inclusion and diversity and not perpetuate a fractured view of the human family.

Photo courtesy of Play Association Tower Hamlets.

Penny Wilson

Better a broken bone than a broken spirit.
　　—Lady Allen of Hurtwood

Background Information

Education　BA Hons Illustration from Camberwell School of Arts and Crafts

Career Information

Position　Play Development Worker for Play Association Tower Hamlets (PATH)

Organization Information　Second-tier organization to support play providers and provide face-to-face play sessions where none exist.

Organization's Mission　To promote high-quality play provision and campaign for a greater awareness of the role of play within local and national consciousness.

Size of Organization　PATH reaches many people throughout Tower Hamlets, a densely populated district of London, but the actual number is impossible to say. PATH employs 9 central staff and 10 playworkers.

Job Description　Coordinate a team of playworkers, who provide inclusive play sessions in local parks and on doorstep spaces on large housing estates. Campaign, train, design, and write about play.

Career Path　Random . . . arts, work with youth and with homeless people. Unemployment during Thatcher's Britain; community employment scheme working with children with disabilities in a play setting. Appointed as a playworker at Chelsea Adventure

Playground, an inclusive site founded by Lady Allen of Hurtwood, who developed Adventure Playgrounds; later appointed as senior playworker. Left that post to join the team at PATH in my home borough.

What I Like About My Job　Every single bit of the work is amazing. Working with a passionate, dedicated, wise, and intelligent team to promote play for children in a deprived area where play has been long neglected is inspirational.

Career Ladder　I am where I want to be and always have been. I have no interest in a career ladder. It is only recently that career development in play has been possible in the United Kingdom.

Personal Statement　The more I study and learn about play, the more convinced I am that it is one of the most important and least valued aspects of human existence. I am not talking about leisure and recreation; I am referring to play that is freely chosen, personally directed and intrinsically motivated, not organized by adults but driven by children.

Creating Inclusive Access to Play

Playgrounds should be for all children. They should be designed to stimulate the imagination, challenge the body, and encourage interaction between all kids. All playgrounds should be fun, safe, and accessible to everyone. Unfortunately, this isn't the case with many older playgrounds and sometimes not even with new ones. Many

times play equipment is set in sand, pea gravel, loose chunks of rubber, or wood chips, all of which are designed to protect kids who may fall; the loose-fill material is surrounded by a big border of railroad timbers designed to contain the loose fill.

This kind of loose safety surface with its border can be very difficult or impossible to negotiate for a child who uses a walker or wheelchair or who has balance difficulties. Was this design meant to intentionally keep kids with disabilities out? Of course not! In the past, some people just never thought about the need for accessibility to playgrounds. Kids with disabilities weren't seen at the playground, so some people figured, why bother? Many people just didn't realize that kids with disabilities probably weren't at the playground because it wasn't accessible. If we make our playgrounds fun, safe, and accessible, all kids will have the opportunity to play together.

The Americans with Disabilities Act tells us that all new construction will be accessible to, and usable by, people with disabilities and that programs, service, and activities will be provided in the most integrated setting. Originally what the law didn't tell us was how to design play facilities that are inclusive and accessible while maintaining safety, fun, and challenge for all children. It became clear that the Accessibility Design Guidelines of the ADA didn't address design in the outdoor and recreation environments very well because of the many unique characteristics of recreation facilities.

The U.S. Access Board convened an advisory committee to develop recommendations for design guidelines for all recreation facilities, including playgrounds. In response to the recommendations, the Access Board then convened a regulatory negotiation committee to develop the final proposed rule for accessibility design guidelines specifically for play facilities. A committee was assembled with representatives from the playground industry, providers of playgrounds (schools and parks and recreation agencies), and people with disabilities. This regulatory negotiation committee reached agreement on the technical requirements (e.g., how wide, high, deep) for accessible design of play areas and play components and the scoping provisions that describe how and when to apply the technical requirements for accessible routes and accessible play components. These technical provisions describe the minimum standards of accessibility. Accessible routes include paths of travel into and around the play facility as well as onto, through, and off play structures.

These design standards to ensure a minimal level of accessibility to all newly constructed playgrounds are final and available (www. access-board.gov). But to make truly inclusive, universally accessible play areas, recreation providers need to work closely with manufacturers and designers to create playgrounds that meet not only the letter of the law (the minimal standard) but also the accessibility and play needs of all children of all abilities. As recreation providers

Photo courtesy of Cindy Burkhour.

The design of this play structures allows this father to interact and play with his daughter on the structure, but the inaccessible sand surface below prevents him from being able to reach his daughter if she falls.

we need to make accessibility a primary consideration and not an afterthought in the planning and design of playgrounds, play areas, and outdoor play spaces. We need to believe that these actions are the right thing to do for all kids. We need to invite parents of children with disabilities to serve on our playground design committees for schools and community parks. Parents can be hugely effective in advocating for universally accessible playgrounds. By ending segregation on the playground, we will open the doors to social and recreation inclusion for all kids.

Play is important to the social and physical development of all children of all abilities. Children with and without disabilities need to climb, rock, swing, slide, pretend, socialize, balance, build strength, test their abilities, spin, dig, splash, and have fun. When children with and without disabilities play together, they learn to appreciate each others' abilities and similarities.

Children are not the only benefactors of accessible design in play areas. When playground surfaces are accessible, parents with disabilities can move around the playground to support and interact with their children as they play. Accessible routes in and around the play area also help parents without disabilities, particularly those pushing younger siblings in strollers, and grandparents who may have a difficult time walking on loose, uneven, or unstable surfaces while playing with their grandchildren. Good universal design is a benefit to adults and children alike.

Because children with disabilities are increasingly included in child care with other children in their neighborhood, in local schools, and community recreation programs such as summer playground programs, accessible play areas are a necessity.

Planning for Accessible Play Areas

Children with disabilities live in every community. Find out who they are and ask them what type of playground would be usable and fun. Children with and without disabilities and their families have very similar expectations for safe, challenging, social, physical, imaginary, and interactive play experiences.

The ADA says that all new and altered play areas must be accessible to and usable by people with disabilities. The ADA accessibility guidelines provide information about technical (how to build play areas) and scoping (when and where to build them) considerations to make play areas accessible to and usable by children with disabilities.

Here are some pointers on universally accessible playground design to go above the minimum requirements of the ADA to create truly inclusive play spaces and places:

- Determine an accessible route to and through the playground.
- Think about how to provide an equitable number and variety of experiences for all children. Show which ground-level and elevated components are accessible, and describe how they meet or exceed the criteria and how children can access them.
- Identify the accessible activities that are physical and social and indicate the equity of opportunities at both elevated and ground levels.
- Identify the activities for children who cannot or choose not to leave their wheelchairs, walkers, or crutches.
- Identify how the design of individual play components and the placement in the layout of the structure meet or exceed the technical and scoping provisions of the rule.
- Ask the designers to sign an agreement stating that they agree to comply with ADA standards and will correct any problems, or better yet require universal design that goes above and beyond the minimum ADA requirements and creates complete accessibility to all play features for all kids of all abilities.

Obtain a copy of the Access Board's requirements; read the rules, the preamble, and the appendix; and use them to guide you throughout the entire planning process. Table 10.2 outlines some elements that you should consider. For a copy of the Accessibility Guidelines for Play Facilities, contact the Access Board at (202) 272-5434 or visit its Web site at www.access-board.gov.

Be able to defend your ideas and designs within the parameters of these requirements and require the designer or playground manufacture representative to do the same, to ensure you not only have met the requirements but have created a play area for all children. Consider parents in your designs. Parents with disabilities need to move around the playground to support and interact with their children as they play. Invite parents of children with disabilities to join the planning process, and ask them which kinds of play components would be most usable and enjoyable for their children.

Table 10.2 Accessible Design

Design element	Specifications
Entry points and seats	Play components, such as slides, spring rockers, or swings, must be at a transferable height. The entry point or seat height must be a minimum of 11 in. (28 cm) and a maximum of 24 in. (61 cm) above the required clear ground or floor space (that's the place a child could leave her chair or walker). This play component must also have a means of support for transfer, such as handholds or gripping surfaces, to help a child move onto the play component.
Play tables	Heights and clearances: Kids need to be able to pull up and under any play tables and reach all the stuff to do like the water spout on a water table. This space must be at least 24 in. (61 cm) high so knees slide right under.
Reach ranges	Interactive features of accessible play components, such as game panels, sound walls, raised sand or water tables, and pretend play props, should be within the reach ranges of children using wheelchairs. For example, components no higher than 36 in. (91 cm) and no lower than 20 in. (51 cm) for children ages 2 to 5 are reachable by most kids. For play components designed for use by children ages 5 to 12, reach ranges no higher than 40 in. (101 cm) and no lower than 18 in. (46 cm) work for most kids using wheelchairs and kids who are standing and don't have disabilities.
Maneuvering space and clear or ground space	A play component must have a maneuvering space (measuring 60 × 60 in. [152 × 152 cm]) so a kid using a wheelchair can get there, play, turn around, and go on to something else. The user must have a clear ground space (measuring 30 × 48 in. [76 × 122 cm]) to sit or stand in to play with the component or leave an assistive device parked in while on the play component (like next to the spring rocker or swing); these spaces must be on the same level as the accessible play component and can overlap.
Accessible route	The accessible route gets you to the play area and onto the play surface and to the accessible play components. The accessible play components must be connected to the accessible route at both entry and exit points, which is particularly important when children traverse the play component. For example, children get on the slide from a deck on a play structure and get off the slide on the ground. If the child arrives to the top of the slide by a ramp, transfers onto the slide leaving his or her chair on the deck, and slides to the ground, the slide end must connect to an accessible route so that the wheelchair can be brought to the child. If the slide ends in the sand, there is no way to bring the child's walker or wheelchair to her.
Surfacing	In the play area, the route surface must be both accessible (firm and stable) and resilient (safe). Some loose-fill materials, such as sand and pea gravel, are definitely not accessible. Other loose-fill materials, such as manufactured wood fibers, can be accessible if maintained to be level at all times even under swings and ends of slides. Significant ongoing maintenance is needed to rake, roll, and compact top surface material to maintain transfer heights at component exits and under swings where the loose-fill material is kicked out of place. Loose-fill materials must be contained by a border, which must have more than one opening to allow for accessible routes onto the play area surface. When there is a combination of loose-fill and unitary surfaces (like mats), special care must be taken so there are no trip or tip hazards at the transition point between the two surfaces. The edges of the unitary surface must be sloped, no steeper than a ramp with a running slope of 8.33%/1:12, and must end below grade; the loose-fill material must be level with the unitary surface so there is not a tip hazard at this transition point. The loose-fill material must also be kept off the unitary surface so that it does not obstruct the accessible route. The most universally accessible surface is unitary, such as manufactured rubber mats or poured-in-place rubber surfacing materials, which require very little upkeep.

Choosing Fun, Accessible Activities

Select different types of play components that can provide a wide variety of comparable experiences. Remember, some children walk using assistive mobility devices such as crutches, walkers, or canes, and others use wheelchairs. Some children who use wheelchairs can also walk, crawl, or scoot when out of their chairs, whereas others need assistance while out of their chairs. Some children who use walkers, crutches, or canes choose not to abandon their assistive mobility devices to crawl or scoot along a play structure where other children are walking; some children who use wheelchairs choose not to get out of their chairs to crawl, drag, or scoot where others walk or climb.

Sometimes, children do not have the strength or skills to move around unassisted; the experience they are trying to achieve is not worth the effort required to move around without assistance, or it may be embarrassing to crawl while others walk or run.

Choose activities that participants can experience while using a wheelchair or assistive mobility device. Choose activities that are physical and social, that can be played alone or with other children. Provide participants with opportunities to rock, spin, play interactive games, swing, slide, make sounds and music, balance, climb, dig, crawl, scoot, and bounce.

Here are some questions to help determine whether a type of play experience component is accessible to and usable by kids with a variety of abilities (see table 10.3):

- Can it be accessed in different ways, such as from the side or end?
- Does accessible surfacing allow for easy entry and exit?
- Is there a route that connects to the other accessible play components?

The big question is whether kids can get to it, get onto or into it, do it, get off it, go on to the

Table 10.3 Determining Accessibility and Usability for Play Components

Play components	Determining factors
Rocking experiences	• Are there transfer supports, such as handles or other gripping devices? • Is the seat space free of obstructions such as raised backs or sides that would impede a transfer from a wheelchair or climbing on once the child has let go of his assistive device? • What types of seating support and single- and multiple-user options are available? • Can the rocker be used alone and with others? • Is the rocker located near other rockers so that the kids can have social interaction? • Is the surface accessible so a child in a wheelchair can get to the swing to get on it?
Swinging experiences	• In which directions do the swings go: to and fro or spinning around? • What types of seating support, like backs and single- and multiple-user options, are available? • Does the swing support the body? • Can kids sit or lie on the swing? • Is the surface accessible so a child in a wheelchair can get to the swing to get on it?
Sliding experiences	• Are there a variety of accessible slides, such as short, straight slides, high spiral slides, tube slides, double slides, and wavy or bumpy slides? • Can kids get to the getting-on point using their wheelchair or walker by a ramp, and is there a transfer system at the top of the slide to make getting onto the slide easy? • Does the slide end where there is accessible surface and a route back to where they got on? • Is there a place near the slide end to leave an assistive device with transfer steps up to the top of the slide, so when users slide down their chair or walker is nearby?
Climbing experiences	• How many handholds and footholds are there, and where are they? • Is there a variety of climbing shapes and angles? • Is the climber shaped so it can support parts of the body while the child is climbing up or down? • Is the surface accessible so a child in a wheelchair can reach the space to get on it and then get off it at the other end?

next fun thing to do, and eventually get back to where they started or left their assistive device.

Play and Playground Advocacy

We all need to work closely with children with disabilities, their families, playground manufacturers, and designers to create playgrounds that provide an accessible environment for all children. As an advocate for accessibility or as a provider of playgrounds, you may come up against two common misconceptions about playground development. The first is that there are no children with disabilities in your community. According to the Americans with Disabilities Act, more than 20% of the people in our communities have disabilities. If you don't currently serve children with disabilities, you will at some point. The second is that accessible playground development is too costly. An accessible play area is not necessarily more expensive if you make good choices about play components and surfacing. For example, a good unitary surface such as rubber tiles requires little to no upkeep to maintain its accessible characteristics while loose-fill safety surfaces require daily leveling and raking to keep them accessible and must be replenished annually. Over the 3- to 5-year life span of the rubber surface, the loose fill actually costs more in labor and material.

People all over the United States are trying to create greater access to play areas. One such effort, the Access to Recreation Initiative, is funded by a $15 million grant from the W.K. Kellogg Foundation (www.AccesstoRecreation. org) is working with recreation providers in the Great Lakes states to create universally accessible recreation opportunities. Several of the grantees have designed play areas that go well above the minimum accessibility requirements of the ADA to create playgrounds that are truly accessible to all kids and parents of all abilities. The unique characteristics of these play area designs include on-deck transfers so a child using an assistive device can transfer directly from a wheelchair onto the entry platform for a slide or climber. Many older play structures are designed with the slide or climbing feature attached to the deck where kids stand, so they sit down on the deck and then go down the slide or climber. Someone who uses a wheelchair would have to "drop" 18 inches (45 centimeters) from the wheelchair

(that's how high the seat is) onto the deck surface in order to slide. The on-deck transfer system allows a child to transfer from a wheelchair or assistive device onto a platform that is 12 to 18 inches (30-45 centimeters) above the deck and serves as the entrance to the slide. All kids walk up or roll up and position themselves on the transfer platform, turn around, and go down the slide or climber. All the Access to Recreation–funded playgrounds use only unitary surfacing such as poured-in-place or rubber tiles and no loose-fill materials; this feature creates complete accessibility to all the surfaces of the entire play area. Each play structure has an accessible route that is connected by ramp to all entry points of all elevated play components. The entire park area is designed to be universally accessible and has accessible amenities such as water fountains, picnic tables, benches, and parking spots. Most designs include interactive play panels that feature braille and sign language. This teaches all playground users about alternate ways of communicating. The designs for each of these play areas are posted on the organization's Web site, as are the designs for many other types of universally accessible recreation experiences (www.accesstorecreation.org). The beauty of these designs is that they allow all people of all abilities to play together, both kids and their families.

We all have an opportunity to improve the quality of life for all kids and families in our communities. Play is essential to the healthy development of all children, including kids with disabilities, and it is vitally important to the health and well-being of families. We must consider universal accessibility at all points in the design process so all kids can play together without barriers or segregation by design.

Summary

Play is vital for the healthy development—cognitive, physical, and social–emotional—of all children. Child-initiated play, often called free play, is different from sports and other activities that are led or created by adults. Free play is vanishing from children's lives, and this can create serious problems for children. Play needs to be restored through advocacy and with the help of adults who know how to support children's play without dominating it. Play takes many forms, but children with and without disabilities need to climb, rock, swing, slide, pretend, socialize, balance, build strength, test their abilities, spin, dig, splash, and have fun. A good play environment allows for a wide range of play types, and the presence of "loose parts" (i.e., open-ended play materials) supports diverse play. Inclusive playgrounds need to be developed that enable children with and without disabilities to play creatively together. Playgrounds must be accessible to all children and their parents or caregivers, some of whom may have disabilities. Parents and children with disabilities should be included in planning new or renovated play spaces.

Discussion Questions

1. What are the characteristics of child-initiated play and what are the differences between it and adult-organized but playful activities?
2. What gains are associated with child-initiated play?
3. What happens if children don't play?
4. Why is play declining today?
5. What can be done to restore play, especially inclusive play, for all children?

Spotlight on Inclusive Programs

Together We Play

Kathleen Scholl
University of Northern Iowa

Susie Lund
YMCA of Black Hawk County

Overview of Program

Together We Play (TWP) is an inclusion service housed at the Family YMCA of Black Hawk County that provides capacity-building supports to community recreation, after-school, and church programs to help them welcome people of all abilities into their activities. This northeast Iowa service has had success in increasing the inclusive recreation opportunities for children and youth with disabilities, ages 3 to 21. TWP serves as a liaison between general recreation service providers and parents of children with disabilities.

Brief History

Since 2001, TWP has partnered with community recreation programs to train and assist staff in including children who have a variety of disabilities. Children have undertaken a variety of community recreation programs, such as summer camp, tee ball, weightlifting, track, karate, taekwondo, swimming lessons, after-school and church activities, gymnastics, art, cooking and acting classes, and Girl Scouts.

Photo by: Family YMCA of Black Hawk County, Together We Play.

Together We Play welcomes people of all abilities into their activities.

Status of Inclusive Recreation in the Program

Community recreation agencies pay a partnership fee for TWP services. TWP's goal is to increase the effectiveness of these agencies and improve their inclusion practices. This partnership includes an agency assessment, training workshops for staff, assistance in hiring staff, and ongoing consultation concerning site improvement and child-specific program adaptations.

In 2008, TWP became a national affiliate of a San Diego–based organization called Kids Included Together (KIT). KIT is a nonprofit organization that provides best-practices training for community-based youth organizations that are committed to including children with disabilities in their programs. KIT established a National Training Center on Inclusion (NTCI) that offers a variety of training and assistance via the World Wide Web, such as delivering onsite training for recreation staff. The affiliation with KIT has given TWP many opportunities to enhance and improve its inclusion efforts. For more information on KIT, see www.kitonline.org. The director of TWP is now a trainer of KIT's four training modules.

Future Directions

In the past, inclusion assistance largely consisted of a TWP staff person who traveled to the site of the recreation activity and acted as a leisure companion for a child. Although this benefited the agency using TWP, it did not effectively promote inclusion. TWP's focus has changed in the past year. The organization will transition from sending leisure companions to agencies to promoting inclusion at each of its partner agencies by teaching strategies for inclusion to partner agency staff, giving them the tools to take ownership and embrace inclusion at their own organization.

Reprinted, by permission, from K. Scholl and S. Lund.

Inclusive Sports

Ronald Davis, PhD

Texas Woman's University

" Sport and recreation are universal; consider the similarities rather than differences between sport for those with and without disabilities. "

—Ronald Davis

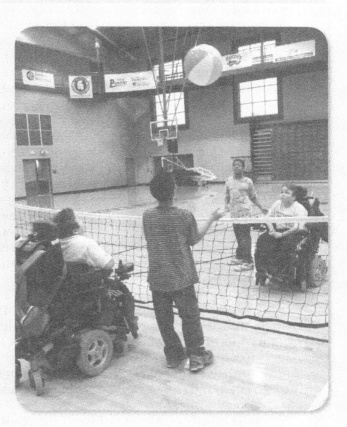

Learning Outcomes

After completing this chapter, learners will be able to do the following:

- Identify a general overview of sport for people with disabilities and a paradigm distinction between disability sport and adapted sport.
- Identify the purpose of classification within sports for people with disabilities.
- Promote inclusion through sport by recognizing similarities, not differences, between sport for participants with and without disabilities.
- Understand the functional approach for modifying movement experiences (FAMME) and game design as they pertain to game modification.

"Sport is sport," a simple statement and one that you will come to understand as you read this chapter. Sport is universal and provides common ground for many societies around the world. Whether you are watching the final set at Wimbledon, the winning touchdown at the Super Bowl, or your local youth soccer league on a Saturday morning, you are enjoying sport. Sport comes to us through the performances of many differently-abled participants. Some of these participants are tall, some are short, some use their legs to run, others use their arms to throw, and some use wheelchairs to play basketball or use beeping balls for baseball. All of these participants engage sport with their own unique set of skills and abilities. As a professional in recreation you have the opportunity to contribute to sport, especially sport for those with disabilities. As you read this chapter think only of "sport" and how different physical, sensory, and cognitive abilities can be summoned to help people participate in sport. Think about the similarities and not the differences between sport for those with and without disabilities, and remember that sport is sport.

This chapter provides the reader with an overview of the sporting world for people with disabilities. It also discusses the structure of disability sport in the United States and how sport for participants with disabilities is becoming more infused into the context of traditional sport; especially school-based programming and recreational settings.

Specifically, the chapter will help the reader understand (a) a general organizational paradigm within sport for people with disabilities; (b) classification within sport for participants with disabilities; (c) opportunities for involvement in sport for people with disabilities for young professionals in general, inclusive, and therapeutic recreation; and (d) ways to modify activities within a sport or game to promote inclusion. Common community-based recreational sports (e.g., basketball, soccer, volleyball, and softball) will be highlighted to share examples of modifications and inclusion strategies.

General Organizational Overview of Sports for People With Disabilities

On an international level, sport for people with disabilities from the United States is represented through the U.S. Olympic Committee (USOC)

and a newly formed suborganization called U.S. Paralympics. The prefix *para* means parallel or equal to, not paraplegic. All sports represented by U.S. Paralympics participate in the Paralympics, but not all national-level sporting organizations participate in the Paralympics.

National-level sporting organizations for people with disabilities are either disability or sport specific. For example, some organizations include a focus on disability in their title (e.g., United States Association of Blind Athletes [USABA]; USA Deaf Sports Federation [USADSF]) and some use a sport reference (e.g., National Wheelchair Basketball Association [NWBA], Special Olympics) to represent athletes with disabilities at the national level. For a detailed explanation of the national and international organizational structures for disability sport, visit these Web sites:

- www.usoc.org
- www.specialolympics.org
- www.paralympic.org
- www.ncpad.org
- www.usdeafsports.org

Paradigm Distinction Within Sports for People With Disabilities

In the United States, sport organizations for those with disabilities will likely fall into two general categories: Paralympic or non-Paralympic. Disability sporting organizations in the Paralympic category generally have as their goal to participate in highly competitive national and international events (e.g., national wheelchair rugby championships, Paralympics). Disability sporting organizations and events in the non-Paralympic category can be described as those representing recreational pursuits (i.e., North American Riding for the Handicapped Association, National Wheelchair Poolplayers Association, American Canoe Association) or interscholastic competition (Georgia Wheelchair Basketball Championship). Whether Paralympic or non-Paralympic, these sporting organizations offer opportunities for participants with amputations, blind or visual impairments, cerebral palsy, deafness, intellectual disabilities (formerly called mental retardation), and spinal cord injuries to engage in sport.

How a person with a disability progresses through her sport career from entry to exit, as a youth, an adolescent, and an adult, is an important paradigm to understand for students studying recreation. Not all sports for participants with disabilities are geared toward high levels of competition.

Two terms, *disability sport* and *adapted sport,* represent a relatively new paradigm shift in sports for people with disabilities. Understanding the distinction between these two terms is key to determining how you are involved in sport for people with disabilities.

Disability Sport

The term *disability sport* is used to describe sporting opportunities and organizations that move a participant from entry level to a high level of competition (national or international) with a strong competitive focus. These sporting organizations usually are considered community based and are not associated with interscholastic sports or school-based sport programs. Examples of traditional sports that are considered club sports are Junior Olympics Volleyball, travel soccer programs, and Amateur Athletic Union [AAU]. Perhaps the best example of a disability sport organization that promotes high-level competition and

could be considered a club sport is BlazeSports. This organization is community based, is funded through donations and fundraising, and strives to produce elite athletes who could compete at an elite level (e.g., Paralympics). BlazeSports has programs designed for lower levels of competition (novice and juniors), but historically has been linked to elite athlete development. Visit BlazeSports at www.blazesports.org to learn more about their programs.

Adapted Sport

The term *adapted sport* refers to sporting opportunities and organizations tied to educational systems. These sports are targeted to promote school-based competition or interscholastic events for participants with disabilities. Think of adapted sport as primarily school based with some emphasis in community-based programming. In school settings, adapted sport participants are considered student-athletes and earn awards from their individual schools or conferences (e.g., most valuable player, letter jackets, and state championships). Adapted sport allows for rule modifications of sports from the

Photo courtesy of Ronald Davis.

Disability sport organizations work within communities and to help athletes achieve an elite level of competition.

disability sport category. For example, wheelchair basketball is played in both disability sport and adapted sport. The rules of wheelchair basketball within disability sport programs (e.g., community based) are taken from the parent organization of the National Wheelchair Basketball Association (NWBA) and are seldom modified. The rules for wheelchair basketball within adapted sport programs (e.g., school based) are taken from the NWBA but are changed or modified to address players' functional and skill development. One of the most successful organizations in adapted sport is the American Association of Adapted Sports (AAASP). This organization began within the DeKalb public schools in Atlanta, Georgia. The AAASP program is infused within the traditional interscholastic athletics around the state of Georgia and is recognized by the Georgia High School Athletics Association. Examples of rule modifications within adapted sport for wheelchair basketball are found in player substitutions, player and team foul limits, playing time (e.g., all players are required to play at least two periods of a six-period game), and the absence of an athlete classification system. Because it has no classification system, AAASP allows the inclusion of players without disabilities on a team, which does not exist in a disability sport competition.

Other states have consulted with AAASP as they consider remodeling their high school athletic associations to include students with disabilities (e.g., Maryland, Alabama). For a more detailed understanding of AAASP, visit www.aaasp.org.

Classification in Sports for People With Disabilities

Within disability sport the most interesting and controversial entity is the use of athlete classification. Few traditional sports use athlete classification, the exceptions including weight classing within wrestling, boxing, and judo.

Athlete classification is targeted at the athlete, not the level of competition (e.g., high school, college, professional) or gender (male or female) or event distance (e.g., 100-meter race). Athlete classification requires an evaluation of the athlete prior to, during, or following competition to help determine an equal playing field among competitors.

There are two systems of athlete classification: medical and functional. Disability sport organizations use one or both classification systems to evaluate their athletes and establish competition schedules. The classification process is simple; the athlete enters a classification area, he is examined by a team of classifiers, results of the classification are recorded, the athlete leaves the classification area, and the results are sent to the competition director to establish lineups for team sports or heat or lane assignments (e.g., track and field or swimming).

Medical System

The medical system of classification is based on the athlete's condition or level of injury; the focus is on the disability. For example, athletes with visual impairments are evaluated on their visual acuity and field of vision, not how well they perform a movement (e.g., throw a javelin). As another example, athletes with amputations are evaluated on location and length of the residual limb (e.g., above or below elbow, AE or BE).

Functional System

In the functional classification system the athlete's disability (medical classification) and skill performance are combined and evaluated. For example, in swimming a functional classification system is used, so athletes in this sport are evaluated based on their medical condition and then asked to swim in the pool using the strokes required in their competition. A team of classifiers record the scores from the medical evaluations and then add their scores from the skill performance in the pool. The two parts of this classification session are added together to produce one score and thus one athlete classification for competition.

Several sports use a functional system (e.g., swimming, track and field, wheelchair rugby), which offers certain advantages and disadvantages. Advantages with the functional system are that (a) it is sport specific and awards training and preparation; (b) it allows the sport to offer cross-disability competition (e.g., those with cerebral palsy compete in the same race as those with spinal cord injury), because participation is based not on medical condition but on performance of skills; and (c) it reduces the number of heats, trials, and semifinal and final races. This system also reduces the administration and organization of competition, as exemplified in a track-and-field meet for those with disabilities. At the national and international level, track and field has approximately 44 classifications that are duplicated by gender for each event. Without the ability to offer cross-disability events, disability-specific events (e.g., all participants with spinal cord compete together, or all those with cerebral palsy compete together) would take a very long to time to complete.

One glaring disadvantage to functional classification is the possibility of cheating. In a functional system, many times the athletes are asked to move an arm or leg through its maximum range of motion. Given that task, the athlete could minimize her effort and decide to only move the arm or leg through a partial range of motion and attempt to fool the classifier. If this deception occurs and a more complete movement of the limbs is later identified by a classifier during competition, the athlete can be taken from the competition, reclassified, or disqualified. A reclassification would apply to the next scheduled competition, not the next event within the current competition.

Opportunities for Involvement of Recreation Leaders

There are two ways young professionals in recreation can get involved with disability sport: through coaching and training and by becoming a classifier.

BlazeSports conducts training camps for future athletes, workshops for coaches, and educational training for professionals, and has established a scientific research component. Certification for recreation professionals is not required to attend any of these training opportunities.

The AAASP offers certification for coaching in four sports: wheelchair football, basketball, team handball, and beep baseball for blind or visually impaired people. Professionals are required to complete a 2- or 3-day coaching clinic, pass a written rules test, and then demonstrate their ability to design and implement a practice plan. AAASP requires its coaches to have a state-approved coaching certification in a traditional sport.

Learning how to become a classifier is another opportunity for young professionals from recreation programs to contribute. As previously mentioned, classification is an evaluation process performed by a group of professionals from several backgrounds (e.g., adapted physical education, physical and occupation therapy, recreation). Students with training in recreation could use their assessment skills as members of

a classification team. Several sporting organizations sponsor classification workshops on how to become a certified classifier. Consider visiting the following Web sites to learn more about how to become a classifier for disability sport: www.ncpad.org, www.blazesports.org, www.usparalympics.org.

Modifying Activities Within Sport to Promote Inclusion

At the beginning of this chapter one simple phrase was used to keep you focused on the theme: sport is sport. No matter whether someone is running on a track while using an artificial leg, pushing a wheelchair on a basketball court, or hitting a pitched ball while blindfolded, you should see this as sport. Think about similarities and not differences; including athletes of all abilities in the same sporting event (those with and without disabilities) embraces the essence of sport.

The purpose of this chapter section is to show you the common ground between sport for those with and without disabilities by sharing a four-step process (Davis, 2002) and present two models for inclusion with a sport or game context, those developed by Kasser and Lytle (2005) and Morris and Stiehl (1999). Both models have similar approaches, which will allow you to choose the one that matches your individual needs.

Common Ground

Inclusion in sport is possible when leaders have a plan and understand how to implement their plan. One of the first steps in using sport to promote inclusion is to consider a systematic approach for including everyone in a sporting activity.

Davis (2002) recommended four steps in this approach:

- Determine the sport the person wants to play and then cross-reference that sport to one from sport for people with disabilities.
- Read and learn about the disability sport to include unique rules and performance skills.
- Make sure you can identify the functional level of all participants with disabilities you are considering for inclusion.
- Implement the game and make skill or rule modifications as needed.

Photo courtesy of Ronald Davis.

Sport is sport, no matter who is playing or what his abilities.

The first step, determine the sport and cross-reference, requires you to do a little homework. You will likely be involved with sports from a general recreation and community setting (e.g., basketball, soccer, volleyball, softball), all of which have a counterpart in sport for those with disabilities. A quick search through the Web sites suggested earlier will help you locate the sports of wheelchair basketball, wheelchair soccer, sitting volleyball, or beep baseball. Once you have read closely about these disability sports you will notice similar skills from the traditional game. Consider the information in table 11.1.

The second step is to learn about the specific rules and skills needed to play the disability sport. You will note a few unique rules specific to a disability sport, but you will also read that many of the same rules exist in traditional sport. The information in table 11.2 is a sample of key rules that have common ground between sport for participants with and without disabilities. Locate, study, and practice all of the rules specific to the sport for those with disabilities before playing the games. Once you

have experience playing a sport for people with disabilities, you will be better equipped to implement an inclusionary approach for these participants because you will know which skills that are needed for the game or activity require modifications.

The third step is to identify the functional level of participants with disabilities. Consider the information presented earlier in this chapter about classification. Each sport has its own classification system; however, learning the specifics of each classification system is beyond the scope of this chapter. Working with a therapeutic recreational specialist, an adapted physical educator, or another specialist, develop your own functional classification system using the information from the official sport system. It can be as easy as using three levels of performance, low, moderate, and high, and then attaching simple rubrics to each of those levels. Establishing your own classification system will help you consider the participant's capabilities first, before she begins the sport. Placing a person in an activity that is beyond her skill

Table 11.1 Skill Similarities Between Traditional and Disability Sports

	Traditional sport	Disability sport
Basketball compared with wheelchair basketball		
Passing (chest, bounce, baseball)	X	X
Dribbling (stationary, moving)	X	X
Shooting (free throw, field goals)	X	X
Soccer compared with wheelchair soccer		
Passing (stationary, moving)	X	X
Dribbling (stationary, moving)	X	X
Throw-ins	X	X
Volleyball compared with sitting volleyball		
Serve (underhand, overhand)	X	X
Passing (underhand, overhand)	X	X
Setting	X	X
Blocking	X	X
Softball compared with beep baseball		
Hitting	X	X
Fielding	X	X
Base Running	X	X

Adapted from Davis 2002.

Table 11.2 Rule Comparison Between Traditional and Disability Sports

	Traditional sport	Disability Sport
Basketball compared with wheelchair basketball		
Passing (chest, bounce, baseball)	All passing done with hands; pass can be made while player is moving or stationary.	Same as in traditional sport.
Dribbling (stationary, moving)	Traveling is prohibited (moving while in possession of the ball and not dribbling with each step).	Traveling: Players are allowed two touches to the hand rim of their wheelchair while in possession of the ball; after two pushes, players must pass, dribble, or shoot the ball.
Shooting (free throw, field goals)	Free throw shooting: feet must be behind the free throw line.	Free throw shooting: small wheels in front of wheelchair (casters) are allowed to be over the free throw line; larger rear wheels must remain behind the line.

(continued)

Table 11.2 *(continued)*

	Traditional sport	Disability Sport
Soccer compared with wheelchair soccer		
Passing (stationary, moving)	All passing done with the feet.	All passing done with the hands.
Dribbling (stationary, moving)	All dribbling done with feet.	Dribbling skills performed similar to basketball; however a player must pass, dribble, or shoot the ball within 3 seconds of possession; once they do so, a new 3-second period starts.
Throw-ins	Players use two-hand overhead throw, keeping both feet on ground and out of bounds.	Players use two-hand overhead throw, keeping all wheels behind the line.
Volleyball compared with sitting volleyball		
Serve (underhand, overhand)	Both feet remain behind the serving line.	Buttocks must stay behind serving line; legs may be inside on court.
Passing (underhand, overhand)	Pass can be made from on or off the court.	Player must remain seated on floor and cannot lift buttocks to gain advantage during play.
Setting	Players must have simultaneous contact with fingers as ball leaves both hands; feet can be off the floor during setting.	Player must remain seated on floor and cannot lift buttocks to gain advantage during play.
Blocking	Players cannot block oncoming serve.	Players are allowed to block at net during serve.
Softball compared with beep baseball		
Hitting	Pitcher and catcher are from fielding team.	Pitcher and catcher are from hitting team; both players are sighted.
Fielding	Players use gloves when throwing to bases for outs.	Gloves are optional; no throwing to bases for outs; fielding players record outs by gaining control of a hit ball and raising it up in the air.
Base running	Players must run all three bases and touch home plate to score a run.	Only two bases are used (first and third) and each has speakers mounted inside to elicit a noise; player hitting the ball must reach the beeping base before the fielding player secures ball; if this occurs, a run is scored.

development or functional performance will not help you implement a successful inclusive game. Consider the general suggestions for identifying functional profiles of people with disabilities presented in table 11.3.

The fourth step is to implement the game and practice the philosophy of placing the person with a disability in a decision-making role. Don't allow participants without disabilities to dominate the game by making all the game decisions. Consider all learning domains (e.g., psychomotor, cognitive, and affective) as you implement an inclusive game. As you learn more about game modifications and creating inclusive settings, psychomotor and cognitive adjustments will become easier to implement. For example, lowering a basket in basketball and playing with a lighter weight ball in volleyball are ideas to address psychomotor modifications and can follow a simple to complex task or motor progression. Allowing someone to move up and down the basketball court without having to dribble could be a rule modification (cognitive domain). Affective behavior is often overlooked when leaders attempt to include those with disabilities in a game or activity. Consider the information in table 11.4 when you address inclusion in a sport or game activity.

Table 11.3 Operationally Defined Functional Profiles for Players With Disabilities

Functional level	Person using a wheelchair	Person blind or visually impaired	Person with intellectual disabilities
Low	Multiple impairments; unable to manually propel a wheelchair; might use a power wheelchair	Total loss of vision; uses guide animal for independent movement; needs sighted guide for activity	IQ 50-55; minimal communication skills; motor coordination appears delayed; needs structured environments to attend to task; extensive support required; difficulty remembering rules during games
Moderate	Able to propel a wheelchair without assistance a short distance; has upper-body coordination and balance and strength to catch, throw, and strike	Able to determine light from dark; functions more independently; good orientation skills; able to move independently with minimal use of cane or sighted guide	IQ 55-70; good receptive and expressive language; fitness and motor performance appears closer to age level; limited support needed for activities of daily living
High	Able to propel a wheelchair independently for long distances; can move continuously for more than 15 min without stopping; able to perform upper-body skills of catching, throwing, and striking without assistance; demonstrates a high degree of functional range of motion	Has some travel vision; able to see using peripheral vision; visual acuity near 20/200; able to move independently and has excellent orientation skills	IQ 70-75; excellent receptive and expressive language; fitness and motor performance at age level; minimal support needed for activities of daily living; could be placed in general education classes with support from paraeducators

Adapted from Davis 2002.

Table 11.4 General Modifications to Promote Inclusion in a Sport or Game Activity

Learning domains and general sport	Person with physical impairment (wheelchair user)	Person with sensory impairment	Person with intellectual disability
Basketball			
Physical (psychomotor)	Passing: Use smaller ball. Shooting: Lower basket or suspend hoop from backboard and shoot through hoop.	Passing: Use ball with bell. Shooting: Designate shooting area with special tape or carpet squares.	Shooting: Create extra distance between defenders. Dribbling: Provide a peer teacher.
Cognitive	Dribbling: Recognize two-push rule limit when dribbling.	Passing: Don't require defense with passing. Dribbling: Require only one bounce per half-court.	Passing: No defense. Dribbling: Not required.
Behavioral (affective)	Allow IWD to recruit players for teams.	Designate IWD as free throw shooter for both teams.	Allow IWD to pick the team she wants to play on.

(continued)

Table 11.4 (continued)

Learning domains and general sport	Person with physical impairment (wheelchair user)	Person with sensory impairment	Person with intellectual disability
Soccer			
Physical (psychomotor)	Passing: Use smaller ball. Shooting: Place alternative goals on either side of official goal as goals for wheelchair user. Dribbling: Allow carrying; allow two-hand dribble.	Passing: Tether sighted player at wrist with shoestring; allow sighted player to stop incoming pass but require IWD to pass. Dribbling: Use ball with bells inside.	Passing: Use deflated ball until skill is developed. Shooting: Allow closer range to shoot at goal. Dribbling: Use ball with bells inside or brightly colored.
Cognitive	Passing: Allow more than 3 seconds before player has to relinquish the ball. Shooting: Don't allow full-court defense.	Passing and dribbling: Require players to keep at least 10 ft (3.5 m) away from IWD when in procession of ball.	Shooting: Require IWD to identify color of ball before shooting.
Behavioral (affective)	Have IWD suggest one modification to game.	Allow IWD to pick the name of the team.	Have IWD repeat the score throughout game.
Volleyball—All players on floor or sitting in wheelchairs			
Physical (psychomotor)	Passing: Use beach ball. All skills: Reduce size of court: 20 × 40 ft and 4 ft net height (6 × 12 m and 1.2 m net height).	Serving: Allow IWD to strike ball off a tee.	Passing: Use beach ball. Serving: Have players stand closer to net.
Cognitive	Passing: Allow ball to bounce once before returning to opponents.	Serving, passing: Allow IWD to catch and throw ball over net.	Rotation: Do not require IWD to rotate position on court.
Behavioral (affective)	Have IWD decide the starting rotations on the floor.	Ask IWD to decide the starting rotations on the floor.	Have IWD decide the starting rotations on the floor.
Softball			
Physical (psychomotor)	Hitting: Use a larger ball. Running: Place a designated area (painted circle) around base for wheelchair user to enter to avoid fielder contact.	Hitting: Use audio ball. Running: Hold guide rope to first base with other players.	Hitting: Allow striking from a batting tee (as needed). Running: Use color-coded bases (red, yellow, blue for first, second, and third base) to help with sequence.
Cognitive	Conduct game on a hard surface (not a grass field).	Allow striking from a batting tee. Require IWD to run only to first base (make noise at base to aid location).	Establish minimal number of pitches before allowing walk (e.g., eight pitches with an attempt to swing).
Behavioral (affective)	Require IWD to umpire one inning.	Have IWD decide the opposing pitcher every inning.	Allow IWD to determine batting order.

IWD = individual with disability.

Adapted from Block 2000 and Davis 2000.

Inclusion and Game Modification Models of FAMME and Game Design

The functional approach for modifying movement experiences (FAMME) developed by Kasser and Lytle (2005) and the game design model by Morris and Stiehl (1999) focus attention on the participant's capabilities, the environment for the activity, and the tasks within the activity. Both are deemed interactive approaches to promote inclusion or address game modification.

The FAMME model is a four-step process leading to inclusive activity. This is a player-centered approach that requires the leader to be familiar with the movement capabilities of the player with a disability.

- Step 1: Determine underlying components of the skills.
  - Consider components like eye–foot coordination for kicking, eye–hand coordination for striking, or strength and balance for shooting a basketball.
- Step 2: Determine the participant's capabilities.
  - Consider how the person will interact with her environment as she plays the game; capabilities are influenced by the person, task, and context of the game.
  - All three (person, task, and game context) are interactive, and changing one will affect the remaining components (e.g., use a lightweight ball in volleyball, and passing might become easier for the participant).
- Step 3: Match modification efforts to capabilities.
  - Make sure your modifications match the capabilities of the participant (e.g., using a ball that is too large or heavy will likely result in errant throws; striking with an object that is too long or heavy will result in missing).
  - Acquire the ability to task analyze the skill and break it down into its simplest components.
- Step 4: Evaluate modification effectiveness.
  - Evaluate your modifications for measures of success, safety, maximum participation, and optimal challenge.

Inclusive recreation makes allowances for the environment and equipment to be modified to match students' abilities.

As you move through the four steps of the FAMME model, use a simple to a complex progression within each step. Table 11.5 on page 204 presents suggestions, modified from Winnick (2005), for moving from simple to complex for a catching and striking activity.

Morris and Stiehl's (1999) game design model uses a three-step process focusing on the components of the game. The key to this model is that all components of a game are interactive; if you change one component it will affect other components. The three-step process for the game design model is (a) understand the structure of the game, (b) modify the basic structure, and (c) manage the game's degree of difficulty.

To understand the structure of a game you must recognize that all games have the following interactive components: purpose, players, movement, objects, organization, and limits. A successful game requires an agreement (mutual interaction) between the first two components: purpose and players.

The purpose of a game can be to develop motor skills, improve fitness, or develop cognitive skills. If the purpose of the game is not

Photo courtesy of Ronald Davis.

Table 11.5 Simple to Complex Progression

Skill	Element	Progression		
		Simple	Moderate	Complex
Catching a ball	Ball size	Large (12 in. [30 cm])	Medium (9 in. [23 cm])	Small (2-4 in. [5-10 cm])
	Distance	Close (2 ft [0.6 m])	Medium (6 ft [1.8 m])	Long (12-15 ft [3.6-4.5 m])
Hitting a ball	Ball size	Large (10 in. [25 cm]) on a tee	Medium (8 in. [20 cm]) tethered swinging	Small (4 in. [10 cm]) pitched
	Striking object	Hand	Plastic bat	Regulation bat

Adapted from Winnick 2005.

clearly defined, the interaction between player and purpose can negatively affect your game. For example, if the leader of the softball game thinks the purpose is to promote fitness by running the bases, but the players think that the purpose is to just score runs, the outcome of the game could be affected.

Different types of movement are used in games, and movement occurs at different locations, has different quality and quantity, and occurs in different sequences. The relationship of these components is critical to the individual's and group's success in the game. When you consider including participants with disabilities in your traditional game, movement abilities become very obvious. Consider the previous example of running in a softball game. People with cerebral palsy might be able to strike a ball from a batting tee in a functional manner, but running to first base could be another story. The player might take longer to reach first base and thus make an out, which might result in negative reaction from teammates. However, a negative reaction can be minimized if the leader clearly defines the purpose of the game for the person with cerebral palsy. If the purpose of the game for the participant with cerebral palsy is to promote fitness through running, then making an out may be acceptable by all players. Different movement abilities in a game can affect the purpose and players.

Objects in a sport or game can be recognized for how they are used. Objects can be moved around, under, over, or through; objects can also be used to move other objects away from your body (e.g., bat, racket). The number of objects used in a game or sport, and the location in the game where the objects are used, should be considered in your inclusion plan. If you consider including a participant with a disability who requires a batting tee, you have increased the number of objects needed to play the game. Although the location of use for the objects (bat and tee) will likely not change, quality of movement and safety will. Consider use, location, and quantity of objects in a sport or activity as you organize and establish your playing areas and rules of play for an inclusive activity.

All sport and games have an organizational pattern (e.g., diamond in softball, rows in soccer, zone in basketball). Each of these patterns dictates a distance or space to be established between players. Some distances between players are close and some are farther away. Think of the distance between an outfielder in softball and the catcher, compared with distance between the pitcher and catcher. Some people with disabilities have attention delays, and positioning them great distances from a source of instruction (e.g., a coach or recreation leader) could be detrimental to successful play. For example, a person with a mild intellectual disability may have a difficult time playing the outfield, especially during long innings, without frequent verbal prompts. Allowing this player to play an infield position may bring greater success. If this player does not have the physical skills to play the infield, perhaps a peer player can stand somewhere nearby in the outfield to help with prompts and cues. Such a modification would have to be established in the rules or what Morris and Stiehl refer to as *limits of the game.*

Here the component of organizational structure is affected by the players' abilities, resulting in change of limits or rules.

Limits of the game can also depend on the movement and participation that are acceptable. It might be acceptable to spit on your hands before grabbing a bat to hit in a softball game but not before serving a volleyball. Some participants with disabilities need a clear explanation of appropriate behaviors expected by players during games. People with intellectual disabilities are sometimes the brunt of jokes because they don't understand sarcasm, so the coach or recreation leader must clearly establish what is and is not acceptable behavior before play occurs. Consider how you will communicate rules and limits in your inclusion planning.

The second step in the game design model is to modify the basic structure of the game. As you just read, the game design model helps you identify game components (i.e., purpose, players, movement, objects, organization, and limits). Morris and Stiehl (1999) recommended modifying one component at a time when changing the structure of the game. Consider how the game design model could be applied to basketball, and then consider what might happen if you modified one component (see table 11.6).

Using table 11.6, consider what would happen if you change the movement component of a basketball game from running to walking; what happens to the other components? One change in the movement component could affect change in the rules and limits component, because more time will be needed to play a game and fewer points will be scored. Requiring all players to walk instead of run might affect how objects are used (e.g., the size of the court might have to be reduced). Notice the interaction of game components: Changing one component forces change in another.

The third step in the game design model is addressing the game's degree of difficulty. Managing a game's degree of difficulty challenges the leader to create modifications that satisfy all players. Much of the logic that goes into managing degree of difficulty uses the information presented earlier in the simple to complex process (see table 11.5).

Addressing the degree of difficulty is central to successful game or sport inclusion. If a player with a visual impairment wants to play traditional softball, several modifications of the degree of difficulty will be required to accommodate the player's abilities. Table 11.7 on page 206 shows how the components of a traditional softball game must be changed to accommodate a player with visual impairment. Including a player with a visual impairment requires that every category of the game be modified.

Table 11.6 Game Design for Traditional Basketball and Softball

Purpose	Players	Movement	Objects	Organization	Limits (rules)
To shoot the ball through the hoop and score points	Five players on a team	Running Jumping Throwing Catching	Basketball Backboard Hoop Court	Players in zone position	Traveling Shooting fouls[a]
To hit pitched ball into field, avoid fielders, run bases, and score runs	Nine players on the field	Running Hitting Throwing Catching Sliding	Softball Gloves Bases Bats	Players in diamond position as infielder or outfielders	Three strikes are out Three outs to inning Four balls to walk Ball thrown to base before runner touches is safe, if not out[a]

[a]Given the extensive rules for each sport, an abbreviated listing of limits (rules) is provided.

Table 11.7 Traditional Softball to Include Player With Visual Impairment

Purpose	Players	Movement	Objects	Organization	Limits
~~Hit pitched ball into field, avoid fielders, run bases, and score runs~~ To hit ball off a batting tee	Nine players on the field Sighted peer	Running Hitting Throwing ~~Catching~~ ~~Sliding~~	Softball Beeper ball[a] Gloves Bases Bats Batting tee[a]	Players in diamond position as infielder or outfielders Sighted peer needed in field	Three strikes are out Three outs to inning ~~Four balls to walk~~ ~~Ball thrown to base before runner touches is safe, if not out~~ Player must reach base before outfielder secures ball in play

Components with strikethrough were deleted from traditional softball rules.

[a]New equipment added.

Summary

This chapter provided an overview of sport for people with disabilities, discussed the use of athlete classification within sport for participants with disabilities, demonstrated a common ground between sport for people with and without disabilities, and provided inclusion ideas for activities and games from sport. After reading this chapter, you should recognize the similarities and not the differences between sport for participants with and without disabilities. Take the challenge to learn more about sports like wheelchair basketball, wheelchair soccer, and beep baseball or enroll in a coaching clinic for disability sports. Remember, sport is sport; using sport to include people with varying degrees of abilities is worthwhile. Promote sport for all.

Discussion Questions

1. Identify five steps you would take to establish an adapted sport program in your local community recreation centers.

2. If you wanted to start an adapted sports program in your recreation program, where would you buy the necessary equipment? Identify the names, manufacturers, and costs of the equipment and how you would order it.

3. What would be your rationale for establishing an integrated (those with and without disabilities) recreation program in your local community for soccer? Softball? Basketball?

4. Your local community recreation program has $5,000 in grants to address adapted recreation; write a proposal for using this money to start a wheelchair tennis program.

Christine Stopka

If I can do this; I can do anything!
—Disabled Sports USA

Photo courtesy of Christine Stopka.

Background Information

Education BS, PhD, MEd, University of Virginia

Credentials

*CTRS *CPRP *ATC *LAT *CSCS *CAPE *MTAA

Special Awards

*John K. Williams Adapted Aquatics Award, International Swimming Hall of Fame (May 2008) *Charles S. Williams Service Award, College of Health and Human Performance (April 2008) *University of Florida Teacher of the Year Award (April 2008) *College of Health & Human Performance Teacher of the Year Award (December 2007) *William A. Hillman Distinguished Service Award from the National Consortium on Physical Education and Recreation for Individuals with Disabilities (2007) *Athletic Training Service Award from the National Athletic Trainers' Association (2007) *Florida-AHPERD (FAHPERD) Educator of the Year (state) Award, University Division (1999) *University of Florida Superior Accomplishment Award, University Winner of Faculty Division (1999) *University of Florida President's Humanitarian Award, University Winner of Faculty Division (1998) *Teacher of the Year Award, College of Health & Human Performance (1998) *Teacher of the Year Award, Department of Exercise & Sport Sciences (1998) *Athletic Trainer of the Year Award, Athletic Trainers' Association of Florida, State's First Winner (1993) *Mabel Lee Award (national) for Outstanding Young Professional in AAHPERD (1989) *Taylor Dodson Award for Leadership, Southern District AAHPERD (1985)

Special Affiliations

*NCPERID *NATA *NSCA

Career Information

Position Professor, University of Florida

Job Description Teaching, research, and service

What I Like About My Job Teaching, research, and service

Career Ladder This is what I do best: teaching, research, and service. I am doing what I should be doing.

Advice to Undergraduate Students Be passionate about what you are learning and what you want to do; this will give you the motivation to do what needs to be done and your enthusiasm will be contagious to your participants. All of you together will change the world for the better.

Personal Statement I work to empower my participants to believe that they can empower others to believe: "If I can do this; I can do anything!" And, indeed, they succeed at doing just that!

Inclusive Recreation, Fitness, and Physical Activity

Sheila Swann-Guerrero, CTRS

University of Illinois at Chicago

Amy Rauworth, MS, RCEP

University of Illinois at Chicago

" A community that excludes even one of its members is no community at all. "

–Dan Wilkins

» Learning Outcomes

After completing this chapter, learners will be able to do the following:

- Understand the importance of inclusive fitness.
- Identify barriers to participation in physical activity.
- Know how to use the International Classification of Functioning, Disability and Health (ICF) to tailor health promotion programs.
- Understand the considerations for disabilities in relation to fitness.

Physical activity is a central component of a healthful lifestyle. All people need some form of activity for their well-being. This is especially important for the 54 million people with disabilities who report lower levels of physical activity participation, are more likely to experience chronic conditions, and are at greater risk for developing secondary conditions than persons without disabilities (Rimmer & Wang, 2005). Data from a recent report published in *Morbidity and Mortality Weekly Report (MMWR)* indicate that approximately twice as many adults with disabilities (25.6%) were physically inactive during the preceding week compared with adults without disabilities (12.8%; CDC, 2007). This finding is consistent with other studies that have reported significantly lower rates of physical activity among people with disabilities compared with people without disabilities (Boslaugh & Andresen, 2006; McGuire et al., 2007). Females report being less active than males and members of minority groups, specifically African Americans and Latinos, as do people of low socioeconomic status. Older people also report having difficulties with physical activity. Approximately 16.5% of American adults age 55 to 64 report difficulty walking a quarter mile, which increases to more than 55% of adults age 85 and older (U.S. Department of Health & Human Services [USDHHS], n.d.).

Given that health promotion initiatives seldom target improving the health of people with disabilities, the low activity status of these people is of concern. Many wellness and health promotion efforts have focused on preventing disabilities rather than promoting a physically active lifestyle for people with disabilities. Additionally, these initiatives often are aimed at the general population, such as the Steps to a Healthier US Initiative, promoted by the U.S. Department of Health & Human Services (USDHHS) to encourage people to walk 10,000 steps a day, yet recommendations for the general population cannot be assumed to apply to people with disabilities. Therefore, a great opportunity exists for recreation and fitness professionals to improve the lives of people with disabilities by providing inclusive fitness services for people with and without disabilities that will empower all people to become healthier and more active.

This chapter begins with an overview of the importance of inclusive fitness and physical activity and explores the definition of disability. It then outlines the barriers to participation,

motivational strategies, and considerations for assisting people with and without disabilities within a recreation or fitness environment. This is followed by a review of exercise basics for people with disabilities, including general guidelines for cardiovascular, flexibility, and strength training. The chapter then discusses strategies for developing fitness programs and creating inclusive accessible environments that promote increased participation. It concludes with resources regarding physical activity, fitness, disability, and inclusion.

Physical Activity and Inclusive Fitness

Engaging in physical activity can improve health and quality of life while reducing the risk of hypertension, diabetes, obesity, asthma, and other serious health problems, including psychological disorders, such as depression (USDHHS, 2000). The U.S. Surgeon General recommends that people participate in at least 30 minutes of moderate-intensity activity 5 days per week or 20 minutes of vigorous activity 3 days per week (USDHHS, 2000). The U.S. Department of Health & Human Services has developed guidelines for physical activity. The *2008 Physical Activity Guidelines for Americans* (USDHHS, 2008) recommend 150 minutes of moderate-intensity activity per week, or 75 minutes of vigorous activity per week, or an equivalent combination of moderate and vigorous physical activity. Increasing to 300 minutes or 5 hours a week of moderate-intensity aerobic physical activity or 2 hours and 30 minutes a week of vigorous physical activity can provide additional health benefits. Increased fitness is becoming increasingly important for all Americans, including people with disabilities. Obesity in the United States has increased dramatically over the past few decades, reaching a critical level and requiring immediate attention (Benson & Marano, 1996; Koplan et al., 2005; Weilet et al., 2002; Wyatt et al., 2006). Results of data from the 1994-1995 National Health Interview Survey (NHIS), the 1994-1995 Disability Supplement (NHIS-D), and the 1995 *Healthy People 2000 Supplement* indicate that there was a 66% higher rate of obesity among adults with physical disabilities compared with people without disabilities. A recent study found that persons with disabilities, regardless of sex, race and ethnicity, or age, had significantly higher rates of overweight, obesity, and extreme obesity compared with the general population (Rimmer & Wang, 2005). Extreme obesity, determined by a body mass index (BMI) greater than 40, was approximately four times higher among persons with disabilities compared with the general population.

There is compelling evidence that moderate levels of physical activity on most days of the week are associated with significant health benefits and an impressive reduction in health risks over the life span. Health promotion efforts targeting people with disabilities, a vulnerable, at-risk population, typically have not focused on developing key health behaviors related to physical activity. A growing body of data suggests that effective health promotion efforts to increase physical activity among people with disabilities could result in significant benefits in health status and quality of life for people with disabilities. This outcome can provide societal benefits in the form of reduced demand on the health care system and a reduction in overall health care costs for this population (Ravesloot et al., 2005).

Participation in physical activity can greatly improve the health of people with disabilities because of the reduction of secondary conditions (CDC, 2006b; USDHHS, 2005). Public policy experts recognize that prevention of secondary conditions is a critical issue among people with disabilities. However, disparities in physical activity levels clearly exist between people with and without disabilities. This is evident in *Healthy People 2010* (see table 12.1), which reports that 56% of people with disabilities do not participate in leisure-time physical activity, compared with 36% of people without disabilities. Intensity of exercise reported is also quite different for people with disabilities compared with people without

disabilities. Only 13% of people with disabilities reported participating in activities identified as vigorous, with a duration of 20 minutes and frequency of three times per week, compared with 25% of people without disabilities. Inactivity levels have also been connected to the severity of disability and to decreased involvement in community activities (Rimmer, 2005a). The reduction of physical independence can be directly associated with low physical fitness, in combination with impairments (i.e., loss of function, spasticity) and secondary conditions associated with the disability. This can limit opportunities to participate in many community events that require moderate to high levels of energy expenditure (e.g., pushing a wheelchair up a ramp or curb), thereby increasing social isolation (CDC, 2006a; Rimmer, 2005b). Physical activity can provide people with disabilities the strength and stamina required to participate in all aspects of life actively and successfully.

Let's define *secondary conditions* in the context of health promotion activities. A secondary condition, as defined in *Healthy People 2010* (chapter 6, Disability and Secondary Conditions), is "a medical, social, emotional, family, or community problem that a person with a primary disabling condition likely experiences" (USDHHS, n.d.). This broad definition of secondary conditions considers the physiological, psychological, and environmental barriers that affect the health of people with disabilities and is helpful in understanding why people with disabilities are more likely to be inactive, develop secondary conditions, and have difficulty meeting daily activity requirements for improved health. To reduce secondary conditions resulting from

Table 12.1 *Healthy People 2010* Physical Activity and Fitness (Values Are Percentages)

	Female	Male	Latino	African American	White	With disabilities	Without disabilities	Healthy People 2010 target
No leisure-time physical activity	43	36	54	52	36	56	36	20
30 min of moderate physical activity ≥5 days per week	13	16	15	10	16	12	16	30
20 min of vigorous physical activity ≥3 days per week	20	26	16	17	25	13	25	30

From http://www.healthypeople.gov

inactivity, recreation and fitness professionals need to increase access to fitness and recreation for all members of the community.

The National Center on Physical Activity and Disability (NCPAD), in collaboration with the American College of Sports Medicine (ACSM), founded the Inclusive Fitness Coalition (www. incfit.org) in January 2007 to make changes in the fitness industry. The coalition addresses policy, environmental, and societal issues associated with the lack of inclusion and access to physical activity among people with disabilities. NCPAD and ACSM are combining with a variety of organizations to create a united effort to make fitness inclusive.

An inclusive community must include fitness for all members. Inclusive fitness gives people the right to participate in any form of health-enhancing activity. Inclusive fitness is not merely a movement to include people with disabilities in a program but rather is a value shared by all participants and the entire community to ensure that fitness services include all members of society. Inclusive fitness involves reaching out to people with disabilities who live in the community but are seldom seen in recreation centers, fitness facilities, and health clubs. It means empowering people with and without disabilities to maintain an optimal level of health by leading physically active lifestyles.

Community members must take an active role to make inclusive fitness a reality as must people with disabilities, who need to be their own self-advocates. Self-advocacy is an important ingredient for the empowerment of people with disabilities. Although access and equal opportunities are central to the Americans with Disabilities Act, people with disabilities continue to struggle for equal rights, including the right to fully participate in fitness opportunities. Being a self-advocate requires people to educate the public about their rights to enjoy successful participation in the community. Self-advocacy also requires that a person understand her disability and be able to clearly communicate what she needs to fully participate in fitness and recreational pursuits (NCPAD, 2006). Self-advocacy means taking charge and making choices that will contribute to vitality and well-being for the enrichment of one's life. These values are expressed in the following comment by the National Recreation and Park Association (NRPA): "Access to recreation sites and programs for people with disabilities contributes to self-confidence, functional ability, independence, and vocational skills."

Defining Disability to Promote Inclusive Fitness

In this section we don't repeat the definitions of disability given earlier in this textbook but rather inform the reader of the approach used to frame this chapter. Promoting physical activity to people with disabilities begins with understanding what disability is and how it may affect successful participation. This may appear to be a simple question with a straightforward answer, yet it is not, because there is no single definition of disability. Disability is defined according to the reason for and source of the definition (Albrecht et al., 2001). Sources include the U.S. Social Security Administration, which defines disability according to gainful employment; the Americans with Disabilities Act (ADA), which defines a person with a disability as one who "has a physical or mental impairment that substantially limits one or more major life activities, a person who has a history or record of such an impairment, or a person who is perceived by others as having such an impairment" to public health; and the World Health Organization, which says that impairment "can be considered any loss or abnormality of bodily function, including physiological, psychological, or anatomical" (p. 27) and which established the International Classification of Functioning, Disability and Health (ICF) to define disability in terms of functional levels. Although definitions vary with sources, clinical definitions of disability, which are associated with medical services, are more commonly known by the general population, and have had the greatest impact on how disability is perceived. This perspective has imposed a specific view of and stigma to disability. The result has generally been a pathological classification of disability with an intention to correct or prevent it.

A very different approach, which considers health, functioning, and social constructs and promotes the inclusion of people with disabilities into society, is the social model of disability. The social model defines disability using the Disabled Person's International definition as the loss or limitation of opportunities to take part in the normal life of the community on an equal level with others due to physical and social barriers (Albrecht, 2001). This model considers a wider spectrum of factors that may limit the participation of people with disabilities in recreation and fitness. It also provides the framework for addressing solutions to these limitations. We use this model because it clearly views the magnitude of a disability in relation to the person's interaction with societal attitudes and the environment. Designing fitness and recreation services based on this premise allows a more tailored approach to program design and, as a result, a greater likelihood of successful adoption and adherence.

Physical Activity Participation and Barriers

For decades, U.S. federal disability rights legislation, such as the Architectural Barriers Act of 1968, Section 504 of the Rehabilitation Act, and the ADA, has mandated equal rights, yet people with disabilities continue to experience significant barriers that limit their involvement in health-promoting opportunities. People with disabilities experience more physical, social, and attitudinal barriers that prevent their participation in work, leisure, and social activities beyond those experienced by the general population. Recent research suggests that people with disabilities are often confronted with so many barriers to participating in the types of physical and recreational activities needed to maintain their health and well-being that they deem such pursuits to be unworthy of the effort involved (Rimmer, 2005a; Scelza et al., 2005). Applying the social model as described in the previous section helps us understand how barriers truly limit community participation. Factors such as pain, fatigue, and deconditioning often significantly affect the ability (and desire) to exercise for persons with disabilities. According to the social model, recreation and fitness professionals have an essential role and responsibility in integrating people with disabilities into society. These professionals can help to eliminate the socially created problems (barriers) that cause disability.

Barriers specific to participation in physical activity for people with disabilities can include inaccessible recreation and fitness environments, lack of knowledge and training on the part of fitness professionals, inadequate supervision, unfriendly or unwelcoming environments, cost of services, transportation, and physical limitations of disability (Rimmer et al., 2004). These barriers reduce the likelihood that people with disabilities will join physical activity programs and adhere to the recommendations of activity leaders. The result is a decline in physical function and a cycle of deconditioning, which produces greater inactivity, further physical decline, and an increase in the number or severity of sec-

ondary conditions. Recreation and leisure professionals' understanding of legislation, awareness of barriers, and commitment to ensuring full and meaningful participation of people with disabilities in the daily operation of fitness facilities and programs can stop this negative cycle and make inclusive fitness a reality.

Using the social model of disability, consider the impact that barriers identified as architectural, attitudinal, and programmatic can have on physical activity. Here are some examples that illustrate how the physical environment or programmatic resources (and not the disability) can be barriers to good health practices. If a person who uses a wheelchair cannot access the cardiovascular equipment on the second floor of the facility because there is no elevator, the primary barrier is not the disability or use of a wheelchair but rather the design of the building. If a fitness facility offers only exercise equipment that uses braille to operate the functions with directional signage, and brochures are only produced in braille to describe the facility layout or program offerings, people who cannot read braille are at a disadvantage. This disadvantage is due to the facility's imposing only one form of communication. If a fitness center provides alternative forms of instructions, printed materials, and signage, the disability (or lack of understanding braille) is no longer the primary barrier to improving health. Eliminating certain programmatic and environmental obstacles greatly enhances health promotion efforts for people with disabilities.

A common barrier is the attitude of recreation and fitness professionals. Feeling welcome in a fitness facility and being treated equally affect a person's perception of the facility and can motivate or encourage a person with a disability to return (or not return) to that facility. People with disabilities often report that negative attitudes are significant barriers to being physically active (Heward, 2000). This includes the attitudes of both facility staff and participants. Promoting accepting attitudes toward people with disabilities requires increased awareness of disability-related issues among recreation professionals and acceptance of varying levels of abilities between participants. Designing recreation programs that address aspects other than disability-specific criteria can enhance health promotion practices. This is a crucial step in developing inclusive fitness opportunities. For a better understanding of the major categories of barriers and their definitions, see table 12.2 on page 214.

Table 12.2 Major Categories of Barriers and Facilitators and Their Definitions

Category	Definition
Built and natural environment	Barriers or facilitators relating directly to aspects of the built or natural environment
Cost, economics	Barriers or facilitators relating to the cost of participating in recreation and fitness activities or costs associated with making facilities accessible
Equipment	Accessibility of exercise and recreation equipment
Guidelines, codes, regulations, and laws	Issues related to the use and interpretation of laws and regulations concerning accessibility of information, particularly building codes and the ADA
Information	Access of information both within the facility (e.g., signs, brochures) and in facility brochures and advertisements
Emotional and psychological	Physical, emotional, or psychological barriers to participation in fitness and recreation activities among persons with disabilities
Knowledge, education, and training	Barriers and facilitators regarding the education and training of professionals in the areas of accessibility and appropriate interactions involving people with disabilities
Perceptions and attitudes	Perceptions and attitudes of both professionals and nondisabled people about accessibility and persons with disabilities
Policies and procedures	Barriers imposed by the implementation of facility or community-level rules or regulations
Resource availability	Needed resources that would allow persons with disabilities to participate in fitness and recreation activities, including transportation and adaptive equipment

From ADA, Americans With Disabilities Act

The ADA, under Title III, ensures that both publicly and privately owned fitness and recreation facilities in the United States are architecturally accessible to people with disabilities in areas such as parking, access routes, and restrooms (U.S. 101st Congress. Americans with Disabilities Act, 1990), although research has demonstrated that many U.S. facilities do not meet ADA standards in these common areas (Cardinal & Spaziani, 2003; Nary et al., 2000; Rimmer, 2005a). Areas often found in recreation facilities that are not covered by the ADA include locker rooms, exercise equipment, and swimming pools. To address these areas, in 2002 the U.S. Architectural and Transportation Barriers Compliance Board (now the U.S. Access Board) created guidelines for recreation facilities (National Archives and Records Administration, 2002). These guidelines are currently under review by the U.S. Department of Justice and, once adopted, will be become standards that all facilities must follow. The guidelines presented by the U.S. Access Board are "minimums," and recreation professionals are encouraged to exceed the guidelines whenever possible. For example, architecturally accessible centers are only as useful as the accessible equipment that is contained in them. What good is an accessible door if you cannot exercise once you get into the center?

Recreation professionals must be proactive in the evaluation of their facilities to determine what changes need to be made and whenever possible should include people with disabilities in the process. Many alterations require little or no cost and can greatly improve the services provided to all participants. According to Ron Mace, founder and former program director of the Center for Universal Design, universal design is the design of products and environments to be usable by all people, to the greatest extent possible, without the need for adaptation or specialized design (National Center on Physical Activity and Disability, 2008). In other words, inclusive design should not even be noticed but rather should be incorporated into the existing environment or structure. A good example of this is the provision of a unisex changing room that provides a private area for a person with a disability who has a personal assistant of the opposite sex or who prefers not to change in a public area. A unisex changing room is also helpful for parents with small children or parents with multiple children of the opposite sex. Other examples of universal design are selecting exercise equipment that has wide seats, which are easier to use for people with limited balance or those with a large body mass index, and choosing equipment that can readily be used for people of short stature. Universal design recognizes that we have an obligation to optimize use for everybody.

Changes to the physical environment can dramatically influence health promotion behavior. Characteristics of the human-made or built environment can either encourage or discourage participation in moderate physical activity (Handy et al., 2002). Many factors that affect the accessibility of a facility go beyond the built environment and include equipment, information, staff training, and policies and procedures (Rimmer, 2005a). To view 24 key changes that can be made at little or no cost, see the before-and-after fitness center makeover, provided by the National Center on Physical Activity and Disability, in figure 12.1.

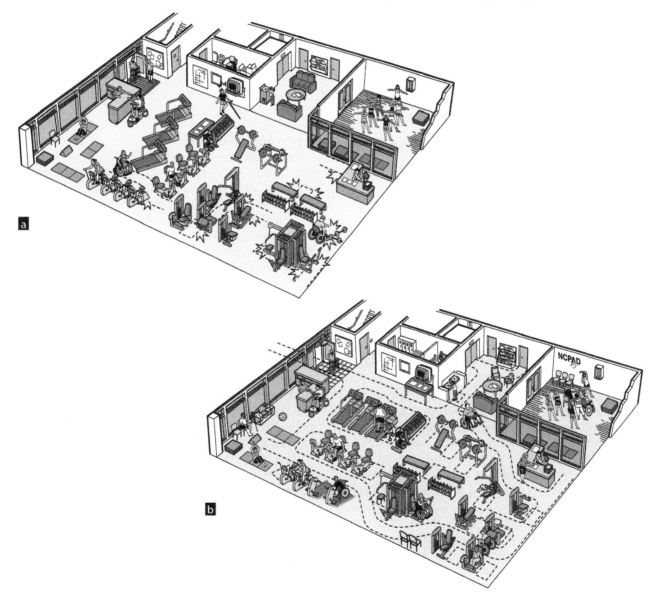

Figure 12.1 *(a)* Before the fitness center makeover and *(b)* after the makeover, with access for all.
Reprinted, by permission, from NCPAD.

Body functions are the physiological functions of body systems (including psychological functions).

Body structures are anatomical parts of the body such as organs, limbs, and their components.

Impairments are problems in body function or structure such as a significant deviation or loss.

Activity is the execution of a task or action by an individual.

Participation is involvement in a life situation.

Activity limitations are difficulties a person may have in executing activities.

Participation restrictions are problems a person may experience in involvement in life situations.

Environmental factors make up the physical, social, and attitudinal environments in which people live and conduct their lives.

Components

Part 1. Functioning and disability

    a. Body functions and structures

    b. Activities and participation

Part 2. Contextual factors

    a. Environmental factors

    b. Personal factors[a]

[a]Not classified in ICF but included in this figure to show contribution and impact.

Reprinted, by permission, from World Health Organization, 2001, *International classification of functioning, disability and health* (Geneva: World Health Organization).

Strategies for Developing Fitness Programs

To design appropriate and successful fitness programs for people with disabilities, we must understand the underlying concept of health promotion and use this concept to tailor the approach for the person. The Ottawa Charter for Health Promotion (1986) offers the most widely accepted definition of *health promotion:* "the process of enabling people to increase control over, and to improve, their health." The important components of health addressed in this definition are empowerment and self-determination. In this context, health is no longer defined as the absence of disease. Because fitness programs are important parts of health promotion, fitness and recreation leaders should tailor health promotion programs to meet individual needs. Disability is only one component of a person's health and should not be the basis on which any relationship is formed but rather a characteristic that is taken into account.

The International Classification of Functioning, Disability, and Health (ICF) provides a framework for the description of health and health-related states and has, over the years, moved from using the medical model to the social model as its premise. The ICF now focuses on "components of health," which provides a background for designing individualized health promotion services based on abilities, not disabilities, to provide optimal health benefits for all (World Health Organization, 2002).

Using the ICF to prepare individualized exercise prescriptions for people with disabilities, recreation professionals can be creative and consider all factors that will contribute to the success of an exercise program. The ICF model not only allows the fitness professional to tailor the program to the needs of the participant but also gives a broader scope and depth to the measure of functional improvements that are an outcome of successful fitness programming. Professionals can use the ICF to identify facilitators of or barriers to physical activity participation, including the participant's level of functioning and other personal factors and environmental factors that are critical to successful adherence.

The ICF provides a comprehensive framework for assessing the relationships among a participant's level of function, activities, and participation while also considering environmental and personal factors that influence the participant's overall health (WHO, 2001). According to the World Health Organization, the overall aim of the ICF is to provide a unified and standard language and framework for the description of health and health-related states. The ICF defines components of health and some health-related components of well-being (such as education and labor). The domains contained in ICF can be seen as health domains and health-related domains (see ICF structure and components sidebar). These domains are described from the perspective of the body, the person, and society in two main categories: (1) body functions and structures (system level) and (2) activities and participation (person level and person–environment interaction). The ICF can be used as a tool in program design to conduct a needs assessment or as an outcome evaluation. The ICF emphasizes function, not the health condition, and categorizes the situation, not the person. Figure 12.2 (see page 218) demonstrates the application of the ICF model for a person who has survived a stroke.

Fostering Motivation

Programs that promote physical activity, healthy eating, and other healthful lifestyle behaviors are not always accepted by people with and without disabilities. Recreation professionals should empower and engage participants to set the agenda for change and, in doing so, allow the people to work through any ambivalence to change and explore self-identified strategies for overcoming barriers. An approach that can assist in this process is motivational interviewing (MI). According to its founders William Miller and Stephen Rollnick, MI is a direct, client-centered approach for eliciting behavior change by helping clients explore and resolve ambivalence. This counseling style includes using reflective listening, setting agendas, eliciting self-motivational statements and change talk, and rolling with resistance (Miller et al., 2002). The effectiveness of MI has been documented in numerous randomized trials. MI has been most effective for people who initially are not ready to change their behavior. The principle of MI is the association of successful behavior change with *motivation*, not *information*. Typical public health messaging often focuses on the risk of the continued behavior, sometimes seen as a scare tactic. For example, the popular smoking commercials that associated smoking with death through the visualization of body bags were meant to shock people into realizing that smoking is a deadly habit. MI provides a nonjudgmental environment in which people can openly discuss the positive and negative aspects of changing or not changing their behavior. Clients are encouraged to express their own opinions and develop plans, and it has been found that people are more likely to accept and take action on ideas that are generated through self-discovery. For more information on MI, visit the Web site at www.motivationalinterview.org.

Considerations for Assisting People With Disabilities

Learning how to work with people who have disabilities will eliminate key barriers, as stated previously, which in turn will increase participation in recreation and fitness programs. The more professionals learn about disability, the more they will transform the field of health promotion. Education and experience are major factors in a client's choice of fitness professionals. However, many recreation and fitness professionals receive very little training, if any, in exercise prescription for people with disabilities, whether in formal degree-seeking programs or otherwise, and those who do often use their own personal initiative to seek out the training or information. The lack of knowledge concerning how to work with people who have physical, intellectual, and sensory disabilities is very troubling and poses a major barrier to these clients' participation in community-based fitness programs. This section provides considerations on how to work with people who have disabilities and chronic conditions.

Important skills in developing successful relationships with people who have disabilities include communication, etiquette, and behavior that reflect a conscious and appropriate approach to a situation. These skills are extremely useful in finding and addressing issues, barriers, and limitations, such as effects on activities of daily living (ADLs), reasonable accommodations, and time involvement for task completion. Being aware of communication techniques and aids that may assist in conveying or receiving messages, knowing how to gather information appropriately, and being willing to seek additional resources to assist with these skills will aid professionals in providing optimal service for clients. One critical tool in effective and appropriate communication with persons with disabilities is the use of person-first language.

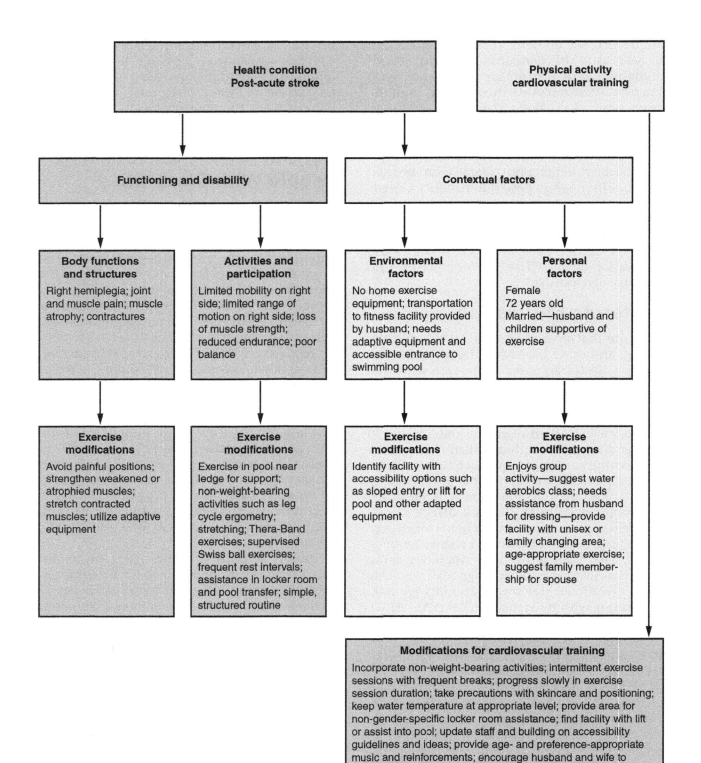

Figure 12.2 An example of how a fitness professional can apply the ICF model for an person who has survived a stroke.

Reprinted, by permission, from NCPAD. Available: http://www.ncpad.org/fitt/fact_sheet.php?sheet=459&section=2451

As described in chapter 8, here are some tips to consider when using person-first language:

- Positive language empowers: When working with or speaking about persons with disabilities or chronic conditions, put the person first. The disability or condition is just a medical diagnosis. It does not define the person!
- Maintain natural language when speaking to persons with disabilities, and to refer to them in the same multidimensional fashion as you would anyone.
- Specify the disability instead of using words such as *abnormal,* which implies a failure.

Here are some tips for interacting and providing services for people with disabilities:

- Always treat people with disabilities or chronic conditions with the same respect as you do anyone else.
- Let the person make his own decisions about what he can and cannot do.
- Be protective but not overprotective.
- Relax; be yourself.
- Speak directly to the person, not the attendant or interpreter.
- Follow the person's cues. Offer assistance, but wait for acceptance before assisting.
- Allow the participant extra time if necessary to perform a task or exercise.
- Establish open communication about abilities and limitations.
- Do not be afraid to ask questions, and ask respectfully. Most people would rather answer a question about protocol than be in an uncomfortable situation.
- Do not be afraid to shake hands if the person appears to have little grasping ability.
- Do not mistake a person's disability for a serious disease or illness. Do not assume a person with a disability is unhealthy!
- Do not assume additional disabilities because of the presence of one.
- Consult with others when you need information on a specific condition. Information sharing is vital!
- Use the same established policies for health forms, membership, and waivers.
- Respect your clients' assistive devices (canes, wheelchairs, crutches, communication boards) as their personal property. Unless given specific and explicit permission, do not move, play with, or use these devices.

The interactions between program staff and people with disabilities have a significant impact on their participation. In fact, negative attitudes and behavior of people without disabilities, both facility staff and participants, are the reasons cited most frequently by persons with disabilities for their hesitation to use fitness and recreation facilities (Rimmer et al., 2004). Research has shown that communication priorities for persons with disabilities include continuity of staff, communication skills, and trust (Murphy, 2006). These issues can be easily and inexpensively addressed through disability awareness training for staff. Staff development and training are necessities in building inclusive fitness and physical activity programs (Dickens-Smith, 1995). Educating professionals on how to interact with people of all abilities can create friendly and supportive environments that motivate people to be active. When facility staff are comfortable interacting with people with disabilities, staff are then in a position to educate their clients without disabilities on how to naturally interact with people with various abilities. The outcome will be a welcoming facility that promotes healthy lifestyles and overall wellness or, in short, inclusive fitness. Please refer to table 12.3 on page 220 for considerations regarding various disabilities.

Here are some tips on gathering information about your clients' and their needs:

- Prior to the discussion, learn about the client's disability as well as any secondary conditions that may affect her goals and activities.
- Use interview techniques and etiquette that help your client feel comfortable.
- Speak to the person throughout the interview, explaining exactly what will happen before touching the person, as well as why information is needed to develop an understanding of their needs.
- Seek specific information. For example, "Do you need adaptive equipment to participate in soccer? If so, what?"
- Use a variety of communication styles including nonverbal communication strategies, such as pictures or activity flash cards.

Table 12.3 Considerations for Persons With Disabilities

Specific disability	Considerations
Blindness or visual impairment	• Visual disabilities vary greatly from partial sight to total blindness. • When communicating, speak in a normal tone of voice when you approach the person and state your name (even if he knows you). • When introducing someone to a new environment or activity, ask him how he would like to be oriented to the environment. • Never touch or distract a service dog without first asking the client. • Do not attempt to lead the client without first asking; use a sighted guide and allow the client to hold your arm and control her own movements. • Be descriptive and detailed when giving directions. • When seating, gently place the client's hand on the back or arm of the chair so that he can locate the seat. • Tell the person when you are leaving.
Cognitive disability	• Some types of cognitive disabilities are not easily noticeable, such as learning disabilities and intellectual disabilities. They affect a person's ability to process information and may cause difficulty with memory or explaining one's needs. • Assistance may be needed to complete forms or understand written instructions. Provide extra time for decision making. Wait for the individual to accept the offer of assistance; do not "overassist" or patronize. • Be prepared to repeat steps to an activity several times if needed. Model activities or exercises whenever possible. • When giving instructions, give one or two steps at a time and ensure that each step is specific. Ask questions that require brief answers, such as yes or no. • If you are in an area with many distractions, consider moving to a quiet or private location. • Do not speak to an adult as if she were a child. Engage her in activities that are age appropriate. • Be aware that individuals with cognitive disabilities may indicate that they understand a task when they really have not grasped the presented information because they may want to please others.
Deafness or hard of hearing	• Levels of hearing loss will vary. Learn the person's preferred method of communication. • Do not assume that everyone with hearing loss can read lips. • When communicating, gain attention first before starting the conversation (i.e., tap the client gently on the shoulder or arm). • Look directly at the individual, face the light, speak clearly and in a normal tone of voice, and keep your hands away from your face. Use short, simple sentences. • If an interpreter is present, speak directly to the individual and not the interpreter. • If you do not have a Text Telephone (TTY), dial 711 to reach the national telecommunications relay service, which facilitates the call between you and the client who uses a TTY.
Mobility disability	• Each disability entails a wide range of mobility disabilities and spectrums. Assess and be aware of the person's ability level. • Position yourself at the wheelchair user's eye level. • Do not assume the client needs assistance with pushing her wheelchair. Ask first. • Offer assistance if the individual appears to be having difficulty opening the door.
Speech disability	• Do not assume that a person with a speech impairment also has a cognitive impairment. Persons with only speech disabilities have normal cognitive functioning. • Be patient; the person may take extra time to communicate. • Do not pretend if you do not understand the individual. Ask the client to repeat what he said, then repeat it back to him. • Ask questions that require only short answers or a nod of the head. • Do not speak for the client or attempt to finish her sentences.

Considerations for Assisting Other Populations

Many of the considerations we use when working with people who have disabilities apply to all of our clients. A universal approach that is based on communication, etiquette, and behavior that accepts and respects a person at her current level of health and ability will welcome and encourage participation. This person-centered approach combined with an understanding of specific issues and recommendations for people of varied abilities will maximize success. Participation in regular physical activity is beneficial to health regardless of the participant's abilities, in most cases. The mode and specific amount of physical activity should be based on individual preferences, abilities, and the severity of any medical condition. Commonalities shared among conditions may affect pain level and fatigue.

Pain can be cyclic, and movement and motion can help to break the cycle of pain. When working with a person who has a painful condition, choose activities that are low impact and have a low risk of joint injury, adjust activities to meet the participant's needs based on his or her pain and endurance levels for a given day, and, if the person is experiencing pain, limit activities to short durations, 10 minutes, when the participant is in the least pain.

Adherence to an exercise program can be challenging for people who have conditions that cause fatigue. It is useful to help people become aware of the level and type of fatigue they are experiencing. Types of fatigue include muscle fatigue, substitution fatigue (strong muscles substituting for weak muscles), depression fatigue, and cardiovascular fatigue (NCPAD, 2009). Identifying the symptoms that lead to the onset of fatigue can help manage energy. Scheduling exercise when one has the most energy, including rest periods, and using appropriate equipment, such as a cane or walker, can relieve or reduce fatigue.

Basics of Exercise and Disability

The benefits of physical activity are vast. Exercise can help build healthy bones, muscles, and joints; may help one's immune system ward off illness and infection; can increase blood flow to all parts of the body; can relieve chronic pain and fibromyalgia; and can improve one's ability to perform activities of daily living. Engaging in physical activity may reduce depression and anxiety, because exercise releases endorphins and can produce feelings of well-being. Physical activity also provides an outlet for socialization and stress release. A regular exercise program helps participants maintain or extend independence and mobility into older age. Physical activity is associated with reduced health care costs, increased productivity, better performance in schools, lower worker absenteeism and turnover, and increased productivity.

The U.S. Surgeon General recommends at least 30 minutes of moderate-intensity physical activity on all or most days of the week (USDHHS, 2000). The U.S. Department of Health and Human Services, in its *2008 Physical Activity Guidelines for Americans* (USDHHS, 2008), recommends 150 minutes of moderate-intensity activity or 75 minutes of vigorous activity per week. The new MyPyramid, developed by the U.S. Department of Agriculture, provides these daily recommendations:

1. To prevent chronic disease, 30 minutes of moderate- to vigorous-intensity exercise
2. To maintain weight, 60 minutes of moderate- to vigorous-intensity exercise while not exceeding recommended caloric intake
3. To maintain weight loss, 60 to 90 minutes of moderate- to vigorous-intensity exercise while not exceeding recommended caloric intake

These recommendations are helpful, yet research is needed regarding exercise for people with disabilities. For example, there is no conclusive evidence on whether 30 minutes of cardiovascular exercise per day will increase the chance of overuse injuries in people who use wheelchairs for mobility. The U.S. Department of Health & Human Services Physical Activity Guidelines Committee has summarized the latest knowledge about activity and health, with efforts directed toward specific population subgroups, such as seniors, children, and people with disabilities. The guidelines, which were released in October 2008, confirm that physical activity is beneficial for almost everyone. These federal guidelines state that adults gain substantial health benefits from 2 1/2 hours a week of moderate aerobic physical activity, and children benefit from 1 hour or more of physical activity per day. The recommendations for adults with disabilities state that "those who are able should get at least 2 1/2 hours of moderate aerobic activity a week, or 1 hour and 15 minutes of vigorous aerobic activity a week. They should incorporate muscle-strengthening activities involving all major muscle groups 2 or more days a week. When they are not able to meet the guidelines, they should engage in regular physical activity according to their abilities and should avoid inactivity" (USDHHS, 2008). People with disabilities or health conditions who are not able to follow the guidelines are encouraged to adapt their physical activity to meet their abilities. Moving is important for everyone, and the evidence indicates that regular physical activity provides important health benefits for people with disabilities.

The following tips are important to consider when designing a physical activity plan for a person with a disability.

- Assess the participant's fitness and ability level for each activity, regardless of whether she does or does not have a disability.
- Learn the precautions and contraindications for exercise associated with medical conditions and medications. Consult a medical professional if needed.
  - Know the participant's medical history and current health status.
  - Find out what medications the person takes, because some medications, such as β-blockers and seizure medications, can affect exercise.

- Check the blood pressure of people who are at risk for cardiovascular conditions.
- Determine whether the participant's range of motion is restricted because of his condition. For example, a person who has Down syndrome is at risk for hypotonia.
- Remember that emotional and behavioral status can have an effect on participation.
- Keep in mind that ability may determine the level of activity or participation.
- When appropriate, use the Borg rating of perceived exertion or other assessments, such as the talk test.
- Require participants to wear appropriate clothing, be properly hydrated, and refrain from participating if they are sick (e.g., if they have a urinary tract or upper-respiratory infection).
- Adhere to the typically recommended stages of exercise (warm-up, activity, stretching, and cool-down) for all people, including those with disabilities.
- It is important to stop any activity immediately and seek medical assistance if a participant experiences any abnormal symptoms such as dizziness, nausea, clammy hands, or shortness of breath.

An exercise program for people with disabilities must start slowly, in terms of difficulty and intensity, and increase gradually. For some people, intermittent exercise may be the best

A successful exercise program will incorporate components that address many elements, including strength and endurance.

Photo courtesy of NCPAD.

choice if prolonged exercise is not sustainable. Physiologically, the body does not know the difference between three 10-minute bouts of moderate-intensity physical activity and 30 minutes of continuous moderate-intensity exercise. The key is maintaining the intensity level during all workouts. A good way to judge exercise intensity is by calculating the client's target heart rate. However, this method is not appropriate for some people, such as persons using β-blockers, people with a spinal cord injury at or above T6, persons who have autonomic dysfunction, or any person with an unstable health status.

Participants can determine their target heart rate using the Karvonen formula. To use this formula, the client must first determine his resting heart rate by taking his pulse before getting out of bed in the morning. Show him how to take his pulse by gently placing his middle and index finger on his wrist or neck. The client will begin counting with zero and continue to count the pulse for 10 seconds and then multiply by 6. The resulting resting heart rate can then be inserted into the following formula:

220 − participant's age = maximum heart rate

Maximum heart rate − resting heart rate = heart rate reserve

Heart rate reserve × (50-70%) = training range

Training range % + resting heart rate = participant's target training zone

The Borg rating of perceived exertion (RPE) can be used if the resting heart rate is not available. This scale is appropriate for all people with disabilities and subjectively allows each person to determine her level of intensity. To use the scale, the participant monitors how she feels while exercising. The recommended RPE is between 11 and 13 on the 6- to 20-point scale. The scale can be provided to the client visually during exercise. The client can then effectively communicate his or her rating of the exercise intensity.

To assist the participant in increasing overall physical activities outside of structured recreation programs, encourage a comprehensive view of physical activity. Figure 12.3 illustrates the different components of activity included in the

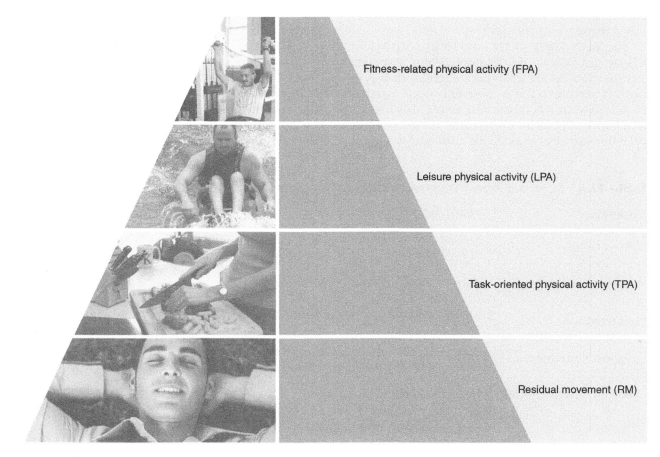

Fitness-related physical activity (FPA)

Leisure physical activity (LPA)

Task-oriented physical activity (TPA)

Residual movement (RM)

Figure 12.3 Physical activity pyramid.

Adapted, by permission, from NCPAD. Residual movement photo: © Istockphoto/Nikada. Leisure physical activity photo and fitness-related physical activity photo courtesy of NCPAD.

National Center on Physical Activity and Disability's physical activity pyramid.

Beginning at the top of the pyramid, fitness-related physical activity can be described as what many of us typically think of when we hear the word *exercise:* structured physical activity. According to updated physical activity guidelines for healthy adults younger than age 65, the American College of Sports Medicine (ACSM) and the American Heart Association (AHA) suggest the following amount of activity to maintain health and reduce the risk for chronic disease: (a) moderately intense cardiovascular exercise 30 minutes a day, 5 days a week, or (b) vigorously intense cardiovascular exercise 20 minutes per day, 3 days per week; for either option, induce 10 strength-training exercises, 8 to 12 repetitions of each exercise, twice per week.

To learn more about these guidelines and what is suggested for adults older than 65, go to www. acsm.org/content/NavigationMenu/Research/ Roundtables_Specialty_Conf/Pastroundtables/ Exercise_for_Older_Adults.htm.

If the client is not ready for structured exercise, choose another category to increase her movement throughout the day.

The next layer of the pyramid consists of leisure physical activity. Many people associate leisure with fun. If structured exercise in a gym sounds terrible to the person, encourage participation in leisure activity, and involve his friends and family. This is an opportunity to learn a new activity, such as kayaking or golf, and is a great way to encourage children and adolescents with disabilities to build skills that will keep them active throughout their lives.

A layer of the pyramid that is often overlooked is the task-oriented activity category. This category can be used to set obtainable goals that will provide a sense of accomplishment and success. For example, if a person walks or rolls to get the mail every day, suggest that he go to the mailbox the same number of times as the number of letters. Making five trips to the mailbox throughout the day can easily increase activity levels and decrease the amount of time that the client is sedentary. Other options are to fold laundry and make a separate trip to put each item away or wash one window at home every day. Items categorized in this area, such as watering the plants or walking a dog, could be considered a task or leisure recreation.

Some movements cannot be labeled as fitness activities, leisure activities, or tasks. This category completes the base of the NCPAD pyramid and is referred to as residual movement. This is the ancillary movement that people perform throughout the day and includes body functions that keep us alive. The amount of energy required to maintain body functions at rest is called the basal metabolic rate. This rate can increase or decrease depending on the person's lean tissue (muscle) mass and fat mass. Physical activity increases the basal metabolic rate by increasing muscle mass. So although the basal metabolic rate decreases as the body ages, we can slow this decrease through physical activity. Exercise is an important factor that influences

Table 12.4 Coronary Artery Disease Risk Factor Thresholds

Risk Factor	Thresholds
Family history	Myocardial infarction, revascularization, or sudden death before age 55 (males) or 65 (females)
Cigarette smoking	Current smoker or quit <6 months ago
Hypertension	≥140/90 observed on two separate occasions, or taking antihypertensive medication
Hypercholesterolemia	Total serum cholesterol >200 mg/dl or high-density lipoprotein <35 mg/dl or low-density lipoprotein >130 mg/dl
Impaired fasting glucose	Fasting ≥110 mg/dl
Obesity	BMI ≥30 or waist girth >100 cm
Sedentary lifestyle	Not engaging in 30 minutes of physical activity most days of the week

Adapted from American College of Sports Medicine, 2006, *ACSM's guidelines for exercise testing and prescription,* 7th ed. (Philadelphia, PA: Lippincott, Williams, and Wilkins.

BMR. When the body is active, it works hard to supply the needed nutrients to the muscles. The more muscle, the greater the need for energy and the higher the BMR. A high BMR has a positive effect on your metabolism and health.

Precautions

Before beginning an exercise program, the participant should consult her primary health care provider. If possible, she should participate in a graded exercise test to determine her current level of fitness. A graded exercise test may be determined medically necessary if a client has elevated risk factors associated with cardiovascular disease. See table 12.4 for a list of coronary artery disease risk factors as determined by the American College of Sports Medicine (2006). If your client has more than three of these risk factors, ask her to consult a physician prior to beginning an exercise program. The effects of any preexisting conditions must be considered, as well as any medications that may have an effect on the person's ability to perform and recover from exercise. A recreation professional may consult a clinical exercise physiologist for exercise testing, prescription, and guidance. The recreation professional may benefit from consulting other health care professionals such as physicians, nurses, or physical therapists should questions arise regarding medical status, condition, or medication.

Encourage the participant to set realistic short-term and long-term goals, and suggest that he monitor his progress by using an exercise log or journal. Encourage him to assess his health status each day and adjust the exercise program accordingly. To increase the likelihood of adherence to the exercise program, review and adjust the program every 8 to 10 weeks to keep it challenging and fun.

Components of a Comprehensive Exercise Program

Physical activity is defined as all forms of bodily movement produced by contraction of skeletal muscle that substantially increases energy expenditure (Caspersen et al., 1985). The subcategories are exercise, leisure-time physical activity, household tasks, and occupational work. Physical fitness is defined as a state characterized by an ability to perform daily activities with vigor and demonstration of traits and capacities that are associated with low risk of premature development of hypo-kinetic diseases (Caspersen et al., 1985). There are six components of physical fitness:

- Cardiorespiratory endurance
- Muscular strength and endurance
- Flexibility
- Body composition (body mass index, bone mineral density)
- Balance
- Pulmonary function

When designing an exercise program, follow the principle of specificity, which states that to improve function of a system through exercise, the exercise must stimulate that system. This means that to improve in a skill or exercise, a person must practice the activity or skill. The common components of an exercise program are cardiovascular, strength (resistance) training, flexibility (range of motion), and balance. Cardiovascular exercise is essential to maintain a healthy heart and the endurance to perform activities of daily living. Strength training maintains or improves skeletal muscle strength and endurance, which also can be crucial to the performance of activities of daily living. Flexibility helps maintain or improve range of motion and avoidance of spasticity and contractures. Balance training can prevent falls and associated injuries. The following sections present guidelines relevant to each exercise component.

Cardiovascular Exercise

For activities involving cardiovascular exercise, be sure that the person exercises at a pace that feels good to her but still provides some cardiovascular benefit. The "conversation rule" can be used to determine whether a person is overexerting herself. If the person exercising cannot carry on a normal conversation during the workout, have her rest or just slow down. Be sure that the client breathes slowly and deeply while exercising. If your client is combating numerous barriers, motivating her to engage in cardiovascular exercise might take creativity, so you must be imaginative, resourceful, and open to alternative methods and styles of exercising. Activities such as walking, cycling, using an ergometer, pushing a wheelchair, or swimming can be beneficial. Teach the participant how to incorporate exercise into her average daily activities: Using a coffee break or lunch break, or even TV commercials, for short bursts of cardiorespiratory activity can be very beneficial if the exercises are done properly (NCPAD, 2006).

Strength (Resistance) Training

Breathing properly is very important during strength exercises. Do not allow participants to hold their breath while training. Breath holding during exercise is termed the *Valsalva maneuver,* and it can cause lightheadedness and dizziness and stress the heart. Participants should exhale while moving against resistance and inhale while letting the weight down. Maintaining good posture is essential. In addition, each movement should be performed through a complete range of motion. Range of motion will vary widely between people and can even fluctuate daily for each person, depending on his disability and secondary conditions (i.e., inflammation), so make note of each client's personal range of motion (NCPAD, 2005).

Flexibility (Range of Motion)

Flexibility improves range of motion, balance, and coordination. Incorporate flexibility training before and after each workout. Participants should hold stretches 10 to 30 seconds and always progress slowly. Stretching should *never* be painful. Activities such as yoga, Pilates, and tai chi can improve flexibility (NCPAD, 2005). Flexibility exercises may be contraindicated for people who have hypotonia (low muscle tone) (e.g., people with intellectual disabilities, such as Down syndrome), who may be at risk for further loosening of the joints and for whom these exercises could cause serious injury or death.

Balance

Before a client begins an exercise program, you must assess his risk for falls. If the client's fall risk is high, he may need one-on-one supervision during activities. If his fall risk is moderate, suggest that he join a group exercise class that provides exercise alternatives, such as seated activities, and offers a supervised setting. If the client's fall risk is minimal, independent exercise may be possible, but you should take precautions to minimize the possibilities of a fall, such as ensuring the space is clear of obstacles and orienting the client to the environment. Balance exercises that can be incorporated into the exercise program involve maintaining standing and postural stability under a variety of conditions, such as walking on sand, standing on foam pads of differing densities while performing the exercise, or closing one's eyes during the exercise.

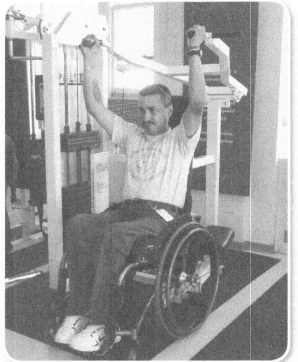

Photo courtesy of NCPAD.

Provide equipment that allows adjustments to be made to allow access to everyone who comes to the fitness center.

Accessible Environments

Environmental access is always important when people with disabilities participate in physical activity. Ensuring that usable equipment is available is a vital step, for example, providing weight machines that have swing-away or removable seats that accommodate a person in a wheelchair. Simple devices, such as Velcro straps, can provide additional support. Participants who have grip strength deficits can use adaptive gloves or mitts to grip handles, and Velcro cuffs can be used as an alternative to traditional grips or handles on machines that use cables. Be sure that the client can use the equipment safely. It may be necessary to hold limbs that are not being used in place and ensure that any pedals or footrests can be reached or secured to the client's feet. A good way to assess whether a machine is potentially beneficial for the client is to determine whether she can perform one repetition of the exercise and still receive benefit (North Carolina Office on Disability and Health [NCODH] and the Center for Universal Design, 2002).

Because weight machines are not always available, consider alternatives. Elastic bands are an inexpensive and portable way for performing strength training; small weights that can be wrapped around the wrists are useful.

Consider alternative types of activities to improve the participant's fitness level. Aquatic activities provide more freedom of movement than land exercise and provide excellent cardiovascular benefits. Be aware of any water temperature sensitivity that a person may have secondary to his disability. Walking or wheeling around the neighborhood on a regular basis is a simple and effective exercise. Activities such as gardening or using a seated aerobics video are excellent choices for those who are more comfortable exercising at home. Seated or standing yoga, tai chi, and martial arts are popular and improve flexibility as well as relieve stress (NCODH and the Center for Universal Design, 2002).

Promoting a positive fitness environment for all involves learning about what setting can best meet a person's needs. For example, seniors who have an orthopedic condition such as arthritis may benefit from aquatic activities; people who are unable to afford program registration fees or who are uncomfortable in a gym environment may prefer to develop a home fitness routine.

Exercise Assessments and Activities

The appropriate frequency, intensity, and duration of physical activity for people without disabilities are well known and provide the basis for exercise training. However, the frequency, intensity, and duration of physical activity necessary to improve fitness and functional health outcomes in persons with disabilities are less clear. An exercise program for a participant with a disability must be designed around the participant's health status and specific ability level. To create a comprehensive exercise program for a client with disabilities, the program designer must have baseline measures of the participant's cardiorespiratory endurance, muscular strength and endurance, flexibility, body composition (body mass index, bone mineral density), and balance. Recreation professionals may not be trained to administer exercise tests, but we must know what tests exist and what they measure.

Graded Exercise Testing

Cardiovascular exercise testing can help the exercise professional determine cardiovascular fitness and create an appropriate exercise prescription. Maximum oxygen consumption is the maximum capacity of a person's body to transport and use oxygen during incremental exercise. Maximal oxygen consumption or uptake ($\dot{V}O_2$max) is widely accepted as the single best measure of cardiovascular fitness and maximal aerobic power. $\dot{V}O_2$max is expressed either as an absolute rate in liters of oxygen per minute or as a relative rate in milliliters of oxygen per kilogram of body weight per minute. A graded exercise test for persons with disabilities often does not determine a true maximal oxygen consumption but does determine the person's peak oxygen consumption. This difference can be identified as the limitation of exercise from fatigue, motivation, pain, or symptoms as a result of the disability or secondary conditions rather than oxygen supply. Graded exercise tests can be performed through several modalities such as a treadmill, a wheelchair ergometer (wheelchair ergometry involves the use of the person's own wheelchair and a wheelchair roller, which locks the chair in place and provides a stationary means of propelling the wheels), a leg cycle ergometer (stationary bicycle), or an arm ergometer. In a nonclinical setting, a recreation professional can use a 6-minute walk test, Rockport Walk test, ergometer, or other field-based test to access aerobic fitness.

Muscular Strength and Endurance

According to the American College of Sports Medicine (ACSM), the best format to determine dynamic strength testing (involving movement of the body or an external load) is the 1-repetition maximum (1RM) (ACSM, 2005). In some cases, a 1RM test is contraindicated, and so a 6RM or 10RM test is used. However, extrapolating these data and estimating one's true 1RM are often problematic, given the marked variations in the number of repetitions that can be performed at a fixed percentage of a 1RM for different muscle groups (e.g., leg press vs. bench press). We can use the Holton curve to estimate the participant's 1RM by determining her 10RM and adjusting the score to estimate the 1RM. An alternative method of testing involves determining the number of repetitions that the participant can complete in 1 minute with performance level graded by individual progression from one testing period to the next. Simple field tests can be used to evaluate the muscular endurance of certain muscle groups. For example, the number of abdominal crunches that can be performed without any rest provides information regarding the endurance of the abdominal muscles. Certain resistance training equipment can be adapted to measure muscular endurance by choosing a submaximal level of resistance and then measuring the number of repetitions that one can perform before fatigue sets in. As an example, the YMCA bench press involves performing standardized repetitions at a rate of 30 lifts per minute. Women are tested using a 35-pound (16-kilogram) barbell, while men are tested with an 80-pound (36-kilogram) barbell. People are scored based on the number of successful repetitions. The weight suggested in the YMCA bench press may not be appropriate for all people and should be determined based on individual strength levels.

Body Composition

Calculating a participant's body mass index (BMI) is a good method for assessing overweight and obesity, and this simple tool only requires height and weight. BMI is a measure of body fat based on height and weight that applies to both adult men and women.

English BMI Formula

$$BMI = (\text{weight in pounds} / [\text{height in inches} \times \text{height in inches}]) \times 703$$

Metric BMI Formula

$$BMI = \text{weight in kilograms} / (\text{height in meters} \times \text{height in meters})$$

BMI Categories

- Underweight = less than 18.5
- Normal weight = 18.5-24.9
- Overweight = 25-29.9
- Obesity = 30 or greater

BMI is not the best tool to establish risk factors in people with spinal cord injury. Many body composition changes occur following a spinal cord injury. A decrease in muscle mass (especially below the level of injury) and bone density often accompanies an increase in body fat. Until research confirms the BMI cut points that are appropriate to determine risk for obesity-related diseases in people with spinal cord injury, waist circumference measures should be used for this population. Table 12.5 illustrates the categories of BMI according to the National Health and Nutrition Examination Survey (NHANES).

BMI is not the same as percent body fat, but it does provide a correlation to body fat and the effect that body weight has on disease and death. BMI differs by sex and age, and it is common for women to have a higher BMI than men. Table 12.5 should not be used for children or teens, as BMI for children and teens is based on gender- and age-specific charts that consider the growth of a child or teen. BMI is a strong indicator of risk for developing certain disease and even an increased chance of death. Some common conditions are related to overweight and obesity:

- Premature death
- Cardiovascular disease
- High blood pressure
- Osteoarthritis
- Some cancers
- Diabetes

BMI is not a diagnostic tool. Many other risk factors are related to the development of chronic disease:

- Poor diet
- Lack of physical activity
- Waist circumference 35 inches (89 centimeters) or greater for women and 47 inches (119 centimeters) or greater for men
- Blood pressure (prehypertensive, 120-139/80-89; hypertensive, ≥140/90)
- Fasting blood glucose (blood sugar) 100 or more
- Cholesterol (total cholesterol >200)
- Family history

Flexibility (Range of Motion)

Maintaining flexibility of joints facilitates movement. Tissue damage can easily occur if an activity moves the structures of a joint beyond its range of motion. Flexibility is joint specific, and to prevent injury, the recreation professional must be aware of any contractures (chronic loss of joint motion) that a participant has. Common devices to measure flexibility include goniometers, electrogonimeters, and tape measures.

Table 12.5 Body Mass Index

BMI	Weight status
<18.5	Underweight
18.5-24.9	Normal
25.0-29.9	Overweight
30.0-39.9	Obese
≥40.0	Extremely obese

Professionals may use a goniometer to measure the range of each joint. Most users make this measurement through passive motion but it can be done through active motion as well. The measurement is done throughout one plane of motion at a time. Other forms of flexibility tests include the sit-and-reach test (measures low back and hip-joint flexibility) and Apley's scratch test.

Balance Assessment

It is important to assess the client's seated and standing balance along with static and dynamic balance control. Balance can be assessed by tests such as the functional reach test or by observing the client stand from a seated position. If a client's balance is poor, alter exercise testing and prescription accordingly to ensure safety. Other tests used to determine balance include timed up-and-go test, Berg balance scale, and physical performance test.

Summary

Numerous studies have reported the benefits of increased physical activity and fitness in reducing cardiovascular and other health risk factors that are associated with chronic disease and disability (Banz et al., 2003; Blair et al., 2001; Donnelly et al., 2000; Eriksson & Lindgärde, 1991). However, although engaging in regular physical activity is critical for maintaining good health and preventing secondary conditions associated with sedentary lifestyles, persons with disabilities encounter major barriers that often prevent full participation in fitness and recreation activities. The preamble to the United Nations Convention on the Rights of People with Disabilities in December 2006 said that states shall "recognize the importance of accessibility to the physical, social, economic and cultural environment, to health and education and to information and communication, in enabling persons with disabilities to fully enjoy all human rights and fundamental freedoms." It also recognized that "persons with disabilities have the right to the enjoyment of the highest attainable standard of health without discrimination on the basis of disability" (United Nations General Assembly, 2006). In the United States, the Inclusive Fitness Coalition stresses the importance of the national priority to battle the effects of obesity and chronic health conditions that have taken such a toll on our society and to provide physical activity opportunities to all Americans.

As indicated by the national and international response to the needs and rights of people with disabilities to have equal and unlimited access to our society's opportunities for self-betterment, the health and wellness of people with disabilities and health considerations is an emerging topic that is reaching its tipping point. Recreation facilities now have the opportunity to address and significantly affect this national and international priority by evaluating the accessibility of their facilities and programs to ensure inclusive opportunities.

Discussion Questions

1. How does leading a physically active life affect one's health status?
2. Explain the recommendations for physical activity as outlined by the Surgeon General's report on physical activity (USDHHS, 2005) and the *2008 Physical Activity Guidelines for Americans* (USDHHS, 2008).
3. Discuss the challenges and barriers people with disabilities may experience when participating in physical activity.
4. Why is the social model of disability a preferred model when developing an inclusive fitness program?
5. Describe an accessible and inclusive environment.

Photo courtesy of Chris Mackey.

Chris Mackey

Luke Skywalker: "I don't believe it!"

Yoda: "That . . . is why you fail."

Background Information

Education BS, Recreation Leisure Studies, Therapeutic Recreation Concentration

Credentials Enrolled in Certified Fitness Trainer Course

Special Awards

   *Named a Youth Leader for the Healthy and Ready to Work Initiative of the Maternal and Child Health Bureau *Several top finishes at the 1997 and 2001 Southeast Regional Wheelchair Games *Three top 10 finishes in the 1997 National Wheelchair Games Swim Meet

Special Affiliations

   *Member of the Transition Subcommittee for the Healthy People 2010 Express National Summit on Children with Special Health Care Needs, Washington, DC (July 2001-December 2001) *Member of the Southeast Disability and Business Technical Assistance Center Regional ADA Training Team *Member of Exceptional Children's Assistance Center Board of Directors (July 2006 to July 2007) *Member, Advisory Council for the University of North Carolina Center for Development and Learning, (June 2008 to present) *Inclusion Subcommittee Co-Chair, NC Outdoor Learning Environments Alliance, NC Office of School Readiness

Career Information

Position Healthy Communities Coordinator, North Carolina Office on Disability & Health

Organization Information NCODH is a collaborative endeavor between the NC Division of Public Health of the Department of Health and Human Services and the FPG Child Development Institute at the University of North Carolina–Chapel Hill.

Organization's Mission Through collaborative partnerships with a variety of stakeholders, the NCODH serves as a catalyst for innovative disability surveillance studies, community interventions, and public and professional education activities designed to build state capacity in responding to the health needs of people with disabilities. The primary mission of the NCODH is to promote the health of people with disabilities, prevent secondary conditions, and eliminate disparities between people with and without disabilities in North Carolina.

Size of Organization The NCODH has four employees, and the FPG Child Development Institute employs approximately 300 people. The NCODH serves people statewide.

Job Description I design and implement health promotion interventions for people with disabilities. One specific area of focus is worksite health promotion programs for people with intellectual and developmental disabilities served in community rehabilitation programs. I deliver presentations on health and wellness for diverse disability service and advocacy groups and organizations. I design and conduct training programs for health professionals that focus on creating inclusive and accessible health promotion services and environments. Specific areas of focus include accessibility of community dental practices, senior centers, and fitness centers and health clubs. These trainings involve didactic presentations, a site accessibility survey, the development of a plan of action to address barrier removal, and ongoing technical assistance. I also work with national colleagues to promote training on inclusive fitness for personal trainers. I assist with the development and distribution of health education materials for persons with disabilities. I am responsible for dissemination of numerous NCODH publications that address accessible environments, women's health, immunization, children's health, and data on persons with disabilities. I coordinate the healthy communities work group and participate in partners advisory groups, including the Eat Smart Move More leadership team and the School Health Matrix Team.

Career Path   After graduation I found out about this job opening through a family member who previously worked with the office on a research project.

What I Like About My Job   It gives me the opportunity to affect a population of underserved citizens in my state and nationally. I enjoy showing people that inclusion is not hard to implement. My work also gives me the opportunity to influence public health policy at various levels.

Advice to Undergraduate Students   Be flexible in your work choices, be inclusive of everyone in your programs, and understand where your clients are coming from and work within that.

Personal Statement   We all work hard so that we are all able to play hard. I enjoy giving people the chance to play hard.

Inclusive Arts and Culture

Kathlyn M. Steedly, PhD

Steedly Consulting

> *Art is amazing because it comes magically from your own thoughts and imagination. Through my art I have learned that the storms outside in the world are like my personal storms and you can get through them.*

—Lisie, Inside Out Artist

Learning Outcomes

After completing this chapter, learners will be able to do the following:

- Define inclusive arts and culture.
- Understand key concepts of inclusive arts and culture programs.
- Identify fundamental aspects of successful inclusive arts and culture programs.

Early one June morning, employees of VSA arts (formerly Very Special Arts) arrived at the Baltimore airport to pick up a group of artists from Iceland. How would the VSA arts group meet up with artists who were possibly blind, had limited mobility, or needed other types of special assistance? What could they do to make sure the artists could get from baggage claim to ground transportation? The usual airport headaches were magnified by issues of language differences, health concerns, and logistical complexities, such as getting wheelchairs specifically designed for dance through U.S. customs. It was VSA arts' responsibility to make sure the artists made it to Washington, DC, safe and sound.

The Icelandic artists were only one group of international artists that VSA arts hosted as part of the 2004 VSA arts International Festival. VSA arts, an international arts organization committed to providing access to the arts for people with disabilities, produced an arts festival in which artists from all art forms, from all over the world, met in Washington, DC, for a week-long celebration of arts and culture. This was a unique event. Venues not traditionally focused on showcasing the work of artists with disabilities included their work front and center alongside permanent exhibits and performance seasons. The John F. Kennedy Center for the Performing Arts opened its stages to musicians and dancers with disabilities. The Smithsonian Institution displayed the work of artists with disabilities. Local arts reviewers had the opportunity to view and respond to the work of artists with disabilities whose work was on display throughout the city. The international arts community, including the community of international artists with disabilities, was represented by juried, professional-caliber artists from all artistic disciplines. Most important, the Washington, DC, community could experience the power and possibility of the arts through witnessing the contribution of artists with disabilities.

The VSA arts International Arts Festival exemplifies inclusive arts and culture programming as mirror, magnifying glass, and microphone. Space was created for artists with disabilities within the larger arts and culture community (participation was determined on the basis of artistic merit through a rigorous selection process). Artists with disabilities were no longer absent from the conversation because artist and audience alike could use an artistic lens to examine commonalities. Issues and challenges of the disability community could be viewed for both their sameness and their difference by the entire arts and culture community.

This chapter sets out to encourage inclusive arts and culture programs in recreational contexts. Toward that end, three primary objectives are outlined: to define inclusive arts and culture programming, to identify inclusive programming across arts disciplines, and to forward fundamental components of successful inclusive arts and culture programming.

Inclusive Arts and Cultural Programming

What makes an inclusive arts and culture program inclusive? Is an inclusive arts and culture program simply a good arts program? Where do inclusive arts and culture happen? These questions frame the central issue addressed in this chapter: How do we encourage inclusive arts and culture programs in recreational contexts? Arts and culture programs occur in a variety of places. Theaters, galleries, museums, studios, live music venues, and school auditoriums are typically the first places people associate with arts and cultural programs; however, some of these places may seem somewhat removed, difficult, expensive, boring, irrelevant, or strange to people who are disconnected from the arts.

If we scratch beneath the surface of mainstream arts and culture, we see that the arts also exist in the cracks and crevasses of everyday life. Arts and culture happen in public parks, community centers, schools, churches, coffee houses, hospitals, living rooms, building lobbies, street corners, and highway viaducts. The arts intersect life where people meet. Inclusive arts and culture programs require that traditional arts and culture program providers shift and mold their practices to include more voices and spaces. Inclusive arts and culture also demand a broader embrace of arts programming by people who may have left the arts off of their agendas. Meaningful reach requires understanding and action across a broad spectrum of stakeholders, including government and business, based on knowledge and commitment.

Erickson (2008) suggests several policy-level actions—such as government subsidy of arts and culture events—in responding to what she terms the "crisis in culture," in which participation and inclusion in arts and culture are limited by socioeconomic constraints. Defining terms, identifying key concepts, and providing tangible examples lay a foundation for new or reinvigorated inclusive arts activities in a variety of communities.

Defining Inclusion

The term *inclusion* is surrounded in legal, cultural, and philosophical meaning. The Civil Rights Act of 1964, the Architectural Barriers Act of 1968, the Rehabilitation Act of 1973, the Fair Housing Amendments Act of 1988, and the Americans with Disabilities Act of 1990 offer legal safeguards to ensure physical accessibility, employment protection, and civil rights support. The Education for All Handicapped Children Act of 1975 (now called the Individuals with Disabilities Education Act) ensures free and appropriate public education within the least restrictive environment for infants, toddlers, children, and youth with disabilities. These laws exist to create a more just society for all people. The long-waged legislative struggle toward inclusion has required a shift of public and political will. Inclusion is defined and required as a matter of law; however, definitions of inclusion must also include cultural and philosophical considerations.

Cultural inclusion recognizes and affirms the presence and contribution of all people in meaningful ways throughout society. Cultural inclusion makes space for a variety of images, and a variety of people, to be publically presented. Cultural inclusion demands that people move beyond pity, fear, and deficit thinking—aspects of "help" that often allow one group of people to remain marginalized and powerless. Cultural inclusion provides for accurate and honest representation of all people. Cultural inclusion seeks to provide equal airtime for all stories to be told. Cultural inclusion views diversity as the golden thread in the fabric of a multicultural society.

Philosophical inclusion speaks to what motivates society to create inclusive environments. Philosophical inclusion involves the ethical notion that all people have the right to fully participate in society. If an inclusive philosophy guides the ways in which society happens, all children are educated soundly, businesses are run fairly, resources are allocated justly, and rules are followed consistently. Within this framework, laws are the product of and the method by which an inclusive philosophy is lived out.

Ultimately, real inclusion involves legal, cultural, and philosophical action. A defined legal system cannot truly protect the rights of people if society does not hold the philosophical belief that all people have rights. Likewise, cultural inclusion can provide the understanding necessary for philosophical and legal inclusion. Real inclusion means that people actively support the rights of others. Inclusive arts and culture programs have the privilege of making visible the powerful beauty of the creative impulse of all people, allowing the voices of all people to be heard, and creating space for understanding across the societal divides of race, class, and ability.

Universal Design

The concept of universal design is central to inclusive arts and culture practice. The way in which environments and objects are developed to increase access, and by extension participation, by the largest group of people is a tenet of universal design. Mace (2008) defines universal design as "the design of products and environments to be usable by all people, to the greatest extent possible, without the need for adaptation or specialized design" (www.design.ncsu.edu/cud/about_ud.htm). Ivey (2001) explained universal design this way:

> The operative point of view for designers (whether architects, landscape architects, interior designers, engineers, industrial designers, web designers, or way finders) becomes one of empathy for the human condition; in universal design, solutions reflect the diversity of human abilities—throughout the range of life. Although codes may assure compliance where the society has improved intransigent, the ultimate answer to the universal design lies in employing our full imaginative and aesthetic gifts in a new way of seeing. (p. xvi)

Universal design is built on the basic belief that all people function better when environmental barriers to participation are removed. The principles of universal design offered by the Center for Universal Design (2008) suggest that a universally designed environment is equitable, flexible, simple, and intuitive. Some everyday examples of universal design include lever handles for opening doors, wide interior hallways, appropriate lighting, and adaptable auditory and visual controls on technology.

Universal design has specific implications within the field of arts and culture. To reiterate, universal design dictates that function and utility yield participation. That includes the entire breadth of the arts and culture field. John Killacky (2005) described the effort to move beyond compliance and make arts programs accessible:

> Accessibility is much more than ramps, seating, listening devices, large print programs, and sign language interpretation. Exhibition lectures, films, interactive computer displays, plays and concerts examine disability, as well as materials about programs—catalogues, labeling, scripts, libretti, brochures, maps, and publicity have become more accessible.

The frame for accessibility into which universal design can be folded acknowledges the specific steps the arts and cultural community has taken to be more inclusive—listening devices, large-print programs, and building spaces that all people can enjoy. Although a great deal of work has been done with respect to universal design and access within the arts and culture community, as evidenced by the work of the Kennedy Center, the National Assembly of State Arts Agencies (2003), and many others, great deal of work remains.

Cultural Economy

Recent years have seen the arts and culture community begin to intensely scrutinize the impact the arts and culture in terms of dollars and cents—making an argument for the arts from an economic perspective. This growing body of literature reveals the important role that the arts and culture community plays in the economic life of society. Best-selling books assert the emergence of a "creative class" in which power and commerce are increasingly controlled by creative, innovative, arts-minded people from arts-friendly communities (Florida, 2002). The data can be particularly persuasive when we communicate with people who may hold the view that the arts are frilly extravagances for easy times.

The data suggest several interesting things with respect to overall economic impact of the arts. Americans for the Arts (2009) reports that 2.98 million people work for 612,095 arts-centric businesses (see figure 13.1.)

The National Endowment for the Arts (2008) found that nearly 2 million Americans identified *artist* as their primary occupation on the U.S. census. Designers are the single largest group of artists, followed by performing artists such as actors, dancers, and musicians.

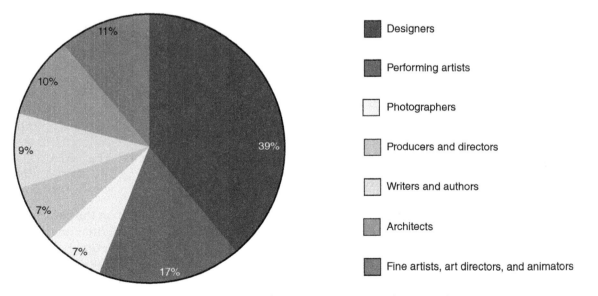

Figure 13.1 Economic impact of the nonprofit arts and culture industry in the United States in 2005.

Data from Americans for the Arts. Available: http://www.americansforthearts.org/pdf/information_services/research/services/economic_impact/aepiii/highlights.pdf and National Endowment for the Arts. Available: www.nea.gov/research/researchreports_chrono.html.

Examples of art-centric employers are these:

- Arts council
- Government agency (e.g., department of cultural affairs)
- Museum
- Arts or science center
- Art school
- Symphony orchestra
- Summer theater
- Opera company
- Theatrical company
- Performing arts center
- Community theater
- Ballet company
- Dance studios, schools, and halls
- Theater (building, ownership, and operation)

Arts & Economic Prosperity (Americans for the Arts, 2009) offers perhaps the most powerful economic case for the arts. In the United States, the nonprofit arts and culture industry generates $166.2 billion in economic activity annually. In 2005, this spending supported 5.7 million full-time jobs (see table 13.1).

The breadth and depth of economic data reveal several important ideas. The arts and culture community is central to economic development—it provides jobs, revenue, and income. The notion that the arts live at the periphery of society may now be challenged with facts that assert a far more comprehensive model of economic involvement. Finally, these numbers give permission for various sectors of society to support systemic arts involvement, including significant funding to ensure comprehensive arts and culture programming.

The economic argument outlined above can be extended to include demographic trends suggesting that the economically valuable arts and culture community embraces inclusive practice. There are 41 million adults and children with disabilities in this country (U.S. Census Bureau, 2004). McNeil reported the following in 1997:

> It is estimated that among the population 6 years and over, 8.6 million people had difficulty with one or more activities of daily living and 4.1 million needed personal assistance. (U.S. Census Bureau, 2008, pp. 70-71)

We must acknowledge the connection between disability and aging, given that there are 37 million people age 65 or older in the United States. By 2030, the population of older adults will reach 71.5 million.

Connecting the demographic and economic dots reveals a direction for arts and culture programs. Society in general, including arts and culture institutions, will have to develop inclusive practice to ensure that people are able to continue to participate and enjoy arts and culture. There will be more demand for inclusive practice: Market forces will dictate arts and culture programming that more clearly reflects a society where accessibility determines involvement. It can also be argued that current levels of participation (as indicated by employment and dollars spent) will not be sustainable without systemic attention to inclusion.

Table 13.1 Economic Impact of the Nonprofit Arts and Culture Industry (2005)*

	Amount
Total expenditures	$166.2 billion
Resident household income	$104.2 billion
Local government revenue	$7.9 billion
State government revenue	$9.1 billion
Federal income tax revenue	$12.6 billion

*Expenditures by audience and organizations.

Note: The nonprofit arts and culture industry in the United States provided 5.7 million full-time-equivalent jobs in 2005. Data from Americans for the Arts (2009).

Based on http://www.americansforthearts.org/pdf/information_services/research/services/economic_impact/aepiii/highlights.pdf and National Endowment of the Arts www.nea.gov/research/researchreports_chrono.html.

Cultural Competency

The ability to successfully understand, live, and work with people from various cultural backgrounds has arguably never been more important. The cultural competence movement can be viewed as a societal response to that need. In a globally focused world with an increasingly multicultural, multi-abled, and linguistically diverse population, culture competence becomes a deeply important skill set. Culture competence can be defined as

> a set of congruent behaviors, attitudes and policies that come together in a system, agency, or among professionals and enables that system agency or professionals to work effectively in cross-cultural situations (Cross et al., 1989, p. iv).

Growing out of the health professions and the desire to appropriately diagnose and treat people from variety of cultures, cultural competence is historically tied to health and well-being. Business and industry have co-opted *cultural competence* as an umbrella term for diversity initiatives within the workplace. Within education, cultural competence can apply to policy circles that seek to understand and confront issues such as the overrepresentation of African American and Latino students within the special education system. Also within education, cultural competence refers to culturally relevant teaching and curriculum.

Inclusive arts and culture programs address cultural competence in several key ways. Programs provide a venue for exploration of different cultures and abilities in artistic, compelling, and responsive ways. Programs that involve instruction and interaction allow for conversation between and among people of various cultures and abilities. Programs draw on the unique texture and nuance of culture—in all its manifestations of materials, language, history, and context. Finally, programs inform and remind communities about the multicultural reality of our society by providing windows into experiences we may not have lived.

Arts and Culture Inclusion in Practice

Common practices are used within the arts and culture community to create more inclusive arts experiences. Inclusive arts and culture programs use tools from the worlds of technology, the arts, and language to bridge the divides created by different abilities. Providing inclusive arts and culture experiences requires program providers to consider the barriers to participation in the artistic event, develop a strategy or approach to overcoming the barrier, and implement a solution to the problem.

Arts and culture within this discussion includes the visual, performing, literary, and media arts. The close relationship shared by the specific art forms, such as music and dance, cannot be underscored enough as inclusive practices are systemically developed. The language used within the arts and culture community reflects the overlap and interdependence of art forms. For example, an exhibit of neon tubes and televisions may be viewed at a museum alongside painting and sculpture—or—a performance artist may play an instrument, recite poetry, and dance during a performance. Art forms are often authentically integrated in practice.

Highlighting a few strategies that arts and culture programmers use to create inclusive arts and culture experiences not only will shine a light on arts and culture but potentially will spur thought about how these strategies might inform work outside the context of arts and culture.

American Sign Language Interpretation and Shadow Interpretation

Many theaters offer performances that are interpreted in American Sign Language (ASL). An interpreter often stands to the side of the stage and translates what is being spoken as part of a play, for example. Often, a few ASL-interpreted performances are offered within a theater company's entire season. ASL interpretation allows people who are deaf and hard of hearing to experience a performance event that would otherwise be inaccessible to them.

Taking ASL interpretation to another level, theaters and performance groups are turning to shadow interpretation as a way to fully integrate aesthetic goals and inclusive practice. Sign language interpreters "shadow" actors on stage and translate the dialog into ASL for deaf audiences or spoken English for hearing audiences. In shadow interpretation, the actors on the stage speak the script in a traditional way (speaking English while performing English scripts) and are shadowed by actors performing in ASL simultaneously to the voiced performances. The approach allows an audience to experience both ASL and the spoken word simultaneously. Reviews of shadow-interpreted shows speak to the power of this approach. A review of a production of *Children of a Lesser God* presented by Pied Piper Players in Lakeland, Florida, explains, "shadow signing allows everyone in the audience to see and understand the play's action as it happens" (Ellis, 2005, www.theledger.com/article/20050420/NEWS/504200308?Title=-Shadow-Signing-Brings-Play-to-Life). A review of Deaf West's *Big River* lauded shadow interpretation:

> What's most striking about this Broadway ensemble is how thoroughly it has intermingled sign-language with the lexicon of musical theater, to the point that we're soon convinced that this singular lingua franca—physical, expressively theatrical, somehow clarifying, even to a hearing audience—is the only way this story of friendship without borders can be told (Kendt, 2003, www.deafwest.org/productions/review.html#lati1mes).

ASL and shadow interpretation exemplify tools for inclusion used in the performing arts. Both specifically create the opportunity for the deaf or hard-of-hearing community to participate in a theatrical event.

Audio Description

Audio description allows people who are blind or visually impaired to enjoy the arts in meaningful ways. Audio description can be delivered live or by a taped narrator. The National Center on Accessible Information Technology in Education (2008) at the University of Washington defines audio description, saying, "Narrators typically describe actions, gestures, scene changes, and other visual information. They also describe titles, speaker names, and other text that may appear on the screen."

Audio description is used across a variety of contexts. In museums, audio description allows a more interactive experience than provided in basic audio tours, which often simply provide information about a particular artist or the historical context of a work of art. An audio-described exhibit gives museumgoers a vivid description of a piece of art. It may provide information about the way in which the artwork is oriented in the museum space, the texture of brush strokes on a painting, or the finish of a statue, for example. Audio description within a television context provides a way in which a program can be watched and understood simultaneously by all viewers. Audio description of a dance performance allows the audience to appreciate the movements as well as the music. Because audio description is used across a breadth of artistic and cultural locales, its implication outside of arts and culture cannot be overlooked.

Assistive Technology

Assistive technology is the broad term used to describe devices that increase access and participation in society. Although often discussed in respect to the disability community—in reference to wheelchairs, for example, or a device that speaks while the user types a message on a keyboard—assistive technology also encompasses the variety of universally designed equipment intended to help all people fully participate in society. Some common types of assistive technology include telecommunications devices, speech recognition software, electronic sensors connected to an alarm system that notifies caregivers of an emergency, and various computer adaptations such as a foot mouse, large monitor, or large-key keyboard. Much like the concept of universal design brings together disparate fields and constituencies under the big tent of access, the field of assistive technology informs and is informed by information technology, health care, product design, and urban planning.

Assistive technology has very specific implications for arts and culture programs. Whether by affording an audience member the opportunity to fully participate in an artistic event (as exemplified by the technology used in audio description) or by providing an artist the tools necessary to create, assistive technology affects arts and culture in real ways. Mouth-sticks can allow an artist to apply paint. Adjustable or motorized easels and tabletop easels make it possible for an artist to create from an optimal position. Adjustable drawing boards and tables, magnification devices, and Verilux lamps are also used by artists as they design a light plot, sew costumes, or draw a set rendering.

ASL interpretation, shadow interpretation, audio description, and assistive technology illustrate practices within the arts and culture community intended to increase participation in and access to the arts for all people. These practices embody the effort to merge the practical and the aesthetic. They acknowledge the fact that all people have the right to fully enjoy the arts. The visible presence of inclusive practices across institutions and contexts also reminds people that different abilities are a fundamental and valuable part of society and that inclusive practice benefits everyone.

Inclusive concepts and practices come together when arts experiences seamlessly, creatively, and deliberately allow for the complete participation, appreciation, and involvement of all people: when the theater troupe decides to cast an actor regardless of ability; when a community builds a museum that all people can enter and move through; when a park secures a piece of public art for the enjoyment of visitors. These actions are concrete manifestations of inclusive arts and culture.

Inclusion and Art Forms

After drawing inclusive arts and culture with broad strokes, we now look at inclusion as it manifests across the art forms. Differences exist in the unique way artistic media communicate using the tools of the body, words, paint, canvas, instruments, and technology. That being said, important overlap can be found in the way dancers move through music, actors portray characters, or a visual artist constructs a mixed-media collage combining materials, words, and images. Providing an inclusive arts experience requires a thoughtful approach that acknowledges the specific needs of artists and the form in which they are working. What follows is not an exhaustive list of inclusive programs. Neither is it necessarily a recommendation of these programs, although the merit of these programs can perhaps be determined by the awards they have received, their longevity, and their ingenious approach to meeting community needs. The programs described here can be considered windows into the practice of inclusive arts programming, conversation starters for artists and others who seek to better understand arts programs, and evidence of the possible breadth and depth of inclusive arts programming. Focusing on several examples of inclusive arts and culture organizations, and specifically on their work, will illuminate the way in which the art forms themselves affect inclusion.

Perspectives and Examples From Performing Arts, Music, and Dance

Deaf West Theatre   Deaf West Theatre (www.deafwest.org) was founded in Los Angeles in 1991 as the first professional, permanent, residential sign language theater west of the Mississippi River. Deaf West's productions involve award-winning artists and have earned more than 60 awards for artistic and technical merit. Deaf West offers a variety of theatrical programming in which the deaf community can engage with theater, and the theater community can experience theater by and with artists and technicians who are deaf. Deaf West produces three main stage shows each season. Deaf West's outreach activities include national touring, in-school workshops, professional acting workshops, and a program called ASL Story Time.

A primary example of Deaf West's overarching impact on the theater community is its production of *Big River*. Deaf West's Broadway production of *Big River* (a musical based on Mark Twain's classic novel *The Adventures of Huckleberry Finn*) was nominated for two Tony Awards, Broadway's highest honor. Following the successful Broadway run, a multicity national tour commenced. The tour crossed the United States throughout the 2004-2005 season. Promotional materials for the tour exclaimed, "Deaf, hard-of-hearing and hearing actors perform each role in a synchronized ballet of speaking and signing. Spoken English and American Sign Language are interwoven with music, dance, and storytelling techniques from both hearing and deaf cultures into a 'third language' creating a unique theatrical event—the adventure of a lifetime!" A *Big River* study guide and deaf sensitivity packet were developed in conjunction with the tour to support the literary and artistic value of the production and bridge the communication divide between people who are deaf and others.

AXIS Dance Company   AXIS Dance Company (www.axisdance.org) began in 1987 as an inclusive movement class for women who use wheelchairs (see figure 13.2). Its press packet explains, "AXIS has been a bridge between contemporary dance and physically integrated dance." AXIS' mission includes creating and performing contemporary dance by dancers with and without disabilities; teaching about collaboration and disability; and promoting physically integrated dance locally, nationally, and internationally. AXIS' commitment to artistic excellence, and its recognized position within the dance world, can be witnessed in its collaborative work with prominent artists and choreographers and its numerous regional national awards. AXIS has created 40 in-house dance pieces, and its educational programs were featured at the Kennedy Center's national Imagination Celebration at the 2002 Olympic Arts Festival. In articulating the power of AXIS Dance, contemporary dance pioneer Bill T. Jones explains, "There is no more defiant a land that I can think of than AXIS. They showed me what dance could be."

Club Wild Club Wild is an Australian community arts organization. Its Web site (www.clubwild.net) explains, "Club Wild runs disability friendly dance parties, training and creative workshops in songwriting, music performance, drumming and dance, hip hop, rapping, DJing,

MCing, and multimedia." Simply stated, "Club Wild supports the creative expression of people with a disability through music, video and performance, and champions their equal participation in society—in seriously funky style!"

Club Wild's work stands uniquely in the middle of artistic, social, and vocational purpose. People of all abilities attend the club's dance parties. Club Wild's workshops develop artists. Its production program graduates theatrical technicians who are equipped with 21st-century techniques. Club Wild artists include DJs, bands, technicians, and more. Akash, a Club Wild DJ, works as a professional performer and composer, having created five film scores and seven albums. The Big Bag Band, another Club Wild act, is a group of artists with and without intellectual disabilities who have been making music since 1989.

Perspectives and Examples From the Visual Arts

VSA arts and Green Light We previously described the scope of VSA arts programming across the breadth of artistic disciplines, and we now focus on one program within this group's visual arts work. In 2001, VSA arts (www.vsarts.org) and Volkswagen Group of America initiated an awards program in which artists with disabilities ages 16 to 25 would receive a significant cash award to further their artistic careers. It is the largest awards program for young artists with disabilities in the United States. This award is particularly important in that it is received at the time in the artist's life when the first professional decisions are being made and support is especially important. Each year a call for entries focused on an arts-related theme is released, and a jury of accomplished leaders from the visual arts community reviews the entries and makes the award. (See figure 13.3 on page 242.)

The theme for the 2008 VSA arts/Volkswagen Group of America award was Green Light. Green Light encouraged young artists to reflect on their artistic motivations and inspirations. Each artist was asked to write an artist's statement as part of the submission process. The statement received from award recipient Michelle Herman explains, "For me, my disability is my 'Green Light.' I am thankful for the experiences I have had as they

Figure 13.2 AXIS Dance in Action.

AXIS Dance Company. Photo by Margot Hartford.

Figure 13.3 *Rustle* won the grand prize in the VSA arts Project Greenlight competition. This piece is a still picture taken from a video in which the sculptural capacity of fabric to illustrate environmental boundaries and movement is explored. The artist, Sara Meuhlbaeur, received her BFA from the University of Wisconsin–Madison.

have shaped me into the artist I am today." The total cash amount for the 2008 competition was $60,000. Fifteen emerging artists with disabilities received individual cash awards of up to $20,000 at a Capitol Hill reception (see figure 13.4). The works of art were then on display at the Smithsonian prior to a 2-year tour of U.S. colleges and universities. The VSA arts/Volkswagen Award, in terms of financial commitment and visibility, stands as an example of the importance and potential of the artists with disabilities when given recognition and support.

Sprout Sprout (http://gosprout.org) is a New York City–based nonprofit organization founded in 1979 to provide travel opportunities for people with disabilities, particularly people with intellectual disability or other developmental disabilities. Sprout programming has grown to include group travel experiences, camps, music festivals, and a film festival. Sprout currently serves more than 1,800 people with disabilities each year. Sprout's promotional materials assert that the organization's age-appropriate recreational and leisure activities enhance mobilization, self-confidence, and socialization

of participants while breaking down societal barriers that prevent the inclusion of people with disabilities.

The Sprout Make-a-Movie program and Sprout Film Festival are unique examples of media programs. The Make-a-Movie program, which began in 1994, offers people with developmental disabilities the opportunity to be involved in developing and producing movies that chronicle and display the life experiences of people who are traditionally marginalized or absent in mainstream film. Since 2005, the Sprout Film Festival has sought to provide a forum for artistic excellence and open discourse about the lives of people with developmental disabilities. Selected movies highlight both the ordinary and the exceptional nature of the day-to-day lives of people with disabilities. The 2008 festival included such titles as *Look Joe I Am in College*, which focused on the stories of four young men with Autism from public schools who are chosen to attend a university pilot program, and *The Gillian Film*, which tells the story of a woman with developmental disabilities who decides to move out of her family home and live on her own.

Still image of *Healing* (film), Michelle Lisa Herman. Image used with artist's permission.

Figure 13.4 *Healing* won the Award of Excellence in the VSA arts Project Greenlight competition. This piece is a still picture from a video in which the artist's mother reflects over the act of preparing bandages. Healing, both physically and emotionally, is the theme explored in this piece. The artist, Michelle Herman, earned her BFA in fine art and art history from the Maryland Institute College of Art in Baltimore.

Inside Out Productions, L.A. Goal Inside Out Productions (www.insideoutproductions.com), a program of L.A. Goal, was established in 1994 "to provide non-traditional creative jobs for adults with developmental disabilities." L.A. Goal maintains a variety of programs focused on developing independent living skills. Inside Out draws on the tradition of "outsider art" in which artists develop an individual style and artistic approach outside of traditional, or formal, artistic style. Inside Out employs part-time artists in a commercial art and sewing studio. Inside Out artists take classes in drawing, painting, ceramics, printmaking, and sewing led by professional artists. Their work is displayed in a virtual gallery online, an annual art show at an art gallery, three exhibitions at a cultural museum, and numerous special exhibitions. Members of Inside Out have been featured on the *NBC Today Show* discussing the publication of their book *Disabled Fables: Aesop's Fables Retold and Illustrated by Artists With Developmental Disabilities* (L.A. Goal, 2004).

The Inside Out artists themselves offer a compelling argument for the value of their artistic endeavors. The artwork featured in the virtual gallery depicts creative explorations of color and theme. Artist statements provide personal insight. Susan simply states, "Painting brings me peace." Jennifer describes, "My art is changing for me because my fingers have grown up." Lisie exclaims:

> Art is amazing because it comes magically from your own thoughts and imagination. Through my art I have learned that the storms outside in the world are like my personal storms and you can get through them.

David sums up his opinion about his artwork by saying, "I feel happy when I do art—proud and safe."

The art forms affect inclusive practice in several important ways. They are inherently inclusive in that they provide avenues for groups of artists to collectively communicate on equal ground. Dancers' bodies move through space in relation to one another, allowing the choreography to showcase the unique physicality of all dancers. The cast of a play creates a production by bringing the words of a script to life on a stage, embracing the abilities of all performers. Troupes, casts, bands, and choirs all encourage inclusion by their very nature. The art forms provide the mechanism by which individual artists can express their unique creative selves. Within this context, inclusion involves the space for a person's story to be told through art, thereby including that story alongside other stories and experiences. All stories are then given the opportunity to be heard. The art forms become a conduit for an inclusive message.

What Makes An Inclusive Arts and Culture Program Successful?

Now that we've defined inclusive arts and culture programs, discussed the fundamentals of inclusive arts and culture programming in terms of concepts and common practices, and highlighted examples across the art forms, it is time to turn our attention to the components of successful arts and culture programs. In general, well-run programs are well-run programs. Sufficient, well-managed resources are critical. Commitment to defined, sustainable, and meaningful impact is also important. But what does all that really mean? In pursuit of those broad and somewhat nebulous goals, it is helpful to break successful inclusive arts and culture programs down into actionable steps.

Maintain Sound Programmatic Practice

Successful inclusive arts and culture programs demand sound programmatic practice. We can draw on wealth of literature and practically gained wisdom about what constitutes good programming (Patton, 2002; Preskill & Catsambas, 2006). Organizational communication is key; this is particularly important in large organizations where many people work on many programs, across many organizational areas. A strategic plan and logic model can provide the backbone for communication and effective program execution. Fiscal responsibility and sound accounting infrastructure are also important. Evaluation—looking closely at how well a program is achieving its stated goals and objectives—plays a central role in programmatic practice, especially in an environment in which funding is often tied to a clearly articulated evaluation plan. These principles hold true across a breadth of organizations and programs.

The arts community has explored the ways in which sound programmatic practice intersects the work of artists. Publications are available that demonstrate sound evaluation practice in arts contexts (Callahan, 2004; National Endowment for the Arts, 2004; VSA arts, 2008). These resources uniformly acknowledge the challenge of arts evaluation, in terms of defining program goals, developing tools that accurately discern the impact of the programs on participants, and maintaining artistic integrity, while looking closely at programmatic elements that may or may not be closely related to the arts.

Integrate Context and Resources

What does it mean to integrate context and resources within an inclusive arts context? One example can be found in the experiences of people who provide programs in rural contexts versus those who work in urban or suburban areas. People who provide arts programming in rural contexts may have to reach out a little further in their search to receive funding. Finding artists trained to implement inclusive programming and obtaining space to conduct inclusive programs may also be barriers.

Providing programs that reflect local arts interest and need, while also maintaining a commitment to inclusion, is not always easy but certainly is possible. For example, you find that your state, city, town, or neighborhood has a community of visual artists with disabilities, and you work at a community center. You might suggest that the center be used as an exhibition space. You may also reach out to those artists to both show their work and possibly develop arts education classes. Similarly, suppose you work at a hospital that has an auditorium, large rooms, or common family areas, and you learn that a local theater troupe offers children's theater classes and performances. You may facilitate an arrangement in which the troupe offers workshops or performs in the hospital.

Integration of context and resources hinges on effective needs assessment. Needs assessment can be used to drive organizational strategy, determine potential funding sources, and guide hiring decisions (Gupta et al., 2007). Needs assessment can provide a solid foundation for providing inclusive programming in that it can map community strengths and needs with respect to the disability community, highlight inclusive resources, and initiate conversation and collaboration among groups in the community that have worked together before.

Provide Meaningful Arts and Culture Experiences

Arts and culture programs exist to provide meaningful arts and culture experiences. A clear focus on the arts needs to be continually reinforced and remembered in environments where program administration, competing organizational priorities, and better-funded programmatic agendas may divert attention. This is particularly important in contexts where resources dictate hiring people to run arts programs who may or may not have a commitment to the arts. Also, attempts to integrate the arts into other programs (such as a basic after-school, homework-focused program) may create the situation in which neither the arts, nor the homework, are well served.

Just what are meaningful arts and culture experiences? That question has perplexed artists, philosophers, theologians, and scholars for centuries. Theoretical explorations of experience abound in the work of prominent scholars in psychology, sociology, and education. "Multiple intelligences" (Gardner, 1983), "dispositional capacities" (Eisner, 1985), "flow" (Csikszentmihalyi, 1990), "aesthetic epistemologies" (Muxworthy Feige, 1999), "wide-awakeness" (Greene, 1977), "an experience" (Dewey, 1934/1980), and "narrative modes of knowing" (Bruner, 1985) are outlined in brilliant detail in an effort to describe the nature of meaningful experience. The science and philosophy of experience center on the idea that meaningful experience is a holistic process, allowing people to engage with themselves and others in unique and powerful ways. Change and evolution occur in the process of art making, pushing the boundaries of communication, investigation, and understanding. A commitment to meaningful arts and culture experiences demands that inclusive arts and culture programs flirt with the edge of identity, perception, and representation, challenging stereotype, privilege, isolation, and prejudice.

Capitalize on Diversity

One beauty of arts and culture programs is that there is no one-size-fits-all approach to making or appreciating art and culture. Within that frame, diversity becomes a reality within which to work—a strength to tap. Artists approach their art form as the product of their lives, using tools and a capacity for expression that allow them to create in individual ways. Similarly, audiences bring a unique and individual cultural background from which to interpret, respond, and participate. The distinction between artist and audience can be blurred when we talk about participatory and educational contexts, but diversity is still central to providing a rich artistic and cultural experience. This heterogeneity, this cacophony of voices, is the foundation on which arts and culture programming is based.

Often diversity gets stuck at the level of bumper sticker notions of Coke commercial unity and sameness, in which all are encouraged to "teach the world to sing in perfect harmony." Inclusion asks that diversity not stop there. Diversity is messy. Inclusion is messy. Real inclusion means that we navigate the world differently, create avenues for different opinions, and open doors for diversity to be explored with glorious contention. It also allows space for healing the wounds that arise when people talk of injustice, anger, pride, and love in the same breath. Inclusive arts and culture programs are in the enviable position of being able, by their very nature, to bring diversity to the front of community conversation.

Focus on Access

We now revisit access as a primary component of inclusive arts and culture programs. Access involves not only bricks and mortar accommodation but also a systemic approach to comprehensive policies and practices that encourage universal participation. Whether we're talking about an after-school arts program that provides support for its arts instructor to attend a professional development program focused on inclusive teaching practice, a nonprofit organization's board of directors that commits to hiring people with disabilities, or a community center that offers a broad variety of inclusive programs in which people of all abilities can participate, decisions must be based on accessibility.

At base, successful inclusive arts and culture programs use sound programmatic practice to increase participation in the arts and culture. Clear strategy and organizational structure are first steps to successful program implementation—that is, beginning with a defined end in mind. The groundwork for inclusion also includes fair hiring, appropriate space, and flexible planning. Decisions must be made based on artistic values and a commitment to diversity and access.

Summary

This chapter set out to encourage arts and culture programs in recreational contexts. Defining the legal, cultural, and philosophical aspects of inclusion provides the connection between general inclusion and inclusion within arts and culture. Learning about universal design, cultural competency, and cultural economy expands our ideas about access to include cultural and economic participation. Examples of inclusive practices and arts programs from across the arts disciplines make the theoretically explored concepts more tangible. Successful arts and culture programs that include all people can guide us in program management. The examples of such groups provided in this chapter reinforce the centrality of the arts experience within the inclusion discussion, support the idea that diversity is an asset, and demonstrate ways in which access can be achieved.

Discussion Questions

1. Describe inclusive arts and culture programs. What makes inclusive arts and culture programs inclusive?
2. Choose one of the highlighted arts and culture program and discuss the ways it is inclusive.
3. In what ways does cultural competency relate to inclusion?
4. What steps have been taken by the arts and culture community to increase inclusive practice and universal participation in arts and culture programs?
5. Identify common aspects of successful arts and culture programs.

›› Professionals in Action

Jaehn Clare

Apply dog logic to life: eat well, be loved, get petted, sleep a lot, dream of a leash-free world.
    –SARK

Reprinted, by permission, from Jaehn Clare. VSA Arts of Georgia.

Background Information

Education

   *BA Theater Arts, University of Minnesota, Minneapolis *MA Dramatic Literature, University of Essex, Colchester, United Kingdom

Credentials

   *CTRS *CPRP

Special Awards

   *Southern Artistry, the online registry of acclaimed artists living and working in the southeastern United States (2008) *Teaching Artist Fellow, VSA arts, the inaugural class of a new initiative, providing a year of high-level professional development for teaching artists with disabilities in the visual and performing arts (2006) *The Chaikin Prize, for outstanding contributions in representing people with disabilities in the performing arts; received the inaugural Chaikin Prize, established by Not Merely Players in honor of the late Joseph Chaikin (2005) *VSA arts of Minnesota establishes the *Jaehny*, an Arts Access Award, Minneapolis, MN, named in recognition of Jaehn's service as the chair of the founding board of directors (1996) *The Indie Award/Outstanding Achievement, *Belle's on Wheels*, *The Independent*, Santa Barbara, California (1995) *Commission Award, *Belle's on Wheels*, the Arts Council of Great Britain, London (1989) *Community Art Fund Grant, Seeing the Being, COMPAS, St. Paul, Minnesota (1987) *Outstanding Achievement/Drama, Rapid City Fine Arts Council, Rapid City, South Dakota (1977) *Best Thespian Award, Stevens High School, Rapid City, South Dakota (1977)

Special Affiliations

*Member, Arts Education Teaching Artist Bank, Georgia Council for the Arts, 2008 to present *Member, Touring Artist Roster, Georgia Council for the Arts, 2008 to present *Member, American Association of People with Disabilities, 2006 to present *Member, Alternate ROOTS, 2000 to present; Regional Representative/Executive Committee, 2003 to 2005 *Golden Key International Honor Society Lifetime Member *Phi Kappa Phi, Lifetime Member

Career Information

Position   Director of Artistic Development, VSA arts of Georgia

Organization Information   VSA arts of Georgia is a fully accredited affiliate of the VSA arts international network.

Organization's Mission   VSA arts of Georgia provides access to the arts for people with disabilities and those with low income. We are a statewide resource working with artists and organizations to fulfill our vision of an inclusive community that encourages everyone to enjoy and participate in the arts.

Size of Organization   VSA arts of Georgia is a medium-sized nonprofit arts organization employing four full-time employees and serving 165,000 people annually.

Job Description   The director of artistic development is the chief contact between VSA arts of Georgia and the artists, teaching artists, and others within those constituencies. The director of artistic development reports directly to the executive director and is responsible for the organization's consistent achievement of its mission as it pertains to artistic programming, education, and relations with community-based artistic organizations.

Following are other duties of the director of artistic development: Provide leadership in implementing organizational plans that pertain to artistic goals with the executive director. Work with the executive director on programming directly related to the artistic goals of the organization, which can include but is not limited to (a) curriculum for artist development and (b) programs and lesson plans for in-school and community residencies, workshops, and master classes. Maintain official records and documents, to assist in grant reporting and application. Maintain a working knowledge of significant developments and trends in the field, including attending and presenting at relevant conferences and gatherings. Publicize the activities of the organization, its programs, and its goals. Establish sound working relationships and cooperative arrangements with community groups and organizations. Represent the programs and point of view of the organization to agencies, organizations, and the general public in partnership with the executive director and especially as they pertain to the artistic goals of the organization. Be responsible, in partnership with the executive director, for the recruitment, employment (contractual), and communications of all artistic personnel, both paid and volunteers. Manage Arts for All Gallery including working, as a peer, with all committees, contractual curators, and artists related to the work of the gallery. Maintain basic marketing efforts for Arts for All Gallery in partnership with the executive director.

Career Path   When I moved to Georgia in 1997, I had a history with the VSA arts network based on my service as the chair of the founding board of directors of the VSA arts of Minnesota affiliate, in 1986. I contacted the Georgia affiliate office when I became a resident in Georgia, offering my services and seeking employment opportunities. In 2000, I moved to Atlanta, and I once again contacted the Georgia affiliate office, seeking opportunities for gainful employment as well as opportunities to contribute to the ongoing work of the VSA arts network around the world. Initially, I was hired as a part-time, temporary employee to serve as the office receptionist while the position was posted and the hiring process was managed. After a month in the position, I was offered a full-time permanent position. Since then,

(continued)

my title has changed four times, and my job description has continued to evolve and expand. I served the organization as interim executive director from February to April 2006.

What I Like About My Job In the current U.S. economy (March 2008) as a person with a disability, as a woman, and as an artist, I very much appreciate being gainfully employed; I like having a job. Additionally, I am employed in a position and with an organization that allows me to combine my personal and professional passions in service to positive social change in my immediate community, the southeastern United States, the United States as a nation, and the global culture. I do not have to stray very far from my authentic self in order to do this work. My job is grounded in providing significant learning opportunities for others, including working with and mentoring aspiring, emerging, developing, and established artists with disabilities who are in pursuit of their own career goals and artistic missions. My position affords me a high degree of flexibility; I enjoy and am honored to have the trust and confidence of a boss and colleague who is quite literally a *humane* being. I take my title of director of artistic development very seriously, and each day on the job I endeavor to apply it to our constituents, my colleagues at VSA arts of Georgia and at our partner agencies and organizations, and to myself as well. I appreciate having a job that feeds my soul.

Career Ladder Although I may not retire from or die in this particular position, working with VSA arts of Georgia is part of my long-term career goals and efforts and my personal and professional artistic mission. Given my history with the larger VSA arts network, no matter where I live I will seek out whatever local nonprofit arts organization that is affiliated with VSA arts to apply for employment opportunities and to contribute to the larger context of the work.

Advice to Undergraduate Students My advice to anyone aspiring to and developing a career path is this: Find a way to secure gainful employment doing something that you genuinely care about, even love. Too many people work at jobs that destroy their souls. Life is too short and (for most of us) our working lives are far too long to be employed doing something that we do not care about and that does not foster our own personal growth.

Personal Statement As a person with an acquired disability, I experienced a very particular form of oppression—the negative social stigma associated with being identified as DISabled. Working in the field of arts and culture allows me to maintain my personal sense of identity as an artist while also earning income with which to support my life. As an artist, I focus my work on the authentic exploration and expression of human experience, in all its myriad forms and manifestations. This is an endlessly fascinating field of study and endeavor. It is a personal choice to (or at least endeavor to) be part of the solution (rather than part of the problem). I have made a personal and professional commitment to working toward the elimination of all forms of oppression, and I believe the arts are uniquely and profoundly well suited to this work.

Inclusive Aquatics

MaryBeth Pappas Baun, MEd

Baun Associates, Wellness-Without-Walls, Center for Health Promotion and Research at the University of Texas, and The Houstonian Club

"*I can't fly but I can swim, and that's the next best thing! The water is my sky.*"

—Unknown

Learning Outcomes

After completing this chapter, learners will be able to do the following:

- Explain at least five ways that water offers an environment uniquely ideal for inclusive recreation.
- Explain the basic legal, attitudinal, marketing, and communication knowledge and skills required to effectively implement inclusive aquatics.
- Describe how to make aquatic facilities and equipment available and accessible to a wide variety of people.
- Explain some ways to tailor group aquatic classes to meet the needs of people with specific conditions and backgrounds.
- Describe how to use the physical properties unique to water, known as the multiple principles of hydrodynamics.
- Understand under what circumstances to apply the benefits associated with each hydrodynamic principle.

Aquatic environments can open the floodgates to joy, fun, accommodation, creativity, and cross-training for most populations and offer a powerful tool for inclusion. Movement in water liberates the body, enhances function and well-being, and allows a playfulness and exhilaration often elusive on land. The dynamics of water produce an inclusive environment by eliminating barriers normally encountered on land. The antigravity traits of buoyancy absorb impact shock and soften falls. Aquatic viscosity creates multidirectional resistance ideal for improving functional capacity, muscle strength and endurance, and range of motion (Koury, 1996). Warm temperatures and hydrostatic pressure can ease painful joints. Water also wicks away body heat and can alleviate the barrier of overheating.

This chapter describes the characteristics of water that make it uniquely inclusive by nature. You will learn about considerations that ensure accessibility, comfort, enjoyment, and productive, meaningful experiences for a wide variety of participants in the same group setting. The chapter outlines delivery strategies, guidelines, and methods that facilitate inclusion and management of risk and can bring about successful, sustainable recreation and fitness, including aquatic exercise and rehabilitation techniques that will appeal to and engage people within mixed groups. The text describes common health and functional conditions that recreation staff members are likely to encounter and ways that people with those conditions can best benefit from aquatic environments. The chapter also lists specific organizations and resources that offer further tools and assistance to enhance the inclusive aquatic experience.

Benefits of Participation in Aquatics

Water activity has many physical, emotional, social, cognitive, intellectual, and even spiritual benefits that make it inviting and popular with both recreation participants and staff. Participants in inclusive aquatics gain valuable motor skills, which can in turn enhance skills in other arenas. The aquatic environment provides freedom of movement and all of the benefits associated with feeling liberated from limitations, and it helps participants improve their fitness, including those with and without limitations.

Everyone who can enter the water can benefit from swimming or water exercise. Everyone can learn to

- float;
- make movements of swim strokes;
- blow bubbles;
- enhance posture, flexibility, and strength;
- improve balance and coordination;
- change body composition;
- support heart health;
- recuperate; or
- enhance function.

All it takes is the equalizing environment of water for partial or full immersion.

What other aspects facilitate universal inclusion in water? Often the area of focus is environmental support.

- Are the coaches and instructors well prepared and trained for inclusion?
- Can participants easily enter the facilities and the pool?
- Do pool temperatures match the needs of participants?
- Is the right kind and array of pool exercise and swimming equipment available?
- Has the facility or program management undertaken to educate and inform members, participants, and the community, as well as the entire range of staff?

This chapter describes in detail many of the issues and conditions to be addressed, and provides information on how to find more in-depth information on many aspects of inclusive water recreation.

Physical

The hydrodynamic properties of water provide buoyancy, hydrostatic pressure, viscosity, multidirectional resistance, eddy drag, and temperature enhancements, elements that can be used to increase participants' safety, function, enjoyment, comfort, relaxation, and fitness. Immersion in warm water (92-96°F or 33-35.6°C) transfers heat to the body, which relieves pain and enhances range of motion. Even activity in somewhat warm temperatures (83-88°F or 28-31°C) will improve the well-being of people with arthritis or fibromyalgia (Baun, 2008). For water exercise among people with arthritis, the water temperature should feel soothing. Temperatures from 83 to 86°F can benefit people with heart disease by preventing arrhythmias. Some people may be prone to overheating. Cooler pool water temperatures in the range of approximately 80 to 85°F (28°C) can be essential for pregnant women and people with lymphedema or multiple sclerosis (MS) and may prevent symptoms and complications. (National MS Society, www. nationalmssociety.org/; American College of Obstetrics and Gynecology). Children as well as adults with many kinds of disabilities benefit from the development and coordination of large muscles and smaller stabilizing core strength muscles used in aquatic exercise and from the coordination of arms, legs, and breathing required for swimming.

Cognitive and Intellectual

Water's motivational and healing properties create a stimulating environment, even for people with severe disabilities (Dulcy, 1983). Studies show that people with fibromyalgia, which often includes symptoms of "foggy thinking" and memory loss, can improve their cognitive and physical function with regular exercise in warm water (Munguia-Izquierdo & Legaz-Arrese, 2007). Research shows that aquatic exercise can reduce depression and anxiety (Piotrowska-Całka & Guszkowska, 2007). Children with autism have been known to be so inspired by the hydrodynamic properties of water that they teach themselves to swim. Swimming is a positive accomplishment for any child. Recreational programs use aquatic environments to teach those who are autistic the cognitive processing of multiple steps or multiple things to do, for example, jump in the water, hold one's breath, move arms and legs to tread water, breathe so as to not inhale water, float when needing a break. Children who have difficulty processing the sensory input in the world often find swimming to be a welcome respite, both relaxing and therapeutic.

Psychosocial

Water creates opportunities to socialize: The fact that we're all in the water together and "stripped down to our skivvies" tends to build rapport and trust. People of all ages, abilities, and disabilities can break down barriers to communication and

Reprinted, by permission, from J. Winnick, 2005, *Adapted physical education and sport*, 4th ed. (Champaign, IL: Human Kinetics), 354.

The fun of blowing bubbles in the water has another advantage: Fun creates enthusiasm and enhances a person's ability to initiate and sustain healthy physical activity habits.

develop social skills in water's equalizing and calming environment. A single water activity can often affect multiple dimensions. For instance, breath control exercises such as holding one's breath, inhaling and exhaling while swimming, and blowing bubbles improve respiratory function and oral motor control, which enhance physical health, social function, and verbal skills. Social interaction has a positive and protective impact on health and well-being, so the enhanced opportunity for interaction benefits all participants.

The ability to move more easily that water provides generates a feeling of independence and control. This asset can be carried over into other areas of life and can have a lasting effect on function and well-being. For instance, children with special needs live day-to-day lives where they often miss the goals that others set for them. These children are usually aware that they don't quite measure up at school or with social interaction with peers. Swimming and water activities offer these children an opportunity to succeed and enhance self-esteem. People with physical disabilities or limitations who feel more independent as a result of their experiences with the liberating qualities of water can improve their body image. Improved body image is in turn a powerful motivator for improved self-image, which builds confidence and self-efficacy (the belief that you can succeed with a given skill or behavior change). One's sense of meaning and purpose, an essential aspect of spiritual health, is greatly enhanced when a person is freed from limitations and can see herself in a new light with a greater and growing scope of capabilities and self confidence.

Sometimes participants express discomfort, even trepidation, about appearing publicly in a swimsuit. The most effective ways to facilitate a participant's process of working through this concern is to acknowledge it with respect, and then ask a few open-ended questions that allow the person to think through their concerns and come up with solutions in order to find a comfort zone that will work for them. Often people decide to wear shorts and a top. It is important to allow this in your policies, within limits (e.g., disallow cut-off shorts in order to protect the pool filtration system, but allow other shorts and tops). Some people decide to purchase the kind of fitness tights and tops that are UV protective, chlorine resistant, and made for water activities. Although in some cases it may require time and patience, when people think about how others likely feel the same way, often they can think beyond their discomfort. Often a simple explanation of the shared experience of similar discomfort suffices (e.g., that everyone is self-conscious at first) and soon their attention is focused on the water activity, most of which is underwater where no one can be seen clearly.

In some cases, gender-specific activities can make participants more comfortable. Physical, emotional, and social comfort is important to successful inclusion. In cases where participants have demonstrated the potential to drift into negative teasing, proactive intervention can help. Interactive group discussion, preferably before commencing the program or series, can focus on the value of everyone's enjoyment. To build awareness, participants might talk about ways they can respect each others' feelings in order to set a tone that builds a supportive environment for treating fellow participants with the same courtesies that would make their own participa-

tion most comfortable and enjoyable. In order to facilitate the kinds of attitude and behavior change that make everyone feel at ease and respected, work with individuals and the group, again with open-ended questions, so that they can come up with what they believe will work to make everyone in the group have a comfortable and enjoyable experience (e.g., ask "What would make you feel most comfortable with your participation in the water program? What would make you uncomfortable? What should we all do about that? Will that work? What else would work?"). This approach works for most ages and stages of development. Those who are too young or early in emotional and social development to participate in this kind of constructive conversation normally do not engage in negative teasing.

Safe, Successful, and Rewarding Programs

Success of an inclusive recreation program begins with strategic planning. The program's or center's values, mission, vision, and goals must explicitly embrace and foster inclusion. The mission statement normally reflects this commitment to inclusion, and it is communicated in brochures and advertisements, Web sites, posters, bulletin boards, and mail of all types. When training programs, including orientation, ongoing service learning, and continuing education, include a deep and meaningful focus on inclusion, staff can successfully deliver effective and rewarding programs. Monitoring and evaluation are required to ensure inclusive quality control. Schleien and Rynders (1998) summed up the concept like this: "Successful inclusion requires the major stakeholders of the service delivery system to adopt a philosophy and value system that reflects the right of every individual to participate" (p. 19).

Instructor Training and Credentialing

Instructor knowledge, attitude, and skill are reported by stakeholders as among important criteria for successful inclusion of diverse people in group settings. This comes up consistently among all groups, including professional evaluators, participants, caregivers, and parents (Suomi & Suomi, 2000). Although some instructors come to your program or facility with the right attitude and skills, most will need the kind of training and leadership that allow them to grow and develop their attitudes, knowledge, and skills so that they can be effective facilitators and advocates for inclusive aquatic recreation (Conaster & Block, 2001; Conaster et al., 2000).

The purpose of inclusion in aquatic activities and classes is to provide opportunities for all people to learn and recreate together and interact as they do in other areas of life. Experts agree that the key factor to successful inclusion is the instructor. Three additional factors that affect successful aquatic inclusion are (1) a coach or instructor's knowledge, beliefs, and attitudes about aquatics for people with disabilities; (2) availability of the right kinds of equipment; and (3) high-quality, hands-on training (Conaster & Block, 2001; Conaster et al., 2000). The benefits to participants with and without disabilities are bountiful: opportunities to learn from healthy role models, enhanced potential for friendships and socialization, a reduction in isolation, the chance to identify aspirations and meet challenges, and the opportunity to become more accepting of, and learn from, people who are different from themselves (DePauw, 2000).

In a study of physical educators' views on preparation for inclusion, hands-on training was identified as the most valuable knowledge source for instructors to teach participants with disabilities (Hardin, 2005) and successfully combine people with diverse needs and backgrounds into group programs and settings (Suomi & Suomi, 2000). Conferences and seminars provide updates on practical techniques, methods, and equipment, and experienced instructors benefit from the continuing education. New or inexperienced instructors, however, can be easily overwhelmed by the massive amount of new information and are better served in multisession training classes and in-service training specific to their objectives. For more information on certification and training in aquatic instruction for people with disabilities, contact the American Association for Physical Activity and Recreation (AAPAR), which is part of the American Alliance for Health, Physical Education, Recreation and Dance (AAHPERD) or the YMCA. The Aquatic Exercise Association (AEA), the Arthritis Foundation (AF), and the Aquatic Therapy and Rehab Institute (ATRI) provide aquatic training and certification for instructors that include serving participants with various medical conditions. Instructors must take it upon themselves, preferably with the support and resources of the recreation facility

or program management, to gain the knowledge, behaviors, and skills needed to become an effective leader of inclusive aquatics.

Essential Coaching Communication Skills

Rapport and trust are built via communication, both verbal and nonverbal. We all express ourselves with body language, tone of voice, posture, gestures, degree and type of eye contact, and facial expressions, and all of this can make more impact than words. The single most important element in essential communication skills is listening. The better you listen, the more effective you will be as a coach, instructor, or leader. Effective leaders, coaches, and instructors begin with a welcoming, accepting, nonjudgmental, and nonauthoritarian attitude and ask open-ended questions (rather than yes-or-no questions) to determine what kind of leadership and coaching each participant needs. Effective leaders listen to the answers and use that information to form their next question. This method helps participants feel heard, respected, empowered, and confident to move forward with their recreation activities.

Go over what you and the individual or group expect from each other. Work together as equals to create and develop programs. Create new and interesting ways to share planning and promote communication. If clients are too young or have cognitive impairments that limit their ability to plan for the future, invite their significant others to join in the planning (Lepore et al., 2007).

Always answer questions with patience, no matter how many times you may have answered that question before, even for the same person. Show receptivity and respect by bending down to listen at the person's eye level. Make contact when appropriate by shaking or touching the participant's hand. Invite participants to make a prioritized list of aquatic activities they would like to accomplish (Lepore et al., 2007).

To reassure yourself of your own capability and confidence, and to foster positive relationships with your participants, familiarize yourself with all aquatic equipment, learn how it works, take it into the water, and become proficient before you use it with participants. Well in advance of your first session, practice procedures and familiarize yourself with transfers, braces, lifts, and any medical equipment used by participants (Lepore et al., 2007). Preparations and practice will lead to more comfortable interactions with participants, especially in the initial stage, during which first impressions are formed.

Trust and rapport develop out of the respect, patience, practice, and preparation you show your participants. Your interactions with participants must demonstrate your integrity, honesty, and commitment (Lepore et al., 2007). Displaying flexibility and patience, for instance, by being prepared and willing to adapt to unexpected circumstances, and by following through on decisions and promises, will build respect. Use language and actions that put people first: Refer to a participant as *a person with arthritis, a person with diabetes,* or *a person with cerebral palsy* rather than as *an arthritic, a diabetic,* or *a CP.* The term *people with disabilities* is considered more respectful than *handicapped people* (Lepore et al., 2007).

To enhance communication or overcome barriers, carefully tune in to participants' expressions, changes of expression, facial flush, body language, gestures, and tone of voice. Be prepared for communication challenges: Learn sign language, and keep pictures, a chalk board, and chalk handy so that participants have alternative ways of sharing their thoughts, interests, preferences, and questions. Good communication enhances safety and comfort, ensures that both leader and participant have a positive experience, and is imperative for avoiding contraindicated activities and medical emergencies.

Collaboration, Integration, and Program Promotion

For a program to be successful, all stakeholders must work together. What program can succeed without the backing and support of the people responsible for communications and marketing? The accountants? The facility supervisors? Stakeholders can include medical staff, physical therapists, communications and marketing professionals, safety and risk management specialists, facilities managers, accounting and finance specialists, trainers, consultants, executive managers, and any other people involved in the program. Sometimes perfectly good programs fall away before they have a chance to begin because of inadequate collaboration in using all possible communication channels creatively and effectively. Support is a critical factor in developing inclusion programs. Lepore and colleagues (2007) listed some critical areas of support to consider, inventory, and cultivate when developing an inclusive aquatic program:

- Resource support, which includes adaptive equipment, financial resources, information resources, and human resources
- Technical support, which can include the services of a consultant who provides strategic assessment and planning, training, in-service education, team teaching, mentoring, and collaboration on development, implementation, evaluation, and growth
- Moral support, which refers to management buy-in and supportive actions, such as experienced aquatic instructors who provide examples and assist other instructors and trainees

Ideas to garner support, network, and collaborate include:

- Identify and inventory your stakeholders and champions. This process builds ownership among stakeholders and can prevent obstacles later on.
- Identify and inventory your community service resources. Explore opportunities for collaboration by networking with representatives from organizations in your community.
- Seek opportunities to collaborate with educational institutions who share your vision or mission. Find out who is conducting research relevant to your projects, and explore possibilities for connections or work with internship programs to give students a chance to learn and grow with your programs.
- Establish mentor programs that pair experienced instructors with new ones for shadowing and supportive relationships.
- Seek out experts who have the credentials and experience to work with you to facilitate the kind of development, guidance, or problem solving that is necessary for your program to succeed.

Aquatic Environments

Implementing inclusive aquatics requires not only welcoming and well-trained staff but also careful attention to physical environment and climate. This section describes basic requirements for inclusive aquatics, including access, transfer, equipment and supplies, facilities, maintenance, and legal issues.

Effects of Legislation on Aquatic Facilities and Activities

The U.S. Congress defined disability in the Rehabilitation Act of 1973. The federal law defines a qualified individual, one who would be covered by laws related to people with disabilities, as someone with a physical or mental impairment that substantially limits one or more of life's major activities (for more information, see www.ada.gov). Over the years, various pieces of federal legislation have been passed to ensure that people with limitations and disabilities have access to aquatic programming. The Americans with Disabilities Act (ADA) standards of 2004 provided guidelines as to what must be accessible in relation to swimming pools, clarifying previous uncertainty and requiring *reasonable accommodation*. The ADA requires that policies, facilities, and programs be adapted so that people with disabilities can participate in mainstream life with people without disabilities.

What is reasonable accommodation may differ from pool to pool. The accommodations must not place *undue hardship* on an organization; in other words, providing access should not lead to profound cost or difficulty for an organization, as determined by its size and financial resources. The pool must be *readily accessible,* meaning easily and immediately usable, where a person with a disability can move around (Scott, 1990). Features of readily accessible facilities include ample parking for people with disabilities, a well-marked route into the facility and to the pool, inclusion of pool hand rails and ramps, signs in braille, family restrooms, and usable lifts or moveable floors. The accommodation must be *readily achievable,* a term that refers to how easily a facility can remove a barrier. Examples of easily achievable modifications that would be required under the act include lowering hooks in locker rooms, unbolting locker-room benches to accommodate wheelchairs, purchasing a transfer tier to help participants into the pool, printing aquatic manuals and other materials in braille, lowering shower door risers so that wheelchairs can enter, and eliminating water collection troughs that would impede access to people with mobility limitations.

There are certain exceptions to the requirement to provide reasonable accommodations:

- When a person does not meet the criteria of a qualified individual with a disability
- When a person does not meet the qualifications to participate in the activity (e.g., able to hold his breath under water)
- When a person's participation creates a reasonable probability of substantial risk to himself or others
- When program modifications significantly alter the primary purpose of the designated aquatic program (e.g., a diving competition would not need to accommodate a person for whom diving is contraindicated)

Pool Access

Many laws apply to inclusive aquatics. To meet the applicable legislation, start by obtaining a copy of *Accessible Swimming Pools and Spas: A Summary of Accessibility Guidelines for Recreation Facilities*, published by the U.S. Access Board (2003).

The following are important considerations recommended in *Accessible Swimming Pools and Spas* (U.S. Access Board, 2003) to reduce barriers to participation in aquatic programs.

Accessibility Guidelines for Swimming Pools and Spas

- Swimming pools with less than 300 linear feet (91.4 meters) of pool wall: The primary means of entry must be either a sloped entry into the water or a pool lift that is capable of being operated independently by a person with a disability.
- Swimming pools with more than 300 linear feet (91.4 meters) of pool wall: A minimum of two means of accessibility are required; the primary means must be either a sloped entry into the water or an independently operated pool lift, whereas the secondary means can be a lift, sloped entry, transfer wall, transfer system, or pool stairs. It is recommended that the secondary means not duplicate the primary means.
- Spas: At least one accessible means of entry is required, which can be a pool lift, transfer wall, or transfer system.
- Wave action pool or leisure river: At least one accessible means of entry, such as a pool lift, sloped entry, or transfer system, must be provided.
- Wading pools: One sloped entry into the deepest part of the pool is required. Handrails are not required.

Reprinted, by permission, from M. Lepore, G.W. Gayle, and S. Stevens, 2007, *Adapted aquatics programming*, 2nd ed. (Champaign, IL: Human Kinetics), 15.

Transfer Capability Guidelines and Biomechanics

Transfer in or out of a wheelchair is potentially dangerous for all involved, and the utmost attention is required. The primary concern is safety of the lifters and the participant. Proper body mechanics and use of appropriate equipment prevent injury. Assess each participant and circumstance before attempting transfer, analyze the answers to the following questions, and design a plan to prevent injury:

- What is the participant's preferred mode of transfer, if any?
- Can you teach the participant to transfer herself?
- Does the participant or caregiver have the knowledge and communication skills to describe how to undertake the transfer most successfully?
- How will the participant help with the transfer?
- If assistance is required, are competent aides available? Do they know their roles, the goals, and who is in charge?
- What equipment is needed, and is it functioning properly?
- What exactly will be done, and what's the easiest way to do it?
- Have obstacles been removed from the transfer area?
- Are transfer assistants' hands placed properly on the participant and on the equipment? (Lepore et al., 2007)

Give the participant and the people assisting a heads up: Say, "On the count of three we're going to lift you up. Ready?" Once the transfer is complete, ensure that the participant is comfortable and positioned correctly and all lifters are ready to relinquish their hold (Lepore et al., 2007).

Proper body mechanics are essential to the safety and efficiency of transfer.

- Keep the load balanced and close to your body.
- Carry the load at a comfortable height.
- Use your legs and hips for lifting, and keep your back straight.
- Avoid twisting or rotating your trunk when lifting and carrying.

- Plan your lift so that the majority of your effort comes from your legs, buttocks, and trunk, which form your base of support.
- Stand with one foot forward to create a wider base of support.
- Make sure that you have unimpeded access to your holds and will not be hindered during the transfer by armrests, footrests, or abduction pommels.
- When all precautions have been taken and everyone is ready, unfasten the participant's seat belt and any other straps.

Pool Entry and Pool Lifts

Entries to the pool and spa determine whether people of many ability levels can participate together in aquatic group programs. In some cases, pool access is the only barrier to participation, and structural changes or lift-and-transfer equipment within the facility is required. Please see figures 14.1 and 14.2 for examples of lift and transfer options that can mitigate barriers to participation involving pool entry.

Figure 14.1a Sloped entries provide a means of access that can make broad inclusion in aquatic programs possible.

Reprinted, by permission, from M. Lepore, G.W. Gayle, and S. Stevens, 2007, *Adapted aquatics programming*, 2nd ed. (Champaign, IL: Human Kinetics), 114.

Figure 14.1b Gradually sloping stairs make access easier for many inclusive aquatic participants who don't use ladders but do not need a lift or graduated slope.

Reprinted, by permission, from M. Lepore, G.W. Gayle, and S. Stevens, 2007, *Adapted aquatics programming,* 2nd ed. (Champaign, IL: Human Kinetics), 115.

Figure 14.1c Portable lift devices take up more deck space than permanent lifts. The advantage is that they can be moved to provide access in various locations.

Figure 14.1d Portable stairs can be moved out of the pool when space is needed.

Reprinted, by permission, from M. Lepore, G.W. Gayle, and S. Stevens, 2007, *Adapted aquatics programming,* 2nd ed. (Champaign, IL: Human Kinetics), 119.

Figure 14.1e Sometimes transfers can be made comfortable simply by placing a mat over the edge of the pool deck to prevent bruises and abrasions.

Reprinted, by permission, from M. Lepore, G.W. Gayle, and S. Stevens, 2007, *Adapted aquatics programming,* 2nd ed. (Champaign, IL: Human Kinetics), 108.

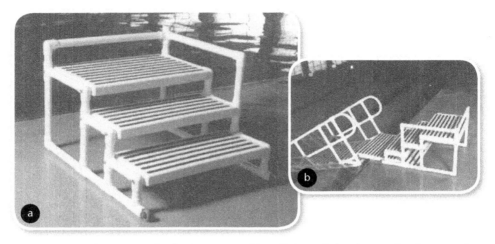

Figure 14.2a-b Aquatek platforms provide a lightweight alternative for transfer into and out of the pool. For more information on lifts and transfer systems, see *Adapted Aquatics Programming: A Professional Guide* by Lepore et al. Human Kinetics, 2007.

Photo courtesy of Rehab Systems, LLC.

Environment, Facilities, Equipment, and Supplies

The Access Board provides information to help existing facilities address issues of accessibility at www.access-board.gov/recreation/guides/pools. htm#Accessible and in the *Federal Register*. To summarize, ADA Title II obliges state and local governments that provide recreation facilities and Title III obliges private recreation facilities to remove architectural barriers in existing facilities when such action is readily achievable. Existing pools have an obligation to the U.S. Justice Department to remove barriers over time and provide access. In addition to addressing pool entries and exits, parking, routes and entrances, and lockers or dressing rooms, the ADA Accessibility Guidelines for Building and Facilities and the Architectural Barriers Act Accessibility Guidelines call for the following pool deck requirements:

- All deck space must meet guidelines for accessible routes with a width of at least 36 inches (91.4 centimeters), with occasional spaces for two wheelchairs to pass, and with a maximum slope of 1:12 (Note: People who use a hand-propelled wheelchair normally appreciate efforts to keep the ratio as far below 1:12 as possible). Access routes are

not required for raised diving boards, raised platforms, and waterslides.

- Clear deck space of 36 inches (91.4 centimeters) wide and 48 inches (121.9 centimeters) length forward is required next to a lift, on the side of the seat opposite the water.

- On transfer walls and near transfer systems there must be a minimum clear deck space of 60 by 60 inches (152.4 by 152.4 centimeters), and slope of clear deck space may be no more than 1:48, or 2% grade.

Creating an environment conducive to inclusion requires more than meeting legal requirements. There are many ways to enhance access and accommodation to suit the variety of needs by people with various conditions. Proactively examine the exercise environment and determine how to best suit participant needs and requirements. The following are some guidelines to help prepare the best environment.

Temperature and Humidity

Temperature governs the participant's comfort in water. Warm water temperatures (80-86°F, or 27-30°C) increase circulation to the muscles, preparing them for stretching and reducing chance of injury. People with arthritis or fibromyalgia will prefer and benefit from water temperatures of 83 to 86°F (28-31°C) for aerobic activity such as swimming, water walking, or flotation jogging.

Temperatures greater than 88°F (21°C) are not appropriate for cardiovascular or aerobic activity because such temperatures do not let the body cool down properly during repetitive, sustained movements of the large muscle groups that use the aerobic energy system. Nonaerobic range-of-motion exercises, such as stationary stretches, ankle or shoulder rolls, or thumb circles, performed while immersed in temperatures from 94 to 104°F (34-40°C) enhance mobility and reduce the joint pain and stiffness associated with arthritis and fibromyalgia. Particularly when the weather is hot, people with multiple sclerosis need to exercise in cooler pool temperatures of 80 to 85°F (27-29°C) in order to decrease the likelihood of exacerbation of symptoms (www.nationalmssociety.org/news/news-detail/index.aspx?nid=1681). Women who are pregnant need to dissipate heat to keep their core temperature in healthy ranges in order to protect the fetus from harmful rises in body temperature, and pool temperatures around 80°F (27°C) will provide a comfortable and safe environment for most women who are expecting. Women with lymphedema have experienced improvements in their condition according to a study that used hydrotherapy at about 89°F (32-33°C; Tidhar & Katz-Leurer, 2009).

Risk Management

Much of what is considered reasonable accommodation falls under the category of risk management. Some examples follow.

Locker Rooms and Restrooms

- Install nonskid carpet from the shower area to the pool ladder to aid participants in balance, crutch traction, orientation, or mobility.
- Provide disability-accessible family and caregiver restrooms and changing areas so that caregivers of the opposite gender can assist.
- Provide disability-accessible private changing and restroom areas, located in the same area as the pool, on the same floor, for people who observe strict modesty (because of cultural tradition or personal inclination) and for people who are transgender. A separate disability-accessible restroom that provides privacy for family and caregivers, with signage identifying it as such, works well.

Aquatic Equipment

- Provide flotation devices for people who cannot stand on the pool bottom, for instance, those with paraplegia or dwarfism.
- Provide a water chair and include upper-body movements in water aerobics classes to accommodate people with lower-body impairments.
- Provide supportive floating equipment designed to aid those with lower-body challenges to walk in the pool, such as the Water Walking Assistant.

Special Accommodations

- Allow a person who has a urine bag to wear long, baggy shorts over her swimsuit to avoid embarrassment.
- Allow participants with obesity and those with financial challenges to wear shorts and a top rather than a bathing suit.
- Allow an aide to participate in the program with a person who needs support; do not charge a fee for the aide to participate.
- Designate an area on the pool deck for assistive companions, guide dogs, crutches, wheelchairs, and other support and mobility equipment.
- Provide special services such as braille or computer disk for registrations, handouts, and certificates.
- Eliminate requirements that discriminate, such as a height requirement for being able to stand on the bottom of the pool, which may not be met by participants who use wheelchairs or have dwarfism.
- Be sensitive to the fact that in some Asian and Middle Eastern cultures it inappropriate for a person to show another the bottom of his feet, make eye contact with the opposite gender, or engage socially with the opposite gender (e.g., be in the pool together). To accommodate the cultural diversity of your participants, consider providing women's-only and men's-only pool time and activities. This arrangement may appeal to others who have no cultural tradition along these lines but would prefer the arrangement for personal reasons.

Nicholas Brown, associate editor
Athletic Business

It is widely acknowledged that people of Muslim faith represent one of the fastest-growing population segments in the United States and Canada. Less appreciated, according to some experts, are their recreation needs.

A glaring example is women's swimming. According to most interpretations of the tenets of Islam, Muslim women are not to be in public without hijab (head and hair coverings and loose-fitting, modest dress that leave only the hands, feet, and face exposed). For safety reasons, the practice is certainly not conducive to swimming. And for particularly conservative Muslims, the idea of donning tight-fitting swimwear in a public recreation environment is almost unthinkable.

It's a problem that Juanita Bueschleb, aquatics supervisor for the city of Mississauga, Ontario, believes every recreation provider with Muslim patrons has a duty to address. "Swimming is different. It's not just a recreation activity, it's a life skill," she says. "And if someone is never provided the opportunity to learn to swim in a comfortable environment, then that person is at risk."

Despite the logistical challenges, some communities have demonstrated that conservative Islam and the freedom to recreate need not be mutually exclusive. In Cary, NC, while organizing swim classes for boys, a group of Muslim parents wondered what it would take to do the same for girls. A local aquatics center offered its standard rental fee for a 15-yard pool ($170 per hour), but windows overlooking a larger pool precluded the kind of women-only privacy required by the group's faith, according to Raleigh *News & Observer* reports.

After a $3,000 private fundraising effort on the part of the Muslim group, and approval from the aquatics center, a retractable shade system was installed. The first learn-to-swim class—involving some 35 women and girls in full-body swimwear, as well as female lifeguards and instructors—took place in December.

"I've wanted to waterproof this community for a long time," Jenny Jaber, a water safety instructor and Islam convert told the *News & Observer's* Yonat Shimron. "We're around water all the time."

Salman Shiekh, a native of Pakistan who helped lead the effort to make the class possible, told the paper, "It makes sense for business and service providers to accommodate the needs of the community. All it takes is dialogue to make it happen."

That very dialogue is what led Bueschleb and her staff to create numerous aquatics programs designed to attract more patrons from one of the city's more ethnically diverse neighborhoods into the pool and, ultimately, make them water-safe.

"There were a lot of people coming into the center, but there were not a lot of people coming into the pool area," says Bueschleb, adding that discussions with various users revealed that many of them—including people with body-image issues, teenage boys and girls, and some Muslim women—simply weren't comfortable in an open swim environment. Thus, new swim programs—including the women-only swim classes that are enjoyed by many Muslim patrons—were created and have boosted the center's attendance figures.

Bueschleb stresses that none of the programs are faith-based or discriminate on the basis of faith. But even limiting participation based on gender has made some waves. "We do run into some resistance to our female-only programming," she says. "There's a segment of the population that thinks it's almost like taking a step backward. But my belief is that it's almost like creating accessibility policies for people with disabilities. Everybody wants to participate in recreation programming, and we should be finding ways to allow everyone to do so."

Al Ellard, an associate professor in the Recreation, Parks, and Leisure Services department at Central Michigan University, says looking backward may not be all bad when evaluating how well recreation providers are serving their Muslim patrons.

"I grew up in a fairly conservative Baptist family, and there were people among the folks I went to church with that didn't believe in mixed bathing—men and women swimming together," says Ellard, who helped develop a National Recreation and Park Association Conference session last year on leisure programming for people of Muslim faith. "Of course there is as much diversity among Muslim people as there is among Baptist or Catholic people—some people are more conservative and some are more secular in their beliefs. The fact is that those people with the more conservative beliefs may not like mixed bathing—and that's a fact that a lot of communities have yet to accommodate."

Simple policy decisions can provide a good starting point. In Dearborn, MI, a Detroit suburb that boasts one of the highest concentrations of Arab-Americans in the country, policies related to dress and poolside access have been created to accommodate Muslim patrons. As opposed to requiring everyone on the pool deck to change and shower, the city created designated "spectator only" areas in which pool attire is not required, allowing mothers in full modest dress to monitor the pool.

As for accommodating actual swimmers without jeopardizing their safety, the city has specified that: a) swimsuits are required, but they may be worn underneath commercially approved full-body swimwear, and all clothing materials must be light enough in weight—as with nylon, polyester, Lycra, or thin cotton—that when waterlogged they do not inhibit in any way the swimmer's movements or ability to stay above the water surface; b) the clothing must not be excessively loose so that it could pose any danger of entanglement, entrapment, or strangulation; and c) bathing caps and other tight-fitting head apparel are permitted.

"We have modified our policy to allow more leniency on full-body attire," explains Greg Orner, the city's recreation director, adding that swimmers in Dearborn's pools often wear suits resembling the full-body racers worn by many competitors at last year's Beijing Olympics. (Several manufacturers now market swimwear specifically to Muslim women.)

Dress accommodations should also be considered for other recreational activities, says Ellard. In fact, many agencies may not realize that they have dress policies—either written or implicit, based on years of practice or available resources—precluding the participation of conservative Muslims. "Do you really have to be wearing a tank top and shorts to participate in a basketball league?" asks Ellard.

Policy issues aside, there are even facility design issues to consider. "We've collectively moved toward designing rec centers so they're like fishbowls, where everybody can see everything," says Ellard. "In a heavily Muslim community, that may not be the way to go. Muslim women like to recreate, but they often don't like to recreate in front of men. You want to ask yourself in the design process, 'Will people of certain beliefs be able to participate?'"

There are instances in which conservative Islamic beliefs are irreconcilable with public policy designed to prevent discrimination. Some women may only participate in aquatics if they can be assured that other participants—as well as lifeguards and instructors—will be clothed from head to toe. In such instances, private facility rentals can be appropriate.

Safety and supervision requirements notwithstanding, often all that's needed to appease groups that wish to be segregated from the rest of the facility are retractable shade systems like the one in Cary, and some Muslim groups have even brought in their own rolls of brown paper to cover windows and expanses of interior glass.

"We have a wide variety of groups that rent our pool, and people can choose what they want to do with their rental," says Bueschleb. "If any rental group requests that they want the blinds closed, we can accommodate that. If they specifically request one gender for staffing, we can try to accommodate that, as well."

"It's not a Muslim issue," says Bueschleb, adding that the city similarly tries to accommodate groups such as the Roaming Bears, composed of nudist men. "You look around and ask, 'Who's missing from the pool area, and how do we get those people to come to the facility,'" she says. "It's about ensuring that everyone in the community has access."

Hydrodynamics: Basic Water Physics

You are about to embark upon a voyage through the uniquely different aquatic laws of physics, how to use them safely and effectively to enhance well-being for all people, and paths to traverse the endless frontier of opportunities for inclusion.

The unique characteristics of water make it an excellent medium for multiple goals and for nearly every type of participant. The term *hydrodynamics* refers to the physical principles associated with moving the body in water. Understanding how best to use those principles can empower recreation professionals to create and provide safe, effective inclusive aquatic programs. Several specific hydrodynamic principles explain the various ways that water affects the movement of the body in the aquatic environment (see table 14.1 on page 262).

Table 14.1 Hydrodynamics Summary: Basic Water Physics

Hydrodynamic principle	Description	Purpose and benefit for inclusive aquatics	Issues and concerns
Buoyancy	The propensity to float	- Reduces impact shock. - Reduces gravity's downward pressure on joints. - Provides resistive force. Note: People with high fat-to-lean ratios may not require buoyancy equipment for flotation aquatics.	- During shallow-water moves, watch for those who have high fat-to-lean ratio, and move them to waist-deep water, rather than-chest deep, to improve control.
Hydrostatic pressure	Equalized pressure of water around a joint	- Can reduce or eliminate pain due to compression in joints. - Improves range of motion and flexibility. - Improves the balance of strength and endurance in muscle groups.	- Guide participants with joint pain to move slowly and within control, using stabilized neutral positioning. - Use hydrostatic pressure (along with buoyancy) to improve balance function.
Movement of force and viscosity	Movement in multiple directions through the increased density of water compared with air	- Creates challenge in dual directions with each completed movement. - Allows for movement in multiple directions of joint function.	- Consider speed of movement to determine degree of intensity. - Perform each exercise at three different speeds.
Progressive overload and FITT principle (frequency, intensity, type, and time)	Gradual increase in force and speed or added resistance equipment to intensify until the exercise is somewhat vigorous without being exhausting	- Can safely improve function, fitness, body composition, and overall health and well-being.	- Increase frequency, intensity, number of repetitions, or length of exercise sessions only after proper stabilization is sustainable at the current level of challenge. - Increase only one aspect at a time and allow for adaptation before adding additional challenges or increasing a different FITT area.
Leverage and eddy drag	Lengthened levers (limbs) increase resistance of force when moving forward and back. Bent limbs or changing direction churn up turbulence when moving side to side, creating greater resistance.	- Allows for variations and creativity in use of resistance.	- Make sure that each person can maintain postural stability (neutral posture) and no one becomes overly challenged by turbulent environments.

Buoyancy

The less dense an object is, the more it is inclined to float. Humans are less dense than water and are therefore inclined to float. Every person has a different propensity to float, based on the percentage of fat to bone and lean muscle tissue and the amount of air the lungs can hold. Therefore, some people experience more exaggerated effects of buoyancy than others. Greater buoyancy may reduce impact shock, but it may also make it more difficult to control movements and posture in water.

The buoyancy that water creates can enhance fitness and function while it decreases the harmful effects of impact shock. The force that buoyancy generates can add either assistance or resistance to movements performed in water. Buoyancy makes it easier to move toward the surface of the water and harder to move away from the surface. It absorbs shock and in the right circumstances can make standing, walking, and running easier for those challenged due to injury or functional condition.

The water displaced when a person enters the water creates buoyancy and produces the non-weight-bearing aspect of exercising in water that makes jumping and running more comfortable. Buoyancy and the hydrostatic pressure around a joint (equalized pressure of water) reduce the pressure of gravity on the joint capsule, working in tandem with the warmth of the water to create a more pain-free environment for increasing range of motion in stiff joints. In water, a person can jump higher, leap farther, run or walk longer, and push harder because of the comfortable, protective environment. That makes water an ideal environment for group programs that include a wide variety of participants in a single program or class: Water's hydrostatic pressure and buoyancy properties, combined with effective cueing and instruction in order to match techniques to goals and concerns, create the opportunity to mix people of many ages, health conditions, fitness levels, and perspectives. With facilitation by well-versed instructors who are committed to inclusion, each student learns to harness specific hydrodynamics principles relevant to her successful participation in the group and to address her own unique styles, preferences, and needs.

Movement of Force, Viscosity, and Hydrostatic Pressure

Pushing or pulling against buoyancy creates resistance that can be increased by adding larger or more buoyancy floats to the working limbs. Participants can use the density of water by using flotation-based resistance equipment that requires pushing against the force created by buoyancy.

The density of water presents resistance, creating a physical conditioning challenge that increases endurance, strength, and power, thereby enhancing function and fitness. When the frontal plane of the body encounters water's viscosity (density), it displaces water and meets with resistance: The faster the speed or the greater the force, the higher the level of resistance. This property is called the *viscosity principle*.

Water creates balanced resistance in multiple directions because immersion in water exerts hydrostatic pressure equally on all the different surfaces of the body. Movement in any direction meets equal resistance in all directions so that opposing muscle groups can be worked equally. A side leg lift, for instance, works the outside of the thigh on the way out and the inside of the thigh on the way in.

The fitness principle of *progressive overload* allows one to intensify results as a participant becomes stronger and more proficient: participants can gradually increase the force and speed or add resistance equipment to intensify the workout until it feels vigorous or somewhat vigorous without being exhausting. Participants should increase only to the point where they can still maintain stable movement control and keep the torso position strong and steady. Avoid increasing both the number of repetitions and the resistance at the same time.

Higher viscosity (or density) in the water means that the faster the move, the greater the resistance that a moving object encounters. To use this training principle, perform each exercise at three speeds. As in all exercise, stay within the limits; if the participants cannot maintain proper stability or the muscle fatigues, they have reached the limit and it is time to switch to another move or to stop and stretch. Respecting the limits, enhancing muscle balance, moving in multiple directions, and moving at multiple speeds are key principles in physical conditioning for healthy function.

Leverage and Eddy Drag

The movable joints in the body function as levers. Participants can change intensity by using the levers in several ways. In most cases, longer levers increase the workload. For example, by bending the knee while gliding the leg forward and back, shorten the lever, decrease the leverage, and reduce the intensity. This is called the *leverage principle*.

A bent limb moved sideways will increase the body's surface area to encounter turbulent *eddy drag* (the circular currents created when the body moves in water). The flow of water may be either streamlined or turbulent. Turbulence is created when you move an unstreamlined shape through the water, thus increasing resistance. On the other hand, streamlined shapes produce a steady, smooth movement of the water. For example, walking with the hands on the hips creates more eddy drag and turbulence than walking with the arms at the sides.

Aquatic Fun and Fitness

Perhaps the best thing about the aquatic environment is that it makes almost anything fun. For most people, disabled or not, the joy of water's liberating environment makes everything easier and more enjoyable. Your participants can experience exhilaration with water raft ball, raft races, water relays, and games like tossing a ball into an inner tube. Noncompetitive activities can be just as much fun (and may be preferred by some people). All of these activities can be done (with some modifications) in water: walking and running, country line dancing, yoga, Pilates, tai chi, kickboxing, plyometrics (jump activities), and hip-hop dancing. These and many other activities can bring out the fun and creativity in people of all ages and abilities (for greater detail and methods to match activities to needs, see Baun, 2008).

Well-trained, experienced instructors and leaders can shape and modify these activities to suit a wide variety of people in an inclusive group setting. Results can be targeted toward fitness and conditioning, functional improvement, social and behavioral enhancement, therapeutic, or just plain fun and positive recreation.

Positioning, Stabilization, and Form

Water activities can strengthen muscles that enhance postural stability—as long as hydrodynamics properties are well understood and used and are tailored to the specific needs of the individual and group. One important consideration is the tendency of buoyancy to alter posture. People with weak core muscle strength, atypical body posture, a high percentage of body fat, or distribution of body fat higher in the chest and buttocks may experience compromised postural stability. This posture is characterized by an increased *lordotic curve*, or an arch at the low back, and can be exaggerated by water's buoyancy. An enlarged lordotic curve at the base of the spine puts stress on the low back if the participant is not guided to contract the abdominals and gluteals (buttocks) firmly to maintain a healthy posture. To protect the low back and to compensate for the tendency to arch at the low back, as well as protect the musculoskeletal integrity of the neck and upper back, encourage participants to adopt the braced neutral position in which the core stability muscles are engaged to maintain proper spinal alignment. At the same time, avoid curling the tailbone under, in order to avoid complications that result from over flattening the normal lordotic curse in the low back.

The braced neutral position uses five steps (see figure 14.3):

- Step 1: Contract (firm) the abdominals from the pelvis to the breastbone and over the rib cage. Visualize shortening the muscles from the pelvis to the belly button to achieve greater low back protection. At the same time, contract the gluteal muscles (buttocks).
- Step 2: Avoid tipping the pelvis under, which can strain the low back.
- Step 3: Bring the shoulders back and down to open the chest, bring the shoulders down and back to open and lift the chest as you draw the shoulder blades together using the scapular stabilizer muscles of the upper back. Visualize putting your shoulder blades "in your back pockets" (See, 2009).

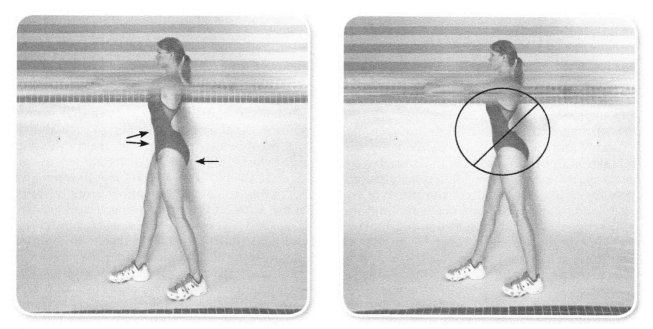

Figure 14.3 The braced neutral position helps prevent and overcome back, hip, and knee pain and is the foundation for all standing and flotation aquatic activities and exercises.

- Step 4: Keep the head level (avoid tilting the head back or forward), with the ears in straight alignment above the shoulders.
- Step 5: Breathe deeply while stabilizing, and practice moving around the pool while maintaining the braced neutral position.

The braced neutral position is important for all participants, because the resistance due to water's viscosity requires that the spine be stabilized. In addition, maintaining the braced neutral position while moving through water can improve core strength and stability—a fundamental objective for fitness and functional improvement. When the muscles in the hips, shoulder girdle, and trunk work together, they form a functional segment referred to as the *core*. Core strength and stability result when the core muscles work in an efficient and coordinated way to maintain correct alignment of the spine and pelvis while the limbs and torso are moving.

Using Hydrodynamics Safely and Effectively

By understanding how the body is affected by the aquatic environment, you can modify techniques to accommodate different needs. Be sure to fully understand the hydrodynamics principles described earlier in this chapter. Then consider these ways to use those principles.

Increase resistance to strengthen and condition by simply increasing movement speed or by adding aqua resistance equipment, both of which increase turbulence and thus the amount of resistance encountered. The top speed is determined by the point at which a participant can no longer maintain healthy body alignment (e.g., braced neutral position). Reduce resistance for participants with low strength by slowing movements (Baun, 2008). Use the characteristics of buoyancy for resistance with special care—too large and, therefore, too buoyant a flotation tool may present too much resistance for a particular person. To increase strength, you can add additional resistance by beginning with smaller, less buoyant equipment. Increase strength very gradually by increasing the number of repetitions and then increasing resistance once the person has demonstrated ease and proficiency with the amount of resistance and can maintain proper form and body alignment. Using the FITT acronym to remember the elements of exercise (frequency, intensity, type, and time [duration]), increase only one dimension at a time, and then allow passage of time for adaptation.

Even if a participant is already fit, increase the intensity of the program gradually, over a period of weeks or months, to avoid injuries, illness, and chronic fatigue. Overuse problems result if the body is not allowed enough time to become adequately conditioned in response to the newly introduced demands of water exercise.

Hydrostatic pressure supplies multidirectional resistance and can improve joint range of motion, but take caution: If a person's joint is unstable, for instance, the knee joint is injured or impaired, allowing that joint to undergo the effects of viscosity and multidirectional force may strain the connective tissue and joint structures, moving the joint beyond normal range of motion or straining the damaged tissue. A participant may need to use a brace while in water until isometric (stationary contractions) and other therapy methods have adequately stabilized the joint. Encourage participants to check with their physician or physical therapist in regard to joint stability.

People with disabilities that impair walking, balance, or sensing can benefit from the buoyant properties of water by using pool guide rails, or they can use flotation equipment, such as the Water Walking Assistant. The Water Walking Assistant is a low-cost tool that can improve balance and gait by increasing proprioception (sense of where your body is in space) as well as leg and torso strength. The flotation frame provides support to arms and upper body and has padded handles for a comfortable grip. The Water Walking Assistant is available through Sprint-Rothhammer International at www.sprintaquatics.com. Ensure that a qualified staff person is near the participant (in the water) at all times and that sound cues are provided to those with sight limitations. To improve walking capabilities in those with degenerative brain conditions or other conditions affecting motor control originating in brain or sensory challenges, instruct participants to visualize each step, each movement in opposition to the legs by the arms, and each postural adjustment as they imagine themselves crossing the pool in good form or standing on one leg to improve balance. These methods originate in sport psychology approaches for elite, competitive athletes and can produce highly successful results for all people. Such methods work well both individually and in mixed groups, because all participants benefit from the qualities of visualization: Enhanced posture, stabilization, and performance are possible for every participant.

The calming environment of the water can ease behavioral, intellectual, or emotional disabilities for many participants. Effective inclusive approaches make aquatic programs work more smoothly. For instance, instead of requiring that each person master an activity in the exact same way, emphasize that people perform the activities to the best of their ability, and, most of all, focus on enjoyment (Mosston & Ashworth, 1986). Using different depths can increase the participant's comfort in water and her ability to control her movements in water (those with less muscle strength and control need shallower water where they encounter less viscosity; those with larger, denser body mass may need to use flotation and move deeper to eliminate impact shock) (Baun, 2008).

Gradually introducing concepts, one at a time, giving time to the participants to adopt and understand the technique before moving on, builds capability and self-efficacy, the belief that one can succeed. People with and without disabilities can be overwhelmed if too many changes or instructions are given all at once.

By using these kinds of inclusive and accommodating modifications, tools, methods, and principles, people with a wide variety of abilities and disabilities can succeed while participating together in a group aquatic activity.

Basic Aquatic Techniques

The water workout is designed to enhance physical fitness, elevate physical capacity, and improve overall health and quality of life. To maximize the participant's gains from a workout—including cardiorespiratory endurance, body composition, flexibility, muscular strength and endurance, agility, coordination, and balance—construct the program according to a physiologically evidence-based format. This format gradually introduces the musculoskeletal and cardiovascular systems to greater challenge, thereby reducing the risk of pain, stiffness, soreness, injury, and illness.

Summary of Workout Structure

1. *Thermal Warm-Up:* At the beginning of each session, start with a warm-up routine with low to moderate speed and range of motion movements. The movements help sharpen body awareness and increase the blood flow to muscles.

Starting Position

Stand upright, with chest lifted, shoulder blades back and down, abdominal muscles firm and buttocks contracted to brace the spine in a healthy neutral position.

Action

Stride forward, then back. Stay upright and maintain the stabilized neutral pelvic position throughout the exercise (see figure 14.4). Slide slightly bent arms forward and back at sides, using arms in opposition to legs: When stepping forward with the right leg, slide left arm forward, and vice versa, palms facing thighs. Most people need to practice this movement using the braced neutral position for some time before it feels natural. This technique strengthens muscles, and the action of synchronizing the alternate arms and legs keeps the torso upright while improving posture, balance, and co-ordination.

Continue striding for several minutes until ready to switch to another move.

Figure 14.4 Water walk.

Variations

- Walk forward and backward with short steps, long steps, average steps, or step kicks.
- Move in the pattern of a circle or square, or in a snakelike pattern. When walking in a circle or square, change directions.
- When participants are ready to increase intensity,
  - stride by taking very large controlled steps, and
  - bound by pushing off with the back foot to bounce up off the pool floor between strides, to perform plyometric movements.

Safety Tips

When circling, turn around midway and circle in the other direction to balance the physical demands on body. Even during the warm-up, postural alignment is very important. Lift upward through the crown of the head and bring shoulder blades back and down. Brace hips and pelvis in a neutral position at the pelvis by contracting abdominal muscles and squeezing buttocks. During the stride, concentrate on maintaining this body alignment to protect and strengthen the muscles that move and protect the spine.

Reprinted, by permission, from M. Pappas Baun, 2008, *Fantastic water workouts* (Champaign, IL: Human Kinetics), 55.

2. *Warm-Up Stretch:* Warm muscles stretch more easily. After the thermal warm-up, complete a stretch sequence to prepare the muscles for more intense exercise and to prevent injury.

3. *Aerobic Exercise:* Aerobic exercise improves cardiorespiratory endurance and body composition. The aerobics component consists of continuously performed large movements that keep the heart rate in the aerobic target zone for an extended period of time. Begin with an aerobic warm-up of mild intensity to let the body adapt to the demands of cardiorespiratory exertion and to prevent an adverse response to the shock of sudden high-intensity activity. A cool-down activity at the end of every aerobic exercise segment is an essential element because it gradually reduces the heart rate and prevents excessive pooling of blood in the limbs.

4. *Muscle Strength and Endurance:* When the aerobic section is placed before muscle conditioning, the muscles responsible for musculoskeletal stabilization will be ready and able to do their job properly during aerobics and will not be fatigued. Muscle strength and endurance exercises take the muscle group to the point of fatigue. The purpose is to increase strength and endurance in specific muscle groups in a balanced manner and to increase lean muscle tissue mass, improve body composition, and enhance rate of metabolism.

5. *Final Cool-Down Stretch:* Each session should end with a final cool-down consisting of stretching and relaxation exercises to reduce heart rate further, prevent muscle soreness, increase flexibility, readjust equilibrium, and leave the participant feeling refreshed.

Appropriate technique, body alignment, joint protection, warm-up, cool-down, stretch, and gradual progression each contribute significantly to the process of injury-free, functional fitness results. If you are interested in learning more about aquatic workouts, see *Fantastic Water Workouts: Proven Exercises and Routines for Toning, Fitness, and Health,* by MaryBeth Pappas Baun, Human Kinetics, 2008. You will also find sample exercises in the sidebar on page 267 and in table 14.2 on page 272.

Additional Safety and Injury Prevention Considerations

Before beginning any new activity or exercise program, participants should see a health care practitioner who can provide recommendations appropriate for each person. In some cases, a customized individual plan (IP) will be required. For more detailed information on IPs, see *Adapted Aquatics Programming: A Professional Guide,* by Lepore, Gayle, and Stevens (2007).

Although most people can benefit from water exercise, there are several situations in which it is advisable to avoid pool activities:

- Fever
- Urinary infection
- Open wound
- Infectious disease that is transmittable through water or with casual contact
- Contagious skin rash
- Extreme fear of water
- Recent heart problems (obtain medical approval and guidance)

Fortunately, most of these conditions tend to be temporary and present only a passing obstacle to beginning an aquatic activity program. If in doubt as to whether water exercise is contraindicated for a client, consult a health professional.

Safety and Injury Prevention Reminders, Cues, and Actions

Risk management requires an in-depth approach to record keeping, reporting, policies, audits, insurance protection, staff training, forms, inspections, and modifications. For a description of ways to address these risk management considerations, see *Adapted Aquatics Programming: A Professional Guide* (Lepore et al., 2007). Simple safety and prevention measures can make a major difference. For instance, provide signage to direct people in wheelchairs how to vacate the facility in case of evacuation emergency. Situate lift and transfer equipment so unauthorized people cannot use it. Assign staff members to monitor and inspect the lift and transfer equipment, or secure the equipment to prevent use by unauthorized parties and post signage on who to contact to access this equipment.

Safety Tips and Cues

Instructors and staff use these cues and techniques to prevent injuries and exacerbation of disabilities in the aquatic environment. Give participants the following guidelines:

- Protect the structures of the body from injury. Maintain the braced neutral position (see figure 14.3 on page 265) during all movements, exercises, and stretches. The braced neutral position helps maintain postural stability and prevents injury, particularly to the spine. An estimated 80% of the general population is vulnerable to back pain. Use of this postural technique can help participants avoid or overcome this debilitating and painful health challenge.

- Frequently return to the braced neutral position to protect the back during jumps, leaps, stretches, resistance work, knee lifts, and many other exercises, particularly those that require reaching overhead or pressing the legs backward.

• Breathe properly. It sounds simple, but it is very easy to inadvertently hold your breath while concentrating on everything else. Oxygen is an essential ingredient in the energy-fueling process. Remind participants to breathe deeply and evenly at all times to prevent injury-causing fatigue and other maladies, such as unhealthy increases in blood pressure.

• Avoid hyperextending the joints. Keep the knees and elbows slightly bent when they extend (straighten) fully. This "softening" of the joints protects the joints from excessive pressure that can cause tendinitis, bursitis, or other painful injuries. Use this same technique to protect the back and the neck. Avoid overarching the back or neck (hyperextension) during kick backs, jumps, and jumping jacks, and keep the abdominal and buttock muscles tightened firmly.

• Maintain balance. To maintain balance and protect the musculoskeletal system during standing and flotation activities, move the limbs in opposition to complement one another. When a participant kicks his right leg forward, he should bring his left arm forward. Instruct participants that when they press one leg back, they should bring both arms forward. When they kick a leg out to the right side, they should bring the arms to the left. Ask participants to move more slowly and reestablish the braced neutral position if they are losing their balance. To increase challenge, add arm and leg movements on the same side.

• Bring the heels all the way down. When participants land with the feet directly underneath them or in front of the body following a step, jump, or other movement, have them bring their heels all the way down to touch the pool floor. Repeatedly raising onto the toes without lowering the heels can cause painful conditions such as shin splints and tight, sore calf muscles.

• Monitor the intensity. Have participants use a perceived exertion scale, check their breathing, or take their pulse two or three times during the aerobic phase to see whether they need to modify their intensity. To lower intensity, they can take smaller steps, slow down, streamline the body, or reduce the height of lifts and jumps. To increase intensity, they can travel more and farther and take larger steps, deeper dips, or higher jumps. To build fitness conditioning, participants can alternate between large and small, high and low moves or add resistance equipment. Faster speed is not necessarily a constructive fitness objective in the water. Working beyond the controllable speed or intensity may result in injury and overuse syndromes that discourage progress.

• Assess the breathing to monitor the intensity. If a participant is not breathing a bit harder than she was when she started, she has not reached aerobic target zone. When the breathing rate increases somewhat, the "respiration rate" indicates that the participant has reached the lower limit of the target zone.

• Use the "talk test." Can the participants talk? If they can still speak during the aerobic exercise phase but are breathing a bit heavier than when they are at rest, they are exercising moderately. If they can comfortably speak a few breathy words, they are exercising at the upper limits of the aerobic target zone. If they cannot speak without gasping, they have passed the anaerobic threshold and have exceeded the aerobic target zone limit; it is time to slow down. If they do not slow down, they risk overuse symptoms.

• Keep the muscles warm during stretching activities, especially when the water is cool. During movement and exercise, the body rids itself of excess heat through sweat evaporation and by transferring heat to the skin, where it is radiated into the environment. This process occurs more quickly in water because water dissipates heat four times more quickly and efficiently than air. Gliding movements of the arms during lower-body stretches generate body heat and keep the muscles warm for more effective stretching. Once participants have developed torso stability, they can jog or march in place while stretching the upper-body muscles. Omit these peripheral movements if they confuse participants, throw off stability, or irritate sensitive shoulder, knee, or hip joints.

• Avoid bouncing stretches during warm-up and cool-down stretching. Hold the stretch position statically (without bouncing) for 10 seconds during warm-up and 20 to 30 seconds during cool-down to lengthen the muscle safely without invoking reflexive shortening, called "the stretch reflex response." The exception to this guideline is to perform warm-up movements that imitate the actions of the activity participants are about to engage in. Participants can perform the same movements of the activity or sport in slow motion. This technique makes for a fun warm-up, prepares the body for more vigorous activity, and improves the condition for the specific activity.

• Increase the challenge gradually. Participants can be spared the pain and aggravation of injury (and even the heartache of "overuse flu," a chronic cold some people experience when they exercise too much or too often) if they start within a comfortable exertion range and schedule and then increase the duration or frequency gradually. Give the body a few weeks to adapt to the new level of exercise before increasing again. Increase only in small increments and vary which component is increased (frequency, intensity, or duration). If participants increase too much or too soon, they may experience pain, which is the body's signal to stop exercising, seek medical attention, or revise the methods.

- Protect the wrist joint. Keep the hand in a straight line with the forearm at all times. Avoid bending the wrist forward or backward during repetitive movements against resistance (see figure 14.5). When pushing the hand against the pressure of the water, always press the palms *facing* the water. The wrist is more resilient to injury in this position and can harness more of the water's resistive qualities. Cup the hand for even greater resistance or use webbed gloves.

- Strengthen the muscles through their full, pain-free, normal range of motion. Short, choppy movements that strengthen only through a limited range of motion increase the risk of injury. Avoid overstraightening, called *hyperextension,* because it involves movement beyond the normal range of motion and leads to injury.

- Exercise the muscles evenly to produce balanced results. Opposing muscle groups sustain an important relationship. Injuries result when one muscle is too strong or less flexible in relation to the opposing muscle. Therefore, work and stretch the opposing muscle groups equally to avoid injury.

- Protect skin from the sun. If participants exercise outdoors, they should wear water-resistant sunscreen to prevent sunburn, premature aging of the skin, and melanoma (skin cancer). They should reapply sunscreen after exiting the pool if they plan to remain outdoors. Wear 100% UV-protective sunglasses to protect the eyes from cataracts and other eye ailments. Avoid being out in the sun between 10 a.m. and 4 p.m., when the sun's rays are the most intense and likely to cause damage.

- Avoid eating during the 1 1/2 hours prior to activity. When participants do eat less than 1 1/2 hours before exercise, they should choose easy-to-digest, low-fat foods such as whole fruit, vegetable sticks, or brown rice. Exercise shunts blood away from the stomach and digestive system and sends it instead to the working muscles. Sour stomach and food putrefaction can result.

- Prevent chlorine from irritating the skin. Shower without soap before getting into the pool. Tap water binds to the skin and helps prevent chlorine from penetrating. Then shower again after leaving the pool, this time soaping all of the skin and rinsing well. Soap helps break down the chemical bonds that link chlorine to the skin. Several manufacturers make soap and shampoo specifically designed to remove chlorine from the body: Ultra Swim, TriSwim, Soap+, WaterGear, Swimmer's Own, Swimmer's OneStep, Aubrey Organics, and Chlor-Off. Finally, use high-quality, light skin lotion after every soap-and-water shower to protect the skin from loss of moisture.

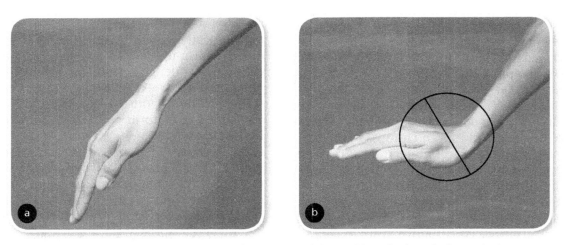

Figure 14.5 Keep the wrist in neutral alignment. While pushing the hands through the water, (*a*) keep the hands in a straight line with the forearm and (*b*) avoid bending the wrist upward.

• Drink water. Although it's not as noticeable as in land-based activity, people do perspire during aquatic activity. The body can become dehydrated during water exercise, and replenishing fluids regularly is vital for safety. To prevent fatigue, it is essential to keep the body hydrated before, during, and after water exercise, particularly in hot or humid environments. The best way to replace lost fluids is by drinking water rather than soda, energy drinks, juice, or coffee.

Safety Considerations

- Avoid using plug-in appliances near the pool. Battery-operated portable musical electronics components are safer, and several manufacturers offer rechargeable players. If using a plug-in appliance, be sure that it is at least 5 feet (1.5 meters) from the pool and elevated on a nonmetallic table or shelf and that the power cord is free from frays or exposed areas. Do not plug in, unplug, or use appliances while standing in a puddle.

- If you must use a plug-in appliance near the pool, buy a ground-fault circuit interrupter (GFCI), a device designed to prevent electrocution that can be purchased for very little cost from hardware and electrical supply stores. It comes as either a portable adapter for plugging into an outlet or as a replacement for the outlet.

Reprinted, by permission, from M. Pappas Baun, 2008, *Fantastic water workouts* (Champaign, IL: Human Kinetics), 55.

Aquatic Exercise for Health and Rehabilitation

Aqua therapy programs use the basic physical properties of hydrodynamics, buoyancy, hydrostatic pressure, temperature, and viscosity. Rehabilitative water exercise uses these properties creatively to increase balance, strength, core stability, range of motion, and flexibility; improve coordination, movement skills, and cardiopulmonary functioning (strengthening the heart, lungs, and circulatory system); improve cognitive function and behavior; enhance the integrated function of the musculoskeletal system; and promote relaxation and well-being.

One water exercise technique is called Watsu. Watsu sessions take place in chest-high warm water and use water's properties to create massage-like effects with a series of flowing, dance-like movements. Harold Dull created Watsu in 1980 when he coined the term *Watsu* from *water* and *Shiatsu*, its two major components. Less experienced Watsu facilitators begin with a learned sequence of moves. Advanced practitioners use a more spontaneous, free-flow method that allows the Watsu facilitator to become increasingly open and free to intuit the client's needs and match them with appropriate movement techniques as the session transpires.

Therapists working with people with disabilities and conditions use the aquatic environment

Watsu session.

Photo courtesy of School of Shiatsu & Massage.

because the properties of water minimize pressure on all of the joints and muscles. For example, when in chest-deep water, the body becomes 90% buoyant so that participants only have to move and support 10% of their body weight. Water makes it possible for people who have many different kinds of disabilities or who are recovering from almost any injury to handle exercise and fitness programs they cannot perform on land, speeding up the often-long process of rehabilitation and healing. The movement of exercise in warm water increases circulation to the injured area, boosting the body's healing mechanisms.

Water offers a safe, protective environment for therapeutic exercise for several other reasons. In water, there is very little negative stress or wear and tear on the body. When a participant performs proper warm-up and cool-down exercises in the pool, water's hydrostatic pressure reduces the likelihood of injuries or exacerbation because it eases the actions of the joints, even though it makes the body work harder against greater resistance. When a person walks on land, there is less resistance to the body's movement and the walker can swing her arms and move her legs freely. In water, the body works against the resistance of the water's viscosity, eddy drag, and turbulence to maintain balance. By working against the resistance (positive stress) of water, participants build strength, coordination, and endurance in a supportive, freeing environment. See table 14.2 for common conditions that can be helped by aquatic rehabilitation.

Table 14.2 Common Conditions and Tips for Aquatic Rehabilitative and Inclusive Exercise

Condition	Types of rehabilitative exercise and considerations
Range-of-motion limitations and joint and tissue pain	
Back and neck pain	Emphasize the braced neutral position and slowly increase the challenge to the stabilizers by using gradually more challenging lever-based movements (i.e., strengthen core stabilization). Focus on stretching, in particular, the buttocks, low back, hamstrings, inner and outer things, hip flexors, calves, and neck. See figure 14.3 on page 265.
Knee pain	Focus on squats and bicycle-type motions. Strengthen and stretch the gluteals, quadriceps, hamstrings, and hip abductors and adductors. Use isometrics of the quadriceps if the knee is in pain. 

Figure 14.6 Partial Squat. Strengthen the muscles around the knee joint with partial squats. Squat only as low as you can without knees moving forward over the toes: Keep knees behind toes and over the heels, use braced neutral position and press the buttocks backward like sitting partway down toward a chair.

Condition	Types of rehabilitative exercise and considerations
	Range-of-motion limitations and joint and tissue pain *(continued)*
Shoulder pain	Emphasize upper-body and pelvic stabilization as well as shoulder range of motion. 

Figure 14.7 Shoulder Circles and Shoulder Internal and External Rotation.

Focus on braced neutral position during all exercises. Slowly performing *(a)* Shoulder Circles and *(b-c)* Shoulder Rotation with stabilized position (see figure 14.3 on page 265) will strengthen the joint and improve range of motion.

Condition	Types of rehabilitative exercise and considerations
Arthritis and fibromyalgia	Immersion in warm water (92-96°F or 33-35.6°C) transfers heat to the body, which relieves pain and enhances range of motion. Warm up and cool down very gradually. Instruct the participant to move slowly, with control, and avoid overdoing it: Do not allow her to exercise to exhaustion. Moderate-level aerobic activity in somewhat warm temperatures (83-88°F or 28-31°C) can improve the health, function, and well-being of people with arthritis or fibromyalgia. 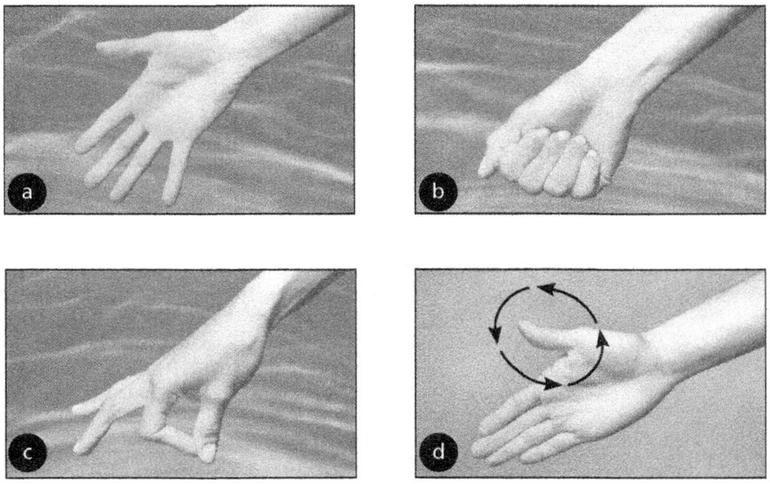

Figure 14.8 *(a)* Finger curl, *(b-c)* finger touch and *(d)* thumb circle, facilitate the relief of hand pain, improve range of motion, and enhance manual dexterity. Writing the alphabet in the water with your foot (see Plantar Fasciitis, or foot pain) or performing ankle circles will relieve foot, ankle, and lower leg stiffness. In cases where participants have arthritis, the range of motion movements should be performed in warmer water.

Please see back pain, knee pain, and shoulder pain entries in the chart for more moves appropriate for people with arthritis or fibromyalgia.

(continued)

Table 14.2 *(continued)*

Condition	Types of rehabilitative exercise and considerations
Range-of-motion limitations and joint and tissue pain *(continued)*	
Plantar fasciitis (foot pain)	Strengthen and stretch muscles of the feet and lower leg. 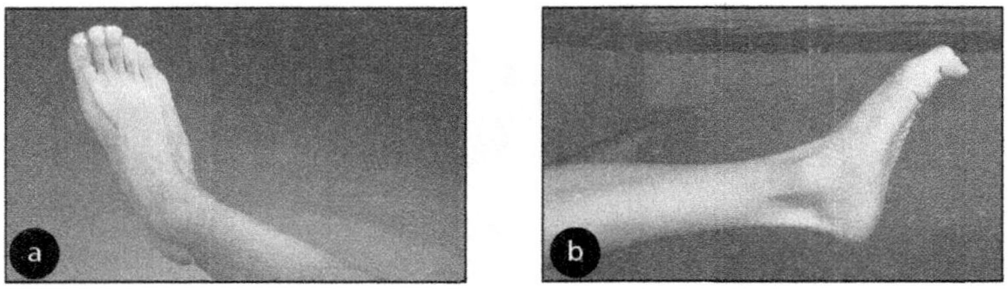 **Figure 14.9** Moving slowly through range of motion at the foot and ankle can relieve foot pain when performed regularly and consistently. Also perform calf and shin stretches, especially bent-knee calf stretches.
Chronic Conditions	
Cardiovascular condition	Use very slow, gradual warm-up and cool-down. Instruct participants to breathe fully throughout activity. Be sure to have doctor's approval and instructions, and match the activity to the phase of recovery. Water at temperatures of 83-86°F, or 28-30°C, can help prevent arrhythmias.
Diabetes	The objective for people with type 2 diabetes is to control weight; therefore, longer, moderately paced aerobic activity and muscle toning to enhance body composition are helpful. Ask the participant to monitor blood glucose before and after activity and adjust food and medication accordingly. Keep a form of quickly ingested food handy in case of emergency. Do not exercise when blood glucose is higher than 240. Diabetes-related numbness in the feet can lead to skin damage, infection, and amputation if properly fitting aqua shoes are not used.
Multiple sclerosis	Warm up and cool down very gradually. Tell the participant to avoid overdoing it: Do not exercise to exhaustion. Use equipment that assists with water walking or use an aide to guide-walk the participant along the length of the pool. On good days, work on balance exercises, such as standing on one foot. If sensitive to heat, avoid hot pool areas.
Osteoporosis	Use shallow water exercises as tolerated to provide the dampened impact shock that can prevent bone loss. Focus on resistance training and postural alignment.
Posture disorders	
Scoliosis (S-shaped curve in the spine)	Swimmer's side stroke, torso range-of-motion stretching and strengthening, and water Pilates can benefit those with scoliosis.
Kyphosis (rounding of the upper back)	Emphasize upper-back stabilization and strengthening and chest stretching. Improve core stability and strength. In the acute stage of juvenile kyphosis, vigorous flexion of the trunk is contraindicated.
Lordosis (hyperextension at the low back)	Emphasize abdominal muscle strengthening; core stability, especially pelvic stabilization (braced neutral position); and stretching the gluteal, hamstrings, low back, outside of hip and thigh, inner thigh, and calf muscles.
Pregnancy	Participant should not exercise on her back. Cool water temperatures can help prevent overheating, which can endanger the fetus. Use slow movements and avoid overstretching the ligaments. Minimize quick directional changes. Participant should wear a bra that fits well and gives lots of support and should not exercise to exhaustion. See the American College of Obstetrics and Gynecology Guidelines.

Condition	Types of rehabilitative exercise and considerations
Sensory disorders	
Balance disorder	Good choices are water yoga, water tai chi, water walking with a Water Walking Assistant, and standing or hopping on one foot. Use the pool edge for fingertip touch in early stages or on days when balance is poor. Use a floating mat to practice various balance positions. Go into deep enough water to avoid injury if the participant falls off the mat. Practice spinning and swinging so that the participant can practice recovery. Participants can straddle long foam noodles or try standing on one like a surfer. Participants can jump up and down or side to side over the lines in the bottom of the pool. Always provide assistance on deck.

Figure 14.10 Water yoga exercises such as the tree pose quiet the mind and improve balance.

Hearing disorder	Teach from pool deck; use sign language as well as visual and tactile cues. When using an interpreter, look at the participant while speaking rather than at the interpreter. Repeat as often as necessary. Short sentences are easier to speech-read.
Vision disorder	Use sound cues, such as voice, noisemaker, or musical cues. Use tactile "touch" cues (touch only after receiving permission, e.g., "May I touch you to indicate which way to go and how to move your leg?"). Provide tactile directions (physically move the participant through the skill or motion) with detailed instructions. Wear dark tights and long-sleeved top to assist those with partial vision to see your position.
Memory and understanding difficulty	Demonstrate the ultimate in patience and kindness. Repeat verbal and visual cues and other cues as often as necessary, but do not use them all at once. Tactile cues may work best. Use visual imagery to facilitate memory stimulation and recall.

(continued)

Table 14.2 *(continued)*

Condition	Types of rehabilitative exercise and considerations
	Sensory Disorders *(continued)*
Paralysis, paresis (partial paralysis), and atrophy	Emphasize balance activities, range-of-motion improvements, and trunk and core stability. Improve aerobic endurance and encourage weight bearing. Use flotation collars as necessary. Encourage independence. Allow extra time. Check for and prevent skin abrasions. Wear aqua shoes. Explore use of hand paddles.

Figure 14.11 Cervical collars.

Photo courtesy of Aquatic Therapy and Rehab Institute, 866-462-2874, atri@atri.org, www.atri.org.

Condition	Types of rehabilitative exercise and considerations
Speech difficulties and oral motor dysfunction	Perform all the vowels using the whole face: Make funny faces and laugh. Blow bubbles, hold the breath under water, blow ping-pong balls across the pool surface. Encourage the participant to say certain sounds or make as much conversation as possible. Provide stability in the pool if needed, because unstable positions will cause the body to stiffen and the mouth to open.

Adapted from Baun 2007 and Lepore et al. 2007.

Summary

Staff of recreation centers and programs have tremendous opportunity to create a culture of acceptance and accommodation by using the dynamically empowering physical properties and principles of the aquatic environment. The benefits to all mirror the definition of health and well-being: Physical, emotional, social, cognitive, intellectual, and spiritual benefits are all derived from successful inclusion in aquatic programming.

Creating successful access amounts to far more than making sure ramps, handrails, and nonskid carpeting are available in the right places. Staff attitudes and professional preparation are critical ingredients in making sure the power of aquatic programming delivers on its capacity for inclusion. The right kind of training includes in-depth, hands-on learning settings, guided by experienced, qualified professionals. It is only through guided experiential learning that staff members learn to plan and respond in a way that enhances the experience for a wide variety of people with a multitude of abilities and disabilities.

Discussion Questions

1. *Hydrodynamics* refers to the physical principles associated with moving the body through water. Understanding how best to use those principles can empower you to create safe, effective, inclusive aquatic programs. For the discussion, keep in mind that your goal is to meet the needs of each

person in your diverse group. Describe an exercise (and its modifications) that would be an example of using each principle or set of principles listed here:

a. Buoyancy
b. Viscosity, movement of force, and progressive overload
c. Hydrostatic pressure
d. Leverage and eddy drag

2. Contemplate and then describe at least three ways that you, as an aquatic exercise coach, could improve your listening skills. Include verbal and nonverbal skills.

3. Who are the stakeholders in your existing (or imagined) aquatic program and facility? Discuss several ways you can gain, maintain, and grow stakeholder support for your inclusive aquatic program.

4. What fun activities and exercise methods can you use to attract, sustain, and grow a diverse group of participants in your aquatic program?

Spotlight on Inclusive Programs

SNAP

Developing and Maintaining Inclusion Groups: A Success Story

An example of a program that has successfully brought together the factors critical to successful inclusion in groups is a swimming program called SNAP. In a pilot project that placed children and youth with developmental disabilities in community recreation activities with nondisabled peers, activity coaches from university teacher education and health education programs received training on use of tailored, individualized accommodations to facilitate participation by all the children (Suomi & Suomi, 2000).

The SNAP philosophy focuses on the major purpose of inclusion: to provide opportunities for all participants to develop skills and attitudes needed to learn, live, work, and recreate together in all aspects of society (Stainback & Stainback, 1990). The program goal is appreciation of and tolerance for inclusion in group settings with people different from ourselves: Children learn to recreate together well when they grow up together in environments such as pools or swimming classes that support individual differences (Suomi & Suomi, 2000).

The name of the program, Special Needs Aquatics Program, was chosen to communicate the concept that all young children have special needs when learning to swim. The special needs addressed in the program include a warm, positive, and safe learning environment; highly qualified staff; age-appropriate activities; and a pool with comfortable water temperatures (88-90°F [31-32°C]).

The age range served (6 months to 7 years) allows for opportunities to create and maintain an inclusive environment using developmentally appropriate practices for each child. *Developmentally appropriate activities* are activities geared to a participant's development status, fitness and skill levels, body size, and chronological age (Council on Physical Education for Children, 1992).

In keeping with the inclusion concept, SNAP advertising uses a reverse marketing strategy, focusing on special needs for all children in a learn-to-swim program, designed to include rather than segment out children with disabilities. Many learn-to-swim instruction programs are marketed by segmenting out children with disabilities as "also welcome." Here is one real-life example: "Deerwood Community Center now offering swim instruction for children ages 6 months to 7 years; children with disabilities welcome." (Note: The community center name is

(continued)

fictitious but the advertisement is not.) The language and descriptions used by SNAP aim to be inclusive of all potential participants. This represents a major departure in marketing strategy compared with typical learn-to-swim programs. An excerpt from the SNAP children's brochure illustrates the marketing concept: "SNAP offers infant and toddler, preschool, and levels 1 and 2 aquatic classes for children between the ages of 6 months and 7 years. The young child's special needs in SNAP are to gain an initial positive water experience, to learn safety skills in and around water, and to have fun."

SNAP organizers assessed the attitudes of parents of the children enrolled in SNAP swim classes. Sixty parents of SNAP participants were randomly selected to respond to a survey. Fifty-six survey responses (93%) were returned and evaluated. Data were categorized into groups: parents who had children in parent–child classes (age range of children 6 months to 4 years); parents who had children in independent swim classes (age range 4-7 years); and parents who had children in both classes. In addition, organizers analyzed parental responses to the following statement: *My child has participated in an aquatic class with a child with a disability: yes _____, no _____.*

Inclusion questions in the survey dealt with quality of aquatic instruction. Parents responded to the following question using a Likert-type scale: *Having a child with a disability in an aquatic class did (would) not affect the amount of instruction given to my child.*

Several trends emerged in the results, including a demonstrated lack of understanding of children with disabilities by parents of children without disabilities. The average response of the 28 respondents who had children with disabilities participating in their child's class indicated they believed that the swim instruction of their child was not affected by the presence of a child with a disability. For the 28 respondents who had never had a child with a disability in an aquatic class with their child, the average response for this question was midway between *agree* and *not sure.* Although this score does not demonstrate a negative parental response to having children with a disability in their child's class, it indicates a lack of confidence or a preconceived idea that instruction may be affected by including a person with a disability alongside their child in the water. Research on inclusive preschool programs has demonstrated that experience with chil-

dren with disabilities has positive effects on parental beliefs about inclusion (Stoiber et al., 1998). Other investigation into parental beliefs about early childhood inclusion has shown that parents of children without disabilities in inclusive preschool programs hold more positive beliefs about inclusion than parents of children without disabilities attending noninclusive preschool programs (Stoiber et al., 1998).

The SNAP research survey results also suggested that in swim programs with higher student-to-teacher ratios, acceptance of a child with a disability may be more negatively viewed in terms of affecting instruction for other children without disabilities. Other research has supported this same conclusion: Studies on inclusive early childhood programs identified high student-to-teacher ratios as a major barrier in preventing effective inclusion (Buysse et al., 1998).

Overall results of the survey, based on this question and several others, led researchers to conclude that introducing children with disabilities into an early childhood swim program helped overcome negative attitudes that nondisabled members of society sometimes hold toward people with disabilities. Provision of age-appropriate activities with suitable levels of support prompted most parents of nondisabled participants to view children with disabilities in a more positive light, which can help parents and children to view as positive their inclusive recreational experiences in later-life (Suomi & Suomi, 2000).

References

Buysse, V., Wesley, P., & Keyes, L. (1998). Implementing early childhood inclusion: Barrier and support factors. *Early Childhood Research Quarterly, 13*(1), 169-184.

Council on Physical Education for Children. (1992). *Developmentally appropriate physical education practices for young children.* Reston, VA: Author.

Stainback, W., & Stainback, S. (Eds.). (1990). *Support networks for inclusive schooling: Interdependent integrated education.* Baltimore: Brookes.

Stoiber, K., Gettinger, M., & Goetz, D. (1998). Exploring factors influencing parent's and early childhood practitioner's beliefs about inclusion. *Early Childhood Research Quarterly, 13*(1), 107-124.

Suomi, J., & Suomi, R. (2000). Creating an inclusive early childhood swim program. *Palaestra 16*(2), 20-30.

Inclusive Outdoor Recreation and Summer Camps

15

" *Awareness is becoming acquainted with environment, no matter where one happens to be. Man does not suddenly become aware or infused with wonder; it is something we are born with.* "

–Sigurd Olson

Learning Outcomes

After completing this chapter, learners will be able to do the following:

- Identify multiple groups that have been traditionally underserved in outdoor activities.
- Describe why a commitment to maintaining our outdoor space is critical to the health and quality of life of all people.
- Identify a variety of popular outdoor recreation activities.
- Describe a strategy for including underserved populations in specific outdoor recreation activities.

Inclusive Outdoor Recreation

Cindy Dillenschneider, MS Ed

Northland College, Ashland, Wisconsin

Frederick Green, PhD, CTRS

University of Southern Mississippi

At this very moment, our natural world is facing the environmental crisis of climate change that will affect every aspect of life for the foreseeable future. Global climate change is primarily caused by the production of greenhouse gases, most of which are being released into the atmosphere through the use of fossil fuels and the internal combustion engine (Hegerl et al., 2007). As recreation providers, you will have the opportunity to influence the next generation of participants. Our hope is that your efforts to help people access, enjoy, and respect the outdoors will also help protect and sustain the diminishing environment that we value so much.

In the United States, many if not most people recreate indoors. Since the development of interactive electronic media, there has been a shift from outdoor play and recreation to leisure pursuits that take place indoors. Additionally, in many areas of the country there has been a transition from smaller family homes with associated outdoor space to large homes that include entire rooms devoted to play and entertainment, with extremely limited outdoor space. However, the joy, sense of accomplishment, and deep connections that develop through outdoor recreation remind us of the personal, communal, spiritual, and environmental importance of connecting with the natural environment. We believe that respecting our environment through ethical use is secondary only to societal acceptance of all people. It is with these shared values that we humbly present this chapter on inclusion and outdoor recreation.

In this chapter we first offer a brief introduction to outdoor recreation to clarify our position on the topic. Although recreation in the outdoors can and does take place in many ways, we have chosen to focus on nonmotorized outdoor pursuits. As you prepare to enter the profession of recreation, we hope you will share our concern

for the environment. Next, the target populations that comprise the myriad of populations that can benefit from inclusive efforts are identified, and the contemporary attitudes and beliefs regarding the values of outdoors and inclusion are discussed. Finally, you will be exposed to a variety of contemporary outdoor pursuits, and the issues related to inclusion for each activity are discussed.

Research has shown that outdoor recreation has enhanced acceptance and inclusion of children and adults with impairments by children and adults without identified impairments, has improved the self-concept of people with and without impairments (Brannan et al., 2003; McAvoy et al., 1989), has contributed to a sense of wholeness and emotional health, and has resulted in improved physical fitness and health (Louv, 2006). Outdoor recreation is one of the easiest and least expensive types of recreation to implement. In the simplest form of outdoor recreation, the only necessary resource is outdoor space. With a little creativity, this space opens opportunities to become an explorer, a scientist, an architect, a musician, a poet, or a dreamer. For the urban explorer, cracks in the sidewalk can become a nature hike, and a visit to a rooftop garden can provide a release from daily stress. For the adventurer who wants to explore distant lands, opportunities abound within every ecosystem. From butterfly migration study to expeditions in remote mountain ranges to meditation by a quiet pool of water, outdoor recreation can take place in urban parks and gardens, backyards, natural areas, forests, swamps, rivers, and of course in wild and wilderness areas. We invite you to journey into the outdoors to discover endless possibilities for recreation and inclusion. As simple as it is to access outdoor recreation, there are inherent risks you must manage in each environment and with each skill area. We strongly encourage you to undertake new experiences in the outdoors with the guidance of skilled outdoor leaders. Becoming a skilled outdoor recreation leader takes time and skilled instruction. Take your time and enjoy the process.

People Who Recreate in the Outdoors

Traditionally, a discussion on inclusive recreation focused on people with disabilities. As our profession has matured, we have come to understand that inclusive practices need not be restricted to one underserved group. A culturally diverse society is a culturally enriched society, and all members of our society need and deserve recreation; however, people with disabilities are not the only group in our society who face barriers to inclusion. In this chapter, we acknowledge recent demographic changes and recognize the barriers to inclusion in the outdoors faced by soldiers and their families, generations of healthy and long-lived adults, children and adults with high rates of obesity, and children who are spending less and less time outdoors. Each of these groups provides us with new outdoor recreation challenges and opportunities. Our intent is to recognize evolving demographics and the value of a culturally diverse society, acknowledge the traditional absence of too many valued members, and provide a foundation on which to build a more universal and truly inclusive outdoor recreation practice. Assisting people of all cultures, abilities, genders, and ages to develop entry-level skills requisite for subsequent competency in outdoor activities will enhance participation in outdoor activities for the future.

Returning Soldiers

Soldiers returning from war need opportunities to reintegrate with their families and be once again included in society. Outdoor recreation can play a significant role in this process. Outdoor recreation provides service people with opportunities to share relaxing moments with their family on a picnic or to reconnect with friends. Additionally, because of the personal and team challenges found in activities such as rock climbing or whitewater rafting, recreation in the outdoors can assist individual soldiers, families, and military communities to reintegrate, recover abilities, learn new skills, and channel energy. Even soldiers undergoing treatment at military hospitals are encouraged to participate in outdoor recreation programs to enhance and speed their recovery. Opportunities for inclusion in outdoor recreation exist on many levels. Soldiers can make the transformation from a soldier who fishes to a fishing enthusiast who once was, and really will always be, a soldier. The skills learned during military service (e.g., orienteering, rope work, leadership, organization) can provide soldiers with opportunities to return to leadership positions within their communities.

Our Grandparents and Boomers

The numbers of U.S. adults remaining active into their 70s, 80s, and 90s is increasing (National Institutes of Health, n.d.). Outdoor recreation for aging adults can play a role in health maintenance, personal enjoyment, and opportunities for meaningful involvement throughout the life span. Additionally, many aging adults spent their childhoods recreating in the outdoors. For them, outdoor recreation with younger generations can offer an opportunity to share lost arts through their knowledge and skill.

People Who Are Overweight

Health data indicate that a significant portion of U.S. citizens are obese. This change accompanies shifts in professions and labor requirements, eating habits, recreation trends, and school curricula, among others (Louv, 2006). Although outdoor recreation experiences can vary from sedentary activities, such as sitting on a pier fishing, to very active pursuits, like backpacking, the process of getting into the outdoors involves movement and activity. Although many people have difficulty getting into a routine of exercise for the sake of exercise, outdoor activities like walking, riding bikes, and boating are intrinsically rewarding, and improved health and fitness are collateral benefits of participating in a preferred activity. The time we spend in outdoor recreation activities can have a direct and beneficial effect on weight reduction for people of all ages and abilities.

Children of the 21st Century

Another group experiencing a move away from outdoor recreation is children. Because of a wide variety of factors, such as perceived safety, liability concerns, an increase in structured recreation, and an increase in access to electronic media,

Help children break free of their video games and reconnect with the earth.

children are spending less time outdoors. Simultaneously, high-adventure outdoor activities are experiencing a rise in media attention through advertising, television shows, and competitive outdoor sports events. This trend started more than a generation ago, so we are developing generations of children who are information rich and experience poor when it comes to the outdoor environment. As a result, outdoor recreation participants are becoming more dependent on technology and are less able to design their own experiences, make good decisions, and use good judgment in outdoor recreation. It is essential for the future of outdoor recreation and the earth that sustains us to reconnect children with the natural environment in healthy ways and to help them develop a sense of stewardship towards the earth.

People With Varied Abilities

In the very recent past, people with impairments were perceived as being incapable of or too fragile to pursue a variety of outdoor pursuits. Impairments were perceived to be disabilities (inabilities) and abnormal rather than a variation experienced within the typical life span of every person. When people with impairments were allowed to participate in outdoor recreation, they were provided segregated programs, and many of those programs were therapeutic rather than recreational. However, with and without the support of the professional recreation provider, people with impairments are regularly engaging in outdoor pursuits of all types and have proven themselves far from being incapable. Examples abound of people who scuba dive and sail independently despite the limitations of quadriplegia; people who are blind who have reached the summit of Mount Everest or independently hiked the entire Appalachian Trail; whitewater paddlers who are missing arms or legs; and countless people who fish, hunt, hike, ski, and ride despite having various physical, cognitive, and health impairments.

Although people of all abilities are participating in the broadest scope of outdoor recreation activities, the inclusion of people of all abilities within most outdoor recreation programs is still very limited. However, great models do exist. One of the best examples of inclusive outdoor recreation in regard to ability has been developed by Wilderness Inquiry (www.wildernessinquiry.org), a nonprofit organization in Minnesota that runs outdoor adventure trips. Wilderness Inquiry has developed its program mission, staff training, marketing information, and group facilitation skills with the goal of successful formation of mixed ability groups for all of their trips. Any recreation provider would be well served to look at this organization's Web site for more information about inclusion of people of all abilities.

Creating Safe Space in Outdoor Recreation

As the field of recreation serves an ever more diverse society, providers must develop skills and techniques to create safe space for recreation participation. Safe space in this context refers to both the physical and emotional safety of the participants. The next sections draw attention to a few specific areas that the professional recreation provider must address in our changing society.

Faith, Spirituality, and Outdoor Recreation

Faith and spirituality play a large part in the lives of many people. The practice of one's faith may be central to the feeling of belonging and security necessary to engage fully in life's activities. As recreation providers who profess to engage in inclusive practices, we need to consider the desires of our clients to adhere to their faith practices while engaging in our programs. Faith practices vary significantly but encompass considerations such as dress, daily worship schedules, holy days of observation, permissible food and drink, fasting, and washing and cleanliness. The mix of practices within each community will vary significantly. However, leaders of faith practices within each community can provide the recreation provider with insights into supportive and inclusive programming considerations that will not alienate others with different beliefs.

Many people find outdoor experiences that lead to or support their own spiritual growth both in and outside of religious traditions. Although secular programs may deem this to be outside the purview of programming considerations, outdoor recreation providers can certainly be involved in the design and leadership of contemplative outdoor experiences that are interpreted and incorporated by the individual participant in her own way.

Gender, Sexual Orientation, and Sexual Identity

Gender, sexual orientation, and sexual identity: How much more personal can it be? Creating environments where each person feels safe to participate and make choices based on his own desires is one of our most important tasks as recreation providers.

Each person has a perception of outdoor recreation activities and how those activities complement or challenge her gender identity. Images of men and women participating in outdoor activities, evident in popular media, shape expectations and norms about how one participates in those activities. In a casual survey of outdoor magazines, men are most commonly represented as rugged adventurers or in leadership roles, and women, if pictured at all, are most often in secondary roles or displayed as part of the scenery. An annual survey of 22 outdoor activities showed that men participate at much higher levels than women in all areas and within all ethnic groups (Outdoor Industry Foundation, 2006b). To allow men, women, girls, and boys to participate freely in outdoor activities, the recreation provider must create an environment that allows everyone to explore desired activities and achieve her potential.

Creating a gender-neutral atmosphere in outdoor experiences can begin with some forethought in language use and staffing. Staff considerations should involve role modeling by both women and men in all outdoor recreation activities. Female leadership of traditionally male-dominated activities can promote the involvement and success of women and girls in new activities. Role modeling behaviors by competent male recreation staff who encourage and support female competence and leadership can improve the gender balance in outdoor recreation activities.

Language use also plays a subtle part in developing a supportive atmosphere for boys, girls, men, and women. In recreation environments it is still common to hear statements that undermine the value of females and males. Recall times you have heard someone say "you run like a girl" or any number of other statements that begin with "you" and end with "like a girl." The majority of the time these phrases were not meant as compliments. If you look up the word *guy* in a dictionary all references are masculine; however, almost daily, it is common to hear a mixed-gender group referred to as guys. Even the thesaurus provides a synonym that supports the use of *guys* to refer to a mixed-gender group (Merriam-Webster Online Thesaurus, n.d.). Although these may be common usages, they carry on a tradition of undermining both males and females. We undermine participants of both genders by denigrating the value of either through derogatory comments and by ignoring the existence of or making an entire group invisible. These are only two examples where gender bias is demonstrated linguistically.

When we modify both role models and language to be inclusive, we have begun to create an environment that promotes equal appreciation of people of all genders and invites greater involvement by those who have previously not found their place in our programs.

Challenging outdoor experiences often stimulate deep and meaningful interactions. Imagine undertaking a difficult task such as backpacking over a period of days while carrying all of life's essentials on your back. During the day, you and your companions struggle with the challenges of reading the map, traversing difficult and dangerous terrain, and at the end of the day hanging all foodstuffs high in the trees to discourage bears from visiting your camp. Add to this the evenings around a small campfire or hours of stargazing from your sleeping bag. In these environments, where you rely on your companions for your safety and well-being and you care equally for them, intimate conversations and friendships arise.

Under these conditions, where most of us feel free to disclose very personal information and know that we will receive support and compassion, people who identify as gay, lesbian, bisexual, or transgender are in a most difficult spot. To share about their loved ones, as a person who identifies as heterosexual can freely do, they put themselves at risk of becoming outcast, avoided, or harassed by the people they have most recently befriended and on whom they depend. And although sexual orientation or identity has nothing to do with the activity, it strongly influences how secure the person may feel in this intimate setting.

No matter the personal beliefs or values the recreation leader holds, it is her responsibility to maintain the safety and security of every person in the group. This responsibility includes maintaining a social environment that is supportive of all participants and one that remains free from exclusion and harassment of any kind. It is the most talented leader who can take this type of challenge and turn it into an opportunity for unquestionable support.

Recognizing Cultural and Ethnic Differences

People of different cultures recreate differently in the outdoors. Each of us has been introduced to the outdoors through family and community norms. What is culturally normative for one person or family may not be the same for another.

For example, the population of Hispanic people in the United States is projected to reach 25% by 2050 (Outdoor Industry Foundation, 2006a). Additionally, people from Hispanic communities traditionally have very strong family and community ties that affect their outdoor recreation participation (Outdoor Industry Foundation, 2006a). Because of these values, recreation providers who wish to serve the Hispanic community will be wise to develop opportunities, such as picnicking, that can be engaged in by extended family groups; to use the strong community connections to promote group outings; and to develop connections with community leaders (Outdoor Industry Foundation, 2006a).

According to research performed for the Outdoor Industry Foundation (2006b), outdoor activities most commonly engaged in by people who self-identify as black or African American are bicycling, fishing, trail running, and camping. Interviews with outdoor leaders who are African American have indicated there are still concerns and fears of race-related violence in remote outdoor settings. One African American author who has studied outdoor recreation use patterns by people of African American descent speculates that the history of violence based on race that has taken place in remote or rural settings, the history of slavery in the United States, and the resulting disaffection of generations of families from recreational and spiritual connections with land influence, and are part of, the culture that encourages younger generations to avoid certain types of outdoor environments (Edmondson, 2006).

American Indians are a bicultural people, many of whom live or work within predominantly nonnative communities while also having ties to centuries-old traditions and values. As such, many American Indians view outdoor recreation much differently than do many people from the dominant culture in

© PhotoDisc

Cultural and ethnic differences cause people to view nature differently, be it with a past that does not support an appreciation of nature or one that encourages a sense of connectedness with the earth.

the United States. In the northern reaches of Wisconsin and Minnesota, for example, hunting, fishing, and harvesting of rice, berries, and maple syrup are still part of the lifestyle of many people, families, and communities. Although children may play outdoors, learning the skills of harvesting the abundance from the land and waters as well as learning values of sharing the harvest with community elders is part of the culture of respect and spirituality rather than recreation. For these Native Americans who are managing to hold onto tradition and culture, outdoor recreation as portrayed in magazines and on television can seem profane. The contradictions create additional challenges for youth living in both worlds.

One significant ethical challenge yet to be adequately addressed in outdoor recreation is that many of our high-adventure activities take place on what is considered sacred ground by indigenous cultures. An example that has seen some press in *Outside Magazine* (Jenkins, 2006) is recreational rock climbing at Bear Lodge, also known as Devils Tower, in South Dakota. This location, which is sacred to several indigenous nations (Hanson, 2000), is used for spiritual cer-

emonies by many tribes and also for recreational and commercial climbing by other national park visitors. In a personal interview, Lakota elder Connie Burditt stated that she and many other Native Americans view this use as someone else might view recreational climbing on one's cathedral or temple (personal communication, October 2007).

Advantages and Challenges to Inclusion in Outdoor Recreation

The great outdoors! Meeting the needs of a diverse population in outdoor recreation presents unique benefits as well as unique challenges. With such a wide range of potential leisure experiences in such a wide variety of leisure environments come barriers for even the most experienced outdoors enthusiast. Efforts to include all people most likely will require individualized solutions to individualized problems.

Consider the unique accessibility challenges. Skilled designers of developed outdoor recreation facilities are expected to design sites to appear in the natural state, unmodified by human hands. Thus modifications that change the natural state seem counterintuitive to the outdoor experience. Outdoor recreation that takes place in less developed settings, where development is restricted, challenges participants of all ability levels to gain access to inaccessible terrain while causing minimal impact on the environment. In other words, modifying, even for accessibility, is considered an unethical outdoor practice. Considering that much of the wilderness can be increasingly challenging for even the most experienced outdoors person, gaining access by people with ability limits poses a similar challenge.

On the other hand, outdoor recreation and the sites used may be considered our most accessible environment. Consider first the developed sites for outdoor recreation, including parks and campgrounds. Many developed sites are built on fairly level ground to accommodate large gatherings, and these may include wide-open spaces. Additionally, these developed sites often accommodate service vehicles, thus justifying the paved roads and ramps not desired in the undeveloped sites. Tables, camp pads, restrooms, and picnic tables can be designed for accessibility without sacrificing on aesthetics. Trails, when paved for accessibility, become multipurpose trails serving cyclists and inline skaters. Maybe most noticeable, settings for outdoor recreation have relatively few doors to navigate between activity areas, and all activities really take place on one floor.

Outdoor recreation in the remote areas creates fewer obvious advantages related to inclusion; however, there are some very unique advantages. First, for many enthusiasts of wilderness activities, it is the personal experience that makes outdoor recreation so attractive. Although some experienced enthusiasts are "turned on" by a 15-mile (24-kilometer) hike with a 2,000-foot (600-meter) elevation change for a chance to be away and sleep under the stars, less experienced outdoors enthusiasts with skill limitations may achieve a similar challenge experience with a 1.5-mile (2.4-kilometer) hike and a 200-foot (60-meter) elevation change. Second, many adventurers in remote outdoor areas travel by water, a medium that is exceptionally accessible with minor modifications. Finally, remote travel is often unforgiving, and enthusiasts often develop a unique style to meet the challenges. This means that everyone "fits in" by the mere fact that no one really fits in.

Outdoor Recreation Activities and Strategies for Inclusion

Understanding inclusion in outdoor recreation may best be accomplished by looking at the relationship among three variables. First and foremost, a discussion on inclusion should center on people—people who have been traditionally excluded and their counterparts who have the responsibility of making them feel welcome. So far in this chapter we have presented several groups that are often left out and have discussed some ways to make them feel more welcome. Second, a discussion on inclusive outdoor recreation should address the meaning of outdoors and the importance of our slowly dwindling outdoor space to quality of life for everyone. Third, as we develop an appreciation of the outdoors and all of its challenges and celebrate a growing movement to include more people in the outdoors, we also should look at the many opportunities for recreation in the outdoors. The diversity of outdoor recreation activities creates opportunities for including an increasingly diverse population, as people try out and select preferred activities. In the next section of this chapter, we present some of the more common outdoor recreation activities and, in doing so, offer recommendations for making the activities more accessible and welcoming to a wider segment of our society.

Water Activities

Water is one of the most inclusive mediums for outdoor recreation. Water travel can take place in a wide variety of craft and on all bodies of water. The multiple options afforded by water travel provide the participant with the opportunity to engage in solo experiences as well as group activities. Participants' roles in water travel can range from passenger to captain, and the opportunity to progress through a range of roles on a range of craft is endless. Next we introduce a few options for water travel.

Canoes

When thinking about canoeing, many of us imagine two people, one at each end of a small, narrow, traditionally shaped boat. In reality, canoes come in a wide variety of shapes and sizes. A functional paddling position in a canoe is either seated or kneeling where the seat is quite a bit above the floor of the boat. Each style of boat can accommodate wide variations in water conditions and a wide range of numbers of participants or paddlers per boat.

The canoe whose design originated from the indigenous people of the United States and Canada is paddled by one or two people who sit or kneel in the bow and stern of the boat. This style of boat is at home in lakes and rivers of all types, but for recreation purposes with novices is best used in inland lakes and less technically challenging rivers. The traditional solo or tandem canoes can be portaged or carried easily and are frequently used for canoe camping throughout many regions of the United States and Canada.

Outrigger canoes were the traditional paddling craft of southeast Asia and the Pacific islands and consist of one or two narrow hulls and one or two stabilizing outriggers. Outrigger canoes are paddled by 1 to 12 paddlers. Paddlers in outrigger canoes sit one person to a seat, and the hull is very narrow. Larger outrigger canoes need larger bodies of water because these boats have a poor turning radius. Outrigger canoes that hold six or more people are typically very heavy and are not easily handled on land. Outrigger canoe racing has become a popular sport in recent years for people of all abilities, and there is some hope that it will become a competition sport in the Paralympic Games. Additionally, organizations that promote outrigger canoeing retain and encourage a strong appreciation for the cultural roots of the sport.

Voyageur canoes, originally used for hauling freight, look like traditional-style canoes but are much larger and have space for 6 to 22 paddlers sitting two to a seat, side-by-side. Voyageur canoes are quite maneuverable and are at home on large lakes and large, slow-moving rivers. Voyageur canoes are a great way for mixed-ability groups and people of all ages and experience to travel and camp in the larger lake regions in the northern part of the U.S. Midwest and in Canada.

The dragon boat of Chinese origin (which is not a type of canoe but can be used for outdoor recreation) carries as few as 10 and as many as 50 paddlers sitting two to a seat. Increasingly, clubs and festivals throughout the United States include dragon boat and outrigger canoe racing. Because of the increasing interest in the continental United States, many events include opportunities for novices to paddle in these larger craft. Groups around the world have included dragon and outrigger teams consisting of people with disabilities or survivors of cancer as a way to improve fitness, maintain health, and celebrate ability. Dragon boat festivals are infused with cultural events that instill a natural appreciation for the origins and history of the culture of the craft.

Rafts

Raft travel relies on the use a soft-sided inflatable boat often with a flat bottom that is propelled and directed by several people using single-blade paddles or by one person who uses a set of large oars in consort with the power of moving water. In a raft, the participant is seated on an inflatable section of the boat and is well off the floor. Rafts are very stable in rough water and can be used to transport a large amount of equipment or a large number of people. Rafting is a popular activity on white-water rivers for day trips and for camping.

Rafting is an excellent medium for including people with disabilities yet offers some unique challenges. The need for propulsion is reduced because the raft travels by force of the current. However, paddling is used with some styles of rafting to control the direction of travel. Much of the steering in these paddle rafts is done by the raft guide from the rear of the raft. Hence, paddlers of all skill and ability levels can contribute successfully to the experience. Maintaining stability in the raft is deceptively difficult. Sitting high on the inflatable sections would be difficult for people with balance limitations, and sitting low on the floor would be dangerous if the raft hits underwater snags or rocks. For people with balance concerns, many raft companies produce oar rigs that are rowed from the center of the raft by a skilled guide. In these rafts, the passengers often sit in the front third of the boat on an inflated cross-tube.

Sailboats

Sailing can be accomplished by one or more people. Small sailboats suitable for one person may have a seat where the sailor controls the sails and a rudder from one position. These sailboats can be outfitted with mouth controls that allow sailors with significant impairments to control the boat independently. Larger boats require the person to move from place to place on the boat. Bench seats or seats with backs are found on many styles of sailboats. Once again, stability is the main barrier to inclusion. This problem is compounded in larger boats by the need to change positions as the sailboat turns. Some sailboats are outfitted with a movable seat, allowing a person with lower-limb impairments to change positions within the boat while remaining seated.

Kayaks

Kayaking differs from canoeing because the paddler uses a double-blade paddle to propel and control the watercraft. Additionally, the paddler sits lower in the boat on a seat that is only slightly raised off the bottom of the boat. This lower positioning creates a lower center of gravity and can improve stability for some paddlers. The paddler in a kayak sits with legs outstretched. Kayaks typically accommodate one or two paddlers; however, some larger kayaks can accommodate three people. A wide range of kayak styles are available that accommodate people of significantly varied abilities and interests. Kayaks can be outfitted with pontoons to increase stability, seats that provide increased torso support, foot pedals for propulsion, and fishing rod holders for the avid angler.

Water Activity Inclusion Challenges and Advantages

Water-based travel poses few barriers to the majority of people. There are no age limits or gender biases, and very few physical, cognitive, or social skills are required to take part in water travel. Water travel has been common to many cultures, can take place in urban or wilderness settings, and can be inexpensive for individual participants. The methods of water travel mentioned here provide options for group participation. Group water travel allows people of all abilities to participate equally, as all contribute and no one gets left behind. Consider a canoe paddled by 12 people. Each person contributes at her level of ability, so the results are accomplished by the whole group. Every person experiences the same sights, sounds, conversations, and movement, and everyone reaches the destination at the same time. This simultaneous accomplishment and arrival create an entirely different experience from that experienced by solo and tandem craft working toward the same destination.

Although water travel is an accessible medium, the challenge for inclusion of people with disabilities, depending on the type of limitations, is comfort and safety in the boat, as well as contribution to the propulsion. Universal design can be accomplished by offering a variety of watercraft, seating options, and propulsion devices. For people who have challenges with sitting stability or grip, adapted seats, paddles, and grip assists can be created or purchased.

The following suggestions may be helpful. Sitting low in the boat, and centered, can reduce some of the problems related to balance, but lowering the position of the paddler can greatly reduce the ability of the participant to implement an effective stroke; each paddler must determine what is best for his participation, comfort, and safety. On some boats, the seats can be temporarily removed. Additionally, side supports of lightweight and floatable material can prevent an excessive lean that would result in capsizing. Any modifications should safeguard the paddler's ability to safely exit the boat if the boat turns over.

Solving the problem of propulsion is not as simple. The barrier is pronounced for people with little upper-body strength or limitations to grip. Although it is possible to allow a person to ride simply as a passenger, this approach can diminish the outdoor experience and eliminate opportunities for solo paddling. The challenge is to find a way for the person to paddle to the great-

© Sport The Library

Water travel can be aided by the use of watercrafts with a more universal design.

est extent possible without jeopardizing safety. Commercial mitts are available that compensate for reduced gripping ability. A single-blade canoe paddle is in development for one-arm use. This design has promise to allow people using one arm the opportunity to generate powerful strokes with skill similar to paddlers who use two arms.

One of the most memorable experiences in our lives was a daylong whitewater rafting trip with a person who spent his adult life with high-level quadriplegia. He used a motorized wheelchair for mobility, breathed using a portable ventilator during the day, and slept in an iron lung at night. On the morning of the trip, we met at the river's edge and helped him transfer to a makeshift seat on an inflated tube in the front of the raft. His ventilator was strapped to the raft, and river guides sat on either side of him to assist in positioning and to provide skilled support in the event of capsizing. We spent the next 6 hours floating downriver, powering through challenging rapids, being splashed by waves, and experiencing the beauty of a wild river canyon. A few years later this man told us it was the only time in his adult life he did not use his mechanical ventilator to breathe. It seems that the movement of the raft on the water allowed his diaphragm to expand and contract, substituting for his mechanical respirator the entire day.

To make water travel activities available to a broader cultural audience, recreation providers must be aware of cultural practices and beliefs that may affect participation. Considerations include full head-to-ankle coverage swim clothing for some women, modesty in dress practiced by groups from various cultures, and the cultural insult of exposing the bottoms of one's feet to another person.

Land-Based Activities

Land travel opportunities include the least expensive methods of travel. From foot travel to animal-powered transportation, a wide range of opportunities are available for the recreation provider to consider. For a significant majority of the U.S. population, foot travel is an excellent form of low-impact exercise. Recreation can involve neighborhood walks, expeditions in wilderness areas, and everything in between.

Water-based activities usually provide many opportunities for accessibility, but activities that are land-based and that adhere to outdoor ethical principles are somewhat at the mercy of the outdoor terrain, which is diverse. Across the United States, outdoor enthusiasts can find flatlands, prairies, hills, mountains, canyons, cliffs, deserts, ice, and snow cover. Each of these provides a different challenge for accessibility for the outdoor enthusiast, and often it is this challenge that the user finds attractive. Hence, the object of participation in land-based activities is not to change the environment but to adapt to it. Land-based activities include hiking, backpacking, rock climbing, orienteering, and many other pursuits common to specific environments (e.g., mountaineering). We have many years of experience with these activities as well as experience modifying activities to meet the needs of people with disabilities.

Hiking

Hiking is a popular activity that requires minimal skills and equipment. Defined by Blanchard and colleagues (2007) as a "walk in a natural setting for less than a day" (p. 325), hiking falls on a continuum between walking and backpacking. People hike for many reasons: to briefly get away from their everyday environment, to see an area in its natural environment, to exercise, or to step up to a personal challenge. As they hike, people experience the climate and terrain and adapt to them.

Backpacking

Backpacking trips are longer hikes with at least an overnight stay, requiring participants to carry all essential gear. Backpacking trips allow people to truly get away from it all, because the extra time away allows the backpacker to make a break from daily routine and find the solitude important for reflection. Backpacking allows one to see their environment in near-pristine form, away from the development of civilization.

Rock Climbing

The allure of rock climbing is in the challenge: a vertical ascent on rock cliffs. Thus, climbs can vary in height and difficulty level. Indoor climbing walls allow for a climbing experience in a controlled environment. Rock climbing requires a considerable amount of strength and agility, along with fine and gross motor control. Universally designed climbing may involve the choice of climbs of graduated difficulty; climbing holds of varied sizes; inset instead of protruding holds; the use of chest harnesses in addition to the seat harnesses; counterweight systems that allow the climber to reduce the amount of weight she must overcome while climbing; and for people whose impairments limit use of arms or legs, mechanical cam devices that allow the climber to ascend, by use of hands or feet, a rope suspended the length of the vertical distance to be climbed.

Orienteering

Orienteering is a land navigation activity, often designed as a timed sport. The object of orienteering is to navigate, using a map and compass, through a series of preset, mapped points in a natural or undeveloped area (U.S. Orienteering Federation, 2008). Orienteering, often defined as a sport for the thinking person, requires a myriad of skills including running and walking over rough terrain, reading maps, navigating by compass, and making decisions. Some orienteering events include trail orienteering and other more accessible designs. Most events have courses designed for beginner through elite participants. The draw for many orienteering enthusiasts is in the challenge of finding a series of control markers, with time added as an additional challenge.

Orienteering competition often takes place during the winter cool and wet months, and experienced competitors adjust to, if not truly relish, cold, damp, miserable weather.

Bicycling

Many states and municipalities have cycling trail systems, such as a single track for the ambitious mountain biking enthusiast, paved surfaces separate from an adjacent roadway, or roadways identified as cycling routes. Options for cycling travel include single-person bicycles, linear model tandems, side-by side tandems, and tricycle and quadcycle models for up to seven people. There are cycles with treadle mechanisms that operate with an up-and-down motion rather than a circular leg motion and hand crank cycles. Riders can find models that allow standing, seated, prone, and recumbent positioning. There is even a busycle that carries 14 peddlers and one driver (for more information, visit the Web site at www.busycle.com).

Horse Power

Horse power opens up opportunities of access to the outdoors in two very distinct ways. A person can travel by horseback, and people and groups can travel by horse-drawn carriages, wagons, or buggies. To ride independently, the rider must be able to sit for relatively long periods of time on a minimally padded surface, to balance on a moving and sometimes unpredictable horse, to mount and dismount with or without assistance, and to independently control the direction and speed of the animal, while considering the well-being of the animal. To travel by wagon, buggy, or carriage, the participant can ride along as a passenger or control the rig through the use of commands and reins. The essential skills for this type of travel are tolerance of movement and occasional jarring. Participants can care for the well-being of the animals through feeding and grooming, and care of tack and other equipment is also part of the experience of horse travel. Wagons and buggies have even been outfitted with solar-powered lifts for wheelchairs, making independent use of wagons or buggies possible for people who would otherwise need assistance and increasing the opportunities for people who use battery-powered wheelchairs that are too heavy to lift.

Horse-powered travel involves some challenges. For example, many people are allergic to horse dander. Another consideration is that horses are expensive to maintain. However, horses make remote outdoor recreation experiences available to a much broader audience than human-powered activities. Other animals are used in the outdoors as well, although they are most often used to carry provisions rather than people. Llamas and goats are notable here; they are often used during hiking to carry some of the load that would otherwise be carried in a backpack.

Dogsledding

An activity with many similarities to horse travel but that takes place in snowy environments is travel by dogsled. Dogsledding provides opportunities to be a musher, who controls and manages the sled and the dog team, or to be a passenger. Essential skills for mushing include dynamic balance and the abilities to hold onto the sled, communicate with and manage the dog team, and periodically assist the dogs by walking or running rather than riding on the sled. Mushing can be a surprisingly aerobic activity, especially in untracked snow or when the team is pulling uphill. Being a passenger requires the ability to tolerate motion and jarring as the dogsled travels over varied terrain. Allergies to dog dander are a consideration for participation. As with horse travel, plentiful opportunities exist to assist in the care and feeding of the dogs and maintenance of the equipment.

Snowshoeing

Snowshoeing has a long history and an active place in today's outdoor recreation world. Today you can find snowshoe hikes and races throughout the winter snow season. Snowshoeing can be a person's way of accessing the silent backcountry of winter, taking on the challenge of a hike in the park, or competing against other athletes. Snowshoes come in a wide variety of shapes and sizes with variations suitable for an endless set of conditions. Modern snowshoes are often narrower and easier to walk with than those made in the tradition of steam-bent wooden frames. New designs often have cleats on the bottom to assist the user in traveling up and down hills, and many people use ski poles while snowshoeing to assist in maintaining balance. Ease of use is partially dependent on the binding that attaches the snowshoe to the user's boot. Some bindings are so user friendly that the snowshoe can be fastened and removed without removing gloves or mittens.

Snowshoeing on unpacked snow can be physically demanding, but snowshoeing on packed conditions is very similar to hiking in summer. Snowshoeing is an excellent low-impact exercise, and the use of ski poles increases both the balance of the participant and the exercise potential of the activity. Snowshoeing is a rather inexpensive outdoor activity requiring very little specialized equipment.

Nordic and Backcountry Skiing

Nordic skiing is another great way to travel on snow. There are several distinct styles of Nordic skiing: Classic-style skiing and backcountry skiing are the most universal styles for the recreational user.

The classic style of cross-country skiing is somewhat similar in movement to walking with the assistance of poles for balance and propulsion. Recreational skiers can travel as slowly as a meandering walk or as quickly as a distance runner. Recreational users often use groomed cross-country ski trails. These trails are groomed with a machine that creates two distinct tracks in the snow deep enough to guide the skis. These tracks are easy to feel even with your eyes closed. Classic ski tracks vary in length and are often created on urban golf courses as well as remote recreation areas. Nordic skiing can be enjoyed by people of all ages and abilities. There are even Nordic skis for people who must ski sitting down because of impairments that affect standing or walking.

Backcountry skiing is similar to hiking and backpacking. Often backcountry skiers carry enough equipment with them in a sled or a backpack to spend one or more nights in the outdoors. Backcountry skiing provides the outdoor enthusiast with access to remote settings. Requisite skills for participation in backcountry skiing are the ability to tolerate cold conditions, proper dressing for cold environments, strength and endurance for hard physical work, and static and dynamic balance for standing on and traveling on skis.

Fishing

Fishing is one of the most popular outdoor activities in the United States, coming in second only to bicycling (Outdoor Industry Foundation, 2006b). According to a study performed in 2005, approximately 43.2% of Americans between the ages of 16 and 24 and 34.5% of Americans 16 and older participate in some type of fishing. Participation in fishing is high in people of all ages, abilities, economic classes, and genders as well as the dominant ethnic groups of people who self-identify as Caucasian, Hispanic, and black or African American (Outdoor Industry Foundation, 2006b). Fishing opportunities abound in many different styles, such as simple cane pole fishing, jigging, fly fishing, spin casting, ice fishing, spearing, deep sea fishing, and netting. The different styles differ significantly in terms of cost, complexity of task, skills needed, physical ability required, and methods of access used.

Many groups in the United States provide assistance to bring new people to the sport of fishing. Examples include fishing days for children sponsored by state-run departments of natural resources; fly fishing programs for women run by sporting goods companies; and Fishing Has No Boundaries, a nonprofit entity devoted to helping people with disabilities gain access to fishing.

Wildlife Watching

For those who want an activity that can be done outdoors at any time and any place, try wildlife and nature watching! Look around or listen closely: What can you find in your neighborhood? Are there any birds, butterflies, ants, or raccoons? What trees and flowers grow there?

Do you know that grasses flower and that some lichens are called *british soldiers* because they have bright red tops? If you visit a local park, you may find many different species common to your ecosystems and your region of the country. In most communities you will find birding clubs and environmental learning centers that can guide your discoveries. People of all ages, abilities, and cultures can find enjoyment in the sights, sounds, smells, and even the tastes of nature. Bring along books with pictures of local flora and fauna, recordings of birds, binoculars, and a magnifying glass. This may be your first opportunity to create your own outdoor recreation program that others can enjoy!

Land-Based Activity Inclusion Challenges and Advantages

Land activities present a unique challenge to inclusion because the inaccessible terrain presents the greatest challenge to inclusion, yet sound environmental practices would discourage modifying the terrain. Nonetheless, people of all levels of ability can experience the outdoors while respecting the environment. The strategy for inclusion should include identifying the desired experience, or what participants would like to get out of their day in the woods, and then finding approaches to achieve this experience.

For example, consider hiking. It is not a sound or desirable practice to pave all hiking trails. Both hikers and backpackers value single-track dirt trails because these require minimal changes to the natural environment. This does not mean that all trails must be single track. Trails designed to be accessible for wheelchair use can vary from packed and consolidated dirt surfaces to those paved for multiple users. This variability allows hikers who use wheelchairs or other mobility supports to experience the outdoors, along with the cyclists and inline skaters who appreciate paved trails through environments in a more natural state.

One should not preclude hikers with mobility impairments from using natural dirt trails. Adjustments in planned distances may be an effective solution. If the allure of hiking is in the challenge, or seeing how far one can get on his own power in natural terrain, the goals for the hike are then personalized, because some people may be fully challenged by a half-mile hike. Developed trails already come with a designation of easy, moderate, and difficult to allow people to find their own degree of challenge. Oddly enough, "easy" is defined by Blanchard and colleagues (2007) as hikes of 6 to 7 miles (9-11 kilometers) with an elevation gain of up to 1,500 feet (450 meters). For the sake of encouraging hikers with mobility impairments, we may need to redefine *easy*.

Rock climbing creates a unique challenge for inclusion of people with mobility impairments because of the inherent difficulty in the sport. It is fairly challenging for the relatively fit participant. Yet it can be a relatively safe sport with trained belay staff. To reproduce the desired outcomes (challenging oneself, traversing a rock face), rappelling may be an acceptable alternative. Rappelling relies on gravity rather than the physical strength to traverse a rock face, yet it still challenges a climber to confront her fear. Selecting an accessible cliff face (ideally with plenty of free fall) would prevent unnecessary bumps and bruises, as would the use of safety clothing and equipment (e.g., helmets).

At first glance, orienteering may appear to be nearly inaccessible, because much of the land traversing is done off of trails. However, orienteering has a history of encouraging participants of all ability levels. Orienteering is considered a sport for the entire family, and most local orienteering meets include courses of varying challenge levels and encourage beginners. Additionally, noncompetitive walking of the course is not only acceptable but encouraged. Even the national "A" meets typically set up seven courses of increasing difficulty levels, opening up the championship events to participants of all ability levels. Additionally, orienteering competition is conducted in canoes, on skis, and at night. Something about the nature of orienteering and the people who embrace it seems conducive to exploring variations that allow for access.

We have briefly introduced a few of the water- and land-based options for outdoor recreation as well as some of the challenges and opportunities that exist. Each activity deserves much greater study, and the provider who chooses to engage others in outdoor recreation must realize that the risks and responsibilities that come with leading others in the outdoors are the paramount considerations. We leave it up to the student as well as the professional recreation provider to choose among these options or to investigate others for further study. You can find resources and program examples on the Internet, in professional texts and journals, and in popular media. In addition to the physical and emotional safety of individuals and the group, the environment in which you travel must be considered. The outdoor user who intentionally or inadvertently degrades the outdoor environment leaves less for the next generation, whereas the provider who teaches and models responsible stewardship may leave more for each new generation to explore.

Professionals in Action

Andy Janicki

I would rather be an optimist and a fool than a pessimist and right.
    –Albert Einstein

Background Information

Education Biology and Water Resources, College of Natural Resources, University of Wisconsin, Stevens Point

Special Awards

  *University Leadership Award (2006) *Chancellor's Leadership Award (2007) *Wisconsin Legislative Affairs Director of the Year (2007)

Career Information

Position Accessibility Coordinator, Wisconsin Department of Natural Resources

Organization The WDNR is a government agency devoted to the management and protection of Wisconsin's natural resources, including fisheries, wildlife, and public lands. The WDNR also provides programs and services for environmental awareness and outreach.

Size of Organization The WDNR employs approximately 2,500 employees and serves the entire state as well as nonresident visitors.

Job Description My position involves creating more outdoor recreation for people with disabilities. This includes a number of things such as establishing accessible trails on state lands, providing necessary services at state parks, and ensuring accommodations are made for disabled hunters and anglers.

Career Path This is my first job out of college.

What I Like About My Job I am extremely passionate about my work. I have been active outdoors for many years and have a strong connection with the natural world. Four years ago, however, I had a spinal cord injury and now use a wheelchair to get around. Being confronted with this new situation has opened my eyes to the challenges faced by people with disabilities when it comes to enjoying the outdoors. It's very fulfilling to help open up the outdoors to this group of people.

Career Ladder I view this position as an interesting stepping stone to a career that I have yet to discover. Although I do love my job, it is definitely not what I had expected to be doing right out of college. I have been an avid environmentalist for quite a while but have developed a strong humanitarian side since my injury. I hope to find a career in the future that meshes both of these ideals, preferably at an international level.

Advice to Undergraduate Students Follow your heart as you pursue a career while working for a cause greater than yourself. Doing something fun as a job has obvious perks, but doing something that benefits something or someone beyond your personal ambitions is far more gratifying.

Personal Statement I have always made it a goal to work for a greater good, for something worthwhile. Working in this field is perhaps the most satisfying and rewarding experience I have ever had. Creating equal opportunities for people with disabilities to access the outdoors, or simply helping to add another small element of independence to someone's life, is truly an indescribable feeling.

Inclusive Summer Camps

Terry Long, PhD

Northwest Missouri State University

Terry Robertson, PhD

Northwest Missouri State University

For camp administrators and staff members, the challenges of providing an inclusive experience to a camper in what is a traditionally rustic and active environment can be overwhelming. Camp in general can be overwhelming, not to mention helping campers who have unique needs or characteristics. As such, it is no surprise that promoting inclusion is sometimes viewed as a problem rather than an opportunity. Still, by learning about ways to promote an inclusive experience, and by challenging fears, apprehensions, and attitudes, camp professionals come to realize that much of the problem is in the eyes of the beholder.

It is naive to think that inclusion is as simple as having a positive attitude and some duct tape. There are real challenges and critical considerations that, if ignored, can lead to very bad outcomes. Campers can be physically and emotionally harmed when inclusion is just thrown to the winds of good intention. Those who provide inclusive camping programs must be professionally competent and must acknowledge the responsibility of caring for all campers' unique needs. Program leaders must also understand the potential of camp environments to open doors to involvement and acceptance that might have been closed in the past. As noted in the outdoor recreation segment of this chapter, the terms *involvement* and *acceptance* are being applied here to all underserved segments of society. Although much of the research presented in this segment focuses on studies of disability-related inclusion research, our intent is for you to apply these concepts to all people.

Providing inclusive camps presents both problems and opportunities simultaneously, or as a more optimistic person might say, "problatunities." Problatunities are situations that present a challenge but, through this challenge, create fantastic opportunities for new ideas and positive change. Camp is the "perfect storm" of problatunities. Campers are challenged every day but are encouraged every day to grow and explore. From this process great things can happen.

Camp Culture

Summer camp is like no other environment: Everybody gets to be a friend, an explorer, a creator, a dreamer, an actor, a comedian, a superstar, and, most important, a camper. The unwritten social code of society that tends to be a real bummer in daily life does not apply at camp. With a little encouragement, campers can let go of the labels and expectations of others and begin to find and enjoy their true selves. Not only is it okay to be different than the flock, but it is encouraged. Campers are taught to let their ambitions go and have fun and to support one another in this pursuit of being their true goofy selves. They are also given a vacation from the worries or burdens of home, a chance to enjoy life 24-7.

A good summer camp can help kids to let go of their worries and focus on just having fun and being kids.

The ultimate goal of camp counseling is to develop this open and accepting culture while ensuring that everyone is physically and psychologically safe. This is why camp is a great opportunity for inclusion of people with disabilities or other differences. Even though there are barriers that need to be addressed, camp is one of the best opportunities in life to foster such genuine acceptance and inclusion.

Building a Culture of Inclusion

The preceding description of summer camp sounds great, but there are some stipulations. There is no magic dust that turns camp into Never-Never Land where kids run free and frolic in the woods. Competent professionals must work hard to ensure that camp is safe, welcoming, and fun for all. This is never easy, and ignoring important considerations when integrating people with differing needs and characteristics into the camp environment will undermine the potential benefits. In contrast, fostering an inclusive environment by addressing such considerations adds significant value to the camping experience. This process starts with creating a camp culture where inclusion is the norm rather than the exception.

An Inclusive Identity

Being recognized as a provider of inclusion is critical to the success of an inclusive camping program. Step 1 in the inclusion process, and in establishing an identity of an inclusive service provider, is informing the public through promotion and advertising (Anderson & Kress, 2003). For camps, promotion of opportunities for inclusion is even more critical, because the general public may not perceive the camping environment as accessible or equipped to meet the needs of campers of all abilities.

Three specific groups of people should be considered in this promotional effort. First, it is important to inform potential donors, sponsors, and partners of the inclusive nature of your camp. Such information can help win the support of partner organizations in the form of money, scholarships, nonmonetary donations, and volunteers. Most of this promotion will occur through direct contact and one-on-one meetings, as opposed to mass mailings or general advertising. Those who handle such contacts must have a good understanding of the camp's philosophy and processes for inclusion and should be able to address concerns and misperceptions related to safety and liability.

A second group that is affected by camp promotion is staff. Developing a reputation for inclusion through brochures, the camp Web page, job announcements, advertisements, and promotional events can be critical in recruiting staff members. Hiring and retaining quality camp counselors is an ongoing challenge for all camps, and clearly communicating camp philosophy and staff expectations from day 1 can be tremendously helpful in separating the prospective camp counselors from the applicants who just want to go camping for the summer.

Finally, promotion and advertising are critical tools for informing the general public, and future campers in particular, of the opportunities for inclusive camping that you provide. Camp advertisements should clearly communicate through both words and images that the camp encourages the attendance of all persons. Furthermore, it should be clear that the camp provides competent services for those with specialized needs and that these services are inclusive rather than segregated.

In cases where prospective camper identities are not likely to be provided directly to the camp, partner agencies can certainly inform their clientele about camp opportunities and recruit participation. Community-serving associations or societies, independent living centers, schools, churches, youth service agencies, and health care providers can be very helpful in spreading the word. Again, sharing an inclusive philosophy with potential partners can help establish common ground that they can identify with and support and should be a core element of the program image that is communicated to the public.

Preparing Camp Staff

A second major element in building a culture of inclusion is staff training. At the top of the list of desirable counselor traits is attitude. As already noted, finding a good fit starts with the message you convey in your job announcements and camp promotional materials. Once you have chosen staff, deliver a clear message regarding the philosophy of the camp and the policies that reflect this philosophy. Staff must have an attitude that allows them to buy into the philosophy and associated policies. Much of this attitude is related to their knowledge and understanding of the people they will work with. Staff training pertaining to attitudes and beliefs regarding disability or other differences can include the following:

- An explanation of people-first philosophy and culturally sensitive language
- An explanation of inclusion, including the importance of social inclusion
- An explanation of the benefits of inclusion
- Success stories and testimonies from former or current campers
- Practical exercises in using equipment, policies, and procedures
- Camp scenarios and role-playing activities

In addition to having a positive attitude and appropriate perception of individual differences, staff members must know how to handle situations. The challenge with providing this knowledge is that no two campers are the same and everyone's needs are slightly different, but it is still useful to establish a set of policies for camp and communicate them to staff. Some examples of common policy areas specific to disability issues include these:

- Showering and toileting
- Managing behavior
- Dispensing medications
- Conducting transfers
- Maintaining special dietary needs
- Accommodating cultural or religious needs

Equally useful, but more difficult, is training for situations where a clear-cut policy is not available to guide the counselor. These scenarios involve counselor responsibilities such as these:

- Talking with campers about their needs
- Addressing incidents of cultural insensitivity between campers or counselors
- Dealing with home sickness and apprehension
- Monitoring how campers treat one another
- Encouraging participation and discouraging self-segregation
- Detecting fatigue, dehydration, heat sensitivity, and medication reactions
- Minimizing embarrassing situations (such as soiled linens)
- Identifying the need for and implementing activity adaptations

Of course, training regarding the inclusion process is critical. Inclusion issues to be addressed in training often are oriented around the logistics of camp and how they are affected by the inclusion process. Staff must be informed in several specific areas:

- Cabin or group placement procedures
- Camper supervision responsibilities
- Strategies for encouraging inclusive social interactions
- Strategies for addressing attitudes campers might hold toward one another

Finally, camp staff will need to know about camper disabilities and what staffers can or cannot do with specific campers in regard to safety. Precamp training sessions usually provide limited time to cover many conditions, and in some cases campers' conditions are not known at the time of the training. The same can be said in regard to cultural or religious needs of campers. As such, it is critical that a detailed intake procedure take place at the time of registration. Registration materials should provide an opportunity for parents to disclose their children's unique needs. This information should be provided to staff as soon as possible. When feasible, preview individual camper needs prior to their arrival, but also talk with staff about how such information can lead to unfair expectations about the camper. Encourage counselors to expect the most from campers and to be creative in finding solutions to barriers while being mindful of both physical and psychological welfare.

Disability-Related Considerations

An important challenge in developing an inclusive camp is determining the best way to support campers with disabilities within the general structure of camp. Historically, segregated camps have been the norm, where campers with similar disabilities attend camp together. These camps are not inclusive, because campers without disabilities do not attend. In other cases, campers with disabilities may be grouped together at a camp with other campers. The campers with disabilities are housed together and may even attend activities in a segregated manner. This also is not an inclusive environment. Furthermore, both of these approaches are completely inappropriate in regard to ethnicity, race, or religion unless self-determined by the participant (e.g., a summer camp for church members).

A third, and truly inclusive, approach is for kids with disabilities or other differences to sleep, eat, and participate alongside the general camper population. This scenario requires camp administrators to devise a strategy for supporting campers with disabilities.

Several approaches to staffing inclusive camps have been described (Blake, 1996). One common approach is to hire specialized counselors who have the sole responsibility for working with campers with disabilities. In such cases, these counselors are the only staff trained to meet the needs of campers with disabilities. These counselors are aware of the individual child's needs and strategies for meeting them, whereas the rest of the staff may not have this information. Other camps train "inclusion counselors" who work alongside regular camp counselors when a child with a disability is assigned to the regular counselor's cabin. Some parents provide a person to assist their child at camp, and sometimes volunteers are trained to assist campers (Blake, 1996; Hutchison, Mecke, & Sharpe, 2008).

A variation of the inclusion counselor approach was described by Hutchison and colleagues (2008). In their case study of an inclusive camping environment (Camp Crystal Sands), all counselors were trained to work as inclusion counselors. Because the camp program offered multiple, week-long camping sessions, the counselors "floated" from week to week, with all counselors working as inclusion counselors at some point during the summer. Thus, all counselors were capable of working with any camper at any time, and counselors were able to fully support one another to facilitate the inclusive camp experience.

As noted earlier, training an entire staff to be inclusion counselors is often challenging, because there is a significant amount to learn in a short time. At Camp Crystal Sands, one full-time inclusion counselor was hired to coordinate the efforts of all other staff. Furthermore, the camp partnered with Project Rainbow, an outside, nonprofit organization that promotes and facilitates inclusive camping. Project Rainbow assists in the development of inclusion policies (e.g., assigning one camper with a disability per cabin), facilitates training of the camp staff, and provides camper referrals. Such partnerships are becoming more common and have proven to be very useful in assisting camps in the development and implementation of inclusive camps.

Disability and Barriers

A major task at hand when working toward inclusion in the camp environment is limiting and, when possible, removing barriers. Barriers come in all forms. Following is a discussion of common barriers to inclusion and how they might be addressed, particularly in regard to those with disabilities.

Often the most restricting barriers are architectural in nature, many of which are addressed in the Americans with Disabilities of 1990 or other related documents such as the ADA Accessibility Guidelines for Play Areas (see www.access-board.gov). Guidelines exist or are being developed for a variety of camp-related elements, including boat docks, beaches, playground equipment, swimming pools, trails, pathways around camp, showers, and dining facilities. Unfortunately, many older camps do not meet the requirements of these standards and do not have funds to address deficits, but camp counselors should always strive to reduce architectural barriers as much as possible. Society's knowledge of and expectations for access in outdoor and recreation environments continue to shift in a positive direction, bringing more and more opportunities for accessible and inclusive camping.

Environmental barriers, or barriers created by the natural environment, are very common in camp settings. These could be related to a natural playing surface such as grass, dirt, or mud. They also can be related to the steepness of that surface and other features of the natural terrain. Tree roots, a steep hill, a rocky mountain trail, a marsh, and a river are all environmental barriers. It is sometimes impossible, or inappropriate, to remove natural barriers. At the same time, the natural environment offers all levels of challenge, so finding a negotiable trail or river can provide an opportunity for a very rewarding experience. As mentioned earlier, watercraft offer advantages for some participants. At the heart of this discussion is the point that the natural environment can be viewed and used as an opportunity for achievement, and people with disabilities can experience the same sense of achievement that others experience when navigating natural barriers. The camp counselor's job is to discover these opportunities and present them to the camper.

Attitudes can be a huge barrier to inclusion. Building a camp culture that thrives on acceptance and celebration of differences was discussed earlier and is the primary weapon against negative attitudes. Still, addressing attitudes is an ongoing process. Administrators may see inclusion as a financial burden or legal liability. Parents may see inclusion as a social and psychological risk for their child. Camp staff can sometimes be indifferent or insensitive to camper needs. Camper attitudes can even be problematic, because campers may see the inclusion setting as threatening or beyond their capabilities. Those leading the inclusion effort must stay in tune with the beliefs and perceptions of all parties involved and constantly work to promote positive attitudes through education and positive exposure.

Camp Logistics

Many architectural and environmental barriers can be addressed through good planning. By considering cabin placement, activity locations, bunk assignments, and even where portable toilets are placed, camp directors can limit many barriers or avoid them together. Camp schedules should also be considered, including the time allotted for bathroom breaks and for moving from activity to activity and the time of the day for indoor, outdoor, active, and passive activities. When scheduling activities, always consider the potential for a particular disability or medication to affect tolerance to heat or cold.

Adapted Equipment

Modern technology and creativity provide a variety of adapted equipment and resources that are useful in the inclusive camp environment. Shooting sports, archery, fishing, water-based activities, swimming, arts and crafts, sports and games, and challenge courses are all more accessible to persons with disabilities because of the availability of adapted equipment and universal design.

Camp Programming

Selecting and structuring programs are critical elements in the development of a high-quality inclusive camp experience. Choosing appropriate camp activities can greatly enhance the potential for genuine social acceptance and reciprocal interactions and friendships. Design and program activities that directly promote inclusion. These are activities that encourage campers to interact with and learn about one another while playing a game or conducting a task that does not allow for a participant to easily exclude others

or himself. Campfire, drama, and evening camp activities are often very conducive to this type of interaction, but all camp programs can be structured in this way.

Program activities that highlight the strengths of campers with disabilities or differences. Discover campers' strengths, and modify your activities so that these campers have the opportunity to demonstrate their unique abilities. A camper who is blind is likely to be very good at listening games. A camper with paraplegia might enjoy and excel at kayaking. Another camper may be good at telling campfire stories. Counselors can introduce traditional Paralympic games such as goal ball or seated volleyball or can modify or create games in a manner that removes barriers. Along with the use of adapted equipment, careful programming adjustments can greatly facilitate inclusion. This same principle can be used with children who have cultural differences. Whatever the situation, counselors can look for opportunities for campers to share and take pride in their uniqueness.

Finally, traditional camp activities can be conducted in a manner that fosters inclusion. Through purposeful interaction with campers, counselors can greatly affect the quality of the camp experience. This can be as simple as walking and talking with a camper on a hike or as direct as shortening the distance of a throw. Much of this involves on-the-spot decisions and adjustments, such as breaking down an art project into simpler steps so that a struggling participant can succeed. Camp counselors are called *counselors* (as opposed to *supervisors)* for a reason. Beyond ensuring the camper's safety, the counselor's role is to see to it that the camper has a good time, and the most powerful tool that the counselor has regarding this task is her ability to develop a relationship with the camper.

Self-Segregation

One important point to mention, which was noted by Hutchison and colleagues (2008), is that even with significant support in an inclusive camp environment, some campers may withdraw from activities. Furthermore, this withdrawal is often viewed as appropriate by staff, because they assume that the camper has no interest in the presented activity. Worse, it has been observed that counselors often offer less encouragement to children with disabilities than to other campers (Hutchison et al., 2008). Hutchison and colleagues identified this as an area for improvement, and we recommend that camp directors address this issue in staff training. Inclusion involves being held to the same participatory expectations as other campers. Removing oneself from camp activities should be discouraged unless attributable to a legitimate reason, such as excess fatigue or cultural restrictions. Counselors must do everything they can to encourage participation, even when doing so requires them to expend great effort and energy.

Types of Camps

This discussion has focused primarily on residential summer camps that involve traditional summer camp activities. This setting was chosen because it presents the broadest range of challenges in regard to inclusion (a residential camp in a natural environment). The principles presented here are relevant to all camp environments including day camps, sports camps, and any other form of structured camp programming. More important than the type of camp are the nature of camper needs, the tasks at hand, and the ability of staff members to consider these two factors and identify areas that facilitate or impede inclusion.

Summary

Professional recreation providers of today recognize the rights of people of all abilities and backgrounds to experience inclusion; however, it will be up to the next generation of recreation providers to implement truly inclusive outdoor recreation programming. Toward that end, we offer the following guidelines as a summary of actions the outdoor recreation provider is encouraged to implement.

Camp presents many challenges for inclusion. These challenges will vary from camp to camp, but you should consider each area thoroughly when developing and implementing an inclusive camp experience. In dealing with these challenges, keep in mind the opportunities that are at hand. Campers and counselors have an opportunity to wipe the slate clean, in terms of attitudes, expectations, past failures, and current apprehensions. Inclusion counselors have a tremendous opportunity to help all campers create expectations for themselves and others. Every camper should leave camp with a deep desire to come back next year. The lessons learned and the memories gained from an inclusive camp culture can make life better for all campers, regardless of their background or situation.

Recreation leaders can ensure inclusion in outdoor recreation by enabling every participant to (1) act as a full participant and be fully engaged in the activity rather than being relegated to a lesser role; (2) operate at a level of competence and independence based on her individual strengths, abilities, and desires rather than the strengths, abilities, and desires assigned or assumed by others; (3) choose from a range of supports that facilitate individual competence and independence rather than be limited to the role of observer because the activity is presented and facilitated with a very narrow set of options and expectations for participation; and (4) be respected as an active and contributing member while holding the same status as all other participants. With these fundamentals in mind, the recreation provider can change attitudes and actions by furthering inclusive programs for all people.

Discussion Questions

1. What would your life be like without access to the outdoors? Develop a list of activities that are common among your classmates, and discuss how you would replace these if you could not be active outdoors. Discuss the groups that have been identified as underserved, and discuss the barriers that keep them away from the outdoors. Discuss what you and your classmates can do, as professionals, to remove the social barriers to participation.

2. Make two lists. On the first list, identify your favorite recreation activities and those of your classmates. On the second list, identify the underserved groups discussed in this chapter. One at a time, match each activity with an underserved group, and discuss strategies for removing barriers that may prevent a positive experience.

3. Ask all members of the class to recall their summer camp and day camp experiences. Discuss the extent to which these camps included children from one of the underserved groups. For those camps that were inclusive, discuss the strategies that were used to facilitate a positive experience for everyone. For those who attended camps with minimal inclusion, ask the students to imagine and discuss with the class how their experiences would have been different if there was a greater attempt at inclusion.

4. Discuss how summer camps have changed over the past 20 years, and focus on the inclusion of underserved people. How would you envision summer camps 20 years from now?

5. Who are the key stakeholders in a successful inclusive camp? What strategies could be used to communicate to each of these different parties the importance of inclusion?

6. What would it take to build a genuine inclusive camp identity?

7. If you worked as a camp counselor, what aspect of inclusion would be most intimidating or concerning to you?

8. What local or regional community resources might be of use if you were providing an inclusive camping program?

9. Is it always necessary or appropriate to provide a fully inclusive camp?

›› Spotlight on Inclusive Programs

Penn State and U.S. Department of Defense Team Up to Provide Training on Inclusive Recreation for Wounded Warriors

Tammy Buckley, CTRS

Coordinator of Professional Development, Internships and Alumni Relations in the department of recreation, park and tourism management, Pennsylvania State University

The willingness with which our young people are likely to serve in any war, no matter how justified, shall be directly proportional to how they perceive veterans of earlier wars were treated and appreciated by our nation.

–George Washington, 1789

Circumstances to Consider

The need to provide inclusive recreation services for active-duty Wounded Warriors is more important now than ever before. Current military policies permit wounded Active Component (AC) and Reserve Component (RC) personnel, including those with amputations, to remain on active duty as opposed to being discharged or medically retired. Additionally, medical advances have dramatically improved battlefield survivability. The time from sustaining injury on the battlefield to receiving "other continent," state-of-the-art medical care has been reduced from 15 days during the Vietnam War to 13 hours during the Iraq War. These advances in medical care have decreased mortalities and increased the survival of wounded and severely wounded service members. Although a positive outcome, increased survival also increases the need to ensure the safe return and full reintegration of Wounded Warriors into family and community life.

Identifying the Need

Recreation personnel working for Morale, Welfare, and Recreation (MWR) at military installations are often "brought up through the ranks" and may or may not have higher education or a recreation background. As a result, many recreation personnel need training regarding the various types of injuries and disorders they will encounter as well as approaches to including active-duty Wounded Warriors in existing MWR programs and services. Because MWR professionals are in a unique position to assist with readjustment to life on the installation, they must be able to recognize the unique needs of military personnel with war-related injuries and take the initiative to assist with healthy reintegration into daily community and family life.

Active participation in MWR services can also benefit the active-duty Wounded Warrior and the Department of Defense by promoting the health and wellness of Wounded Warriors; increasing combat readiness; reducing incidents of suicide and destructive behaviors associated with posttraumatic stress disorder (PTSD)

Kortney Clemons, retired U.S. Army combat medic, was the first Wounded Warrior from Iraq to qualify for the U.S. Paralympic Games.

(e.g. substance abuse) and secondary problems (e.g., domestic violence, social isolation, depression); facilitating the adjustment of spouses and family members to injured personnel; complying with legal mandates (i.e., Americans with Disabilities Act); and supporting the President's commitment to provide the best care to military personnel and veterans. However, to fully engage active-duty Wounded Warriors in programs and services, the MWR professional must be able to recognize the characteristics of injuries (e.g., PTSD, traumatic brain injury, amputation) and the needs created by those injuries and must acquire the knowledge, tools, and resources to promote inclusion.

Development of Customized Training

In response to the identified need to train MWR personnel, faculty members Tammy Buckley and Ralph Smith from Penn State's department of recreation, park and tourism management collaborated with the School of Hospitality Management and Outreach's Management Development Programs and Services to develop a highly customized 4-day course titled Inclusive Recreation for Wounded Warriors. Beginning in 2009, Penn State has been funded to provide 12 courses across all branches of military service over the next 3 years.

The purpose of the course is to train MWR staff on methods for including wounded active-duty service members in existing MWR programs and services, adapting and modifying programs and services as appropriate. For example, military personnel with amputations may require different prosthetic feet to rock climb, stabilization straps to lift weights, and flotation aids to swim, while those with PTSD who experience adverse reactions to crowds and loud noises may need recreation activities structured in quieter settings to enable participation.

The course, which is available across all branches of service, aims to broaden recreation personnel's understanding of the characteristics and contraindications of the physical and psychological outcomes of war. Course participants learn the importance of providing programmatic access as well as physical access. They learn how to create accessible programs, how to adapt and modify programs, and how to use recreation-related adaptive and specially designed equipment to facilitate participation. At course conclusion, attendees perform an inclusive recreation needs analysis for their installation and develop an inclusive recreation action plan to be implemented upon the participant's return to the installation.

Course Methods

Approximately 30 people attend each course, and instructors are certified therapeutic recreation specialists (CTRS) by the National Council for Therapeutic Recreation Certification. The course uses subject matter experts in each area of injury including, but not limited to, PTSD, traumatic brain injury, amputation,

The return of so many Wounded Warriors to active-duty status underscores the importance of providing inclusive recreation services on military installations.

(continued)

spinal cord injury, inclusive recreation, and accessible design. A hands-on presentation of adaptive and specially designed equipment that can be used to adapt or modify existing MWR programs and services is also offered. Guest speakers with related injuries augment the course by interacting with participants and offering personal perspectives on life and the influence of recreation before and after injury. Guest speaker Joshua Watson, a Penn State senior studying recreation, park, and tourism management, understands the value of recreation for military personnel.

Summary

The Iraq War has created several challenges for MWR staff to address the needs of Wounded Warriors returning to active duty. We hope that recreation personnel who take this course will be able to design, adapt, and modify recreation programs and services to enable greater participation by Wounded Warriors and their family members. The over-arching goal of this course is to enable the Wounded Warrior transition from the battlefield to a healthy community and family life on the installation.

If your organization could benefit from disability awareness or inclusive recreation training, please feel free to call 814-867-1756 or e-mail tbuckley@psu.edu for more information.

In part from Penn State Department of Defense.

Inclusive Adventure and Challenge Courses

> *We should come home from adventures, and perils, and discoveries every day with new experience and character.*
> —Henry David Thoreau

>> Learning Outcomes

After completing this chapter, learners will be able to do the following:

- Define and differentiate the terms *adventure, therapeutic outdoor programs, wilderness therapy, adventure therapy,* and *challenge education.*
- Describe the significant benefits associated with inclusive adventure activities.
- Understand the participation and management issues of inclusive adventure for persons with specific needs.
- Delineate important staff and training considerations for leading inclusive outdoor adventure programs, including potential activity modifications and adaptations for specific populations.
- Describe several risk management components essential to the delivery of safe outdoor adventure activities.
- Define a challenge course.
- Understand how challenge courses work.
- Know how people are kept safe on a challenge course.
- Identify two factors that prevent and two that limit participation in a challenge course.
- Identify four techniques to encourage participation in a challenge course.

Inclusive Adventure

Alison Voight, PhD, CTRS

Indiana University

Alan Ewert, PhD

Indiana University

The adventure industry in the United States has experienced continued growth in terms of both the number of participants and the types of activities and experiences engaged in. More and more persons want to be involved with adventure or high-risk activities, as evidenced by the increased popularity of climbing, snow boarding, bungee jumping, and indoor climbing walls (Ewert et al., 2006). Participation in adventure activities has evolved beyond the small segment of our society deemed daredevils or risk-takers to a point where these activities are considered a fairly legitimate form of recreation and leisure. Participants in adventure activities today transcend the traditional image of young males in their 20s and 30s and include a much broader segment of our society. Women as well as men seek out adventure activities that involve mountaineering, heli-skiing, white-water rafting and kayaking, hang gliding, base jumping, and more. Additionally, participants in their 40s, 50s, and 60s have become much more common in the pursuit of adventure.

The gap is also closing between adventure participation of persons with and without disabilities. People who have disabilities are often choosing, if not mandating, their right to seek and participate in all types of activities, including adventure activities. (See the Americans with Disabilities Act [ADA] Web site for more information regarding the rights of persons who have disabilities: www.ada.gov/publicat.htm#Anchor-14210.) Adventure activities are becoming an inclusive enterprise for those who seek to push their personal limits (Brannan et al., 2003).

What Is Adventure?

Activities that involve adventure, or are defined as adventure activities, usually possess specific elements that are different from traditional recreation activities such as swimming, painting, horseback riding, playing at the beach, biking, and playing tennis. Adventure activities are different in that they often involve risk, fear, personal challenge, and an unknown outcome (Yerkes, 1985). These activities usually take place outdoors, with elements of real or perceived danger, and include the purposeful use of stress, skill testing, and challenge (Ewert, 1989; Ford & Blanchard, 1993). Adventure activities are often deliberately sought out because they involve the elements of risk, fear, and the unknown. They may be used for group purposes in a therapeutic context, broadly referred to as therapeutic outdoor programs, or may be used for personal growth and challenge by an individual.

Therapeutic Outdoor Programs

Adventure recreation or adventure programs are often used in conjunction with therapeutic purposes. *Wilderness therapy* historically has focused on the use of remote wilderness locations, and often intense personal challenges, to bring about positive social and psychological changes for adolescents. *Adventure therapy* uses risk and uncertainty, brought about through adventure-based activities in outdoor or emulated outdoor environments, to promote positive life changes for persons with disabilities and psychological issues. *Challenge education* uses group problem-solving activities such as "initiatives" (i.e., ground games) or ropes courses with both high and low obstacles and is usually a one-time planned event to promote bonding within a specific group (e.g., students, business groups, educators). Challenge courses usually take place outdoors and, if processed correctly, can be an effective tool in reaching therapeutic or educational goals. In the second part of this chapter, Brent Wolfe discusses challenge courses in greater detail. (For an example of a challenge education program, see http://departments.weber.edu/wrc/Challenge_Education/index.htm.) *Renewal* or *special* focus courses are offered through Outward Bound (see www.outwardboundwilderness.org/specialfocus.html). These programs focus on personal development, change, violence, crises, or issues for specific groups such as families, veterans, or women. *Wilderness experience programs* include a variety of outdoor experiences (e.g., www.cnr.uidaho.edu/wrc/Publications/wrcreport9900.pdf). *Outdoor behavioral health* is considered "an emerging treatment modality in mental health practice that is used with adolescents who have emotional, behavioral, psychological, and substance use disorders" (Woodbury Reports, 2003, www.strugglingteens.com/archives/2003/7/obhrc2.html). Outdoor behavioral health is considered a treatment program, similar to outpatient treatment in clinics or hospitals or residential treatment, and is different from traditional therapies such as family therapy, cognitive–behavioral therapy, wilderness therapy, or adventure therapy (for more information, see http://cehd.umn.edu/Kin/research/OBHRC/).

Although each type of program has a different focus, all of which are beyond the scope of this chapter to explore in depth, they all use some aspect of the adventure experience to bring about change within the individual or group. McCormick and colleagues (2000) defined therapeutic outdoor programs as direct, experientially structured programs, with specific goals and objectives, designed to bring about therapeutic changes within a person, for the purposes of rehabilitation as well as psychological, social, and physical development, in outdoor or emulated outdoor settings (p. 157). The trend of using adventure programs for therapeutic purposes has grown tremendously in the last few decades. Typing the term *adventure therapy* into an Internet search will return more than 250,000 hits. This trend reflects not only the excitement and interest in adventure activities but also the recognition of inclusive rights for all persons to participate in adventure programs, regardless of ability or disability. People who have a limiting condition or impairment are seeking the same types of outcomes and benefits from adventure activities as anyone else.

Goals for Inclusive Adventure Programs

As indicated previously in this chapter, people seek adventurous activities for many reasons. Some of these may be to test oneself through exciting challenges, to live on the edge, to improve group dynamics, or simply to experience something new or different. Inclusive adventure programs are as varied in their goals and objectives as there are inclusive adventure programs available. These goals may include purely recreation and social enjoyment, personal enrichment, or education and skill building. The most important goal of any inclusive adventure program is to welcome all persons to the group, regardless of whether or not they have a disability. This attitude must be fostered from the top of management down to the program staff. If the proper attitude toward the inclusion of all participants, regardless of limitations, is not in place, then the adventure program has no chance to truly be an inclusive experience. The mission, goals, and objectives of inclusive adventure programs are often based on the types of outcomes or benefits that participants seek.

Benefits of Inclusive Adventure Participation

Most inclusive adventure programs have specific mission statements, goals, and objectives that attract a specific client or type of participant. Clients who seek out adventure programs often have specific outcomes or benefits in mind that they wish to achieve. For instance, some participants want to be a part of a group that is attempting something exciting and demanding, such as climbing or white-water skills. Others may seek personal growth or wish to experience more challenge in their life, make new friends in a diverse setting, or become more physically fit. The outcomes or benefits that participants seek are a very important component of inclusive adventure programs. Many of the benefits can be categorized, for clarity, according to several well-established behavioral domains. These include psychological and cognitive, sociological, physiological, and spiritual domains. Each area, and its potential benefits, is briefly described in the next section.

Psychological–Cognitive Benefits

These types of benefits relate to one's psychological development or personality, thought processes, and learning ability. Benefits in the psychological–cognitive areas can include:

- Improvements in self-systems: Many components of adventure activities increase self-concept, esteem, confidence, and control.

Adventure activities can provide participants the opportunity to face a challenging or fearful experience and know that they tried their best or attempted something they would never have thought possible before the adventure program.

● Potential increases in competence, empowerment, determination, resilience: Research has shown that completing a challenging adventure program or activity has carryover value in other areas of a person's life. A person who attempts difficult outdoor adventure challenges may say, "I was able to climb the crag, or paddle the rapids, so I think I can handle these difficulties on my job, or at school, too."

● Locus of control shift: Shifting from negative perceptions, negative thoughts about one's ability, or feelings of helplessness to greater perceptions of success and ability has true potential in adventure activities. This shift in perception is rooted in the theoretical context of attribution theory (Weiner, 1974, 1980), which attempts to explain, or attribute, outcomes of behavior. Most people develop perceptions about why they are successful or unsuccessful in different areas of their lives. Some people attribute their success in life to factors outside their control (unstable attributions), such as chance, fate, or luck. They do not attribute success to a perceived sense of skill or hard work, or they blame others for their failure. Conversely, others learn that they have to try harder to achieve success and that it is within their control to be successful (stable attributions). Inclusive adventure programs, if managed correctly, can help shift negative, unstable self-perceptions, or attributions, to more stable, positive attributions. This is particularly important for persons with disabilities who have had little chance to experience success elsewhere in their lives (Austin, 2004).

● Increased knowledge of outdoor skills: Inclusive adventure activities can provide an opportunity to learn a multitude of skills specifically related to outdoor activities, such as knot tying, climbing, canoeing, hiking, and map and compass skills.

● Potential decreases in depression and anxiety: Inclusive adventure programs and activities allow the participant to focus on an area of her life that is different from everyday issues. Learning new skills and activities and accomplishing difficult challenges can help reduce depression and refocus thoughts in a more positive direction.

Adventure participation can bring participants a sense of challenge and excitement.

Photo courtesy of Alison Voight.

Sociological Benefits

Sociological benefits relate to those areas of a person's life that involve social situations. These situations include the social dynamics of one's family, social interaction at school, social or peer relationships with friends, and social isolation from friends and family members. Social circumstances also relate to a person's adult interactions in the workplace and sometimes involve a legal context, if antisocial behavior becomes destructive, such as can be the case with adolescents or young adults in their 20s. Benefits from a sociological standpoint might include several opportunities:

- Being a team member: Most inclusive adventure programs operate within the "group process" or group framework. For many persons who have disabilities, being able to positively contribute to a group may have a profound impact and might be a first-time experience for some. Adventure activities can allow for group input and contributions, where everyone can play a part. The group can also reinforce positive behavior from participants and extinguish socially inappropriate behaviors.

- Eliminating negative perceptions of people with disabilities: Inclusive adventure programs provide the perfect platform from which to turn around misconceptions about persons with disabling conditions. A person who has a limitation can dispel myths about her condition and capabilities as she becomes a contributing group member.

- Learning decision-making skills: Inclusive adventure activities can provide an opportunity for leadership development and decision making during challenging or stressful adventure situations. Adventure activities often require decisions to be made quickly and with group cooperation.

Physiological Benefits

Physiological, or physical fitness, benefits relate to the biological aspects of a person. The very nature of most outdoor adventure activities, especially for people who have reduced strength and endurance or for those who have not been active, can be quite physically demanding. Participating in adventure activities has an almost immediate impact on one's ability to perform and opportunities to persevere and physically challenge oneself. Like any exercise or physical exertion, adventure activities carry many benefits:

- Increased strength, endurance, and cardiovascular fitness: These physical benefits are sometimes underrated but are important to overall health.

- Increased agility and skill base: Adventure participants learn to work with a variety of outdoor equipment, manipulating and handling ropes, paddles, and backpacks, and so on. These skills can carry over to other areas of a person's life.

- Improved health parameters: Weight, stress, and blood pressure can be improved by the physical demands of the adventure activity if sustained over a period of time (see Driver et al., 1991). These benefits will vary according to the length of the program and changes maintained once the program is over.

Spirituality

Spiritual benefits refer to intangible beliefs that a person considers important in his life. These beliefs may be religious in nature, or they may take the form of gratitude, compassion, personal revelations, or an epiphany that occurs through inclusive adventure recreation activities. Spiritual outcomes or benefits from participation may provide several opportunities:

- Opportunities for a greater connectedness to nature and the outdoors: We can become aware that we are a part of a much larger world and can better appreciate the greater cycle of life in natural surroundings and the beauty of nature.

- Opportunities to learn new personal insights and reflection: This may not always be possible within routine, everyday experiences. For instance, we might recognize that we can be self-sufficient in our life without material goods—that we can exist without technology! Inclusive adventure activities allow us look beyond our own personal needs and assist those around us who may have greater problems, concerns, and issues.

- Opportunities for higher level learning: We can learn through the struggles of outdoor adventure that we possess strengths we didn't realize, resulting in new levels of learning, such as self-actualization, and we can develop greater insights and understanding, or "meta-needs" (i.e., truth, justice, uniqueness, order), that we never examined before.

Participation Issues

Leaders must know the type of adventure activity a participant is seeking, what skill levels are required, and the consequences of ill-advised or potentially dangerous situations. Several important points to consider for inclusive adventure participation are (a) types of adventure activities and skill demands, (b) training and background needed to perform the activity, and (c) level of engagement. Each of these issues is discussed in more detail in the sections that follow.

Types of Adventure and Skill Demands

People with limitations, and staff members as well, are often concerned with a number of issues regarding participation in inclusive adventure activities. For example, are participants' skills adequate for the demands of the activity? Extending far beyond the traditional "flow" model (Csikszentmiháli, 1975), the intersection of skill and demand is an important component in determining whether an activity is too dangerous or risky for a participant. The adventure industry has addressed some of the uncertainty about the levels of skill needed by creating guidebooks that describe a specific area, climbing or hiking route, scuba dive, or section of river or ocean, thus alerting readers to the demands of some activities. A person might find this type of information through national organizations such as Outward Bound (www.outwardbound.org), the American Canoe Association (www.americancanoe.org), and PADI (Professional Association of Diving Instructors, www.padi.com/padi/default.aspx). Also consider local agencies in your area such as park service offices, land management agencies, city and county parks and recreation offices, local outdoor equipment stores, and national chain outdoor stores such as REI (www.rei.com) and Gander Mountain (www.gandermountain.com). These agencies can provide valuable information on a wide range of topics including equipment needs, safety, maps, and skills training.

Participant Training and Background Considerations

Another issue, somewhat related to the previous issue, involves training. The adventure participant often asks what level and type of training she will need to be successful and safe with the activity. Will this training need to be specific to the activity or more generalized? For example, if one is interested in going on a hike, will she need specialized training such as cold weather skills, or will basic outdoor skills suffice?

Level of Engagement

Another issue is who will be a part of the inclusive adventure activity. In other words, is this activity done as part of a group or team or individually? Moreover, will this activity involve a group of friends or acquaintances, or will it be part of a structured class or program? For example, a person might want to canoe in the boundary waters canoe area (BWCA) with a group of friends, without special assistance or professional guides. Conversely, adventure participants may want to go canoeing as part of a group with an organization. Many considerations will "weigh in" on the ultimate level of engagement in an adventure activity—whether to engage in the activity alone, with a group of friends, or with a group of people who may or may not know one another. Groups can be organized through a church, community or university recreation department, or professional guide services or by interest in a specific activity through a nationally organized group of persons with similar interests (e.g., hiking, snowboarding, kayaking). Wilderness Inquiry (see www.wildernessinquiry.org) is an organization that connects persons who are interested in outdoor adventure activities, regardless of ability or disability, with other interested people for a guided adventure experience.

Ewert and Hollenhorst (1989) developed a useful model describing the different types of adventure experiences sought out by people as a function of their level of engagement. As depicted in figure 16.1, people who are relatively low on the engagement scale (e.g., first-timers or people just trying the activity out) often seek different types of adventure activities than those who have a higher level of engagement. Once the type of participation (alone, group, guided) and skill level needed are established, the leader of inclusive adventure activities must determine how accessible an area is, and what accommodations might be needed for successful participation.

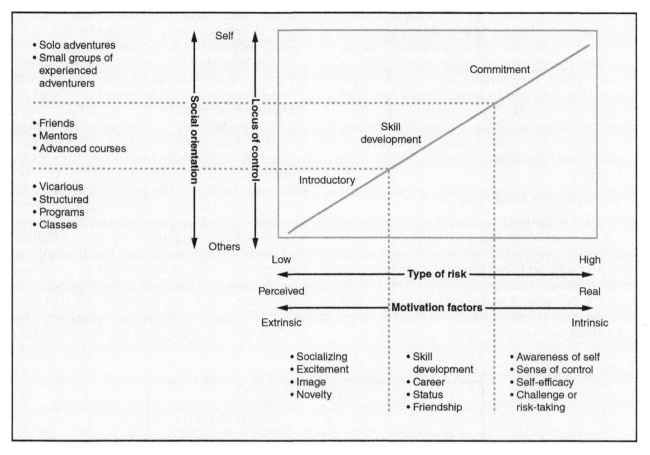

Figure 16.1 The adventure model depicts the interaction between engagement in an adventure activity and the impact of risk on skill and motivation.

Reprinted, by permission, from A. W. Ewert and S. Hollenhorst, 1989. *Outdoor adventure pursuits: Foundations, models, and theories* (Scottsdale, AZ: Publishing Horizons). © A.W. Ewert.

Access and Accommodation Issues in Inclusive Adventure Activities

Access and accommodation are important considerations to ensure full participation in inclusive adventure programs. Leaders must investigate several important points before planning, leading, or offering inclusive adventure activities: (a) remote outdoor access, (b) staff training considerations, (c) activity modifications and specific accommodation needs, and (d) participants' rights to participation. These points are discussed in the following sections.

Remote Outdoor Access

Physical access to an outdoor area is critical to inclusive participation in adventure activities. Access is an especially salient issue for persons who have mobility, strength, or endurance issues. Debates continue regarding just how much of an outdoor area should be made accessible, and issues related to every person's right to access the beauty and uniqueness of outdoor locations are discussed as well. However, adventure activities, by their very nature (e.g., remote, rugged, poor weather, uncertain terrain) do not always lend themselves to inclusion. There will be occasions for exclusion in difficult-to-access outdoor areas, for example, if it is not possible to provide paved, smooth trails for wheelchair users. Pertinent information should be placed at the beginning of an outdoor trail or outdoor area in the form of trail signage. Signage that is clearly posted at entrances of trails can allow a professional leader, or a participant, to determine whether this is an appropriate adventure endeavor. The following section describes in greater detail how trail signage can benefit all interested patrons (e.g., elderly participants, those with mobility issues, or families with small children) who visit an outdoor area or consider a challenging outdoor activity.

Trail Signage and Access

The U.S. Department of the Interior has delineated classification systems for outdoor trails in many national parks to inform users how long an outdoor trail is and what type of terrain it entails. Such information can greatly reduce problems for both the participant and the leader. Figure 16.2 is an example of trail-head information that can inform the outdoor participant of what types of trails are ahead. More information can be found at the National Center on Accessibility, in Bloomington, Indiana (see www.ncaonline.org).

As can been seen in figure 16.2, the gradient of the trail, possible hazards along the way, length of the trail, and type of trail use are well laid out on the signs, which are placed at the head of the trail (see the following Web link for more information about accessible outdoor areas: www.access-board.gov/outdoor/outdoor-rec-app.htm). Using these signs, participants can determine in advance how far they want to go on the trail or whether they want to try the trail at all. Figure 16.3 shows some information, such as types of users and level of accessibility, that might be used on trail signs at trail heads. These signs indicate that the trails are designed for hiking, that wheelchair users will have an accessible trail, and that the person who uses a chair will be entering a wooded trail area. The ADA Access Guidelines, or ADAAG, founded in 1991, are guidelines for buildings and facili-

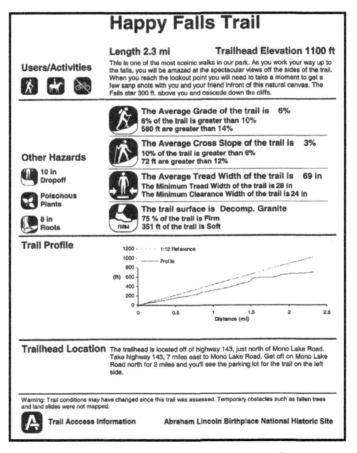

Figure 16.2 An example of universal signage for outdoor trails.

Reprinted from http://www.access-board.gov/outdoor/outdoor-rec-app.htm

Figure 16.3 Universal trail signage allows for personal and group decision making.

Reprinted from http://www.access-board.gov/outdoor/outdoor-rec-app.htm

ties (for more details visit the ADAAG Web site at www.access-board.gov/adaag/html/adaag.htm). Recreation facilities were addressed in an amended section of ADAAG in 2002.

The U.S. Department of the Interior has designated a classification system of trails and published these in *A Guide to Designing Accessible Outdoor Recreation Facilities* (1980). This publication describes in great detail the five classes of trails. These classifications range from class I (the shortest and least difficult, with pavement and rest areas) to class V (more than 10 miles [16 kilometers] in length, no defined width of trail, and no developed rest areas). This information allows participants and staff to make informed decisions about participation.

Staff Training Considerations

Designers and leaders of adventure programs should consider some important questions:

1. What will the staff-to-participant ratio be? Can the adventure activity be carried out safely with available staff? The ratio will often depend on the ability level of the participants and whether any participants will require one-on-one attention. Sometimes other participants who have no specific needs are willing to help other participants. Expectations of whether nonstaff participants should assist others must be established prior to the start of the adventure

activity. If enough staff members are not available to safely carry out an activity, without the assistance of the other group members, the program manager must decide whether to hire more staff or redesign the activity.

2. How will participants be assessed in terms of skill level and ability? How a leader or staff member determines the abilities of clients often depends on the type of program and how much is going to be required of its participants. An activity conducted in a remote location, without immediate emergency access, presents a different set of concerns than would an adventure program conducted in a local outdoor area with ready access to emergency care. Leaders must assess and document participants' skill level, experience, medical needs, personal hygiene and toilet care needs, medication needs, balance issues, endurance issues, dietary restrictions and necessities, or cognitive limitations.

3. What type of background knowledge is needed by staff to lead inclusive adventure programs? Staff must have a certain level of training and knowledge regarding disabling conditions before leading inclusive adventure activities. This could involve knowing how to communicate with participants who are deaf or visually impaired; how to safely guide a person who is blind; how to handle persons who display inappropriate behavior or social skills; how to transfer participants from wheelchairs to canoes, kayaks, or other locations; how to help participants who use wheelchairs and other assistive devices; and how to assist with personal hygiene needs if warranted. Specific certifications may also be required of staff, depending on the group with whom they'll work. Several desirable certifications include Wilderness First Responder, American Canoeing Association Certification; and National Therapeutic Recreation Certification. Often, graduate degrees in psychology, counseling, or social work are desirable when working in inclusive adventure programs.

4. How will you promote an inclusive adventure experience for participants? Conducting an inclusive adventure activity will require more than bringing participants of varying skill and ability levels together for an adventure activity. A truly inclusive experience requires the acceptance of all the group members, their abilities as well as their limitations. It also requires social interaction between the group members, where no one becomes a social isolate because of a

disabling condition or appearing to be different. But it also means recognizing that all persons in the activity can make a positive contribution while avoiding patronizing behavior or assigning participants to make token contributions to the group. A skilled leader will bring together the group members through appropriate processing of group issues, for both its challenges and successes.

When developing or updating a training program for outdoor adventure personnel, pay particular attention to the issues previously described. Staff must be aware of how to safely conduct programs while at the same time foster a sense of inclusiveness, where all interested participants have the opportunity to experience adventure as well as contribute to the group process.

Activity Accommodations and Modifications

When possible, activities should be modified in advance of conducting an inclusive adventure activity. Furthermore, most activities can be modified with very few major changes to the activity and without methods or equipment. For instance, some simple modifications for a canoeing activity could include using duct tape to better grip a paddle or providing extra cushions for support and balance. Consider the following suggestions to accommodate groups that require minor adjustments for a successful inclusive adventure experience: (a) people with sensory impairments (visual and hearing) and (b) those with mobility limitations (wheelchair users, elderly persons, people with paralysis or multiple sclerosis). As a cautionary note, prior to assisting a person with a disability or limitation, always ask the person *first* whether she needs assistance and, if needed, how best to provide it.

Visual Limitations

- Always provide an orientation to the outdoor environment. This will help a person with limited vision understand her surroundings, location of restrooms, and possible hazards. Describe the area in detail by specifically pointing out the number of steps to a ledge, rock face, or campsite, for instance, or how to distinguish these areas by differences in trail texture such as grassy areas, gravel, or woodchips.
- Determine the person's preferred method of mobility. For a person who is visually

impaired, this may be a guide dog, a cane, or a sighted guide whose elbow is held by the participant while being guided. Sometimes, the person who is visually impaired will use a combination of these mobility methods. Be sure to find out his preference.

- Consider outdoor locations and alternatives. Excessive exposure to bright sunlight can cause problems for persons with low vision or other visual impairments. Consider adventure activities in alternative areas where shade is also available or tell participants to use dark sunglasses or wide-brim hats.
- Consider how you will describe the adventure activity or possible risks. Persons who have visual impairments will need an exact description of what is involved with the adventure activity, because they may not be able to see the demonstration. Modeling portions of the activity can be helpful, as can letting the person feel the object needed to participate in the adventure activity, such as a paddle, rock face, or belay system. Also describe how tall, deep, or far away something is, so the participants can decide whether they would like to continue with the adventure activity.

Hearing Impairments

- For those with hearing impairments or deafness, communication is paramount in adventure activities. Because a participant who is hearing impaired cannot hear what you are saying, find a method of communication, such as writing or drawing instructions, using sign language, or using an interpreter.
- Include visual cues such as pointing.
- Never assume that someone with a hearing impairment reads lips or knows sign language.
- Avoid shouting at someone who is deaf or hearing impaired.

Mobility Impairments

- Mobility can affect many areas of movement in adventure activities. Consider what may be required during the adventure activity; a person who has mobility issues may need assistance with balance, agility, strength, endurance, and coordination. These are critical areas to assess in order to ensure a safe and positive inclusive experience.

- Be considerate of those who have fluctuations in performance. A person with mobility impairments may tire easily during a strenuous adventure activity and may need accommodations. Ability can change from one day to the next: Do not interpret this as lack of enthusiasm or laziness.

- Be familiar with the condition of inclusive adventure participants and the limitations they face. Different mobility conditions present varying issues during an adventure activity. For example, a person with cerebral palsy may be affected by coordination or balance difficulties. Participants with multiple sclerosis may have issues with strength and endurance. People who use wheelchairs may need specific considerations for transfers, access to areas, and toileting care. Persons with mobility impairments can be as varied in their abilities as anyone else. Never make assumptions about the abilities of someone with physical or motor impairments: Each person is different.

- Keep open communication about pain or problems. A participant may feel uncomfortable about discussing any problems or pain she is experiencing and may not want to hold up the group. Make the group members comfortable enough to openly communicate about pain or other problems that occur before they become too serious or threaten the safety of the group. Be aware of any special conditions or any problems that arise.

Make as few modifications as needed for persons who have specific needs. Keep the essence of the adventure activity intact—don't modify it to the point of nonrecognition. Activity modifications should never alter the basic purpose of the adventure experience. Modifications can often be made very simply, without major specialized adaptive equipment, and should be done only to safely carry out the activity. Always ask a participant whether he wants or needs any modifications—don't assume anything. The purpose of inclusive adventure activities is for everyone to be part of the activity and for no one, whether with or without disabilities, to stand out from the group or be defined solely by his impairment.

Participants' Rights to Participation—Challenge by Choice/No Discounting

Developed a number of years ago (Rohnke, 1989), the concept of "challenge by choice/no discounting" seeks to preserve the dignity of participants

Photo courtesy of Alison Voight.

Develop programs that will get everyone participating at the same time, but also leave room for people to decide whether they want to participate.

by allowing them to choose the level and type of participation in a particular challenge or activity. Implicit in the concept of challenge by choice are the following assumptions:

- Participants build trust and confidence knowing that they are part of a group that supports their choice and that their choice will be honored by the rest of the group.
- Instructors can nudge and encourage individual participation, but ultimately each person has the right and obligation to decide her own level of participation (Martin et al., 2006).
- Instructors need to develop programs that maximize the probability of participation by everyone but should have alternative plans in the event that a student or client decides not to participate in a specific activity. These alternative plans are often critical to keeping the participant engaged in the program and part of the group.

Full-value contracts involve integrating each participant with the success of the group. That is, for the group to achieve its goals, everyone in the group will need to cooperate and be engaged to the extent they are comfortable (see the description of challenge by choice/no discounting). Although full-value contracts vary with the program, many contracts involve making participants aware of several things:

- They have to work together to achieve individual and group goals.
- They have to follow specified safety and normative behavior guidelines.
- They have to be willing to give and receive feedback, whether positive or negative.

Risk Management in Inclusive Adventure Settings

Although persons with specific needs may desire to participate in inclusive adventure activities, recreation leaders must manage the risk associated with these activities. In some instances, a person may not be able to participate in adventure activities if the leader believes it is risky or unsafe. Inherent in many adventure experiences and activities are a number of issues associated with risk management common to people with

and without disabilities, and several issues are mostly relevant to the person with a disabling condition. The following section addresses some of the risk management issues associated with disabilities within an adventure context.

Common Issues

Risk management issues common to both people with disabilities and those without include the following:

- Risk awareness and assessment: Ewert (1989) differentiated between actual risk and apparent risk. That is, some risks such as falling from a rock, getting caught in a hydraulic on a stretch of white water, or being thrown from a horse are present and possible—they are *actual risks*. These things often do happen, and there is a real possibility of serious injury or death. Other accidents, such as falling off an indoor climbing wall or ropes course, often look like they could occur but are very unlikely, particularly when proper equipment and techniques are used. These types of risks are often termed *apparent* or *perceived risks*. Indeed, many adventure-based programs will seek to avoid real risks but emphasize the apparent risks through their programmed activities and experiences. Thus, any risk management process involves being aware of what risks actually exist and accurately assessing those risks. Are they real or are they somewhat illusory?

- Waivers and assumption of risk: Many adventure-based programs use both an assumption of risk form and liability waiver as part of their risk management plan. The essential component of this approach is making sure the participant is aware that there are risks and dangers associated with the upcoming activity and that the safety of the participant cannot be completely guaranteed. Waivers and similar types of release forms tend to be invalid if they do not specify the dangers and the expectations that leaders have for the participant. Waivers usually are not valid if signed by a minor, nor can constitutional or legislative rights be waived away by the use of a particular form.

- Negligence and standard of care: Liability waivers are primarily concerned with issues related to negligence or failure to practice due care with the participant or client. In the case of negligence, four factors must be present: (1) a legal duty to provide care, (2) a failure to perform that care, (3) a connection between this lack of care and injury to the client, and (4) actual damages or injury. With respect to the concept of standard of care, adventure organization managers need to be aware of the type of activity their clients are engaged in, the abilities of these clients, and the appropriate level and type of supervision provided.

- Components of the risk management plan: Effective risk management plans involve a number of components. Here is a sample of these elements:
  - Dates, times, and location of the program and activity
  - Goals and objectives
  - Hazards and dangers
  - Transportation
  - Participants and their individual needs
  - Equipment and logistics
  - Staff abilities and skills
  - Conduct of the activity
  - Emergency action plans

Several issues are specific to adventure participants who have disabilities. According to McAvoy and colleagues (2006), the following three concerns need to be considered:

- Challenges to accommodation: Will the program or adventure experience allow for specific accommodations relative to the disability? Will some specialized equipment or changes in the program provide for the participant with a better experience?

- Monitoring and assessment: Will the participant be able to self-monitor and assess his physical and emotional conditions and, based on these assessments, make accommodations? Will the instructors or specifics of the experience allow for this monitoring and assessment with possible changes? For example, will the group stop to allow someone to check his blood sugar level?

- Social acceptance: How will the participant be accepted within the group? Will he be perceived as slowing the group down or incapable of helping the group reach its objectives? The social interface between participants with disabilities and their peers without disabilities can be a major concern within inclusive programs (Devine & Dattilo, 2000).

Dillenschneider (2007) listed several principles for accommodating participants in inclusive programs:

- Inform all participants about the attributes associated with the activity or planned experience. Participants should understand the upcoming experience, the demands that will be placed on them, and the skills and techniques needed to successfully deal with the activity.

- Encourage participants to inform the program staff about their specific needs and the adaptations that have worked in the past.

- Be innovative in thinking of ways to accommodate specific needs and issues, and encourage participants to do the same.

- Provide adequate and appropriate support by considering the social, emotional, physical, cognitive, and spiritual needs of the client.

The considerations described here make it clear that both staff and the design of the activity play important roles in the conduct of inclusive programs.

Adventure Summary

Inclusive adventure activities involve a wide range of definitions, issues, and possibilities. Inclusive adventure programs may be sought for their inherent therapeutic value through group processing and opportunities for personal growth, such as therapeutic outdoor programs, or these programs may be well-integrated activities, where people both with and without disabilities come together to experience the risky, exciting, and sometimes unknown outcomes in adventure activities. Participants can glean many benefits from appropriately managed inclusive adventure activities, including positive physical changes, inherent challenge, personal testing, and an increased sense of empowerment, self-esteem, and confidence. These programs also offer opportunities for leadership, decision making, and friendship. To provide a truly inclusive venue, however, staff must value and positively regard persons with specific needs and allow them to be contributing members of the group. Staff must consider the risks involved as well as the skill level of the participant versus the demands of the activity. When designing inclusive adventure activities, programming staff must be concerned with access to outdoor areas, must be familiar with any condition or impairment that may require additional assistance, and must determine how best to accommodate a person's need with as little modification as the adventure activity will safely permit. The establishment of a sound risk management plan is paramount for inclusive adventure programs. When the program is properly managed, all people, regardless of ability, can have the dignity and occasion to experience risk. But the most important step in creating inclusive adventure opportunities is maintaining a positive attitude and promoting an inclusive mission, thus allowing all interested persons the chance to discover the compelling rewards of outdoor adventure.

>> Professionals in Action

Greg Lais

Wilderness Inquiry.

Background Information

Education

*BS Psychology, St. John's University, Collegeville, Minnesota *MBA, Carlson School of Management, University of Minnesota

Credentials

*CTRS *CPRP

Special Awards

*Full Community Inclusion Award, American Association on Mental Retardation (AAMR) (2005) *Community Building Award, American Network of Community Options and Resources (ANCOR) (2005) *Boggs-Mitchell Award for Integrated Recreation Programs, Arc Minnesota (2005, 1996) *Jim Renne Leadership Award, Association of Outdoor Recreation and Education (May 2000) *Minnesota State council on Disability Distinguished Service Award (November 1992) *St. John's University Alumni Achievement Award (1990) *Honored at the White House for service for people with disabilities (April 1989)

Career Information

Position Founder and executive director of Wilderness Inquiry, Inc.

Organization Information Wilderness Inquiry (WI) is an organization dedicated to sharing the outdoors with others. We provide all kinds of outdoor adventures for a wide variety of people. We offer canoe, kayak, hiking, horse pack, dogsled, and raft trips throughout the world.

We are a nonprofit organization founded in 1978 and headquartered in Minneapolis, Minnesota. We are not a subsidiary of anything, nor are we officially affiliated with any group or organization. We partner with many organizations, and our trip participants come from all 50 U.S. states and from around the world.

Our passion is making high-quality outdoor experiences accessible for everyone, including those who do not typically get out and enjoy the wilderness. In addition to trips, a variety of programs and activities that help are conducted to fulfill our mission. We train staff for other organizations and provide outdoor skills workshops at community events. We also raise money to provide scholarships to make our programs financially accessible to everyone.

Organization's Mission

Our mission is to provide outdoor adventure experiences that inspire personal growth, community integration, and awareness of the environment. Wilderness Inquiry adventures encourage people to open themselves to new possibilities and opportunities.

Size of Organization

WI is run with 10 full-time staff, 60 part-time staff, and a volunteer board of directors of 21 people. Each year we conduct more than 250 events serving more than 9,000 people.

Job Description Strategic planning with board and tactical planning with board and staff. Managing organizational growth rate averaging 35% annually. Hiring, training, and supervising 10 full-time office staff and 45 field staff. Fundraising for general operating support, scholarships, and capital campaigns. Program development, promotion, and media relations.

Personally guide more than 80 extended wilderness adventures involving people with disabilities throughout North America, Australia, and the Soviet Union.

What I Like About My Job Changing lives.

Advice to Undergraduate Students Be prepared to work hard.

Personal Statement I love working in the recreation and leisure field!

Inclusive Challenge Courses

Brent Wolfe, PhD, CTRS

Georgia Southern University

Challenge courses have long been used as successful interventions for a multitude of participants; however, as participants become more diverse, additional thinking regarding implementation and adaptation of challenge courses for use by all people is needed. Specifically, challenge course managers and facilitators are encouraged to rethink the entire concept of a challenge course in relation to participants with disabilities and inclusion of diverse groups (in terms of age, ethnicity, race, gender). This section addresses five concepts related to challenge courses and the inclusion of all who desire to participate.

This section begins with a discussion of challenge courses and explores components involved in typical challenge course experiences. The second topic focuses on how challenge courses work and examines some of the research about successful challenge course programs. If we desire to include all people in challenge course experiences, it is helpful to recognize the process participants go through during their experience and potential outcomes from those experiences. The third topic presented is safety—both physical and emotional. Through the discussion of how people stay safe we will explore the idea of physical and emotional safety as well as the concept of challenge by choice (mentioned earlier in the chapter on page 313). The fourth topic

area focuses on what prevents participation in challenge courses. At this point the concept of disability begins to formally enter the section. Although a participant's disability may prevent her from participating, it is more likely that her attitude and the attitudes of those around her play a larger role in limiting participation. The section concludes with a discussion of how we can encourage participation of all people on a challenge course.

Defining a Challenge Course

Challenge course is a term synonymous with *ropes course* and has been described as a series of physical and psychological challenges (Quezada & Christopherson, 2005) where a group of participants are asked to work together to solve numerous problems posed by a person known as a *facilitator*. The challenges presented typically come in three forms:

- Initiatives
- Low elements
- High elements

These three components, used collectively (in most situations), are known as a challenge course experience. Challenge courses come in many different shapes, sizes, and locations but are typically located in a wooded, relatively remote area and use some combination of the three components.

The first experience many people have with a challenge course is *initiative activities*. These activities typically involve little equipment or even no equipment and focus on group interaction. Facilitators may ask participants to work together to collectively solve a contrived problem that typically involves moving the group or an object from one point to another while negotiating a constraint (e.g., inability to talk, see, move). Examples of initiatives include warp speed (passing a small ball around a circle as quickly as possible), turnstile (moving a group of people from one side of a spinning jump rope to the other), and antigravity (having a group of people keep an inflatable ball in the air for as long as possible).

The second component of a challenge course is made up of *low elements*. Low elements are typically permanently constructed obstacles that a group must work together to overcome. As with initiative activities, low elements focus on group interaction but these activities introduce human-made challenges for the group to conquer. Examples of low elements include whale watch (asking the group to stand on and balance a platform that totters back and forth), telephone pole (TP) shuffle (reordering a group of people on a horizontal log without stepping off), and islands (moving a group across three small platforms using 2- × 6-foot [0.6- × 1.8- meter] boards).

The third component of a challenge course is made up of *high elements*. High elements are permanently constructed obstacles that, as the name suggests, are elevated 10 to 40 feet (3-12 meters) above the ground. These elements typically require the individual participant to complete the task with physical independence and psychological and verbal support from other group members. Some high elements incorporate more than one person; however, many of the goals of these elements still involve some component of overcoming personal fears. All people who participate in high elements are connected to a safety system known as a *belay system* that is designed to protect participants in case of falling. Examples of high elements include pamper pole (ascending a 20-foot [6-meter] pole, standing on top, and jumping to catch a trapeze swing), giant's ladder (working with a partner to climb a

High elements in a challenge course can help participants face and overcome fears.

ladder with rungs approximately 3-5 feet [0.9-1.5 meters] apart), and zip line (sliding down a wire while suspended from a trolley).

How Challenge Courses Work

Understanding how challenge courses work requires understanding the following concepts:

- Dissonance
- Change zones
- Risk
- Disequilibrium
- Transference

The effectiveness of challenge courses depends on a sense of *dissonance* within participants. The idea behind creating dissonance is to challenge participants' ways of thinking and doing. Traditionally educators create this dissonance by developing situations where learners must think creatively because of a level of perceived imbalance between past knowledge and future implementation; this dissonance may help develop participants' ways of thinking (Wang & Rodger, 2006). In literature related to challenge courses, dissonance is also referred to as *dynamic tension* (Luckner & Nadler, 1997), where challenge course educators encourage learning by creating environments where disequilibrium exists. Although challenge courses certainly do not fit the idea of a traditional classroom, connections between growing through discomfort and growing through dissonance are applicable in multiple settings.

In the challenge course literature, the idea of dissonance or growth through discomfort is explained using *change zones* (Luckner & Nadler, 1997). The three zones presented for growth include the comfort zone, groan zone, and growth zone. Luckner and Nadler suggested that by participating in activities such as challenge courses, participants experience a sense of disequilibrium that can lead to growth, but the participant must embark on a safely facilitated journey and experience opportunity for success and failure. By participating in activities (e.g., initiative activities, low elements, and high elements) that may cause some level of discomfort or distress, people have the opportunity to move from their comfort zone to a zone where they experience growth. Luckner and Nadler suggested that for participants to experience this growth zone, they must explore and work on the "edge." It is on the edge between their comfort zone and groan zone that people either retreat and turn back or experience a breakthrough into the unknown territory that is the groan zone. The learning process is greatly enhanced when people participating in a challenge course program experience the opportunity to safely do this "edgework" (Luckner & Nadler, 1997).

When discussing the issue of disequilibrium, the conversation naturally turns to *risk* and understanding the appropriate amount of risk to present to people participating in challenge course programs. Risk is inherent in challenge courses (Davis-Berman & Berman, 2002); however, the manner in which risks are managed becomes extremely important when including people of all ability levels in challenge course programs. According to Davis-Berman and Berman (2002) and Wolfe and Samdahl (2005), there are two types of risk—real and perceived (i.e., actual and apparent risk as mentioned earlier in the chapter on page 314). Real risk involves the

inherent dangers involved in an activity, such as twisting an ankle when stepping down from a low element, falling from a high element, or being stung by a bee while outside. "Perceived risks involve an individual's perceptions of tasks that face him or her, such as the anxiety created as a result of being asked to crawl through a hole that is smaller than one's body" (Wolfe & Samdahl, 2005, p. 32). Recognizing that these different types of risk exist is pertinent if we desire to provide an inclusive environment in our challenge course programs.

Simon Priest (an influential researcher who studied challenge course programs, particularly as they are used by organizations) attempted to explain the concepts of *disequilibrium* and risk by using the adventure experience paradigm (1992). Building from Csikszentmiháli's (1975) concept of flow, Priest contrasted a person's skill level with the competence necessary to complete an activity and developed a five-component adventure experience paradigm. According to Priest, when a participant's competence is significantly greater than the risk involved in the activity, she is likely to experience the component called *exploration and experimentation*. When a participant's competence level is only slightly higher than the risk involved, that person is likely to experience *adventure*. When there is a match between the risk involved and a participant's competence, that person will experience the component termed *peak adventure*. When the risk of an activity begins to outweigh a participant's competence, the component of *misadventure* is the likely result. Finally, when the risk of an activity significantly outweighs a person's competence, the component *devastation and disaster* is the likely result. Priest's premise was that with the exception of devastation and disaster, all of the categories of the adventure experience paradigm were acceptable because they likely lead to growth, and growth through dissonance is a tenet of challenge courses.

The final concept that is important for the success of challenge courses is *transference*. As mentioned previously, for challenge courses to be effective, learning must occur even in the midst of difficulty; however, this learning does not simply occur on its own. Authors have suggested that some transference should occur, and a trained facilitator can enhance this process (Kolb, 1984; Luckner & Nadler, 1997). To enhance transference, facilitators should encourage participants who have completed a challenge course program to discuss their thoughts and feelings related to their experience. The formal process as advocated by several researchers and theorists includes the following components and is recognized as the experiential learning cycle:

- Provision of an experience (in this case, the challenge course)
- Provision of a time to reflect on the particular experience
- Opportunity to generalize lessons learned during the experience to real-life settings
- Opportunity to put the newly learned lessons into practice in real-life settings

Through this process, participants can experience growth and can transfer ideas and concepts learned during the challenge course to their daily lives.

Safety on Challenge Courses

Safety is of the utmost importance in a challenge course. Safety on challenge courses has two separate but equal components:

- Physical safety
- Emotional safety

The need for *physical safety* is apparent from the description of a challenge course. When participants are engaged in physical activities that require them to move their bodies into awkward or unusual positions and place their bodies in the hands of others (literally), issues of physical safety become readily apparent. Likewise, when participants are elevated off the ground by other participants, by climbing ladders and trees, or by being attached to ropes, protecting the physical body is easily seen as a priority.

To physically protect participants on challenge course elements, several pieces of equipment connected to the sport of rock climbing are used. A plethora of specific, technical safety devices exist for challenge courses. When creating an inclusive environment, program designers must explore the type of equipment used and the size of the equipment (e.g., various sized harnesses to allow participants of different sizes to attempt high elements). Technical devices include harnesses, carabiners, figure eights, dynamic ropes, belay systems, ascenders. Mechanical advantage systems (4:1 pulley systems), slings, counterbalance

systems, and full-body harnesses are also all excellent ways to include participants with various levels of abilities (Rohnke et al., 2003).

Participants' *emotional safety*, while less frequently mentioned when discussing challenge courses, is equally as important as their physical safety. Earlier we discussed how a challenge course worked and used words like *dissonance, disequilibrium,* and *groan zone*. These words all indicate a level of discomfort that participants experience. When we intentionally place participants into situations where they will be physically and emotionally challenged, it is our responsibility and duty to protect both their physical safety and their emotional safety. The greatest challenge for some participants may be the emotional risks that they take throughout the challenge course program as they do their edgework. A brief personal story may enforce this idea.

While conducting research on a challenge course, I had the opportunity to observe interactions between facilitators and participants and then interview the participants after the completion of their program. While interviewing a female participant who had self-identified as obese, I asked her about putting her harness on in preparation for the high elements. She told me that putting on the harness was the most difficult part of the day for her because she was embarrassed by how she looked. In her words, her "thighs were squishing out like marshmallows." This made me pause and really consider the concept of emotional safety. If we place our participants into emotionally difficult situations (disequilibrium), our participants should demand that we protect them emotionally during the challenge course experience.

One technique used to protect the emotional and physical safety of challenge course participants is "challenge by choice." There are three components to challenge by choice (Carlson & Evans, 2001). First, participants in challenge course programs must be able to establish their own goals. Every participant in our programs, regardless of ability level, will have different needs and ideas of what qualifies as success. When fostering an inclusive environment we should allow participants to determine what qualifies as success rather than impose a preconceived notion of success. Consider the example of a man who has just had knee surgery and is present at a challenge course. Because of a physical condition (recent knee surgery), his goals will likely be different from others in his group. By giving him the opportunity to establish his own goals and determine his own level of success, we provide him with "safety equipment" to protect him emotionally as he participates in the course. He does not have to feel like an outcast because of his decisions; he can feel embraced and part of the group because he has been given permission to make personal decisions.

The second component of challenge by choice suggests that participants should be the ones to determine "how far" and "how much." Each element on a challenge course is designed with a starting and ending point (either figuratively or literally); however, to keep our participants physically and emotionally safe, provide opportunities for growth, and foster an inclusive environment, we must allow them to determine how much of each activity or element they would like to complete. This concept can be very freeing for participants. Consider a female participant who has been physically, sexually, or emotionally abused in previous relationships. Her participation in a challenge course program could have a tremendous positive or negative outcome for her. If she is allowed to determine how far to go, in both the literal and figurative senses, she gains power. If she is not provided with the opportunity to determine how much of an activity she would like to complete, facilitators can become representations of her past abusers.

The final component of challenge by choice states that it is the facilitators' responsibility to provide participants with enough information to make an informed decision about their level of participation. Although this is an area where many challenge course facilitators excel, it does take on a slightly different look and meaning when working with people with diverse abilities. For example, if your program includes a participant in a wheelchair who would like to ascend the climbing wall, he should be provided with enough information regarding the experience to make an informed decision about participating. He could certainly ascend the wall by using a mechanical advantage system and with the assistance of his group, but he should be informed that on a pitched wall (depending on ability level), he may bounce over the handholds and scrape along the wall as he ascends. Facilitators must inform participants of what they are likely to encounter so they can make informed decisions about participation.

Some of these ideas about emotional safety may concern some facilitators who feel that participants may elect to avoid activities that are difficult for them. We as facilitators need to realize that that is okay. It is okay if participants do not elect to do their edgework but elect to remain in their comfort zone. Although these participants may not move to the groan or growth zones during our challenge course program, they may make these transitions at other times in their lives. It is better to have a participant leave your challenge course program wishing he had taken on more challenges than have that same participant leave angry and frustrated with the facilitator because the participant was pushed too hard and did not feel emotionally safe.

Allowing participants to determine how far or how much they will do gives them a sense of control over the situation, which can lead to a strong sense of power and accomplishment.

Photo courtesy of Brent Wolfe.

Limits to Participation on a Challenge Course

In a section exploring the idea of inclusion and challenge courses, it is only fitting to spend some time understanding what might prevent or limit participation in a challenge course program. Two primary factors limit participation:

- Attitudes
- Course design

Attitudes That Limit Participation

As with participation in any activity, the attitudes of those involved are intimately connected to continued participation and enjoyment levels. When we consider developing an inclusive environment in our challenge courses, we should think about three categories of attitudes:

- Individual attitudes
- Intra-individual attitudes
- Interindividual attitudes

Individual attitudes are the attitudes that a participant holds about herself. These are attitudes of the self and are directly connected to past experiences. If participants have had positive experiences with risk in general and challenge courses specifically, then they are more likely to participate in future challenge course programs. Alternatively, if their experiences have been negative in the past, they will be less likely to participate or enjoy participating in future challenge course programs. Specific attitudes could range from "I love challenge courses! The activities are the best!" to "I hate these programs. We always do the same things and I don't learn anything." Regardless of whether participants are self-defeating, fearful, excited, or anxious, their individual attitudes can limit their participation in challenge courses. By practicing challenge by choice and allowing participants to make their own decisions about participation, we can greatly reduce negative attitudes and uncertainty about challenge course participation regardless of a person's ability.

Intra-individual attitudes are attitudes of current group members. These are attitudes outside of an individual participant that can limit his participation during a challenge course program. By its very design, a challenge course program is social in nature; unfortunately, some of the social interactions that occur during a challenge course program may hinder participation. Even unrelated comments from others in the group that might hint at inability to complete an activity or element may discourage a person from participating. Even comments made with the best intentions may make participants feel unable to participate. For example, in a group of adolescents with emotional and behavioral disorders, one group member may say to another, "Even you should be able to do this." We can see how this might be taken as condescending, but more important, the comment implies that the participants will not be able to participate in other activities and elements as well. This mentality flies directly in the face of both inclusion and challenge by choice.

Participants may have encountered *interindividual attitudes* before joining the current group or challenge course program. These are attitudes that other people have expressed about the capabilities of people who have disabilities, and these attitudes can have a profound influence on challenge course participants. The concept that is most relevant here is that of learned helplessness. If participants in our programs have been taught (and, more important, believe) that they are unable to do certain activities, this mindset can limit their participation in challenge courses. Learned helplessness occurs when people believe that the environment is not responsive to individual actions (Dattilo, 2002). Participants who have learned to become helpless believe that they will fail regardless of what they try. This feeling of helplessness will certainly limit participation in challenge courses and is extremely difficult to combat because it results from a longstanding pattern of comments and behaviors. One method to help participants regain a sense of control and autonomy is to provide them with opportunities for choice and for control of their environment. Facilitators of challenge courses must promote the concept of challenge by choice as they encourage participants to complete their edgework.

Course Designs That Limit Participation

Obviously, a challenge course must contain certain components, but the traditional way of thinking about challenge courses, their location, their design, and their purpose may need an overhaul for our programs. As mentioned at the beginning of the section, challenge courses are designed to promote growth. Traditionally, that has meant outcomes focused on communication, cooperation, teamwork, and trust (the typical challenge course buzzwords) (cf. Bronson et al., 1992; Maxwell, 1997; Meyer, 2000; Priest, 1995, 1996a, 1996b, 1998; Priest & Lesperance, 1994; Vincent, 1995). However, Goldenberg and colleagues (2000) offered additional outcomes including critical thinking, decision-making skills, leadership, confidence, self-esteem, coordination, agility, and expression of thoughts and feelings that might be addressed through challenge course programs. By expanding the potential areas of growth for participants in challenge course programs, we can create a more inclusive environment.

Some additional design areas to rethink as they pertain to limiting participation include construction of the elements themselves. During an interview, one challenge course participant referred to the manner in which physical safety was protected on the high elements. To climb these particular high elements, participants first ascended a ladder before they reached the permanent holds on the tree. Once a participant was fully off of the ladder and on the permanent holds, the ladder was removed. During my interview with this participant he stated that participation might have been limited because the "way down" had been removed. In this instance, participants could perceive that choice had been removed because the ladder had been removed and, as a result, their desire to participate may have been reduced. This concept runs directly in contradiction to challenge by choice. Participants should be able to determine how much of an element to complete and, in this case, whether their "way down" should be removed or retained.

Other design factors can limit access and participation of all people in challenge course programs:

- Restroom facilities
- Distance from parking to the course
- Existence or number of handicapped parking spaces
- Trails connecting elements
- Outdoor temperature

Next we explore some potential solutions to these and other issues so we can create inclusive challenge course programs.

Encouraging Participation of All People on a Challenge Course

The overarching concepts in this book are those of accessibility and accommodation for all people, and this section is much less philosophical and much more practical in nature. Four steps will help us encourage participation of all people on a challenge course:

- Focus on ability rather than disability
- Change the psychological environment
- Change the social environment
- Change the physical environment

To this point, disability has entered the conversation minimally, and this has been intentional. I have instead addressed more philosophical issues related to the way we understand implementation of challenge courses. If we do not understand what challenge courses are, how they work, what safety issues are involved, and what limits participation, then we cannot talk about the idea of inclusion. Once we have explored these topics, we can begin to explore specifically how to include people of all abilities.

Focusing on Ability Rather Than Disability

To talk about encouraging participation of all people in a challenge course, we must focus on our participants' abilities rather than disabilities; this shift of focus changes our questions regarding inclusion. Questions about details like adapting an element to make a course inclusive overlook larger issues related to inclusion. We can take many steps that will help us to create an inclusive environment. This is a paradigm shift as discussed by Kuhn (1970): not simply a brief change in thought but a radical departure from the old way of thinking, a departure that promotes changes in thought and behavior.

Changing the Psychological Environment

The second step to encouraging participation of all people on a challenge course involves changing the psychological environment that surrounds the challenge course. To change the psychological environment, we must do three things:

- Create an environment that provides opportunities for success and failure.
- Practice challenge by choice.
- Provide opportunities for dignified risk.

Challenge courses are excellent forums to provide opportunities for both success and failure. Many (but certainly not all) challenge course programs promote the idea of success, which does not sound like a bad thing; however, as mentioned earlier, we have to consider whose definition of success we are using. We want to promote the participant's definition of success, and sometimes that means changing the language that we use to describe the activities and elements on a challenge course. Staff of some challenge course programs dislike the idea of failure, but failure is a part of life and people must be taught how to deal with failures. Trying to protect people with disabilities, some program staff establish goals that are incredibly easy or refuse to acknowledge failure. Why this level of protection? If we allow participants to establish their own goals and then either succeed or fail at those goals, we have an opportunity to teach extremely important lessons.

Challenge course experiences should be about creating an environment that fosters learning. We can promote this idea by encouraging learning in all situations—regardless of success or failure. If our participants fail, the responsibility of the facilitator is to teach through that failure. John Maxwell's book *Failing Forward: How to Make the Most of Your Mistakes* (2000) explores the idea that, to be successful, people must learn to embrace and learn from their mistakes. He suggests that "the difference between average people and achieving people is their perception of and response to failure" (p. 2). That is the concept presented here. Through the failed attempt, learning occurs and participants are able to move forward in their understanding of life and themselves.

To practice the idea of "failing forward" we can implement the concept of challenge by choice as was presented earlier. If we provide our participants opportunities to determine their own goals, to decide how much of an element to complete, and to make informed decisions, then they may experience success or failure but they will experience it on their own terms and,

more important, learn through the experience. Using challenge by choice in this way requires a psychological shift in the manner in which administrators and facilitators present challenge course experiences.

The final way we can change the psychology of a challenge course is by providing our participants the opportunity for dignified risk (Rohnke et al., 2003). When people who have disabilities participate on our courses, we want them to experience risk (as mentioned earlier, a tenet of a challenge course); however, we want all of our participants to experience risk in a dignified manner. This means communicating with our participants before they begin activities or elements so we understand what their abilities are and what levels of risk they are comfortable with. Consider the case of Rick, a challenge course participant with cerebral palsy who had significant mobility and communication limitations (Carlson & Evans, 2001). During the challenge course, Rick ascended a climbing wall with complete assistance from the program facilitators. He did not have the ability to climb, but the wall was designed with a counterweight system to aid group members in their ascent. Rick was completely dependent on those pulling him up the wall and literally slid up the entire face of the wall. Carlson and Evans struggled with the issue of dignified risk as they explored the manner in which the situation had been handled. Regardless of our participants' abilities, we want to allow for risk, but that risk must be dignified.

Changing the Social Environment

Changing the social environment will encourage people to participate in challenge courses. There are three suggestions for changing the social environment:

- Provide a variety of role opportunities for participants.
- Provide opportunities for challenge course staff to interact with participants of different abilities.
- Change participant and staff attitudes about people with disabilities.

One technique that has been used extensively on challenge courses to promote involvement of group members is to allow for people within the group to determine the role they would like to fill. In some cases this means that participants assume more of a cognitive role, where they attempt to mentally work through the problem to find a solution, but take a less active role in the physical actions needed to put the solution into practice. In other cases, participants elect to encourage other group members from the sidelines rather than actively take part in either the solution or implementation phases. Allowing for multiple roles that fit the needs and desires of our participants is necessary to encourage all participants to engage in challenge courses. There are three steps that will allow for the development of valued roles for our participants.

First, we must ask participants what they can do. If we don't know what they can do, assisting them in finding meaningful roles becomes difficult. Second, we should ask participants what they want to do. Just because a participant is able to do something doesn't mean that she wants to do it. Finally, we should create opportunities for participants to do would they would like to do. Although this may take some additional planning and thinking on the part of facilitators, creating a social environment that provides meaningful roles for our participants is extremely valuable. Consider the example of a participant with a severe visual impairment who is participating with a group on your course. Creating an inclusive social environment for her would involve allowing her to determine the role she would like to have within the group. This role is likely to change from activity to activity and element to element. Providing an environment where she is comfortable saying what she is able to do and what she would like to do can show her that she is a welcome, valued, and needed member of the team.

The second suggestion for changing the social environment involves providing opportunity for challenge course staff members to interact with people with different abilities during training, observation, and programming. For many people, new situations with new people can be very intimidating. In many cases, simply having the opportunity to interact with people who are different from traditional challenge course participants can encourage a change in the social environment. Creating opportunities for challenge course staff members to interact with people with different abilities may create a social environment where people of all abilities are respected and welcomed. If we promote interaction with people of different abilities,

we may be able to encourage and promote an atmosphere and culture that are accepting of all people, regardless of ability level (Dattilo, 2002).

Once we have provided a variety of role opportunities for participants and have provided staff with opportunities to interact with people with disabilities, the final step for changing the social environment is to change staff and participant attitudes about people with different abilities.

Nine strategies can be used to change attitudes (Dattilo, 2002). First, we can structure interactions. This concept closely follows the previous suggestion that we create opportunities for staff and participants to interact with people of different abilities; however, these interactions must be structured so they are beneficial. "Simply placing people in the same environment does not ensure positive interactions between them" (Dattilo, 2002, p. 80). The second suggestion offered by Dattilo is to encourage extensive personal contact. The more extensive the interactions, the more likely communication and understanding will be increased, thus creating a social environment that is supportive of all participants. Promoting joint participation is Dattilo's third suggestion, and it implies that the more frequently people participate in inclusive settings, the less likely they are to develop stereotypes that limit participation. Earlier, the suggestion was offered to provide opportunities for a variety of roles. The fourth strategy to change participant and staff attitudes toward people with disabilities relates to this idea but recommends development of roles that are of equal status. If those without disabilities consider themselves the caretakers of those with disabilities, then honest respect and interaction will be difficult to develop. Fostering cooperative interdependence, the fifth strategy for changing attitudes, is particularly suited to the strengths of a challenge course program. By its very design, a challenge course requires cooperation and interdependence. Fostering these ideals will promote an environment that is inclusive of all people. Dattilo's sixth strategy is to develop effective communication. As we seek to influence attitudes in an effort to change the social environment found at challenge courses, we must keep open lines of communication among all invested parties. One area where challenge courses are uniquely situated to promote inclusion relates to the seventh strategy— encourage age-appropriate behaviors. Although challenge courses are used by participants of all ages, providing activities within a challenge course program that are age-appropriate will aid in the inclusion process. Creating naturally proportioned groups is the eighth strategy for changing attitudes. Groups that Dattilo considers naturally proportioned, that is, in which about 10% of the group's members have disabilities, are more likely to promote positive attitudes toward those in attendance. The final suggestion provided by Dattilo is to model positive interactions. As mentioned previously, providing staff with opportunities to interact with people with different abilities is likely to promote a welcoming social environment. If our staff have positive attitudes toward people and these positive attitudes are modeled, then other participants are likely to support a socially accepting environment for people of all abilities.

Changing the Physical Environment

The final method for encouraging participation of all people is to change the physical environment. When we consider changing the physical environment, there are four areas for contemplation:

- Universal design
- Course adaptations
- Element adaptations
- Design considerations

Universal design involves making activities usable and accessible by all people so no one feels separate or "special." Challenge courses that are universally designed will offer multiple, meaningful levels of challenge. In many courses, this concept is already in existence. For instance, a facilitator may present the spider's web feature to a group of participants with cognitive disabilities and say that if anyone touches the web at anytime, then the entire group must start over. A simple method of offering multiple levels of challenge is to make the adaptation that for every three touches, one person must go to the other side and start over, a very simple adaptation that follows the spirit of universal design. One key word in the description of universal design is *meaningful*. To change the physical environment and encourage participation of all people on a challenge course, we cannot simply make activities and elements easier: We must also make them meaningful.

The second step in changing the physical environment involves course adaptations. These might be some of the easiest changes to make and

observe. Suggestions include widening trails and pathways to allow for a wheelchair to pass and to allow two people to walk side by side (e.g., a participant walking with a guide or assistive device). We must also consider the surfaces of those trails: Durable material that makes a smooth and solid surface free of tree roots and stumps will increase physical access to our courses.

Other considerations are the amount of shade at our challenge courses and the location and condition of restroom facilities. Wide-open areas with direct sunlight may pose difficulties for some who wish to participate in our challenge courses. Likewise, although portable toilets may be an economical choice for restroom facilities, they are certainly not inviting to participants who need extra space (or any people with olfactory senses). Other course adaptations could involve the manner in which information is

Photo courtesy of NCA.

Adapting the physical environment of a challenge course creates an environment that allows for maximum participation.

delivered and disseminated. Braille brochures, large-print materials, and telephone typewriter/telecommunications device for the deaf (TTY/TDD) communication systems are three simple suggestions for opening our courses and advertising to a new clientele, a clientele who may be very interested in participating if the physical environment is adapted to their needs. An interesting note about all of these suggestions is that not only do they create a physical environment that is more inclusive for people with disabilities, but they also create a more comfortable environment for all participants.

In addition to adapting our courses, we can also adapt our elements to provide a more inclusive environment. For an excellent discussion of this idea, review the text by Rohnke and colleagues (2003). These authors provide an in-depth discussion of the adaptation of certain elements; however, designing activities that cater to participant strengths is the best way of making element adaptations. For instance, if you are working with a group of participants with severe physical impairments, try providing activities that are more cognitive than physical in nature. Brain teasers that require problem solving, thoughtful consideration, and creative solutions may be very acceptable activities for those who have limited physical mobility. Similarly, if participants have impairments in their lower extremities, providing activities that require more upper-body strength may be a viable adaptation. Regardless of the group we are working with, we traditionally select activities and elements that emphasize participant strengths; when we work with people of varying abilities, this idea must not change. What must change is our way of thinking about activity

Assessing Challenge Course Access

Elements

Initiatives

- Physical accessibility
- Presence of multiple levels of challenge
- Specific skills needed for each activity
  - Physical
  - Social
  - Cognitive
  - Emotional

Low elements

- Physical accessibility
- Number of elements requiring physical skills
- Number of elements requiring social skills
- Number of elements requiring cognitive skills
- Number of elements requiring emotional skills
- Specific skills needed for each element

High elements

- Physical accessibility
- Presence of multiple levels of challenge
- Number of fudge harnesses
- Number of full body harnesses
- Number of slings
- Availability of mechanical advantage systems

Staff

- Trained in challenge by choice
- Trained in element adaptation
- Trained for disability specific adaptations
- Trained in disability awareness
- Trained with presence of people with varying abilities
- Employment of people with varying abilities

Environment

Restrooms

- Number
- Type
- Location

Parking

- Distance from parking lot to course
- Number of handicapped parking spaces

Trails

- Surface types
- Design of trails leading to challenge course
- Design of connecting elements
- Design of trails at the base of elements

Temperature

- Accessible shaded areas
- Accessible drinking water
- Accessible rain shelter
- Accessible wind break

choices. If the "traditional" challenge course activities are the only ones we consider, we will have difficulties adapting our elements for our participants. Recently a challenge course facilitator described to me some of his frustrations and difficulties with trying to adapt current elements on our challenge course to include people with different abilities. In our conversation I came to understand that he was trying to use the existing elements that had not been created with universal design in mind. We were able to explore several new initiative activities that would work very well, but the more important result of the conversation was that we had to rethink the concept of challenge course elements that were specific to our course.

The final area of physical adaptations involves specific design considerations. Rohnke and colleagues (2003) provide an extensive discussion of issues such as determining platform height for transfers of people in wheelchairs, designing handholds that allow for different gripping abilities, changing the angles of ascent and descent for high elements and climbing walls, using trolley and scooters for mobility, incorporating belay systems on low elements, and using pulley systems. By designing our courses with these concepts in mind, we can create challenge courses that are physically designed to encourage people of all ability levels to participate.

Clearly, our challenge courses must be accessible. See the Assessing Challenge Course Access sidebar on page 327 for a summary of components to keep in mind when planning a challenge course. But regardless of the physical accessibility of courses, if attitudes of staff and other participants are not welcoming and inclusive, it doesn't matter how many physical changes we make to our courses. We must start with our thinking and our attitudes.

Challenge Summary

This section began by defining challenge courses as physical and psychological challenges that include initiative activities, low elements, and high elements. Next we explored how challenge courses work and discussed the concepts of dissonance, change zones, risk, disequilibrium, and transference. Then we presented the ideas of emotional and physical safety and their importance. The conversation then turned to understanding why some people do not participate in challenge courses and two reasons were provided—attitudes

and course design. Finally we explored how we can encourage all people to participate in challenge courses by making adaptations to the psychological, social, and physical environments. The central theme for this section was threefold. First, many of the techniques that we should use when leading and planning challenge course programs are already inclusive in nature (e.g., challenge by choice). Second, many of the suggestions for including all participants in our challenge courses make sense not only for purposes of inclusion but for all of our participants. Finally, creating an inclusive atmosphere does not start with the physical environment; creating an environment that is welcoming of people of all ability levels begins with the attitudes of all of us.

Discussion Questions

1. How might access issues in outdoor recreation areas affect inclusive programming and participation for the following populations: persons who use wheelchairs; young children; persons with mobility or strength issues; participants with developmental delays; non-English-speaking people; people over the age of 65; and those with sensory impairments, such as visual impairments or deafness?

2. What are several important components of a risk management plan for an inclusive outdoor adventure program? What role do waivers and assumption of risk forms play in the leadership of adventure activities?

3. Should all persons, even those with specific limitations, be allowed the opportunity to participate in a high-risk adventure experience? Why or why not? What are some advantages and disadvantages for inclusive versus noninclusive adventure recreation programs?

4. Can people with different abilities experience perceived and real risk?

5. Can people with different abilities experience growth through discomfort?

6. Can people with different abilities learn through an experience?

7. How can we keep participants with different abilities safe on a challenge course? What is the difference between keeping participants with and those without disabilities safe on challenge courses?

8. What is the difference between physical and emotional safety? Is one (physical or emotional safety) more important than the other?

9. Does a person's ability influence how challenge courses work? Do different ability levels prevent participation in a challenge course?

10. How do your attitudes, the attitudes of your staff, and the attitudes of your participants encourage or discourage participation in your course?

11. What psychological, social, and physical adaptations can you make to your challenge course to include people of all ability levels?

>> Spotlight on Inclusive Programs

Inclusive Recreation Programs and Services in Japan

Aya Hayashi

The term *inclusive recreation* isn't widely used in Japan. Instead, *sport and recreation for all, adapted sport and recreation,* and *therapeutic recreation* are used when we discuss the concepts of normalization and integration.

The Paralympics following the Tokyo Olympics in 1964 could be considered the start of sport and recreation programs for people with disabilities in Japan. In the 1960s and 1970s, several laws were passed to support rehabilitation and active participation in community activities, and facilities and support organizations were established. Since the Winter Paralympics in Nagano, Japan, in 1998, adapted sport has received more attention. As the population of Japan has aged, a need has arisen for recreational options for older people. Tourism, art and culture, and outdoor recreation for elderly people have become very popular. The main purposes of sport and recreation for participants with disabilities and elderly people are providing rehabilitation and increasing the quality of life.

Since the 1990s, nonprofit organizations (NPOs) and associations have been established that have specific focuses, especially outdoor recreation such as canoeing, camping, and skiing. Campwith is the NPO founded in 1998 that promotes "camping for all." This organization strives to improve the well-being of all people (with or without disabilities) through outdoor and recreational activities. Campwith provides monthly and seasonal camp programs in Japan and overseas for people with disabilities (physical and

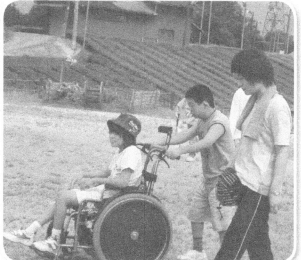

Photo courtesy of Yasunori Ishida.

The Campwith organization in Japan provides recreation programs that are geared for all participants.

mental) and for elderly people, and the organization has staff training programs as well.

Monkey Magic is an NPO with the slogan "No Sight, But On Sight!" The organization encourages interactions among participants with and without visual disabilities through rock-climbing schools (indoor and outdoor) and events to promote independence and socialization of people with disabilities.

(continued) ▶

Participants in Japan's Monkey Magic program.

Photo courtesy of Koichiro Kobayashi.

Although more recreational opportunities have become available for various populations, further efforts are needed. Many programs are offered only occasionally, and more efforts are needed to make inclusive recreation a lifelong activity. There aren't many opportunities for people with severe disabilities; we lack instructors who are knowledgeable and skilled in inclusive recreation, and we lack long-term support from the government and communities.

Inclusive Travel, Tourism, and Amusements

Alison Voight, PhD, CTRS

Indiana University

Shu Cole, PhD

Indiana University

" The World is a book, and those who do not travel read only a page. "

–St. Augustine

Learning Outcomes

After completing this chapter, learners will be able to do the following:

- Define and differentiate the terms *inclusion, inclusive tourism, inclusive travel, inclusive amusements,* and *universal design.*
- Explain how the Americans with Disabilities Act affects tourism professionals in the delivery of their services to the public.
- Identify several means of accommodating tourists with specific needs.
- Identify major barriers that may prevent persons with special needs from fully participating in tourism activities.
- Identify four major areas of accessibility that are critical to inclusive participation in tourism.

The travel and tourism industry is one of the largest industries in the world, with an estimated 900 million international tourist arrivals worldwide in 2007 (United Nations World Tourism Organization, 2008), and grosses billions of dollars each year. Students seeking careers in service industries, such as tourism and hospitality, will encounter people with a variety of interests, skill and ability levels, cultural backgrounds, age ranges, and specific needs. To provide the most satisfying experiences in the travel and tourism arena, professionals must have a sound grasp and understanding of the clients they serve and, more important, how clients with specific needs can be accommodated.

In many countries, serving clients with specific needs is not an option but rather a legal and ethical obligation to assist and accommodate all persons in their recreational and tourism pursuits, regardless of ability. Societies with tourism activities must create travel and tourism opportunities that are inclusive. This chapter discusses several important topics related to inclusive travel and tourism, including (a) the terms used to describe inclusive travel, tourism, and amusements; (b) accommodation of people who have disabilities, those who require longer time periods to participate in certain activities, families with small children, persons who are deaf or visually impaired, non-English-speaking persons, or those with mobility issues; (c) barriers often encountered by people with disabilities or people from minority groups or ethnic cultures that prevent full participation in tourism; (d) accessibility issues and universal design; and (e) international legislation affecting tourism and travel.

The key terms discussed in this chapter cover a wide array of topics and issues, some of which are beyond the scope of this chapter to fully explore. For the purpose of clarity, we define the terms *inclusive travel, inclusive tourism,* and *inclusive amusements* in a rather broad context that will be used and referenced throughout the chapter. The terms *inclusive* refers to the fundamental belief that all persons have value, have the right to participate in tourism activities, and should be included in these activities regardless of ability or disability. Inclusiveness is a concept, as well as a practice, whereby professionals who provide tourism activities to clients recognize the inherent capacities and contributions of people who have impairments and do not exclude these people from participation based solely on ability.

There are certain circumstances, however, where persons may be excluded from participating in tourism activities if it would be unsafe or inappropriate for them to do so. Examples are a person who is too small, someone who is underage, a person unable to safely balance herself, someone who doesn't have the strength and endurance to participate in an activity, or a person who is unable to follow instructions. However, exclusion should be based on well-established policies that are in place before a person is excluded from a tourism-related activity.

Most tourism providers in the United States are mandated by laws set forth by the Americans with Disabilities Act (ADA) to establish these policies and make them publicly available (see the ADA for more details: www.ada.gov). In addition, most recreation organizations have "essential eligibility rules" to safely and fairly deliver their services to the public (Smith et al., 2005). Examples of eligibility rules include factors such as residency, age, skill level, capacity, and safety (McGovern, 1992). Any agency that delivers tourism and recreation activities should have as its primary mission to be as inclusive as possible—to include all persons who wish to participate.

Inclusive Travel

Before we describe *inclusive travel* and what this entails, it is important to distinguish the term from *travel* in general. Travel refers to the act of leaving one's usual area of residence to proceed to another destination. To be considered a tourist one must be traveling for pleasure, not for business, and must spend at least one night away from home, but not more than 6 months in one's own country and not more than a year internationally (Fennel, 1999). Traveling can involve a host of other activities along the way to another destination including recreation activities, restaurants, hotel or resort stays, and unique methods of transportation (e.g., trains, watercraft). Inclusive travel, as we define it in this chapter, should not be confused with prepaid, all-inclusive travel packages that include all activities and services provided for tourists during a trip. In this chapter, *inclusive travel* refers to the accommodation of all persons, especially those who have certain needs or disabling conditions during the period of time—or travel—from their residence to a tourist destination. For example, if a person who uses a wheelchair wants to travel from his home to a resort hotel on the beach, he needs transportation that allows him to get to public air terminals, transfer from there to accessible public transportation or car rentals, and arrive at a physically accessible hotel. In this scenario, the traveler with a motor impairment can pursue his desire to take a holiday on the beach and not be turned away because of inaccessible transportation or lodging.

Travel services constantly strive for service excellence. Providing services that are convenient to as many customers as possible allows tourist businesses to differentiate themselves from competitors whose services exclude certain groups of people. Although many tourists do not have disabilities, today's customers prefer services that are easy to access and use. Airports with parking within walking distance are more attractive than those that shuttle people to and from the parking lots. As people age, they are more likely to have mobility, visual, or hearing impairments. As a result, they prefer attractions with fewer stairs, captioned media presentations, flatter trails, or more places to sit and rest. Travel professionals must realize the importance of providing accessible products and services, because when people with disabilities or their families make travel decisions, accessibility determines whether they will choose a given service (Israeli, 2002). For example, a person without disabilities may participate in a highly sought after tourist activity even though the activity takes place in a crowded facility. However, a person using a wheelchair will not even consider this activity if the site does not have accessible parking or an accessible entrance to the facility.

Inclusive Tourism

Tourism can be defined as the interrelated system that includes tourists and the associated services that are provided and used, such as facilities, attractions, transportation, and accommodation (Fennel, 1999). The term *inclusive tourism* also refers to business practices and tourism development efforts that provide travel opportunities for all people, regardless of their ages, abilities, and disabilities. In this context, the essence of inclusive tourism is to design and develop travel services that are accessible for all—young and old, able or disabled. Accessibility of tourism sites influences the travel decisions of not only people with disabilities but also their families. Tourism sites that are not suitable for strollers, or restau-

The use of an interpreter for sign language for the deaf can create a more inclusive tourism experience.

rants that do not offer kids' menus, may not be attractive to families with young children, and these businesses may lose potential customers to competitors whose facilities and services are more accessible.

Tourists represent a wide range of people: *mass tourists* (e.g., those who visit Disney World, Las Vegas, Florida beaches, resorts), *tour groups* (e.g., those who travel by bus or cruise ship), *do-it-yourself tourists* (e.g., those who tour alone without a guide or group), and *adventure tourists* (e.g., those who seek risk, unknown areas, and unknown outcomes; see Fennel, 1999). Travel and tourism—to be truly inclusive—should not be a privilege of certain groups of people but rather a right for all, including those with disabilities or specific needs.

Disability Statistics in Tourism

Inclusive tourism makes not only humanitarian sense but also good business sense. Although teens are major target markets for many U.S. businesses, the spending power of Americans with disabilities is four times that of American teens (U.S. Department of Justice, 2008). People with disabilities are reported to spend $13.6 billion annually for travel (Open Doors Organization, 2005). The disability community is a largely untapped market in the United States (Digh, 1998), and as this population continues to increase as America ages, the demand for inclusive travel will increase and expand to all segments of tourism. Consider that almost 600 million people worldwide (WHO, 2003) and 50 million people in the United States have some type of disabling condition (about 1 in 5 Americans; U.S. Census Bureau, 2000). Also consider that 40% of persons age 65 years or older in the United States (about 12% of the U.S. population) have some type of disability (Smith et al., 2005) and that about 21 million American families have at least one family member with a disability (U.S. Census Bureau, 2005). Another staggering statistic to note is that by the year 2030, approximately 20% of the U.S. population will be 65 years or older (Smith et al., 2005) —a population cohort that the recreation and tourism industries cannot discount. Despite these statistics, only about 31.7 million trips were made by people with disabilities in 2002 (Open Doors Organization, 2005), whereas the total number of domestic trips in the United States was 1.9 billion in the same year (Travel Industry Association, 2008).

Visits to U.S. national parks during 2002 were most frequent among white, non-Hispanic people, much less frequent among Hispanic Americans, and least frequent among African Americans. Nonwhite visitors cited lower visitation to the national park system because of barriers like costs of food and hotels and distance they would have to travel to parks (National Park Service, 2003).

Inclusive Amusements

The term *inclusive amusements* is distinguished from the term *amusements* only by the efforts of tourism and business operators to plan and develop services for people with disabling conditions or special needs. Amusements, in general, are activities that people seek for enjoyment and recreation. Common categories of amusements are theme parks, water parks, video arcades, cinemas, carnivals, and miniature golf.

The remaining sections of the chapter discuss concepts and methods to make travel, tourism, and amusements inclusive of, and pleasurable for, people who have disabilities. We examine how to accommodate clients who have specific needs, define the legal aspects of a disability and a person's right to be accommodated, explain how to identify and eliminate barriers that prevent people from fully participating in tourism activities, discuss access rights and the impact of the principles of universal design in tourism facilities, and provide some examples of international legislation that has helped other countries recognize the rights of travelers with disabilities.

Accommodating People With Specific Needs

The term *accommodation* can be somewhat confusing when used in the context of travel and tourism. In this chapter, *accommodation* refers to how persons with disabilities might be assisted or accommodated by tourism professionals. Those who deliver tourism services must consider many factors, such as lodging, transportation, dining and food facilities, and attractions or amusements. In many instances, accessibility of all areas of a tourism product is mandated by legislation. It is the responsibility of the professional and the tourism agency to be aware of the rights of persons with disabilities (see ADA for more details) and how to appropriately provide services. This also makes the best business sense, because professionals won't be faced with unsatisfied customers or court costs, lawyers' fees, or lengthy civil rights trials.

Lodging

Travelers with disabilities spent $4.2 billion on hotels and lodging annually according to a 2002 study (Open Doors Organization, 2005). One of the most critical factors for inclusive tourism and travel is ensuring that lodging is accessible for persons who have special needs or mobility issues. The worst-case scenario would be to book hotel or motel accommodations for a person with an impairment, who discovers on arrival that the facility is *not* truly inclusive. The following points should be considered when planning inclusive lodging for tourist clientele:

- Never assume a lodging site is truly accessible, even if its promotional materials say that it is.
- Contact the hotel manager ahead of time to ensure that the hotel property is indeed accessible.

- Ask for specific accessible amenities (e.g., elevators, restrooms, beach access, TDD phone services).

- Inform hotel staff when you arrange accommodations for a person with a visual impairment. When booking the room, specify whether the client uses a service dog (also known as a "seeing eye" or guide dog). Hotel staff may readily agree to assist persons with visual impairments but are often taken by surprise when a guest arrives with a guide dog. Although most lodging is required by law to accommodate service dogs, staff may be unfamiliar with this legal mandate. Informing hotel management in advance will ensure an uneventful and inclusive stay.

- Even when you have verified that a hotel or resort property is accessible and can readily accommodate your clients, be sure that accessible rooms are actually *available* when booking. Having accessible rooms on the property, but none available at check-in time, can create a true crisis for tourists with special needs. Also consider the needs of a family with small or infant children when reviewing a hotel, such as children-friendly restaurants and menus, babysitting services, play care, or activities for young children or teenagers.

- When planning international travel, investigate conditions in the destination country for people with disabilities. Some countries have no legislation or policies in regard to inclusion, or their policies may differ from the United States in regard to accommodating persons with impairments. Do not assume that the same standards of accessibility and legislation protecting persons with disabilities will be available in all countries. Some countries will have better standards regarding accessibility than the United States (see international legislation later in the chapter). The important point is to do your research ahead of time and plan accordingly.

- Considerations for special accommodations that might be needed for the following disabling conditions in tourism settings are described in table 17.1 on page 336. A tourism professional must be familiar with accessibility issues for these groups:
  - People who are visually impaired or legally blind
  - People who are deaf

- People who have mobility restrictions
- Elderly people
- Families with small children
- People who have cognitive limitations

Transportation

Every aspect of the trip has to be accessible. If a person cannot physically access a vehicle or boarding area, she will be unable to continue with her travel plans. This will be especially significant if the person has a mobility impairment, such as paralysis or muscle weakness (e.g., multiple sclerosis, muscular dystrophy, arthritis, or similar condition), and uses a wheelchair. Accessible travel is also important for persons who require longer periods of time for transferring from one place to another, walking, climbing ramps, getting in and out of buildings, and using vehicles such as buses, trains, cruise ships, airplanes, or automobiles. Other groups who may require special assistance or extra time when traveling include persons who are elderly, have reduced strength or endurance, have reduced cognitive capacity, or require extra attention in interpreting signage or instructions. Some persons with cognitive impairments (e.g., mental retardation, brain injuries, autism, dementia) may need information repeated or shown to them in alternative formats (e.g., pictures or written information in simpler forms). Other people with motor or cognitive limitations may require one-on-one assistance throughout the travel period. Careful planning is essential if a person requiring additional assistance is to have a positive inclusive travel experience.

Dining and Food Facilities

People with disabilities are reported to have spent $36 billion in restaurants in 2002 (Open Doors Organization, 2005), which is indicative of the tremendous attraction to dining out. Dining at restaurants provides a great deal of pleasure for people and continues to grow as a tourism-related experience each year. To be a truly inclusive activity, however, the restaurant must be accessible. In this instance, accessibility means that a person with an impairment can fully enjoy the eating experience with family or friends and cannot be turned away because the restaurant is not accessible. Additional consideration should be paid to menu formats for children and people with sensory impairments or menu choices that provide people from various ethnic or religious

Table 17.1 Inclusive Tourism Considerations and Accommodations

Groups with specific needs	Inclusive tourism considerations and accommodations		
	Mobility	**Access**	**Communication**
People who are visually impaired	• Know preferred method of mobility (e.g., cane, guide dog, sighted guide). • Determine whether guide dogs will be an issue. (Legally they must be allowed, but sometimes they may create unexpected barriers.)	• Be aware of possible hazards entering and exiting and within tourism site. • Provide verbal and physical orientation of facility or attraction. • Provide support, if needed, at tourism site.	• Provide verbal cues often. • Indicate whether audio devices are provided. • Permit modeling or touching of objects and exhibit materials where appropriate. • Provide large-print information when available.
People who are hearing impaired	• Mobility is usually not an issue unless indicated by the person. • When traveling, walking, and biking, alert person to sounds (e.g., oncoming traffic, trains, birds, other visitors, dogs).	• Signage at sites and facilities will provide added information. • Provide additional literature if needed to supplement verbal or audio information. • Determine whether facilities have flashing lights for fire alarms, phones, exits, and other warnings.	• Provide visual cues. • Determine preferred method of communication (e.g., written, sign language, interpreter, lip reading). • During emergencies, determine whether persons with hearing impairments have been alerted and know to exit hotel or site. • Ask whether captioning is available.
People who have mobility restrictions	• Know best method of mobility for person (e.g., wheelchair, cane, crutches, personal assistant). • Consider transportation needs and possibilities between tourism sites and facilities (e.g., cars, golf carts). • Determine whether the person will be traveling alone, in a tour group, or with an assistant or family member.	• Determine whether elevators are available to all levels and areas on site. • Determine whether accessible ramps to site, parking, and entrances are provided. • Determine whether the hotel or attraction has accessible facilities available or whether special arrangements will need to be made.	• Keep communication open about problems or issues, like pain and fatigue. • Never assume persons with similar mobility issues (e.g., paralysis, cerebral palsy, multiple sclerosis, arthritis) have the same level of ability, needs, or disability.
Older adults	• Determine whether pace should be slower. • Determine whether assistive devices are needed for mobility (e.g., canes, walkers, personal assistant, wheelchairs, golf carts). • Consider possible balance issues.	• Know distances between sites, resting areas, level of emergency care available. • Determine whether parking areas are close by. • Determine whether elevators are available.	• Inform elderly persons of distances between, and within, tourism facilities; time and endurance needed; types of accommodations available at site. • Determine whether the person has hearing or vision issues. • Never assume elderly people are incapable or need help. Always ask first.

Groups with specific needs	Inclusive tourism considerations and accommodations		
	Mobility	Access	Communication
Families with children	• Families with younger children and infants will need more time getting to sites and moving within other tourism areas. • Know whether strollers, buggies, or other mobility devices for kids will be needed, permitted, or provided by the site.	• Determine whether strollers can access site. • Determine whether there are age or height restrictions for kids at site. • Be aware of hazards for small children, such as cliffs, traffic, crowds, deep water, insects, sun. • Know how much supervision is needed. Can children touch exhibit items?	• Explain time elements needed and distance between tourism sites. • Explain climate concerns of heat, sun, and cold exposure at site. • Explain expectations of child behavior where appropriate. • Discuss possible needs for kids (e.g., snacks, drinks, rest, entertainment).
People who have cognitive limitations	• Mobility usually is not an issue unless indicated by the person. • Consider any balance issues when traveling at sites. • Determine whether a personal assistant or family member will accompany the person.	• Point out potential hazards of accessing sites (e.g., getting lost, dangerous areas). • Determine whether the person can read signage, get to restrooms, and understand exhibits and information provided at the site.	• Don't treat adults as children. • Repeat information or instructions as needed. • Use simple, step-by-step instructions. • Model desired behavior. • Explain signage or other information if needed.

The best way to make tourism and recreation activities inclusive is to include the person with specific needs in the planning process, ahead of time if possible.

groups or who have special dietary needs with a wide range of choices. More detail regarding access of tourism sites and attractions are provided later in the chapter.

Amusements

When determining the accessibility of a tourism destination site such as Disney World or other amusement-related venues, most of the items previously listed will also apply. However, the larger and more internationally known an amusement venue is (e.g., Disneyland, Sea World, King's Island), the greater the obligation and the legal mandate to serve the public and those persons with limitations or impairments. Most of these destinations now have in place policies and procedures to better assist people with specific needs. Many accessibility issues can be answered via online services. For instance, Disney World has an online disability link (www.wdwinfo.com/wdwinfo/disabgeneral.htm) for discussion, questions, and answers regarding a specific disability, measurements, and access. The following excerpt is a response from a professional staff member at Disney World to a tourist inquiring about the best time to visit, how accessible the park is, and how to get around:

The best time to visit (during your dates) is the second week in January! The first week in November is very busy. The first week in January is also busy with the runover from the holidays. The second week in January is a little bit better if you can avoid the Disney Marathon weekend. If you can plan around these dates, you may want to try to visit January 6 to 11. The Disney Marathon & Half is on January 12 and 13, so this weekend also gets a little busy. Once you arrive to the Disney Theme Parks, you can stop by guest services to talk with them about your situation. The use of separate waiting areas, backdoor access, and front-of-the-line access is based on a

Large and established amusement parks should have policies and procedures in place for making their parks and facilities as accessible as possible.

case-by-case situation decided by guest services. You do need to have a medical letter signed by your doctor with more information about your situation. Guest services will need this letter to make their decision. Universal Studios has this same service, since this park also has lots of rides and attractions. Sea World, which offers mostly shows but also a few rides, has the same service. The parks do not have manual wheelchairs: All scooters and wheelchairs are electric. Most of the companies that deliver medical supplies have basic wheelchairs and scooters. One of the most popular companies is Walker Mobility. You may want to call this company to request an electric wheelchair instead of the scooters. This company is very reasonable in regard to prices for wheelchairs and scooters. Enjoy your visit!

As can be seen from the online response, a patron needs to be aware of some very specific items if he has special needs. To receive special consideration when visiting Disney World (each attraction may be different in its policies), a visitor must have a letter from a medical doctor indicating a legitimate limitation or disabling condition. In this case, you must contact guest services in advance, and the staff will determine the level of inclusive services to provide and how to best accommodate a guest with special needs.

Again, it is always best to call a venue and ask specific questions if you are not able to get the information you need online or from a brochure. Questions about wheelchair use, accessibility, guide dogs, family-friendly environments and activities, restaurants that accommodate certain religious observances, language options available, or emergency medical treatment concerns should be answered before the visit takes place.

Barriers in Recreation and Tourism Activities

People face barriers, discrimination, and challenges every day. But those who have a limitation or disability face challenges that people without disabilities cannot even imagine. Most people with disabilities do not want pity or special treatment. But many travelers who have disabilities face prejudice or the deliberate exclusion from activities simply because they have an impairment. This same type of bias or exclusion may be experienced by people who do not understand the language or who dress in clothing not typical of the region, those who are unable to communicate about a specific need or problem they may be encountering, and those who are elderly. Many barriers are still encountered during travel and prevent persons with disabilities or other particular needs from access and enjoyment of tourism opportunities (Turco et al., 1998). People with disabilities may be excluded because a tourism operator or manager believes these people might be harmed during a trip or activity. For example, a person who is blind wants to try skydiving or parasailing but is declined service because the operator does not believe the person could participate successfully. The Americans with Disabilities Act prevents unjust or unreasonable exclusion from recreation activities based solely on a disabling condition or the perception that a person may be unsuccessful in an activity.

There are major barriers that prevent a person from fully participating in recreation and tourism activities. Some of these barriers are briefly discussed in terms of their impact on tourism participation: personal barriers, attitudinal barriers, and communication barriers.

Personal Barriers

Personal barriers are those barriers that may come from within the person who has a disability. As a recreation and tourism professional, you may encounter a person with a lifelong impairment or a recent disabling condition that is difficult to accommodate, even with the best intentions by you or your staff. Sometimes, it is helpful to understand that certain barriers are intrinsically based. In other words, the barriers are created by the person and not by others. And although these barriers are not easily resolved or changed, recognizing them can be helpful when we attempt to accommodate a person in a tourism activity. Typical personal barriers may include:

- Lack of knowledge: People are unaware of available resources or where to find information about a tourism activity or venue.

- Social skills: People are not able to speak for themselves, make feelings known, or act appropriately in social situations.

- Physical or psychological dependency: Some people come to depend solely on others for assistance; sometimes referred to as "learned helplessness."

- Lack of skills: Persons with disabilities may not have skills that allow for full and enjoyable recreation participation or, because of recently acquired limitations, must relearn new skills in order to participate in tourism or recreation activities.

- Health issues: Problems related to the person's impairment may create difficulties in participating due to reduced strength, pain, or medications (Smith et al., 2005).

Attitudinal Barriers

Unlike personal barriers that exist within a person with a disability, attitudinal barriers are created by others. Several studies (Avis et al., 2005; Bi et al., 2007; Takeda & Card, 2002) have found that when traveling, people with disabilities often encounter not only accessibility barriers but also attitudinal barriers from business staff and employees. These barriers have hindered travelers' access to certain tourist attractions and diminished their levels of enjoyment while traveling. People with disabilities have fought a long, hard battle to be accepted as persons within their own right and *not* to be defined by their disability. But people, including professionals who serve the public through tourism and recreation venues, are still wary of those whom they perceive to be "different" and are unsure how to accommodate them. These perceptions may also apply to persons who dress differently, people from a country or cultural background that is perceived to be hostile or negative, those who cannot communicate well in the local language, those who are cognitively impaired, and persons of different ethnic or racial groups.

Although employees' negative attitudes toward tourists with disabilities or other perceived differences can be related to a societal bias, oftentimes they are a result of businesses' ignorance of the special needs of these tourists. As a result, a relatively small number of people with disabilities participate fully in mainstream tourism (Yau et al., 2004). Attitudinal barriers persist when people-first language is ignored by service providers (e.g., incorrectly saying, "the disabled man, Mr. Davis," rather than correctly saying, "Mr. Davis, the man with a disability"), when staff are not willing to help people with special needs or knowledge about services available is reduced, or when employees provide travelers with inaccurate information. Staff must realize that the needs of tourists with disabilities are just as important as those of any other tourist. Examples of attitudinal barriers that may prevent or inhibit travel by persons with disabilities include these:

- Perceptual barriers: Misinformation or fear often engenders negative attitudes about people who have disabilities. Many people fear what they do not understand, such as a disability or other "difference." Negative perceptions often prevent persons with specific needs from fully participating in tourism activities.

- Omission barriers: This type of barrier happens when professionals conveniently omit information or fail to enforce legislation, rules, or regulations that would assist persons with disabilities or other specific needs; tourism professionals may unintentionally or deliberately eliminate persons with disabilities from involvement in planning tourism activities or fail to make minor changes that would make activities more accessible for someone (e.g., a tour guide might choose an inaccessible site rather than find an accommodating location in the same area).

- Paternalistic barriers: These types of attitudes happen when a tourism professional assumes, wrongly, that people with an impairment cannot function independently, that they must be given special treatment, or that they should be addressed in a patronizing manner (such as people who are elderly); paternalistic barriers perpetuate myths about people with disabilities as being helpless, objects of pity, or even burdens.

Communication Barriers

Barriers in communication occur when one person cannot understand or communicate with another person (Tamparo and Lindh, 2008). This lack of exchange in information presents an important barrier to overcome during travel and tourism activities. Being able to accurately communicate information during travel is a critical component of the tourism experience. People have to be aware of time schedules, regulations regarding international travel, transportation to and from a site, and what to expect once they travel to a site in terms of potential hazards, dining, restrooms, and accessibility. Reasons for barriers in communication or a lack of information exchange can be due to several factors, including sensory impairments, cognitive limitations, and language barriers.

- Sensory impairments: These types of barriers can be present when a person is deaf, has a hearing impairment, or is visually impaired or legally blind. People with visual impairments need to accurately receive information when traveling if they are unable to read signs, brochures, or exhibit displays. The ADA legislation in the United States mandates that barriers to communication must be removed and alternative formats must be provided for those persons who want additional information in travelling or tourism venues. These alternatives can be audiotapes for a person who is blind, additional reading materials or an interpreter for a traveler who is deaf, or adaptive devices that can accom-

modate specific needs for those with sensory impairments.

- Cognitive limitations: Conditions such as autism, attention-deficit/hyperactivity disorder, dementia, or cognitive limitations, including intellectual disability and learning disabilities, can make travel difficult. Using easy-to-understand instructions or explanations that are short and concise is often helpful for persons with cognitive limitations. Repeat information often if necessary.

- Language barriers: International travelers often face language barriers that prevent accurate information from being communicated. This has been a longstanding barrier for any traveler who leaves her native country. Sometimes this barrier can be eliminated by learning some simple phrases in the language of the country, employing guides from a tourism agency, or hiring a resident to accompany the tourist group and provide translations. American Sign Language is an official language and the fourth most spoken language in the United States (Valli, 2005). Regardless of the language spoken, one element of inclusion in regard to tourism is the provision of a quality interpreter (for more information regarding barriers, see Smith et al., 2005).

Access Rights and Universal Design in Tourism Areas

Despite national legislation established to protect the rights of persons with disabilities, problems and barriers are still encountered by people that can prevent their full participation in tourism activities. Access to buildings, attraction sites, or visitor areas remains a major issue that can cause difficulty for patrons, especially those with mobility impairments. Many persons with physical disabilities avoid traveling because they are not sure of access to sites and hotels. Research conducted by the American Hotel and Lodging Association (AHLA) indicates that the demand for hotels and other facilities to be accessible is rather low, regardless of legal mandates (AHLA, 2000). This low demand may be attributable, in part, to perceptions held by persons with mobility issues that their needs will not be accommodated and that traveling is not worth the effort. Accessibility is more than simply being able to *enter* a tourism facility. It is not uncommon for people who use wheelchairs to be able to get into their hotel rooms but unable to get into the restroom or a crowded hotel restaurant. The next section describes four main areas from which accessibility should be considered when planning truly inclusive tourism and travel experiences. The principles of universal design, as they relate to tourism activities and accessibility, will also be discussed.

Four Main Areas of Accessibility

Entrances, parking, ramps, and restrooms are extremely important when considering inclusive environments and activities for tourists who have limitations (see the National Center on Accessibility Web site for more details: www.ncaonline.org/index.php?q=node/317/). Although each area carries with it a tremendous amount of detail regarding accessibility, it would be beyond the scope of this chapter to explore every aspect and measurement of accessibility. Instead, we review each area briefly in terms of issues of accessibility that tourism providers should consider.

- Entrances: This area relates to door widths, types of doors, and their physical layout in terms of thresholds, incline, and flush levels from outside the door to the inside. Door widths should be 32 inches (91 centimeters) minimum, there should not be a steep incline to the door, and there should be no lip or edge at the entrance. Doors should be opened by handles, if possible, and the door itself should not require more than 5 pounds (2.2 kilograms) of pressure to open it.

- Parking: Anyone who needs an accessible entrance will not be able to participate in an activity or enter a facility if they cannot park a vehicle and easily access a building or site. Most facilities are mandated by law to provide at least one accessible parking space per 25 spots or less. These spots are ideally located close to the building and have an access aisle next to the parking spot so people can get in and out of a car relatively easily. Always check ahead to determine whether there are accessible spaces in the parking lot of a tourism destination. Never assume this will be a sure thing.

- Ramps and routes: This refers to how steep the grade is along routes to and from a tourism site or building. The incline for walks should not exceed a ratio of 1:20 inches (1:50 centimeters). When there are very steep ramps, railings should be in place along the routes as well as a place to rest. When clients have mobility or strength and endurance issues (such as chair users, small children, people who are obese, people with multiple sclerosis, elderly people), knowing what types of routes and walkways are in place at a tourism facility will be of paramount importance. Also consider whether the surface of the walkways promotes accessibility.

- Restrooms: Restroom facilities are a critical factor for any tourism venue. Restrooms should be accessible for chair users and others with specific issues or needs. Call in advance to ask about restroom availability. Find out the turning radius in a restroom stall for a chair user, making sure it is 5 feet (1.5 meters) in diameter. Also, ask whether there are ramps to the restroom, lightweight doors and door levers, and handrails around the toilet.

Determining accessibility can mean the difference between a successful versus unsuccessful tourism experience for clientele. Although tourism professionals are not always able to see a facility first-hand, asking a few simple questions of the staff or site managers ahead of time can resolve problems before persons with special needs arrive. The reverse is true as well—when people inquire about accessibility in *your* facility or tourism site, give them as much information about the site as possible. When someone asks you about specific assistance, find out what type of needs certain tourists have. An informed tourist, or tourism professional, can make the best decision regarding whether to attend an event or facility.

Finally, *accessibility* and *usability* are not necessarily synonymous terms. A tourist destination that is described as accessible, following minimum established standard guidelines, may not necessarily be usable by a person with a disability. A person might be able to enter a tourism site but once inside cannot use the restroom, cannot understand exhibits or guides, or cannot find information. Only when facilities and services are usable are they truly accessible and inclusive.

Betty Siegel

Where, after all, do universal human rights begin? In small places, close to home—so close and so small that they cannot be seen on any map of the world. Yet they are the world of the individual person: The neighborhood he lives in; the school or college he attends; the factory, farm or office where he works. Such are the places where every man, woman, and child seeks equal justice, equal opportunity, equal dignity without discrimination. Unless these rights have meaning there, they have little meaning anywhere. Without concerted citizen action to uphold them close to home, we shall look in vain for progress in the larger world.

> *–Eleanor Roosevelt*

Photo courtesy of John W. Merck, Jr.

Background Information

Education

BA Theater Arts, Virginia Tech, Blacksburg, Virginia

Credentials

JD, Columbus School of Law, Catholic University

Special Awards

*Northern Virginia Resource Center for the Deaf and Hard of Hearing award for promoting access to the arts (2002) *Friends of the Library for the Blind and Physically Handicapped, DC Public Library award for opening doors for people with disabilities (2000) *Gallaudet University award for expanding theater accessibility for the deaf community (1988) *Helen Hayes Award, VA Tech Theater Department (1981)

Career Information

Position   Director of Accessibility, John F. Kennedy Center for the Performing Arts

Organization Information   The Kennedy Center, which opened in 1971, is the living memorial to President John F. Kennedy and is the national performing arts center. From its very beginnings, the Kennedy Center has represented a unique public–private partnership. The center receives federal funding each year to pay for maintenance and operation of the building, a federal facility. However, the center's artistic programs and education initiatives are paid for almost entirely through ticket sales and gifts from individuals, corporations, and private foundations.

Organization's Mission   The center continues its efforts to fulfill President Kennedy's vision by produc-

ing and presenting an unmatched variety of theater and musical productions; dance and ballet performances; orchestral, chamber, jazz, popular, and folk music concerts; and multimedia performances for all ages. Every year the institution that bears President Kennedy's name brings his dream to fruition, touching the lives of millions of people through thousands of performances by the greatest artists from across America and around the world. The center also nurtures new works and young artists, serving the nation as a leader in arts education and accessibility, and creating broadcasts, tours, and outreach programs.

Size of Organization   The center employs approximately 300 full-time employees and serves upwards of 4 million people every year.

Job Description   I am responsible for ensuring that people with disabilities and older adults have access to all the programs, performances, and activities of the Center and for ensuring compliance with federal disability discrimination laws. I direct, supervise, and have oversight over or assist with accessibility programs and projects through the Kennedy Center Accessibility Program.

Career Path   I always wanted to be in the theater, originally as an actress. But during college I realized my skills lay more behind the scenes, and I went into costume design. After working for Houston Grand Opera with top-notch international designers, I realized that I was a good designer but not a great one and that I cared more for doing something that involved people and had a lasting impact. So I became a house manager, and it was in that position that I begin to work with people with disabilities and older adults in the field of accessibility to the cultural arts.

What I Like About My Job It is never boring; it is always challenging—solving problems, being innovative, and being creative. Most important, it has a significant impact on the lives of performers, employees, interns, volunteers, audience members, others across the nation.

Career Ladder I am currently finishing a law degree, which I hope will allow me to do what I already do only better.

Advice to Undergraduate Students No matter what you do and where you do it, you need to have a passion for your work.

Personal Statement I truly believe that making things accessible to people with disabilities and older adults shapes the way our society sees itself and the way our society grows to be more inclusive.

Using Universal Design With Travel and Tourism

The concept and principles of universal design presented in chapter 8 have greatly advanced the issues of usable facilities, especially in the areas of travel and tourism (Center for Universal Design, 1997). The seven principles of universal design were designed by a group of concerned professionals to accommodate all persons with specific needs as well as persons who have disabilities. Recall that the central philosophy of universal design is that products or environments should not be designed for particular groups of people but rather should be designed with optimum economic efficiency so they can be used by as many people as possible. Seven principles form the premise for universal design: These include equitable use, flexibility of use, simple and intuitive use, low physical effort, perceptible information, tolerance for error, and size and space for approach and use. See the NCA Web site at ncaonline.org for more information.

Applying the principles of universal design in tourism settings not only will encourage participation of people with diverse abilities but also is likely to improve tourists' levels of overall satisfaction with the services. For example, if the exhibits in a museum are designed at heights that are appropriate for adults, people who use wheelchairs, and small children, parents with small children will not need to lift their kids up at each exhibit and thus the parents will have a more enjoyable experience. Another familiar example of universal design is seen in airport restrooms. Most restrooms in airports have no external doors to maneuver or open. This design is very convenient for people with luggage on rollers, persons who use wheelchairs, and families with baby strollers.

Photo courtesy Ragen E. Sanner.

Simply lowering a sign so that it is accessible to more people can have an impact on how enjoyable an experience is for people at your facility.

International Legislation Regarding the Rights of Persons With Disabilities

The United States has protected the rights of persons with disabilities from discrimination in the workplace, and other areas of society, since 1990 through the Americans with Disabilities Act. As has been indicated throughout this chapter, laws in the United States protect its citizens from discrimination as they live their lives, go to work, recreate, and travel. Not all countries have such legislation in place. A tourism professional must be familiar with legislation in other countries in order to plan services for clients who need special assistance or accommodations.

Countries that have legislation for persons with disabilities include China (discussed in the next section) and the United Kingdom, whose Disability Discrimination Act was established in 1995. This act makes it unlawful "to discriminate against people in respect of their disabilities in relation to employment, the provision of goods and services, education and transport." Several Web sites provide information for persons traveling in Europe. In particular, the Web site called Accessible Europe is a valuable link to accessible tourist areas and other information regarding access: http://europeforvisitors.com/europe/planner/blp_accessible_countries.htm.

For persons using wheelchairs or family and friends accompanying them, several countries with specific information for disabilities and travel are listed through Disability Links at www.globalaccessnews.com/linksnew.htm.

For persons interested in traveling to virtually any country in the world, the Disabled Travelers Guide lists information for travelers with disabilities: www.disabledtravelersguide.com/contact.htm.

Legislations Regarding People With Disabilities in China

The first Law of the People's Republic of China on the Protection of the Rights of Persons with Disabilities was passed by the National People's Congress on December 28, 1990. This law was recently revised in April 2008. The purpose of the law is to safeguard "the lawful rights and interests of persons with disabilities, promoting the work on disability, ensuring the equal and full participation of persons with disabilities in social life and their share of the material and cultural wealth of society" (CDPF, 2009). The law designates the third Sunday in May, every year, as the National Day for Supporting People with Disabilities. China Disabled Persons Federation (CDPF), established in 1988, is the government agency that represents and protects the interests of people with disabilities in China. CDPF and its local organizations are responsible for providing education and services for people with disabilities in accordance with this law.

The law addresses the rights of people with disabilities, including rights to rehabilitation, education, employment, cultural life, accessible environment, and social security, as well as their legal rights. Under the provisions of accessible environment, the law mandates that new constructions and renovations of infrastructure and superstructure should follow the engineering codes set by the state. To minimize physical barriers, public service facilities should gradually meet all accessible requirements and provide accessible parking lots wherever possible. The law mandates the local governments should encourage and assist people with disabilities in their participations in cultural, sports, and recreational events and activities.

After the first passage of the Law of the People's Republic of China on the Protection of the Rights of Personas with Disabilities, a series of rules and regulations were set to provide guidance for local governments to implement the law. For example, specific design codes and standards were developed for accessible roads and buildings, special education campuses, train stations, and airports.

Summary

This chapter introduced key terms in inclusive travel, tourism, and amusements and discussed accommodating people who have disabilities, people who have cultural and language barriers, families and young children, and elderly persons in tourism settings. The chapter discussed accessibility rights and common barriers encountered in tourism settings. In tourism areas, persons with special needs or those perceived to be different from "normal" populations often encounter barriers, including personal barriers, attitudinal barriers, and communication barriers. The chapter also discussed ways to enhance accommodation for people in the areas of lodging, transportation, amusements, and dining. To be truly inclusive, tourism services and businesses in the United States must meet the standards set by laws (the ADA) to uphold and protect the rights of full participation for persons who have disabilities or special needs.

Truly inclusive tourism settings and activities should be accessible and usable. Four main areas of accessibility that are of extreme importance to inclusive travel, tourism, and amusements are entrances, parking, ramps and routes, and restrooms. Applying the principles of universal design when designing and developing tourism services and activities will likely result in truly inclusive environments. Tourism services and activities should not be designed for particular groups of people but rather should be designed with optimum economic efficiency so these services and activities can be used by as many people as possible.

Tourism service professionals must realize that not all countries have established laws and regulations to protect the rights of persons with disabilities. When planning for travel to countries that do have legislations for persons with disabilities, specific needs, or other cultural and ethnic issues (e.g., travel to China and the United Kingdom), tourism service professionals need to be familiar with these legislations. The chapter provides several online sources for additional information regarding accommodation of persons with specific needs in the travel industry.

Discussion Questions

1. Compare and discuss the implications of the terms *accessible* versus *useable* in inclusive tourism activities.

2. Describe three major barriers that certain populations often encounter when attempting participation in tourism-related activities. Discuss how these barriers translate to noninclusive participation.

3. How might the four main areas of accessibility—entrances, parking, ramps and routes, and restrooms—affect people who visit an amusement park? Give examples from each of the four areas.

4. Discuss how applying the principles of universal design in tourism settings can benefit both tourists and tourist businesses.

>> Spotlight on Inclusive Programs

Open Doors Organization

Opening Doors for People With Disabilities

Open Door Organization is a Chicago-based nonprofit organization whose mission is to help large and small businesses tap into the disability market through research, training, and guidance and at the same time provide information and services to people with disabilities. This organization was established in 2000 by Eric Lipp, who became disabled after a surgery removing a tumor in his spinal cord. While using a wheelchair after the surgery, Eric found that many businesses were not wheelchair friendly, although they all met the minimum ADA standards. This experience inspired him to help businesses effectively implement the law.

ODO staff have worked with businesses, community groups, government agencies, and other organizations. ODO has offered staff training and marketing strategies to airlines, airports, hotels, restaurants, cruise lines, and state and national transportation services. At the community level, ODO is also an advocate for people with disabilities. Since 2003, ODO has worked with the Girl Scouts of Chicago to raise awareness of disability issues among girls ages 8 to 14. In these programs, youths learned first-hand about the lives of people with disabilities, with the intention of reducing the attitudinal bias that exists in society.

Another function of ODO is to conduct and facilitate research on disability-related issues. This market research has demonstrated the profit potential of the disability market. Through focus groups of people with disabilities, ODO is able to give feedback to stakeholders in tourism about their perceptions and expectations of travel services and facilities. ODO also hosts a biannual Universal Access in Airports conference, which serves as a platform for airport-related businesses and services to exchange ideas about improving accessibility in and around airports.

Adapted, by permission, from Open Doors Organization.

Appendix A

Healthy People 2010 and the International Classification of Functioning, Disability, and Health Model

David Howard, PhD, MSW, CTRS

Indiana State University

Healthy People 2010

Healthy People 2010 (HP2010) serves as the health agenda of the United States and is run by the U.S. Department of Health and Human Services. At the core of HP2010 lies a focus on changing behaviors, and with this in mind, recreation and leisure professionals can capitalize on what is known about behavioral medicine as a health-related field that strives to study and explore health as a function or result of behavior.

HP2010 consists of two main goals, 10 leading health indicators, and 28 different chapters or areas that focus on specific health conditions. Comprising hundreds of national health objectives, this body of work identifies what are thought to be the most significant preventable threats to health. HP2010 is based on the principle that each citizen of the United States deserves equal access to community-based health care systems and that these are comprehensive, culturally relevant, and focused on serving the needs of individuals and promote community health. It is known that individual health and community health are often interrelated; thus, HP2010 encourages multi-faceted community-based efforts that create healthy environments that promote healthy behaviors and therefore increase access to quality health (U.S. Department of Health and Human Services, 2000).

The principle goals of HP2010 are first, to increase quality and years of healthy life. This goal directs health care providers and health promotion specialists to increase life expectancy and quality of life by empowering individuals to gain and implement the knowledge, motivation, and opportunities necessary to make informed decisions about their health. The second primary goal of HP2010 is to eliminate health disparities. A health disparity is defined as an inequality or gap that exists between two or more groups. These gaps likely result from a complex interaction between personal, societal, and environmental factors. It is believed that the greatest opportunity for reducing health disparities exists within community-wide safety and education programs, through access to health care, and through the empowerment of individuals (regardless of age, gender, race or ethnicity, level of education, income, disability, or sexual orientation) to make informed decisions and engage in healthier behaviors (U.S. Department of Health and Human Services, 2000).

Within HP2010, leading health indicators (see table A.1) form a set of health priorities that reflect 10 major public health concerns in the United States. These indicators were identified by an interagency work group of the U.S. Department of Health and Human Services. The indicators were chosen because of their importance as public health issues, the existence of data needed to measure progress, and the likelihood that individuals could be motivated to action. It is thought that within any given community, acting on even just one of these indicators and increase quality of life and reduce health disparities.

The reader is encouraged to see the U.S. Department of Health and Human Services Web site for Healthy People 2010 at www.healthy-people.gov for more information.

Table A.1 Healthy People 2010 Leading Health Indicators

Health Indicator	Rationale	Goal
Physical activity	Regular physical activity throughout life is important for maintaining a healthy body, enhancing psychological well-being, and preventing premature death. Regular physical activity decreases the risk of death from heart disease, lowers the risk of developing diabetes, and is associated with a decreased risk of colon cancer. Regular physical activity helps prevent high blood pressure and plays a role in decreasing existing high blood pressure.	Promote regular physical activity
Overweight and obesity	Overweight and obesity raise the risk of illness from high blood pressure, high cholesterol, type 2 diabetes, heart disease and stroke, gallbladder disease, arthritis, sleep disturbances and problems breathing, and endometrial, breast, prostate, and colon cancers. Obese individuals may also suffer from social stigmatization, discrimination, and lowered self-esteem.	Promote healthier weight and good nutrition
Tobacco use	Cigarette smoking is the single most preventable cause of disease and death in the United States. Smoking is a major risk factor for heart disease, stroke, lung cancer, chronic lung diseases, and complications with pregnancy. Environmental tobacco smoke increases the risk of heart disease and significant lung condition, especially asthma and bronchitis in children.	Prevent and reduce tobacco use
Substance abuse	Alcohol use and illicit drug use are associated with many of this country's most serious problems, including child and spousal abuse; sexually transmitted diseases including HIV infection; teen pregnancy; school failure; motor vehicle crashes; rising health care costs; low worker productivity; and homelessness. Alcohol and illicit drug use also can result in substantial disruptions in family, work, and personal life.	Prevent and reduce substance abuse
Responsible sexual behavior	Unintended pregnancies and sexually transmitted diseases (STDs), including infection with the human immunodeficiency virus (HIV) that causes AIDS, can result from unprotected sexual behaviors.	Promote responsible sexual behavior
Mental health	Mental health is a state of successful mental functioning, resulting in productive activities, fulfilling relationships, and the ability to adapt to change and cope with adversity. Mental health is indispensable to personal well-being, family and interpersonal relationships, and one's contribution to society.	Promote mental health and well-being
Injury and violence	More than 400 Americans die each day primarily because of motor vehicle crashes, firearms, poisonings, suffocation, falls, fires, and drowning. The risk of injury is so great that most persons sustain a significant injury at some time during their lives.	Promote safety and reduce violence

Health Indicator	Rationale	Goal
Environmental quality	An estimated 25% of preventable illnesses worldwide can be attributed to poor environmental quality. In the United States, air pollution alone is estimated to be associated with 50,000 premature deaths and an estimated $40 billion to $50 billion in health-related costs annually.	Promote healthy environments
Immunization	Vaccines are among the greatest public health achievements of the 20th century. Immunizations can prevent disability and death from infectious diseases for individuals and can help control the spread of infections within communities.	Prevent infectious disease through immunization
Access to health care	Strong predictors of access to quality health care include having health insurance, a higher income level, and a regular primary care provider or other source of ongoing health care. Persons with health insurance are more likely to have a specific source of care and to have received appropriate preventive care.	Increase access to quality health care

From *Healthy People within Healthy Communities*, U.S. Department of Health and Human Services, 2000.

International Classification of Functioning, Disability, and Health Model

The World Health Organization's (WHO) International Classification of Functioning, Disability, and Health (ICF) model assists us in identifying and taking into consideration the myriad of factors that can be associated with any given disability or health condition. The WHO defines health as "a state of complete physical, mental and social well-being and not merely the absence of disease or infirmity" (World Health Organization, 1946). The ICF is a conceptualization that applies not only to health care but to health promotion as well and the large proportion of recreation and leisure professionals who work within the context of health promotion.

Published in 2001, the ICF is part of the WHO's Family of International Classifications (FIC), a companion volume to the *International Classification of Diseases* (ICD, 10th edition). The ICF is a conceptualization that has four primary aims: (a) to provide a scientific basis for understanding and studying health and health outcomes; (b) to establish a common language for describing health in order to improve communication at all levels of health and society; (c) to permit comparison of data across countries, health care disciplines, and health-related services; and (d) to provide a systemic coding scheme for health information systems (World Health Organiza-

tion, 2001). As seen in figure A.1, the ICF shows components that interact with one another. One's daily activity or level of participation is affected by proper function of body structures and functions. Environment and personal factors also play important roles, as does the presence (or absence) of activity limitations or participation restrictions that lead to perceived or real disability.

The majority of the ICF's nearly 300 pages is devoted to chapters that delineate specific components of body functions and structures, activities, and participation and environmental factors. Within the ICF, body functions and structures are divided into eight areas:

1. Mental functions (e.g., orientation, personality, attention, memory, cognition)
2. Sensory functions (e.g., sight, hearing, taste, smell, touch, sensation of pain)
3. Voice and speech functions (e.g., articulation, fluency, rhythm)
4. Functions of the cardiovascular system
5. Functions of the digestive system
6. Genitourinary and reproductive functions
7. Neuromuscular and movement-related functions
8. Functions of the skin

Activities and participation chapters of the ICF cover nine areas:

1. Learning and applying knowledge (e.g., listening, thinking, reading, solving problems)

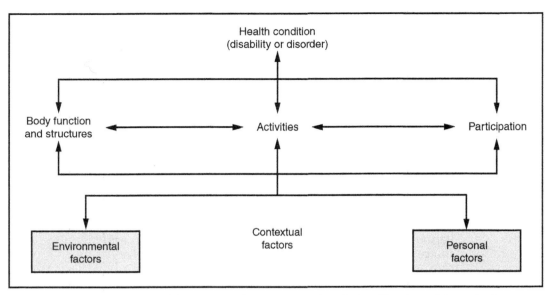

Figure A.1 The World Health Organization's International Classification of Functioning, Disability and Health model.

Reprinted, by permission, from World Health Organization, 2001.

2. General tasks and demands (e.g., daily routine, handling stress)

3. Communication (e.g., conversing, discussion, written messages)

4. Mobility (e.g., body positioning, lifting objects, moving around, using transportation)

5. Self-care (e.g., washing, dressing, eating, drinking, looking after one's health)

6. Domestic life (e.g., acquiring a place to live, preparing meals, assisting others)

7. Interpersonal interactions and relationships (e.g., with strangers, formal, family)

8. Major life areas (e.g., education, work, economics)

9. Community, social, and civic life (e.g., recreation and leisure, religion, human rights)

The five chapters related to environmental factors are as follows:

1. Products and technology

2. Natural environment and human-made changes to environment

3. Support and relationships

4. Attitudes

5. Services, systems, and policies

Within each of these chapters are numerous definitions and descriptors (each with its own code number) that delineate aspects of health and level of functioning. The framework of the ICF provides corresponding scales to help identify the degree to which a person experiences impairments, limitations, or barriers. Environment factors (such as the existence of settings policies supportive of recreation) are unique inasmuch as they can be classified in a positive manner and are labeled as "facilitators" when thought to be beneficial and supportive of individual or community health. Environment factors that are not supportive or actually impede an individual's ability to participate or have access to participate are called "barriers." According to the WHO, the applications of the ICF are many.

1. As a statistical tool for collecting and recording data

2. As a research tool to measure outcomes and quality of life or environmental factors

3. As a clinical tool during assessment or to assist matching treatments with a person's health condition

4. As a social policy tool when designing, for example, social security or compensation systems

5. As an educational tool for design of curriculum or to raise awareness or undertake social action for the betterment of society and its individuals (WHO, 2001)

The reader is encouraged to see the WHO/ICF Web site, www.who.int/classifications/icf/en, or recent articles and books within therapeutic recreation and health-related literature for more information (Howard et al., 2007; Howard et al., 2008; Porter & Burlingame, 2006; Porter & Van Puymbroeck, 2007).

Resources

World Health Organization: www.who.int/en

WHO/ICF: www3.who.int/icf/icftemplate.cfm

Healthy People 2010: www.healthypeople.gov

Healthy People 2010 (Chapter 6): www.healthypeople. gov/Document/HTML/Volume1/06Disability.htm

ICF Clearinghouse E-Newsletter: www.cdc.gov/nchs/ about/otheract/icd9/icfactivities.htm

References and Resources

Centers for Disease Control and Prevention. (2000). *Healthy People Chapter 6: Disability and secondary conditions.* www.healthypeople.gov/document/ HTML/Volume1/06Disability.htm

Colditz, G. (1999). Economic costs of obesity and inactivity. *Medicine and Science in Sports and Exercise, 31*(Suppl 11), S663-667.

Davis, J. (1952). *Clinical applications of recreational therapy.* Springfield, IL: Charles C Thomas.

DeJong, G., Palsbo, P., Beatty, P., Jones, G., Kroll, T., & Neri, M. (2002). The organization and financing of health services for persons with disabilities. *.Milbank Quarterly, 80*(2), 261-301.

Field, M., & Jette, A. (2007). The future of disability in America (free executive summary). www.nap.edu/ catalog/11898.html.

Flegal, K., Carroll, M., Ogden, C., & Johnson, C. (2002). Prevalence and trends in obesity among US adults, 1999-2000. *Journal of the American Medical Association, 288*, 1723-1727.

Fontaine, K., Redden, D., Wang, C., Westfall, A., & Allison, D. (2003). Years of life lost due to obesity. *Journal of the American Medical Association, 289*, 187-193.

Freedman, D., Khan, L., Serdula, M., Galuska, D., & Dietz, W. (2002). Trends and correlates of class 3 obesity in the United States from 1990 through 2000. *Journal of the American Medical Association, 288*, 1758-1761.

Gray, D., Hollingsworth, H., Stark, S., & Morgan, K. (2006). Participation survey/mobility: Psychometric properties of a measure of participation for people with mobility impairments and limitations. *Archives of Physical Medicine and Rehabilitation, 87*(2), 189-197.

Howard, D. (2006, June 5-7). *The significance of environmental factors for older men diagnosed with prostate cancer.* Paper presented at the 12th Annual North American Collaborating Center Conference on ICF, Vancouver, British Columbia.

Howard, D., Browning, C., & Lee, Y. (2007). The International Classification of Functioning, Disability, and Health: Therapeutic recreation code sets and salient diagnostic core sets. *Therapeutic Recreation Journal, 41*(1), 61-81.

Howard, D., Nieuwenhuijsen, E., & Saleeby, P. (2008). Health promotion and education: Application of the ICF in the U.S. and Canada using an ecological perspective. *Disability & Rehabilitation.* Accepted for publication.

Larsson, U., Karlsson, J., & Sullivan, M. (2002). Impact of overweight and obesity on health-related quality of life-a Swedish population study. *International Journal of Obesity Related Metabolic Disorders, 26*, 417-424.

Leschin-Hoar, C. (2007). Targeting obesity. *Parks & Recreation, 42*(4), 62-65.

McCormick, B., Lee, Y., & Jacobson, J. (2004, June 1-4). Operationalizing community integration via the ICF. Paper presented at the 10th Annual North American Collaborating Center Conference on ICF, Halifax, Nova Scotia.

McNeil, J. (1997). *Americans with disabilities 1994-95*: Current Populations Report P7061:3-6.

National Center on Birth Defects and Developmental Disabilities. (2001). *Healthy People 2010 Chapter 6, Vision for the Decade: Proceedings and Recommendations of a Symposium.* Atlanta: Author.

National Instituted of Health. (2000). *The practical guide: Identification, evaluation, and treatment of overweight and obesity in adults* (NIH publication 04-4084). Bethesda, MD: Author

Noreau, L., Desrosiers, J., Robichaud, L., Fougeyrollas, P., Rochette, A., & Voscogliosi, C. (2004). Measuring social participation: The liability of the LIFE-H in older adults with disabilities. *Disability & Rehabilitation, 26*(6), 346-352.

Office of Disease Prevention and Health Promotion. (2000). *Healthy People 2010.* www.healthypeople. gov

Ogden, C., Flegal, K., Carroll, M., & Johnson, C. (2002). Prevalence and trends in overweight among US children and adolescents, 1999-2000. *Journal of the American Medical Association, 288*, 1728-1732.

Ostir, G., Granger, C., Black, T., Roberts, P., Burgos, L., Martinkewiz, P., et al. (2006). Preliminary results for the PAR-PRO: A measure of home and community participation. *Archives of Physical Medicine and Rehabilitation, 87*(8), 1043-1051.

Pi-Sunyer, F. (1993). Medical hazards of obesity. *Annals of Internal Medicine, 119*, 655-660.

Pope, A., & Tarlov, A. (Eds.). (1991). *Disability in America: Toward a national agenda for prevention.* Washington, DC: National Academy Press.

Porter, H., & Burlingame, J. (2006). *Recreational therapy handbook of practice: ICF based diagnosis and treatment.* Enumclaw, WA: Idyll Arbor.

Porter, H., & Van Puymbroeck, M. (2007). Utilization of the International Classification of Functioning, Disability, and Health within recreational therapy practice. *Therapeutic Recreation Journal, 41*(1), 47-60.

Russoniello, C. (1997). Behavioral medicine: A model for therapeutic recreation. In D. Compton (Ed.), *Issues in therapeutic recreation* (pp. 461-488). Champaign, IL: Sagamore.

Russoniello, C., & Howard, D. K. (2005). The prescription of recreational activity in mental health promotion and disease prevention. *Recreational Activity for Disease Prevention, 4*(1), 31-34.

Seidell, J. (1995). The impact of obesity on health status: some implications for health care costs. *International Journal of Obesity Related Metabolic Disorders, 19*(Suppl 6), S13-S16.

Simeonsson, R., Leonardi, M., Lollar, D., Bjorck-Akesson, E., Hollenweger, J., & Martinuzzi, A. (2003). Applying the International Classification of Functioning, Disability and Health (ICF) to measure childhood disability. *Disability & Rehabilitation, 25*(11-12), 602-610.

Society of Behavioral Medicine. (2003). *Definition of Behavioral Medicine.* www.sbm.org/about/definition.html.

Stark, S., Hollingsworth, H., Morgan, K., & Gray, D. (2007). Development of the measure of receptivity of the physical environment. *Disability & Rehabilitation, 29*(2), 123-137.

Stucki, A., Daansen, P., Fuessl, M., Cieza, A., Huber, E., Atkinson, R., et al. (2004). ICF Core Sets for obesity. *Journal of Rehabilitation Medicine, 44*(Suppl), 107-113.

U.S. Department of Health and Human Services. (2000). *Healthy People 2010: Understanding and Improving Health* (2nd ed.). Washington, DC: U.S. Government Printing Office.

Whiteneck, G., Harrison-Felix, C., Mellick, D., Brooks, C., Charlifue, S., & Gerhart, K. (2004). Quantifying environmental factors: A measure of physical, attitudinal, service, productivity, and policy barriers. *Archives of Physical Medicine and Rehabilitation, 85*, 1324-1335.

Wolf, A. (2002). Economic outcomes of the obese patient. *Obesity Research, 10*(Suppl 1), 58S-62S.

World Health Organization. (1946). *Constitution of the World Health Organization.* Geneva, Switzerland: Author.

World Health Organization. (1986, November 21). *The Ottawa Charter for health promotion.* www.who.int/healthpromotion/conferences/previous/ottawa/en/.

World Health Organization. (1998a). *Preventing and managing the global epidemic of obesity: Report of a WHO Consultation on Obesity.* Geneva: WHO/NUT/NCD98.1.

World Health Organization. (1998b). *World health report—life in the 21st century: A vision for all.* Geneva: Author.

World Health Organization. (2001). *International classification of functioning, disability and health.* Geneva, Switzerland: Author.

World Health Organization. (2003). *Diet, nutrition and the prevention of chronic diseases: Report of a Joint WHO/FAO Expert Consultation.* Geneva: Author.

World Health Organization. (2005). *The Bangkok Charter for health promotion in a globalized world.* www.who.int/healthpromotion/conferences/6gchp/bangkok_charter/en/.

Appendix B

National Recreation and Park Association Position Statement on Inclusion

(Approved by the NTRS Board of Directors, October 30, 1997 and the NRPA Board of Trustees in 1999)

Diversity is a cornerstone of our society and culture and thus should be celebrated. Including people with disabilities in the fabric of society strengthens the community and its individual members. The value of inclusive leisure experiences in enhancing the quality of life for all people, with and without disabilities, cannot be overstated. As we broaden our understanding and acceptance of differences among people through shared leisure experiences, we empower future generations to build a better place for all to live and thrive.

Inclusive leisure experiences encourage and enhance opportunities for people of varying abilities to participate and interact in life's activities together with dignity. It also provides an environment that promotes and fosters physical, social, and psychological inclusion of people with diverse experiences and skill levels. Inclusion enhances individuals' potential for full and active participation in leisure activities and experiences. Additionally, the benefits of this participation may include:

- Providing positive recreational experiences that contribute to the physical, mental, social, emotional, and spiritual growth and development of every individual
- Fostering peer and intergenerational relationships that allow one to share affection, support, companionship, and assistance
- Developing community support and encouraging attitudinal changes to reflect dignity, self-respect, and involvement within the community

Purpose

The purpose of the National Therapeutic Recreation Society's (NTRS) Position Statement on Inclusion is to encourage all providers of park, recreation, and leisure services to provide opportunities in settings where people of all abilities can recreate and interact together.

This document articulates a commitment to the leisure process and the desired outcomes. Accordingly, the NTRS Position Statement on Inclusion encompasses these broad concepts and beliefs:

- **Right to leisure:** The pursuit of leisure is a condition necessary for human dignity and well-being. Leisure is a part of a healthy lifestyle and a productive life. Every individual is entitled to the opportunity to express unique interests and pursue, develop, and improve talents and abilities. People are entitled to opportunities and services in the most inclusive setting. The right to choose from the full array of recreation opportunities offered in diverse settings and environments and requiring different levels of competency should be provided.

- **Quality of life:** People grow and develop throughout the life span. Through leisure an individual gains an enhanced sense of competence and self-direction. A healthy leisure lifestyle can prevent illness and promote wellness. The social connection with one's peers plays a major role in one's life satisfaction. The opportunity to choose is an important component in one's quality of life; individual choices will be respected.

• **Support, assistance, and accommodations:** Inclusion is most effective when support, assistance, and accommodations are provided. Support, assistance, and accommodations should be responsive to people's needs and preferences. Support, assistance, and accommodations should create a safe and fun environment, remove real and artificial barriers to participation, and maximize not only the independence but also the interdependence of the individual. People want to be self-sufficient. Support, assistance, and accommodations may often vary and are typically individualized. Types of support, assistance, and accommodations include, but are not limited to, qualified staff, adaptive equipment, alternative formats for printed or audio materials, trained volunteers, or flexibility in policies and program rules.

• **Barrier removal:** Environments should be designed to encourage social interaction, risk-taking, fun, choices, and acceptance that allow for personal accomplishment in a cooperative context. Physical barriers should be eliminated to facilitate full participation by individuals with disabilities. Attitudinal barriers in all existing and future recreation services should be removed or minimized through education and training of personnel (staff, volunteers, students, or community at large).

The National Therapeutic Recreation Society is dedicated to the four inclusion concepts of:

- Right to leisure (for all individuals)
- Quality of life (enhancements through leisure experiences)
- Support, assistance, and accommodations
- Barrier removal in all park, recreation, and leisure services

Properly fostered, inclusion will happen naturally. Over time, inclusion will occur with little effort and with the priceless reward of an enlightened community. Encouraged in the right way, inclusion is the right thing to plan for, implement and celebrate.

Reprinted, by permission, from NRPA.

Appendix C
Person-Related Factors Influencing Capability

This appendix serves as supplementary information to the text regarding individual factors that might influence capability in movement experiences. Although classifications such as these can be helpful in providing general information, they do not provide deep insight into any one person's capability to perform. The task demands and nature of the context significantly affect performance outcomes and benefit. This information is provided so that practitioners are aware of the possible influences on performance and, more important, to give them insight into the implications for physical activity participation, potential safety concerns, and activity recommendations and contraindications. It is important that practitioners do not generalize specific factors to all individuals nor make assumptions about capability should any given factor exist. Individuals will differ in terms of their functional capabilities regardless of any specific factor, thus assumptions about individuals based on categorical labels must be avoided.

Note: The information provided in this appendix has been compiled from the Web sites referenced for each section.

Amputee

Definition

Amputation refers to removal or loss of an entire limb or particular limb segment. Amputation can be congenital or acquired resulting from disease, tumor, complications of frostbite, injury, diabetes, arteriosclerosis (hardening of the arteries), or any other illness that impairs blood circulation.

Selected Facts

- Problems with thermoregulation could be present as a consequence of decreased skin surface.
- Prosthetic devices are typically used to increase functional use of the limb or body part.

Tips and Techniques

- Participants should be encouraged to increase fluids during physical activity to prevent overheating.
- Allow time for participants with new prostheses to become familiar with them as necessary for performing an activity or task.

Informative Web Site

www.amputee-coalition.org

Amyotrophic Lateral Sclerosis (ALS)

Definition

Amyotrophic lateral sclerosis (ALS) is a progressive neurodegenerative disease that attacks nerve cells in the brain and spinal cord. The progressive degeneration of the motor neurons in ALS eventually leads to their death. When the motor neurons die, the ability of the brain to initiate and control muscle movement is lost. With all voluntary muscle action affected, individuals in later stages of ALS become totally paralyzed.

Selected Facts

- Often referred to as Lou Gehrig's disease.
- At the onset of ALS the symptoms can be so slight that they are overlooked.
- As motor neurons degenerate, functional differences might include muscle weakness in one of the hands, arms, legs; weakness in the muscles involving speaking, swallowing, or breathing; cramping of muscles; difficulty in projecting the voice; shortness of breath; and difficulty in breathing and swallowing.
- Because ALS attacks motor neurons only, the sense of sight, touch, hearing, taste, and smell are not affected.

- For the vast majority of people, their mind and thoughts are not affected by ALS, and they remain sharp despite the progressive degenerating condition of the body.

Tips and Techniques

- Range of motion and stretching exercises can help prevent painful spasticity and shortening (contracture) of muscles.
- Gentle, low-impact aerobic exercise (e.g., walking, swimming, stationary bicycling) can strengthen unaffected muscles and improve cardiovascular health.

Informative Web Site

www.lougehrigsdisease.net/

Arthritis

Definition

Arthritis is a rheumatic disease that causes pain in the joint or the muscle. The word "arthritis" is derived from the roots arth (joint) and itis (inflammation). The two most prevalent forms of arthritis are osteoarthritis, a degenerative joint disease that leads to deterioration of cartilage and formation of bone in the joint, and rheumatoid arthritis, a chronic and systemic inflammatory disease.

Selected Facts

- Many people report that regular exercise reduces the experience of pain and weakness from arthritis and provides a general feeling of well-being.
- Some arthritis medications might affect the cardiopulmonary systems and inhibit performance levels.

Tips and Techniques

- Heat or ice treatments (e.g., shower, ice, massage, whirlpool) before and after exercise can reduce pain and discomfort.
- It is best to do a variety of aerobic activities to avoid overstressing joints.
- Choose activities that expend less stress on joints, such as aquatherapy, biking, rowing, cross-country skiing, walking on soft surfaces, or low-impact aerobics. Choose activities depending on which joints are arthritic.
- Individuals with rheumatoid arthritis who experience morning stiffness should exercise later in the day.

- Strength training should focus on increasing number of repetitions rather than amount of weight.
- A complete warm-up and cool-down stretching program should be done before and after each exercise program.

Informative Web Site

www.arthritis.org

Arthrogryposis

Definition

Arthrogryposis (arthrogryposis multiplex congenita) involves the presence of multiple joint contractures at birth. A contracture is a limitation in the range of motion of a joint.

Selected Facts

- In some cases, few joints are affected, and full range of motion might exist. In other cases, the hands, wrists, elbows, shoulders, hips, feet, and knees are affected. In the most severe cases, nearly every body joint is involved, including the jaw and back.
- Frequently, the joint contractures are accompanied by muscle weakness that further limits movement.

Tips and Techniques

- Physical and occupational therapy as well as exercise have proven very beneficial in improving muscle strength and function and increasing the range of motion of affected joints.
- Stretching exercises are extremely important to increase range of motion. Emphasize achieving as much joint mobility as possible.

Informative Web Site

http://sonnet1.sonnet.com/avenues/

Asthma

Definition

Asthma is a lung disorder characterized by wheezing, coughing, breathing difficulty, and lengthened expiration (prolonged exhaling).

Selected Facts

Wheezing, coughing, tightness in the chest, and general fatigue are signs of an impending asthma attack.

Tips and Techniques

- When individuals with asthma exercise (particularly in cold weather), they can become short of breath and have an attack.
- Remind individuals with asthma to use their medication before exercising.

Informative Web Sites

www.asthma.org.uk

www.aaaai.org/

Attention Deficit/ Hyperactivity Disorder (ADHD)

Definition

Attention deficit/hyperactivity disorder (ADHD) is a condition in which individual differences include inattentiveness or distractibility, impulsivity, or hyperactive behavior, or a combination of the three. These difficulties usually begin before the person is seven years old but in some cases are not noticed until the child is older.

Selected Facts

- The behavioral differences of ADHD can be managed through helping the individual manage his or her behavior; creating a structured physical activity program that fits the learner's individual needs; and providing medication, if necessary.
- One effective strategy for people with ADHD is exercise, preferably vigorous exercise. Exercise helps work off excess energy, focuses attention, and stimulates beneficial hormones and neurochemicals.

Tips and Techniques

- Practitioners must be clear, consistent, and positive. Set clear rules and expectations.
- Have a reinforcement program for good behavior.
- Employ effective strategies for managing behavior, such as charting, starting a reward program, ignoring behaviors, and using consistent consequences related to the behavior.
- Help individuals stay focused by making activities fun and rewarding.

Informative Web Sites

www.add.org/

www.chadd.org/

Autism and Pervasive Developmental Disorder (PDD)

Definition

Autism and PDD are developmental disabilities that share many similar functional differences. Usually evident by age three, autism and PDD are neurological disorders that affect a child's ability to communicate, understand language, play, and relate to others. Other functional differences often associated with autism are engagement in repetitive activities and stereotyped movements, resistance to environmental change or disruption in daily routines, and unusual responses to sensory experiences, such as loud noises, lights, or certain textures. This description may also include individuals with high functioning autism and Asperger's syndrome.

Selected Facts

- Children with autism or PDD vary widely in abilities, intelligence, and behaviors.
- Autism is no longer considered a form of emotional disturbance but is now considered under "other health impaired" according to IDEA. "Other health impaired" means having limited strength, vitality, or alertness, or a heightened alertness to environmental stimuli that limits alertness within the educational environment and is caused by chronic or acute health problems.
- Children with autism might also experience seizures or display differences in intellectual capabilities.

Tips and Techniques

- When teaching children with autism, try using physical guidance as the children learn movement skills; also try verbal and visual cues and prompts.
- Physical activity helps children with autism reduce self-stimulatory behavior and increase play behavior.
- Use behavior-management techniques to promote on-task and safe behavior.

- Hypersensitivity to touch can be desensitized through firmly but gently stroking a child with different cloth textures.
- Teach with gentle methods, such as whispering softly to the child.
- Provide a stable, structured environment for the child. Limit the amount of relevant stimuli or activity focus initially.
- Teach to the preferred learning mode.
- Minimize unnecessary external stimuli or distractions.
- Sensory stimulation through activities such as music, dance, and aquatic activities might be successful for on-task and attentive behavior.

Informative Web Site

www.autism.org/

Blindness and Low Vision

Definition

Individuals who are legally blind have less than 20/200 vision in the better eye or a very limited field of vision (20 degrees at its widest point). Those who have low vision generally have a severe visual impairment, not necessarily limited to distance vision. Low vision applies to all individuals with sight who are unable to read a newspaper at a normal viewing distance, even with the aid of eyeglasses or contact lenses. They use a combination of vision and other senses to learn, although they might require adaptations in lighting or the size of print, and, sometimes, Braille.

Selected Facts

- A young child with vision loss might have little reason to explore interesting objects in the environment and thus might miss opportunities to experience and learn about interaction with other people and other things. They might also miss opportunities to learn how to move in a variety of ways.
- Because the child cannot see parents or peers, he or she might be unable to imitate social behavior or understand nonverbal cues.

Tips and Techniques

- A sighted guide (peer tutor) can help an individual who is blind in any physical activity for positive learning.

- Make sure individuals know the size, shape, and boundaries of an activity area before they use it for sport or physical activity. Allow them to explore the area without others present.
- Arrange mats around the out-of-bounds area so participants know when they go out of bounds.
- Use beeper cones or music to mark boundaries. Use different surfaces to mark various playing areas.

Informative Web Sites

www.nfb.org

www.afb.org

Cerebral Palsy (CP)

Definition

Cerebral palsy is a nonprogressive but chronic disorder of movement and posture caused by a defect or lesion to the brain occurring before, during, or within two years after birth. The condition might be accompanied by associated differences in intellectual functioning, vision, hearing, communication, and seizures.

Selected Facts

- Movement differences might involve lower extremities (diplegia), one side of the body (hemiplegia), all four extremities (quadriplegia), or three extremities (triplegia).
- Motor differences might involve spasticity or increased muscle tone and tightness, athetosis or fluctuating muscle tone, or ataxia or low muscle tone and balance and coordination differences. Postural reactions and reflexive activity can influence movement efficiency and outcomes.

Tips and Techniques

- Flexibility is one of the important fitness goals for individuals with CP.
- Aquatic activity is often a preferred physical activity experience for movement, balance, and fitness development.
- Weight-bearing activity is important for bone density and reduced risk of osteoporosis.

Informative Web Sites

www.ucpa.org

www.nichcy.org

Deafness and Hearing Loss

Definition

Deafness is defined as a hearing difference so severe that the individual cannot process linguistic information through hearing, with or without amplification. Deafness might be viewed as a condition that prevents an individual from receiving sound in all or most of its forms. In contrast, a person with a hearing loss can generally respond to auditory stimuli, including speech.

Selected Facts

- Loss in hearing can occur in loudness or intensity or in both areas; the condition might exist in one ear or both ears.

- Hearing loss is generally described as slight, mild, moderate, severe, or profound, depending on how well a person can hear the intensities or frequencies associated with speech.

- There are four types of hearing loss: conductive hearing loss caused by diseases or obstructions in the outer or middle ear; sensorineural hearing loss resulting from damage to the delicate sensory hair cells of the inner ear or the nerves that supply it; a mixed hearing loss or a combination of conductive and sensorineural loss; and a central hearing loss resulting from damage or impairment to the nerves or nuclei of the central nervous system.

- Hearing loss or deafness does not affect a person's intellectual capacity or ability to learn. However, children who are either hard of hearing or deaf generally require some form of support in order to receive an adequate education.

Tips and Techniques

- When planning a lesson, use visual cues, fewer rules, and less equipment. Creating peer tutor programs for the individuals helps keep individuals from isolating themselves from social gatherings. Teach your younger deaf students neighborhood games such as jump rope and hop scotch. Knowing how to play these games helps them interact better with their peers.

- For those who are deaf or have severe hearing losses, early, consistent, and conscious use of visible communication modes (such as sign language, fingerspelling, and cued speech) or amplification and aural/oral training can help facilitate language development and communication.

- People with hearing loss use oral or manual means of communication or a combination of the two. Oral communication includes speech, lip reading, and the use of residual hearing. Manual communication involves signs and fingerspelling.

- Practitioners should attempt to learn some sign language in order to communicate directly with participants. If interpreters are used, be sure to speak to the participant and not to the interpreter.

Informative Web sites

www.nad.org/

www.deafchildren.org

www.asha.org

http://clerccenter.gallaudet.edu/infotogo/index.html

www.nidcd.nih.gov

Deaf-Blindness

Definition

Deaf-blindness is a combination of vision and hearing loss, not necessarily complete deafness and complete blindness.

Selected Facts

Individuals who are deaf-blind sign tactually on the hand of the person with whom they are communicating.

Tips and Techniques

- Introduce an individual to roller-skating, swimming, biking, skiing, and gymnastics that allow for increased physical activity without the unpredictability of other players and equipment required in team activities.

- Modifications need to be made, such as changing the rules, equipment, or environment. For example, allow choices of activity and equipment. Link movement to language; teach the word for each skill learned.

Informative Web Sites

www.tr.wou.edu/dblink/aadb.htm

www.deafblind.com

Diabetes

Definition

Diabetes is a disease in which the body does not produce or use insulin. Insulin is a hormone that converts sugar, starches, and other food into energy required for daily life. The condition results in too much glucose (sugar) in the blood.

Selected Facts

- When blood sugar is elevated or when basal insulin levels are low, exercise generally causes blood sugars to rise further.
- Symptoms of insulin shock are sudden fatigue, weakness, tremors, hunger, sweating, and double vision. If an individual with diabetes exhibits any of these during physical activity, have the person stop exercising immediately and take a quick-acting sugar, such as sugar cubes or a regular soft drink.

Tips and Techniques

- Encourage exercise and participation in sports for individuals with diabetes.
- Be familiar with the signs, symptoms, and treatment of low blood sugar (insulin reaction).
- Make sure participants drink plenty of fluids. Dehydration can adversely affect blood glucose levels.

Informative Web Site

www.diabetes.org

Down Syndrome

Definition

Down syndrome is the most common and readily identifiable chromosomal condition associated with mental retardation. It is caused by having 47 instead of the usual 46 chromosomes, which changes the orderly development of the body and brain. Down syndrome might result in slow physical development and cognitive differences.

Selected Facts

- There is a wide variation in mental abilities, behavior, and developmental progress in individuals with Down syndrome.
- There are over 50 clinical signs of Down syndrome, but it is rare to find all or even most of them in one person. Some common differences include poor muscle tone, hyper-flexibility at the joints, and a variety of physical differences.
- Children with Down syndrome frequently have specific health-related problems, such as a lowered resistance to infection, making them more prone to respiratory problems.
- Differences in vision and hearing might exist.
- About 15 percent of people with Down syndrome have atlantoaxial instability, a misalignment of the first two cervical vertebrae. This condition makes these individuals more prone to injury if they participate in activities that overextend or flex the neck.
- Some individuals might have congenital heart defects or cardiac problems.

Tips and Techniques

- Because of individual differences, it is impossible to predict future achievements of children with Down syndrome. It is important for families and practitioners to place few limitations on potential capabilities.
- For some individuals it can be effective to emphasize concrete concepts rather than abstract ideas.
- Teach physical activity tasks in a step-by-step manner with frequent reinforcement and consistent feedback.
- Find out what the individual enjoys most and begin with this activity first to promote increased involvement.
- Avoid activities that place undue pressure on the neck (e.g., gymnastics, diving, the butterfly stroke) unless otherwise informed by the child's physician that these activities are appropriate.
- Be sure to obtain medical information regarding risks associated with cardiac or respiratory difficulties.

Informative Web Site

www.ndss.org

Dwarfism

Definition

Dwarfism is defined as a medical or genetic condition that usually results in an adult height of 4 feet 10 inches or shorter. In some cases a person with dwarfism might be slightly taller than this.

Selected Facts

- Although achondroplasia accounts for the majority of all cases of dwarfism, there are approximately 200 diagnosed types.
- Although such terms as dwarf, little person, and person of short stature are all acceptable, most people would rather be referred to by their name than by a label. The term "midget" is not well-received and considered offensive by most.
- There are three complications sometimes found in infants and toddlers with achondroplasia: compression of the brain stem, hydrocephalus, and obstructive apnea. These conditions do not always occur, but children should be evaluated.

Tips and Techniques

- Individuals are able to participate in physical activity and athletic events within the limits of their individual medical diagnoses. Swimming and bicycling are often recommended for people with skeletal dysplasias because these activities do not put pressure on the spine.
- Long-distance running or even extensive walking can be harmful because of the constant pounding or trauma to joints, although, as a rule, healthy individuals without any unusual orthopedic problems should be allowed to engage in typical activities and running games or sports.

Informative Web Sites

www.lpaonline.org

www.dwarfism.org/

www.nlm.nih.gov/medlineplus/dwarfism.html

Emotional Disturbance

Definition

According to the Individuals with Disabilities Education Act, emotional disturbance is defined as "a condition exhibiting one or more of the following characteristics over a long period of time and to a marked degree that adversely affects a child's educational performance: (A) An inability to learn that cannot be explained by intellectual, sensory, or health factors. (B) An inability to build or maintain satisfactory interpersonal relationships with peers and teachers. (C) Inappropriate types of behavior or feelings under normal circumstances. (D) A general pervasive mood of unhappiness or depression. (E) A tendency to develop physical symptoms or fears associated with personal or school problems." [Code of Federal Regulations, Title 34, Section 300.7(c)(4)(i)].

Selected Facts

- Children who have emotional disturbances might exhibit hyperactivity and a short attention span, might show aggression or self-injurious behavior, might be withdrawn or have excessive fear or anxiety, might have poor coping skills, and might have learning difficulties.
- Children with the most serious emotional disturbances might exhibit distorted thinking, excessive anxiety, bizarre motor acts, and abnormal mood swings. Some are identified as children who have a severe psychosis or schizophrenia.
- Many children who do not have emotional disturbances might display some of these same behaviors at various times during their development, but these behaviors do not continue over long periods of time.

Tips and Techniques

- It is important to provide students with positive behavioral support (PBS) so that problem behaviors are minimized and positive, appropriate behaviors are promoted.
- Physical activity settings should be highly structured with consistent routines and expectations that are frequently shared with participants.
- Repetition and small sequential, progressive steps should be incorporated into activity plans.
- Removal of distractions, reduction of wait time, and consideration of spacing and groupings can help maintain on-task behavior.

Informative Web Sites

www.nichcy.org

www.dbpeds.org

Epilepsy

Definition

Epilepsy is a neurological condition in which nerve cells of the brain occasionally release abnormal electrical impulses. Individuals with epilepsy have seizures that might be related to brain injury or family tendency, but the cause is usually unknown.

Selected Facts

- About 50 percent of people who have one seizure without a clear cause will likely have another one, usually within 6 months. If a person has two seizures, there is about an 80 percent chance he or she will have more.
- Recent research indicates that up to 70 percent of children and adults with newly diagnosed epilepsy can be successfully treated.
- Seizures can vary from mild to severe. Single brief seizures do not cause brain damage.

Tips and Techniques

- There must be a balance between safety and the desire to pursue a full life of activity.
- For persons with rare or fully controlled seizures, most activities can be safely pursued.
- For those with frequent seizures with loss of consciousness or a brief period of confusion afterward, certain activities might need to be restricted. Activities that include aquatics, high speed, or high places should be supervised and carefully monitored. Helmets should be worn when appropriate.
- Practitioners should be aware of safety and first aid procedures for seizures.

Informative Web Sites

www.epilepsy.com
www.epilepsyfoundation.org

Fetal Alcohol Syndrome (FAS)

Definition

FAS is a lifelong set of physical, mental, and neurobehavioral birth differences associated with maternal consumption of alcohol during pregnancy. Alcohol-Related Neurodevelopmental Disorder (ARND) describes the functional or mental impairments linked to prenatal alcohol exposure, and Alcohol-Related Birth Defects (ARBD) describes malformations in the skeletal and major organ systems.

Selected Facts

- Individuals with FAS have evidence of central nervous system dysfunction. In addition to

mental retardation, individuals with FAS, ARND, and ARBD might have other neurological deficits, including poor motor skills and poor eye–hand coordination.
- They might also have a complex pattern of behavioral and learning problems, including difficulties with memory, attention, judgment, and problem solving, as well as problems with mental health and social interactions.

Tips and Techniques

- Keys to working successfully with learners who have FAS are structure, consistency, variety, brevity, and persistence.
- It is important to provide external structure and to be consistent in response and routine. Give the learner lots of advance warning of activity changes or transitions.
- Because of attentional difficulties, it is important to give brief explanations and directions. Incorporate different ways to get and keep attention.
- Repetition of learning is critical. Break work down into small pieces so that the learner is not overwhelmed.
- Establish a few simple rules with consistent language.
- Allow the learner choices and encourage decision making.

Informative Web Site

www.nofas.org

Fragile X

Definition

Fragile X syndrome is the most common inherited cause of mental retardation. A person with fragile X syndrome has a mutation in the FMR1 (fragile X mental retardation 1) gene in the DNA that makes up the X chromosome.

Selected Facts

- Individuals with fragile X syndrome might have significant intellectual differences. The spectrum ranges from subtle learning disabilities to severe mental retardation and autism.
- Individuals might have a variety of physical and behavioral differences, including attention deficit disorders, speech disturbances,

autistic behaviors, poor eye contact, and aversion to touch and noise.

- Connective tissue problems might lead to ear infections and skeletal problems.

Tips and Techniques

- Multidisciplinary approaches and therapy are helpful in addressing many of the physical, behavioral, and cognitive impacts of fragile X syndrome.
- Sensory integration activities and calming activities are useful when teaching some individuals with fragile X.
- Try to reduce sensory overload when considering the setting or context in which activities will be performed.
- See "Mental Retardation" for additional tips and techniques.

Informative Web Site

www.fragilex.org

Learning Disability

Definition

Learning disability is a neurological condition that causes a difference in one or more psychological processes that presents an individual with difficulty in listening, thinking, speaking, reading, writing, spelling, or doing mathematical calculations.

Selected Facts

- People with learning disabilities generally have average or above average intelligence.
- There are different types of learning disabilities. Each person is unique and might show a different combination and degree of difficulties.
- Learning disabilities might be accompanied by attentional difficulties.
- People with learning disabilities can be successful at school, work, and in the community given appropriate supports.

Tips and Techniques

- Teach using a multisensory approach (visual, auditory, and kinesthetic).
- Establish a routine and incorporate repetition.
- Break learning down into small sequential steps.

- Provide regular prompts and quality feedback.
- Allow sufficient time for processing and ample time for practice.
- Employ various techniques for memory and organization.

Informative Web Sites

www.ldonline.org/

www.ldanatl.org/

Mental Retardation

Definition

Mental retardation is a term used when a person has specific differences in intellectual functioning and adaptive functioning in skills such as communicating, daily living, and social skills manifested during the developmental period.

Selected Facts

- These differences might cause an individual to learn and develop more slowly.
- Individuals with mental retardation will learn, but it takes them longer. There might be some things they cannot learn.

Tips and Techniques

- Divide tasks into small, meaningful steps and present them to the student sequentially. Limit distractions. Keep the activity area clean and well ordered; store equipment not currently in use out of sight.
- Encourage independence. Use reinforcement strategies and motivational techniques.
- Break tasks down into smaller steps.
- Demonstrations, verbal cues, and physical prompts are useful but should gradually fade to encourage increased independence.
- Teach individuals tasks across settings to promote generalization of skills.
- Physical activities and sports can improve fitness, increase confidence, and help build social skills.
- Programs should focus on age-appropriate activities.

Informative Web Site

www.aamr.org/

Multiple Sclerosis

Definition

Multiple sclerosis is a demyelinating disease of the central nervous system. Myelin, the fatty material surrounding the nerves, is destroyed, leading to symptoms such as muscle weakness, paresis, paralysis, spasticity, tremors, impaired balance, discoordination, heat sensitivity, and fatigue.

Selected Facts

* Some individuals with MS have cardiovascular dysautonomia in which irregular function of the autonomic nervous system (ANS) leads to a blunted heart rate and decreased blood pressure in response to exercise.
* Some people with MS have oversensitivity to heat. This might lead to fatigue, loss of balance, and visual changes.
* Balance and coordination difficulties can lead to dangerous falls.
* Be aware of side effects of medication and how this might affect exercise programming. Medication can affect energy level, muscle coordination, and muscle strength.

Tips and Techniques

* If cardiovascular dysautonomia exists, heart rate and blood pressure must be monitored throughout the exercise program; intensity might need to be decreased.
* Choose exercises and equipment that provide maximum support (e.g., swimming, recumbent cycling) and have participants work out in a safe environment (e.g., avoid slippery floors, poor lighting, and throw rugs).
* For those who are heat sensitive, create a cool environment with fans, air temperature between 72 and 76 degrees Fahrenheit, and pool temperature between 80 and 85 degrees Fahrenheit. If exercising outdoors in hot weather, exercise during early morning or evening hours. Wear clothing that "breathes," and use cooling aids as needed (e.g., cool vests, ice packs, cool baths).

Informative Web Sites

www.nationalmssociety.org

www.ncpad.org

Muscular Dystrophy

Definition

Muscular dystrophies are genetic disorders characterized by progressive muscle wasting and weakness that begin with microscopic changes in the muscle. As muscles degenerate over time, the person's muscle strength, power, and endurance decline. There are several types of muscular dystrophy, including Duchenne muscular dystrophy, the most common, Becker muscular dystrophy, facioscapulohumeral dystrophy (FSHD), and myotonic muscular dystrophy.

Selected Facts

* Muscular dystrophies are inherited, progressive disorders that gradually weaken the respiratory muscles as they do the muscles that move the limbs and trunk. The spinal muscular atrophies and many other neuromuscular disorders can also lead to breathing problems and lung complications.
* Contractures and muscle atrophy are common.

Tips and Techniques

* Maintenance and improvement in muscular strength for performing activities of daily living, maintaining ambulation, and preventing contractures are important.
* Maintaining sufficient respiratory capacity is critical. Work with appropriate medical personnel to assess cardiovascular condition and potential complications.
* Strengthening postural muscles, which can slow the formation of scoliosis, should be included in the exercise program.
* Set reasonable goals involving activities that are achievable and enjoyable.
* Avoid overfatigue of muscles.

Informative Web Site

www.mdausa.org

Obesity

Definition

Obesity is an excess of body fat frequently resulting in a significant impairment of health.

Selected Facts

- Obesity is defined as being over 30 percent above ideal body weight.
- Being overweight or obese might cause little or no inconvenience to a person's career, lifestyle, daily activities, and so on. Over time, however, a disability might occur from obesity. When obesity becomes severe, it can inflict bodily pain and affect normal daily activities.
- Obesity is a chronic disease with a strong familial component.
- Obesity increases a person's risk of developing high blood pressure, diabetes (type 2), heart disease, stroke, gallbladder disease, and cancer of the breast, prostate, and colon.
- Health insurance providers rarely pay for treatment of obesity despite the condition's serious effects on health.
- The tendency toward obesity is promoted by an environment that includes lack of physical activity combined with high-calorie, low-cost foods.
- If maintained, even small weight losses (as small as 10 percent of body weight) can improve health significantly.
- People with obesity are often victims of employment and other kinds of discrimination; they are frequently penalized for their condition despite many federal and state laws and policies.

Tips and Techniques

- During physical activity, frequently monitor blood pressure and heart rate of individuals who are obese to ensure appropriate exercise intensity.
- Offer fun, achievable activities that increase a participant's chances of succeeding in an activity program.
- Use the cool-down phase of class to chat about nutritious foods that taste good.

Informative Web Site

www.obesity.org/

Osteogenesis Imperfecta

Definition

Osteogenesis imperfecta (OI) is caused by a genetic defect that affects the body's production of collagen. Collagen is the major protein of the body's connective tissue and can be likened to the framework around which a building is constructed. In OI, a person has either less collagen than normal or a poorer quality of collagen than normal, leading to weak bones that fracture easily.

Selected Facts

- There are at least four recognized forms of OI, making for extreme variation in severity from one individual to another. A person might have just a few or as many as several hundred fractures in a lifetime.
- Individuals might have loose joints and low muscle tone.
- Some individuals might have underdeveloped lungs and respiratory problems.
- Spinal curvature is possible with the more severe types of OI.
- Hearing loss is also possible.

Tips and Techniques

- Treatment for OI is directed toward preventing or controlling the symptoms, maximizing independent mobility, and developing optimal bone mass and muscle strength.
- Use of wheelchairs, braces, and other mobility aids is common, particularly among people with more severe types of OI.
- People with OI are encouraged to exercise as much as possible to promote muscle and bone strength, which can help prevent fractures. Swimming and water therapy are common exercise choices, as water allows independent movement with little risk of fracture.
- Walking (with or without mobility aids) is excellent for those who are able.
- Individuals with OI will also benefit from maintaining a healthy weight, eating a nutritious diet, and avoiding activities such as smoking, excessive alcohol or caffeine consumption, and taking steroid medications—all of which might deplete bone and exacerbate bone fragility.

Informative Web Site

www.oif.org

Parkinson's Disease

Definition

Parkinson's disease is a chronic, progressive neurological disease. In Parkinson's, neurons in a specific region of the brain degenerate and result in the lack of a neurotransmitter responsible for the control of muscle movement. This can lead to tremors, muscle stiffness, and slower movements. Postural instability can also occur.

Selected Facts

- The functional differences of Parkinson's occur mainly between the ages of 50 to 65 years. Young-onset Parkinson's can occur in persons younger than 50.
- Signs and symptoms of Parkinson's change as the disease progresses.
- With Parkinson's, there might be behavioral and psychological changes including cognitive or memory difficulties, depression, anxiety, apathy, and fatigue.
- Medication plays a significant role in the treatment of Parkinson's.

Tips and Techniques

- Exercise and physical activity are strongly recommended to maintain functional ability and psychological well-being.
- Physical activity should be planned with consideration of medication schedules.
- Walking, swimming, and cycling are particularly good activities for maintaining health.
- Tai chi can promote postural control, balance, and smooth movement.
- Stretching exercises are particularly beneficial.
- Use light weights for maintaining as much strength and muscle tone as possible. Strengthening should focus on the extensor and postural control muscles.

Informative Web Site

www.parkinson.org/

Post-Polio Syndrome

Definition

Poliomyelitis (polio), an acute viral disease, affects the lower motor neurons and causes muscle paresis, paralysis, and sometimes death.

Post-Polio syndrome, or PPS, is a name that has been adopted to indicate a constellation of new symptoms that occur between 20 to 40 years after the onset of the initial polio infection and after a period of "recovery" of at least 10 years. These symptoms often include new weakness, pain, breathing or swallowing difficulties, a variety of sleep disorders, muscle twitching, gastrointestinal problems, muscle fatigue, or "central" fatigue.

Selected Facts

- Symptoms can occur in previously affected muscles or in what were previously thought to be muscles unaffected at onset.
- Complications of PPS often include neuropathies, nerve entrapments, arthritis, scoliosis, osteoporosis, and, sometimes, additional atrophy.
- Onset of PPS is usually gradual, over a period of years, but sometimes abrupt, with major losses of function suffered over several months or a couple of years. Onset often occurs after a physical or emotional trauma, illness, or accident.

Tips and Techniques

- Physical activity is recommended for improvement in cardiovascular capacity and in performing activities of daily living.
- Energy management is important and achieved by striking a balance between rest and activity.
- Short-term exercise is indicated for affected muscles showing no signs of weakness and a full exercise program for muscles that have not been affected. Exercise is contraindicated for affected, severely weakened muscles.

Informative Web Site

www.ott.zynet.co.uk/polio/lincolnshire/
www.post-polio.org
www.ninds.nih.gov

Prader-Willi Syndrome

Definition

Prader-Willi is a disorder of chromosome 15 that leads to low muscle tone, cognitive impairment, and behavioral differences.

Selected Facts

- There is likely developmental delay before age six and mild to moderate mental retardation or learning problems in older children.
- Children with Prader-Willi might have excessive or rapid weight gain between one and six years of age; central obesity can occur in the absence of intervention.
- Behavioral problems might include temper tantrums, violent outbursts, obsessive or compulsive behavior, and a tendency to be argumentative, oppositional, and rigid.

Tips and Techniques

- Compounding the pressure of excessive appetite is a decreased calorie utilization in those with PWS as a consequence of low muscle mass and inactivity. Daily exercise (at least 30 minutes) is essential for weight control and health.
- Motor milestones are typically delayed one to two years; although hypotonia improves, deficits in strength, coordination, balance, and motor planning might continue. Exercise and sports activities should be encouraged.

Informative Web Sites

www.pwsausa.org

www.ipwso.org/

Rett Syndrome

Definition

Rett Syndrome (RS) is a neurological disorder in which a child usually shows an early period of apparently typical development until 6 to 18 months of life. A period of temporary stagnation or regression follows during which the child loses communication skills and purposeful use of the hands. Stereotyped hand movements, gait difficulties, and slowing of the rate of head growth might then occur.

Selected Facts

- A child with RS might experience seizures and disorganized breathing patterns.
- Apraxia (dyspraxia), the inability to program the body to perform motor movements, and other motor problems are common occurrences and might interfere with ambulation, speech, and gaze.

- RS is most often misdiagnosed as autism, cerebral palsy, or non-specified developmental delay.
- Scoliosis might develop and range from mild to more severe.

Tips and Techniques

- A combination of interventions are recommended to maintain or improve function, prevent deformities, and promote mobility.
- Practitioners should be familiar with possible alternative communication methods, including eye-gaze response; picture, letter, and word boards; and touch- or switch-operated voice output devices.
- Physical therapy, exercise, and aquatic therapy are useful for preventing or treating scoliosis.
- Walking, standing, and assistive positioning techniques are also recommended.

Informative Web Site

www.rettsyndrome.org

Spina Bifida

Definition

Spina bifida is an incomplete closure of the spinal column during the first month of fetal development. In general, the three types of spina bifida (from mild to severe) are spina bifida occulta, an opening in one or more of the vertebrae (bones) of the spinal column without apparent damage to the spinal cord; meningocele, in which the meninges, or protective covering around the spinal cord, has pushed out through the opening in the vertebrae but the spinal cord remains intact; and myelomeningocele, in which a portion of the spinal cord itself protrudes through the back. In some cases, sacs are covered with skin; in others, tissue and nerves are exposed. Generally, people use the terms "spina bifida" and "myelomeningocele" interchangeably.

Selected Facts

- Myelomeningocele might include muscle weakness or paralysis below the area of the spine where the incomplete closure occurs, loss of sensation below the cleft, and loss of bowel and bladder control.
- A large percentage (70 to 90 percent) of children born with myelomeningocele have

hydrocephalus or a buildup and accumulation of fluid in the brain. Hydrocephalus is controlled by a surgical procedure called "shunting," which relieves the fluid buildup in the brain. If a drain (shunt) is not implanted, the pressure buildup can cause brain damage, seizures, or blindness. Hydrocephalus might occur without spina bifida, but the two conditions often occur together.

- Children with spina bifida who also have a history of hydrocephalus might experience learning problems and difficulty paying attention, expressing or understanding language, and grasping concepts.

Tips and Techniques

- Participants might not have the ability to sweat and thus should take appropriate precautions to prevent overheating.
- Individuals with shunts should avoid activities that might result in physical contact to the head (e.g., soccer heading, boxing, headstands, forward rolls, tackles).
- Be aware of symptoms such as headaches, dizziness, seizures, irritability, swelling, and redness along the shunt tract, which might indicate a blocked shunt.
- Flexibility in scheduling might need to occur to accommodate bowel and bladder management programs.
- Some individuals with spina bifida have latex allergies. If so, latex equipment (e.g., some types of rubber balls and balloons) should be avoided.
- Children with myelomeningocele need to learn mobility skills and often require the aid of crutches, braces, or wheelchairs. Even if the participant can ambulate on long leg braces, a wheelchair might make sport and game participation easier.

Informative Web Sites

www.sbaa.org

www.easter-seals.org

www.modimes.org

www.naric.com

Spinal Cord Injury (SCI)

Definition

Spinal cord injury (SCI) is a complete or partial lesion to the spinal cord that results in functional loss of sensory, motor, and autonomic systems. The extent of functional differences depends on the level and completeness of the lesion. The physical ability of individuals with SCI is classified according to the amount of function retained. Common categories are paraplegia (SCI affecting level T2 and below, trunk and lower extremities involved) and quadriplegia/tetraplegia (SCI affecting level T1 or above, all four extremities and trunk involved).

Selected Facts

- Individuals with lesions above the sacral level experience a loss of control with their bowel or bladder.
- Spasticity or high muscle tone and hyperactive stretch reflexes might occur in the muscles below the site of injury and be exacerbated by exposure to cold air, urinary tract infections, and physical exercise.
- Autonomic dysreflexia or a sudden rise in blood pressure resulting from an exaggerated autonomic nervous system response to noxious stimuli such as bladder or bowel overdistension or a blocked catheter below the level of injury might occur.
- Individuals with SCI often experience irregular body temperatures.
- Pressure sores (decubitis ulcers) or damage to the skin or underlying tissue caused by a lack of blood flow to the area might be problematic for individuals with SCI.

Tips and Techniques

- In extreme heat, individuals with spinal cord injuries at the 6th thoracic level and above have difficulty sweating. Some individuals with spinal cord injuries should avoid exercising in extremely cold or hot environments because of difficulty with thermal regulation.
- In response to autonomic dysreflexia, monitor signs of profuse sweating, sudden elevation in blood pressure, flushing, shivering, headache, and nausea; seek medical attention immediately if these symptoms occur.
- Monitor blood pressure throughout exercise, avoid quick movements, perform orthostatic training (if available), maintain proper hydration, and use compression stockings and an abdominal binder to avoid significant drops in blood pressure.

Informative Web Site

www.spinalcord.org

Stroke

Definition

Stroke, often called cerebrovascular accident (CVA), is a sudden central nervous system impairment in which the flow of oxygen and nutrients to the brain is halted through a blood clot (ischemia) or bleeding (hemorrhage).

Selected Facts

* Risk factors associated with stroke include hypertension, coronary artery disease, hyperlipidemia, diabetes, obesity, and high amounts of alcohol, caffeine, and nicotine.
* Motor ability and control, sensation and perception, communication, and emotions might be influenced. Individuals might have partial or total paralysis on one side of the body.

Tips and Techniques

* Check with the participant's primary physician before starting an exercise program, and conduct exercise screening and assessments to ensure a safe and effective program.
* Know the implications of necessary medications (e.g., hypertension medications, water pills) on the body's ability to exercise or participate in physical activity.
* Monitor blood pressure periodically throughout an exercise program.
* Be aware of occurrences of orthostatic hypotension, which is dizziness, nausea, and lightheadedness from suddenly sitting or standing up.
* To avoid dangerous falls, make sure you have adequate support for balance while using exercise machines.
* If muscle groups are not functional because of spasticity, the opposing muscle groups might be strengthened to help normalize the spasticity. Any muscle groups incapable of being strengthened should be stretched.
* Spasticity can affect the respiratory muscles of the involved side. Cardiovascular exercise and deep rhythmical breathing can help strengthen respiratory muscles.

Informative Web Sites

www.hemikids.org/stroke.htm

www.stroke.org/

Traumatic Brain Injury (TBI)

Definition

Traumatic brain injury is an acquired insult or injury to the brain caused by an external force. TBI might result in a diminished physical and cognitive capacity or psychosocial difficulties. The term applies to open or closed head injuries resulting in changes in one or more areas, such as cognition; language; memory; attention; reasoning; abstract thinking; judgment; problem-solving; sensory, perceptual, and motor abilities; psychosocial behavior; physical functions; information processing; and speech. The term does not apply to brain injuries that are congenital or degenerative or to brain injuries induced by birth trauma.

Selected Facts

* Traumatic brain injuries often result from motor vehicle, sports, and recreation accidents.
* Brain injuries can range from mild to severe, as can the changes that result from the injury. It is hard to predict how an individual will recover from the injury.
* In the case of children, as a child grows and develops, functional capabilities might change as he or she is expected to use the brain in new and different ways. The damage to the brain from the earlier injury can make it hard for the child to learn new skills that come with getting older. For an adult, brain injury can result in the loss of, or difficulty with, previously learned skills.

Tips and Techniques

* Give the participant more time to finish tasks.
* Break lessons down into small components and give directions one step at a time. For tasks with many steps, give the individual both visual and verbal cues.
* Show the participant how to perform new tasks. Give examples to go with new ideas and concepts.
* Have consistent routines. This helps the participant know what to expect. If the routine is going to change, let him or her know ahead of time.
* Assist the individual with organizational strategies, such as color-coding activities,

using an assignment book, and keeping to a daily schedule.

- Realize that the participant might get tired quickly. Because of fatigue levels, avoid "overloading"; let the participant rest as needed.
- Reduce distractions.
- Offer choices, and be flexible about expectations.

Informative Web Sites

www.neuroskills.com/
www.biausa.org
www.headinjury.com

Reprinted, by permission, from S.L. Kasser and S. Lytle, 2005, *Inclusive physical activity: A lifetime of opportunities* (Champaign, IL: Human Kinetics).

References and Resources

Chapter 1

da Gama, G., Hironaka-Juteau, J.H., & Nir, D. (2003, summer). Inclusivity: The philosophy and process on inclusion in recreation. *California Park and Recreation Society Magazine, 59,* 3.

Stringer, E.T. (2007). *Action research* (3rd ed.). Thousand Oaks, CA: Sage.

University of Maryland College Park. (1995). *Diversity at UMCP: Moving toward community plan.* College Park, MD: Author.

U.S. Census Bureau. (2005-2007). American community survey. http://factfinder.census.gov.

U.S. Department of Justice Americans with Disabilities Act of 1990. www.ada.gov.

U.S. Department of Justice, Civil Rights Act of 1964. www.usdoj.gov/crt/cor/coord/titlevi.php.

U.S. Department of Labor Section 504, Rehabilitation Act of 1973. www.dol.gov/oasam/regs/statutes/sec504.htm.

Chapter 2

Addams, J. (1908/2002). The home and the special child. In J.B. Elshtain (Ed.), *The Jane Addams reader* (pp. 224-228). New York: Basic Books. (Reprinted from the National Education Association, *Journal of Proceedings and Addresses*, 1908, p. 99-102)

Avedon, F.M. (1974). *Therapeutic recreation service: An applied behavioral science approach.* Englewood Cliffs, NJ: Prentice Hall.

Architectural Barriers Act of 1968. Statutes at Large. Vol. 82.

Bogus, C. (2001). *Why lawsuits are good for America: Disciplined democracy, big business and the common law.* New York: New York University Press.

Brinckerhoff, L.C., Shaw, S.F., & McGuire, J.M. (1992). Promoting access, accommodations and independence for college students with learning disabilities. *Journal of Learning Disabilities 25*(7), *417-429.*

Bryan, M.L.M., & Davis, A.F. (Eds.). (1990). *100 years at Hull House.* Bloomington & Indianapolis: Indiana University Press.

Bullock, C.C., & Howe, C.Z. (1991). A model therapeutic recreation program for the reintegration of persons with disabilities into the community. *Therapeutic Recreation Journal, 25*(1), 7-17.

Bullock, C.C., & Mahon, M.J. (2000). *Introduction to recreation services for people with disabilities: A person-centered approach* (2nd ed.). Champaign, IL: Sagamore.

Chronology of the Disability Rights Movements. (n.d.). www.sfsu.edu/~hrdpu/chron.htm.

Calasanti, T., Slevin, K., & King, N. (2006). Ageism and feminism: From et cetera to center. *NWSA Journal, 18*(1), 13-30.

Camurat, D. (1993). *The American Indian in the great war: Real and imagined.* Masters Thesis: Institut Charles V of the University of Paris VII. net.lib.byu.edu/~rdh7/wwi/comment/Camurat1.html.

Civil Rights Acts. Amusement park is covered by Public Accommodations Section of the Civil Rights Act of 1964. *Miller v. Amusement Enterprises, Inc.,* 394 F.2d 342 (5th Cir. 1968) (en banc). (1969). *Harvard Law Review, 82*(3), 686-691.

Cohen, P. (2001). Being reasonable: Defining and implementing a right to community based care for older adults with mental disabilities under the Americans with Disabilities Act. *International Journal of Law and Psychiatry, 24*(2-3), 233.

Cone, K. (1996). Section 504 history—overview. http://dredf.org/504site/histover.html.

Cozzens, L. (1995). *Brown v. Board of Education. Welcome to African American history!* www.watson.org/~lisa/blackhistory/early-civilrights/brown.html.

DBTAC. (n.d.) *ADA structure.* www.adata.org/about/structure.html.

Dieser, R.B. (2005). Jane Addams and Hull-House: Understanding the role of recreation and leisure in bridging cross-cultural differences in human service work. *Human Service Education, 25*(1), 53-63.

Dieser, R.B. (2008). History of therapeutic recreation: In T. Robertson & T. Long (Eds.), *Foundations of therapeutic recreation* (pp. 13-30). Champaign, IL: Human Kinetics

Dieser, R.B., Hutchinson, S., Fox, K., & Scholl, K. (2005). Reflecting upon covert frameworks in clinical therapeutic recreation practice: Becoming aware. In C. Sylvester (Ed.), *Philosophy of therapeutic recreation: Ideas and issues* (Vol. III, pp. 23-39). Ashburn, VA: National Recreation and Park Association.

Disability history timeline. http://isc.temple.edu/neighbor/ds/disabilityrightstimeline.htm.

Dower, J.W. (1986). *War without mercy: Race and power in the pacific war.* New York: Pantheon Books.

Edginton, C.R., DeGraaf, D.G., Dieser, R.B. & Edginton, S. (2006). *Leisure and life satisfaction: Foundational perspectives* (4th ed). Boston: WCB McGraw-Hill

Evans, D.P. (1983). *The lives of mentally ill retarded people.* Boulder, CO: Westview Press.

Foucault, M. (1965). *Madness and civilization: A history of insanity in the age of reason.* (R. Howard, Trans.). London, UK: Tavistock.

Foucault, M. (1998). *Aesthetics, method, and epistemology.* In J.D. Faubion (Ed.), *Essential works of Foucault 1954-1984* (Vol. 2). New York: The New Press.

Fox, K.M., & van Dyck, J. (1997). Embrace the wrongs that we have committed and celebrate that there is time to start anew. *Journal of Leisurability, 24*(3), 3-22.

Howe-Murphy, R., & Charboneau, B. G. (1987). *Therapeutic recreation interventions: An ecological perspective.* Englewood Cliffs, NJ: Prentice Hall.

Hutchison, P., & McGill, J. (1998). *Leisure, integration and community* (2nd ed). Toronto, ON: Leisurability.

Lopiano, D. (2000). Modern history of women in sports: Twenty-five years of Title IX. *Clinics in sports medicine, 19*(2), 163-173.

Mahon, M.J., Bullock, C.C., Luken, K., & Martens, C. (1996). Leisure education for persons with severe and persistent mental illness: Is it a socially valid process? *Therapeutic Recreation Journal, 30*(3), 197-212.

McBride, P. (1989). Jane Addams. In H. Ibrahim (Ed.), *Pioneers in leisure and recreation* (pp. 53-64). Reston, VA: American Association for Leisure and Recreation.

Midgely, J. (1995). *Social development: The developmental perspective in social welfare.* Thousand Oaks, CA: Sage.

Nirje, B. (1969). The normalization principle and its human management implications. In R. Kugel & W. Wolfensberger (Eds.), *Changing patterns in residential services for the mentally retarded.* Washington, DC: President's Committee on Mental Retardation.

Nirje, B. (1972). The right to self-determination. In W. Wolfensberger (Ed.), *Normalization: The principle of normalization in human services* (pp. 194-200). Toronto, ON: The National Institute on Mental Retardation.

Nirje, B. (1992). *The normalization principle paper.* Uppsala, Sweden: Centre for Handicapped Research.

Pedlar, A., & Gilbert, A. (1997). Normalization for individuals with disabilities: The Canadian model. In D.M. Compton (Ed.) *Issues in therapeutic recreation: Toward the new millennium* (2nd ed., pp. 489-506). Champaign, IL: Sagamore.

Perrin, B., & Nirje, B. (1985). Setting the record straight: A critique of some misconceptions of the normalization principle. *Australian and New Zealand Journal of Developmental Disabilities, 11*(2), 69-74.

Peregoy, J.J., & Dieser, R.B. (1997). Multiculturalism in therapeutic recreation: Living in hamlets. *Therapeutic Recreation Journal, 31*(3), 173-188.

Polacheck, H.S. (1989). *I came a stranger: The story of a Hull-House girl.* Urbana, IL: University Press.

Rich, N.P., & Alperin, D.E. (2002). *Innovation and change in the human services* (2nd ed.). Springfield, IL: Charles C. Thomas.

Scholl, K., Dieser, R., & Schilling, A. (2004). Leisure educational systems: The "Together We Play" initiative. *Expanding Horizons in Therapeutic Recreation, 21*, 68-77.

Schram, B., & Mandell, B.R. (2000). *An introduction to human services: Policy and practice* (4th ed). Boston: Allyn & Bacon.

Searle, M.S., Mahon, M.J., Iso-Ahola, S.E., Sdrolias, H.A., & van Dyck, J. (1995). Enhancing a sense of independence and psychological well-being among the elderly: A field experiment. *Journal of Leisure Research, 27*(2), 107-124.

Searle, M.S., Mahon, M.J., Iso-Ahola, S.E., Sdrolias, H.A., & van Dyck, J. (1998). Examining the long term effects of leisure education on a sense of independence and psychological well-being among the elderly. *Journal of Leisure Research, 30*(3), 331-340.

Still, M., & Williams, J. (2005). A legal perspective on family issues at work. In M. Pitt-Catsouphes, E. Ernst Kossek, & S. Sweet (Eds.), *The work and family handbook: Multidisciplinary perspectives and approaches* (pp. 309-326). London: Routledge.

Sylvester, C. (1989). Therapeutic recreation and the practice of history. *Therapeutic Recreation Journal, 23*(4), 19-28.

Sylvester, C., Voelkl, J.E., & Ellis, G.D. (2001*). Therapeutic recreation programming: Theory and practice.* State College, PA: Venture.

Thomas, J. (April, 2008). U.S. gender-equity law led to boom in female sports participation. http://www.america.gov/st/educ-english/2008/April/200804011633001CJsamohT0.2589533.html.

Trimble, J.E. (1981). Value differentials and their importance in counseling American Indians. In P.B. Pedersen, J.G. Draguns, W.J. Lonner, & J.E. Trimble (Eds.), *Counseling across cultures* (pp. 203-226). Honolulu, HI: East-West Culture Learning Institute, University of Hawaii.

Weir, R. F. (1984). *Selective nontreatment of handicapped newborns: Moral dilemmas in neonatal medicine.* New York: Oxford University Press.

Welch, P. (1995). *Strategies for teaching universal design.* Boston: Adaptive Environments.

Welsford, E. (1935). *The fool: His social and literary history.* London: Faber & Faber.

Wolfensberger, W. (1972). *The principle of normalization in human services*. Toronto, ON: National Institute on Mental Retardation.

Wolfensberger, W. (1983). Social role valorization: A proposed new term for the principle of normalization. *Mental Retardation, 21*(6), 234-239.

Wolfensberger, W. (1985). An overview of social role valorization and some reflections on elderly mentally retarded persons. In M.P. Janicki & H.M. Wisniewski (Eds.), *Aging and development disabilities: Issues and approaches* (pp. 61-76). Baltimore: Brookes.

Wolfensberger, W., & Thomas, S. (1983). *PASSING (Program Analysis of Service System's Implementation of Normalization Goals): Normalization criteria and rating manual* (2nd ed). Toronto, ON: National Institute on Mental Retardation.

Zames-Fleischer, D., & Zames, F. (2001). *The disability rights movement: From charity to confrontation*. Philadelphia: Temple University Press.

Chapter 3

Atkinson, D.R., Morten, G., & Sue, D.W. (1993). *Counseling American minorities: A cross-cultural perspective* (4th ed.). Dubuque, IA: Brown.

Axelson, J.A. (1985). *Counseling and development in a multicultural society*. Belmont, CA: Wadsworth.

Barna, I.M. (1994). Stumbling blocks in intercultural communication. In L.A. Samovar & R.E. Porter (Eds.), *Intercultural communication: A reader* (7th ed., pp. 337-346. Belmont: CA: Wadsworth.

Bennett, M.J. (1986). A developmental approach to training for intercultural sensitivity. *International Journal of Intercultural Relations, 10*(2), 179-196.

Bennett, M.J. (1993). Towards ethnorelativism: A developmental model of intercultural sensitivity. In R.M. Paige (Ed.), *Education for the intercultural experience* (pp. 21-71). Yarmouth, ME: Intercultural Press.

Bennett, M.J. (1998). *Basic concepts of intercultural communication*. Yarmouth, ME: Intercultural Press.

Bryan, H. (2000). Recreation specialization revisited. *Journal of Leisure Research, 31*, 18-21.

Cross, T.L. (1988, summer). *Focal point: Services to minority populations: What does it mean to be a culturally competent professional?* Portland, OR: Research and Training Center, Portland State University.

Cross, T.L., Bazron, B.J., Dennis, K.W., & Isaacs, M.R. (1989). *Toward a culturally competent system of care*. Washington, DC: Georgetown University Development Center.

Derman-Sparks, L. (1993-1994). Empowering children to create a caring culture in a world of differences. *Childhood Education, 90*, 66-71.

Devore, W., & Schlesinger, E.G. (1981). *Ethnic sensitive social work practice*. St. Louis: Mosby.

Diller, J.V., & Moule, J. (2005). *Cultural competence: a primer for educators*. Belmont, CA: Thomson Wadsworth.

Frielich, M. (1989). Introduction: Is culture still relevant? In M. Frielich (Ed.), *The relevance of culture*. New York: Morgan & Garvey.

Gobster, P. (2002). Managing urban parks for a radically and ethnically diverse clientele. *Leisure Sciences, 2A*, 143-159.

Godbey, G. (1991). Planning for leisure in a pluralistic society. In T.L. Goodale & P.A. Witt (Eds.), *Recreation and leisure: Issues in an era of change* (pp. 137-148). State College, PA: Venture.

Goldsmith, J. (1994). Designing for diversity. *National Parks, 68*(5/6), 20-21.

Green, J. W. (1982). *Cultural awareness in the human services*. Englewood Cliffs, NJ: Prentice Hall.

Gudykunst, W.B., & Kim, Y.Y. (1992). *Communicating with strangers: An approach to intercultural communication*. (2nd ed.). St. Louis: McGraw-Hill.

Hammer, M.R., Bennett, M.J., & Wiseman, R. (2003). Measuring intercultural sensitivity: The intercultural development inventory. *International Journal of Intercultural Relations, 27*, 421-443.

Harrison, R. (1966). The design of cross-cultural training: An alternative to the university model. In *Explorations in human relations training and research*,(NEA, vol. 2). Bethesda, MD: National Training Laboratories, 4.

Healey, J.F. (1995). *Race, ethnicity, gender, and class: The sociology of group conflict and change*. Thousand Oaks, CA: Pine Forge Press.

Hofstede, G. (1980). *Culture's competence*. Beverly Hills, CA: Sage.

Hofstede, G. (1983). Dimensions of national cultures in fifty countries and three regions. In J. Oeregowski, S. Duirawiec, & R. Annis (Eds.), *Explications in cross-cultural psychology*. Lisse, Netherlands: Swets and Zeitlinger.

Hoopes, D.S. (1972). *Reader in intercultural communication* (Vols. 1 & 2). Pittsburgh: Regional Council for International Education.

Horley, J. (19.92). A longitudinal examination of lifestyles. *Social Indicators Research, 26*, 205-219.

Kalmijn, M., & Bernasco, W. (2001). Separated lifestyles in married and cohabiting relationships. *Journal of marriage and the family, 63*, 639-654.

Katz, J.H. (1989). The challenges of diversity. In C. Woolbright (Ed.), *Valuing diversity on campus* (pp. 1-21). Bloomington, IN: Association of College Unions International.

Kniker, C.R. (1977). *You and values education*. Columbus, OH: Merrill.

Kottak, C. (2008). *Mirror for humanity: a concise introduction to cultural anthropology*. (6th ed.). Burr Ridge, IL: McGraw-Hill.

Kottak, C.P., & Kozaitis, K.A. (2008). *On being different: Diversity and multiculturalism in the North American mainstream.* (3rd ed.). Burr Ridge, IL: McGraw-Hill.

Kroeber, A.L., & Kluckhohn, C. (1952). *Culture: A critical review of concepts and definitions* (Papers of the Peabody Museum No. 47). Cambridge, MA: Peabody Museum Press.

Lum, D. (1986). *Social work practice and People of Color: A process-stage approach.* Monterey, CA: Brooks/Cole.

McAdoo, H.P. (Ed.). (1993). *Family ethnicity: strength in diversity.* Thousand Oaks, CA: Sage.

Marin, G., & Marin, B.V. (1991). *Research with Hispanic populations.* Thousand Oaks, CA: Sage.

Olsen, M. (1978). *The process of social organization* (2nd ed.). New York: Holt, Rinehart & Winston.

Pedersen, P. (1994). *A handbook for developing multicultural awareness* (2nd ed.). Alexandria, VA: American Counseling Association.

Petrick, J., Backman, S., Bixler, R., & Norman, W. (2001). Analysis of golfer motivations and constraints by experience use history. *Journal of Leisure Research, 33,* 56-70.

Petersen, P.B., Draguns, J.G., Lonner, W.J., & Trimble, J.E. (1989). *Counseling across culture.* Honolulu: University of Hawaii Press.

Ponterotto, J.G., Casas, J.M., Suzuki, L.A., & Alexander, C.M. (1995). *Handbook of multicultural counseling.* Thousand Oaks, CA: Sage.

Pope, R.L., Reynolds, A.L., & Mueller, J.A. (2004). *Multicultural competence in student affairs.* San Francisco, CA: Jossey-Bass.

Rokeach, M. (1972). *Beliefs, attitudes, and values.* San Francisco: Jossey-Bass.

Scott, D., & Thigpen, J. (2003). Understanding the birder as tourist: Segmenting visitors to the Texas Hummer/Bird Celebration. *Human Dimensions of Wildlife, 8,* 199-209.

Stodolska, M. (2000). Changes in leisure participation patterns after immigration. *Leisure Sciences, 22,* 39-63.

Sue, D.W., Arredondo, A., & McDavis, R.J. (1992). Multicultural counseling competencies and standards: A call to the profession. *Journal of Counseling and Development, 70,* 477-486.

Thomas, R.R., Jr. (1991). *Beyond race and gender: Unleashing the power of your total workforce by managing diversity.* New York: AMACOM.

Ting-Toomey, S. (1999). *Communicating across cultures.* New York: Guilford.

Trompenaars, F., & Hampden-Turner, C. (1998). *Riding the waves of culture: Understanding diversity in global business* (2nd ed.). New York: McGraw-Hill.

Vaske, J., Carothers, P., Donnelly, M., & Baird, P. (2000). Recreation conflict among skiers and snowboarders. *Leisure Sciences, 22,* 297-313.

Veal, A.J. (1993). The concept of lifestyle: A review. *Leisure Studies, 12,* 233-252.

Wolffe, K., & Sacks, S.Z. (1997). The lifestyles of blind, low vision and sighted youths: a quantitative comparison. *Journal of Visual Impairment & Blindness, 91,* 245-258.

Chapter 4

Americans with Disabilities Act of 1990, Public Law No. 101-336.

Anderson, L., & Kress, C. (2003). *Including people with disabilities in parks and recreation opportunities.* State College, PA: Venture.

Ajzen, I. (1991). The theory of planned behavior. *Organizational Behavior and Human Decision Processes, 50,* 179-211.

Chavez, D. (2000). Invite, include, involve! Racial groups, ethnic groups, and leisure. In T.M. Allison & I.E. Schneider (Eds.), *Diversity and the recreation profession: Organizational perspectives* (pp. 179-191). State College, PA: Venture.

Boyte, H. (2000, spring). *Creating the commonwealth: A newsletter for the Center for Democracy and Citizenship.* Minneapolis: Humphries Center.

Boyte, H., Kari, N.N., Lewis, J., Skelton, N., & O'Donoghue, J. (1999). *Creating the commonwealth.* Dayton: Kettering Foundation.

Bullock, C.C., & Mahon, M.J. (2001) *Introduction to recreation services for people with disabilities: A person-centered approach* (2nd ed.). Champaign, IL: Sagamore.

Dattilo, J. (2002). *Inclusive leisure services: Responding to the rights of people with disabilities* (2nd ed.). State College, PA: Venture.

Deci, E. L., & Ryan, R. M. (1985). *Intrinsic motivation and self-determination in human behavior.* New York: Plenum Press.

Deci, E.L., & Ryan, R.M. (2000). The "what" and "why" of goal pursuits: Human needs and the self-determination of behavior. *Psychological Inquiry, 11,* 227-268.

Devine, M.A., O'Brien, M.B., & Crawford, T. (2004). Inclusion: Beyond simply sharing the same space. In M.A. Devine (Ed.), *Trends in therapeutic recreation* (pp. 201-229). Washington, DC: National Recreation and Park Association.

Ellis, W.K. (1993). Accessibility: A balancing act. *Disabled Outdoors Magazine, 7*(4), 7-8.

Fishbein, M., & Ajzen, I. (1975). *Belief, attitude, intention and behavior: An introduction to theory and research.* Reading, MA: Addison-Wesley.

Montgomery, S., & Kazin, M. (2005). *Fun and leisure: Providing inclusive recreation opportunities: The Cincinatti model.* Retrieved from http://www.ncpad.org/fun/fact_sheet.php?sheet=66&view=all.

Nolan, C.V. (2005, winter). *Best practices of inclusive services: The value of inclusion.* Bloomington, IN: National Center on Accessibility, Indiana University-Bloomington. www.ncaonline.org.

Robertson, T. (2004, September). *Issues of access: Successful models for change.* Paper presented at the 8th World Leisure Congress/Issues of Access and Accommodation, Brisbane, Australia.

Robertson, T.P., & Long, T. (2002, September). *Hey, you can't play, but neither should I.* Paper presented at the 2nd Annual National Institute on Recreation Inclusion, Las Vegas, NV.

Robertson, T.P., & Long, T.D. (2001, April). *Measuring inclusion.* Paper presented at the Midwest Therapeutic Recreation Symposium, St. Louis.

Robertson, T., Chambers, J., & Holmes, D. (2000). *Social accessibility and inclusion: A plea for policy and shared responsibility.* Paper presented at Leisure and Human Development, the 5th World Leisure and Recreation Congress, Bilbao, Spain.

Schleien, S., Ray, M., & Green, F. (1988). Community recreation and people with disabilities: Strategies for integration. Toronto, ON: Paul H. Brooks Publishing.

Scholl, K.G., Dieser, R.B., & Davison, A. (2005). Together we play: An ecological approach to inclusive recreation. *Therapeutic Recreation Journal, 39*(4), 299-311.

Chapter 5

Fisk, R., Grove, S., & John, J. (2007). *Interactive services marketing* (3rd ed.). Boston: Houghton Mifflin.

North Carolina Office of Disability and Health (NCODH) & Woodward Communications. (2002). Removing barriers: Tips and strategies to promote accessible communication. www.fpg.unc.edu/~ncodh/removingbarriers/index.cfm.

Pride, W., & Ferrell, O.C. (2008). *Marketing: Concepts and strategies* (14th ed.). Boston: Houghton Mifflin.

U.S. Census Bureau. (2000). Disability status. www.census.gov/prod/2003pubs/c2kbr-17.pdf. Zeithaml, V., Bitner, M.J., & Gremler, D.D. (2005). *Services marketing: Integrating customer focus across the firm* (4th ed.). Boston: McGraw-Hill.

Scholl, K., Smith, J. & Davidson, A. (2005). Agency readiness to provide inclusive recreation and after-school services for children with disabilities. *Therapeutic Recreation Journal, 39*(1), 50-65.

Sherrill, C. (Ed.). (2004). *Adapted physical activity, recreation, and sport: Crossdisciplinary and lifespan* (6th ed.). Boston: McGraw-Hill.

Wagner, G., Wetherald, L., & Wilson, B. (1994). A model for making county and municipal recreation departments inclusive. In M.S. Moon (Ed.), *Making school and community recreation fun for everyone* (pp. 181-192). Baltimore: Brookes.

Chapter 6

Allison, M.T., & Geiger, C.W. (1993). Nature of leisure activities among the Chinese-American elderly. *Leisure Sciences, 15,* 309-319.

American Community Survey. (2006a). Data profile highlights. http://factfinder.census.gov/servlet/ACSSAFFFacts?_event=&geo_id=01000US&_geoContext=01000US&_street=&_county=&_cityTown=&_state=&_zip=&_lang=en&_sse=on&ActiveGeoDiv=&_useEV=&pctxt=fph&pgsl=010&_submenuId=factsheet_1&ds_name=null&_ci_nbr=null&qr_name=null&reg=null%3Anull&_keyword=&_industry=.

American Community Survey. (2006b). S2301 Employment status. http://factfinder.census.gov/servlet/STTable?_bm=y&-geo_id=01000US&-qr_name=ACS_2006_EST_G00_S2301&-ds_name=ACS_2006_EST_G00_&-_lang=en&-redoLog=false&-format=&-CONTEXT=st.

American Community Survey. (2006c). S2001. Earnings in the past 12 months (in 2006 inflation-adjusted dollars). http://factfinder.census.gov/servlet/STTable?_bm=y&-geo_id=01000US&-qr_name=ACS_2006_EST_G00_S2001&-ds_name=ACS_2006_EST_G00_&-_lang=en&-redoLog=false&-format=&-CONTEXT=st.

Anderson, A.B., & Frideres, J.S. (1981). *Ethnicity in Canada: Theoretical perspectives.* Toronto: Butterworth.

Barth, F. (1969). *Ethnic groups and boundaries.* Boston: Little, Brown.

Berry, B. (1958). *Race and ethnic relations.* Boston: Houghton Mifflin.

Bialeschki, D., & Henderson, K.A. (2000). Gender issues and recreation managements. In M.T. Allison & I.E. Schneider (Eds.), *Diversity and the recreation profession: Organizational perspectives* (pp. 73-93). State College, PA: Venture.

Blahna, D., & Black, K. (1993). Racism: A concern for recreation resource managers. In P. Gobster (Ed.), *Managing urban and high-use recreation settings: Selected papers from the 4th North American Symposium on Society and Natural Resource Management* (pp. 11-118). St. Paul, MN: USDA Forrest Service GTR NC-163.

Crave. (2007). The Internet refrigerator has arrived. http://crave.cnet.com/8301-1_105-9681568-1.html.

Cronan, M.K., Shinew, K.J., & Stodolska, M. (2008). Trail use among Latinos: Recognizing diverse uses among a specific population. *Journal of Park and Recreation Administration, 26,* 62-86.

Cross, G. (1990). *A social history of leisure since 1600.* State College, PA: Venture.

Dawson, D. (2000). Social class and leisure provision. In M.T. Allison & I.E. Schneider (Eds.), *Diversity and the recreation profession: Organizational perspectives* (pp. 99-114). State College, PA: Venture.

Doherty, A., & Taylor, T. (2007). Sport and physical recreation in the settlement of immigrant youth. *Leisure/Loisir, 31,* 27-55.

Dye, J.L. (2005). Fertility of American women: June 2004. *Current Population Reports* (p. 4). www.census.gov/prod/2005pubs/p20-555.pdf.

Floyd, M.F. (1998). Getting beyond marginality and ethnicity: The challenge for race and ethnic studies in leisure research. *Journal of Leisure Research, 30,* 3-22.

Floyd, M.F., & Gramann, J.H. (1995). Perceptions of discrimination in a recreation context. *Journal of Leisure Research, 27,* 192-199.

Freysinger, V.J. (1999). Life span and life course perspectives on leisure. In E.L. Jackson & T.L. Burton (Eds.), *Leisure studies: Prospects for the twenty-first century* (pp. 253-266). State College, PA: Venture.

Freysinger, V.J. (2000). Acting our age: The relationship between age and leisure. In M.T. Allison & I.E. Schneider (Eds.), *Diversity and the recreation profession: Organizational perspectives* (pp. 139-155). State College, PA: Venture.

Gobster, P.H. (2002). Managing urban parks for a racially and ethnically diverse clientele. *Leisure Sciences, 24,* 143-159.

Hawkins, B.A., May, M.E., & Rogers, N.B. (1996). *Therapeutic activity intervention with the elderly: Foundations and practices.* State College, PA: Venture.

He, W., Sengupta, M., Velkoff, V.A., & DeBarros, K.A. (2005). 65+ in the United States: 2005. Washington, DC: U.S. Government Printing Office. Health United States. (2006). www.cdc.gov/nchs/data/hus/hus06.pdf#027.

Henderson, K.A. (1990). The meaning of leisure for women: An integrative review of research. *Journal of Leisure Research, 20,* 228-243.

Henderson, K.A. (1996). One size doesn't fit all: The meanings of women's leisure. *Journal of Leisure Research, 28,* 139-154.

Henderson, K.A., Hodges, S., & Kievel, B. (2002). Context and dialogue in research on women and leisure. *Journal of Leisure Research, 34,* 253-271.

Henderson, K.A., & Hickerson, B. (2007). Women and leisure: Premises and performances uncovered in an integrative review. *Journal of Leisure Research, 39,* 591-610.

Hutchison, R. (1988). A critique of race, ethnicity, and social class in recent leisure-recreation research. *Journal of Leisure Research, 20,* 10-30.

Irwin, P.N., Gartner, W.C., & Phelps, C.C. (1990). Mexican-American/Anglo cultural differences as recreation style determinants. *Leisure Sciences, 12,* 335-348.

Isajiw, W.W. (1990). Ethnic identity retention. In R. Breton, W.W. Isajiw, W. Kalbach, & J.G. Reitz (Eds.), *Ethnic identity and equality: Varieties of experience in a Canadian city* (pp. 34-91). Toronto: University of Toronto Press. Iso-Ahola, S.E., Jackson, E.L., & Dunn, E. (1994). Starting, ceasing, and replacing leisure activities over the life-span. *Journal of Leisure Research, 26,* 227-249.

James, K. (2000). "You can feel them looking at you": The experiences of adolescent girls at swimming pools. *Journal of Leisure Research, 32,* 262-280.

Johnson, C.Y., Bowker, J.M., English, D.B.K., & Worthen, D. (1998). Wildland recreation in the rural South: An examination of marginality and ethnicity theory. *Journal of Leisure Research, 30,* 101-120.

Kelly, J., & Godbey, G. (1992). *The sociology of leisure.* State College, PA: Venture.

Kim, E., Kleiber, D.A., & Knopf, N. (2001). Leisure activity, ethnic preservation, and cultural integration of older Korean Americans. *Journal of Gerontological Social Work, 36,* 107-129.

Klitzing, S.W. (2003). Coping with chronic stress: Leisure and women who are homeless. *Leisure Sciences, 25,* 163-181.

Klitzing, S.W. (2004). Women living in homeless shelter: Stress, coping, and leisure. *Journal of Leisure Research, 36,* 483-512.

Martin, P., & Midgley, E. (2003). Immigration: Shaping and reshaping America. *Population Bulletin, 58,* 3-46.

McDonald, D., & McAvoy, L. (1997). *Racism, recreation and Native Americans.* Paper presented at the 1997 Leisure Research Symposium, Salt Lake City, Utah, October 29-November 2.

National Coalition for the Homeless. (2007a). Who is homeless? http://www.nationalhomeless.org/factsheets/who.html.

National Coalition for the Homeless. (2007b). How many people are homeless? from http://www.nationalhomeless.org/factsheets/How_Many.html.

National Coalition for the Homeless. (2007c). Why are people homeless? http://www.nationalhomeless.org/factsheets/why.html.

Philipp, S. (1999). Are we welcome? African American racial acceptance in leisure activities and the importance given to children's leisure. *Journal of Leisure Research, 31,* 385-403.

Podymow, T., Turnbull, J., Coyle, D., Yetsir, E., & Wells, G. (2006). Shelter-based managed alcohol administration to chronically homeless people addicted to alcohol. *Canadian Medical Association Journal, 174,* 45-49.

Pollard, K.M., & O'Hare, W.P. (1999). America's racial and ethnic minorities. *Population Bulletin, 54,* 1-48.

Rublee, C., & Shaw, S.M. (1991). Constraints on the leisure and community participation of immigrant women: Implications for social integration. *Loisir et Société, 14,* 133-150.

Shaull, S.L., & Gramann, J.H. (1998). The effect of cultural assimilation on the importance of family-related and nature-related recreation among Hispanic Americans. *Journal of Leisure Research, 30,* 47-63.

Shaw, S.M. (1994). Gender, leisure, and constraint: Towards a framework for the analysis of women's leisure. *Journal of Leisure Research, 26,* 8-22.

Shinew, K.J., Floyd, M.F., & Parry, D. (2004). Understanding the relationship between race and leisure activities and constraints: Exploring an alternative framework. *Leisure Sciences, 26,* 181-199.

Smith, A.C., & Smith, D.I. (2001). Emergency and transitional shelter population: 2000. Census 2000 Special Reports. www.census.gov/prod/2001pubs/censr01-2.pdf.

Stewart B. McKinney Act. (1994). 42 U.S.C. § 11301, et seq.

Stodolska, M. (2000). Changes in leisure participation patterns after immigration. *Leisure Sciences, 22,* 39-63.

Stodolska, M. (2007). Social networks, ethnic enclosure, and leisure behavior of immigrants from Korea, Mexico, and Poland. *Leisure/Loisir, 31,* 277-324.

Stodolska, M., & Livengood, J.S. (2006). The effects of religion on the leisure behavior of American Muslim immigrants. *Journal of Leisure Research, 38,* 293-320.

Stodolska, M., & Santos, C.A. (2006). Transnationalism and leisure: Mexican temporary migrants in the United States. *Journal of Leisure Research, 38,* 143-167.

Terrazas, A. & Batalova, J. (2008). U.S. in focus: The most up-to-date frequently requested statistics on immigrants in the United States. www.migrationinformation.org/USFocus/display.cfm?ID=714.

The Urban Institute. (2000). Millions still fear homelessness in a booming economy. www.urban.org/publications/900050.html.

Tinsley, H.E.A., Tinsley, D.J., & Croskeys, C.E. (2002). Park usage, social milieu, and psychological benefits of park use reported by older urban park users from four ethnic groups. *Leisure Sciences, 24,* 199-218.

Tirone, S., & Shaw, S.M. (1997). At the center of their lives: Indo Canadian women, their families and leisure. *Journal of Leisure Research, 29,* 225-244.

U.S. Census. (2006a). Poverty thresholds in 2006. www.census.gov/hhes/www/poverty/threshld/thresh06.html.

U.S. Census. (2006b). Occupation group of the employed population in the civilian labor force by sex and age: 2006. Table 12. www.census.gov/population/www/socdemo/men_women_2006.html.

U.S. Census. (2006c). Marital status of the population 15 years and over by age and sex: 2006. Table 2. http://www.census.gov/population/www/socdemo/men_women_2006.html.

U.S. Census. (2006d). S0103. Population 65 years and over in the united states. http://factfinder.census.gov/servlet/STTable?_bm=y&-qr_name=ACS_2006_EST_G00_S0103&-geo_id=01000US&-ds_name=ACS_2006_EST_G00_&-_lang=en&-format=&-CONTEXT=st.

U.S. Census. (2007a). How the Census Bureau measures poverty (official measure). www.census.gov/hhes/www/poverty/povdef.html.

U.S. Census. (2007b). Poverty: 2006 highlights. www.census.gov/hhes/www/poverty/poverty06/pov06hi.html.

Washburne, R.F. (1978). Black under participation in wildland recreation: Alternative explanations. *Leisure Sciences, 1,* 175-189.

Webster, B. H., & Bishaw, A. (2007). Income, earnings, and poverty data from the 2006 American Community Survey. *American Community Survey Reports,* p. 22. www.census.gov/prod/2007pubs/acs-08.pdf.

Woodard, M.D. (1988). Class, regionality, and leisure among urban black Americans: The post Civil Rights era. *Journal of Leisure Research, 20,* 87-105.

Chapter 7

Anderson, L., & Kress, C. (2003). *Inclusion: Including people with disabilities in parks and recreation opportunities.* State College, PA: Venture.

Bronfenbrenner, U. (1979). *The ecology of human development.* Cambridge, MA: Harvard University Press.

Cameron, S.J. (1994). What is an inclusion specialist? A preliminary investigation. Unpublished manuscript, University of Oregon. http://www.eric.ed.gov/ERICDocs/data/ericdocs2sql/content_storage_01/0000019b/80/16/7e/70.pdf.

Community: Introduction and Model for Community Programming and Evaluation. (n.d.). Evaluating the national outcomes. U.S. Department of Agriculture. http://ag.arizona.edu/fcs/cyfernet/nowg/comm_index.html.

Couchenour, D., & Chrisman, K. (2004). *Families, schools and communities: Together for young children.* Albany, NY: Delmar Learning.

Devine, M.A., O'Brien, M.B., & Crawford, T. (2004). Inclusion: Beyond simply sharing the same space. In M.A. Devine (Ed.), *Trends in therapeutic recreation: Ideas, concepts, and applications* (pp. 201-232). Ashburn, VA: National Recreation and Park Association.

Devine, M.A., & McGovern, J. (2001). Inclusion of individuals with disabilities in public park and recreation programs: Are agencies ready? *Journal of Park and Recreation Administration, 19*(4), 60-82.

Dunlap, T., & Shea, M. (2004). *Together we're better: A practical guide to including children of all abilities in out-of-school time programs.* Unpublished manuscript.

Frazeur Cross, A., Traub, E., Hutter-Pishgahi, L., & Shelton, G. (2004). Elements of successful inclusion for children with significant disabilities. *Topics in Early Childhood Special Education, 24,* 169-184.

Howe-Murphy, R., & Charboneau, B.G. (1987). *Therapeutic recreation intervention: An ecological perspective.* Englewood Cliffs, NJ: Prentice Hall.

Intercultural Center for Research in Education and National Institute on Out-of-School Time. (2005). *Pathways to success for youth: What counts in afterschool? Massachusetts After-School Research Study (MARS).* Boston: Author.

Küpper, L. (2000). *A guide to the individualized education program.* Jessup, MD: U.S. Department of Education. www.ed.gov/about/offices/list/osers/index.html?src=mr.

Kretzman, J.P., & McKnight, J.L. (1993). *Building communities from the inside out.* Chicago: ACTA.

Lynch, E., & Hanson, M. (1998). *Developing cross-cultural competence: A guide for working with children and their families.* Baltimore: Brookes.

Mainstreaming—-Implications for therapeutic recreation. (1979). *Therapeutic Recreation Journal, 8*(4).

McDonnell, L., & Elmore, R. (1987). Getting the job done: Alternative policy instruments. *Education Evaluation and Policy Analysis, 9*(2), 133-152.

Melaville, A.I., Blank, M.J., & Asayesh, G. (1993). *Together we can: A guide for crafting a profamily system of education and human services.* Chevy Chase, MD: PrismDAE.

Miller, K., & Schleien, S. (1999). *A community for all children: A guide to inclusion for out-of-school time.* Unpublished manuscript.

Mulvihill, B., Cotton, J., & Gyaben, S. (2004). Best practices for inclusive child and adolescent out-of-school care: A review of literature. *Family and Community Health, 27,* 52-65.

Mulvihill, B., Shearer, D., & VanHorn, M. (2002). Training, experience, and child care providers' perceptions of inclusion. *Early Childhood Research Quarterly, 17,* 197-215.

National Child Care Information Center. (NCCIC). (2003). *Passages to inclusion: Creating systems of care for all children, monograph for state, territorial and tribal child care administrators.* Vienna, VA: Author.

National Council for Therapeutic Recreation Certification (NCTRC). (n.d.). www.nctrc.org.

Scholl, K., Glanz, A., & Davison, A. (2006). Importance-performance analysis of supportive recreation services: Community agency perspective. *Journal of Park and Recreation Administration, 24*(2), 102-124.

Stumbo, N., & Peterson, C. (2009). *Therapeutic recreation program design: Principles and procedures* (5th ed.). San Francisco: Pearson Education.

Yohalem, N., & Pittman, K. (2006). *Putting youth work on the map: Key findings and implications from two major workforce studies.* www.forumfyi.org.

Chapter 8

Access to Recreation. (2009). Recreation opportunities for people of all ages and abilities. www.AccesstoRecreation.org.

Acrey, C., Johnstone, C, & Milligan, C. (2005). Using universal design to unlock the potential for academic achievement of at-risk learners. *Teaching Exceptional Children, 38*(2), 22-31.

The Center for Universal Design. (1997). The principles of universal design, version 2.0. Raleigh: North Carolina State University. www.design.ncsu.edu/cud/about_ud/udprinciples.htm.

Government of Alberta, Human Resources and Employment. (2003, May). Workplace health and safety: Good product design—avoiding the average. *Ergonomics.* http://employment.alberta.ca/documents/WHS/WHS-PUB_erg030.pdf.

Institute for Human Centered Design. (2008). History of universal design. www.adaptenv.org/index.php?option=Content&Itemid=26.

Lais, G. (2000). *Staff training manual.* Minneapolis: Wilderness Inquiry.

National Center on Accessibility. (2004). *Principles of universal design for challenge course programming.* Bloomington, IN: Indiana University. www.indiana.edu/~nca/challenge/pro_universal_design.htm.

National Center on Physical Activity and Disability. (2009). www.ncpad.org.

Osborne, H. (2001). In other words . . . Communicating across a life span . . . Universal design in print and Web-based communication. www.healthliteracy.com/article.asp?PageID=3812.

Outdoor Industry Foundation. (2006, June). *Outdoor recreation participation study* (8th ed. for year 2005). Boulder, CO: Leisure Trends Group.

Reclaim Civil Rights. (2007). www.reclaimcivilrights.org/resources/timeline/.

Rogers, D. (2000, March). To the top—Designing disabled-friendly challenge courses. *Parks & Recreation.* http://findarticles.com/p/articles/mi_m1145/is_3_35/ai_61793380.

Sousa, D. (2000). *How the brain learns* (2nd ed.). Thousand Oaks, CA: Corwin Press.

U.S. Department of the Interior, Fish and Wildlife Service, and U.S. Department of Commerce, U.S. Census Bureau. (2006). 2006 national survey of fishing, hunting, and wildlife-associated recreation. www.census.gov/prod/2008pubs/fhw06-nat.pdf .

Ventegodt, S., Merrick, J., & Anderson, N.J. (2003). Quality of life theory III. Maslow revisited. *Scientific World Journal, 3,* 1050-1057.

Weisman, L. (1999). Creating justice, sustaining life: The role of universal design in the 21st century www.adaptiveenvironments.org/index.php?option=Resource&articleid=151.

Winter, P.L. (2007). Equity in access to recreation opportunities: A synthesis of research and management implications. In L.E. Kruger, R. Mazza, & K. Lawrence (Eds.), *Proceedings: National Workshop on Recreation Research and Management* (General Technical Report PNW-GTR-698) (pp. 167-180). Portland, OR: U.S. Department of Agriculture, Forest Service, Pacific Northwest Research Station.

Chapter 9

Geiser, R.L. (1976). *Behavior modification and the managed society.* Boston: Beacon Press.

History. (2008). Fresno, CA: Break the Barriers. www.breakthebarriers.org/history.htm.

Lavay, B.W., French, R., and Henderson, H.L. (1997). *Positive behavior management strategies for physical educators.* Champaign, IL: Human Kinetics.

Stensrud, C. (1993). *A training manual for Americans with disabilities act compliance in parks and recreation settings.* State College, PA: Venture.

Wehmeyer, M.L. (1998). National survey of the use of assistive technology by adults with mental retardation. *Mental Retardation, 36*(1), 44-51.

Chapter 10

Access to Recreation. (2009). Recreation opportunities for people of all ages and all abilities. www.AccesstoRecreation.org.

Adventure playground. (2009). Irvine, CA: City of Irvine. www.ci.irvine.ca.us/depts/cs/commparks/specialfac/ap/default.asp.

Adventure playground. (n.d.). Berkeley, CA: City of Berkeley. www.ci.berkeley.ca.us/ContentDisplay.aspx?id=8656.

American Academy of Pediatrics. (n.d.). *New AAP report stresses play for healthy development.* Elk Grove Village, IL: Author. www.aap.org/pressroom/play-public.htm.

American Academy of Pediatrics via Kenneth R. Ginsburg and the Committee on Communications and the Committee on Psychosocial Aspects of Child and Family Health. (2007). The importance of play in promoting healthy child development and maintaining strong parent-child bonds. *Pediatrics, Vol. 119,* p. 182-191.

Brown, S., with C. Vaughan. (2009). *Play: How it shapes the brain, opens the imagination, and invigorates the soul.* New York: Avery-Penguin.

Gill, T. (2007). *No fear: Growing up in a risk averse society.* London: Calouste Gulbenkian Foundation. www.gulbenkian.org.uk/publications/education/no-fear.

Henry J. Kaiser Family Foundation. (2005). *Generation M: Media in the lives of 8–18-year-olds.* Menlo Park, CA: Author.

Hofferth, S. (2008). American children's outdoor and indoor leisure time. In E. Goodenough (Ed.), *A place for play* (p. 42). Carmel Valley, CA: National Institute for Play.

Huntington beach adventure playground. (2009). www.beachcalifornia.com/adventure-playground-kids-vacation.html.

Montague, A. (1981). *Growing young.* New York: McGraw-Hill.

Play. (2006). Cardiff, Wales: Play Wales. www.play-wales.org.uk/landing.asp?id=3.

Play deprivation. (2006). Cardiff, Wales: Play Wales. www.playwales.org.uk/landing.asp?id=3.

Playwork. (n.d.). College Park, MD: Alliance for Childhood. www.allianceforchildhood.org/playwork.

U.S. Access Board. (2009). A federal agency committed to accessible design. www.access-board.gov.

Wenner, M. (2009, January). The serious need for play. *Scientific American Mind,* pp. 22-29. www.sciam.com/article.cfm?id=the-serious-need-for-play.

Wild Zones. (2008). www.wild-zone.net.

Wilson, F. (1998). *The hand.* New York: Pantheon Books.

Wilson, P. (2009). Playworkers and the adventure play movement. In E. Goodenough (Ed.), *Where do the children play?* College Park, MD: Alliance for Childhood.

Chapter 11

Block, M. (2000). A teacher's guide to including students with disabilities in regular physical education (3rd ed.). Cincinnati, OH: Brookes.

Davis, R. (2002). Inclusion through sports: A guide to enhancing sport experiences. Champaign, IL: Human Kinetics.

Kasser, S.L., & Lytle, R.K. (2005). Inclusive physical activity: A lifetime of opportunities. Champaign, IL: Human Kinetics.

Morris, D., & Stiehl, J. (1999). Changing kids's games (2nd ed.). Champaign, IL: Human Kinetics.

Winnick, J. (2005). Adapted physical education and sport (4th ed.). Champaign, IL: Human Kinetics.

Chapter 12

Albrecht, G.L., Seelman, K.D., & Bury, M. (Eds.). (2001). *Handbook of disability studies.* Thousand Oaks, CA: Sage.

American College of Sports Medicine. (2005). *ACSM's guidelines for exercise testing and prescription* (7th ed.). Philadelphia: Lippincott Williams & Wilkins.

Banz, W.J., Maher, M.A., Thompson, W.G., Bassett, D.R., Moore, W., Ashraf, M., Keefer, D.J., & Zemel, M.B. (2003). Effects of resistance versus aerobic training on coronary artery disease risk factors. *Experimental Biology and Medicine, 228*(4), 434-440.

Benson, V., & Marano, M.A. (1996). Vital and health statistics: Current estimates from the National Health Interview Survey, 1995. *Data From the National Health Survey, 10*(199). www.cdc.gov/nchs/data/series/sr_10/sr10_199acc.pdf.

Blair, S.N., Cheng, Y., & Holder, J.S. (2001). Is physical activity or physical fitness more important in defining health benefits? *Medicine and Science in Sports and Exercise, 33*(6), S379-S399.

Boslaugh, S.E., & Andresen, E.M. (2006). Correlates of physical activity for adults with disability. *Preventing Chronic Disease, 3*(3), A78.

Cardinal, B.J., & Spaziani, M.D. (2003). ADA compliance and the accessibility of physical activity facilities in Western Oregon. *American Journal of Health Promotion, 18*(3), 197-201.

Caspersen, C.J., Powell, K.E., & Christenson, G.M. (1985). Physical activity, exercise, and physical fitness: Definitions and distinctions for health-related research. *Public Health Reports, 100*(2), 126-131.

Centers for Disease Control and Prevention. (2006a). Environmental barriers to health care among persons with disabilities—Los Angeles County, California, 2002-2003. *Morbidity and Mortality Weekly Report, 55,* 1300-1303.

Centers for Disease Control and Prevention. (2006b). *The imperative of public health in the lives of people with disabilities.* Atlanta: Author.

Centers for Disease Control and Prevention. (2007). Physical activity among adults with a disability—United States, 2005. *Morbidity and Mortality Weekly Report, 56*(39), 1021-1024.

Dickens-Smith, M. (1995). *The effect of inclusion training on teacher attitude towards inclusion.* http://eric.ed.gov/ERICDocs/data/ericdocs2sql/content_storage_01/0000019b/80/13/d1/99.pdf.

Donnelly, J.E., Jacobsen, D.J., Snyder Heelan, K., Seip, R., & Smith, S. (2000). The effects of 18 months of intermittent vs. continuous exercise on aerobic capacity, body weight and composition, and metabolic fitness in previously sedentary, moderately obese females. *International Journal of Obesity and Related Metabolic Disorders, 24*(5), 566-572.

Eriksson, K.F., & Lindgärde, F. (1991). Prevention of type 2 (non-insulin dependent) diabetes mellitus by diet and physical exercise. The 6-year Malmö feasibility study. *Diabetologia, 34*(12), 891-898.

Handy, S.L., Boarnet, M.G., Ewing, R., & Killingsworth, R.E. (2002). How the built environment affects physical activity: Views from urban planning. *American Journal of Preventive Medicine, 23*(2), 64-73.

Heward, W.L. (2000). *Exceptional children. An introduction to special education.* Englewood Cliffs, NJ: Prentice Hall.

Koplan, J.P., Liverman, C.T., & Kraak, V.L. (2005). Preventing childhood obesity: Health in the balance: Executive summary. *Journal of the American Dietetic Association, 105*(1), 131-138.

McGuire, L.C., Strine, T.W., Okoro, C.A., Ahluwalia, I.B., & Ford, E.S. (2007). Healthy lifestyle behaviors among older U.S. adults with and without disabilities: Behavioral risk factor surveillance system, 2003. *Preventing Chronic Disease, 4*(1), A09.

Miller, W.R., Rollnick, S., & Conforti, K. (2002). *Motivational interviewing: Preparing people for change.* New York: Guilford.

Murphy, J. (2006). Perceptions of communication between people with communication disability and general practice staff. *Health Expectations, 9,* 49-59.

Nary, D.E., Froehlich, A.K., & White, G.W. (2000). Accessibility of fitness facilities for persons with disabilities using wheelchairs. *Topics in Spinal Cord Injury Rehabilitation, 6*(1), 87-98.

National Archives and Records Administration. (2002, September 3). Americans with Disabilities Act accessibility guidelines for buildings and facilities (ADAAG). www.access-board.gov/recreation/final.htm.

National Center on Physical Activity and Disability. (2005). Exercise guidelines for people with disabilities. www.ncpad.org/exercise/fact_sheet.php?sheet=15&view=all.

National Center on Physical Activity and Disability. (2006). You're here? Now what? Making self-advocacy work for you in recreation settings. www.ncpad.org/fun/fact_sheet.php?sheet=318.

National Center on Physical Activity and Disability. (2008). Designing for inclusive play: Applying the principles of universal design to the playground. www.ncpad.org/fun/fact_sheet.php?sheet=592&view=all.

National Center on Physical Activity and Disability. (2009). Multiple sclerosis: Designing an exercise program. www.ncpad.org/disability/fact_sheet.php?sheet=187&section=1442.

North Carolina Office on Disability and Health (NCODH) and Center for Universal Design. (2002). Removing barriers to health clubs and fitness facilities: A guide for accommodating all members, including people with disabilities and older adults. www.fpg.unc.edu/~ncodh/pdfs/rbfitness.pdf.

Ottawa Charter for Health Promotion. (1986, November 21). First International Conference on Health Promotion. www.who.int/hpr/NPH/docs/ottawa_charter_hp.pdf.

Ravesloot, C., Seekins, T., & White, G. (2005). Living Well With a Disability health promotion intervention: Improved health status for consumers and lower costs for health care policymakers. *Rehabilitation Psychology*, 50(3), 239-245.

Rimmer, J.H. (2005a). The conspicuous absence of people with disabilities in public fitness and recreation facilities: Lack of interest or lack of access? *American Journal of Health Promotion*, 19(5), 327-329.

Rimmer, J.H. (2005b). Exercise and physical activity in persons aging with a physical disability. *Physical Medicine and Rehabilitation Clinics of North America*, 16(1), 41-56.

Rimmer, J.H., Riley, B., Wang, E., Rauworth, A., & Jurkowski, J. (2004). Physical activity participation among persons with disabilities: Barriers and facilitators. *American Journal of Preventive Medicine*, 26(5), 419-425.

Rimmer, J.H., & Wang, E. (2005). Obesity prevalence among a group of Chicago residents with disabilities. *Archives of Physical Medicine and Rehabilitation*, 86(7), 1461-1464.

Scelza, W.M., Kalpakjian, C.Z., Zemper, E.D., & Tate, D.G. (2005). Perceived barriers to exercise in people with spinal cord injury. *American Journal of Physical Medicine & Rehabilitation*, 84(8), 576-583.

U.S. 101st Congress. Americans with Disabilities Act, 1990.

U.S. Department of Health & Human Services. (2000). *Healthy People 2010*. (2nd ed.) Washington, DC: U.S. Government Printing Office.

U.S. Department of Health & Human Services. (2005). *The 2005 Surgeon General's call to action to improve the health and wellness of persons with disabilities*. Washington, DC: Office of the Surgeon General.

U.S. Department of Health and Human Services. (2008). *2008 physical activity guidelines for Americans*. http://pag.airhealthprojects.org/paguidelines/guidelines/summary.aspx.

U.S. Department of Health & Human Services. (n.d.). *Healthy People 2010*. Chapter 6: Disability and secondary conditions. www.healthypeople.gov/document/HTML/Volume1/06Disability.htm.

United Nations General Assembly. (2006, December 13). *United Nations convention and optional protocol on the rights of persons with disabilities*. UN Doc. A/61/611. http://untreaty.un.org/English/notpubl/IV_15_english.pdf.

Weil, E., Wachterman, M., McCarthy, E.P., Davis, R.B., O'Day, B., Lezzoni, L.I., et al. (2002). Obesity among adults with disabling conditions. *Journal of the American Medical Association, 288*(10), 1265-1268

World Health Organization. (1980). International classification of impairments, disabilities and handicaps: A manual of classification relating to the consequences of disease. Geneva: Author.

World Health Organization. (2001). The world health report 2001: Mental health: New understanding, new hope. www.who.int/entity/whr/2001/en/whr01_en.pdf.

World Health Organization. (2002). The world health report 2002: Reducing risks, promoting healthy life. www.who.int/whr/2002/en/whr02_en.pdf.

Wyatt, S.B., Winters, K.P. & Dubbert, P.M. (2006). Overweight and obesity: Prevalence, consequences, and causes of a growing public health problem. *American Journal of the Medical Sciences, 331*(4), 166-174.

Chapter 13

Americans for the Arts. (2009). Arts & economic prosperity. www.artsusa.org/information_services/research/services/economic_impact/default.asp.

Bruner, J. (1985). Narrative and paradigmatic modes of thought. In E. Eisner (Ed.), *Learning and teaching the ways of knowing: Eighty-fourth yearbook of the National Society for the Study of Education* (pp. 97-116). Chicago: University of Chicago Press.

Callahan, S. (2004). *Singing our praises: Case studies in the art of evaluation*. Washington, DC: Association of Performing Arts Presenters.

Center for Universal Design. (2008). Principles of universal design. Raleigh, NC: Center for Universal Design. www.design.ncsu.edu/cud/pubs_p/docs/poster.pdf.

Cross, T., Bazron, B., Dennis, K., & Isaacs, M. (1989). *Towards a culturally competent system of care, Vol. I*. Washington, DC: Georgetown University Child Development Center.

Csikszentmihalyi, M. (1990). *Flow: The psychology of optimal experience*. New York: Harper & Row.

Dewey, J. (1980). *Art as experience*. New York: Perigee. (Original work published 1934)

Diller, J., & Moule, J. (2005). *Cultural competence: a primer for educators*. Belmont, CA: Thomason Learning.

Ellis, R. (2005, April 20). Shadow signing brings play to life [review of the play *Children of a Lesser God*]. *Florida Ledger Correspondent*, www.theledger.com/article/20050420/NEWS/504200308?Title=-Shadow-Signing-Brings-Play-to-Life.

Eisner, E. (Ed.). (1985). Aesthetic modes of knowing. *Learning and teaching the ways of knowing: Eighty-fourth yearbook of the National Society for the Study of Education*. Chicago: University of Chicago Press.

Erickson, B. (2008). The crisis in culture and inequality. In S.J. Tepper & B. Ivey (Eds.), *Engaging art: The next great transformation of America's cultural life* (pp. 343-363). New York: Routledge.

Florida, R. (2002). *The rise of the creative class*. New York: Harper Collins

Gardner, H. (1983). *Frames of mind: The theory of multiple intelligences*. New York: Basic Books.

Greene, M. (1977). Toward a wide awakeness: An argument for the arts and humanities in education. *Teacher's College Record, 79*(1), 119-125.

Gupta, K., Sleezer, C., & Russ-Eft, D. (2007). *A practical guide to needs assessment* (2nd ed.). San Francisco: Wiley.

Ivey, R. (2001). Foreword. In W. Preisser & E. Ostroff (Eds.), *Universal design handbook* (pp. xvi-xvii). New York: McGraw-Hill.

Kendt, R. (2005, January 14). Review of the musical *Big River. Los Angeles Times*, www.deafwest.org/productions/review.html#latimes.

Killacky, J.R. (2005, October). The emergent ability discourse. Keynote address presented at the Kennedy Center Leadership Exchange in Arts and Disability Training Conference, Scottsdale, AZ. www.sff.org/programs/arts-culture/Disability_Keynote.pdf

L.A. Goal (2004). *Disabled fables: Aesop's Fables retold and illustrated by artists with developmental disabilities*. New York: Star Bright Books.

Mace, R. (2008). Center for Universal Design, College of Design, North Carolina State University. Accessed on the Web August 19, 2009. http://www.design.ncsu.edu/cud/about_ud/about_ud.htm

McNeil, J.M. (1997). *Americans with disabilities: 1994-1995*. U.S. Bureau of the Census Current Population Reports, P70-61. Washington, DC: U.S. Government Printing Office.

Muxworthy Feige, D. (1999). The legacy of Gregory Bateson: Envisioning aesthetic epistemologies and praxis. In J. Kane (Ed.), *Education, information, and transformation: Essays on learning and thinking* (pp. 77-111). Upper Saddle River, NJ: Prentice Hall.

National Assembly of State Arts Agencies. (2003) *Design for accessibility: A cultural administrator's handbook*. Washington, DC: Author.

National Center on Accessible Information Technology in Education. (2008). www.washington.edu/accessit/articles?1079.

National Endowment for the Arts. (2004). *Outcome-based evaluation: A working model for arts projects*. www.nea.gov/grants/apply/out/faq.html#16.

National Endowment for the Arts. (2008). *Artists in the workforce, 1990-2005*. www.nea.gov/research/researchreports_chrono.html.

Patton, M. (2002). *Qualitative research and evaluation methods* (3rd ed.), Thousand Oaks, CA: Sage.

Preskill, H., & Catsambas, T. (2006). *Reframing evaluation through appreciative inquiry*. Thousand Oaks, CA: Sage.

U.S. Census Bureau. (2008). Number of Americans With a Disability Reaches 54.4 Million. *U.S. Census Bureau Press Release, December 18, 2008*. Retrieved August 9, 2009, from www.census.gov/Press-Release/www/releases/archives/income_wealth/013041.html.

VSA Arts. (2008). *The contours of inclusion: Frameworks and tools for evaluating arts in education*. www.vsarts.org/x1370.xml.

Chapter 14

Baun, M.B.P. (2008). *Fantastic water workouts: Proven exercises and routines for toning, fitness, and health* (2nd ed.). Champaign, IL: Human Kinetics.

Block, M.E., & Conatser, P. (2002). Adapted aquatics and inclusion. *Journal of Physical Education, Recreation & Dance, 73(5)*, 31-34.

Conaster, P., & Block, M.E. (2001). Factors that improve aquatics instructor's belief's toward inclusion. *Therapeutic Recreation Journal, 35*(2), 170-184.

Conaster, P., Block, M.E., & Lepore, M. (2000). Aquatic's instructor's attitude toward teaching students with disabilities. *Adapted Physical Activity Quarterly, 17*, 173-183.

DePauw, K.P. (2000). Social-cultural context of disability: Implications for scientific inquiry and professional practice. *Quest, 52*, 358-368.

Dulcy, F.H. (1983). Aquatic programs for disabled children. *Physical and Occupational Therapy in Pediatrics, 3*, 21-38.

Hardin, B. (2005). Physical education teachers' reflections on preparation for inclusion. *The Physical Educator, 62*(1), 45-56.

Koury, J.M. (1996). *Aquatic therapy programming*. Champaign, IL: Human Kinetics.

Lepore, M., Gayle, G.W., & Stevens, S. (2007). *Adapted aquatics programming: A professional guide* (2nd ed.). Champaign, IL: Human Kinetics.

Mossten M., & Ashworth, S. (1986). *Teaching physical education* (3rd ed.) Columbus, OH: Merrill.

Munguia-Izquierdo, D., & Legaz-Arrese, A. (2007). Exercise in warm water decreases pain and improves cognitive function in middle-aged women with fibromyalgia. *Physical Education and Sports, 25*(6), 823-830.

Piotrowska-Całka, E., & Guszkowska, M. (2007). Effects of aqua-aerobic on the emotional states of women. *Physical Education and Sport, 51*,11-14.

Schleien, S., & Rynders, J. (1998). Inclusive recreation: A parent's guide to quality. *TASH Newsletter, 24*(4), 18-19.
Scott, K. (Ed.) (1990). *The Americans with Disabili-*

ties Act: An analysis. Silver Springs, MD: Business Publishers.

See, Julie. (2009). DCAC Fitness Education Conference, Houston, TX.

Tidhar D, Katz-Leurer M. Aqua lymphatic therapy in women who suffer from breast cancer treatment-related lymphedema: a randomized controlled study. Support Care Cancer. 2009 Jun 3.

U.S. Access Board (2003). *Accessible swimming pools and spas: A summary of accessibility guidelines for recreation facilities.* Washington, DC: U.S. Access Board. www.access-board.gov/recreation/guides/pools.htm#Accessible.

Chapter 15

Anderson, L., & Kress, C. (2003). *Inclusion: Including people with disabilities in parks and recreation purposes.* State College, PA: Venture.

Blake, J. (1996). Opening doors: Integration of persons with a disability in organized children's camping in Canada. *Journal of Leisurability, 23*(2), 3-10.

Blanchard, J., Strong, M., & Ford, P. (2007). *Leadership and administration of outdoor pursuits.* State College, PA: Venture.

Brannan, S., Fullerton, A., Arick J., Robb, G., & Bender, M., (2003). *Including youth with disabilities in outdoor programs: Best practices, outcomes and resources.* Champaign, IL: Sagamore.

Edmondson, D. (2006). *Black and brown faces in America's wild places: African Americans making nature and the environment a part of their everyday lives.* Cambridge, MA: Adventure Publications.

Hansen, E. (2000, summer). Sacred Lands. *Points West Online.* www.bbhc.org/pointsWest/PWArticle.cfm?ArticleID=72.

Hegerl, G.C., Zwiers, F.W., Braconnot, P., Gillett, N.P., Luo, Y., Marengo, J.A., Orsini, N., Nicholls, N., Penner, J.E., & Stott, P.A. (2007). Understanding and attributing climate change. In S. Solomon, D. Qin, M. Manning, Z. Chen, M. Marquis, K.B. Averyt, M. Tignor, & H.L. Miller (Eds.), *Climate change 2007: The physical science basis. Contribution of Working Group I to the Fourth Assessment Report of the Intergovernmental Panel on Climate Change* (pp. 663-745).Cambridge, UK, and New York: Cambridge University Press.

Hutchison, P., Mecke, T., & Sharpe, E. (2008). Partners in inclusion in a residential summer camp: A case study. *Therapeutic Recreation Journal, 42*(3), 181-198.

Jenkins, M. (2006, August). The hard way: Because it's sacred. *Outside Magazine.* http://outside.away.com/outside/features/200608/devils-tower-national-monument-1.html.

Louv, R. (2006). *Last child in the woods: Saving our children from nature-deficit disorder.* Chapel Hill, NC: Algonquin Books.

McAvoy, L.H., Schatz, E.C., Stutz, M.E., Schleien, S.J., & Lais, G. (1989). Integrated wilderness adventure: Effects on personal and lifestyle traits of persons with and without disabilities. *Therapeutic Recreation Journal, 23*(3), 51-64.

Merriam-Webster Online Thesaurus (n.d.). www.merriam-webster.com/thesaurus/guy.

National Institutes of Health. (n.d.). *Fact sheet: Disability in older adults.* www.nih.gov/about/researchresults-forthepublic/DisabilityinOlderAdults.pdf.

Outdoor Industry Foundation. (2006, March 22). *Hispanic community and outdoor recreation.* Boulder, CO: UCLA Anderson School of Management Applied Management Research Program.

Outdoor Industry Foundation (2006, June). Outdoor Recreation Participation Study (8th edition for year 2005). Boulder, CO: Leisure Trends.

United States Orienteering Federation. (2008). Orienteering: The sport of a lifetime. www.us.orienteering.org.

Chapter 16

Austin, D.R. (2004). *Therapeutic recreation processes and techniques* (5th ed.). Champaign, IL: Sagamore.

Brannan, S., Fullerton, A., Arick, J., Robb, G., & Bender, M. (2003). *Including youth with disabilities in outdoor programs.* Champaign, IL: Sagamore.

Bronson, J., Gibson, S., Kishar, R., & Priest, S. (1992). Evaluation of team development in a corporate adventure training program. *Journal of Experiential Education, 15,* 50-53.

Carlson, J.A., & K. Evans. 2001. Whose choice is it? Contemplating challenge-by choice and diverse-abilities. *Journal of Experiential Education, 24,* 58-63.

Csíkszentmiháli, M. (1975). *Beyond boredom and anxiety.* San Francisco: Jossey-Bass.

Dattilo, J. 2002. *Inclusive leisure services: Responding to the rights of people with disabilities.* State College, PA: Venture.

Davis-Berman, J., & D. Berman. 2002. Risk and anxiety in adventure programming. *Journal of Experiential Education, 25,* 305-310.

Devine, M., & Dattilo, J. (2000). The relationship between social acceptance and leisure lifestyles of people with disabilities. *Therapeutic Recreation Journal, 34,* 306-322.

Dillenschneider, C. (2007). Integrating persons with impairments and disabilities into standard outdoor adventure education programs. *Journal of Experiential Education, 30*(1), 70-83.

Driver, B.L., Brown, P.J., & Peterson, G.L. (Eds.). (1991). *Benefits of leisure.* State College, PA: Venture.

Ewert, A. (1989). *Outdoor adventure pursuits: Foundations, models, and theories.* Scottsdale, AZ: Publishing Horizons.

Ewert, A., Attarian, A., Hollenhorst, S., Russell, K., & Voight, A. (2006). Evolving adventure pursuits on public lands: Emerging challenges for management and public policy. *Journal of Park and Recreation Administration, 24*(2), 125-140.

Ewert, A., & Hollenhorst, S. (1989). Testing the adventure model: Empirical support for a model of risk recreation participation. *Journal of Leisure Research, 21*(2), 124-139.

Goldenberg, M.A., Klenosky, D.B., O'Leary, J.T., & Templin, T.J. (2000). A means-end investigation of challenge course experiences. *Journal of Leisure Research, 32,* 208-224.

Kolb, D.A. (1984). *Experiential learning: Experience as the source of learning and development.* Englewood Cliffs, NJ: Prentice Hall.

Kuhn, T.S. (1970). *The structure of scientific revolutions* (2nd ed.). Chicago: University of Chicago Press.

Luckner, J.L., & Nadler, R.S. (1997). *Processing the experience: Strategies to enhance and generalize learning* (2nd ed.). Dubuque, IA: Kendall/Hunt.

Martin, B., Cashel, C., Wagstaff, M., & Breunig, M. (2006). *Outdoor leadership: Theory and practice.* Champaign, IL: Human Kinetics.

Maxwell, J. (1997). Increasing work group effectiveness: Combining corporate adventure training with traditional team building methods. *Journal of Experiential Education, 20,* 26-33.

Maxwell, J.C. (2000). *Failing forward: How to make the most of your mistakes.* Nashville, TN: Nelson.

McAvoy, L., Smith, J., & Rynders, J. (2006). Outdoor adventure programming for individuals with cognitive disabilities who present serious accommodation challenges. *Therapeutic Recreation Journal, 40*(3), 182-199.

McCormick, B., Voight, A., & Ewert, A. (2000). Therapeutic outdoor programming: Theoretical connections between adventure and therapy. In K. Richards & B. Smith (Eds.), *Therapy within adventure* (pp. 155-174). Augsburg, Germany: Ziel.

Meyer, B.B. (2000). The ropes and challenge course: A quasi-experimental examination. *Perceptual and Motor Skills, 90,* 1249-1257.

Priest, S. (1995). The effect of belaying and belayer type on the development of interpersonal partnership trust in rock climbing. *Journal of Experiential Education, 18,* 107-109.

Priest, S. (1996a). Developing organizational trust: Comparing the effects of challenge courses and group initiatives. *Journal of Experiential Education, 19,* 37-39.

Priest, S. (1996b). The effect of two different debriefing approaches on developing self-confidence. *Journal of Experiential Education, 19,* 40-42.

Priest, S. (1998). Physical challenge and the development of trust through corporate adventure training. *Journal of Experiential Education, 21,* 31-34.

Priest, S., & Lesperance, M.A. (1994). Time series trends in corporate team development. *Journal of Experiential Education, 17,* 34-39.

Quezada, R.L., & Christopherson, R.W.. (2005). Adventure-based service learning: University students' self-reflection accounts of service with children. *Journal of Experiential Education, 28,* 1-16.

Rohnke, K., Wall, J.B., Tait, C.M., & Rogers, D. (2003). *The complete ropes course manual* (3rd ed.). Dubuque, IA: Kendall/Hunt.

Rohnke, K. (1989). *Cowtails and cobras II.* Dubuque, IA: Kendall/Hunt.

U.S. Department of the Interior, Conservation and Recreation Service. (1980). *A guide to designing accessible outdoor recreation facilities.* Ann Arbor, MI: Heritage.

Vincent, S.M. (1995). Emotional safety in adventure therapy programs: Can it be defined? *Journal of Experiential Education, 18,* 76-81.

Wang, Y, and R. Rodgers. (2006). Impact of service-learning and social justice education on college students' cognitive development. *NASPA Journal, 43,* 316-337.

Weiner, B. (1974). (Ed.). *Achievement motivation and attribution theory.* Morristown, NJ: General Learning Press.

Weiner, B. (1980). *Human motivation.* New York: Rinehart & Winston.

Wolfe, B.D., & Samdahl, D.M. (2005). Challenging assumptions: Examining fundamental beliefs that shape challenge course programming and research. *Journal of Experiential Education, 28,* 25-43.

Woodbury Reports. (2003). *Outdoor Behavioral Healthcare Research Cooperative (OBHRC) launches second research study.* Bonners Ferry, ID: Woodbury Reports.

Yerkes, R. (1985). High adventure recreation in organized camping. *Trends, 22*(3), 10-11.

Chapter 17

American Hotel and Lodging Association. (2000). *2000 summary report of the survey of usage of accessible hotel guestrooms by travelers with disabilities.* Washington, DC: AHLA.

Avis, A.H., Card, J.A., & Cole, S.T. (2005). Accessibility and attitudinal barriers encountered by travelers with physical disabilities. *Tourism Review International, 8*(3), 239-248.

Bi, Y.H., Card, J.A., & Cole, S.T. (2007). Accessibility and attitudinal barriers encountered by Chinese travelers with physical disabilities. *International Journal of Tourism Research, 9,* 205-216.

Center for Universal Design. (1997). *The principles of university design, version 2.0*. Raleigh, NC: North Carolina State University.

China Disabled Persons' Federation. (2009). Law on the protection of persons with disabilities. www.cdpf.org.cn/english/lawsdoc/content/2008-04/10/content_25056081.htm.

U.S. Department of Justice. (2008). Customers with disabilities mean business. www.ada.gov/busstat.htm.

Digh, P. (1998, March). America's largest untapped market: Who they are, the potential they represent. *Fortune Magazine*. www.lbln.org/news/Eletwhoarethey.doc.

Fennel, D.A. (1999). *Ecotourism: An introduction*. New York: Routledge.

Israeli, A.A. (2002). A preliminary investigation of the importance of site accessibility factors for disabled tourists. *Journal of Travel Research, 41*(1), 101-104.

McGovern, J.N. (1992). *The ADA self-evaluation: A handbook for compliance with the Americans with Disabilities Act by parks and recreation agencies*. Arlington, VA: National Recreation and Park Association.

National Park Service. (2003, December). *Ethnic and racial diversity of National Park System visitors and non-visitors technical report*. Flagstaff, AZ: National Park Service Social Science Program, Northern Arizona University.

Open Doors Organization. (2005). Details of the market studies. http://opendoorsnfp.org/_wsn/page3.html.

Smith, R.W., Austin, D., Kennedy, D.W., Lee, Y., & Hutchinson, P. (2005). *Inclusive and special recreation: Opportunities for persons with disabilities*. Boston: McGraw-Hill.

Takeda, K., & Card, J.A. (2002). U.S. tour operators and travel agencies: Barriers encountered when providing package tours to people who have difficulties walking. *Journal of Travel & Tourism Marketing, 12*(1), 47-61.

Tamparo, C., & Lindh, W. (2008). *Therapeutic communications for health care* (3rd ed.). Clifton Park, NY: Thomson Delmar Learning.

Travel Industry Association. (2008). U.S. travel market overview: travel volumes and trends. www.tia.org/researchpubs/us_overview_volumes_trends.html.

Turco, D., Stumbo, N., & Garncarz, J. (1998). Tourism constraints for people with disabilities. *Parks & Recreation, 33*, 78-84.

United Nations World Tourism Organization. (2008, January). UNWTO World Tourism Barometer, 6(1). www.unwto.org/facts/eng/pdf/barometer/UNWTO_Barom08_1_en.pdf.

U.S. Census Bureau. (2000). Disability status: 2000. www.census.gov/hhes/www/disability/disabstat2k/disabstat2ktxt.html.

U.S. Census Bureau. (2005, July). Disability and American families: 2000. *Census 2000 Special Reports*. Washington, DC: Author.

Valli, C. (2005). *The Gallaudet dictionary of American Sign Language*. Washington, DC: Gallaudet University Press.

World Health Organization. (2003). *Access to rehabilitation for the 600 million people living with disabilities*. www.who.int/mediacentre/news/notes/2003/np24/en/index.html.

Yau, M., McKercher, B., & Packer, T. (2004). Traveling with a disability: More than an access issue. *Annals of Tourism Research, 31*(4), 946-960.

Index

Note: The italicized *f* and *t* following page numbers refer to figures and tables, respectively.

play spaces. *See* playgrounds
post-polio syndrome 366
poverty
   constraints on participation in leisure and 106, 107-108
   number and characteristics of people in 106, 107f
   poverty thresholds 106
   provision of leisure services for 108
Power of 504, The (www.npr.org/programs/wesun/features/2002/504/) 32
Prader-Willi syndrome 366-367
Priest, Simon 319
program management issues
   behavior management 169, 170t-171t, 171-172
   communication style 168-169, 169t
   fees 167
   scholarships and sliding fees 167
   site selection 167, 168
   transportation 168
public perceptions inclusion
   attitudes 65-67, 65f, 66f
   humanistic and ecological philosophies 64-65
   legal mandates 64
public policies of sport and leisure in Brazil
   award for social inclusion in Brazilian sports and leisure 38
   Bolsa-Athletes Program 37-38
   Law of Incentive to Sports 37
   Ministry of Sports 36
   Program Painting the Citizenship 38
   Program Painting the Freedom 38
   Program Sport and Leisure of the City (PELC) 36-37
   Second Time Program 37
   social rights 36

R

Rabinowitz, Erik 81
race and ethnicity
   defining 94
   ethnic and racial minorities, spatial distribution of 95, 96f-99f
   leisure participation patterns and styles 98, 99, 100
   segregation among 97, 98
   sociodemographics of U.S. 94-95
   socioeconomic profile of 96, 97
Rauworth, Amy 209
recreation leaders
   awareness of clients' worldview 25-26
   cultural values and biases 24-25
Reis, Arianne 36
Rett syndrome (RS) 367
Robertson, Terry 61, 294
Rodrigues, Rejane Penna 36
Rustle (Meuhlbaeur) 241, 242f

S

Salman, Shiekh 260
Scholl, Kathleen G. 19, 119, 190
Scientific American 178
"The Serious Need for Play" (Wenner, *Scientific American*) 178
Shimron, Yonat 260
Siegel, Betty 342-343
Smith, Ralph 301
social barriers, removing
   Maslow's hierarchy of needs 143
   sense of empowerment 145
   sense of safety and belonging 143-144
   social acceptance 143
spina bifida 367-368
spinal cord injury (SCI) 368
sport activities for inclusion, modifying
   FAMME and game design models 203-205, 204t-206t
   including everyone, steps for 197-198, 199t-202t, 200
sports for people with disabilities. *See also* sport activities for inclusion, modifying
   adapted sport 195, 196
   classification in 196-197
   differently-abled participants 194
   disability sport 195
   functional classification system 196-197
   medical system of classification 196
   overview of 194
   paradigm distinction within 194-196
   recreation leaders, opportunities for 197
Sports 'n Spokes (www.pvamagazines.com/sns/) 85
Sprout 242
staff training for inclusion. *See also* inclusion in recreation setting; inclusion processes
   accommodations 126-127
   biases 126
   collaborating with community 127, 128
   practices, committing to 124
   recreation provider, role of 120
   respect, language for 124-125, 125t
   social ecological theory 120-121, 120f
   training, importance of 124-128
Starr, Ellen Gates 22
Steedly, Kathlyn M. 233
Stodolska, Monika 93
Stopka, Christine 207
stroke 369
summer camps
   camp culture 294-295
   camp logistics and adapted equipment 298

   camp programming 298
   camp staff, preparing 295-296
   camps, types of 299
   culture of inclusion 295
   disability and barriers 297-298
   disability-related considerations 296-298
   inclusion, challenges with promoting 294
   inclusive identity 295
   program leaders and problatunities 294
   self-segregation 298-299
Swann-Guerrero, Sheila 209

T

Therapeutic Recreation Journal 121
traumatic brain injury (TBI) 369-370
travel and tourism. *See also* accommodation for people with special needs; barriers in recreation and tourism
   access rights and universal design 340-343
   disability statistics in tourism 333-334
   inclusive tourism 333-334
   inclusive travel 332-333
   industry 332
   international legislation and rights of people with disabilities 343-344

U

universal design. *See also* barriers, removing; universal recreation access process
   for challenge course programming 141-142, 141t
   civil rights legislation for 145-147
   concept of 138
   defining 12, 13
   environments built prior to mid 1990s 138-139
   for a just society 142
   principles of 139, 139t-140t, 140
   social factors, considerations for 140-141
universal recreation access process
   Access to Recreation Initiative 147
   ADA minimal technical requirements 149
   archery range and beaches and waterfronts 154
   boardwalks 154
   canoe, kayak, and boat launches and campgrounds 154
   design concepts, applying 149, 150
   environments, designing 147-150, 149t
   fishing dock or pier and observation or viewing decks 152
   hiking trails, nature trails, walkways, pathways 150

About the Contributors

Joan Almon was a Waldorf preschool and kindergarten teacher in Maryland for nearly 20 years and then spent 10 years traveling internationally, teaching about early childhood and the importance of play. In 1999 she became co-founder and director of the U.S. branch of the Alliance for Childhood, which addresses the decline in children's health and well-being. Through public education and advocacy, the Alliance works with educators, health professionals, recreation workers, parents, and others to restore creative play to the lives of children. It has introduced the role of playworkers in the United States and co-hosts workshops across the country on play and playwork, with a special focus on inclusive play.

Cindy Burkhour, MA, CTRS, CPRP, is a certified therapeutic recreation specialist and certified park and recreation professional who has consulted around the country on a variety of recreation issues. Cindy has consulted in the areas of inclusive recreation, universal design, and the Americans with Disabilities Act (ADA). She helps recreation providers to design universally accessible recreation facilities, programs, and services, to include persons with disabilities in typical recreation programs and to comply with the ADA. She has worked with many municipal, county, and state agencies as well as school districts, private industries, and advocacy organizations.

Cindy has been the director of parks and recreation and coordinator of therapeutic recreation services for her community. She has taught therapeutic recreation and adapted physical education on the adjunct faculties of Grand Valley State University, Aquinas College, and Wayne State University and as a visiting professor at Eastern Michigan University. She has volunteered and consulted with a variety of sports organizations for persons with and without disabilities. Cindy has chaired several leisure and recreation–related committees for state and national disability advocacy and recreation organizations. She served on the U.S. Access Board's Recreation Accessibility Advisory Committee and the Regulatory Negotiation Committees on Access to Play Facilities and Access to Outdoor Developed Areas to establish the ADA compliance rules for recreation facilities.

Cindy has been active working with persons with disabilities her entire life. She has a sibling who has multiple physical and mental impairments. She also is the parent of a child who experienced several massive strokes and now faces a variety of challenges. She advocates professionally and personally for the rights of people of all abilities to be included in all aspects of community life.

Shu Cole, PhD, obtained her doctorate in recreation, park and tourism sciences from Texas A&M University in 1998 and is currently associate professor in the Department of Recreation, Park and Tourism Studies at Indiana University, Bloomington. Her research expertise is in tourism marketing with a focus on visitors' and tourists' travel experiences. She has published in *Journal of Travel Research, Journal of Leisure Research, Journal of Travel and Tourism Marketing, Tourism Management, Tourism Review International, Journal of Vacation Marketing, Asia Pacific Journal of Tourism Research,* and *China Tourism Research.* She has presented at numerous regional, national, and international professional conferences. Currently, her research interest is on understanding the impact of leisure travel on the quality of life of people with mobility impairments. Specific topics include leisure travel motivations of people with mobility impairments, barriers they encounter while traveling, and their travel needs.

Tracey Crawford, CTRS, CPRP, is employed at Fox Valley Special Recreation Association (FVSRA) which is a partnership of seven western suburban Illinois Park and Recreation agencies. FVSRA provides leisure and recreation opportunities for people with disabilities and also provides inclusion support for the park and recreation agencies in those communities.

Crawford earned a Bachelor of Science degree in therapeutic recreation from the University of Iowa in Iowa City. She is a certified therapeutic recreation specialist (CTRS) and a certified park and recreation professional (CPRP). She is certified as a trainer in crisis prevention techniques from the Non-Violent Crisis Prevention Institute, Brookfield, WI, and a trainer for the Illinois Park and Recreation Association's "Benefits are Endless" marketing program. She was awarded the Meritorious Service Award from NTRS for her work and dedication in the field of therapeutic recreation, particularly in the area of inclusion.

Ronald W. Davis, PhD, is a professor of adapted physical education at Texas Woman's University in Denton. Dr. Davis has more than 2 decades of experience teaching, researching, and advocating for persons with disabilities in the areas of physical education, sport, and recreation. He spent 20 years at Ball State University creating and directing the adapted physical education undergraduate preparation program before joining TWU's faculty in January 2007. A former disability sport coach, referee, and director of athlete classification for 1996 Atlanta Paralympics, Dr. Davis continues his contribution to the field while training graduate students in adapted physical activity. He has published and presented at the national and international levels, served as chair of the AAHPERD Adapted Physical Activity Council and president of the National Consortium of Physical Education and Recreation for Individuals with Disabilities, and received a distinguished alumni award from the University of Wisconsin–LaCrosse. He has authored a book titled *Inclusion Through Sports,* which provides practical ideas for teaching disability sport in general physical education curriculums. His research interests include collaboration training of paraeducators for adapted physical education, training of athletes with disabilities, and improving bone mineral density in persons with spinal cord injuries.

Rodney B. Dieser, PhD, is an associate professor in the School of Health, Physical Education, and Leisure Services at the University of Northern Iowa (UNI). His research and teaching interests include cross-cultural therapeutic recreation and leisure practice; therapeutic recreation as an adjunctive therapy for people with mental illnesses and disabilities; historical and philosophical foundations of leisure, youth, and nonprofit human services, including Hull-House from 1889 to 1953; representations of health in popular culture; and hegemonic masculinity and youth development in leisure, sport, and physical activities. Rod currently serves as the program coordinator for the master's degree program in philanthropy and nonprofit development at UNI and is involved in nonprofit community engagement services.

Rod has coauthored two textbooks in leisure studies and has published extensively in the field of leisure studies (e.g., *Journal of Leisure Research, Leisure Science, Leisure Studies, Leisure/Loisir, Therapeutic Recreation Journal*) and in other academic fields such as counseling psychology, education, and nonprofit human services (e.g., *Alberta Journal of Education Research, Human Service Educator, Journal of College Student Development, Journal of Progressive Human Services, Transactional Analysis Journal*).

Rod has served as an associate editor for the *Therapeutic Recreation Journal* and as an editor for the academic newsletter *SPRE Professor* and was awarded a Presidential Citation by the Society of Parks and Recreation Educators for his work as the editor of *SPRE Professor*. In 2006 he received the Outstanding Professional Research Award by the National Therapeutic Recreation Society in the United States. He has also received outstanding research and writing awards from the Alberta Therapeutic Recreation Association and the Canadian Therapeutic Recreation Association, respectively.

Cindy Dillenschneider, MS Ed, has been a professor of outdoor education at Northland College in Ashland, Wisconsin, since 1989, where she teaches undergraduate students to implement universal design in outdoor curricula and experiences and to apply outdoor experiences to enhance therapeutic gains. She received her BS in physical education with a specialization in corrective therapy at Texas A&M University and an MS in experiential education from Mankato State University. She began her career in outdoor education as a raft guide with Environmental Traveling Companions, providing outdoor experiences to underserved populations. Cindy enjoys sharing the knowledge and experience gained from years in the field as an instructor for the Breckenridge Outdoor Education Center, the National Outdoor Leadership School, and Outward Bound and as a trips assistant with Wilderness Inquiry. Cindy is actively engaged in design and development of equipment to improve outdoor access for people of all abilities and recently received a patent for a canoe paddle for one-arm use.

Torrie Dunlap, CPLP, began her career in the field of arts administration, and for 16 years developed and implemented theater and dance programs in both K-12 education and after-school agencies. Torrie received her degree in theater for young audiences from San Diego State University. She worked for 11 years as the education director for the prestigious San Diego Junior Theatre (the country's oldest theater by and for children), always including children with disabilities in classes and stage productions. In this capacity Torrie served on the executive board of the American Alliance for Theatre & Education (AATE) and has won national awards for her arts education programs. Torrie joined the staff of Kids Included Together (KIT) in 2003 and now serves as the director of KIT's National Training Center on Inclusion, based in San Diego. She regularly presents workshops at national and regional conferences, sits on a variety of committees dedicated to improving access for people with disabilities, and has written several manuals on inclusion. KIT has been adopted by the U.S. Navy Child & Youth Programs, and Torrie manages the development of inclusion materials and training for naval bases worldwide. Torrie has extensive experience developing curriculum and has led the creation of KIT's eLearning program. Torrie is a member of the American Society for Training and Development (ASTD).

Alan Ewert, PhD, received his doctorate at the University of Oregon in recreation and park management and is currently a professor and holder of the Patricia and Joel Meier Endowed Chair in Outdoor Leadership at Indiana University. Dr. Ewert's expertise resides in outdoor adventure education, where he has served as an instructor with Outward Bound and the National Outdoor Leadership School (NOLS), as well as a U.S. Air Force survival instructor. He has also served as the branch chief of recreation and wilderness research in the USDA Forest Service in Washington, DC, and as director of professional development for Outward Bound. He has written several textbooks on adventure education and natural resource management, including Outdoor Adventure Pursuits, and is a seasonal instructor for Outward Bound. Dr. Ewert is the faculty supervisor for the semester-long program on conservation in outdoor recreation education (CORE), and he conceptualized and developed the Therapeutic Outdoor Programs Certificate Program in the department of recreation, park, and tourism studies at Indiana University in Bloomington.

Frederick Green, PhD, is a professor in therapeutic recreation at the University of Southern Mississippi. He received his BS in outdoor recreation and MS in rehabilitation administration from Southern Illinois University and his PhD in therapeutic recreation from the University of Minnesota. Throughout his professional career, Rick has advocated for and planned inclusive recreation opportunities for people with disabilities. He served as the coordinator of recreational Sports at Southern Illinois University, where his primary responsibilities were to provide recreation opportunities for traditionally underserved students, including students with disabilities, international students, and students with children. He has eight summers of camp experience, with positions ranging from camp counselor to waterfront director to camp director. He continues pursuing his interest in the outdoors as an avid bicyclist, canoeist, and orienteerer.

Jody Hironaka-Juteau, EdD, CTRS, RTC, is professor and chair of the department of recreation administration at California State University, Fresno. She regularly presents at regional, national, and international conferences and writes on topics such as culture and diversity, inclusion, experiential education, and action research. With more than 20 years experience as a Certified Therapeutic Recreation Specialist (CTRS) working with children, teens, adults, and older adults in hospital and community-based settings, Jody has worked in the areas of physical medicine and rehabilitation, mental health, sensory impairment, and developmental disability. She currently hosts a regular segment titled Fun Family Activities for the KVPT Valley Public Television parenting show *0-5 in 30 Minutes*. She earned a doctoral degree from Fielding Graduate University, a master's degree in education, and bachelor's degree in recreation administration from California State University, Fresno.

David Howard, PhD, MSW, CTRS, is an assistant professor in the College of Nursing, Health and Human Services at Indiana State University. He received his PhD in rehabilitation science from the University of Florida in 2004 and completed master's and undergraduate degrees from the University of Utah in clinical social work (1998) and recreation and leisure studies (1995), respectively. David has worked with the American Therapeutic Recreation Association (ATRA) and has served as chair of the Public Health World Health Organiza-

tion team, coordinator of the General Medicine and Oncology Treatment Network, and member of the Public Health Healthy People 2010 committee. He previously served the National Therapeutic Recreation Society as chair of committees related to youth at-risk and corrections. His interests include the study of: (a) psychosocial factors related to coping after cancer diagnosis and treatment; (b) the World Health Organization and global conceptualizations of functioning, health, and disability; (c) complementary and integrative therapies; and (d) implications of leisure constructs related to sexuality and intimacy inclusive of factors of disability and/or spirituality. He serves on the Advisory Board of the Center for the Study of Health, Religion and Spirituality at his university. As a practitioner, David has experience in mental health, substance abuse, and corrections settings. As a part-time consultant, David is the executive director of the Maple Center, a nonprofit organization that supports maternal and integrative health care services.

Terry Long, PhD, is an associate professor at Northwest Missouri State University. His primary responsibilities are teaching in the therapeutic recreation curriculum and coordinating graduate studies. Dr. Long has been involved with several organizations and initiatives that promote inclusive recreation and community life. He has most recently served on the Kansas City advisory board for the National Sports Center for the Disabled and as a board member for Midland Empire Resources for Independent Living, an independent living center in northwest Missouri. His personal interests include collecting music, attending festivals, and spending time with family. Terry also wrote the online ancillaries for this text.

Pamala V. Morris, PhD, is an assistant dean and the director of the Office of Multicultural Programs in the College of Agriculture at Purdue University in West Lafayette. She is an associate professor in the Department of

Youth Development and Agricultural Education. Pamala has worked in the area of multiculturalism for more than 17 years. She has taught the upper elementary school grades for many years and served as an elementary school principal in the innercity of Indianapolis for several years before completing a PhD in curriculum and instruction at Purdue University. She developed and currently teaches a course titled Communicating Across Cultures to prepare students to communicate effectively in diverse environments. She serves as the project leader for a virtual Community of Practice, CoP through eXtension. The CoP Diversity Across Higher Education can be accessed at www.extension.org/diversity. In November 2002, Pamala received the United States Department of Agriculture National Diversity Award for her work in service learning, diversity, and international programs. Her research focuses on identity development.

Nancy Nisbett, EdD, CTRS, RTC, is an associate professor in the department of recreation administration at California State University, Fresno. She coordinates the community recreation and youth services specialization as well as the Serving At-Risk Youth certificate. Dr. Nisbett is certified, both state and nationally, as a recreation therapist and has been practicing for more than 15 years. Her past work experiences include working at youth ranches, camps, and hospitals and as the inclusion director for a municipal recreation agency.

MaryBeth Pappas Baun, MEd, is the author of *Fantastic Water Workouts: Proven Exercises and Routines for Toning, Fitness and Health, Second Edition,* a popular guidebook that has been translated into several languages and distributed internationally. For more than 25 years, she has focused on empowering people to make sustainable healthy lifestyle changes. A professional author,

educator, trainer, wellness coach, and consultant with a mission of enhancing wellness opportunities for everyone, she has done just that for the thousands of people who have participated in her training programs and workshops, used her electronic curricula, and read her books and articles. Pappas Baun has operated her own training company since 1987; has worked in several university, health care, and recreational facility settings; and was employed in-house in health promotion staff roles for Kaiser Permanente, Goodrich Aerospace, and the University of Texas M.D. Anderson Cancer Center. She currently operates a wellness consulting and training firm and a private wellness coaching practice that serves clients internationally.

She is a certified wellness practitioner and a member of the National Wellness Association and the Houston Wellness Association. In 2008, she received the National Wellness Institute's Service and Leadership Circle award. She received certifications as a personal fitness trainer in 1995 from the National Academy of Sports Medicine, as aquatic exercise instructor in 1990 from the Aquatic Exercise Association and the Arthritis Foundation, as health & fitness specialist in 1988 from ACSM, and as a Group exercise instructor in 1988 and in 1986 from ACE and AFAA, respectively. In her leisure time, Pappas Baun enjoys being active through swimming, hiking, biking, kick scooter-biking, and kayaking, among other activities. She enjoys dance, yoga, tai chi, and reading.

Erik Rabinowitz, PhD, is assistant professor of recreation management at Appalachian State University and has taught previously at Oklahoma State University and Southern Illinois University. Erik received a PhD in educational psychology and a master of science in recreation at Southern Illinois University and a bachelor's in social science from Colorado State University. Previous significant work experiences for Erik are assistant to the director of university assessment at SIUC; manager of a community radio station, WDBX 91.1, with more than 100 volunteers; and assisting individuals with learning disabilities for Project Achieve and Brehm Preparatory School. He is interested in two major lines of research, one in recreational interventions for individuals with learning disabilities and the other in extreme sports participation. He spends his leisure time chasing his two little girls, which makes him very happy. He loves skiing, soccer, canoeing, chess, playing his mandolin like David Grisman (he wishes), and attending Dead shows.

Amy Rauworth, MS, RCEP, is the associate director of the National Center on Disability and Physical Activity. She is a Registered Clinical Exercise Physiologist with the American College of Sports Medicine. Ms. Rauworth has applied exercise physiology experience in the areas of orthopedic and cardiac rehabilitation, health promotion, and corporate wellness. Ms. Rauworth conducts inclusive fitness trainings nationally on behalf of NCPAD and specializes in accessible fitness center design. Ms. Rauworth has more than 14 years of personal training experience, focusing on the delivery of physical activity programming to older adults and people with disabilities.

Terry Robertson, PhD, is a full professor at Northwest Missouri State University and serves as department chair for the Department of Health, Physical Education, Recreation, and Dance. Terry is a recognized and respected leader, teacher, and friend to many. He enjoys meeting new people, further developing the relations he has, traveling (recently to China, Australia, Spain, and Finland), trying new things, and spending time outdoors with family and friends. Dr. Robertson has worked in clinical settings, community settings, research centers, and in higher education. Dr. Robertson believes that educating others about inclusion (in theory and in practice) is an important opportunity. He further hopes that readers will support inclusion as a concept and apply it in daily life. He believes that individual rights, when combined with shared values and shared responsibility, will help create a common

good that transcends race, gender, belief systems, and history. He hopes that as future professionals, you will continue the pursuit of ensuring human rights and social justice for all.

Kathleen G. Scholl, PhD, CTRS, is a faculty member of the Leisure, Youth and Human Service Division within the School of HPELS and a research associate for Recreation, Research & Service (R2S) at UNI. She teaches courses in outdoor recreation management, research and evaluation, and social psychology of leisure. Dr. Scholl integrates practical experiences for her students to apply current best practices to outdoor recreation planning and programming. For example, outdoor recreation students are involved in the design and development of interpretative trail for the UNI Biological Preserves Committee. Dr. Scholl is a Certified Therapeutic Recreation Specialist (CTRS). She is committed to the provision of recreation opportunities for all individuals. Dr. Scholl provides her expertise in inclusive recreation services to community agencies in order that they may increase their capacity to provide recreation services to individuals with disabilities. Her research interests are inclusive recreation, accessibility, parent advocacy and support for families with disabilities, outdoor leadership and communication effectiveness, outdoor recreation, and community development. Dr. Scholl is currently sits on five agency boards: Together We Play; Friends of Hartman Reserve; Cedar Valley Resource, Conservation & Development; Cedar River Festival Group, and Iowa Conservation Education Coalition.

Kathlyn M. Steedly, PhD, has 15-plus years working on a variety of education issues, primarily the arts and special education. Dr. Steedly has viewed the education landscape as a high school drama teacher, researcher, professor, evaluator, and program administrator.

Dr. Steedly established Steedly Consulting in October of 2008. Her work at Steedly Consulting has focused on curriculum development and program evaluation for a breadth of non-profit, private, and governmental organizations. Clients include the Blue Man Group, the Federal Consulting Group, and the Council of Chief State School Officers.

Prior to Steedly Consulting, Dr. Steedly worked as a research officer at the Academy for Educational Development and was primarily responsible for project evaluation and research dissemination at the National Dissemination Center for Children and Youth with Disabilities.

As the director of evaluation and outcomes at VSA arts, Dr. Steedly investigated the way in which the arts impact students with disabilities. Dr. Steedly developed arts education research databases, evaluated the efficacy of arts organizations, investigated the social, academic, and artistic impact of VSA arts programs, presented at national and international conferences, and published on the arts, disabilities, and evaluation.

Dr. Steedly received her PhD in curriculum and instruction with a focus on the arts from the University of Texas at Austin. She holds an MA in theatre from Western Washington University, and a BA in English and theatre and a teaching credential in English, theatre, and speech communications from Indiana University, Bloomington, IN.

Monika Stodolska, PhD, is an associate professor with the Department of Recreation, Sport and Tourism, University of Illinois at Urbana–Champaign. Her research focuses on leisure behavior of ethnic and racial minorities and on constraints on leisure. She explores subjects such as the effects of race and ethnicity on leisure behavior of immigrants, issues of cultural change and adaptation among minority groups, and transnationalism. Other subjects that are prominent in her research include ethnic and racial discrimination in leisure settings, recreation behavior of minority populations in natural environments, physical activity among minority groups and constraints on leisure. Dr. Stodolska has published the results of her work in journals such as *Journal of Leisure Research, Leisure Sciences, Leisure/Loisir, Loisir et Société, Journal of Park and Recreation Administration, Cultural and Social Geography,* and *Journal of Immigrant and Refugee Studies.* She teaches classes on diversity in leisure behavior for undergraduate and graduate students at the University of Illinois.

Sheila Swann-Guerrero, CTRS, is a senior information specialist at the National Center on Physical Activity and Disability. Sheila is a Certified Therapeutic Recreation Specialist (CTRS), who has worked for more than 25 years with children and adults with disabilities and their families. She has coached adapted sports, directed day camps, and managed community-based recreation and inclusion programs. Ms. Swann-Guerrero coordinates Sibshops for siblings of children with disabilities. Sheila believes in providing services for all family members to promote wellness for the entire family. She has co-authored several book chapters and factsheets on disability, recreation, physical activity, and inclusive fitness. Sheila also consults on health promotion and disability for Leadership Education in Neurodevelopment Disabilities and has adapted a statewide curriculum in physical activity for the inclusion of children with disabilities in Safe Routes to School programs. Sheila is completing her master's degree in disability studies with an emphasis on health promotion and disability policy at the University of Illinois Department of Disability and Human Development. She is an avid swimmer and loves participating in outdoor activities and spending time with her family and friends.

Alison Voight, PhD, CTRS, received her doctorate at the University of Oregon in leisure studies and services, with a minor concentration in educational psychology and counseling. Dr. Voight served as a recreational therapist for psychiatry at the University of Kentucky Medical Center in Lexington and as a recreation therapist for emotionally disturbed youth at a private hospital in Columbus, Ohio. She has taught recreation courses at several universities in the United States and Canada and is currently an assistant professor in the department of recreation, park, and tourism studies at Indiana University in Bloomington. Dr. Voight teaches in the areas of therapeutic recreation, resource-based tourism, visitor behavior, therapeutic outdoor programs, and inclusive recreation services. She serves as the coordinator of the Therapeutic Outdoor Certificate Program (TOP) for the department. Her research interests and publications have involved motivation, theory-based processing, social psychology of leisure, and best practices in accessibility of recreation programs and facilities. Dr. Voight is vice-chair of the Inclusive Recreation Advisory Council for the City of Bloomington and a Certified Therapeutic Recreation Specialist (CTRS) through the National Council on Therapeutic Recreation Certification.

Stephanie West, PhD, received a bachelor's degree from Auburn University and a master's degree from Georgia Southern University, both in recreation management. Her PhD is from Texas A&M University, where she worked with Dr. John Crompton. Prior to completing her PhD, Stephanie worked full-time in campus recreation for 3 years at the University of North Florida and for 5 years at Texas A&M University. Other noteworthy experiences include running a summer day camp in Blackville, South Carolina, as part of the Rural Recreation Development Project and completing an internship as a transportation hostess at Walt Disney World. She is currently an assistant professor at Appalachian State University, where she teaches in the recreation management program. The classes she enjoys teaching most are leisure promotions, program planning, and a course on the cruise line industry, where she takes students onboard cruise ships for a behind-the-scenes look at their operations. Her research focuses on leisure-time physical activity, and when she is not at work, she enjoys traveling, road cycling, running (very slowly), reading, watching television shows recorded on Tivo, and spending time with her cats.

Brent Wolfe, PhD, CTRS, is assistant professor of recreational therapy at Georgia Southern University and is the president of the National Therapeutic Recreation Society (NTRS). Prior to employment at Georgia Southern University, Dr. Wolfe was an assistant professor of therapeutic recreation at the University of Southern Mississippi. Dr. Wolfe received his BS in 1996 from Houghton College, where he majored in outdoor recreation and minored in English and psychology. Upon graduation, Dr. Wolfe became a certified therapeutic recreation specialist (CTRS), and he worked for 2-1/2 years as a CTRS in a locked residential facility for adolescents with severe emotional and behavioral disorders. In 1998, Dr. Wolfe enrolled in graduate studies at the University of Georgia and he graduated with his MA in therapeutic recreation in 2001. In 2004, Dr. Wolfe received his PhD for studying a preexisting team's perception of their challenge course experience. He enjoys playing disc golf and spending time with his wife, two-year-old daughter, and long-haired Chihuahua.

You'll find other outstanding
recreation resources at
www.HumanKinetics.com